que's

COMPUTER & INTERNET DICTIONARY

6th Edition

By Bryan Pfaffenberger, Ph.D.
with David Wall

D0109358

que®

Que's Computer & Internet Dictionary, 6th Edition

Copyright © 1995 by Que® Corporation

Library of Congress Catalog No.: 95-078878

ISBN: 0-7897-0356-4

98   97   96   95   4   3   2   1

Interpretation of the printing code: the rightmost double-digit number is the year of the book's printing; the rightmost single-digit number, the number of the book's printing. For example, a printing code of 95-1 shows that the first printing of the book occurred in 1995.

President: Roland Elgey

Publisher: Stacy Hiquet

Editorial Services Director: Elizabeth Keaffaber

Publishing Director: Brad R. Koch

Managing Editor: Sandy Doell

Director of Marketing: Lynn E. Zingraf

Senior Series Editor: Chris Nelson

Credits

Publishing Manager
Thomas H. Bennett

Acquisitions Editor
Cheryl Willoughby

Product Development Specialist
Mark Cierzniak

Production Editor
Nanci Sears Perry

Copy Editors
Andy Saff, Paige Widder

Technical Writer
David Wall

Technical Editors
Lori Leonardo, Jim O'Reilly

Acquisitions Coordinators
Ruth Slates, Andrea Duvall

Book Designer
Barbara Kordesh

Cover Designer
Dan Armstrong

Graphic Image Specialist
Cari Skaggs

Production Team
Gary Adair, Kim Cofer, David Garratt, Aleata Howard,
Kevin Laseau, Shawn MacDonald, Joe Millay, Erika Millen,
Nancy Price, Gina Rexrode, Erich J. Richter, SA Springer,
Suzanne Tully, Christine Tyner, Robert Wolf

Dedication

For Suzanne, always
—BP

For my family
—DW

About the Authors

Bryan Pfaffenberger, the author of more than 50 books on personal computing and the Internet, teaches technical writing and the sociology of technology at the University of Virginia's pioneering Division of Technology, Culture, and Communication. When he's not doing such serious things, he enjoys backpacking, wine tasting, anime, and driving his white Probe GT. He lives with his family in the country near Charlottesville, Virginia.

David Wall is a Charlottesville, Virginia-based freelance writer. He has collaborated with Bryan Pfaffenberger on parts of *The World Wide Web Bible*, *PCs in Plain English*, and *Publish It on the Web*. His articles have appeared in *The Wall Street Journal*, *The Washington Post*, and have been broadcast worldwide by the Bloomberg Business News wire service. He enjoys the novels of W. Somerset Maugham and the music of Bruce Springsteen.

Acknowledgments

A dictionary as comprehensive as this one, embracing personal computing and spanning the riches of the Internet, requires help from many able hands. Thanks to all the readers who submitted suggestions for terms to include; they're too numerous to list here, but I'd like to especially thank Arthur J. Guertin, who supplied no fewer than 10 single-spaced pages of acronyms and their meanings. I'd like to thank Cheryl Willoughby for thinking grand thoughts about this sixth and very much expanded edition, and providing me with the time and encouragement to bring it to fruition. Thanks again to Judy Peterson, who revised and expanded the fifth edition. I would also like to thank this book's technical editors, and the people at Que, who used their considerable knowledge of computing and the Internet to make sure that this book meets the highest standards of technical accuracy. Thanks to all, but the responsibility for what follows is mine alone—and if I've slipped up somewhere, or omitted terms that you think should have been included, please let me know (**bp@virginia.edu**).

Trademarks

All terms mentioned in this book that are known to be trademarks or service marks have been appropriately capitalized. Que cannot attest to the accuracy of this information. Use of a term in this book should not be regarded as affecting the validity of any trademark or service mark.

Preface

Just a couple of years ago, that computer on your desk—or the notebook in your briefcase—was an isolated creature, capable—at most—of linking with on-line services, bulletin boards, and maybe a local area network (LAN). A computer user's dictionary, one focused on the computer user's needs, could restrict itself to desktop computer terms. But all that's changed, thanks to the sudden, dramatic arrival of the Internet. And this dictionary's changed, too—to the tune of more than 1,000 new definitions, covering the new Internet terms as well as everything that's new in desktop computing.

An academic network originally, the Internet has exploded into the big time. Growing at an estimated pace of 10 percent per month, the Internet now provides the de facto standard for wide area networking. An estimated 45 million people worldwide can communicate with one another via Internet electronic mail. And the World Wide Web (WWW), growing at an even more explosive rate, adds multimedia—and ease of use—to the Internet's many attractions. Soon, the Web will provide secure channels for on-line credit-card ordering—and with this development, even more rapid growth is anticipated.

By the time you read this book, the Internet will have become another option on your computer's graphical desktop—just as you'd click a drive icon to view the files on a drive, you'll click an Internet icon to gain entry to the vast resources of a global computer system. (It's not quite that simple, of course; you'll need an Internet connection, but this is increasingly easy to come by.)

For computer users, the Internet's arrival is a mixed blessing—there's a whole new world of new Internet terms to master. The terminological challenges of desktop computing are burden enough, as you'll conclude after reading any computer magazine: What's so great about this computer's four-way set associative cache, and do I need to care whether my monitor is interlaced or not? Now, one must also worry about an avalanche of Internet terms. Is SLIP sufficient for my connectivity needs, or should I look for a PPP connection? And what's all the fuss about public key cryptography? If the key's public, then how can your message be secret?

The Internet isn't the only new arrival on the scene. The publication of this book coincides (approximately) with the release of Microsoft Windows 95. Perhaps the most significant innovation in the history of personal computer operating systems, Windows 95 brings with it a host of new, confusing terms. For instance, is *cooperative multitasking* really sufficient for your computing needs, or is *preemptive multitasking* required? You'll find a complete guide to Windows 95 terms in the pages to follow.

This book's coverage isn't restricted to Microsoft Windows systems. Youll also find full coverage of Macintosh and OS/2 terms, as well. If you use a personal computer of any brand or model, you'll find this book to be a valuable reference and learning tool.

Use this dictionary to help you navigate your way through such terminological trials as the following:

- **Buying your computer system.** Do I need a *four-way set associative cache* or will a *two-way* design do? What's EDO RAM, and why does this salesperson say it's so hot?

- **Understanding application program capabilities.** You say this program can serve as a *client* for *OLE*, but not as a *server?*

- **Reading computer manuals.** What in the world does Remove the *SIMMs*, which are located just above the *SRAM cache* on the *motherboard*, mean?

- **Using the Internet.** I think I want to *delurk*, but I'm afraid I'll be *flamed* because I don't know *netiquette*. What should I do?

- **Using Microsoft Windows 95.** I never thought this would happen, but I'm longing for the days of Standard Mode and Program Manager. Now I'm faced with *Windows Explorer* and a *Recycle Bin*. What's the story on this new *operating system*?

Keep this dictionary handy when you're buying or upgrading your computer system, reading computer magazine articles or computer books, and reading computer manuals. Reach for it when you're trying to figure out what's available on the Internet and on-line services. Happy computing!

How to Use This Book

This dictionary is designed to be easy to use. The conventions used in this book are as follows:

- **Terms.** Each term is listed alphabetically, in boldface type.

- **Pronunciation.** Some terms have a phonetic spelling.

- **Cross References.** In many definitions, you'll find italic cross-references. For more information, just flip to the corresponding entry.

- **Acronyms.** Looking for an acronym? If you don't know what the acronym stands for, just look for the acronym itself. You'll see a cross-reference that guides you to the correct entry.

 - **Internet Icon.** You'll find an icon that identifies Internet terms.

 TIP: *Cool tricks that you can try.*

 CAUTION: *Things to watch out for.*

Let Us Hear from You

Trying to keep up with the language of desktop computing and the Internet is like trying to change a tire on a moving truck—hardly a day goes by without some new, impenetrable term or acronym. That's why Que puts out a new edition of this dictionary every year, and that's also why this dictionary is the most up-to-date you'll find. Still, you may encounter computer or Internet terms that aren't defined here. If so, please let us know. If you're on the Net, write to us at **bp@virginia.edu**, or send snail mail to the address given at the end of this book.

Bryan Pfaffenberger

David Wall

Earlysville, VA

@function   See *built-in function*.

^   See *caret*.

0.5-micron technology   A means by which *semiconductor* manufacturers can pack more electronics onto *chips*, while at the same time making the chips run faster and cooler. Some components on chips that employ 0.5-micron technology are as little as one-half-millionth of a meter in width.

1-2-3   See *Lotus 1-2-3*.

2X   See *double speed drive*.

2 1/2-inch disk   A defunct *floppy disk* standard once used on a few Zenith *portable computers*. Many *hard disks* for *portable computers* are 2 1/2 inches in diameter, though.

3-D graph   See *three-dimensional graph*.

3-D spreadsheet program   See *three-dimensional spreadsheet*.

3 1/2-inch disk   A *floppy disk*, originally developed by Sony Corporation, used for magnetically storing data. The disk is enclosed in a hard plastic case with a sliding metal access door.

High-density 3 1/2-inch disks, capable of storing $1.44M$, are most common. Older, *double-density* disks hold $720K$, while new, somewhat rare 3 1/2-inch disks store 2.88M. *Macintosh* 3 1/2-inch disks hold either 800K (double density) or 1.4M (high density).

4X   See *quad speed drive*.

5 1/4-inch disk   A *floppy disk* enclosed in a flexible plastic *shell*. The most widely used floppy disk before 1987, 5 1/4-inch disks have been almost entirely replaced by *3 1/2-inch floppy disks*.

6X   In *CD-ROM disk drives*, a drive that can transfer data at up to 600 *K* per second, six times as fast as the first CD-ROM disk drives. 6X CD-ROM disk drives, unlike *double speed* and *quad speed* drives, are considered state-of-the-art for personal computers.

8-bit microprocessor   A *microprocessor* that can handle only one *byte* of data at a time. The *Intel 8088*, used in the first IBM personal computers, is an 8-bit microprocessor and has an *internal data bus* 8 bits wide.

8-bit sound board   An obsolete type of *sound board* that can process and generate sounds recorded with 8-bit resolution. 8-bit sound boards have output quality too poor for music reproduction, and barely adequate for voice reproduction and system sounds.

8-bit video adapter   A color *video adapter* that can display 256 colors simultaneously.

8.3 filename   A filename corresponding to the standard *MS-DOS* file-naming conventions, which restrict *file names* to 8 characters and optional *extensions* to 3 characters.

12-bit sound board   A *sound board*, generally considered sufficient for *business audio* applications, that can process and reproduce sound recorded with 12-bit resolution. Though 12-bit sound boards can handle simple music, they are far from capable of generating *Compact Disc-Digital Audio (CD-DA)* quality sound.

14-inch monitor   A *monitor* with an overall diagonal *display* measurement of 14 inches. In reality, the edges of the display are hidden by the monitor housing and the area of the screen actually used measures 12.8 to 13.5 inches diagonally. 14-inch monitors are too small for the high *resolutions* and large screen areas that *graphical user interfaces (GUIs)* demand.

15-inch monitor   A *monitor* with an overall diagonal *display* measurement of 15 inches and an area measuring 13.3 to 14 inches diagonally actually available for display tasks. Though 15-inch monitors are better than *14-inch monitors*, *17-inch monitors* are much preferred over both.

16-bit computer   A *computer* that uses a *central processing unit (CPU)* with a 16-*bit internal data bus* and processes two bytes (16 bits) of information at a time.

16-bit microprocessor   A *microprocessor* that can handle two *bytes* of data at a time, making it significantly faster than an *8-bit microprocessor*. The *Intel 8086* and *Intel 80286* are 16-bit microprocessors. See *external data bus, internal data bus,* and *register.*

16-bit sound board   A high-quality *sound board* capable of processing and reproducing sounds and music recorded with 16-*bit resolution*—the resolution of the *Compact Disc-Digital Audio (CD-DA)* standard. Most 16-bit sound boards can process sounds recorded at resolutions lower than 16-bits, too.

17-inch monitor   A *monitor* with an overall diagonal *display* measurement of 17 inches and an area measuring 15.4 to 16.6 inches diagonally actually available for display tasks. 17-inch monitors are becoming the standard for *desktop computers,* since they allow high *resolutions* and make it easy to see many windows at the same time.

21-inch monitor   A *monitor* with an overall diagonal *display* measurement of 21 inches and an area measuring 19 inches diagonally actually available for display tasks. 21-inch monitors are too big and expensive for everyday desktop use, but they are ideal for *desktop publishing* applications, in which large expanses of page layouts need to be seen at once.

24-bit video adapter   A *video adapter* that can display more than 16 million colors simultaneously. With a 24-bit video adapter and monitor, a computer can display beautiful, photographic-quality images. Such video cards and full-color monitors, however, can add hundreds of dollars to the cost of a computer system.

30-pin SIMM slot   A socket, usually on the *motherboard,* for 30-pin *single in-line memory modules (SIMMs).* Such SIMMs are obsolete and have been replaced with 72-pin versions. See *72-pin SIMM slot.*

32-bit microprocessor   A *microprocessor* that can handle four *bytes* of data at a time, making it much faster than *16-bit microprocessors.* 32-bit microprocessors like the *Intel 486* and *Intel 386DX* have *internal data buses* 32 bits wide that connect to 32-bit *external data buses,* while the *Intel 386SX,* another 32-bit microprocessor, connects to a 16-bit external data bus.

32-bit operating system   An *operating system* that takes full advantage of the *32-bit microprocessors*, which can perform operations on 32 bits of information at a time. Among the many advantages of 32-bit operating systems are their ability to set up a *flat address space*, in which the operating system can map out the available memory without restrictions imposed by segmentation (see *segmented memory architecture*). In addition, a 32-bit operating system can use lengthy file names (in *Microsoft Windows 95,* you can use file names up to 255 characters in length). *Microsoft Windows NT* and *UNIX* are true 32-bit operating systems; Microsoft Windows 95 is a hybrid, retaining some 16-bit code so that users can continue to run their Windows 3.1 applications.

32-bit video adapter   An obsolete type of *video adapter* with an *internal data bus* 32 bits wide. 32-bit video adapters cannot handle the high resolutions that make *Microsoft Windows 95* easy to use, and are too slow for most modern *graphics* tasks. *64-bit* and *128-bit video adapters* have replaced 32-bit video adapters.

64-bit microprocessor   A *microprocessor* that can handle eight *bytes* of data at the same time, and the fastest microprocessor ever mass-produced for personal computer use—much faster than 8-, 16-, or *32-bit microprocessors*. The *Pentium* is a 64-bit microprocessor whose 64-bit *internal data bus* connects to a *32-bit external data bus*. The difference in bus width at the 64-bit level does not cause a significant performance decrease.

64-bit video adapter   A *video adapter* with an *internal data bus* 64 bits wide. Though *128-bit video adapters* are faster, 64-bit video adapters represent the best balance between cost and performance for *personal computers* today.

83-key keyboard   The type of *keyboard* found on the original IBM Personal Computer. The 83-key keyboard was panned because of its odd *key* layout. It was replaced by the *AT keyboard*.

84-key keyboard   See *AT keyboard*.

100% column graph   See *one hundred percent (100%) column graph*.

101-key keyboard   See *extended keyboard*.

128-bit video adapter   A *video adapter* with an *internal data bus* 128 bits wide, making it the fastest kind of video adapter available for *personal computer monitors* today. A 128-bit video adapter can significantly speed up *graphics*-intensive tasks such as *computer-aided design (CAD)* and animation.

680x0   The generic designation of the *Motorola microprocessor* architecture that is *binary compatible* with Macintosh software. See *Motorola 68000, Motorola 68020, Motorola 68030*, and *Motorola 68040.*

765   A *chip* that controls the flow of *data* and instructions be-tween the *central processing unit (CPU)* and the *floppy disk drive*. The 765, because it is easily programmed with *basic input-output system (BIOS)* instructions, has been used in personal computers for many years.

6845   A *video controller* chip that has appeared on or been simu-lated on all *video adapters* since IBM's early-1980s *MDA* standard. *Video drivers* can program the 6845's *registers*, and define the char-acteristics of the video signal the 6845 sends to the screen.

8250   The *Universal Asynchronous Receiver/Transmitter (UART)* chip found on the original IBM Personal Computer, the IBM Personal Computer XT, and compatible machines. The 8250, now obsolete, will experience *overrun errors* if used with modern machines, since it cannot handle the fast data transfers they demand.

8514/A   An IBM *video standard* for 1024 *pixel* by 768 line *resolution*. Largely because it was designed for the doomed *Micro Channel Architecture (MCA)*, 8514/A is obsolete.

16450   The *Universal Asynchronous Receiver/Transmitter (UART)* chip found on IBM Personal Computer AT machines and compatibles. The 16450 is better than the *8250*, but is technically inferior to the *16550A* because of its tendency to cause *overrun errors* under fast data-transfer conditions.

16550A   The *Universal Asynchronous Receiver/Transmitter (UART)* chip found on fast, modern computer systems. As the state-of-the-art UART, the 16550A has a much larger storage buffer than the obsolete *8250* and *16450*, making it less prone to *overrun errors.*

abandon   To clear a *document, spreadsheet,* or other work from the screen—and therefore from memory—without saving it to a *floppy* or *hard disk.* The work is irretrievably lost.

abort   To cancel a *program, command,* or procedure while it's in progress. You can often abort a procedure manually, or a procedure may abort by itself because of a *bug* in the program, power failure, or other unexpected cause.

A-B roll editing   In *multimedia,* a method for creating a master edited video sequence by directing selected portions of video signals from two video sources (VCRs or camcorders) to a destination recording device, usually a VCR.

absolute address   In a *program,* specifying a location in *random-access memory (RAM)* by its address instead of using an expression to calculate the address.

absolute cell reference   A *spreadsheet cell reference* that doesn't adjust when you *copy* or move a *formula.* An absolute cell reference includes the $ symbol before both the *column* letter and the *row* number (A6). Use absolute cell references when you refer to cells containing *key variables,* such as the inflation rate or a standard discount. See *relative cell reference.*

absolute value   The positive value of a number, regardless of its sign (positive or negative). The absolute value of −357, for example, is 357. In *Microsoft Excel* and other *spreadsheet* programs, the @ABS *built-in function* returns the absolute value of a number.

accelerator board   A circuit board designed to speed up some function of your computer. A *graphics accelerator board,* for example, contains a *microprocessor* that relieves the *central processing unit (CPU)* of many video chores, enabling it to get to other work sooner.

accent   A mark that forms one of the special characters of many languages. The following accents are used frequently:

´	Acute	˘	Breve	ç	Cedilla
^	Circumflex	¨	Diaeresis	`	Grave
°	Macron	˜	Tilde	¨	Umlaut

Accented characters are included in most *font* sets, and some application programs include commands or keystrokes that insert accented characters for you. See *compose sequence* and *extended character set*.

Acceptable Use Policy (AUP)   A *service provider's* policy statement that indicates which types of uses are permissible. Epitomized by the *AUP* of *NSFNet,* the backbone network formerly funded by the U.S. *National Science Foundation (NSF)*, the AUPs of publicly funded *networks* sharply restrict commercial use. To foster commercial development of the *Internet*, an organization called the *Commercial Internet Exchange (CIX)* provides an AUP-free international backbone for commercial Internet traffic.

acceptance test   A final demonstration of a new *software* or *hardware* product that illustrates the product's capabilities and special features. When companies or other entities hire *systems analysts* or other computer consultants to do work for them, the acceptance test serves to show that the consultants have satisfied their contract obligations.

Access   See *Microsoft Access*.

access   To retrieve *data* or *program* instructions from a *hard* or *floppy disk drive* or another computer connected to your computer by a *network* or a *modem*.

access arm   See *head arm*.

access code   An identification number or *password* you use to gain access to a computer system.

access control   In a *network*, a means of ensuring the system's *security* by demanding that users supply a *login name* and *password*.

access control list (ACL)   In a *network*, a *database* that lists the valid users of the systems and the level of network access that they have been granted.

access hole See *head access aperture.*

access privileges On a *network*, the extent of a user's capability to use and modify *directories*, *files*, and *programs* located on other computers in the network. See *local area network (LAN).*

access time The amount of time that lapses between a request for information from *memory* and the delivery of the information. Access times apply to disks and to *random-access memory (RAM)*. RAM access times are much shorter than disk access times, so adding extra RAM can dramatically improve a computer's overall performance.

account In a *network,* a contractual agreement between the user and the service provider. In return for network access, the user agrees to abide by the service provider's regulations and, in some cases, pay a fee.

accounting package A *program* or group of programs intended to help a small-business owner automate a firm's accounting procedures. Though accounting packages have grown easier to use recently, they still often require a level of accounting expertise that small-time entrepreneurs usually lack, and require tedious *data* entry. See *integrated accounting package* and *modular accounting package.*

accumulator A *register* in a *central processing unit (CPU)* that holds values to be used later in a computation. Computer multiplication, for example, frequently is done by a series of additions; an accumulator holds the intermediate values until the process is completed.

accuracy A statement of how correct a measurement is. Accuracy is different from *precision,* which describes the number of decimal places to which a measurement is computed.

ACM See *Association for Computer Machinery (ACM).*

acoustic coupler A *modem* with cups that fit around the earpiece and mouthpiece of a standard (not cellular) telephone receiver. The cups contain a *microphone* and a speaker that convert the computer's digital signals into sound, and vice versa. With the almost-universal use of *modular jacks, direct-connect modems* have supplanted acoustic modems in general use.

acoustical sound enclosure   An insulated cabinet for noisy *impact printers* that reduces the noise such *printers* make.

acronym   A new word made from the first or other important letters in a descriptive phrase; used to help people remember technical phrases. For example, *RAM* is an acronym for *Random Access Memory*. To pronounce acronyms, spell out the letters unless the acronym contains enough vowels to make it pronounceable as a word (*BASIC, SIMM*).

active area   In a *spreadsheet* document, such as a *Lotus 1-2-3* worksheet, the area bounded by *cell* A1 and the lowest rightmost cell containing *data*.

active cell   In a *spreadsheet*, the *cell* in which the *cell pointer* is located. Synonymous with *current cell*.

active configuration   The way you configure a *modem*, usually with an *initialization string*, at the beginning of a communications session. The active configuration supersedes the *factory configuration* and remains in effect until you turn off the modem or *reboot* the computer.

active database   In *database management*, the *database file* in use and present in *random-access memory (RAM)*.

active file   The *worksheet* on-screen when you're working with *Lotus 1-2-3*.

active index   In *database management systems (DBMSs)*, the *index* file being used to determine the order in which *data records* are displayed.

active matrix   See *active matrix display*.

active matrix display   In *portable computers*, a full-color *liquid-crystal display (LCD)* in which each of the screen's *pixels* is controlled by its own transistor. Active matrix displays offer higher *resolution*, *contrast*, and *vertical refresh rate* than cheaper *passive matrix displays*.

active sensing   In *multimedia*, a *Musical Instrument Digital Interface (MIDI)* message that tells a device to monitor its channels to determine whether messages occur on the channels within a predetermined time frame (called a time window).

active termination   Like *passive termination* and *forced perfect termination*, a means of ending a chain of *Small Computer System Interface (SCSI)* devices. Active termination is noted for its ability to reduce electrical interference in a long string of SCSI devices.

active window   In a *program* or *operating system* that displays multiple *windows*, the window in which the *cursor* is located and where text appears if you type (see fig. A.1). See *windowing environment*.

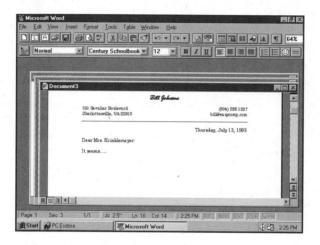

Fig. A.1   *An active document window superimposed on other document windows in Microsoft Word.*

 TIP: *The color of the active window's title bar is usually different from the other windows' title bars.*

activity light   On the front panel of a computer's *case*, a small colored light that flickers when a *hard* or *floppy disk drive* is reading or writing data.

actuator   See *head actuator*.

Ada   A high-level *programming language* developed by the U.S. Department of Defense and required by the DoD for all military programming applications. Ada uses the principles of *structured programming*, including the use of program *modules* that can be compiled separately. Ada programs are designed to be highly readable so they're easy to maintain. See *compiler, high-level programming language, Modula-2, Pascal,* and *structured programming.*

adapter   A *circuit board* that plugs into an *expansion slot* in a computer, giving the computer additional capabilities. Synonymous with card. Popular adapters for personal computers include *video adapters* that produce video output, memory expansion boards, internal *modems;* and *sound boards.*

adapter segment   See *upper memory area.*

Adaptive Differential Pulse Code Modulation (ADPCM)   In *multimedia,* a method of digital *waveform* compression where the difference between successive samples rather than their actual values is encoded. Using ADPCM, the quantity of audio information that can be stored on a *single CD-ROM* increases from 1 hour to about 16 hours, while maintaining or improving fidelity. ADPCM is the storage technique used by *CD-ROM eXtended Architecture (CD-ROM XA),* and *Compact Disk-Interactive (CD-I)* disks. See *pulse code modulation (PCM).*

ADB   See *Apple Desktop Bus (ADB).*

add-in program   An accessory or *utility program* designed to work with and extend the capabilities of an *application program.* Add-in programs can be created by other software developers, such as Allways by Funk Software, or included with the application, such as the auditors, file viewers, and "what-if" programs included in many *spreadsheet* programs.

address   See *memory address.*

address bus   An internal electronic channel from the *microprocessor* to *random-access memory (RAM),* along which the addresses of memory storage locations are transmitted. Like a post office box, each memory location has a distinct number or address; the address bus provides the means by which the *central processing unit (CPU)* can *access* the contents of every location in memory.

 Address Resolution Protocol (ARP)   An *Internet* standard that provides *IP addresses* to *workstations* on a *local area network (LAN).*

 address resolution   In a *local area network (LAN)* that is connected to the *Internet,* the automated process by which the

LAN address of each workstation is converted into an *IP address.* The translation is needed because the Internet and LANs handle workstation addresses in different ways. Programs based on the *Address Resolution Protocol (ARP)* handle the translation.

addressability A somewhat irrelevant measure of *monitor* performance. Ignoring the critical role of the *shadow mask,* addressability describes the number of positions on the display at which a monitor's *electron guns* can be pointed. *Dot pitch, resolution,* and *refresh rate* are more important specifications of monitor performance.

ADI See *Apple Desktop Interface (ADI).*

Adobe Acrobat An *application program* that creates richly formatted *portable documents* that can be accessed and read on a wide variety of computers. To read an Acrobat document, you need a copy of the Adobe Acrobat Reader that is designed to run on your computer. The Reader is freely available for downloading on the *Internet.* Once you have installed the Reader, you can display any Adobe Acrobat document, and you will see the fonts, graphics, and other document design elements that the original author chose. Increasingly popular on the *World Wide Web,* Acrobat documents enable publishers to overcome the formatting limitations of *HyperText Markup Language (HTML).* Adobe Acrobat 2.0 introduced hypertext-like features that enable authors to create navigable paths through the various sections of their documents.

Adobe Photoshop A very powerful *image-editing program* that enables you to alter a photograph much more extensively than you could in a darkroom. Elaborate (and customizable) filters, lighting effects, and editing tools allow you to prepare images for publication. Some critics don't like the fact that Adobe Photoshop requires a fast *microprocessor* and lots of *random-access memory (RAM),* but others say the capabilities of the program are worth the *hardware* investment.

Adobe PostScript See *PostScript.*

ADPCM See *Adaptive Differential Pulse Code Modulation.*

ADSL See *asynchronous digital subscriber loop.*

Advanced Interactive eXecutive (AIX) An *IBM* version of the *UNIX* operating system. AIX runs on PS/2 computers equipped with the *Intel 80386* microprocessor, IBM *workstations*, *minicomputers*, and *mainframes*.

Advanced Micro Devices (AMD) A manufacturer of *microprocessors* and other *integrated circuits*. Based in Sunnyvale, California, AMD is the fifth-largest U.S. chipmaker and is known for the *Am386*, the *Am486*, and the developmental *AMD K5*.

Advanced Research Projects Agency (ARPA) An agency of the U.S. Department of Defense (DoD), now called Defense Advanced Research Projects Agency (DARPA), and a major source of funding for important computer innovations. In the late 1960s and early 1970s, ARPA funded the development of the *ARPAnet*, the *Internet's* predecessor, and the *TCP/IP* protocols, which have since provided the foundation for the emergence of a *wide-area network (WAN)* of global proportions.

Advanced Run-Length Limited (ARLL) A method of storing and retrieving information on a *hard disk* that increases the density *of Run-Length Limited (RLL)* storage by more than 25 percent and offers a faster data-transfer rate (9 megabits per second). See *data-encoding*.

Advanced SCSI Programming Interface (ASPI) A standard that states how *Small Computer System Interface (SCSI)* devices work with each other and the rest of the computer system.

advanced setup options Options in the *BIOS setup program* that let you choose PCI interrupts, port addresses, and *hard disk* setup options. Because bad advanced setup option settings can cripple a computer, make sure you know what you're doing before you alter them.

Advanced Technology Attachment Packet Interface (ATAPI) A standard that makes it very easy to connect a *CD-ROM disk drive* to an *Enhanced IDE host adapter*.

aftermarket The market for *software* and *peripherals* created by the sale of large numbers of a specific brand of computer or software. See *add-in program*.

agate A 5.5-*point* type size used in newspaper classified advertisements and financial tables, but too small for most other uses.

agent A *program* that is designed to operate on the user's behalf, performing a specific function in the background. When the agent has achieved its goal, it reports to the user. In the future, agents may roam the world's computer networks, looking for information and reporting only when the information has been retrieved.

aggregate function   In *database management* programs, a command that performs arithmetic operations on the values in a specific *field* in all the *records* within a *database*, or in one *view* of the database. *dBASE*, for example, performs the following aggregate functions:

Function	Description
Average	Computes the arithmetic mean of the values
Sum	Adds all the values
Minimum	Finds the smallest value
Maximum	Finds the largest value
Count	Counts the number of records that meet the specified criteria

aggregate operator   In a *database management* program, a command that tells the program to perform an aggregate function.

Suppose that you own a videotape rental store and want to know how many tapes are more than two weeks late. Because the date is May 19, you want to know how many rentals were due on or before May 5 (less than 05/06/95). The following dBASE expression finds the information:

```
COUNT FOR due_date <05/06/95
```

You see a response such as the following:

```
2 records
```

AI   See *artificial intelligence (AI)*.

AIFF   An 8-bit monaural sound *file format* developed by *Apple Computer* for storing digitized *wave sounds*. The format is also widely found on Silicon Graphics *workstations* and is often encountered on the *Internet*.

Air Mosaic   A *Web browser* created by Spry, Inc., using technology licensed from the *National Center for Supercomputing Applications (NCSA)*. Air Mosaic features a well-designed system for storing and organizing hotlist items. Air Mosaic is available separately or as part of the award-winning *Air Series* package, which provides *TCP/IP* support and a variety of Internet applications for IBM PC-compatible computer users.

AIX   See *Advanced Interactive eXecutive (AIX)*.

Aldus PageMaker   A *desktop publishing (DTP)* program that, like *QuarkXPress*, offers extensive, professional-level *typography* tools. With Aldus PageMaker, it is easy to create long, elaborate documents that include both text and graphics. Aldus PageMaker includes Aldus Additions that automate certain tasks (such as creating *drop capitals*) but are difficult to create. Aldus PageMaker, available for both *Macintosh* and *IBM-compatible* computers, is not as customizable as QuarkXPress, but it is easier to learn.

alert box   In a *graphical user interface (GUI)*, a *dialog box* that appears on-screen to warn you that the *command* you've given may result in lost work or other errors, or that explains why an action can't be completed. Alert boxes remain on-screen until you take some action—usually clicking an OK button—to remove the box or cancel the operation.

algorithm   A mathematical or logical procedure for solving a problem. An algorithm is a recipe for finding the right answer to a difficult problem by breaking down the problem into simple steps. Algorithms also are used to improve the performance of your computer. Algorithms are used, for example, in *caches* to determine what *data*, if any, should be replaced by incoming data.

alias   A secondary or symbolic name for a *file,* a collection of *data,* or a computer device. In a *spreadsheet,* a *range* name, such as Income, is an alias for a range, such as A3..K3. In *networks,* group aliases provide a handy way to send *electronic mail* to two or more people simultaneously.

> **TIP:** *With the Macintosh System 7 software, you can create aliases for commonly accessed program and document icons. If you drag an alias to the Apple Menu Items folder within the System Folder, the alias appears on the Apple pull-down menu, allowing fast access to that item.*

aliasing   In *graphics,* the undesirable jagged or stair-stepped appearance of diagonal lines in computer-generated images. A *low-resolution monitor* causes aliasing. Bit-mapped characters, especially when they are enlarged, have aliasing. Synonymous with the jaggies. See *anti-aliasing.*

alignment   The placement of hard and floppy disk drives *read/write heads* over the disk *tracks* they must read and write. In *desktop publishing,* synonymous with justification.

> **CAUTION:** *Because a jolt can knock a disk drive's heads out of alignment, be careful not to drop or knock your computer around when moving it. A drive slightly out of alignment may have trouble reading floppy disks, especially those formatted by a different computer. If your machine can't read an important floppy disk, don't assume that the disk is bad. Try reading the disk on another computer.*

Aliweb   A search engine for locating *World Wide Web (WWW)* documents that is provided by NEXOR, a U.K.-based service provider. Aliweb does not use a *spider* (an automated document discovery program), instead, it relies on forms that Web authors themselves submit to the Aliweb database. Other *search engines,* such as *Lycos,* provide far more comprehensive coverage.

allocate   To reserve sufficient *memory* for a *program's* operation. In *Microsoft Windows 95,* use the *PIF* Editor to set a minimum, desired, and maximum amount of memory to ensure the best performance from DOS applications running in Windows. *Macintosh* users can use the *Finder* to see the suggested memory size and the current memory allocation for each program.

all points addressable (APA) graphic   See *bit-mapped graphic.*

AlterNet   A major national *backbone service provider* with head-quarters in Falls Church, Virginia, and a founding member of the *Commercial Internet Exchange (CIX)*.

alt hierarchy   In *UseNet,* one of several top-level classifications (hierarchies) of *newsgroups.* Alt (short for alternative) newsgroups can be created by anyone who knows the appropriate newsgroup origination commands, thus bypassing the voting procedures required to originate newsgroups in the *standard newsgroup* hierar-chies (such as *comp, soc,* and *talk*). However, UseNet administra-tors are not compelled to carry alt newsgroups, and they are not available at all UseNet sites. Although there are many worthwhile alt newsgroups, this category contains many frivolous groups (such as `alt.barney.dinosaur.die.die.die`) and the infamous `alt.sex.*` newsgroups, which have raised difficult issues regard-ing censorship.

Alt key   On *IBM PC-compatible keyboards,* a key used in combi-nation with other keys to select commands from the menu or as shortcut keys to execute commands. In *WordPerfect,* for example, pressing Alt+F2 begins a search-and-replace operation. See *Control (Ctrl) key* and *Shift key.*

alphanumeric characters   Characters available on a *key-board,* including upper- and lowercase letters A through Z, num-bers 0 through 9, punctuation marks, and special keyboard sym-bols. See *data type.*

alpha test   The first stage in the testing of computer products before they are released for public use. Alpha tests usually are conducted by the *hardware* manufacturer or *software* publisher. Later tests, called *beta tests,* are conducted by selected users.

ALU   See *arithmetic-logic unit (ALU).*

Am386   A *microprocessor* manufactured by *Advanced Micro Devices (AMD)* that is *binary compatible* and *pin compatible* with the *Intel 80386.* AMD sold more 386-class *chips* than any other manufacturer, including Intel.

Am486   A *microprocessor* manufactured by *Advanced Micro Devices (AMD)* that is *binary compatible* and *pin compatible* with the *Intel 80486.* See *Am486DX2* and *Am486DX4.*

Am486DX2   A *clock-doubled* version of the *Am486* that competes with the *Intel 486DX2*. The fastest Am486DX2 runs at 80 *megahertz (MHz)*.

Am486DX4   A *clock-tripled* version of the *Am486* that competes with the *Intel 486DX4*. The fastest Am486DX4 runs at 100 *megahertz (MHz)*.

AMD   See *Advanced Micro Devices (AMD)*.

AMD K5   A developmental microprocessor that *Advanced Micro Devices (AMD)* claims will be both *binary compatible* with and significantly faster than the *Pentium*. Unlike the Pentium, which can begin processing two instructions simultaneously, the K5 allegedly will be a *quad-issue microprocessor*, capable of initiating four instructions at one time. By employing *reduced instruction-set computer (RISC)* design and *a register renaming* scheme that allows 40 *registers,* AMD claims the K5 will exceed the Pentium's performance by 30 percent.

America Online (AOL)   The largest *online information service* (with 2.5 million subscribers), headquartered in Vienna, Virginia. Offering the usual mix of news, sports, *electronic mail,* computer support, *Internet* access, and fee-based services, AOL targets new computer users. *Macintosh* and *Windows 95* users can take advantage of the freely-distributed AOL *graphical user interface (GUI)* that enables the user to access AOL services using *point-and-click* techniques. AOL's major competitors include *CompuServe* and the *Microsoft Network*.

American National Standards Institute (ANSI)   A non-profit organization devoted to the development of voluntary standards designed to improve the productivity and international competitiveness of American industrial enterprises. ANSI committees have developed recommendations for computer languages such as *COBOL, C,* and *FORTRAN* and the DOS *device driver ANSI.SYS.* ANSI is the U.S. representative of the *International Standards Organization (ISO)*.

American Standard Code for Information Interchange   See *ASCII*.

Amiga   A computer system developed by Commodore International, based on the *Motorola 68000 microprocessor*. Though the Amiga is no longer manufactured, it has a rabid following among graphic artists and musicians, who laud its strong graphics and sound capabilities. The Amiga, with *aftermarket* Video Toaster hardware, is used extensively in television production. See *Musical Instrument Digital Interface (MIDI)*.

Ami Pro   See *Lotus Word Pro*.

ampersand   A character (&) sometimes used in place of the English word "and." The ampersand was originally a *ligature* of et, which is Latin for "and." The ampersand is used as an operator in *spreadsheet programs* to include text in a *formula*.

analog   A representation of the changing values of a property using an indicator that can vary continuously.

A speedometer is an analog device that shows changes in speed using a needle indicator that can move over an infinite range of speeds up to the maximum limit of the vehicle. Analog techniques also are used for the reproduction of music in standard LP records and audio cassettes. See *digital*.

analog computer   A computer used to measure conditions that change constantly, such as temperature, heartbeat, or atmospheric pressure. Analog computation is used widely in laboratory settings to monitor ongoing, continuous changes and to record these changes in *charts* or *graphs*. See *digital computer*.

analog device   A *peripheral* that handles information in continuously variable quantities rather than digitize the information into discrete, *digital* representations. An *analog monitor,* for example, can display millions of colors with smooth, continuous gradations.

analog modem   The most common kind of *modem* available today. Analog modems, unlike *digital modems,* are designed to communicate over *plain old telephone service (POTS)* lines.

analog monitor   A *monitor* that accepts a continuously *varied video signal* and consequently can display a continuous range and infinite number of colors. In contrast, a *digital monitor* can display only a finite number of colors. Most analog monitors are designed to accept input signals at a precise frequency; however, higher frequencies are required to carry higher-resolution images to the monitor. For this reason, *multiscanning monitors* have been developed that automatically adjust themselves to the incoming frequency. *Video Graphics Array (VGA)* monitors are analog monitors.

analog-to-digital converter   An adapter that allows a *digital computer* to accept *analog* input, such as that from laboratory instruments. Analog-to-digital converters are frequently used when monitoring temperature, movement, and other conditions that vary continuously. A *sound board* is an analog-to-digital converter.

analog transmission   A communications scheme that uses a continuous signal varied by amplification. See *broadband* and *digital transmission.*

analogical reasoning   A form of *analysis* in which the dynamics of something in the real world—such as the aerodynamics of a proposed airplane—are understood by building a model and exploring its behavior. One of the computer's greatest contributions has been to lower the cost (and increase the convenience) of analogical reasoning. See *model.*

analysis   A method of discovery in which a situation is broken down to its component parts, and the parts are studied to try to understand how they affect one another. In personal computing, a common form of analysis is sensitivity testing, or "what-if" analysis, using a *spreadsheet* program. In sensitivity testing, you alter the variables in a formula to see how changing each variable affects the outcome of the calculation.

analytical graphics   The preparation of *charts* and *graphs* to help in the understanding and interpretation of *data.* The graphs available with spreadsheet programs fall into this category since they're useful for clarifying trends in worksheet numbers, but *presentation graphics* packages still have the edge in creating stunning charts.

anchor   See *hyperlink.*

anchor cell   In *Lotus 1-2-3* and *Quattro Pro*, the *cell* in a *range* in which the *cell pointer* is located.

anchored graphic   A *graph* or picture fixed in an absolute position on the page rather than attached to specific text. See *floating graphic* and *wrap-around type.*

animation   Creating the illusion of movement in a *program* by saving a series of images that show slight changes in the position of the displayed objects, and then displaying these images back fast enough that the eye perceives smooth movement. See *cell animation.*

annotation   An explanatory note or comment inserted into a *document*.

With some *application programs*, you can insert an annotation as an *icon* that, when clicked by the person who reads the *document*, opens a separate *window* containing the note. Users of personal computers equipped with *sound boards* and *microphones* can add voice annotations to their documents.

TIP: *Microsoft Windows 95 users can use the Annotate command on the Help Options menu to add comments to Help topics. A paper clip to the left of the topic title indicates an annotation.*

 anonymity   In *UseNet*, the concealment of the identity of a person posting an article to a *newsgroup*. Anonymity cannot be assured by simply omitting one's signature or typing a phony name; the article's header information, constructed automatically by the UseNet software, shows where the message originated. Anonymity can be guaranteed only by sending the message through an *anonymous server* (such as the infamous anon.petit.fi)—and even then it cannot be absolutely guaranteed, because the anonymous server must keep a record of the e-mail address of each message that it receives (this is necessary for the server to handle replies to anonymous messages).

 anonymous FTP   In systems linked to the *Internet*, the use of a file-transfer program to contact a distant computer system to which you have no access rights, log on to its public *directories*, and transfer files from that computer to your own. When logging on to an anonymous FTP server, you should type anonymous as your name and your *electronic mail* address as your password. For help in finding files to access via anonymous FTP, you can use *archie*, *Gopher*, a *Wide Area Information Server (WAIS)*, or the *World Wide Web (WWW)*.

anonymous post   In *UseNet*, an article that has been posted through an *anonymous server* so that the identity of the person posting the article is impossible to determine.

 anonymous server   An *Internet*-connected computer that has been programmed to function as a relaying station for *anonymous*

UseNet posts. To post anonymously to *UseNet,* you send an electronic mail message to the anonymous server, which strips the message of any header data that might reveal its origin. The server then posts the message to a UseNet newsgroup. Anonymous servers are detested by some UseNet participants, who believe that *anonymity* encourages posters to break UseNet posting guidelines (called *netiquette*). Others believe that valid reasons exist for anonymous posts to groups such as **alt.whistleblowing**.

ANS CO+RE   An *Internet service provider* and *backbone* operator that formerly provided the *NFSnet* backbone subsidized by the U.S. *National Science Foundation (NSF).*

ANSI See *American National Standards Institute (ANSI).*

ANSI graphics   A set of *cursor*-control codes, developed by the *American National Standards Institute (ANSI),* that enables a *bulletin-board system (BBS)* to display *graphics* and colors on a remote computer's *monitor.* To use ANSI graphics, put the line DEVICE=ANSI.SYS in the computer's *CONFIG.SYS* file and set your communications program to emulate an ANSI terminal.

ANSI screen control   A set of standards developed by the *American National Standards Institute (ANSI)* to control the display of information on computer screens and enable *ANSI graphics.* See *ANSI.SYS.*

ANSI.SYS   Pronounced *an-see-sis.* In *MS-DOS,* a configuration file containing instructions needed to display *ANSI graphics* and to control *cursor* location, line wrapping, and the behavior of the *keyboard,* following the recommendations of the *American National Standards Institute (ANSI).* Some programs require that you include the instruction DEVICE=ANSI.SYS in the *CONFIG.SYS* file so the program displays properly.

answer mode   See *auto-dial/auto-answer modem.*

answer/originate   In *modems,* the capability of a communications device to receive (answer) and send (*originate*) messages.

antialiasing   The automatic removal or reduction of stair-step distortions *(aliasing)* in a computer-generated *graphic* image. This is accomplished by filling the jagged edges with gray or color to make the *aliasing* less noticeable. Unfortunately, the result is a fuzzy display, an effect some users find unpleasant or uncomfortable.

anti-glare   Any procedure or treatment used to reduce the reflection of outside light sources on a *monitor,* ranging from repositioning the monitor in relation to windows to coating the *display* with a light-damping chemical. Chemical anti-glare treatments can reduce the *brightness* of a display.

antistatic mat   A mat or pad placed on or near a computer device. The mat absorbs static electricity, which can damage *semiconductor* devices if the devices aren't properly grounded.

antivirus program   A utility designed to check for and remove computer *viruses* from *memory* and disks.

An antivirus program detects a virus by searching code recognized as that of one of the thousands of viruses known to afflict computer systems. An antivirus program also can be used to create a *checksum* for vulnerable files on your disk, save the checksums in a special file, and then use the checksums to determine whether files have been modified, perhaps by a new virus. Special *terminate and stay resident (TSR)* programs can check for unusual attempts to access vital disk areas and system files, and check files you copy into memory to be sure they aren't infected. See *Trojan horse,* *vaccine,* and *worm.*

APA graphic   See *bit-mapped graphic.*

aperture grille   The equivalent of a *shadow mask* in Sony *Trinitron monitors* and *monitors* of similar design. Aperture grilles use vertical wires to direct electron beams to *phosphors* of a particular color. *Slot pitch* and *screen pitch* are the Trinitron equivalent of *dot pitch,* so compare monitors on those specifications.

API   See *application program interface (API).*

APL (A Programming Language)   A *high-level programming language* well-suited for scientific and mathematical applications. APL uses Greek letters and requires a *display* device that can display these letters. Once used only on IBM *mainframes,* the language is now available for IBM PC-compatible computers.

append   To add *data* at the end of a *file* or a *database. In database management,* for example, to append a record is to add a new record after all existing records.

Apple Computer   A Cupertino, California-based company best-known for manufacturing the *Macintosh* line of computers. Unlike *International Business Machines (IBM)*, its main competitor, Apple kept the *architecture* of its computers *proprietary*—a move that many analysts say cost it market share in the business computing community. Regardless, Apple established a strong following among artists and musicians, for whose purposes Macintoshes are especially well-suited.

As *IBM PC-compatible* computers improved, though, Apple's market share eroded. Apple recently licensed a handful of other companies to make Macintosh *clones*, which may boost the companys market position.

Apple Desktop Bus (ADB)   An interface for connecting *keyboards, mice, trackballs,* and other input devices to *Macintosh* computers. These computers come with an ADB *serial port* capable of a maximum *data transfer rate* of 4.5 *kilobits* per second. You can connect up to 16 devices to one ADB port, with each additional device daisy-chained to the previous device. See *asynchronous communication.*

Apple Desktop Interface (ADI)   A set of *user-interface* guidelines, developed by *Apple Computer* and published by Addison-Wesley, intended to ensure that the appearance and operation of all *Macintosh* applications are similar.

Apple File Exchange   A *utility program* provided with each Macintosh computer that allows Macs equipped with suitable *floppy disk drives* to exchange *data* with IBM PC-compatible computers.

AppleShare   A *network operating system (NOS)* developed by *Apple Computer* for the *Macintosh* computer. To use the *local area network (LAN)*, each user installs the AppleShare *driver* and at least one computer is configured as the *server.* Users then choose a server and begin working. The Macintosh being used as the server can't be used for other applications; that computer becomes a "slave" of the network. See *AppleTalk, LocalTalk,* and *virtual device.*

AppleShare file server   In an *AppleTalk local area network (LAN),* a *Macintosh* computer running *AppleShare* file server *software* so that all *network* users can share the *programs* and *data* stored on the Macintosh.

applet   A small, often free, *application program* that performs a simple task. Calculator and Phone Dialer, which come with *Microsoft Windows 95,* are applets.

An applet can be designed to be accessible only from within a program, such as Microsoft Graph packaged with *Microsoft Word* and *Microsoft Excel.* The work that you create with this kind of applet becomes an *embedded object* within the document you are creating. See *object* and *object linking and embedding (OLE).*

AppleTalk   A *local area network (LAN)* standard developed by *Apple Computer.* AppleTalk can link as many as 32 *Macintosh* computers, *IBM PC-compatible* computers, and *peripherals* such as *laser printers.* Every Macintosh computer has an AppleTalk port through which you can quickly and easily connect the machine to an AppleTalk network. The only hardware required for an AppleTalk network is connectors and ordinary telephone wire for cables (called *twisted-pair* cable). AppleTalk networks are simple and inexpensive but quite slow—capable of transmitting only up to 230 *kilobits* per second compared to *EtherTalk,* which is capable of speeds of up to 10 million *bits per second (bps).*

application   The use of a computer for a specific purpose, such as writing a novel, printing payroll checks, or laying out the text and *graphics* of a newsletter. The term application also is frequently used instead of *application software* or *application program.*

application control menu   In *Microsoft Windows 95* and Windows applications, a *menu* displayed by selecting the control button on the far left of the *title bar.* You can use this menu with the *keyboard* to *minimize, maximize,* and restore the application window; to move and resize the application window; to switch to other active Windows applications; and to close the application in the window.

application development system   A coordinated set of program development tools, typically including a *full-screen editor;* a *programming language* with a *compiler, linker,* and *debugger;* and an extensive library of ready-to-use program modules. The use of an application development system lets experienced users develop a stand-alone application more easily than writing a program using a language such as *C++* or *COBOL.*

application heap   In a *Macintosh,* the area of memory set aside for user *programs.* Synonymous with *base memory.*

application icon   In *Microsoft Windows 95*, an on-screen graphic representation of a *minimized program*. The *icon* appears at the bottom of the desktop to remind you that the application is still present in memory (see fig. A.2). *Double-click* the application icon to switch to that program.

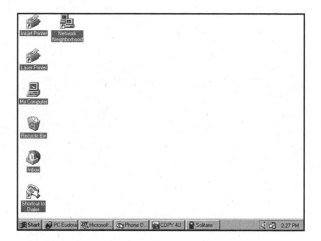

Fig. A.2   *Application icons of several minimized applications.*

application program   See *application software*.

application program interface (API)   System software that provides a complete set of functions and resources on which *programmers* can draw to create user interface features, such as *pull-down menus,* command names, *dialog boxes, keyboard* commands, and *windows*. In *network* systems, an API establishes how programs use various network features.

application shortcut key   In *Microsoft Windows 95,* a *shortcut key* you assign to launch or bring an application to the foreground. You assign the keyboard shortcut, such as Alt+Ctrl+W for Word for Windows, using the Properties command on the File *menu*. Application shortcut keys are also available in applications such as DESQview, *PerfectOffice,* and PC Tools Desktop to launch and switch among programs.

application software   *Programs* that perform specific tasks, such as *word processing* or *database management;* unlike *system* *software* that maintains and organizes the computer system and utilities that help you maintain and organize the system.

application window   In a *graphical user interface (GUI)*, an application's main *window*, containing a *title bar*, the application's *menu bar*, and a work area. The work area can contain one or more *document windows*.

Approach   See *Lotus Approach*.

A Programming Language   See *APL*.

Archie   An *Internet* tool for finding specific files that are available in publicly accessible *File Transfer Protocol (FTP)* archives. A major drawback of Archie is that you must know the precise spelling of some or all of the file names in order to retrieve the file. It's much easier to find software by using the *Virtual Software Library (VSL)*. See *anonymous FTP*.

Archie gateway   In the *World Wide Web (WWW)*, a Web page that provides an easy-to-use interface to the *Archie* search service.

architecture   The physical structure or design of a computer and its components, from its internal operating structure and specific *chips* to the *programs* that make it usable.

The term architecture is frequently used to describe the internal data-handling capacity of a *microprocessor*. The 8-bit architecture of the *Intel 8088* microprocessor, for example, is determined by the 8-bit *internal data bus* that transmits only one byte of data at a time.

archival backup   A *backup* procedure in which a *backup utility* backs up all files on the *hard disk* by copying them to *floppy disks, tape,* or some other backup medium. See *incremental backup*.

archive   A compressed *file* designed for space-efficient storage that contains one or more files.

Programs for compressing and decompressing IBM PC-compatible files are readily available as *shareware*. Look for the ARC program created by Systems Enhancement Associates and PKZIP by PKWare, Inc. The *file compression utility* of choice for *Macintosh* users is StuffIt, a shareware program created by Raymond Lau.

In the *Internet*, a file directory accessible by File Transfer Protocol (FTP) or a directory that has been set aside for public dissemination of stored files. See *anonymous FTP*.

archive attribute   In DOS, a hidden *code,* stored with a *file's* directory entry, that indicates whether the file has been changed since it was last copied using XCOPY or a *backup utility.*

DOS always sets the archive attribute to ON when you save a file. When you back up files using XCOPY or a backup utility, you can have the archive attribute turned off. If you later modify the file, DOS turns on the archive attribute when you save the file. The next time you back up files, you can tell the backup utility or XCOPY to back up only files that have changed, which is determined by checking the archive attribute.

 TIP: *When the archive attribute is off, you can't use XCOPY to copy a large directory of files to floppy disks without resetting the archive attribute. Use the ATTRIB command to turn the archive attribute back on.*

ARCnet   See *Attached Resource Computer Network (ARCnet).*

area graph   In *presentation graphics,* a *line graph* in which the area below the line is filled in to emphasize the change in volume from one time period to the next. The *x-axis* (categories axis) is the horizontal axis, and the *y-axis* (values axis) is the vertical axis.

When more than one data series are displayed, each series is shown in a distinctive cross-hatching pattern or shade of gray (as shown in fig. A.3). See *column graph.*

areal density   The tightness with which data can be packed onto a *hard disk* or *floppy disk.* Both the smoothness of the disk surface and the nature of the recording medium affect areal density, which is expressed in megabits per square inch (Mb/in^2). Areal densities of between 100 and 200 Mb/in^2 are typical for modern hard disks.

argument   Words, phrases, or numbers you enter on the same line as a *command* or a statement to expand or modify how that command or statement operates.

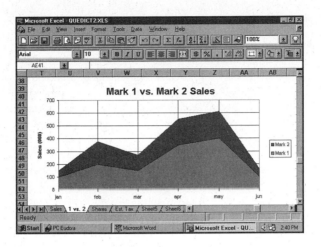

Fig. A.3 *An area graph.*

argument separator   In *spreadsheet* programs and *programming languages,* a comma or other punctuation mark that sets off one *argument* from another in a *command* or statement.

> **TIP:** *If you're having trouble getting a command or function to work, make sure that you know exactly how many arguments the command or function requires and that you've separated the arguments with the correct separator. Some programs don't allow spaces after the separator. If you're used to pressing the space bar after typing a comma, you may have to delete unnecessary spaces.*

arithmetic-logic unit (ALU)   The portion of the *central processing unit (CPU)* that makes all the decisions for the microprocessor, based on the mathematical computations and logic functions it performs.

arithmetic operator   A symbol that tells a *program* the arithmetic operation to perform, such as addition, subtraction, multiplication, and division.

In most computer programs, addition is represented by a plus sign (+), subtraction by a hyphen or minus sign (–), multiplication by an asterisk (*), division by a slash (/), and exponent by a caret (^). See *logical operator* and *relational operator*.

ARLL See *Advanced Run-Length Limited*.

ARPAnet A *wide area network (WAN)*, created in 1969 with funding from the Advanced Research Projects Agency (ARPA). Undergoing constant research and development in the early- to mid-1970s, ARPAnet served as the testbed for the development of *TCP/IP* (the protocols that make the *Internet* possible). A major goal of the ARPAnet project was to increase the military's command and control capability by enabling communication across a variety of physically dissimilar media, including satellites. An allied goal was to create a robust network capable of withstanding outages, such as those that might result from a nuclear exchange. ARPAnet met these objectives, but it also surprised its creators: It was found in short order that most ARPAnet users preferred to use the network for communication, such as *electronic mail* and discussion groups. Initially, the ARPAnet was available only to government research institutes and to universities holding Department of Defense (DoD) research contracts. In 1983, ARPAnet was divided into a high-security military network (Milnet) and an ARPAnet that was recast as a research and development network.

array In *programming*, a fundamental data structure consisting of a single- or multidimensional table that the program treats as one data item. Any information in the array can be referenced by naming the array and the location of the item in the array.

arrow keys See *cursor-movement keys*.

article In *UseNet*, a contribution that an individual has written and posted to one or more *newsgroups*. There are two kinds of articles: original articles on new subject, and *follow-up posts*. By means of *cross-posting*, an article can appear in more than one newsgroup.

article selector In *UseNet*, a *newsreader* feature in which the newsreader groups and displays the *articles* that are currently available for reading. The best newsreaders, called *threaded newsreaders*, automatically sort the articles in such a way that you can see the *thread* of discussion: an article is followed immediately by all its *follow-up articles*.

artificial intelligence (AI) A computer science field that tries to improve computers by endowing them with some of the characteristics associated with human intelligence, such as the capability to understand *natural language* and to reason under conditions of uncertainty. See *expert system*.

artificial life   A scientific research area devoted to the creation and study of computer simulations of living organisms.

Computer *viruses* have forced a renewal of the debate on the definition of life. Besides forcing us to re-examine our definition of life, artificial life research may create more effective technology. By applying artificial life concepts to real-life problems, we can program computer-generated solutions to compete for survival based on their capability to perform a desired task well.

ascender   In typography, the portion of the lowercase letters b, d, f, h, k, l, and t that rises above the height of the letter x. The height of the ascender varies in different *typefaces*. See *descender*.

ascending order   A *sort* in which items are arranged from smallest to largest (1, 2, 3) or from first to last (a, b, c). Ascending order is the default sort order for virtually all applications that perform sorting operations. See *descending sort*.

ASCII   (Pronounced *as-kee)* Acronym for American Standard Code for Information Interchange. See *ASCII character set* and *extended character set*.

ASCII art   Low-brow art in a high-tech medium, using only *the ASCII character set* (see fig. A.4). *Smileys*, sideways faces, such as a :-) happy face and :-(frowning face, provide emotional and social context for *electronic mail* messages, and provide yet another genre for ASCII art. See *smiley*.

```
        (__)                (__)                (__)
        (oo)                (@@)                (xx)
 /--------\/         /--------\/         /--------\/
/ |     ||         / |     ||         / |     ||
*  ||----||       *  ||----||       *  ||----||
   ^^    ^^          ^^    ^^          ^^    ^^
```

Fig. A.4   *Examples of ASCII art (cows).*

ASCII character set   A standard character set consisting of 96 upper- and lowercase letters, plus 32 non-printing *control characters,* each of which is numbered to achieve uniformity among different computer devices. Most modern computers use an *extended character set* containing accented, technical, and illustrative characters.

ASCII file   A *file* that contains only characters drawn from *the ASCII character set*. No special *formatting* (such as boldface or underlining) is in an ASCII file. See *binary file*.

ASCII sort order   A *sort order* determined by the sequence used to number the standard *ASCII character set*. Words or lines that begin with spaces or punctuation come first, followed by those beginning with numbers. Next sorted are words or lines that begin with uppercase letters, followed by those that begin with lowercase letters.

CAUTION: *Programs that sort data in ASCII sort order may violate publication guidelines; all capitalized words, for instance, come before words beginning with lowercase letters. Also, an ASCII sort doesn't alphabetize foreign language characters properly. See* dictionary sort.

ASCII transfer   A *file transfer protocol* that employs *no error-correction protocol* or *flow control*. ASCII transfers are inferior to protocols like *XMODEM,* but they are the only type of transfer some older computers, particularly *mainframes,* support.

A-sized paper   What Americans often call letter-sized paper. The *American National Standards Institute (ANSI)* defines A-sized paper as a page 8.5 by 11 inches (210 by 297 millimeters).

ASM   See *Association for Systems Management (ASM)*.

.ASM   The *MS-DOS file name extension* usually attached to a *file* containing *assembly language source code*.

aspect ratio   In *graphics,* the ratio of the width of an image to its height. When changing the size of a graphic, maintaining the width-to-height ratio is important to avoid distortions.

ASPI   See *Advanced SCSI Programming Interface (ASPI)*.

assembler   A *program* that transforms an *assembly language* program into *machine language* so the computer can execute the program.

assembly language   A *low-level programming language* in which each *program* statement corresponds to an instruction that the *microprocessor* can carry out.

Assembly languages are *procedural languages.* They tell the computer what to do in precise detail, requiring as many as two dozen lines of code to add two numbers. Assembly language programs are difficult and tedious to write. On the other hand, assembly language code is compact, operates quickly, and, when assembled, is more efficient than a compiled program written in a *high-level language.* See *BASIC, C, compiler,* and *Pascal.*

assign   To give a *value* to a named *variable.*

assignment statement   In *programming,* a program statement that places a *value* into a *variable.* In *BASIC,* for example, the statement LET A=10 places the value 10 into the variable A.

associated document   A *file* linked at the system level with the *application* that created it. You can start an application by choosing one of its associated documents.

Association for Computer Machinery (ACM)   The oldest professional society for computer experts. ACM was founded in 1948 and sponsors conferences, journals, book publishing, and student groups at colleges and universities. The ACM is known for its annual Computer Science Conference.

Association for Systems Management (ASM)   A professional society for *systems analysts* and other computer professionals. The ASM has chapters in most cities and offers many short courses in systems analysis and other information-systems topics. The ASM was formerly known as the Systems and Procedures Association (SPA).

asterisk   In DOS, the *wild-card* symbol (*) that stands for one or more characters; unlike the *question mark* (?) wild card, which stands for only one character. An asterisk is also the arithmetic symbol for multiplication. See *arithmetic operator.*

astonisher   See *ball bat.*

Asymetrix ToolBook   An *application development system* and *hypertext* authoring tool for *Microsoft Windows 95* that lets non-*programmers* develop Windows *applications* quickly. Asymetrix Corporation publishes the program, which resembles the *HyperCard* application in the *Macintosh* environment.

asynchronous communication   A method of *data commu-nication* in which the transmission of bits of data isn't synchro-nized by a clock signal, but is accomplished by sending the bits one after another, with a *start bit* and a *stop bit* to mark the begin-ning and end, respectively, of each data unit. Telephone lines can be used for asynchronous communication. See *baud rate, modem, synchronous communication, and Universal Asynchronous Receiver/ Transmitter (UART)*.

asynchronous digital subscriber loop (ADSL)   A *data communication* method that can deliver through existing tele-phone lines a single, compressed, high-quality, video signal at a rate of 1.5*M* per second in addition to an ordinary telephone conversation.

ADSL may provide the key to *a National Information Infrastruc-ture (NII),* in which high-*bandwidth* intercommunity services connect to low-bandwidth *copper pair* wiring for service delivery to the home.

ATA-2   See *Enhanced IDE.*

ATA-3   An experimental standard for attaching many different recording media—such as *disk drives* and *tape drives*—to a PC. ATA-3, when it is released in late 1995 or early 1996, should have much better *throughput* than *Enhanced IDE* and will likely re-place it.

ATAPI   See *Advanced Technology Attachment Packet Interface.*

ATA packet interface (ATAPI)   See *Advance Technology Attachment Packet Interface..*

AT Attachment (ATA)   See *Integrated Drive Electronics (IDE).*

AT bus   The 16-*bit expansion bus* used in the IBM Personal Computer AT, as distinguished from the 8-bit bus of the original IBM Personal Computer and the 32-bit bus of computers using the *Intel 80386* and *486 microprocessors.* Most 80386 and 486 machines contain AT-compatible *expansion slots* for *backward compatibility.* See *local bus, and Micro Channel Bus.*

AT command set   See *Hayes command set.*

AT keyboard   An 84-key *keyboard* introduced with the IBM Personal Computer AT in response to complaints about the original IBM Personal Computer keyboard, which used a layout different from that of office typewriters. The AT keyboard is considered a minimal standard today; most IBM and IBM-compatible computers come equipped with a 101-key *enhanced keyboard*. See *keyboard layout*.

AT-size case   A type of *desktop* (that is, flat-lying) case that matches the design of the case IBM used for its Personal Computer AT in 1984. AT-size cases, with their horizontally mounted *motherboards*, provide lots of room for *adapters* and other components, but as a result have very large *footprints*. See *mini-AT-size case*, *mini-tower case*, and *tower case*.

attached document   In *electronic mail (e-mail)*, a *binary file* (such as a program or a compressed word processing document) that has been attached to an e-mail message. The contents of the file do not appear within the e-mail message itself. Instead, on the *Internet*, they are encoded following the specifications of the *Multipurpose Internet Multimedia Extensions (MIME)*. To include an attached document with an e-mail message, both the sender and receiver must have e-mail programs, such as *Eudora*, that are capable of working with MIME.

Attached Resource Computer Network (ARCnet)   A popular *local area network (LAN)* originally developed by Datapoint Corporation for *IBM PC-compatible* computers and now available from several vendors. ARCnet interface cards are inexpensive and easily installed. ARCnet networks use a *star topology*, a *token-passing protocol*, and *coaxial* or *twisted-pair cable*. The network can transmit data at speeds of 2.5 *M* per second. See *network interface card* and *network topology*.

attenuation   In *local area networks (LANs)*, the loss of signal strength when cables exceed the maximum length stated in the network's specifications. Attenuation prevents successful data communications. You can use a device called a *repeater* to extend a network's cable range.

attribute   In many *word processing* and *graphics programs*, a character emphasis, such as *boldface* and *italic*, and other characteristics, such as *typeface* and *type size*.

In *MS-DOS* and *Microsoft Windows 95*, information about a file that indicates whether the file is a *read-only* file, a *hidden file*, or a *system file*. See *archive attribute* and *file attribute*.

AU   An 8-bit *monaural sound file format* that is widely used on *UNIX workstations,* including Sun and NeXT machines for storing digitized *wave sounds.* The format employs an advanced storage technique that enables 14-bit sounds to be stored in only 8 bits of data, with minimal loss.

audible feedback   The capacity of a *keyboard* to generate sounds each time a key is pressed. Audible feedback makes it easier for some people to determine when a key has been depressed sufficiently for a character to be generated on-screen. See *tactile feedback.*

 audio helper   A *program* that is designed to play sounds that have been found and downloaded while browsing the *World Wide Web (WWW).* To use an audio helper, you must configure your Web browser to start the helper program once the downloading has been completed. The audio helper then appears on-screen, and plays the sound file.

audio monitor   Any speaker, but especially a speaker mounted on a *modem* that lets you hear what is happening on the telephone line. They let you hear a busy signal, or the hissing sound of two modems establishing a *carrier.*

audit trail   In an *accounting program,* any program feature that automatically keeps a record of transactions so that you can backtrack to find the origin of specific figures that appear on reports.

 AUP   See *Acceptable Use Policy.*

(AUP) authentication   In a *network,* the process by which the system attempts to ensure that the person logging on is the same person to whom the *account* was issued. The sole means of authentication in most networks is the demand for a *password.*

AUP-free   Not limited to non-commercial activity by an acceptable use policy (AUP). Publicly funded *networks,* such as the *NSFNet,* are intended for research and educational uses, and commercial use is discouraged or forbidden. To promote commercial use of the *Internet,* service providers have created a national *backbone* that is AUP-free.

TIP: *If you're using a networked computer in a public facility, such as a computer lab at a college or university, be sure to log off the network before leaving the computer. Somebody else might sit down at the computer, discover it's still logged on, and send threatening or harrassing messages—and the police will come hunting for you!*

authoring   In *multimedia*, the process of preparing a presentation. This involves not only writing the text, but also preparing the sound, graphic, and video components.

authoring language   A *computer-assisted instruction (CAI) application* that provides tools for creating instructional or presentation *software*. A popular authoring language for *Macintosh* computers is *HyperCard*, provided free with every Macintosh computer. Using HyperCard, educators can develop instructional programs quickly and easily.

auto-answer mode   See *auto-dial/auto-answer mode.*

AutoCAD   A *computer-aided design (CAD)* program developed by AutoDesk and widely used for professional CAD applications.

auto-dial/auto-answer modem   A *modem* that can generate tones to dial the receiving computer and can answer a ringing telephone to establish a connection when a call is received.

auto-dial mode   See *auto-dial/auto-answer mode.*

AUTOEXEC.BAT   In *MS-DOS*, a *batch file* containing instructions that DOS executes when you start the system. AUTOEXEC.BAT files commonly include *PATH* statements that tell DOS where to find *application programs* and the commands to install a *mouse* or operate your *printer*. All this information must be provided at the start of every operating session; AUTOEXEC.BAT does the task for you. See *CONFIG.SYS, path, and path statement.*

auto-logon   A feature of *communications programs* that lets you automate the process of logging on to a *bulletin board system (BBS)* or *on-line service*. Think twice about including your *password* in an auto-logon *script*, though—such a script enables anyone with access to your computer to log on in your name.

TIP: *Although you may need to add commands to AUTOEXEC.BAT yourself, most programs come with an installation program that adds any needed commands, even creating the file, if necessary. Because these changes can be difficult to reconstruct, be careful to leave AUTOEXEC.BAT undisturbed and to keep a copy of the file in a safe place. Should you accidentally erase the file, you can copy it into the root directory of your hard disk.*

automatic backup An *application program* feature that saves a *document* automatically at a period the user specifies, such as every 5 or 10 minutes. After a power outage or *system crash,* you can retrieve the last automatic backup file when you restart the application. This feature can help you avoid catastrophic work losses.

CAUTION: *The automatic backup feature isn't a substitute for regularly saving your work.*

automatic emulation switching In *printers,* the ability to *change printer control languages* without human intervention. Printers with automatic emulation switching sense the language, such as *PostScript* or *PCL5,* used by incoming documents and adjust automatically.

automatic font downloading The transfer of *downloadable fonts* from the *hard disk* to the *printer* by a *utility program* as the *fonts* are needed to complete a printing job.

automatic head parking A *hard disk* feature that moves the *read/write head* over the *landing zone*—preventing a *head crash*—whenever power is shut off. To move the head of older hard disks over the landing zone, you must issue a special command.

automatic hyphenation See *hyphenation.*

automatic mode switching In *video adapters,* the automatic detection and adjustment of a video adapter's internal circuitry to the video output of a *program* on an IBM PC-compatible computer. Most *Video Graphics Array (VGA)* adapters, for example, switch to adjust to *Color Graphics Array (CGA), Monochrome Display Adapter (MDA), Extended Graphics Array (EGA),* or VGA output from applications.

automatic network switching   A feature of *departmental laser printers* and *workgroup printers* that allows them to serve several different kinds of computers and several different kinds of *networks*. A printer equipped with automatic network switching can receive data from *Ethernet, AppleTalk,* or *TCP/IP* networks and print it without human attention. See *automatic emulation switching.*

automatic recalculation   In a *spreadsheet,* a mode in which *cell* values are recalculated every time any cell changes in the worksheet. Automatic recalculation can be switched to *manual calculation* while you're entering data into a large spreadsheet if recalculation takes a long time. See *background recalculation.*

automatic speed sensing   A *modem* feature that lets the modem automatically determine the maximum speed at which a connection can be made. Performed during the *handshaking* period at the beginning of a call, modems with automatic speed sensing will *fall back* to the fastest speed the two connected modems, and line conditions, can support.

automation   The replacement of human skill by automatic machine operations. *Word processing software* is an example of the potential of automation. These programs automate tasks as simple as centering text and as complex as sorting a mailing list into ZIP code order.

AutoPlay   A *Microsoft*-initiated standard for *CD-ROM*s. When an AutoPlay disk is inserted into a CD-ROM drive, *Microsoft Windows 95* will detect that the disk is an AutoPlay disk. A program will start automatically.

autorepeat key   A *key* that repeatedly enters a character as long as you hold it down.

autosave   See *timed backup.*

autosizing   A *monitor* feature that allows a monitor to size an image to fit the *display,* regardless of its *resolution.* Autosizing monitors maintain the *aspect ratio* of an image, but enlarge or reduce it to fit in the space available.

autostart routine   A set of *instructions* contained in *read-only memory (ROM)* that tells the computer how to proceed when you switch on the power. See *basic input/output system (BIOS)* and *power-on self-test (POST).*

A
B

autotrace   In a *graphics* program, such as Adobe Illustrator, a *command* that transforms an imported *bit-mapped graphic* into an *object-oriented graphic*. Object-oriented graphics print at the printer's maximum resolution (up to 300 dots per inch for *laser printers*). Using the autotrace tool, you can transform low-resolution graphics into art that prints at a higher *resolution*.

AUX   In *MS-DOS,* an abbreviation for the auxiliary *port*, the communications (*COM*) port DOS uses by default (usually COM1).

A/UX   *Apple Computer's* version of the *UNIX operating system.* To use A/UX, you need a Macintosh with a *Motorola 68020* or *68030 microprocessor* and 4 *M* of *random-access memory (RAM).*

auxiliary battery   In a *portable computer,* a small, built-in battery that can power the computer for a few minutes while you insert a freshly charged *battery pack.*

auxiliary speakers   Two or more stereo speakers that connect to the *sound board* and allow you to hear its output. Auxiliary speakers replace a computer's *on-board speaker* and are usually magnetically shielded to prevent interference with the monitor.

auxiliary storage   See *secondary storage.*

average access time   See *access time.*

average seek time   See *seek time.*

axis   See *x-axis, y-axis,* and *z-axis.*

backbone In a *wide area network (WAN)* such as the *Internet*, a high-speed, high-capacity medium that is designed to transfer data over hundreds or thousands of miles. A variety of physical media are used for backbone services, including microwave relay, satellites, and dedicated telephone lines.

backdoor An undocumented way to gain access to a *program*, some *data*, or an entire *computer system*, often known only to the *programmer* who created it. Backdoors can be handy when the standard way of getting at information is unavailable, but usually they constitute a *security* risk.

back end The portion of a *program* that accomplishes the processing tasks that the program is designed to perform. In a *local area network (LAN)* with *client/server architecture*, the back-end application may be stored on the *file server* while *front-end* programs handle the *user interface* on each workstation.

background In computers that can do more than one task at a time, the environment in which tasks (such as printing a *document* or *downloading* a *file*) are carried out while the user works with an *application* in the *foreground*.

In computers that lack *multitasking* capabilities, background tasks are carried out during brief pauses in the execution of the system's primary (foreground) tasks.

background communication *Data communication,* such as *downloading* a file from an *online information service,* that takes place in the *background* while the user concentrates on another application in the *foreground*. See *multitasking*.

background noise See *noise*.

background pagination See *pagination*.

background printing The printing of a *document* in the *background* while a *program* is active in the *foreground*. Background printing is particularly useful if you frequently print long documents or use a slow printer. With background printing, you can continue to work while the document prints. See *multitasking, print queue,* and *print spooler.*

background recalculation   In *spreadsheet programs,* such as *Quattro Pro,* an option that causes the program to perform recalculations in the *background* while you continue to work in the spreadsheet.

background tasks   In a *multitasking operating system,* the operations occurring in the *background* (such as printing, sorting a large collection of *data,* or searching a *database*) while you work in another *program* in the *foreground.*

backlighting   A *display* design that involves shining light at a *liquid crystal display (LCD)* from behind, increasing the contrast between light and dark *pixels.* Though backlighting increases power consumption, it makes LCDs much more readable in bright-light conditions, such as those outdoors.

backlit display   A *display* design that incorporates *backlighting.*

backplane   A *motherboard.* Originally, the term described a main *circuit board* mounted vertically at the rear of the *case.*

backspace   A *key* used to delete the character to the left of the *cursor's* position, or the act of moving one space to the left by using the backspace or *cursor-movement keys.*

backup   A copy of installed *application software* or of *data files* you've created. Also, the act of copying files to another *disk.* Regular *backup procedures* are required for successful use of a *hard disk* system. See *archival backup, full backup,* and *incremental backup.*

TIP: *Make copies of all software installation disks whenever you buy new software. Use the copies to install the program and keep the originals in a safe location away from your computer.*

backup procedure   A regular maintenance procedure that copies all new or altered *files* to a *backup storage medium,* such as *floppy disks* or a *tape drive.*

Whether you use your computer for home or business purposes, you should back up your *hard disk* on a regular basis—at least weekly. If you don't, you expose yourself to the possibility of professional embarrassment, lost customers and profits, and lost time while you re-create *documents.* See *backup utility.*

backup utility   A *utility program* designed to back up program and data files from a *hard disk* to a backup medium such as *floppy disks* or a *tape drive.*

Backup utility programs include *commands* to schedule regular *backups,* to back up only selected directories or files, and to restore all or only a few files from a backup set.

TIP: *Rather than use floppy disks for backups, consider buying a more convenient* quarter-inch cartridge (QIC) *or* digital audio tape (DAT) tape drive. *Tape drives with a 250 M capacity are available for less than $200. See* archival backup, backup procedure, incremental backup, quarter-inch cartridge (QIC), *and* save.

Backus-Naur form (BNF)   A set of rules for describing the organization of a *program* without actually writing instructions in any particular *programming language.* BNF is useful for teaching programming concepts and for comparing procedures written in different languages.

backward chaining   In *expert systems,* a commonly used method of drawing inferences from IF/THEN rules. A backward chaining system starts with a question such as "How much is this property worth?" and searches through the system's rules to determine which ones allow the system to solve the problem and what additional data you must provide. A backward-chaining expert system asks questions of the user, engaging him or her in a dialogue. See *forward chaining* and *knowledge base.*

backward compatible   Compatible with earlier versions of a *program* or earlier models of a computer. *Microsoft Windows 95,* for example, is backward compatible with *application programs* designed to run on Windows 3.1, but won't run on IBM PCs and PC compatibles equipped with the *Intel 8088 microprocessor,* even though millions of those machines exist.

backward search   In a *database, spreadsheet,* or *word processor document,* a search that begins at the *cursor's* location and proceeds backward toward the beginning of a database or *document* (rather than searching forward to the end).

bad break   An improperly *hyphenated* line break.

bad page break   In a *document* or *spreadsheet,* a *soft page break* that divides text at an inappropriate location. Headings can be left dangling at the bottom of pages (*widows*); *data tables* can be split; and a single line of text (*orphans*) can be left at the top of a page. A common flaw in documents produced on computers, bad page breaks can be caught by a final, careful review of the document using the program's print preview command or with widow/orphan protection features in some software. See *block protection.*

bad sector   An area of a *floppy* or *hard disk* that won't reliably record *data.* Almost all hard disks have some bad sectors as a result of manufacturing defects. The *operating system* locks these *sectors* out of reading and writing operations so you can use the disk as though the bad sectors don't exist. See *bad track table.*

bad track   A *hard disk* or *floppy disk track* that contains a *bad sector.* Marked as unusable in the *file allocation table (FAT),* bad tracks are harmless—unless Track 0 is bad, in which case the disk must be replaced.

bad track table   A document attached to or packaged with a *hard disk* that lists the *bad sectors* of the disk. Almost every hard disk comes off the assembly line with some defects. During the *low-level format,* these defective areas of the disk are locked out so system software can't use them.

.BAK   The *MS-DOS file name extension* usually attached to a *file* containing *backup* data. Many *application programs* assign the .BAK extension to the old version of a file any time you change the file's name.

ball bat   In *UNIX,* a common slang term for an exclamation point (!). Also called a bang character or an *astonisher.* See *bang path.*

band   In a *database management* program's *report* function, an area set aside for a certain type of information, such as a header area or *data* from *fields.* Also, the track on which a *band-stepper actuator* travels.

band-stepper actuator   A mechanism, incorporating a *stepping motor* and a track (a band), that positions the *read/write head* of a *hard disk* over a *track.* Band-stepper actuators are not as common as *servo-voice coil actuators* on today's hard disks.

bandwidth A frequency measurement, expressed in cycles per second (*hertz*) or *bits per second (bps)*, of the amount of information that can flow through a channel. The higher the frequency, the higher the bandwidth.

bang See *ball bat.*

bang character See *ball bat.*

bang path In *UNIX-to-UNIX Copy Protocol (UUCP)*, an *electronic mail* address that specifies the location of a specific computer on a UUCP-based *network*. The address is called a bang path because the various units of the address are separated by exclamation points (bang characters, or *ball bats*).

bank switching A way of expanding memory beyond an *operating system's* or *microprocessor's* address limitations by switching rapidly between two banks of memory. See *expanded memory (EMS).*

bar code A printed pattern of wide and narrow vertical bars used to represent numerical codes in machine-readable form. Computers equipped with *bar-code readers* and special software can interpret bar codes.

Supermarkets use bar codes conforming to the Universal Product Code (UPS) to identify products and ring up prices, while the U.S. Postal Service uses POSTNET bar codes to make ZIP codes machine-readable. The latest versions of word processing programs such as *WordPerfect* and *Microsoft Word* include options to print POSTNET bar codes on envelopes.

bar code reader An input device that scans *bar codes* and, with special *software*, converts the bar code into a number on-screen.

bar graph In *presentation graphics,* a *graph* with horizontal bars commonly used to show the values of unrelated items (see fig. B.1). The *x-axis* (categories axis) is the vertical axis, and the *y-axis* (values axis) is the horizontal axis. Though often confused with a *column graph,* which uses vertical bars, a bar graph is best for conveying quantities while a column graph is best for conveying changes over time. See *line graph* and *paired bar graph.*

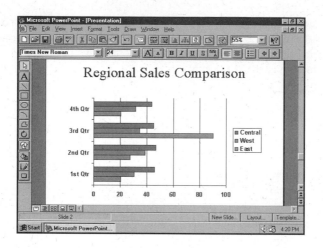

Fig. B.1 *A bar graph.*

.BAS The *MS-DOS file name extension* usually attached to a *file* containing *BASIC source code.*

baseband In *local area networks (LANs),* a communications method in which the information-bearing signal is placed directly on the cable in *digital* form without *modulation.*

Because many baseband networks can use *twisted-pair* (ordinary telephone) cables, they're cheaper to install than broadband networks that require *coaxial* cable. However, a baseband system is limited in its geographic extent and provides only one channel of communication at a time. Most personal computer local area networks are baseband networks. See *broadband.*

base font The *font* that's used in a document. Changes such as *italics* or *bold* and larger or smaller sizes are variations of the base font. You can change to a different *typeface* at any point in the document, but if you change the base font while working in a document, the font change is applied for the entire document. In most *word processing* programs, you can choose a default base font for all documents or for just the document you're editing.

base-level synthesizer In *multimedia,* the minimum capabilities of a music synthesizer required by *Microsoft Windows 95* and its *Multimedia Personal Computer (MPC)* specifications. A base-level synthesizer must be capable of playing at least six simultaneous notes on three melodic instruments, and three simultaneous notes on three percussion instruments. See *extended-level synthesizer* and *Musical Instrument Digital Interface (MIDI)*.

baseline   In *typography*, the lowest point that characters reach (excluding *descenders*). For example, the baseline of a line of text is the bottom of letters such as a and x, excluding the lowest points of p and q, which have descenders.

base memory   See *conventional memory*.

BASIC   An easy-to-use (but widely criticized) *high-level programming language* available on personal computers. Developed in 1964, BASIC (Beginner's All-Purpose Symbolic Instruction Code) is a *procedural language* that tells the computer what to do step by step.

BASIC is easy to learn, but programs written in it execute slowly, making the language a poor choice for professional applications. *C* is far more popular for professional program development.

New programming techniques are giving BASIC a new lease on life. For example, Microsoft's *Visual BASIC,* designed for *Microsoft Windows 95* programming, uses the Windows *graphical user interface (GUI)* and *event-oriented programming* to create impressive applications. See *BASICA, compiler, control structure, debugger, interpreter, Pascal, QuickBASIC, spaghetti code,* and *structured programming*.

BASICA   An *interpreter* for the Microsoft *BASIC programming language.* BASICA is supplied on the *MS-DOS* disk provided with IBM-maufactured personal computers. See *GW-BASIC.*

basic input/output system (BIOS)   A set of *programs* encoded in *read-only memory (ROM)* on IBM PC-compatible computers. These programs handle startup operations such as the *power-on self-test (POST)* and low-level control for hardware such as *disk drives, keyboard,* and *monitor.*

The BIOS programs of IBM personal computers are copyrighted, so manufacturers of IBM PC-compatible computers must create BIOSs that emulate the IBM BIOS or buy an emulation from companies such as Phoenix Technologies and American Megatrends, Inc. Some system components have a separate BIOS. The BIOS on a *hard disk controller,* for example, stores a table of *tracks* and *sectors* on the drive.

Basic Rate ISDN   In the *Integrated Services Digital Network (ISDN)* specification, the basic digital telephone and data service that is designed for residences. Basic Rate ISDN offers two 64,000 *bit per second (bps)* channels for voice, graphics, and data, plus one 16,000 bit per second channel for signalling purposes.

.BAT   The *MS-DOS file name extension* attached to a *batch file.* See *AUTOEXEC.BAT.*

batch file   A *file* containing a series of MS-DOS *commands* executed one after the other, as though you had typed them. The mandatory .BAT file extension causes *COMMAND.COM* to process the file one line at a time. Batch files are useful when you need to type the same series of MS-DOS commands repeatedly. Almost all *hard disk* users have an *AUTOEXEC.BAT* file, a batch file that MS-DOS loads at the start of every operating session.

The following example shows how a simple batch file can help you back up your precious data files to floppy disks using the XCOPY command. Add the /M *parameter* to copy only changed files and to mark each file when it's copied, /S to copy the contents of any *subdirectories,* and /V to verify that each copy matches the original file. Name the file BACKUPS.BAT and run it daily or weekly.

```
ECHO OFF
ECHO Insert a blank disk in drive A: Press Enter when
 ready.
PAUSE
MKDIR A:\wp
MKDIR A:\123
XCOPY C:\WP60\WPDOCS A:\WP /S/M/V
XCOPY C:\123R24\FILES A:\123 /S/M/V
```

If you get a disk full message, insert a blank disk and run BACKUPS.BAT again. Continue until all files have been copied.

batch processing   A *mode* of computer operation in which *program instructions* are executed one after the other without user intervention.

Batch processing efficiently uses computer resources but isn't convenient—especially if you discover a *programming* or data input error while the computer is spewing out reams of useless printout. In *interactive processing,* you see the results of your commands on-screen so that you can correct errors and make necessary adjustments before completing the operation. Reserve batch processing for well-tested routines such as system *backups.*

battery pack   A rechargeable battery that supplies power to a computer, usually a *portable computer,* when external (main) power isn't available. Most battery packs use nickel-cadmium (NiCad) batteries, which have two significant drawbacks: they're prone to becoming incapable of accepting a full charge, and, because of their cadmium content, are extremely toxic. Increasing in use are nickel metal hydride (NiMH) and lithium-ion battery packs, which provide increased capacity without either drawback. See *auxiliary battery.*

baud   A variation or change in a signal in a communications channel. See *baud rate* and *bits per second (bps).*

baud rate   The maximum number of changes that can occur per second in the electrical state of a communications circuit.

Under *RS-232C communications protocols,* 300 *baud* is likely to equal 300 *bits per second (bps),* but at higher baud rates, the number of bits per second transmitted is usually twice the baud rate because two bits of data can be sent with each change. Therefore, the transfer rate of modems, for example, is usually stated in bps. See *asynchronous communication, modem, serial port, serial printer,* and *telecommunications.*

bay   See *drive bay.*

BBS   See *bulletin board system (BBS).*

BCD   See *binary coded decimal (BCD).*

bed   In *multimedia,* the instrumental or choral music that provides the enveloping background for a presentation.

Bell 103A   In the United States, a *modulation protocol* for computer *modems* governing sending and receiving data at a speed of 300 *bits per second (bps).* See *ITU-TSS protocol.*

Bell 212A   In the United States, a *modulation protocol* for computer *modems* governing sending and receiving data at a speed of 1200 *bits per second (bps).* See *ITU-TSS protocol.*

bells and whistles   An *application program's* or *computer system's* advanced—or superfluous, depending on your interpretation—*features*. Many people say that bells and whistles, such as *mail-merging* capabilities in a *word processing* program, aren't desirable for novices, and they recommend programs that lack such features. This notion not only requires that you buy additional software as your skills improve, it actually discourages learning by eliminating the opportunity to explore more complex features. If advanced features don't clutter the user interface, you should buy full-featured software you can grow into. A feature that seems hopelessly advanced right now may turn out to be vital.

benchmark   A standard measurement, determined by a *benchmark program*, that is used to test the performance of different brands of equipment.

benchmark program   A *utility program* used to measure a computer's processing speed so that its performance can be compared to that of other computers running the same program.

A variety of standard benchmark tests are available. You should look for results of tests that are applicable to the way you work. Tests such as Dhrystone and Whetstone, for example, test the *central processing unit (CPU)* thoroughly but don't test the performance of system components such as *disk drives* and internal communications. The speed of components and application programs also affect performance. Look for benchmark tests such as *Winstone* and SPECmark, or try using those included with *Norton Utilities* or PC Tools. See *cache memory* and *throughput.*

Berkeley Software Distribution (BSD)   A version of the *UNIX operating system* that was developed and formerly maintained by the University of California, Berkeley. BSD helped to establish the *Internet* in colleges and universities because the distributed software included *TCP/IP.*

Berkeley UNIX   A version of the *UNIX operating system*, developed at the University of California at Berkeley, that takes full advantage of the *virtual memory* capabilities of Digital Equipment Corporation (DEC) *minicomputers.*

Bernoulli box   An innovative removable *secondary storage* device developed by Iomega Corporation for IBM PC-compatible and Macintosh computers. Bernoulli boxes have removable cartridges containing flexible disks that can hold up to 44*M* of *data*. Bernoulli boxes are extremely resistant to *head crashes*, but *removable hard disks* have stolen some market share from Iomegas one-time flagship product.

beta site   The company, university department, or individual authorized to *beta test* software. When developing a program or a version of an existing program, a company chooses out-of-house beta sites where the program is subjected to demanding, heavy-duty usage. This process reveals the program's remaining *bugs* and shortcomings.

beta software   In *software* testing, a preliminary version of a *program* that's widely distributed before commercial release to users who test the program by operating it under realistic conditions. See *alpha test, beta site,* and *beta test.*

beta test   The second stage in the testing of computer software, after *alpha test* but before commercial release. Beta tests are at *beta sites*. Also used as a verb, as in, the software is ready to be beta-tested.

Bézier curve   (Pronounced *beh-zee-ay*)   A mathematically generated line that can take the form of non-uniform curves. In a Bézier curve, the locations of two midpoints—called control *handles*—are used to describe the overall shape of an irregular curve. In *graphics* applications, by dragging the control handles (shown as small boxes on-screen), you manipulate the complexity and shape of the curve.

bibliographic retrieval service   An *on-line information service* that specializes in maintaining huge computerized indexes to scholarly, scientific, medical, and technical literature.

The two leading information firms are BRS Information Technologies (Latham, NY) and DIALOG Information Services (Menlo Park, CA). Serving mainly corporate and institutional customers, these companies' fees average more than $1 per minute. Personal computer users can access, at substantially lower rates, special menu-driven night and weekend versions of these services, BRS/After Dark and Knowledge Index.

TIP: *Before signing on, find out whether your local library makes databases available on CD-ROMs. If so, you can search these databases for free. Because no clock is ticking away, you can make full use of these resources interactive searching potential.*

bidirectional communication A quality of new *parallel port* designs that enables a computer and a peripheral device to exchange messages through a parallel cable. Both the *enhanced parallel port (EPP)* and the *extended capabilities port (ECP)* offer bidirectional communication.

bidirectional parallel port A *parallel port,* capable of both sending and receiving detailed messages, that can transfer data much faster than a standard parallel port. In its standard *IEEE 1284,* the Institute of Electrical and Electronics Engineers (IEEE) established the technical rules governing bidirectional parallel ports. Both the *enhanced parallel port (EPP)* and the *extended capabilities port (ECP)* conform to IEEE 1284, and one of the two standards—probably the ECP, experts say—will replace the standard parallel port in the next few years.

Big Blue Slang for *International Business Machines (IBM)* Corporation, which uses blue as its corporate color.

big red switch *Programmers* slang for the main power switch on a computer. Usage: He dug the machine so deep into an *infinite loop,* the only way out was the big red switch.

bin Common abbreviation for *binary file.*

binary coded decimal (BCD) A method of coding long decimal numbers so that they can be processed with great *precision* in a computer, which uses a fixed number of places, such as 8 or 16, to code numerical values.

Also, a very early code, similar in function to *ASCII,* that was used in the early 1960s to enable printers to print numeric characters. See *binary coded information (BCI)* and *extended binary-coded decimal interchange code (EBCDIC).*

binary coded information (BCI) An improvement on *binary coded decimal (BCD)* that included codes for capital letters and some punctuation. See *extended binary-coded decimal interchange code (EBCDIC).*

binary compatible   In *microprocessors,* capable of running software designed for another company's *central processing unit (CPU).* In *software,* a program will run on any *microprocessor* with which it is binary compatible.

binary file   A *file* containing data or program instructions in a computer-readable format. Using the *MS-DOS* TYPE command or a *word processing* program, you can't display the actual contents—ones and zeroes—of a binary file in a useful form. The opposite of a binary file is an *ASCII file.*

TIP: *Don't panic if you open a strangely named file and see an appalling collection of happy faces, spades, clubs, and other odd symbols: chances are you've opened a binary file accidentally.*

binary newsgroup   In *UseNet,* a *newsgroup* in which the articles contain (or are supposed to contain) binary files, such as sounds, *graphics,* or movies. These files have been encoded with *uuencode,* a program that transforms a *binary file* into coded ASCII characters so it can be transferred via the *Internet.* In order to use these files, it is first necessary to decode them (using a program called *uudecode*).

binary numbers   A number system with a base (radix) of 2, unlike the number systems most of us use, which have bases of 10 (decimal numbers), 12 (measurement in feet and inches), and 60 (time).

Binary numbers are preferred for computers for *precision* and economy. Building an electronic circuit that can detect the difference between two states (high current and low current, or 0 and 1) is easy and inexpensive; building a circuit that detects the difference among 10 states (0 through 9) is much more difficult and expensive. In fact, the word *bit* derives from the phrase BInary digiT.

binary search   A search *algorithm* that avoids a slow search through hundreds or thousands of *records* by starting in the middle of a sorted *database* and determining whether the desired record is above or below the midpoint. Having reduced the number of records to be searched by 50 percent, the search proceeds to the middle of the remaining records, and so on, until the desired record is found.

binary transfer   A *file transfer protocol* that allows you to transfer *binary files* to a *remote* computer using *terminal software.*

binder   Before the invention of *thin-film magnetic media,* the adhesive that held a *recording medium* on the surface of a *hard disk.* Binder was mixed with the medium (and sometimes a lubricant, too) and applied to the *substrate,* by *sputtering* or some other means.

binding offset   In *word processing* and *desktop publishing (DTP),* a gap left on one side of a printed page to allow room for binding the *document.* Binding offset is used only for documents printed or reproduced on both sides of the page (*duplex printing*); the text is shifted to the left on *verso* (left, even-numbered) pages and to the right on *recto* (right, odd-numbered) pages. Synonymous with *gutter.* If you're planning to bind a document printed or reproduced on only one side of the page, just increase the left margin to make room for the binding.

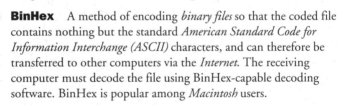

BinHex   A method of encoding *binary files* so that the coded file contains nothing but the standard *American Standard Code for Information Interchange (ASCII)* characters, and can therefore be transferred to other computers via the *Internet.* The receiving computer must decode the file using BinHex-capable decoding software. BinHex is popular among *Macintosh* users.

BIOS   See *basic input/output system (BIOS).*

bit   The basic unit of information in a binary numbering system (BInary digiT). The electronic circuitry in computers detects the difference between two states (high current and low current) and represent these states as one of the two numbers in a binary system: 1 or 0. These basic high/low, either/or, yes/no units of information are called bits. Because building a reliable circuit that tells the difference between a 1 and a 0 is easy and inexpensive, computers are accurate in their internal processing capabilities, typically making fewer than one internal error in every 100 billion processing operations. Eight bits comprise an *octet,* sometimes called a *byte.*

bit map   The representation of a video image stored in a computer's memory as a set of *bits.* Each picture element *(pixel),* corresponding to a tiny dot on-screen, is controlled by an on or off code stored as a bit (1 for on or 0 for off) for black-and-white displays. Color and shades of gray require more information. The bit map is a grid of rows and columns of the 1's and 0's that the computer translates into pixels to display on-screen. See *bit-mapped graphic* and *block graphics.*

bit-mapped font   A *screen* or *printer font* in which each character is composed of a pattern of dots. To display or print bit-mapped fonts, the computer or *printer* must keep a full representation of each character in memory.

When referring to bit-mapped fonts, the term font should be taken literally as a complete set of characters of a given *typeface, weight, posture,* and *type size.* If you want to use Palatino (Roman) 12 and Palatino Italic 14, for example, you must load two complete sets of characters into memory. You can't scale bit-mapped fonts up or down without introducing grotesque staircase distortions, called *aliasing* (see fig. B.2). See *antialiasing.*

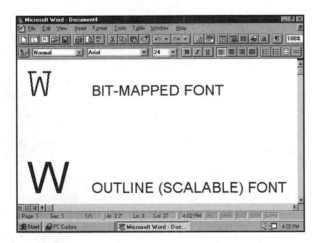

Fig. B.2   *Aliasing visible in the diagonal lines of a bit-mapped font compared with an outline font.*

bit-mapped graphic   A *graphic* image formed by a pattern of *pixels* and limited in *resolution* to the maximum resolution of the *display* or *printer* on which it is displayed. Bit-mapped graphics are produced by *paint programs* such as MacPaint, SuperPaint, GEM Paint, PC Paintbrush, and some scanning programs.

Considered inferior to *object-oriented graphics* for most applications, bit-mapped graphics may have *aliasing* caused by the square shape of pixels. The irregular patterns are visible when the image includes diagonal lines (refer to fig. B.2) and curves. Additionally, resizing a bit-mapped graphic image without introducing distortions is almost impossible, and bit-mapped graphics are notorious memory hogs. See *Encapsulated PostScript (EPS) file* and *object-oriented graphic.*

BITNET   A *wide area network (WAN)* that links *mainframe* computer systems at approximately 2,500 universities and research institutions in North America, Europe, and Japan. BITNET (an acronym for Because It's Time Network) does not use the *TCP/IP* protocols but can exchange *electronic mail* with the *Internet.* BITNET is operated by the Corporation for Research and Educational Networking (CREN), with headquarters in Washington, D.C. To become a member of the *network*, an organization must pay for a *leased line* that connects to the nearest existing BITNET site—and it must also agree to let another institution connect with this line in the future. Faced with competition from the Internet, BITNET is slowly dying.

bits per second (bps)   In *asynchronous communications,* a measurement of *data* transmission speed. In *personal computing,* bps rates frequently are used to measure the performance of *modems* and *serial ports.* The bps rates are enumerated incrementally: 110 bps, 150 bps, 300 bps, 600 bps, 1200 bps, 2400 bps, 4800 bps, 9600 bps, 14400 bps, 19200 bps, 38400 bps, 57600 bps, and 115200 bps. See *baud rate.*

BIX   An *on-line information service* owned by the parent company of *Delphi* but operated as an independent entity. BIX offers *electronic mail;* more than 200 conferences, including conferences for more than 90 *hardware* manufacturers and *software* publishers; real-time conferencing; software *downloads; Internet* access; and direct access to the WIX (Windows Information Exchange) on-line service, which features a number of Windows-related conferences.

black hole   In the *World Wide Web (WWW)*, a *hyperlink* to a document that has been erased or moved. Synonymous with *stale link.*

black letter   In *typography,* a family of *typefaces* derived from German handwriting of the medieval era. Black letter typefaces often are called Fraktur (after the Latin word fractus, meaning broken) because the medieval scribes who created this design lifted their pens from the line to form the next character—fracturing the continuous flow of handwriting.

black-write technique   See *print engine.*

blank cell   In a *spreadsheet program,* a *cell* that contains no *values, labels,* or *formatting* different from the *worksheet's global formats.*

bleed   In *desktop publishing,* a photograph, text box, or other page-design element that extends to the edge of the page, such as the thumb tab index at the edge of this page. This usually isn't possible if you're printing with a *laser printer,* which can't print in a 1/4-inch strip around the page's perimeter.

bleed capability   The ability of a *printer* to print *bleeds.*

blessed folder   The *Macintosh folder* containing a *System* file and a *Finder* file. The blessed folder is like a *MS-DOS directory* named in the *PATH* command because the System Folder is the only folder the System consults when it can't find a file. Macintosh users, therefore, are obliged to place all the configuration files required by their application programs in this folder, which can quickly grow so large that keeping track of its contents is difficult.

TIP: *Moving the System and Finder files into another folder is called* blessing *a folder. The procedure of changing the blessed folder can be automated using a free utility called Folder Blesser, available in the Macintosh Systems forum (GO MACSYS) on* CompuServe.

blessing   The act of moving *System* and *Finder* files to a new *folder,* creating a *blessed folder.*

blind courtesy copy (BCC)   In *electronic mail,* a copy of a message that is sent to one or more persons without the knowledge of the recipient.

bloatware   See *fatware.*

block   A unit of information that's processed or transferred. The unit may vary in size.

In *modems,* a unit of information passed from one computer to another is a block. If, for example, you use *XMODEM,* a *file transfer protocol,* 128 bytes are considered a block. Under *MS-DOS,* a block transferred to or from a *disk drive* is 512 bytes in size.

In *word processing,* a unit of text that you mark so that you can use a *block operation* to move, copy, or otherwise affect that text.

block definition   See *selection.*

block graphics   On IBM PC-compatible computers, *graphics* formed on-screen by *graphics characters* in the *ASCII extended character set.*

The graphics characters in the ASCII extended character set are suitable for creating and shading rectangles but not for fine detail. Because the block graphics characters are handled the same way as ordinary characters, the computer can display block graphics considerably faster than *bit-mapped graphics.*

block move   A fundamental editing technique in *word processing* in which a marked *block* of text is cut from one location and inserted in another. Synonymous with *cut* and *paste.*

block operation   The act of transferring a *block* of information from one area to another. In *word processing,* an editing or formatting operation—such as copying, deleting, moving, or underlining—performed on a marked block of text. See *block move.*

block protection   In *word processing* and *page layout programs,* a *command* that prevents the insertion of a *soft page break* in a specific block of text, preventing a *bad page break.*

block size   The size of an individual piece of data transmitted by a file transfer protocol or *error-correction protocol* over a *modem.* *XMODEM* uses a block size of 128 *bytes,* for example.

blurb   In *desktop publishing,* a brief explanatory subheading that's set below or next to a headline.

.BMP   In *Microsoft Windows 95,* an extension indicating that the file contains a Windows-compatible *bit-mapped graphic.*

BNF   See *Backus-Naur form (BNF)*.

board   See *adapter* and *circuit board*.

body type   The *font* (usually 8- to 12-*point*) used to set paragraphs of text, distinguished from the font used to set headings,
captions, and other typographical elements.

Serif typefaces, such as Century, Garamond, and Times Roman, are
preferred over *sans serif* typefaces for body type because they're
more legible. See *display type.*

bogus newsgroup   In *UseNet,* a *newsgroup* that does not
correspond to the site's list of approved newsgroups. Most
newsreaders are programmed to detect such newsgroups and delete
them automatically. Bogus newsgroups may originate from programming errors or somebody's effort to create the group by skirt-
ing the normal newsgroup creation process.

boilerplate   A block of text used over and over in letters,
memos, or reports.

> **TIP:** *Use boilerplates to achieve big speed gains in your writing. If
> your job involves answering routine inquiry letters, develop
> boilerplate responses to questions on such matters as warranty, sales
> terms, and the like, and attach these passages to glossaries or save the
> text in a file. Then you can write a letter just by inserting two or
> three glossaries or files, and then adding a few personalized touches.*

boldface   A character *emphasis* visibly darker and heavier in
weight than normal type. Each entry word in this dictionary is in
boldface type.

bomb   See *crash.*

bookmark   In general, a code inserted at a particular point in a
document so that point can easily be found later. You might insert
a bookmark in a part of a novel you're writing that needs to be
revised, or at an often-used point in a *Microsoft Windows 95* Help
file.

In *Netscape* or other *Web browser,* a bookmark is one of your favorite places on the *World Wide Web,* someplace you'd like to visit
again.

Bookshelf See *Microsoft Bookshelf.*

book weight A *typeface* that's darker and heavier than most typefaces, but not so dark and heavy as *boldface.* Book weight *fonts* are used to set lengthy sections of text so that they're easy to read and produce a pleasing gray tone on the page. See *weight.*

Boolean operator See *logical operator.*

Boolean search A search that involves the use of Boolean operators (AND, OR, and NOT). In a Boolean search, you can use these operators to refine the scope of your search. A search for "Chardonnay or Cabernet" returns all the items that mention either Chardonnay or Cabernet. A search for "Chardonnay and Cabernet" returns only those documents that mention both of these wines. A search for "Chardonnay and Cabernet not Merlot" returns only those items that mention both Chardonnay and Cabernet, but omits those that also mention Merlot. Boolean searches are often used in *bibliographic retrieval services.*

boot To initiate an automatic routine that clears the memory, loads the *operating system,* and prepares the computer for use.

Included in the computer's *read-only memory (ROM)* is the *power-on self-test (POST),* which executes when the power is switched on (a *cold boot*). After a system crash or lockup occurs, you usually must boot the computer again, or reboot, by pressing the Reset button or Ctrl+Alt+Del (a *warm boot*).

boot sector The first track on an IBM PC-compatible *hard* or *floppy disk* (track 0). During the *boot* process, *read-only memory (ROM)* tells the computer to read the first block of data on this track and load whatever *program* is found there. If *system files* are found, they direct the computer to load *MS-DOS.*

boot sequence The order in which a computers *basic input-output system (BIOS)* searches *disk drives* for *operating system* files. Unless programmed otherwise, IBM PCs and compatibles look for the operating system on drive A first, then search drive C. To speed up your computers *boot* procedure, you can use the BIOS *setup program* to make it search drive C first.

bot In *multi-user dungeons (MUDs)* and *Internet Relay Chat (IRC),* a character whose on-screen actions stem from a *program* rather than a real person. The term is a contraction of robot. The most famous of all bots, Julia, inhabits a MUD called *LambdaMoo,* and has tricked thousands into thinking that she is a real human being. See *MOO.*

bounced message   An *electronic mail* message that comes back to the sender after a failed delivery attempt. The failure may be due to an incorrectly-typed e-mail address or to a *network* problem.

bowl   In *typography,* the curved strokes that enclose or partially enclose a blank space, called the *counter,* that's part of a letter, such as the blank space in the letter a or c.

bps   See *bits per second (bps).*

brain-dead design   *Programmers* slang for *microprocessors* or other *hardware* devices that have features that prevent them from being as useful as they might otherwise be.

branch   In *MS-DOS,* one or more *subdirectories* located within a *directory.* In *Microsoft Windows 95 Explorer* and other graphical *file* manager utilities, directory branches can be displayed or hidden, depending on your needs (see fig. B.3).

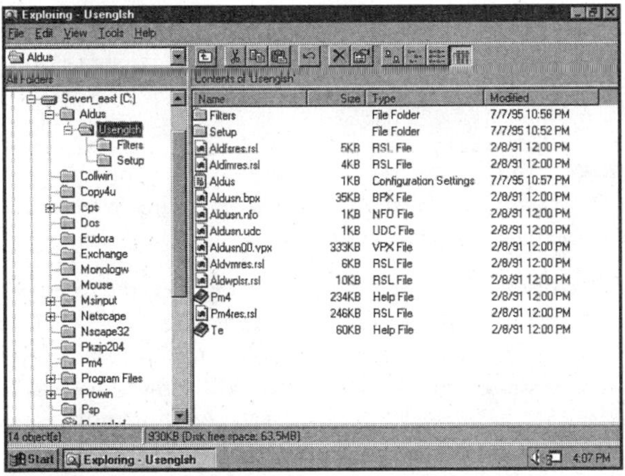

Fig. B.3   *A directory tree with a branch in the Windows Explorer.*

branch control structure   In *programming,* a *control structure* that tells a *program* to branch to a set of *instructions* only if a specified condition is met. If a program detects that a vital data file has been irretrievably corrupted, for example, the program branches to display a message that says something like, "The file you want to open is corrupted." Synonymous with *selection*. See *IF/THEN/ELSE*.

branch prediction   An educated guessing method employed by *microprocessors* that use *superscalar architecture*. By looking at a *program* and predicting how a true/false test will turn out, a microprocessor that employs branch prediction can get ready to execute the code that follows a certain test outcome. The *Pentium* microprocessor employs branch prediction and guesses correctly 90 percent of the time.

break   A user-initiated signal that interrupts processing or receiving *data*. See *Control+Break*.

break-out box   A testing device inserted into a communications cable or between a *serial port* and a serial cable that allows each signal to be tested separately.

breakpoint   A location in a *program* where it pauses to let the user decide what to do next.

TIP: *If you're writing a complex macro, include several breakpoints so that you can check progress and decide whether to continue.*

bridge   In *local area networks (LANs)*, a device that allows two *networks* (even ones dissimilar in *topology*, wiring, or *communications protocols*) to exchange *data*.

brightness   A *monitor* control that regulates the strength of electron beams striking the rear of a *cathode ray tube (CRT) display*. A high brightness setting increases the strength of the beams and makes the on-screen image brighter, while a low brightness setting weakens the beams and dims the image. *LCD* and other types of displays have similar controls that have the same effects.

broadband   In *local area networks (LANs)*, an *analog* communications method characterized by high *bandwidth*. The signal usually is split, or *multiplexed,* to provide multiple communications channels.

Because a computer's signals are *digital* signals, they must be transformed by a process called *modulation* before they can be conveyed over an analog signal network. A *modem* at each end of a *network* cable performs this task. Broadband communications can extend over great distances and operate at extremely high speeds. See *baseband.*

broadcast message In a *network,* a message to all system users that appears when you *log on* to the system. For example, broadcast messages are used to inform users when the system will be shut down for maintenance.

brownout A period of low-voltage electrical power caused by unusually heavy demand, such as that created by summertime air-conditioner use. Brownouts can cause computers to operate erratically or to *crash,* either of which can result in *data* loss. If brownouts frequently cause your computer to crash, you may need to buy a *line-interactive uninterruptible power supply* to work with your machine.

browse To use a *dialog* or *list box* to look for a *document* or *directory* (see fig. B.4). In a *database management program,* to use a dialog or list box to look for a *data record.*

Fig. B.4 *A Microsoft Windows 95 Browse dialog box.*

 TIP: *When you use the Browse dialog box, restrict the display of files by choosing an appropriate option in the List Files of Type list box.*

Browse mode In a *database management program,* a mode in which *data records* are displayed in columns for quick, on-screen review. Synonymous with list view or table view in some programs. See *edit mode.*

browser   See *Web browser*.

browsing   An information-seeking method that involves manually searching through linked documents. In the *World Wide Web (WWW)*, browsing is rarely effective for finding information on a specific topic (it's much better to use subject trees and search engines), but it's lots of fun. Browsing, for no particular reason, is called *surfing*. See *search engine* and *subject tree*.

brush style   In *typography*, a typeface design that simulates script drawn with a brush or broad-pointed pen.

brute force   In *programming*, a crude technique for solving a difficult problem by repeating a simple procedure many times. Computer spell-checkers use a brute-force technique. They don't really "check spelling"; they merely compare all the words in a *document* to a dictionary of correctly spelled words.

BSD UNIX   See *Berkeley UNIX*.

B-size paper   A page that measures 11 × 17 inches, as specified by the American National Standards Institute (ANSI). See *A-size paper*.

B-size printer   A printer capable of printing on *B-size* (11 × 17 inch) and smaller paper.

BTW   In *on-line* conferences, an *acronym* for By The Way.

bubble-jet printer   A variation on the *ink jet printer* concept that uses heating elements instead of piezoelectric crystals to shoot ink from nozzles.

buckyball toner   *Toner* made of large molecules of a synthetic carbon called buckminsterfullerene. Buckyball toner, named after engineer Buckminster Fuller, is easier to control than toner made of other types of carbon.

buffer   A unit of memory given the task of holding information temporarily, especially while waiting for slower components to catch up.

bug   A *programming* error that causes a *program* or a computer system to perform erratically, produce incorrect results, or *crash*. The term bug was coined when a real insect was discovered to have fouled up one of the circuits of the first electronic *digital* computer, the ENIAC. A *hardware* problem is called a *glitch*.

built-in font   A *printer* font encoded permanently in the *printer's read-only memory (ROM)*. All *laser printers* offer at least one built-in *typeface*, also called a resident font. You should consider buying printer with several typefaces, including a Roman-style *serif* font such as Times Roman or Dutch, and a clean *sans serif* font such as *Helvetica* or Swiss. Check a printer's literature for a list of the built-in fonts and whether they're *scalable*. See *cartridge font*, *downloadable font*, and *screen font*.

built-in function   In a *spreadsheet program,* a ready-to-use formula, also called an @function, that performs mathematical, statistical, trigonometric, financial, and other calculations

A built-in *function* begins with a special symbol (usually @ or =), followed by a *keyword,* such as AVG or SUM, that describes the formula's purpose. Most built-in functions require one or more *arguments* enclosed in parentheses and separated by commas (*argument separators*).

built-in pointing device   In *portable computers,* a *trackball* or *pointing stick* that's built into the computer's *case* in a fixed position. See *clip-on pointing device, freestanding pointing device, mouse,* and *snap-on pointing device.*

CAUTION: *Before buying a portable computer that has a* built-in pointing device, *try it out to make sure that you're happy with its position and performance. Some pointing devices are especially uncomfortable for left-handed people.*

bulk storage   *Magnetic media* that can store *data.* Synonymous with mass storage. See *secondary storage.*

bullet   Originally, a hollow or solid circle about the height of a lowercase letter, used to set off items in a list. Today, squares, triangles, pointing fingers, and a variety of other *graphic* characters are used as bullets.

Often combined with indentation, bullets are used when listing items whose content is roughly equal in emphasis or significance. When listing items that vary in significance or are arranged chronologically, using numbers is more effective. See *hanging indent.*

bulleted list chart   In *presentation graphics,* a text *chart* that lists a series of ideas or items of equal weight (see fig. B.5).

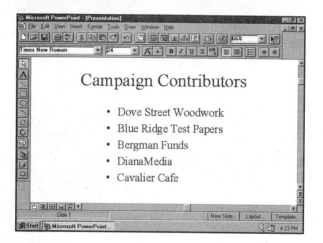

Fig. B.5   *A bulleted list chart.*

bulletin board system (BBS)   A *telecommunications utility,* usually set up by a personal computer hobbyist for the enjoyment of other hobbyists.

Late at night, you can dial a BBS, leave messages, *upload* and *download* public domain *software* and *shareware,* and play Space Invaders. However, a little caution is necessary since the advent of computer *viruses.* Nowadays, most BBSs scan all uploaded files before writing the file to the host computer's *hard disk.* If you find no virus checking on a certain BBS, don't use it as a source to download files—look elsewhere for a software source. See *chat forum, communications program, cybersex,* and *Fidonet.*

bulletproof   Capable, because of high *fault tolerance,* of resisting external interference and recovering from situations that would crash other programs.

bundled software   *Software* included with a *computer system* as part of the system's total price. Also, several programs that are packaged and sold together, now frequently called *software suites.*

burn-in   Operating a newly assembled *computer system* to screen for failures. *Semiconductor* components such as memory chips and *microprocessors* tend to fail either in the first few hours of operation or late in their lives. Responsible computer retailers, therefore, run systems continuously for 24 to 48 hours before releasing the systems to customers.

Sometimes used incorrectly to refer to permanently burning, or etching, the screen phosphors of a *display* when the same image is constantly on-screen. This phenomenon is really called *ghosting*.

bus An internal electrical pathway along which signals are sent from one part of the computer to another. Personal computers have a processor bus design with three pathways:

- The *data bus* sends data back and forth between the memory and the *microprocessor* divided into an *external data bus* and an *internal data bus.*

- The *address bus* identifies which memory location will come into play.

- The *control bus* carries the control unit's signals.

An extension of the data bus, called the *expansion bus,* connects the computer's expansion slots to the processor. The data, address, and expansion buses are wired in parallel rows so that all the bits being sent can travel simultaneously, like cars side by side on a 16- or 32-lane freeway.

Three bus architectures are commonly found in today's IBM PC and PC-compatible marketplace:

- *Industry Standard Architecture (ISA) bus.* Synonymous with AT bus, this is the 16-*bit* bus initially developed for IBM's AT computers. The bus includes 8-bit expansion slots for compatibility with earlier *adapters,* and 16-bit slots for AT-compatible adapters.

- *Micro Channel Architecture (MCA) bus.* A proprietary, 32-bit bus used in *high-end* IBM PS/2 computers.

- *Enhanced Industry Standard Architecture (EISA) bus.* A 32-bit bus that, unlike the MCA bus, is backward compatible with ISA adapters.

- *Peripheral Component Interconnect (PCI) bus.* A 32-bit bus designed for use with the Pentium. PCI buses usually co-exist with ISA buses on new motherboards for purposes of backward compatibility, but most experts agree that PCI has replaced EISA buses.

> **TIP:** *Confused about which bus to choose when you're buying a new PC? If you're running* Microsoft Windows 95, *choose a system with* PCI. *Such systems offer significantly faster performance than those with other bus designs.*

business audio   A category of sound hardware that supports sounds useful in business applications, such as putting background music into presentations, adding voice annotations to *word processing* documents, and voice-checking *spreadsheets.* *12-bit sound boards* are generally considered acceptable for business audio, but higher-quality *16-bit sound boards* are not much more expensive.

bus mouse   A *mouse* connected to the computer by a dedicated mouse *adapter* inserted into an available expansion slot. See *serial mouse.*

bus network   In *local area networks (LANs),* a decentralized *network topology* used by *AppleTalk* and *EtherNet,* for example, in which a single connecting line, the bus, is shared by a number of *nodes,* including workstations, shared *peripherals,* and *file servers* (see fig. B.6).

In a bus network, a workstation sends every message to all other workstations. Each node in the network has a unique address, and its reception circuitry monitors the bus for messages being sent to the node, ignoring all other messages.

Fig. B.6   *An illustration of a bus network.*

TIP: *Bus networks have a significant advantage over competing network designs (star topology and ring topology): the failure of a single node doesn't disrupt the rest of the network. Extending a bus network also is a simple matter; just lengthen the bus and add nodes, up to the system's maximum (about 1,000 feet without a repeater).*

button In *graphical user interfaces (GUIs),* a *dialog box* option used to execute a command, choose an option, or open another dialog box. See *Cancel button, default button, OK button, pushbutton,* and *radio button.*

button bar See *icon bar* and *toolbar.*

byline In *desktop publishing,* the author's name (often including organizational affiliation and address) positioned directly after the article's title.

byte Eight contiguous *bits,* the fundamental data unit of personal computers. Storing the equivalent of one character, the byte is also the basic unit of measurement for computer storage. Because computer *architecture* is based (for the most part) on *binary* numbers, bytes are counted in powers of two. Many members of the *Internet* community prefer to call groups of eight bits *octets.*

The terms kilo (in *kilobyte,* abbreviated as K) and mega (in *megabyte,* abbreviated as M) are used to count bytes but are misleading: they derive from decimal (base 10) numbers. A kilobyte actually is 1,024 bytes, and a megabyte is 1,048,576 bytes. Many computer scientists criticize these terms, but the terms give those who think in decimal numbers a nice handle on the measurement of memory.

C A *high-level programming language* widely used for professional *programming* and preferred by most major software publishers. A general-purpose *procedural language,* C combines the virtues of high-level programming languages with the efficiency of an *assembly language.* Most big-name programs, such as *Quattro Pro,* are written in C or *C++,* while many *shareware* programs are written in other languages, such as *Visual BASIC.*

Because the *programmer* can embed instructions that directly reach the *bit*-by-bit representation of data inside the *central processing unit (CPU),* compiled C programs run significantly faster than programs written in other high-level programming languages. C programs are highly *portable,* being easily and quickly rewritten to run on a new computer as long as the target environment has a C *compiler.*

C: In *IBM PC-compatible* personal computers, the *default* letter assigned to the first *hard disk.*

C++ A *high-level programming language* developed by Bjarne Stroustrup at AT&T's Bell Laboratories. Combining all the advantages of the *C* language with those of *object-oriented programming,* C++ has been adopted as the standard house programming language by several major software vendors, such as *Apple Computer.*

cache A storage area that keeps frequently accessed *data* or *program instructions* readily available so that you don't have to retrieve them repeatedly from slow storage.

Caches improve performance by storing data or instructions in faster sections of memory and by using efficient design to increase the likelihood that the data needed next is in the cache. See *hardware cache* and *internal cache.*

cache controller A *chip,* such as the *Intel 82385,* that manages the retrieval, storage, and delivery of *data* to and from *cache memory* or a *hard disk.*

When data or instructions are requested by the *central processing unit (CPU)*, the cache controller intercepts the request and handles the delivery from *random-access memory (RAM)*. The cache controller then determines where in the cache to store a copy of the just-delivered data, when to fetch data or code from adjacent addresses in RAM in case it's needed next, where in the cache to store this new data, and which data to discard if the cache is full. The cache controller also keeps an up-to-date table of the addresses of everything it's holding. Despite the magnitude of these duties and the small amount of memory actually used (32K to 256K), a well-designed cache controller must predict and have stored in the cache what the CPU needs next with an accuracy greater than 95 percent.

cache memory A special section of fast memory chips set aside to store the information most frequently accessed from *random-access memory (RAM)*. Synonymous with external cache.

Cache memory is a small section, usually 32*K* to 512K, of ultra-fast *static random-access memory (SRAM)* chips with its own *bus* to the *central processing unit (CPU)*, used to store data and code requested by the CPU. Cache memory is distinguished from a *software cache*, an area of ordinary RAM set aside to store information frequently retrieved from disk drives. See *wait state*.

cache settings Options in the *setup program* that enable or disable a *motherboard's secondary cache*. Sometimes disabling the secondary cache will make a game designed for a slow computer easier to play on a computer that would otherwise run it so fast as to make it unplayable.

CAD See *computer-aided design (CAD)*.

CADD See *computer-aided design and drafting (CADD)*.

caddy A tray, usually plastic, into which a *CD-ROM disk* is inserted before it is placed in certain *CD-ROM disk drives*. Caddies prevent fingerprints from getting on the disk surface, but it can be a hassle to load and unload caddies every time you want to change CD-ROMs.

CAI See *computer-assisted instruction (CAI)*.

calculated field   In a *database management* program, a *data field* that contains the results of calculations performed on other fields. Current balance and total score are examples of calculated fields. Synonymous with derived field.

call   In *programming,* a statement that transfers *program* execution to a *subroutine* or procedure. When the subroutine or procedure is complete, program execution returns to the command following the call statement. Also, a statement that invokes a *library routine.*

callback   A feature of some *communications programs* that enables the program to originate a call to a pre-cleared telephone number after an authorized user calls the program, informs it that he or she wants to exchange data, and hangs up. Callback features enhance *security,* since the program calls only certain numbers, but can be a problem for salesmen and field engineers who are often on the road and use a variety of telephone numbers.

Call for Votes (CFV)   In the standard *UseNet newsgroups,* a voting procedure that controls the creation of new newsgroups. Following a period of discussion, the call for votes is posted to the newsgroup news.announce.newgroups. During the voting period, 21 to 31 days in length, any UseNet participant may vote for or against the new newsgroup's creation by sending *electronic mail* to an independent tabulator (a volunteer). To pass, a newsgroup must receive at least 100 more Yes votes than No votes, and the number of Yes votes must be at least two-thirds of the total. If the newsgroup passes the vote, the newsgroup creation commands are issued and UseNet administrators are expected to carry the newsgroup, but there is no mechanism to force them to do so. The voting procedure does not apply to newsgroups outside the *standard newsgroup hierarchy,* such as the *alternative newsgroup hierarchy.*

callout   In *desktop publishing (DTP),* items of text that name parts of an illustration, usually with a line or arrow pointing to the part of the illustration the text describes.

call waiting   A service provided by the telephone company that's handy for voice communications—it lets you put one call on "hold" while you answer another—but that can play havoc with *modem* communications. Disable call waiting before dialing a number (try entering *70 and a comma before the number in your *communications program*, or call your phone company for other instructions).

camera-ready copy   A finished, printed manuscript or illustration ready to be photographed by a printing company for reproduction.

campus-wide information system (CWIS)   An information system that provides students, faculty, staff, and the public with all the information pertinent to a large college or university, including registration information, events, faculty and staff telephone numbers, and access to the library catalog. The need to create user-friendly navigation software for a CWIS led to the development of *Gopher* at the University of Minnesota. Increasingly, colleges and universities are abandoning Gopher in favor of systems based on the *World Wide Web (WWW)*.

cancelbot   In UseNet, a program that can hunt down a given individual's posts, and remove them from the network. Cancelbots, such as the one used by the storied *Cancelmoose,* are frequently wielded against *spammers*, those who post unwanted messages to dozens or even hundreds of newsgroups, but they have also been used to try to silence unwanted opinion.

Cancel button   An option in a *graphical user interface (GUI)* *dialog box* that you use to cancel a command and return to the active document. Equivalent to pressing *Esc*.

Cancelmoose   In *UseNet*, an individual, whose identity remains unknown, who takes upon himself the task of cancelling articles that are inappropriately posted to a large number of *newsgroups* (this is called *spamming*). Although *UseNet* software ordinarily permits only the author of an article to cancel it (remove it from *UseNet*), Cancelmoose has devised ingenious software (called a *cancelbot*) that gets around this restriction, allowing him or her to cancel any person's articles. Although the Cancelmoose's actions are controversial, many *UseNet* participants believe that his or her actions are fully justified.

canonical form   In mathematics and *programming,* an expression that conforms to established principles learned only through practice, apprenticeship, and interaction with experts. It's possible to write a programming expression that's entirely functional but not in canonical form, thus preventing social acceptance in learned mathematical and computer science societies. Most people, however, are concerned with getting the right answer.

cap height   In a *typeface,* the height of capital letters, measured in *points,* from the *baseline.*

Caps Lock key   A toggle *key* that locks the *keyboard* so that you can enter uppercase letters without pressing the *Shift* key. When you're in uppercase mode, most keyboards have a light that illuminates; many programs also display a message, such as CAPS LOCK or CAPS. The Caps Lock key has no effect on the number and punctuation keys.

caption   In *desktop publishing (DTP),* a descriptive phrase that identifies a figure, such as a photograph, illustration, or graph.

capture   In *modem* communications, to record what happens on the *monitor* and store it in a *file* that can be viewed later. Capturing data is useful if you're paying a per-minute connection charge.

Also, to copy all or part of an image on-screen and convert it to a *graphics file format* to insert in a *document* or save on a disk.

In *NetWare* network software, a command used to create a connection between the LPT1 port of a *workstation* and a *network printer.* If you have a *local printer* attached to LPT1, you can redirect LPT2 to the network printer.

card   See *adapter.*

caret   A symbol (^) commonly found over the 6 *key* on computer *keyboards.* In *spreadsheet* programs, the caret is the symbol for exponent, or "to the power of." Caret also can be used to stand for the *Ctrl* key in computer documentation, as in "Press ^C."

carpal tunnel syndrome   See *repetitive strain injury (RSI).*

carpet bomb   See *spam.*

carriage return   A signal that tells the *printer* to move to the left margin. Some printers also perform a *line feed* when executing a carriage return; such distinctions are handled by *printer drivers.* See *Enter/Return.*

carrier   A continuous tone established by two connected *modems.* Data is communicated by altering the carrier.

carrier detect signal   A signal sent from the *modem* to the rest of the computer to indicate that a connection has been made and the *carrier* tone has been established. The carrier detect (CD) light on *external modems* will illuminate when the carrier detect signal is sent.

carrier sense multiple access with collision detection (CSMA/CD)   In *local area networks (LANs),* a method used by *EtherNet, AppleTalk,* and other *network protocols* for controlling a computer's access to the communication channel. With CSMA/CD, each component of the *network* (called a *node*) has an equal right to access the communication channel. If two computers try to access the network at the same time, the network uses a random number to decide which computer gets to use the network first.

This channel access method works well with relatively small- to medium-sized networks (two or three dozen nodes). Large networks use alternative channel access methods, such as *polling* and *token passing* to prevent overloading or locking up the system.

Cartesian coordinate system   A method, created by 17th century French mathematician René Descartes, of locating a point in a two-dimensional space by defining a vertical axis and a horizontal axis. A *mouse* uses the Cartesian coordinate system to locate the *pointer* on-screen. In some *graphics applications,* you can display the coordinates so the pointer can be located precisely.

cartridge   A removable module containing data *storage media* such as magnetic tape or disks. In *printers,* a removable module that expands the printer's memory or contains *fonts,* called *cartridge fonts.*

cartridge font   A *printer font* supplied in the form of a *read-only memory (ROM) cartridge* that plugs into a receptacle on Hewlett-Packard LaserJet *laser printers* and *clones.*

Unlike *downloadable fonts,* a cartridge font is immediately available to the printer and doesn't consume space in the printer's *random-access memory (RAM),* which can be used up quickly when printing documents loaded with *graphics.* The popular cartridges contain multiple fonts, often more than 100. Most laser printers now use *built-in fonts* or software-generated fonts.

cascade In *follow-up messages* posted to *UseNet,* the accretion of quotation markers in messages that have been repeatedly quoted. Each time a message is quoted in a follow-up message, a newsreader adds quotation markers, as in the following:

```
>>>>>>Let's stop this thread.
>>>>>I agree.
>>>>Me too.
>>>You shouldn't post just to say, "Me too."
>>I agree.
>Me too.
Aargh!
```

cascading menu A *menu* system where selecting a command on a *pull-down menu* causes another menu to appear, or cascade, next to the selected command. The presence of a cascading menu is usually indicated by a triangle at the right edge of the menu. Synonymous with submenu.

cascading windows In a *graphical user interface (GUI),* two or more *windows* displayed so they overlap. This mode is convenient because you still can see the *title bar* and an edge of all the other windows you've opened (see fig. C.1). See *overlaid windows* and *tiled windows.*

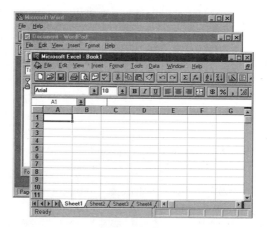

Fig. C.1 *Cascading windows in Microsoft Windows 95.*

case   The metal cabinet that contains the *motherboard, adapters,* and any internal components, such as *disk drives.* There are several types of cases, but the most basic distinction is between *desktop cases,* which lie flat, and *tower cases,* which stand vertically. Cases typically are sold with a *power supply* installed. See *AT-size case* and *mini-AT-size case.*

case-sensitive   Distinguishing the difference between upper- and lowercase letters. *MS-DOS* isn't case-sensitive; you can type MS-DOS commands in upper- or lowercase letters. *UNIX* is case-sensitive, so you must be careful not to interchange upper- and lowercase letters.

case-sensitive search   A search in which a *program* tries to match the exact pattern of upper- and lowercase letters. A case-sensitive search for Porter, for example, matches Porter but not PORTER, porter, or porTer.

cast-based animation   In *multimedia,* an animation method in which each object in a production is treated as an individual *graphic* image (a cast member). You can manipulate each cast member individually by means of a *script.*

catalog   In *database management,* a list of related database *files* you've grouped together so that you can easily distinguish them from others.

All *relational database management systems* can work with more than one file at a time. Frequently, the results of relational operations (such as a *join*) produce a new file. Also, you create several *indexes* and other files that support the application. A *catalog* helps you track all these related files in a unit.

catch up   In *UseNet,* a command commonly implemented in *newsreaders* that marks all the current *articles* in a *newsgroup* as read, even if you have not actually read them. When you access the newsgroup again, you will only see the articles that have come in since the last time you accessed the newsgroup.

catenet   An obsolete term for an *internet:* a *wide area network (WAN)* composed of physically distinct *local area networks (LANs),* which are connected by means of *routers.* The term is a contraction of "concatenated network." The *Internet* (note the capital "I") is a world-wide catenet based on the *TCP/IP* protocols.

cathode ray tube (CRT)   In a *monitor,* a vacuum tube that uses an *electron gun* (cathode) to emit a beam of electrons that illuminates *phosphors* on-screen as the beam sweeps across the screen repeatedly. The monitor is often called a CRT. The same technology is used in television sets.

CAV   See *constant angular velocity (CAV).*

CBT   See *computer-based training (CBT).*

CCITT   See *Comité Consultatif International Téléphonique et Télégraphique (CCITT)* and *International Telephone Union— Telecommunications Standards Section (ITU-TSS).*

CCITT protocol   A number of standards for the transmission of data using a computer *modem, serial port,* or a *network.* The following protocols are in the V series: *V.17, V.21, V.22, V.22bis, V.27ter, V.29, V.32, V.32bis, V.34, V.42,* and *V.42bis.*

CCP   See *Certified Computer Programmer (CCP).*

CD   See *compact disk (CD).*

CD-DA   See *Compact Disk-Digital Audio (CD-DA).*

CDEV   See *control panel device (CDEV).*

CD-I   See *Compact Disk-Interactive (CD-I).*

CDP   See *Certified Data Processor (CDP).*

CD-R   A recordable *CD-ROM.* CD-R technology is useful to law offices and other business that must permanently *archive* large amounts of information, and it enables individuals to manufacture saleable CD-ROMs. Unlike most other storage media, though, CD-R disks can be recorded upon only once.

CD-ROM   *Acronym* for compact disk-read only memory, a read-only optical storage technology that uses compact disks.

CD-ROMs can store up to 650 *M* of data. CD-ROM technology was originally used for encyclopedias, dictionaries, and software libraries, but now they often are used in *multimedia* applications.

If you're buying a CD-ROM drive for a *Microsoft Windows 95* system, make sure that you look for a drive that conforms to the *Multimedia Personal Computer 2 (MPC-2)* standard.

CD-ROM changer   A machine that will robotically load any of up to 100 *CD-ROMs* into a *CD-ROM disk drive.* Synonymous with jukebox, a CD-ROM changer usually requires about five seconds to locate and load a requested disk.

CD-ROM disk drive   A read-only disk drive designed to read the data encoded on *CD-ROMs* and to transfer this data to a computer.

Unlike audio compact disk players, CD-ROM disk drives contain circuitry optimized to locate *data* at high speeds; audio CD players need to locate only the beginning of audio tracks, which they play sequentially.

CD-ROM drives retrieve data much more slowly than computer disk drives. If you're buying your drive for a Multimedia Personal Computer (MPC) system, make sure that the CD-ROM drive can play CDs that store up to 650 *M* of data, transfer data at rates of at least 300 *kilobits* per second, and have access times of 200–300 milliseconds (ms).

CD-ROM interface   A feature of a *sound board* that lets you connect *a CD-ROM disk drive* directly to the sound board, thereby easing installation and enabling you to send audio from a *CD-ROM disk* directly to the sound circuitry, without taxing the rest of the computer.

CD-ROM/SD   See *CD-ROM/Super Density (CD-ROM/SD).*

CD-ROM/Super Density (CD-ROM/SD)   A little-used standard for packing up to 9.6 *G* onto a *CD-ROM.* The CD-ROM/SD standard uses both sides of disks and is not compatible with any mass-produced *CD-ROM disk drives.* See *Multimedia Compact Disk (MMCD).*

cell   In a *spreadsheet,* a rectangle formed by the intersection of a row and column in which you enter information in the form of text (a *label*) or numbers (a *value*).

cell address   In a *spreadsheet,* a letter and number combination that identifies a cell's location on the worksheet by column and row (A3, B9, C2, and so on). If you refer to a cell in a formula, the cell address is called the *cell reference.*

cell animation   An *animation* technique in which a background painting is held in place while a series of transparent sheets of celluloid containing objects are placed over the background painting, producing the illusion of movement.

Cell animation is much easier than drawing a new background for every frame in the animation sequence. A *Macintosh* animation program that uses a computerized version of cell animation is Macromedia Director.

cell definition   The actual contents of a *cell* in a *spreadsheet,* as displayed on the *entry line.* If you place a *formula* in a cell, the program displays the result of the calculation rather than the formula itself.

cell format   In a *spreadsheet,* the way the *program* displays the contents of *cells. Label* formats include aligning the text on the left, right, or center. *Numeric formats* include currency, percent, including commas, setting a number of decimal places, and date and time display. You can change the *font* and *font size,* and make *values* and labels *bold* and *italic.* See *current cell, global format, graphics spreadsheet, label alignment,* and *range format.*

cell pointer   In *spreadsheet* programs, the rectangular highlight that indicates the *current cell.* When you enter *data* in the spreadsheet, it's recorded in the current cell.

cell protection   In a *spreadsheet* program, a *format* applied to a cell, a *range* of cells, or an entire *file* that prevents you from altering the contents of protected cells.

TIP: *With most spreadsheets, you can use a two-step process to create a worksheet in which the cell pointer can move only to cells where you want values entered. After you enter column and row labels and titles, unprotect the cells that will contain values (protected is the default format). Second, protect the rest of the worksheet, including those cells containing labels. The worksheet can then be saved to use as a data-entry form.*

cell reference   In a *spreadsheet formula,* the address of the *cell* that contains a value needed to solve the formula. To take full advantage of your spreadsheet's power, use cell references rather than *values* to write a formula, such as +B1+B2, where B1 and B2 are cell addresses. When used in a formula, they tell the program to go to the named cell (such as B1) and use the value in that cell to perform the calculation.

A cell reference can refer to a cell containing a formula, which may contain its own cell references to other cells, which can themselves contain formulas, and so on. A change made to any constant in such a worksheet affects intermediate values and, ultimately, the bottom line. See *recalculation method*.

Center for Innovative Computer Applications (CICA)   An Indiana University-based research center that fosters innovative research in computer visualization and artificial intelligence. For *Internet* users, CICA is better known as the home of a massive Windows *shareware archive*, accessible by means of *File Transfer Protocol (FTP)* and the *Virtual Software Library (VSL)*.

central mass storage   See *file server*.

central processing unit (CPU)   A computer's internal storage, processing, and control circuitry, including the *arithmetic-logic unit (ALU)*, the *control unit, read-only memory (ROM)*, and *random-access memory (RAM)*. The ALU and control unit are wholly contained on a chip called the *microprocessor;* the memory is elsewhere on the *motherboard* or an adapter on the *expansion bus*.

Centre Universitaire d'Informatique (CUI)   A unit of the University of Geneva, located in Geneva, Switzerland, that has played a leading role in the development of the *World Wide Web (WWW)*. See *CUI W3 Catalog*.

Centronics interface   The *parallel port* of IBM PC-compatible computers, named after the company that designed a predecessor to this interface standard.

Centronics port   See *parallel port*.

CERN   See *European Laboratory for Particle Physics (CERN)*.

certified   Guaranteed by the manufacturer to accurately hold a certain quantity of data. For example, a disk might be certified for 2.88 *M* of data.

Certified Computer Programmer (CCP)   A person who has earned a Certificate in Computer Programming from the *Institute for Certification of Computer Professionals (ICCP)*. CCPs must pass an examination in *programming* rules and concepts. CCP certification is considered equivalent to Certified Public Accountant status for accountants, though it is rarely an employment requirement.

Certified Data Processor (CDP)   A person who has earned a Certificate in Data Processing from the *Institute for Certification of Computer Professionals (ICCP)*. CDPs must pass an examination in *hardware, software, programming,* and systems analysis. CDP certification is considered equivalent to Certified Public Accountant status for accountants, though it is rarely an employment requirement.

CGA   See *Color Graphics Adapter (CGA).*

CGI   See *Common Gateway Interface (CGI).*

CGM   See *Computer Graphics Metafile (CGM).*

chain printing   The printing of separate *files* as a unit by placing commands at the end of the first file to direct the program to continue printing the second file, and so on. Full-featured *word processing* programs such as *Microsoft Word* allow chained printing with continuous pagination and, in some cases, the generation of a complete table of contents and index for the linked files. See *master document.*

chamfer   In *desktop publishing (DTP)* and *presentation graphics,* a beveled edge between two intersecting lines.

channel access   In *local area networks (LANs),* the method used to gain access to the data communication channel that links the computers. Three common methods are *contention, polling,* and *token passing.*

character   Any letter, number, punctuation mark, or symbol that you can produce on-screen by pressing a *key* on the *keyboard.* A character uses one *byte* of memory.

character-based program   A *program* that relies on the *ASCII* and *extended ASCII character sets* that includes *block graphics* to create its screens and display the text you enter.

character graphics   See *block graphics.*

character-mapped display   A method of displaying characters in which a special section of *memory* is set aside to represent the displayed image; programs generate a display by inserting characters into the memory-based representation of the screen. Therefore, the whole screen—not just one line—remains active, and the user or the program can modify characters anywhere on-screen. See *teletype (TTY) display.*

chart **83**

character mode   In *IBM PC-compatible* computers, a *display* mode in which the computer displays only those characters contained in its built-in *character set*. Synonymous with text mode. See *character view* and *graphics mode.*

character set   The fixed set of *keyboard* codes that a particular computer system uses. See *ASCII character set, code page,* and *extended character set.*

characters per inch (cpi)   The number of *characters* that fit in an inch of type of a given *font*. Standard sizes drawn from typewriting are pica (10 cpi) and elite (12 cpi).

characters per second (cps)   A measurement of the speed of a *modem* (though modem speed is most often measured in *bits per second [bps]*), *impact printer* or *inkjet printer.*

character string   Any series of *characters* (including spaces) that a *program* treats as a group. In *programming* and *database management,* you distinguish character strings from reserved words (command names) by enclosing strings in quotation marks; as a result, the characters in the string give no instructions to the computer. In a database management query language, for example, the expression FIND "Wyoming" causes the computer to search for the first record that exactly matches the character string Wyoming. Synonymous with string.

character view   In some *MS-DOS application programs,* a mode in which the program switches the *display adapter* circuitry to character mode; also called draft mode by some programs. In character mode, the computer can display only those characters contained in the computer's built-in *character set*. See *character mode* and *graphics view.*

charge-coupled device   A device used in a *scanner* or *digital camera* to convert light into electrical signals readable by the computer. A scanner's horizontal resolution is determined by the number of CCDs it packs into a row—usually 300, but in some high-end scanners, 600.

chart   A representation of data in pictoral form. Charts make it easier to discern the significance of data and identify trends.

chat forum In a *bulletin board system (BBS)* or *on-line informa-tion service,* a special forum or conference that allows two or more callers, on-line at the same time, to engage in conversation with each other by taking turns typing.

Bulletin boards usually feature conferences for specific *software,* such as *WordPerfect* or various games, and chat lines can be used by two aficionados swapping information and hints. Other BBSs, such as SeniorNet, a San Francisco-based board designed to serve senior citizens' needs, includes a number of computer conference groups and chat lines where users can gather via computer. See *cybersex.*

check box In a *graphical user interface (GUI) dialog box,* a square box that you choose to *toggle* an option on or off. When the option is turned on, an X appears in the check box. A check box can appear alone or with other check boxes in a list of items. Un-like *radio buttons,* you can choose more than one check box.

checksum An acronym for SUMmation CHECK. In *data* communications, an *error-checking* technique in which the number of *bits* in a unit of data is summed, transmitted along with the data, and checked by the receiving computer. If the sum differs, an error probably occurred in transmission and the transmission is repeated. A commonly used personal computer communications protocol called *XMODEM* uses the checksum technique.

In *virus* scanning software, such as Central Point Anti-Virus, checksums are calculated for every file in a directory and the results saved in a file stored in the directory. When the program is scan-ning, it compares the checksum information stored in the direc-tory with the current checksum for each scanned file. A difference in the sum may indicate that the file has been infected by a virus that doesn't leave a recognized signature.

checkwriting program An *accounting program* designed to help individuals and small-business owners keep track of checking accounts, credit card accounts, tax records, and budgets using a blank check as its basic data entry form. See *Intuit Quicken Deluxe.*

Chiclet keyboard A *keyboard,* frequently found on calcula-tors, that uses small rectangular keys the size of Chiclet chewing gum. Chiclet keys are difficult to use because the keys are too small and offer little *tactile feedback*. A Chiclet keyboard was featured on one of *IBM's* most notorious marketing failures, the PCjr home computer.

chip A miniaturized electronic circuit mass-produced on a tiny wafer of silicon.

Chips are made out of semiconducting materials and duplicate the function of several transistors and other electronic components. The first *integrated circuits* contained only a few components, but the same manufacturing techniques now can generate 16 million components on a chip smaller than a fingertip.

Today's *Pentium*, for example, sells for less than $500, but is the electronic equivalent of a *mainframe* computer priced at several million dollars just 20 years ago. The achievement of chip-manufacturing technology has spread the use of computer technology throughout society.

chip set The collection of *chips* that work together to perform a function, such as helping a *microprocessor* access memory or update a *display*. The chips that comprise a chip set must be designed to work together and typically come from a single manufacturer. Synonymous with chipset.

choose In a program that uses *menus* and *dialog boxes,* the process of picking an option that begins an action.

Highlighting or selecting an option is often different from choosing it. To choose a highlighted option, press Enter. In *Microsoft Windows 95* and many *MS-DOS* applications, to choose using the *keyboard,* move the selector or highlight to the item and then press Enter; or press the Alt key plus the underlined letter in the item name. To choose with the *mouse,* click buttons and menu commands; *double-click* icons and file names to execute commands or launch applications.

TIP: *If you use a mouse, look for ways you can save time by double-clicking an option. In many applications, double-clicking an option highlights and chooses it in one quick action.*

Chooser A *Macintosh desktop accessory (DA)* supplied by *Apple Computer* with the Mac's *operating system*—the *System*. The Chooser governs the selection of *printer* and *network drivers,* the programs that control communication with the *printer* and *local area network (LAN)*. The Chooser displays the *icons* of the printer and network drivers installed in the *System Folder*.

chord In *desktop publishing* and *presentation graphics,* a straight line that connects the end points of an arc.

chrominance In *multimedia*, the portion of a composite video signal that contains color information.

CICA. See *Center for Innovative Computer Applications*.

ciphertext In *cryptography,* a message that has been encrypted so that it can be read only by the intended recipient, who possesses the *key* needed to decode the message. See *encryption* and *public-key cryptography*.

circuit board A flat plastic board on which electrically conductive circuits are laminated. Synonymous with printed circuit board. See *adapter* and *motherboard*.

circuit switching network A type of *wide-area network (WAN)*, epitomized by the world telephone system, in which the originating and receiving stations are linked by a single, physical circuit, created by complex switching mechanisms. The connection is maintained until the communication is finished. Compare to *packet-switching network*.

circular reference In a *spreadsheet,* an error condition caused by two or more *formulas* that refer to one another. A circular reference occurs, for example, when the formula +B5 is placed in *cell* A1, and the formula +A1 is placed in cell B5. Spreadsheet programs usually have a *command* that displays a screen that includes a list of the cells containing circular references.

Circular references don't always result in errors. They can be used deliberately, for example, to create an iterative function in a worksheet: each recalculation increases the values of the two formulas.

CISC See *complex instruction set computer (CISC)*.

clari   In *UseNet*, an *alternative newsgroup hierarchy* that includes dozens of read-only *newsgroups* containing wire service articles—the same ones that will appear in today's newspapers. These wire services include United Press International (UPI), Newsbytes, and TechWire. The Clari hierarchy is available only at those UseNet sites that have paid a fee to ClariNet, the organization that collates the wire service articles and posts them to the dozens of clari newsgroups. The articles posted to the clari newsgroups are copyrighted and cannot be redistributed without ClariNet's written approval.

Class 1   A standard for *fax modems* that describes the way in which the *Hayes command set* is modified to send faxes. Class 1 fax modems, unlike *Class 2* fax modems, leave most of the tasks relating to digitizing images and preparing faxes for transmission to software, which is perfectly fine in most computers.

Class 2   A standard for *fax modems* that describes the way in which the *Hayes command set* is modified to send faxes. Class 2 fax modems handle most of the fax-preparation tasks that *Class 1* fax modems leave to software, which makes Class 2 modems very expensive. Class 2 isn't even a true industry standard, so you're better off buying a Class 1 fax modem.

Class A certification   A Federal Communications Commission (FCC) certification that a given make and model of computer meets the FCC's Class A limits for *radio frequency interference (RFI),* which are designed for commercial and industrial environments.

Class A network   On the *Internet,* a participating *network* that is allocated up to 16,777,215 distinct Internet addresses (called *IP addresses*). Current Internet addressing limitations define a maximum of 128 Class A networks.

Class B certification   A Federal Communications Commission (FCC) certification that a given make and model of computer meets the FCC's Class B limits for *radio frequency interference (RFI),* which are designed for homes and home offices. Class B standards are tougher than Class A and are designed to protect radio and television reception in residential neighborhoods from excessive (RFI) generated by computer usage. Class B computers are also shielded more heavily from external interference.

Class B network   On the *Internet*, a participating *network* that is allocated up to 65,535 distinct Internet addresses (called *IP addresses*). Current Internet addressing limitations define a maximum of 16,384 Class B networks.

 Class C network   On the *Internet*, a participating *network* that is allocated up to 256 distinct Internet addresses (called *IP addresses*). Current Internet addressing limitations define a maximum of 2,097,152 Class C networks.

clear   To remove *data* from a *document*. In the *Microsoft Windows 95* and *Macintosh* environments, the Clear command (Edit *menu*) completely wipes out the selection, as opposed to Cut, which removes the selection to the *Clipboard* (from which you can retrieve the selection, if you later discover that you deleted it by mistake). Synonymous with delete.

 TIP: *Most applications can recover cleared data if you choose Undo immediately after performing the clear. In Lotus 1-2-3, press Alt+F4 to Undo; in other programs, Undo is usually on the Edit menu. Don't move the pointer, choose another command, or type any other text before choosing Undo, or the deletion may be lost irretrievably.*

click   To press and quickly release a *mouse* button. You frequently see this term in instructions such as "Click the Bold check box in the Fonts dialog box." For users of *IBM-compatible PCs*, this instruction means, "Move the mouse pointer so its tip touches the Bold check box and then click the left mouse button." See *double-click* and *Shift+click*.

client   In a *network*, a workstation with processing capabilities, such as a personal computer, that can request information or applications from the *network server*. In *Object Linking and Embedding (OLE)*, an *application* that includes data in another application, called the *server application*. See *client application*.

client application   In *Object Linking and Embedding (OLE)*, an *application* in which you can create a linked object or embed an object.

client-based application   In a *client/server network*, an *application* that resides on a *workstation* and isn't available for use by others on the *network*. *File server* crashes don't affect client-based applications. Also, individual packages of software must be installed on workstations if network licenses haven't been bought. See *local area network (LAN)* and *server-based application.*

client/server architecture   A design model for *applications* running on a *network,* in which the bulk of the *back-end* processing, such as performing a physical search of a *database,* takes place on a *server.* The *front-end* processing, which involves communicating with the user, is handled by smaller programs distributed to the client workstations. See *local area network (LAN)* and *wide area network (WAN).*

client/server model   See *client-server architecture.*

client/server network   A method of allocating resources in a *local-area network (LAN)* so computing power is distributed among the computers in the network, but some shared resources are centralized in a *file server.* See *client/server architecture* and *peer-to-peer network.*

clip art   A collection of *graphics,* stored on disk and available for use in a *desktop publishing* or *presentation graphics program.* The term clip art is derived from a graphics design tradition in which packages of printed clip art are sold in books and actually clipped out by layout artists to enhance newsletters, brochures, and presentation graphics. Most page layout or presentation graphics programs can read *graphics file formats* used by clip art collections available on disk (see fig. C.2).

Fig C.2   *Print preview of a document using clip art.*

Clipboard In a *windowing environment* such as *Microsoft Windows 95* or the *Macintosh Finder*, a temporary storage area in memory where material cut or copied from a document is stored until you paste the material elsewhere (see fig. C.3).

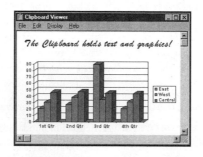

Fig C.3 *The Clipboard window in Microsoft Windows 95.*

clip-on pointing device A *trackball* that clips on the side or front of a *portable computer*. See *built-in pointing device, freestanding pointing device, mouse, pointing stick,* and *snap-on pointing device.*

Clipper A *compiler* developed by Nantucket Systems, Inc., for the *dBASE* software command language. Many application developers consider Clipper superior to the compiler offered by dBASE's publisher.

Clipper Chip A U.S. government-backed encryption technology, housed on a semiconductor that could be manufactured in massive quantities, that would provide private individuals with the means to encrypt their messages. However, the Clipper Chip includes a *back door* that would enable law enforcement agencies to eavesdrop on the message. In order to do so, law enforcement personnel would have to obtain a warrant, as is now required to eavesdrop on telephone communications. Privacy advocates fear that the government would abuse its power, eavesdropping on conversations without having obtained the proper certification, while law enforcement personnel fear that encryption technologies will prevent the detection of terrorist and drug-dealing activity.

clock An electronic circuit that generates evenly spaced pulses at speeds of millions of *hertz (Hz)*. The pulses are used to synchronize the flow of information through the computer's internal communication channels. Most computers also contain a circuit that tracks the time of day. See *clock/calendar board* and *clock speed.*

clock/calendar board   An *adapter* that includes a battery-powered clock for tracking the time and date and is used in computers that lack such facilities on their *motherboards.*

clock cycle   The time between two ticks of a computer's *system clock.* A typical personal computer goes through millions or even billions of clock cycles each second.

clock doubled   Operating twice as fast as the *system clock.* A 50 *MHz* 486DX2 operates on a *motherboard* with a 25 MHz system clock, for example, and completes internal *microprocessor* operations faster than a 25 MHz 486DX on the same motherboard. A clock-doubled chip, though, does nothing to speed up operations outside the microprocessor.

clock speed   The speed of the internal clock of a *microprocessor* that sets the pace—measured in *megahertz (MHz)*—at which operations proceed within the computer's internal processing circuitry.

Higher clock speeds bring noticeable gains in microprocessor-intensive tasks, such as recalculating a *spreadsheet,* but isn't the only feature that determines performance. Disk-intensive operations proceed slowly, regardless of clock speed, if *hard* and *floppy disks* are sluggish. When comparing clock speeds, compare only computers that use the same microprocessor, such as the *Pentium* 90, which runs at 90 Mhz, and the *Pentium* 120, which runs at 120 Mhz.

clock tripled   Operating three times as fast as the *system clock.* Clock-tripled microprocessors perform internal *microprocessor* functions faster than *clock-doubled* or standard microprocessors, but do nothing to speed up the rest of the system.

clone   A functional copy of a *hardware* device, such as a *personal computer* that runs the *software* and uses all the peripherals intended for the IBM Personal Computer. Also, a functional copy of a *program,* such as a *spreadsheet* program that reads *Lotus 1-2-3* files and can recognize most or all Lotus commands. See *IBM PC-compatible computer.*

close In a *program* that can display more than one *document window,* to exit a file and remove the window from the *display.*

 CAUTION: *In many applications, you must save your work before you close a window. If you haven't saved your work, the program probably displays an alert box warning you to save. To abandon your work, confirm that you don't want to save the document.*

close box In a *graphical user interface (GUI),* a box at the left end of the *title bar* of a *window,* which may include a *pull-down menu,* that is used to close the window. A close box available in all *Macintosh* windows is used only to close the window. Similar boxes in *Microsoft Windows 95* applications are called *control menu* boxes.

closed bus system A design in which the computer's *data bus* doesn't contain receptacles and isn't easily upgraded by users. See *open bus system.*

closed-loop actuator A mechanism that moves the *read/write head* of a *hard disk,* then sends messages to the *hard disk controller* confirming its location. Closed-loop actuators, since the read/write head can be positioned with greater accuracy over the recording medium, improve *areal density.*

cluster On a *floppy* or *hard disk,* the basic unit of *data* storage. A cluster includes two or more *sectors.*

When *Microsoft Windows 95* stores a *file* on disk, MS-DOS writes the file into one or even hundreds of *contiguous* clusters. If enough contiguous clusters aren't available, MS-DOS locates the next empty cluster and writes more of the file to the disk, continuing this process until the entire file is saved. The *file allocation table (FAT)* tracks how files are distributed among the clusters on a disk. See *file fragmentation.*

CLV See *constant linear velocity (CLV).*

CMOS See *Complementary Metal-Oxide Semiconductor (CMOS).*

CMOS reset jumper A *jumper* on the *motherboard* that, when moved, clears the *advanced setup options.* The CMOS reset jumper is useful if poor setup-option choices render your computer unable to start.

CMYK   A *color model* that makes all colors from combinations of cyan, magenta, yellow, and black. The CMYK model supports device-independent color better than the *RGB* and *HSB* models.

coated paper   Specially treated paper that enhances the output of *color printers*. *Thermal wax-transfer printers* require coated paper, which is much more expensive than standard *printer* paper. See *consumables*.

C ◄
D
E

coaxial cable   In *local area networks (LANs)*, a high-*bandwidth* connecting cable in which an insulated wire runs through the middle of the cable. Surrounding the insulated wire is a second wire made of solid or woven metal.

Coaxial cable is much more expensive than *twisted-pair cable* (ordinary telephone wire) but can carry more *data*. Coaxial cables are required for high-bandwidth *broadband* systems and for fast *baseband* systems such as *EtherNet*.

COBOL   A *high-level programming language* specially designed for business applications.

Short for COmmon Business Oriented Language, COBOL is a compiled language that was released in 1964 and was the first language to use the *data record* as a principal data structure. Because COBOL is designed to store, retrieve, and process corporate accounting information and to automate such functions as inventory control, billing, and payroll, the language quickly became the language of choice in businesses. COBOL is the most widely used programming language in corporate mainframe environments.

Versions of COBOL are available for personal computers, but business applications for personal computers are more frequently created and maintained in *C* or *Xbase*. See *high-level programming language*.

CODASYL   See *conference on data-systems languages (CODASYL)*.

code   To express a problem-solving *algorithm* in a *programming language*. Also a synonym of *source code*.

codec   In *multimedia*, a program that compresses audio, video, or graphics files for efficient storage or transmission, and decompresses them for playback purposes. Codec is an abbreviation of *compression*/decompression. See *lossless compression* and *lossy compression*.

code page   In *MS-DOS*, a table of 256 codes for an IBM PC-compatible computer's *character set*. The two kinds of code pages are classed as follows:

- *Hardware* code page. The character set built into the computer's ROM.

- Prepared code page. A disk-based character set you can use to override the hardware code page.

codes   See *hidden codes.*

code snippet   One or more lines of *source code* embedded in a user-defined *menu* option or *button.* The instructions define what the button or option does.

cold boot   Starting a computer by turning on the system's power switch. See *boot* and *warm boot.*

cold link   A method of copying information from one *document* (the source document) to another (the target document) so that a link is created. To update the link, choose a command that opens the source document, reads the information, and recopies the information if it has changed. See *dynamic data exchange (DDE), hot link,* and *Inter-Application Communication (IAC).*

collaboratory   In scientific networking, a shared workspace, including shared scientific *databases,* facilities for teleconferencing, and network-accessible facilities for collaborative experimentation. See *federated database* and *Grand Challenge.*

collapse   When creating an outline or viewing a *directory tree* (such as in the *Windows Explorer*), the process of hiding all the outline levels or *subdirectories* below the selected outline heading or directory.

TIP: *In the* Windows Explorer, *you can double-click the directory icon to collapse or expand a directory quickly.*

collate   See *sort.*

collating sequence   See *sort order.*

collision   In *local area networks (LANs),* a garbled transmission that results when two or more workstations transmit to the same network cable at exactly the same time. Networks have means of preventing collisions.

color   In *typography,* the quality of the printed portion of the page, which should be perceived by the eye as an even shade of gray. Defects such as *rivers, bad breaks,* poor character spacing, or uneven line spacing disrupt this even appearance.

To maintain good color, use consistent word spacing, avoid *widows* and *orphans,* use *kerning* as necessary (especially for display type), and avoid *hyphen ladders.*

color depth   In *monitors,* the number of colors a *video adapter* can display at one time. The *Video Graphics Array (VGA)* standard, for example, allows a color depth of 256.

In scanners, the number of data bits with which a *scanner* records each *pixel* of a scanned image. The greater its color depth, the more colors or shades of gray a scanner can distinguish. A 24-bit scanner can depict 16.7 million colors and 256 shades of gray. A 30-bit scanner can record more than a billion colors and 1,024 levels of gray.

Color Graphics Adapter (CGA)   A *bit-mapped graphics display adapter* for *IBM PC-compatible* computers. The CGA *adapter* displays four colors simultaneously with a resolution of 200 *pixels* horizontally and 320 *lines* vertically, or displays one color with a resolution of 640 pixels horizontally and 200 lines vertically.

color ink jet printer   An *ink jet printer* that can generate color output. Some color ink jet printers create all colors from cyan, magenta, and yellow inks, but better ones use black ink, too, to fully conform with the *CMYK* model.

color laser printer   A *laser printer* that can generate output that includes color, but that (for now, anyway) cannot match the output quality of *thermal wax transfer, dye sublimation,* or *thermal dye transfer* printers. Color laser printers are less expensive, faster, and have lower *consumables* costs than other color-capable printers, but they are more expensive than *monochrome* laser printers.

C
D
E

color model   The way in which colors are described and altered. Three popular color models exist: the *HSB* model, the *RGB* model (used in *monitors*), and the *CMYK* model, which can support *device-independent color* systems such as the *Pantone matching system (PMS)*.

color monitor   A *display* device that can display an image in multiple colors, unlike a *monochrome monitor* that displays one color on a black or white background.

color scanner   A *scanner* that records colors as well as shades of gray. Color scanners are distinguished mainly by their *color depth,* and are not significantly more expensive than *grayscale scanners.*

color scheme   A named collection of screen colors you can select from a menu to change a program's on-screen appearance.

In *Microsoft Windows 95*, you can alter screen colors in the Display *dialog box,* in the *Control Panel folder* (see fig. C.4). If Microsoft's color schemes don't suit you, you can paint each element of the screen to your liking.

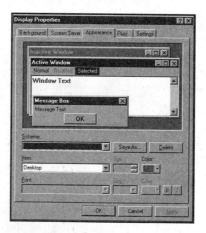

Fig. C.4 *The Display Properties dialog box.*

color separation   The separation of a multicolor *graphic* into several layers of color, with each layer corresponding to one of the colors that will be printed when a professional printer reproduces the graphic. See *Pantone Matching System (PMS).*

column   In character-based video displays, a vertical one-character-wide line down the screen. In a *spreadsheet,* a vertical block of *cells* usually identified by a unique alphabetical letter. In a *database management* program, the terms column and *field* are sometimes used synonymously.

column graph   In analytical and *presentation graphics,* a *graph* with vertical columns. Column graphs are commonly used to show the values of items as they vary at precise intervals over a period of time (see fig. C.5). The *x-axis* (categories axis) is the horizontal axis, and the *y-axis* (values axis) is the vertical axis. Such graphs are often called *bar graphs,* but technically speaking, bar graphs have horizontal bars.

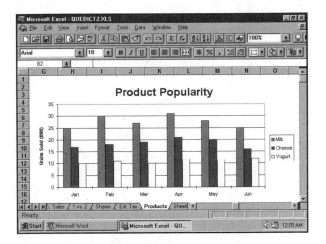

Fig. C.5   *A column graph with clustered columns.*

When you display more than one data series, clustering the columns (as in fig. C.5) or overlapping them (see fig. C.6) is helpful. With caution, you also can create a three-dimensional effect to differentiate the columns, if it really helps clarify the data (see fig. C.7). See *histogram* and *stacked column graph.*

column indicator   In *word processing programs,* such as *Microsoft Word,* a message in the *status bar* that shows the number of horizontal spaces, or columns, the *cursor* has moved across the screen.

column text chart In *presentation graphics*, a chart showing related items as side-by-side columns of text (see fig. C.8).

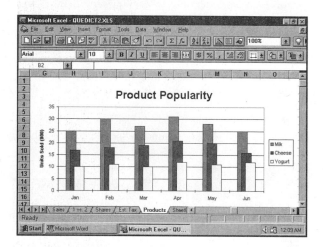

Fig. C.6 *Overlapped columns.*

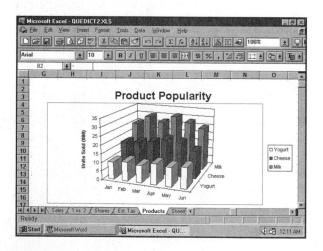

Fig. C.7 *A three-dimensional column graph.*

column-wise recalculation In *spreadsheet programs*, a *recalculation order* that calculates all the values in column A before moving to column B, and so on.

CAUTION: *If your spreadsheet program doesn't offer natural recalculation, use column-wise recalculation for worksheets in which columns are summed and the totals are forwarded. Row-wise recalculation may produce erroneous results. See* optimal recalculation.

C
D
E

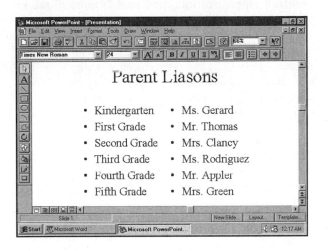

Fig. C.8 *A column text chart.*

COM In *MS-DOS*, a device name that refers to the *serial ports* available in your computer. Your computer can have up to four COM ports, designated as COM1, COM2, COM3, and COM4.

When used as a file name extension, .COM indicates an *executable program* file limited to 64K. To run a .COM file, type the file name and press Enter.

 com On the *Internet*, a top-level domain name that is assigned to a corporation or business. Top-level domain names come last in a given Internet computer's domain name (such as **www.apple.com**).

combinatorial explosion A barrier to the solution of a problem that occurs when the possibilities that must be computed are too numerous.

Combinatorial explosions vex the designers of chess software, which must frequently compute and analyze tens of thousands of alternative moves in a turn. Because people rely on as-yet poorly understood intuitive processes to narrow down the range of possibilities to a manageable number, the best chess champions can still beat the best chess programs. See *artifical intelligence.*

COMDEX   See *Computer Dealers Exhibition (COMDEX).*

Comité Consultatif International Téléphonique et Télégraphique (CCITT)   A defunct international organization that designed standards for *analog* and *digital* communications involving *modems,* computer *networks,* and *fax* machines. For computer users, CCITT's most important role lay in the establishment of international standards for modem connectivity, the famous "V-dot" standards (such as *V.32bis* and *V.34*). The CCITT has been replaced by the *International Telecommunications Union-Telecommunications Standards Section (ITU-TSS).*

comma-delimited file   A *data file,* usually in *ASCII* format, in which a user or *program* separates the data items by commas to facilitate the transfer of data to another program. See *tab-delimited file.*

command   A user-initiated signal given to a *program* that initiates, terminates, or otherwise controls the execution of a specific operation. In *command-driven programs,* you type the command statement and its associated syntax and press Enter. In a *menu-driven program,* you choose a command from an on-screen *menu.*

command button   In *graphical user interfaces (GUIs)* such as *Microsoft Windows 95* or the Macintosh *Finder,* a *pushbutton* in a *dialog box* that initiates an action such as carrying out a command with the options chosen, cancelling a command, or displaying another dialog box. You can quickly choose the default button just by pressing Return (for Macintoshes) or Enter (for Windows systems).

COMMAND.COM   In *MS-DOS,* a *file* that contains the *command processor.* This file must be present on the startup disk for MS-DOS to run.

command-driven program   A *system, utility,* or *application program* that requires you to type *command* statements, with the correct *syntax* and nomenclature, to use the program's features. See *graphical user interface (GUI)* and *menu-driven program.*

Command key On *Macintosh keyboards,* a key marked with " that's frequently used in combination with alphabetical keys to provide keyboard shortcuts for *menu* options. Apple standardized these shortcuts so all Macintosh *applications* support them.

command language See *software command language.*

command-line operating system A *command-driven* operating system, such as *MS-DOS,* that requires you to type commands using the *keyboard.* See *graphical user interface (GUI).*

command mode A *modem* mode in which it takes instructions from other parts of the computer, such as the *keyboard,* instead of transmitting everything over the phone line. *Communications programs* usually handle the distinction between command mode and *communications mode.*

command processor The part of an *operating system* that accepts input from the user and displays prompts and messages, such as confirmation and error messages. Also referred to as the command interpreter. See *COMMAND.COM* and *command-line operating system.*

comment See *remark.*

comment out In *programming,* to place a symbol (such as a semicolon) or a command at the beginning of a line that marks the line as documentation. The *compiler* or *interpreter* ignores any lines preceded with this symbol.

Commercial Internet Exchange (CIX) An organization of *Internet* service providers, who collaborate to provide a national Internet *backbone* service that is free from Acceptable Use Policies (AUPs), which bar commercial activity. There are no restrictions on commercial use of the CIX backbone network. See *NSFnet.*

Common Gateway Interface (CGI) A standard that describes how *HTTPD*-compatible *World Wide Web (WWW)* servers should access external programs, so that this data is returned to the user in the form of an automatically generated Web page. CGI programs, called scripts, come into play when a Web user fills out an on-screen *form;* the form generates output that is handled by the script, which brings other programs into play as necessary. These may include a database search engine or a mailer program.

In any case, the result is that the user sees a new Web page, which may contain the results of a database search or a confirmation that a mail message has been sent. Common applications of CGI include providing a means for users to type and mail feedback, enabling database searches, and creating *gateways* to other Internet services that are not directly accessible through the Web.

Common User Access (CUA) Interface in *Microsoft Windows 95 application programs*, a set of basic *menu* items, the arrangement of items on the menus, and basic *keystrokes*. These include Alt+F4 to close an *application,* Ctrl+F6 to switch to another *window,* and the location of File, Window, and Help on the *menu bar*. See *application program interface (API).*

communications mode A *modem* mode in which everything sent to the modem, such as text from the *keyboard,* is put onto the telephone line. See *command mode.*

communications parameters In *telecommunications* and serial printing, the settings (parameters) that customize serial communications for the *hardware* you're contacting. See *baud rate, communications protocol, full duplex, half duplex, parameter, parity bit,* and *stop bit.*

communications program An *application program* that turns your computer into a *terminal* for transmitting data to and receiving data from distant computers through the telephone system.

A good communications program includes a *software command language* you can use to automate cumbersome *log-on* procedures, several *file-transfer protocols* (such as *XMODEM* and *Kermit*), *terminal emulation* of several popular mainframe terminals (such as the DEC VT100), on-screen timing so you can keep track of time charges, and a phone book for storing and retrieving telephone numbers.

communications protocol The standards that govern the transfer of information among computers on a *network* or using *telecommunications.* The computers involved in the communication must have the same settings and follow the same standards to avoid errors.

When you use a *modem* to access a *bulletin board system (BBS)* or *on-line information service,* such as *America Online* or *CompuServe,* choose the communications protocol established by the host computer system, including *baud rate, data bits, duplex, parity,* and *stop bits.* Most communications services use eight data bits and one stop bit; full duplex is also common. Review any documentation you have for an on-line service to find out which settings to use.

You may have to specify an additional parameter called *handshaking.* This parameter establishes the way one computer tells the other device when to wait. Almost all computers and many peripheral devices use *XON/XOFF* handshaking, the default for most communications programs. If you're having trouble establishing communication with an on-line service, press Enter twice and try these settings:

    Parity: No

    Data bits: 8

    Stop bits: 1

    Duplex: Full

If you can't see what you're typing, switch to half duplex. If the preceding settings don't work, hang up and dial again with these settings:

    Parity: Even

    Data bits: 7

    Stop bits: 1

    Duplex: Full or half

If you're using half duplex and see any typed text echoed, such as HHEELLLLOO, switch to full duplex.

See *asynchronous communication.*

communications settings   See *communications parameters* and *communications protocol.*

comp   In *desktop publishing (DTP),* a complete mock-up of a page layout design, showing what the final printed page will look like.

comp hierarchy   In *UseNet,* one of the seven *standard newsgroup hierarchies;* the comp.* newsgroups deal with every conceivable aspect of computing, including *artificial intelligence*, *computer-aided design (CAD)*, *database* systems, digital telephony, *graphics*, the *Internet*, professional organizations, *programming languages*, *networks*, *operating systems*, specific *computer systems*, and theory. The comp.binaries.* newsgroups contain *freeware* and *shareware* programs.

Compact Disk-Interactive (CD-I)   A *compact disk (CD)* standard designed for interactive viewing of audiovisual recordings with a television set and a CD-I player. Designed for education, training, and entertainment, CD-I has been slow to find a market.

compact disk (CD)   A plastic disk, 4.75 inches in diameter, that uses optical storage techniques to store up to 72 minutes of music or 650*M* of digitally encoded computer data.

CDs originally provided read-only data storage. The computer can read information from the disk, but you can't change this information or write new information to the disk. Therefore, this storage medium accurately is termed *Compact Disc-read-only memory (CD-ROM)*. Erasable optical disk drives are now available and are expected to have a major impact on secondary storage techniques in the next decade. See *erasable optical disk drive, optical disk,* and *secondary storage.*

Compact Disk-Digital Audio (CD-DA)   The sort of *CD-ROM* you can buy in a record store. Based on an early-1980s standard for recording sounds on compact disks, CD-DA is one of the most popular music-recording media around.

company network   A *wide area network (WAN),* such as DEC ENET (the internal engineering network of Digital Equipment Corporation), that often has automatic gateways to cooperative networks such as *ARPAnet* or *BITNET* for functions such as *electronic mail* and file transfer.

comparison operator   See *relational operator.*

compatibility   The capability of a device, *program,* or *adapter* to function with or substitute for another make and model of computer, device, or program. Also, the capability of one computer to run the *software* written to run on another computer.

To be truly compatible, a program or device should operate on a given system without changes; all features should operate as intended and run, without changes, all the software the other computer can run. See *clone*.

TIP: *In IBM PC-compatible computing, a frequently used index of 100 percent IBM compatibility is a computer's capability to run Microsoft Flight Simulator.*

C
D
E

compiler   A program that reads the statements written in a human-readable *programming language,* such as *Pascal* or *Modula-2,* and translates the statements into a machine-readable executable program. Compiled programs run significantly faster than interpreted ones because the program interacts directly with the *microprocessor* and doesn't need to share memory space with the *interpreter.* See *machine language.*

Complementary Metal-Oxide Semiconductor (CMOS)   An energy-saving *chip* made to duplicate the functions of other chips, such as memory chips or *microprocessors.* CMOS chips are used in battery-powered *portable computers* and in other applications where reduced electrical consumption is desired.

CMOS also refers to a special CMOS chip that operates the real-time clock included on a motherboard and stores the basic *system configuration,* including the *floppy* and *hard disk* types, amount of installed memory, and *wait state* settings. These settings are retained while the computer is off with only nominal battery support.

complex instruction set computer (CISC)   A type of *central processing unit (CPU)* that can recognize as many as 100 or more instructions, enough to carry out most computations directly.

Most microprocessors are CISC chips. The use of *reduced instruction set computer (RISC)* technology, however, is becoming increasingly common in professional workstations and is expected to migrate to personal computers in the mid 1990s.

compose sequence   A series of *keystrokes* that lets you enter a *character* not found on the computer's keyboard. In *Lotus 1-2-3,* for example, you can enter é by pressing Alt+F1 and then typing 233.

composite   See *comp.*

composite color monitor   A *monitor* that accepts a standard video signal that mixes red, green, and blue signals to produce the color image. Display quality is inferior to that of *RGB monitors.* See *composite video.*

composite video   A method for broadcasting video signals in which the red, green, and blue components, as well as horizontal and vertical synchronization signals, are mixed together.

Composite video, regulated by the U.S. *National Television Standards Committee (NTSC),* is used for television. Some computers have composite video outputs that use a standard RCA phono plug and cable such as on the backplane of a hi-fi or stereo system. See *composite color monitor* and *RGB monitor.*

compound device   In *multimedia,* a device, such as a *Musical Instrument Digital Interface (MIDI) sequencer,* that reproduces sound or other output that you recorded in a specific media file.

compound document   In *Object Linking and Embedding (OLE),* a single *file* created by two or more applications. When you use OLE to embed a *Microsoft Excel* chart into a *Microsoft Word* document, for example, the resulting file contains the Word text as well as the Excel *object.* The object contains all the information Excel needs to open the chart for editing. This information results in file sizes considerably larger than normal.

compress   A *UNIX compression utility* that creates files with the *.Z extension. A copyrighted program, compress cannot be freely redistributed, so many UNIX users prefer to use the Open Software Foundation's gunzip, which creates compressed files with the *.gz extension.

 TIP: *Need to decompress *.Z files? Get a copy of Niko-Mak Computing's shareware WinZip 5.6, which can decompress *.Z, *.gz, and *.tar archives as well as *.zip files.*

compressed file   A *file* converted by a *file compression utility* to a special format that minimizes the disk storage space required.

 compressed SLIP (CSLIP)   An optimized version of the *Serial Line Interface Protocol (SLIP),* commonly used to connect

PCs to the *Internet* by means of dialup connections, that includes compression and produces improved throughput.

compression The reduction of a *file's* size by means of a compression program. The two types of compression are *lossless compression* and *lossy compresion.* In lossless compression, the compression process allows for the subsequent decompression of the file with no loss of the original data. Lossless compression is used for program and dat files. Lossy compression, in which the compression processes remove some of the data in a way that is not obvious to a person using the data. Lossy compression is used for sounds, graphics, animations, and videos. Many modems offer on-the-fly compression, and often use the *MNP5* or *V.42bis* protocols.

CompuServe The second-largest *on-line information service.* A for-profit version of a *bulletin board system (BBS),* CompuServe offers file *downloading, electronic mail,* news, up-to-the-minute stock quotes, an on-line encyclopedia, and conferences on a wide variety of topics. The outmoded and challenging character-based user interface, however, has encouraged the creation of front-end programs such as CompuServe Navigator and TAPCIS, either of which you should consider using. See *America Online, GEnie,* and *Prodigy.*

compusex See *cybersex.*

computation The successful execution of an *algorithm,* which can be a textual search or *sort,* as well as a calculation.

computer A machine that can follow instructions to alter *data* in a desirable way and to perform at least some operations without human intervention. Computers represent and manipulate text, *graphics,* symbols, and music, as well as numbers. See *analog computer* and *digital computer.*

computer addiction See *computer dependency.*

computer-aided design (CAD) The use of the *computer* and a CAD program to design a wide range of industrial products, ranging from machine parts to homes. CAD has become a mainstay in a variety of design-related fields, such as architecture, civil engineering, electrical engineering, mechanical engineering, and interior design. CAD applications are *graphics*- and calculation-intensive, requiring fast *microprocessors* and high-*resolution* video *displays.*

Like many other professional computer applications based on expensive *mainframe* or *minicomputer* systems, CAD is migrating to powerful personal computers, such as those based on the *Pentium* and *Motorola 68040* microprocessors. CAD software for personal computers blends the *object-oriented graphics* found in *draw programs* with precision scaling in two and three dimensions, to produce drawings with an intricate level of detail.

computer-aided design and drafting (CADD)   The use of a *computer system* for industrial design and technical drawing. CADD software closely resembles *computer-aided design (CAD)* software, but has additional features that allow the artist to produce drawings conforming to engineering conventions.

computer-assisted instruction (CAI)   The use of programs to perform instructional tasks, such as drill and practice, tutorials, and tests.

Unlike human teachers, a CAI program works patiently with bright and slow students alike. Ideally, CAI can use sound, graphics, and on-screen rewards to engage a student in learning with huge payoffs.

With the advent of *multimedia,* CAI may be entering a new era. Multimedia machines equipped with *compact disks, video adapters,* and *sound boards* may function to open new worlds to students by placing immense reservoirs of knowledge and experience in every classroom. *Authoring languages,* such as *HyperTalk,* make developing high-quality instructional software much easier.

computer-based training (CBT)   The use of *computer-aided instruction (CAI)* techniques to train for specific skills, such as operating a numerically controlled lathe.

Computer Dealers Exhibition (COMDEX)   A huge computer-industry trade show at which hardware manufacturers and software publishers display their wares for customers, the computer press, and each other. Held twice annually (in the spring in Atlanta and in the fall in Las Vegas), the fall COMDEX is regarded as the more important show.

computer dependency   A psychological disorder characterized by compulsive and prolonged computer usage. For example, medical authorities in Denmark have reported the case of an

18-year-old who spent up to 16 hours a day with his computer. Doctors found that he was talking to himself in a *programming language.*

 Computer Emergency Response Team (CERT)   An *Internet* security task force that is designed to detect and respond rapidly to Internet security threats. Formed by the *Defense Advanced Research Project Agency (DARPA)* in 1988 in response to the infamous *Internet Worm,* CERT monitors Internet security and alerts system administrators concerning the activities of computer *crackers.*

Computer Fraud and Abuse Act of 1984   A U.S. federal law that criminalizes the abuse of U.S. government computers or *networks* that cross state boundaries. Fines and/or prison sentences are spelled out for unauthorized access, theft of credit data, and spying with the intent to aid a foreign government.

Computer Graphics Metafile (CGM)   An international graphics file format that stores *object-oriented graphics* in device-independent form so you can exchange CGM files among users of different computer systems (and different *programs*). A CGM file contains the graphic image as well as the instructions required for another program to create a file.

Personal computer programs that can read and write to CGM file formats include Harvard Graphics and Ventura Publisher. It's the standard format used by *Lotus 1-2-3.* See *Windows Metafile Format (WMF).*

Computer Professionals for Social Responsibility (CPSR)   A non-profit, public advocacy organization, based in Palo Alto, California, that brings together computer scientists, computer educators, and interested citizens who are broadly concerned about the impact of computer technology on human welfare. Issues of CPSR concern include worker health and safety, the impact of computer technology on modern warfare, and civil liberties in the electronic age. The group's activities include education, conferences, publications, lobbying, and litigation.

computer system   A complete computer installation—including *peripherals,* such as *hard* and *floppy disk drives, monitor, mouse, operating system, software,* and *printer*—in which all the components are designed to work with each other.

CON In *MS-DOS,* the device name for *console,* which refers to the *keyboard* and *monitor.* The *command* COPY CON C:AUTOEXEC.BAT, for example, creates a file called AUTOEXEC.BAT and stores in this file all the characters you type after giving the command. To finish copying text from the keyboard, press Ctrl+Z and then press Enter.

concatenation To link together two or more units of information, such as *strings* or *files,* so that they form one unit. In *spreadsheet* programs, concatenation is used to combine text in a formula by placing an ampersand between the formula and text.

concordance file A *file* containing the words you want a *word processing* program to include in the index the program constructs.

concurrency control In a *local area network (LAN)* version of an *application program,* the features built into the program that govern what happens when two or more people try to access the same program feature or *data file.*

Many programs not designed for networks can run on a network and allow more than one person to access a *document,* but it may result in one person accidentally destroying another person's work. Concurrency control addresses this problem by enabling multiple access where such access can occur without losing data and by restricting multiple access where access could result in destroyed work. See *file locking, LAN-aware program,* and *LAN-ignorant program.*

concurrency management See *concurrency control.*

concurrent processing See *multitasking.*

condensed type Type narrowed in width so more characters can fit into a linear inch. In *dot-matrix printers,* condensed type usually is set to print 17 *characters per inch (cpi).*

conference on data-systems languages (CODASYL) A professional organization dedicated to improving and standardizing *COBOL.*

confidentiality In *electronic mail,* the protection of a message from being read or intercepted by persons other than the intended recipient. An essential element in the privacy people expect from digital communications, confidentiality is illusory in most electronic mail systems—a fact that users should appreciate. Although the U.S. Electronic Communications Privacy Act (ECPA) prevents federal investigators from intercepting electronic mail messages while they are en route, ECPA does not forbid investigators from retrieving copies of your mail that are stored on backup tapes, and it does not forbid employers from accessing employee electronic mail. Some states provide varying degrees of protection, but in general one should never send an electronic mail message that you wouldn't want to see on your boss's desk the next morning—or on the front page of your local newspaper.

CONFIG.SYS   In *MS-DOS*, an *ASCII* text *file* in the *root directory* that contains *configuration* commands. MS-DOS consults this file at system startup.

configuration   The choices made in setting up a *computer system* or an *application program* so that it meets the user's needs.

Properly configuring your system or program is one of the more onerous tasks of personal computing and, unfortunately, hasn't been eliminated by the arrival of *windowing environments.* In *Microsoft Windows 95,* for example, you must perform some manual configuration to obtain maximum performance from Windows and to take full advantage of the memory available on your system. When established, the configuration is saved to a *configuration file,* such as *WIN.INI* or *AUTOEXEC.BAT.*

configuration file   A *file* created by an *application program* that stores the choices you make when you install the program so that they're available the next time you start the program. In *Microsoft Word,* for example, the file MW.INI stores the choices you make from the Options menu.

TIP: *More than a few users have accidentally erased configuration files when trying to free up disk space. Make copies of files with extensions such as .CFG, .INI, or .SET. To avoid re-creating erased configuration files, you can use the copy of the configuration file.*

To avoid disturbing configuration and other vital program files, don't store your documents in your application's directory. If you store them elsewhere, you're less likely to erase vital application files when you're deleting unwanted documents.

configuration manager   In Microsoft Windows 95, the utility program that keeps track of the software drivers associated with hardware devices. See *hardware tree.*

confirmation message   An on-screen message asking you to confirm a potentially destructive action, such as closing a *window* without saving your work. See *alert box.*

 connectionless protocol   In *wide area networks (WANs),* a standard that enables the transmission of data from one computer to another even though no effort is made to determine whether the receiving computer is on-line or able to receive the information. This is the underlying protocol in any *packet-switching network,* such as the *Internet,* in which a unit of data is broken down into small-sized packets, each with a header containing the address of the data's intended destination. In the Internet, the connectionless protocol is the *Internet Protocol (IP).* IP is concerned only with breaking data down into packets for transmission, and reassembling the packets after they have been received. A *connection-oriented protocol* (on the Internet, TCP) works at another level to assure that all the packets are received. Research on computer networks has disclosed this design is highly efficient. See *Transmission Control Protocol (TCP).*

 connection-oriented protocol   In *wide area networks (WANs),* a standard that establishes a procedure by which two of the computers on the *network* can establish a physical connection that lasts until they have successfully exchanged data. This is accomplished by means of *handshaking,* in which the two computers exchange messages that say, in effect, "OK, I'm ready," "I didn't get that; please re-send," and "Got it, bye." In the *Internet,* the *Transmission Control Protocol (TCP)* is a connection-oriented protocol; it provides the means by which two Internet-connected computers can enter into communication with each other to ensure the successful transmission of data. In contrast, the *Internet Protocol (IP)* is a *connectionless protocol,* which enables the transmission of data without requiring handshaking. See *X.25.*

connectivity   The extent to which a given computer or *program* can function in a *network* setting.

connectivity platform   A *program* or *utility* designed to enhance another program's capability to exchange *data* with other programs through a local area network (LAN). Oracle for the

Macintosh, for example, provides *HyperCard* with the connectivity required to search for and retrieve information from large corporate *databases.*

connector conspiracy A computer manufacturer's cynical plot to force its customers to buy its products, which contain bizarre connectors that work only with peripherals made by the same company. Vastly unpopular with users, connector conspiracies nevertheless spring up eternally, fueled by greed. The most recent version: Proprietary *CD-ROM* connectors on *sound cards,* which force you to buy a *CD-ROM disk drive* made by the same manufacturer (unless you're willing to live with reduced functionality).

connect speed The data-transmission rate at which a *modem,* after performing a *handshaking sequence* with another modem and determining the amount of *line noise,* establishes a connection. The connect speed may be lower than the modem's top speed.

console A *terminal,* consisting of a *monitor* and *keyboard.* In *multiuser systems,* console is synonymous with *terminal,* but console also is used in *personal computer* operating systems to refer to the keyboard and display. See *CON.*

constant In a *spreadsheet program,* a number you type directly into a *cell* or place in a *formula.* See *cell definition* and *key variable.*

constant angular velocity (CAV) In *data storage media* such as *hard* and *floppy disk drives,* a playback technique in which the disk rotates at a constant speed. This technique results in faster data retrieval times as the *read/write head* nears the *spindle;* retrieval times slow as the read/write head moves toward the perimeter of the disk. See *constant linear velocity (CLV).*

constant linear velocity (CLV) In *CD-ROM disk drives,* a playback technique that speeds or slows the rotation of the disk to ensure that the velocity of the disk is always constant at the point where the disk is being read. To achieve constant linear velocity, the disk must spin more slowly when reading or writing closer to the *spindle.* See *constant angular velocity (CAV).*

consumables The supplies a *printer* uses up as it operates. Consumables expenses, such those for ink cartridges and paper, can quickly add up. Consumables costs are usually expressed as a *cost per page,* which for some *high-end* color-capable printers can exceed $3.00!

contact head   In a *hard disk,* a *read/write head* that skates on the surface of a *platter* instead of flying over it. Contact heads offer resistance to *head crashes* and improved *areal density.*

container   See *compound document.*

contention   In *local area networks (LANs),* a channel access method in which access to the communication channel is based on a first-come, first-served policy. See *carrier sense multiple access with collision detection (CSMA/CD).*

context-sensitive help   In an *application program,* a user-assistance mode that displays documentation relevant to the *command, mode,* or action you are now performing. Context-sensitive help reduces the time and keystrokes needed to get on-screen help. After pressing Format (Shift+F8) in WordPerfect 6 for *MS-DOS,* for example, rather than search for the desired information manually from an index or menu, press Help (F1) to see a help screen explaining the options available on the Format menu.

context switching   Changing from one *program* to another without exiting either program. A multiple-loading program enables context switching.

Unlike the true *multitasking* possible with *Microsoft Windows 95* and *DESQview,* a multiple-loading program doesn't allow *background* programs to continue executing, but does allow you to switch rapidly from one program to another. When combined with a *graphical user interface (GUI)* and cut-and-paste facilities provided by a *clipboard,* context switching lets you move data rapidly and easily from one application to another. See *multiple program loading.*

contiguous   Adjacent; placed one next to or after the other. A *range* of *cells* in a *spreadsheet* is often, but not always, made up of contiguous cells.

continuous paper   Paper manufactured in one long strip, with perforations separating the pages, so you can feed the paper into a *printer* with a *tractor-feed* mechanism. Synonymous with continuous-feed paper.

continuous-tone image   *Printer* output in which colors and shades of gray blend smoothly together, as they would in a chemically printed photograph.

continuous-tone printer   A *printer* that can generate *photorealistic output,* with smooth gradations between colors or shades of gray.

contrast   In *monitors,* the degree of distinction between dark and light *pixels.* A contrast control regulates contrast. Bright light, especially sunlight, can wash out low-contrast displays, so you should turn up the contrast control under such conditions.

C ◄
D
E

control   In a *Microsoft Windows 95* program, a *dialog box* feature (such as a *check box, radio button,* or *list box*) that allows the user to choose options.

Control+Break   In *MS-DOS,* a *keyboard command* that cancels the execution of a *program* or command at the next available *breakpoint.*

Control (Ctrl) key   In *IBM PC-compatible* computing, a *key* frequently pressed in combination with other keys to issue *program commands.* In *Microsoft Word,* for example, pressing Ctrl+F calls up the Find *dialog box.*

control character   See *control code.*

control code   In *American Standard Code for Information Interchange (ASCII),* a code reserved for *hardware*-control purposes, such as advancing a page on the printer. ASCII has 32 control codes.

controller   See *hard disk controller* and *floppy disk controller.*

controller card   An *adapter* that connects *hard* and *floppy disk drives* to the computer. Most personal computer controller cards contain circuitry to connect one or more *floppy disks* and a *hard disk.*

control menu   In *Microsoft Windows 95,* a *pull-down menu,* found in all *windows* and *dialog boxes,* that contains options for managing the *active window* (see fig. C.9). The control menu *icon,* a button containing a bar shaped like a hyphen, is on the left end of the *title bar.* The contents of the menu vary, but the menu usually includes commands to move, size, *maximize,* and *minimize* windows, as well as to close the current window or switch to another application window or the next document window.

> **TIP:** *To display the control menu of an application window or a dialog box quickly, press Alt+space bar. To open a document window's control menu, press Alt+hyphen. You can use the keyboard to select commands on the control menu.*

control menu

| Microsoft Excel - QUEDICT2.XLS |

Restore
Move
Size
Minimize
Maximize
Close   Alt+F4

	C	D	E	F	G	H	I
May							
1							
2			Month	Estimate			
3			Jan	25		Tax Rate:	0.4
4			Feb	60		Inflation:	0.05
5			Mar	95			
6			Apr	130			
7			May	165			
8			Jun	200			
9			Jul	235			
10			Aug	270			
11			Sep	305			
12			Oct	340			
13			Nov	375			
14			Dec	410			
15							
16							
17							

Sales / 1 vs. 2 / Shares \ Est. Tax / Sheet5 / Sheet6

Move, size, or close window

Start | Microsoft Word | Microsoft Excel - QU... | 11:57 PM

Fig. C.9   *The control menu.*

control panel   In *Lotus 1-2-3*, the top three lines of the screen. The top line contains the *current cell* indicator and the mode indicator. The second is the entry line and the third line is blank. When you press the slash key to use menu mode, the second and third lines contain *menus* and prompts.

In the *Macintosh* and *Microsoft Windows 95* operating environments, the control panel is a utility window that lists options for *hardware* devices, such as the *mouse, monitor,* and *keyboard.*

control panel device (CDEV)   Any *Macintosh utility program* placed in the *System Folder* that appears as an option in the *Control Panel.*

control structure   A logical organization for an *algorithm* that governs the sequence in which *program* statements are executed.

Control statements govern the flow of control in a program by specifying the sequence in which the steps in a program or *macro* are carried out. Control structures include branch structures that cause a special set of instructions to be executed if a specified situation is encountered; loop structures that execute over and over until a condition is fulfilled; and procedure/function structures that set aside distinct program functions or procedures into separate modules, which are invoked from the main program.

control unit   A component of the *central processing unit (CPU)* that obtains program instructions and emits signals to carry them out. See *arithmetic-logic unit (ALU)*.

convenience copier   A *printer/scanner* combination or a *fax* machine that can be used to make small numbers of photocopies.

conventional memory   In any IBM PC-compatible computer, the first 640K of *random-access memory (RAM)*.

The *Intel 8086* and *Intel 8088 microprocessors,* which were available when the IBM Personal Computer (PC) was designed, can directly use 1*M* of *random-access memory (RAM)*. The PC's designers decided to make 640*K* of RAM accessible to programs, reserving the rest of the 1M memory space for internal system functions. *Microsoft Windows 95* gives programs direct access to all of a system's RAM

conventional programming   The use of a *procedural programming language,* such as *BASIC, FORTRAN,* or *assembly language,* to code an *algorithm* in machine-readable form. In conventional programming, the programmer must be concerned with the sequence in which events occur within the computer. Nonprocedural programming languages let the programmer focus on the problem without worrying about the precise procedure the computer must follow to solve the problem. *See declarative language.*

 convergence   In a *packet-switching network*, an automatic process of network mapping that occurs after a router is switched on. A *router* is a device, usually a dedicated computer, that "reads" each incoming packet and determines where to send it next. In order to do its job correctly, the router needs an accurate map of the networks to which it is directly connected. If this map had to be updated manually, organizations would have to devote a considerable amount of time and human resources to the job.

Convergence software enables to router to detect changes to the network, such as the addition or removal of workstations, and to adjust its map automatically. The process is called convergence because it takes a few minutes for the router's map to "converge" to reality (the current state of the network).

In *monitors*, the alignment of the red, blue, and green *electron guns* to create colors on-screen. If they aren't perfectly aligned, poor convergence results, causing a decrease in image sharpness and *resolution*. White areas also tend to show colors around their edges.

cooperative multitasking   In an *operating system*, a means of running more than one *program* at a time. In cooperative multitasking, one *application program* cannot force another to do something. An application yields to another voluntarily, but only after checking the electronic equivalent of a message box to see if any other applications have made a request. If the application is involved in a lengthy processing operation, however, it may not check the message box until the operation is completed. See *pre-emptive multitasking*.

cooperative network   A *wide-area network (WAN)*, such as *BITNET* or *UUCP,* in which the costs of participating are borne by the linked organizations. See *company network* and *research network.*

copper pair   Standard telephone cable that cannot handle high-speed *digital* communications services such as the *Integrated Services Digital Network (ISDN).* The copper pair wire that pervades American residences and businesses will have to be replaced before high-speed digital communication can become commonplace. See *twisted pair.*

coprocessor   A *microprocessor* support *chip* that takes over a specific processing operation, such as handling mathematical computations or displaying images on the video display. See *numeric coprocessor.*

copy   The material—including text, *graphic* images, pictures, and artwork—to be assembled for printing. Also, to reproduce part of a *document* at another location in the document or in another document.

copy fitting   In *desktop publishing (DTP),* a method used to determine the amount of copy (text), in a specified *font,* that can fit into a given area on a page or in a publication.

copyleft   A type of copyright promoted by the Free Software Foundation that is intended to promote the free distribution of copyrighted software for noncommercial purposes.

copy protection   Hidden instructions included in a *program* intended to prevent you from making unauthorized copies of *software.* Because most copy-protection schemes impose penalties on legitimate owners of programs, such as forcing them to insert a specially encoded "key disk" before using a program, most business software publishers have given up using these schemes. Copy protection is still common, however, in recreational and educational software.

core dump   In *mainframe* computing, a *debugging* technique that involves printing out the entire contents of the computer's core, or memory. In slang, the term refers to a person who, when asked a simple question, recites everything he or she remembers about a subject. See *dump.*

core-logic chip set   A collection of integrated circuits that allows a *central processing unit (CPU)* to work with an *external cache, random-access memory (RAM),* and an *expansion bus.*

core set of modulation protocols   The methods for transmitting data that are built into *modems.* The core set of modulation protocols in modern modems typically includes *Bell 103, Bell 212, V.22, V.22bis, V.32,* and *V.32bis,* and enables virtually any pair of modems to communicate successfully.

corona wire   In *laser printers,* a wire that applies electrostatic charge to paper.

corrupted file   A *file* that contains scrambled and unrecoverable data. Files can become corrupted due to bad *sectors* (surface flaws on the disk), *hard* or *floppy disk drive controller* failures, or *software* errors.

cost-benefit analysis   A projection of the costs and benefits of buying certain equipment or taking certain action.

CAUTION: *Cost-benefit analyses of computer equipment often involve overly optimistic assumptions about the tangible cost. With a word processing program, for example, you can revise a document faster, but you may keep working to achieve perfection, spending more time than you originally would have. See* re-engineering.

cost per page   In *printers,* an estimate of the cost of *consumables* for each page of output generated. Since consumables can ultimately cost more than the printer, pay attention to cost per page figures when shopping for printers. Some high-end color-capable printers have costs per page of $3.00 or more.

counter   In *typography,* the space fully or partially enclosed by a *bowl,* the strokes that form a letter, such as the blank space inside the letter a or o.

Courier   A *monospace typeface,* commonly included as a *built-in font* in *laser printers,* that simulates the output of office typewriters. For example: `This is Courier type.`

courseware   Software developed for *computer-assisted instruction (CAI)* or *computer-based training (CBT)* applications.

courtesy copy (CC)   In *electronic mail,* a copy of an e-mail message that is sent to one or more addresses. These addresses are included in the header information that the message's recipient sees. In a *blind courtesy copy* (BCC), the recipient does not know who, if anyone, has received copies of the message.

cpi   See *characters per inch (cpi).*

CP/M (Control Program for Microprocessors)   An early *operating system* for personal computers that used the 8-bit Intel *8080* and Zilog Z-80 *microprocessors.* CP/M was created in the late 1970s as *floppy disk drives* became available for early personal computers.

CPM   See *critical path method (CPM).*

cps   See *characters per second (cps).*

CPU   See *central processing unit (CPU).*

CPU fan   A fan that mounts directly on top of the *microprocessor chip* to keep it cool. Newer *microprocessors,* such as the *Pentium,* get extremely hot and can malfunction if allowed to overheat.

cracker A computer hobbyist who gets kicks from gaining unauthorized access to computer systems. Cracking is a silly, egotistical game in which the object is to defeat even the most secure computer systems. Although many crackers do little more than leave a "calling card" to prove their victory, some attempt to steal credit card information or destroy data. Whether or not they commit a crime, all crackers injure legitimate computer users by consuming the time of system administrators and making computer resources more difficult to access. In the press, the term "cracker" is used synonymously with *"hacker,"* but *hacking* has a completely different meaning and plays a valuable role in computing. See *hacker ethic* and *security*.

crash An abnormal termination of *program* execution, usually (but not always) resulting in a frozen *keyboard* or an unstable state. In most cases, you must *cold boot* the computer to recover from a crash.

CRC See *cyclic redundancy check (CRC)*.

creator type In the *Macintosh*, a four-letter code that identifies the program used to create a *document*. The code associates the document with the application so that you can start the application by opening the document. See *associated document*.

creeping featurism An unfortunate tendency in *programming* where *software* developers add more and more *features* in an attempt to keep up with the competition. The result is a program that's hopelessly complex, sluggish, and hogs disk space.

crippled version A freely distributed version of a *program* that lacks one or more crucial features, such as printing, that have been deliberately disabled in an attempt to introduce the user to the program in the hope that the user will buy the full version. Synonymous with working model. See *demo*.

criteria range In a *spreadsheet program* that includes *database* functions, the *range* of *cells* that contains the conditions, or criteria, you specify to govern how a search is conducted or an *aggregate function* is calculated.

critical path method (CPM) In *project management*, a technique for planning and timing the execution of tasks where you identify a critical path—a series of tasks that must be completed in a timely fashion if the entire project is to be completed on time.

Project management *software* helps project managers identify critical paths.

cropping   A *graphics* editing operation in which you trim the edges from a graphic to make it fit into a given space or to remove unnecessary parts of the image.

cross-hatching   A pattern of parallel and crossed lines added to areas solid in a *graph* to distinguish one data range from another.

 CAUTION: *In graphs, the overuse of cross-hatching may create moiré vibrations, which result from visual interference between cross-hatching patterns. If your graph seems to flicker, reduce the cross-hatching. See* moiré effect.

cross-linked files   In *Microsoft Windows 95,* a file-storage error that occurs when the *file allocation table (FAT)* indicates that two *files* claim the same disk cluster. Like *lost clusters,* cross-linked files occur when the computer is interrupted (by a *crash* or a power outage) while it's writing a file.

To repair cross-linked files, run ScanDisk frequently. Repairing files quickly can minimize the extent of data loss.

cross-platform computing   The use of virtually identical *user interfaces* for programs running on a variety of different (and often incompatible) computer architectures. The *Microsoft Windows 95* and *Macintosh* versions of *Microsoft Word,* for example, resemble each other very closely.

 cross-post   In a computer newsgroup such as *EchoMail* (*Fidonet*) or *UseNet* (*Internet*), to mail a contribution to two or more discussion groups simultaneously. Cross-posting is rarely warranted and is often taken as a *netiquette* violation by someone who doesn't care to get involved in the give-and-take of discussion within a specific group.

cross-reference   In *word processing programs,* a code name used to refer to material discussed elsewhere in a *document.*

Cross-references, such as "See the discussion of burnishing methods on page 19," are helpful to the reader, but they can become a nightmare if you add or delete text. The best word processing programs (such as *WordPerfect* and *Microsoft Word*) contain cross-reference features, enabling you to mark the original text and assign a code name to the marked text, such as BURNISH. Then you type the code name (not the page number) when you want to cross-reference the original text. When you print your document, the program substitutes the correct page number for the code name. If you add or delete text later and print again, the cross-references are updated to reflect the new page numbers.

crosstalk   The interference generated by cables too close to one another. You sometimes hear crosstalk on the telephone. When speaking long-distance, hearing other voices or entire conversations in the background of your conversation isn't uncommon. Crosstalk often prevents error-free transmission of *data.*

CRT   See *cathode ray tube (CRT).*

cryptoanalysis   The science of breaking encrypted messages, both to determine the strength of encryption techniques and to provide the nation with a military advantage.

cryptography   The science of coding messages so that they cannot be read by any person other than the intended recipient. Cryptography dates back to ancient Rome, but it has always been plagued by the messenger problem: If you want to send an encrypted message to somebody, then you must also somehow send the key that is needed to decode the message. There is always the threat that the key could be intercepted en route without your knowing, thus defeating the purpose of encryption. Possibly the most significant event in the history of cryptography is the recent invention of *public key cryptography*, which completely eliminates the need to send a key via a separate, secure channel, and enables two people who have never before communicated to exchange virtually unbreakable messages. See *cryptoanalysis.*

CSMA/CD   See *carrier sense multiple access with collision detection (CSMA/CD).*

CSO name server   An *Internet*-accessible white pages directory that an organization makes available. Listing the names, telephones, and *electronic mail* addresses of all the organizaton's employees, a CSO name server provides an alternative to the telephone directory. The acronym CSO stands for Computing Service Office (CSO), a unit of the University of Illinois, where the original name server software was developed.

Ctrl   See *Control (Ctrl) key.*

Ctrl+Break   See *Control+Break.*

CTS/RTS   Also called hardware *handshaking,* a method of flow control used between the *modem* and the computer in which it is installed. When ready to send data, the computer will send a Request To Send (RTS) signal, to which the modem will reply with a Clear To Send (CTS) signal when it is ready to receive data. CTS/RTS prevents the computer from sending more data than the modem can handle.

CUA   See *Common User Access (CUA).*

CUI   See *Centre Universitaire d'Informatique (CUI).*

CUI W3 Catalog   A *search engine* for locating *World Wide Web (WWW)* documents that is provided by the Centre Universitaire d'Informatique (CUI), a unit of the University of Geneva, Switzerland. The CUI W3 catalog does not rely on an automated search routine (*spider*); instead, the CUI database indexes all the documents that are manually added to the *National Center for Supercomputing Applications (NCSA) "What's New"* database, the *Virtual Library,* and a variety of additional Internet indexes. Although the CUI W3 Catalog indexes far fewer documents than competing search engines such as *Lycos,* it provides an excellent way to search for new documents that may not have appeared yet in the databases of other search engines.

cumulative trauma disorder   See *repetitive strain injury (RSI).*

Curie temperature   A distinct temperature at which a material's *coercivity* changes drastically. *Magneto-optical disk drives* take advantage of the Curie temperature by recording data at high temperatures but storing and reading it at low temperatures, ensuring a long shelf life for the data.

current cell   In a *spreadsheet* program such as *Lotus 1-2-3,* the *cell* in which the *cell pointer* is positioned. Synonymous with active cell.

current cell indicator   In *Lotus 1-2-3,* a message in the upper-left corner that displays the *address* of the *cell* in which the *cell pointer* is positioned.

current directory   The *directory* that *MS-DOS* or an *application program* uses by default to store and retrieve *files.* Synonymous with default directory.

Within an application, the current directory is usually determined by the application program defaults and is often the directory in which the program's files are saved. Some applications, however, let you specify another directory where you want to save *data* files, which then becomes the current directory.

current drive   The *hard* or *floppy disk* the *operating system* uses for an operation unless you specify otherwise. Synonymous with default drive.

current graph   In *Lotus 1-2-3,* the *graph* that the program creates when you open the Graph menu and choose View, which is retained in memory until you save the graph or quit the worksheet.

cursor   An on-screen blinking *character* that shows where the next character will appear. See *pointer.*

cursor-movement keys   The *keys* that move the *cursor* on-screen. Synonymous with arrow keys.

The arrow keys move the cursor in the direction indicated by the arrow on each key—one character left or right or one line up or down. The *enhanced keyboard* includes separate cursor keys that perform the same function as the arrow keys on the numeric key-pad. Some programs configure additional keys so that they move the cursor. These keys include Home, End, Tab, Page Up, and Page Down, and are often combined with other keys, such as Shift+Tab. See *scroll.*

cut and paste   See *block move.*

cut-sheet feeder   A paper-feed mechanism that feeds separate sheets of paper into the printer, where a friction-feed mechanism draws the paper through the printer.

You can buy cut-sheet feeding mechanisms as optional accessories for *dot-matrix* and *letter-quality printers,* but they're standard equipment with *laser printers* and high-quality *ink jet printers.* See *friction feed* and *tractor feed.*

CWIS   See *Campus Wide Information System (CWIS).*

cyberphobia   An exaggerated and irrational fear of computers. Noted by the psychotherapist Craig Brod and others, cyberphobia stems from the stress individuals encounter as they try to cope with an increasingly computer-driven society. Alert employers that offer training to employees new to computers can help ease employee transition to a computerized work environment.

cyberpunk   A genre of science fiction that depicts a dystopian future dominated by worldwide computer *networks,* battling *artificial intelligences,* monopoly capitalism, and a world culture as ethnically eclectic as it is politically apathetic and alienated. On this stage are chronicled the exploits of *hackers* who use hallucinogenic drugs, cyborg implants, and trance states to carry out criminal and heroic missions within the networks' fabulous realms of *virtual reality.*

The originator of the genre is William Gibson in his 1982 book *Neuromancer,* which coined the term cyberspace. Curiously, Gibson knew little about computing when he wrote the book—on a typewriter.

cybersex   A form of long-distance eroticism made possible by a *real-time* computer *chat forum;* synonymous with compusex. To stimulate your virtual partner, you relay a favorite sexual fantasy or describe in vivid terms what you would be doing if the person were actually present.

Cybersex occurs in "chat" lines on adult *bulletin board systems (BBSs),* in which you exchange messages with another person who is also connected to the same system. These chat lines offer explicit sex—one of the reasons people call them. See *teledildonics.*

cyberspace   The virtual space created by *computer systems.*

One definition of space is "a boundless three-dimensional extent in which objects and events occur and have relative position and direction." In the 20th century, computer systems are creating a new kind of space that fits called cyberspace. (The prefix "cyber" refers to computers.)

Cyberspace can take the form of elaborate *virtual reality* worlds or relatively simple *electronic mail.* Electronic mail advocates will readily testify that the ability to communicate with other users, located all over the world, breaks down social and spatial boundaries in an exhilarating way. See *cyberpunk, Internet,* and *virtual reality.*

cyclic redundancy check (CRC)   An automatic error-checking method used by *MS-DOS* when writing data to a *hard* or *floppy disk*. When MS-DOS later reads data from the disk, the same error-check is conducted, and the results of the two checks are compared to make sure that the data hasn't changed. If you see an error message such as CRC ERROR READING DRIVE C, it signals serious problems with the disk. A similar CRC checking procedure also is commonly used by file compression utilities (such as PKZIP) and when transferring files using *data communications*. See *XMODEM-CRC*.

cylinder   In *hard* and *floppy disk drives*, a unit of storage consisting of the set of *tracks* that occupy the same position on opposite sides of the *platter*. On a double-sided disk, a cylinder includes track 1 of the top and the bottom sides. On hard disks in which several disks are stacked on top of one another, a cylinder consists of track 1 on both sides of all the disks.

Cypherpunk   A *programmer* who strongly believes that private citizens possess the right to send a secure, encrypted message to anyone they please, and that *encryption* technology should not be regulated.

Cyrix   A manufacturer of computer chips.

Cyrix 486DLC   A *microprocessor* that is *binary compatible* with *software* written for *x86* computers and *pin-compatible* with the *Intel 386DX*, making the 486DLC an option for 386DX owners who want to upgrade their machines. Unlike the Intel 486DX, the 486DLC—which runs at clock speeds up to 33 *megahertz (MHz)*, does not have a *numeric coprocessor*, so to upgrade fully, computer owners have to install a Cyrix 83D87 chip as well. Internet reports say the 486DLC will not work with the *NeXTStep* operating system. See *Cyrix CX486DRu2*.

Cyrix 486DX2   A *microprocessor* that is both *binary compatible* with *x86 software* and *pin-compatible* with the *Intel 486DX2* microprocessor. Though it is *clock-doubled* like the Intel 486DX2, the Cyrix part has a smaller *internal cache* and is therefore slower.

Cyrix 486SLC   A *microprocessor* that is *binary compatible* with software written for x86 computers and *pin-compatible* with the *Intel 386SX* chip and is designed to upgrade 386SX systems to near-486 performance levels. The 486SLC is available in 16 *megahertz (MHz)* and 25 MHz versions.

Cyrix CX486DRu2   A clock-doubled version of the Cyrix 486DLC microprocessor, designed to run at a clock speed of 66 *megahertz (MHz)*.

Cyrix M1   An unreleased *microprocessor* designed to compete with—and claimed to outperform—the *Pentium*. With its *superscalar architecture,* the M1 is generally similar in design to the Pentium, and the two *chips* are supposed to be *binary compatible.* But the M1 is rumored to offer several advantages over the Pentium, including *superpipelining, register renaming,* and fewer *issue restrictions. Cyrix* claims that the M1 will be 50 percent faster than existing Pentiums.

DA See *desk accessory (DA)*.

daemon A program, usually on a computer running UNIX, that serves some obscure function (such as routing *electronic mail* to its recipients) and usually has a very limited user interface. There's some debate about the origins of the word, but most say it derives from the devilish spirits of Greek mythology.

daisy chain A method of connecting together several devices along a *bus* and managing the signals for each device. Devices that use a *Small Computer System Interface (SCSI)*, such as a *CD-ROM*, hard disk, and scanner, can be daisy-chained to one *SCSI port*.

daisy chaining In displays, the act of linking several *monitors* together so they all show the same thing. Daisy chaining is convenient when large numbers of people must see the output of a computer simultaneously, such as at a convention or trade show.

daisywheel printer An *impact printer* that simulates the typescript produced by a typewriter. The term daisywheel refers to the metal or plastic disk consisting of characters mounted on spokes connected to a hub, resembling a daisy. To produce a character, the printer spins the wheel until that character is in front of a hammer that strikes the character against an inked ribbon, transferring the image to paper. Daisywheel printers can print many typefaces, but changing fonts within a document is tedious, because you must change the daisywheel manually.

DASD See *Direct Access Storage Device (DASD)*.

data Factual information such as text, numbers, sounds, and images, in a form that can be processed by a computer. Although data is the plural of the Latin word datum, data is commonly used to represent both singular and plural.

database A collection of related *information* about a subject organized in a useful manner that provides a base or foundation for procedures such as retrieving information, drawing conclusions, and making decisions. Any collection of information that serves these purposes qualifies as a database, even if the information isn't stored on a computer. In fact, important predecessors of today's sophisticated business database systems were files kept on index cards and stored in file cabinets. Information usually is divided into *data records*, each with one or more *data fields*.

database design The choice and arrangement of *data fields* in a *database* so that fundamental errors (such as *data redundancy* and *repeating fields*) are avoided or minimized.

database driver In *Lotus 1-2-3*, a program that lets 1-2-3 exchange *data* with other *database* programs, such as *dBASE*.

database management Tasks related to creating, maintaining, organizing, and retrieving information from a *database*. See *data manipulation*.

database management program An *application program* that provides the tools for *data retrieval*, modification, deletion, and insertion. Such programs also can create a *database* and produce meaningful output on a *printer* or on-screen. In *personal computing*, three kinds of *database management programs* exist: *flat-file*, *relational*, and *text-oriented*. See *band* and *table-oriented database management program*.

database management system (DBMS) A program that organizes *data* in a *database*, providing information storage, organization, and retrieval capacities, sometimes including simultaneous access to multiple databases through a *shared field* (*relational database management*). See *flat-file database management program*.

database structure In *database management*, a definition of the *data records* in which information is stored, including the number of *data fields*; a set of field definitions that specify the type, length, and other characteristics of the data that can be entered in each *field*; and a list of *field names*. See *data type*.

CAUTION: *Rare is the database structure that doesn't require changes after you start entering data. Many database management programs, however, either don't let you redefine the database structure, or require a cumbersome procedure that may corrupt the data. If you're using such a program, perform exhaustive tests on sample data before typing hundreds of data records.*

data bits   The number of *bits* a computer uses to represent a character of data. When two computers communicate by *modem*, they must use the same number of data bits—usually 8, but sometimes 7. See *parity* and *stop bits*.

data bus   An internal electronic pathway that allows the *microprocessor* to exchange data with *random-access memory (RAM)*. The width of the data *bus*, usually *16* or *32 bits,* determines how much data can be sent at one time.

data communication   The transfer of information from one computer to another. The transfer can occur via direct cable connections, as in *local area networks (LANs),* or over telephone lines using *modems*. See *telecommunications*.

Data Communications Equipment (DCE)   The term used by the specification that defines the standard *serial port* to describe the electronics that connect the computer to a *modem* or *fax modem*.

data-compression protocol   In *modems,* a standard for automatically *compressing* data when it's sent and *decompressing* data when it's received. With data compression, you can realize gains of up to 400 percent in effective transmission speed. The two most common data-compression protocols are *V.42bis* and *MNP-5.* See *CCITT protocol.*

> **TIP:** *If you use your modem frequently to exchange lengthy files with others, consider a modem that offers automatic data compression, which is much more convenient than manually compressing files using programs such as PKZIP.*

data deletion   In a *database management program,* an operation that deletes records according to specified criteria.

Many *database* programs don't actually delete the *records* in such operations; they merely mark the records so that they aren't included in *data retrieval operations.* Therefore, you usually can restore the deleted records if you make a mistake. Check your program manual.

data dependency   A situation in which a *central processing unit (CPU)* using *superscalar architecture* and multiple *pipelines* must have the result of one calculation before beginning another. See *false dependency*.

data dictionary   In a *database management program,* a list of all the *database* files, indexes, views, and other *files* relevant to a database application. A data dictionary also can include data structures and any information pertinent to the maintenance of a database.

data-encoding scheme   The technique a *disk drive controller* uses to record bits of data on the magnetic surface of a floppy disk or hard disk. Disk drives are categorized by the data-encoding scheme the drive uses. See *Advanced Run-Length Limited (ARLL), disk drive controller, Modified Frequency Modulation (MFM),* and *Run-Length Limited (RLL).*

Data Encryption Standard (DES)   A controversial IBM-developed *encryption* technique that was adopted by the U.S. government for non-classified information, and widely used by financial institutions to transfer large sums of money electronically. Critics charge that DES technology was deliberately weakened so the government would be able to break DES-encoded messages when it chose to do so.

data-entry form   In a *database management program,* an on-screen form that makes entering and editing *data* easier by displaying only one *data record* at a time. The data fields are listed vertically, as in figure D.1. You also can create a custom data-entry form (see fig. D.1).

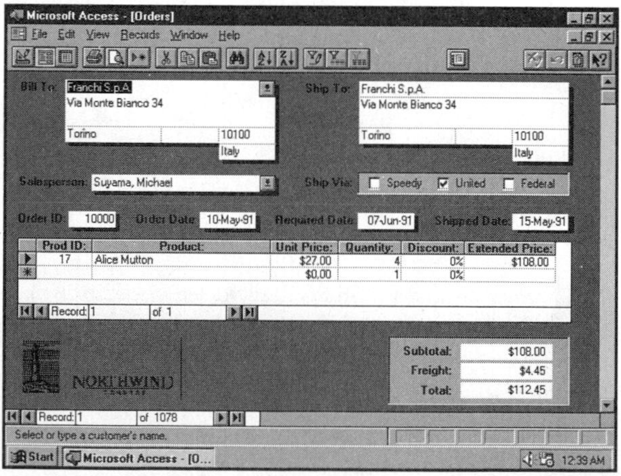

Fig. D.1   *A data-entry form in Microsoft Access.*

data field In a *database management program,* a space reserved for a specified piece of information in a *data record.* In a *table-oriented database management program,* in which all *retrieval operations* produce a table with rows and columns, data fields are displayed as vertical columns.

Data fields in a simple mailing list database might be FIRSTNAME, LASTNAME, COMPANY, ADDRESS, CITY, ST, and ZIP. *Field definitions* determine what sort of data can go into each field..

data file A *file* containing the work you create with a program; unlike a *program file* that contains instructions for the computer.

data independence In *database management,* the storage of data in a way that allows you to access that *data* without knowing exactly where it's located or how it's stored. Newer *database management programs* include command languages, called *query languages,* that let you phrase questions based on content rather than the data's physical location. See *Structured Query Language (SQL).*

data insertion In a *database management program,* an operation that adds new records to the database. Unlike appending records, however, insertion lets you add records anywhere in the database. See *append.*

data integrity The accuracy, completeness, and internal consistency of the information stored in a *database.* A good *database management program* ensures data integrity by making it difficult (or impossible) to accidentally erase or alter data. *Relational database management programs* help to ensure data integrity by eliminating *data redundancy.*

data interchange format (DIF) file In *spreadsheet programs* and some *database programs,* a *standard file format* that simplifies importing and exporting data between different spreadsheet programs. Originally developed by Software Arts—the creators of *VisiCalc*—DIF is supported by *Lotus 1-2-3, Quattro Pro,* and most other spreadsheet programs.

data manipulation In database management, the use of the basic database manipulation operations—*data deletion, data insertion, data modification,* and *data retrieval*—to make changes to data records.

data mask   See *field template*.

data modem   A *modem* that can send and receive *data*, but not faxes. Data modems are bad buys, since for little or no extra money, you can get a *fax modem*.

data modification   In *database management*, an operation that updates one or more records according to specified criteria. You use a *query language* to specify the criteria for the update. For example, the following statement, written in a simplified form of *Structured Query Language (SQL)*, tells the program to find records in which the supplier field contains CC, and then increase the value in the price data field by 15 percent:

```
UPDATE inventory
SET price = price * 1.15
WHERE supplier = "CC"
```

datapac   A type of *packet-switching network*. Datapac networks use the *TCP/IP network protocol*.

data privacy   In *local area networks (LANs)*, limiting access to a file so that other users in the network can't display the contents of that file. See *encryption, field privilege, file privilege,* and *password protection*.

data processing   Preparing, storing, or manipulating *information*.

Data Processing Management Association (DPMA)   A professional society, specializing in business computing issues, for *programmers, systems analysts,* and managers. DPMA established the *Certified Data Processor (CDP)* recognition process in the 1960s, but later turned the responsibility for certification over to the *Institute for Certification of Computer Professionals (ICCP)*.

data record   In a *database management program*, a complete unit of related *data* items stored in *named data fields*. In a *database*, data record is synonymous with *row*.

A data record contains all the information related to the item the database is tracking. Most programs display data records in two ways: as *data-entry forms* and as *data tables*. In a *table-oriented relational database management system*, the data records are displayed as horizontal rows and each data field is a column.

data redundancy   In *database management,* the repetition of the same data in two or more *data records.*

Generally, you shouldn't enter the same data in two different places within a database—someone may mistype just one character, destroying accurate retrieval. To the computer, Acme isn't the same as Acmee. The program fails to retrieve both data records if you search for all the records with Acme in the COMPANY field. Integrity is a serious issue for any database management system, and careful system design can help reduce *redundancy-related problems.*

data retrieval   In *database management programs,* an operation that retrieves information from the database according to the criteria specified in a *query.*

A database management program is most useful when you want to access only a few records: all the customers in Florida or those who haven't been contacted in the last 90 days. By using queries, you can tell the program to sort the data, perhaps by customer last name, or to select only certain records, such as customers in Atlanta. In some programs, the query can specify which *fields* to display after the matching records are selected.

data series   In business and *presentation graphics,* a collection of *values* that all pertain to a single subject, such as the third-quarter sales of three products.

In *spreadsheet* programs, a *column, row,* or block of values that increases or decreases a fixed amount. When creating a data series, you indicate a beginning value, the amount to increase or decrease the value, and an ending value.

data striping   An important method employed by *redundant arrays of inexpensive disks (RAID)* in which a single unit of data is distributed across several *hard disks,* increasing resistance to a failure of one of the drives.

data table   In a *database management program,* an on-screen view of information in a columnar (two-dimensional) format, with the field names at the top. Most database management programs display data tables as the result of sorting or querying operations (see fig. D.2). See *data-entry form.*

In spreadsheet programs, a form of what-if analysis where a formula is calculated many times using different values for one or two of the arguments in the formula. The results are displayed in a table.

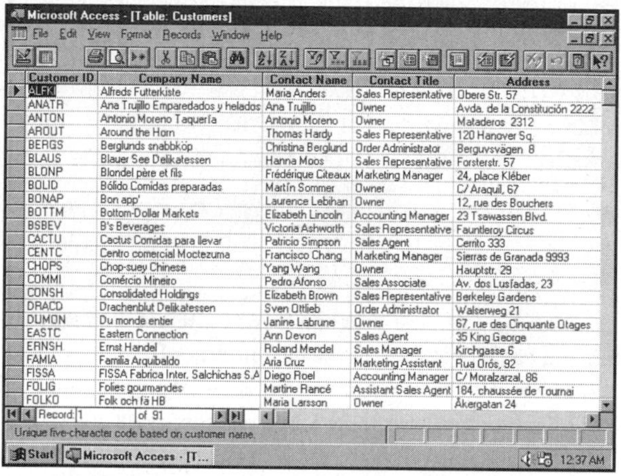

Customer ID	Company Name	Contact Name	Contact Title	Address
ALFKI	Alfreds Futterkiste	Maria Anders	Sales Representative	Obere Str. 57
ANATR	Ana Trujillo Emparedados y helados	Ana Trujillo	Owner	Avda. de la Constitución 2222
ANTON	Antonio Moreno Taquería	Antonio Moreno	Owner	Mataderos 2312
AROUT	Around the Horn	Thomas Hardy	Sales Representative	120 Hanover Sq.
BERGS	Berglunds snabbköp	Christina Berglund	Order Administrator	Berguvsvägen 8
BLAUS	Blauer See Delikatessen	Hanna Moos	Sales Representative	Forsterstr. 57
BLONP	Blondel père et fils	Frédérique Citeaux	Marketing Manager	24, place Kléber
BOLID	Bólido Comidas preparadas	Martín Sommer	Owner	C/ Araquil, 67
BONAP	Bon app'	Laurence Lebihan	Owner	12, rue des Bouchers
BOTTM	Bottom-Dollar Markets	Elizabeth Lincoln	Accounting Manager	23 Tsawassen Blvd.
BSBEV	B's Beverages	Victoria Ashworth	Sales Representative	Fauntleroy Circus
CACTU	Cactus Comidas para llevar	Patricio Simpson	Sales Agent	Cerrito 333
CENTC	Centro comercial Moctezuma	Francisco Chang	Marketing Manager	Sierras de Granada 9993
CHOPS	Chop-suey Chinese	Yang Wang	Owner	Hauptstr. 29
COMMI	Comércio Mineiro	Pedro Afonso	Sales Associate	Av. dos Lusíadas, 23
CONSH	Consolidated Holdings	Elizabeth Brown	Sales Representative	Berkeley Gardens
DRACD	Drachenblut Delikatessen	Sven Ottlieb	Order Administrator	Walserweg 21
DUMON	Du monde entier	Janine Labrune	Owner	67, rue des Cinquante Otages
EASTC	Eastern Connection	Ann Devon	Sales Agent	35 King George
ERNSH	Ernst Handel	Roland Mendel	Sales Manager	Kirchgasse 6
FAMIA	Familia Arquibaldo	Aria Cruz	Marketing Assistant	Rua Orós, 92
FISSA	FISSA Fabrica Inter. Salchichas S.A	Diego Roel	Accounting Manager	C/ Moralzarzal, 86
FOLIG	Folies gourmandes	Martine Rancé	Assistant Sales Agent	184, chaussée de Tournai
FOLKO	Folk och fä HB	Maria Larsson	Owner	Åkergatan 24

Fig. D.2 *A data table in Microsoft Access.*

Data Terminal Equipment (DTE) The term used by the specification that defines the standard *serial port* to describe the computer that is connected to a *modem* or *fax modem.*

data transfer rate In *modems,* the speed, expressed in *bits per second (bps),* at which a *modem* can transfer, or is transferring, data over a telephone line. See *connect speed.*

In *hard disks,* the theoretical speed at which a hard disk can transfer data to the rest of the computer. Data transfer rate is established by laboratory tests; *throughput* is a better indication of how well a hard disk performs.

data type In a *database management program,* a classification you give to a *data field* that governs the kind of data you can enter. In *dBASE for Windows,* for example, you can choose among the following data types:

- Character field (or text field). Stores any character you can type at the keyboard, including numbers. The program can't, however, perform computations on character fields. A character field can contain approximately one line of text.

- Memo field. Stores any type of text; useful for entering notes about the information contained in a record. A memo field can contain more text than a character field.

- Numeric field. Stores numbers in such a way that the program can perform calculations on them.

- Logical field. Stores information in a true/false, yes/no format.

- Date field. Stores dates so that the program can recognize and compare them.

See *field template*.

dBASE for Windows   A *database management program*, published by Borland International for the *Microsoft Windows 95* operating environment, that achieves a good blend of usability, flexibility, and power. People developing *applications* in dBASE for Windows can use *object-oriented programming* techniques, and can just as easily alter *source code* by manipulating graphical objects as by editing the code directly.

Though dBASE for Windows isn't as good as *Lotus Approach* for setting up databases quickly, it is more powerful. It also provides a way for the millions of people who learned to work with dBASE's earlier versions to apply their skills to graphical environments.

DBMS   See *database management system (DBMS)*.

DCE   See *Data Communications Equipment (DCE)*.

DCE speed   The speed, measured in *bits per second (bps)* at which *Data Communications Equipment (DCE)* devices can communicate over a telephone line.

DDE   See *dynamic data exchange (DDE)*.

debugger   A *utility program*, often included in *compilers* or *interpreters,* that helps programmers find and fix *syntax errors* and other errors in *source code*.

debugging   The process of locating and correcting errors in a *program*.

decimal tab   In a *word processing* or *page layout program*, a *tab stop* configured so that values align at the decimal point.

declarative language A *programming language* that frees the *programmer* from specifying the exact procedure the computer needs to follow to accomplish a task. Programmers use the language to describe a set of facts and relationships so that the user may then query the system to get a specific result.

For example, *Structured Query Language (SQL)* allows you to perform a search by asking to see a list of records showing specific information instead of by telling the computer to search all records for those with the appropriate entries in specified fields. See *data independence, expert system,* and *procedural language.*

declarative markup language (DML) In text processing, a markup language—a system of codes for marking the format of a unit of text—that indicates only that a particular unit of text is a certain part of the document, such as an abstract, a title, or an author's name and affiliation. The actual formatting of the document part is left up to another program, called a parser, which displays the marked document and gives each document part a distinctive format (fonts, spacing, etc.). An international standard DML is the *Standard Generalized Markup Language (SGML),* which was little-known until a subset of SGML, the *HyperText Markup Language (HTML),* came into widespread use on the *World Wide Web (WWW).* HTML is a declarative markup language, and the Web browsers in use by millions today are parsers for HTML.

decrement To decrease a value. See *increment.*

decryption In *cryptography,* the decoding of an encrypted message by means of a *key.* See *encryption.*

dedicated file server In a *local area network (LAN),* a computer dedicated exclusively to providing services to the users of the network and running the *network operating system (NOS).*

Some *file servers* can be used for other purposes. In *peer-to-peer networks,* for example, all the networked computers are potential file servers, although they're being used for stand-alone applications.

dedicated line A telephone line, devoted to data communications, that has been specially conditioned and permanently connected. Dedicated lines are often *leased lines* from regional telephone companies or *public data networks (PDN).*

default button   In *graphical user interfaces* such as *Microsoft Windows 95,* the highlighted button automatically selected as your most likely choice in a dialog box. You can press Enter to choose this button quickly. See *pushbutton.*

default directory   See *current directory.*

default editor   In a *UNIX* system, the text editor (such as *emacs* or *vi*) that the system automatically starts when the services of a text editor are needed. PC users will find these programs to be difficult and counter-intuitive; you'll need to read the programs' documentation carefully.

default extension   The three-letter extension an *application program* uses to save and retrieve *files* unless you override the default by specifying another extension.

Using the default extension makes retrieving files easier. During retrieval operations, programs that use a default *extension* display a list of only the files that use their default extension, making retrieving a file easier, unless you give a file a different extension. You still can retrieve the file, but you must remember the file's name or change the *file name* entry to *.* so that all files are listed.

default font   The font that the printer uses unless you tell it otherwise. Synonymous with *initial base font.*

default home page   In a *Web browser,* the *World Wide Web (WWW)* document that appears when you start the program or click the Home button. Most Web browsers are set up to display the browser publisher's *home page,* but you can easily change this setting so that the browser displays a more useful default home page.

default numeric format   In a *spreadsheet* program, the *numeric format* that the program uses for all *cells* unless you choose a different one.

default printer   The *printer* a *program* automatically uses when you tell it to print. If you change printers for a single *print job,* some programs return to the printer designated as the default when the document is closed. Others treat the currently selected printer as the default printer until you select another printer.

default setting   The setup a program uses unless you specify another setting. In *Lotus 1-2-3,* for example, the default column width is nine characters.

An important step toward the mastery of an application program is learning the program defaults and how to change these settings so the program works the way you want. Most programs save the changes you make so they're the default settings thereafter, but some options can't be saved under any circumstances.

default value A value a *program* uses when you don't specify one.

Defense Advanced Research Projects Agency (DARPA) A unit of the U.S. Department of Defense (DoD), the successor to the *Advanced Research Projects Agency (ARPA)* that played a key role in the development of the *ARPAnet,* the *Internet's* predecessor. DARPA is one of several U.S. agencies that participate in the *High Performance Computing and Communications Program (HPCC).*

deflection yoke See *yoke.*

defragmentation A procedure in which all the *files* on a *hard disk* are rewritten on disk so that all parts of each file are written to contiguous *sectors.* The result is an improvement of up to 75 percent in the disk's speed during retrieval operations. During normal operations, the files on a hard disk eventually become fragmented so that parts of a file are written all over the disk, slowing down retrieval operations.

TIP: *Microsoft Plus! includes Disk Defragmenter, which you can schedule to run at whatever time you wish. Run Disk Defragmenter no more than once a month to obtain maximum system performance without undue wear on your hard disk.*

Delete key (Del) A *key* that erases the character to the right of the cursor. Use the *backspace* and Delete keys to correct mistakes as you type.

delimiter A code, such as a space, tab, or comma, that marks the end of one section of a *command* and the beginning of another section. Delimiters also are used to separate data into fields and records when you want to export or import data using a *database* format. For example, using delimiters makes it easy to *export* a *merge file* created using a *word processing program* or to *import* data into a *spreadsheet program* and have lines of *data* divided logically into columns.

DELPHI   A full-service *on-line information service,* established in 1982 as an on-line encyclopedia.

Today, DELPHI has grown to offer a variety of business and financial services; news and analysis; special interest group forums for every major category of computer; a range of real-time conferences; entertainment in the form of games; Hollywood gossip and movie reviews; trivia tournaments; and astrological predictions. There are also forums on many topics of interest; news, weather, and sports information; a gateway to the DIALOG Information Service and Grolier's Academic American Encyclopedia; shopping, travel support services, and special regional gateways to major cities (note that DELPHI/Miami and DELPHI/Argentina are Spanish-language versions of DELPHI).

Delrina Communications Suite   A suite of programs that includes Delrina WinFax Pro, a best-selling *fax program*, and Delrina WinComm, a *communications program.* Though the two programs are not especially well integrated (they have very different *menu* structures and are only superficially alike), they are both useful. Future editions of the Delrina Communications Suite are supposed to include a *scanner* for sending hard copy by *electronic mail* or *fax.*

   delurk   In *UseNet,* to post a message in which you reveal your identity and confess that you have been reading the newsgroup for a long time without contributing anything. See *lurk.*

demo   An animated presentation or a preview version of a *program* distributed without charge in an attempt to acquaint potential customers with a program's features. See *crippled version.*

demodulation   In *telecommunications,* the process of receiving and transforming an analog signal into its digital equivalent so that a computer can use the information. See *modulation.*

demount   To remove a *disk* from a *disk drive.* See *mount.*

density   See *areal density.*

departmental laser printer   A *high-end laser printer* designed to serve large groups of people and print 12,000 pages or more each month. Departmental laser printers often feature *automatic emulation switching, automatic network switching, bidirectional communication, duplex printing,* and *remote management.*

dependent worksheet   In *Microsoft Excel,* a worksheet that contains a link, or reference formula, to data in another Excel worksheet, called the source worksheet, on which it depends for the data. More than one worksheet can depend on a single source worksheet. In other spreadsheet programs, such as Lotus 1-2-3 and Quattro Pro, a worksheet containing a link is called a target worksheet. See *external reference formula* and *source worksheet.*

TIP: *If you include links in worksheets, group the dependent worksheet and the source worksheet as a workbook or workspace to ensure that the changes you make in the source worksheet are always reflected in the dependent worksheet.*

derived field   See *calculated field.*

DES.   See *Data Encryption Standard (DES).*

descender   The portion of a lowercase letter that hangs below the baseline. Five letters of the English alphabet have descenders: g, j, p, q, and y. See *ascender.*

descending sort   A *sort* that reverses the normal *ascending sort* order. Rather than sort A, B, C, D and 1, 2, 3, 4, for example, a descending sort lists D, C, B, A and 4, 3, 2, 1.

descriptor   In *database management,* a word used to classify a data record so that all records containing the word can be retrieved as a group. In a video store's database, for example, the descriptors Adventure, Comedy, Crime, Horror, Mystery, or Science Fiction can be entered in a field called CATEGORY to indicate where the film is shelved in the store. See *identifier* and *keyword.*

desk accessory (DA)   In a *graphical user interface (GUI),* a set of *utility programs* that assists with day-to-day tasks such as jotting down notes, performing calculations on an on-screen calculator, maintaining a list of names and phone numbers, and displaying an on-screen calendar (see fig. D.3). See *Font/DA Mover.*

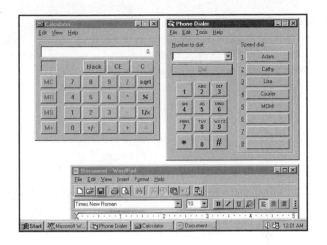

Fig. D.3   *Desk accessories in Microsoft Windows 95.*

desktop   In a *graphical user interface (GUI),* a representation of your day-to-day work, as though you were looking at an actual desk with folders full of work to do. In *Microsoft Windows 95,* this term refers specifically to the background of the screen, on which *windows, icons,* and *dialog boxes* appear. You can change the desktop color and pattern by choosing Colors in the *Control Panel.*

desktop computer   A *personal computer* or professional *work-station* designed to fit on a standard-sized office desk that's equipped with sufficient memory and disk storage to perform business computing tasks. See *portable computer.*

Desktop Management Interface (DMI)   A system for *printers* developed by the *Desktop Management Task Force (DMTF)* that warns users when printers need attention, such as when *toner* runs low, paper jams occur, or paper is exhausted. DMI is expected to supersede the *Simple Network Management Protocol (SNMP).*

Desktop Management Task Force (DMTF)   A consortium of computer-equipment manufacturers that has established standards for the *Desktop Management Interface (DMI)* and *Plug and Print.*

desktop pattern   In *Microsoft Windows 95*, a graphical pattern—called wallpaper—displayed on the *desktop* (the background "beneath" *windows, icons,* and *dialog boxes*). To change the desktop pattern, choose Display from the *Control Panel.*

desktop presentation   The use of a *slide show* feature available in a *presentation graphics* program (and some spreadsheet programs) to create a display of *charts* or other illustrations that can be run on a desktop computer. You can tell the program to run the presentation automatically or to give you a menu of options. See *presentation graphics program.*

desktop publishing (DTP)   The use of a personal computer as an inexpensive production system for creating typeset-quality text and *graphics.*

Desktop publishers often merge text and graphics on the same page and print pages on a *high-resolution laser printer* or typesetting machine (see fig. D.4). Desktop publishing software lets one person produce typeset-quality text and graphics with a personal computer, enabling an organization to reduce publication costs by as much as 75 percent.

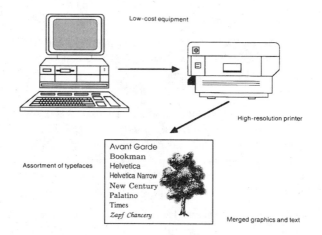

Fig. D.4   *The elements of desktop publishing.*

desktop video   A *multimedia application* in which a *personal computer,* coupled with a videocassette recorder or *laser disk player,* is used to control the display of still or motion images.

destination   The record, file, document, or disk to which information is copied or moved, as opposed to the *source.*

destination document   In *object linking and embedding (OLE),* the document in which you insert or embed an object. When you embed a *Microsoft Excel* object (such as a chart) into a *Microsoft Word* file, for example, the Word document is the destination document. See *source document.*

destination file   In many DOS commands, the file into which data or program instructions are copied. See *source file.*

device   Any *hardware component* or *peripheral,* such as a *printer, modem, monitor,* or *mouse,* that can receive and/or send data. Some devices require special software, called *device drivers.*

device contention   The technique that *Microsoft Windows 95* uses to handle simultaneous requests from multitasked *programs* to access devices.

device-dependent color   An annoying but common feature of output devices, including *printers* and *monitors,* that makes it very difficult to accurately match a color generated by one device with a color generated on another. *Device-independent color* overcomes these hassles.

device driver   A program that provides the *operating system* with the information needed for it to work with a specific device, such as a *printer.*

device independence   The capability of a *program, operating system,* or *programming language* to work on a variety of computers or *peripherals,* despite their electronic variation. *UNIX,* an operating system for multiuser computer systems, is designed to run on a wide variety of computers, from *personal computers* to *mainframes. PostScript,* a *page description language* for high-quality printing, is used by many printer manufacturers.

device-independent color   A method of describing colors in a standard way, such as with the *Pantone matching system (PMS),* then modifying output devices, such as *printers* and *monitors,* to conform to the standard. Though rare and expensive, device-independent color is far superior to *device-dependent color*—and is essential if you're in the publishing business.

device name In *DOS,* a three-letter abbreviation that refers to a peripheral device. See *AUX, CON,* and *LPT.*

device node In *Microsoft Windows 95,* an *object* in the *hardware tree* that represents a piece of *hardware.* Synonymous with *Plug and Play* object.

diagnostic program A *utility program* that tests computer hardware and software to determine whether they're operating properly.

 CAUTION: *Most computers initiate a diagnostic memory check at the start of every operating session. If any errors are found, you see an error message, and the computer doesn't proceed. If you run into this problem, start the computer again. If you see the error message again, write down the location of the faulty chip—the number you see in the message.*

 dialer program In *SLIP* and *PPP,* a program that dials an *Internet* service provider's number and establishes the connection. A dialer program is unlike a *communications program,* which transforms your computer into a *terminal* of a *remote computer.* Instead, the dialer program establishes the connection that fully integrates your computer into the Internet. Many service providers distribute preconfigured dialer programs that enable users to connect to their service without configuring or programming the dialer; if you cannot obtain a *preconfigured dialer,* you may have to write your own *login script,* which can be tedious for people who lack *programming* experience.

dialog box In a *graphical user interface (GUI),* an on-screen message box that conveys or requests information from the user (see fig. D.5).

 dialup access A means of connecting to another computer, or a network like the *Internet,* with a *modem*-equipped computer. Internet service providers will sell you dialup access to the Internet, which is useful and economical but prohibits you from using the graphical programs that *dialup IP* access lets you use.

dialup IP A method of accessing the *Internet* over a *plain old telephone service (POTS)* line. By means of dialup IP (in conjunction with Point to Point Protocol [PPP] or Serial Line Internet Protocol [SLIP]), you can use graphical programs like *Netscape*

Navigator and *Eudora* to browse the *World Wide Web (WWW)* and collect *electronic mail.* Though dialup IP Internet access is better than *dialup access,* transfer rates may still be too slow to enjoyably browse the Web.

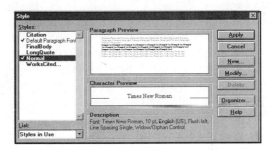

Fig. D.5 *A typical dialog box (Style) in Microsoft Windows 95.*

dialup modem   In contrast to a *modem* designed for use with a *leased line,* a modem that can dial a telephone number, establish a connection, and close the connection when it is no longer needed. Most *personal computer* modems are dialup modems.

dictionary flame   In *UseNet,* a *follow-up post* that initiates or prolongs a controversy over the meaning of a word or phrase, such as "Second Amendment" or "right to life." Dictionary *flames* are usually pointless because the controversy has roots far deeper than the present discussion and is not likely to be resolved on UseNet, or anywhere else.

dictionary sort   A *sort order* that ignores the case of characters as data is rearranged. See *sort.*

DIF   See *data interchange format (DIF) file.*

digest   In *UseNet,* an article that appears in a moderated *newsgroup* summarizing the posts received by the newsgroup's *moderator.* An excellent example: Risks Forum, a digest that appears in comp.risks.

digital   A form of representation in which distinct objects, or digits, are used to stand for something in the real world—temperature or time—so that counting and other operations can be performed precisely. *Data* represented digitally can be manipulated to produce a calculation, a *sort*, or some other *computation*. In digital electronic computers, two electrical states correspond to the 1s and 0s of *binary numbers*, which are manipulated by computer programs. See *algorithm, analog,* and *program*.

digital camera   A portable camera, incorporating one or more *charge-coupled devices (CCDs)*, that records images in a machine-readable format. Though digital cameras are expensive and generate output of far lesser quality than that of film-based cameras, they eliminate the potentially expensive and time-consuming film-processing and photo-scanning steps involved in getting photos into computer-readable form. Digital cameras are sometimes used to manufacture security badges quickly.

digital cash   A proposed method of ensuring personal privacy in a world in which electronic commerce becomes common. In digital cash commerce, a person who maintains an electronic bank account could make on-line purchases, which would be debited automatically and transferred to the payee. The transactions would be secure for all three parties concerned—the bank, the payer, and the payee—yet none of these parties, nor any outside investigator, would be able to determine just what has been done with the money. Relying on *public key cryptography,* this technology alarms government and law enforcement officials, who see it as an open invitation to tax cheats and drug dealers. Lacking U.S. Department of Commerce certification, digital cash schemes are currently in an experimental stage; one *World Wide Web (WWW)* accessible service allows you to obtain $5 of pretend money that you can "spend" at participating Web pages.

digital computer   A computer that uses the digits 0 and 1 to represent *data*, and then uses at least partly automatic procedures to perform computations on this information. See *analog computer* and *computer*.

digital controls   *Monitor* controls that, instead of knobs or dials, consist of pushbuttons. Digital controls, like analog controls, can adjust *brightness, contrast,* and image size.

Digital Darkroom   An image-enhancement program developed by Silicon Beach Software for *Macintosh* computers. The program uses computer processing techniques to edit and enhance scanned black-and-white photographic images.

digital modem A communications *adapter* designed to connect one computer to another digitally. *Digital* modems are not really modems at all, since *modulation* and *demodulation* are necessary only for *analog* connections. Digital modems, such as IBM's WaveRunner, work with digital telephone systems such as the *Integrated Services Digital Network (ISDN)*, and therefore have not achieved widespread use.

digital monitor A *monitor* that accepts digital output from the display adapter and converts the digital signal to an analog signal. Digital monitors can't accept input unless the input conforms to a digital standard, such as the IBM *Monochrome Display Adapter (MDA), Color Graphics Adapter (CGA),* or *Enhanced Graphics Adapter (EGA)* standards. All these adapters produce digital output, but, unlike *Video Graphics Array (VGA)* and other *analog monitors*, can display a limited number of colors.

digital signal processor (DSP) A programmable sound-processing circuit, used in both *modems* and *sound boards*. Sound boards use DSPs to handle a variety of sound *resolutions*, formats, and sound-altering filters without requiring separate circuits for each one, while modems use DSPs to handle several *modulation protocols*.

digital transmission A *data communications* technique that passes information encoded as discrete on-off pulses. Digital transmission doesn't require digital-to-analog converters at each end of the transmission; however, *analog transmission* is faster and can carry more than one channel at a time.

digitize The process of transforming *analog* data into *digital* form. A *scanner* converts *continuous-tone images* into *bit-mapped graphics. CD-ROMs* contain many digital measurements of the pitch and volume of sound. See *digitizing tablet.*

digitizing tablet In *computer-aided design (CAD),* a *peripheral* device, usually measuring 12×12 or 12×18 inches and 1/2 inch thick, that is used with a pointing device called a cursor to convert graphics, such as pictures and drawings, into digital data that a computer can process. The location of the cursor on the tablet is sensed magnetically in relation to a wire grid embedded within the tablet, and the position is tracked on-screen. Synonymous with *graphics tablet.* See *Cartesian coordinate system.*

dimmed　The display of a *menu* command, *icon*, or *dialog box* option in a different color or shade of gray to indicate that the selection isn't available.

dingbats　Ornamental characters—such as *bullets*, stars, pointing hands, scissors, and flowers—used to illustrate text. Dingbats originally were used between columns or, more commonly, between paragraphs, to provide separation. See *Zapf Dingbats*.

DIP　See *dual in-line package (DIP)* and *document image processing (DIP)*.

DIP switch　One or more toggle switches enclosed in a small plastic housing, called a *dual in-line package (DIP)*. This housing is designed with downward-facing pins so it can be inserted into a socket on a *circuit board* or soldered directly to the circuit board. DIP switches are frequently used to provide user-accessible configuration settings for computers, *printers*, and other electronic devices.

CAUTION: *If you must remove the computer or printer case to change DIP switch settings, ALWAYS unplug the computer or printer first. Although your computer's electronic circuits use low-voltage DC, the power supply uses high voltages and may contain a capacitor that stores extremely high voltages for system start-up purposes. DON'T TOUCH THE POWER SUPPLY, even when the system is unplugged! To change a DIP switch, use a toothpick or another small pointed device. Don't use a pencil; lead shavings can damage the internal workings of a DIP switch. See* dual in-line package (DIP).

Direct Access Storage Device (DASD)　Any storage device, such as a *hard disk*, that offers *random access* or direct access to the stored data; in contrast to a *sequential access* device (such as a tape drive).

direct-connect modem　A *modem* equipped with a jack like the standard jack found in a telephone wall outlet, both of which accept an *RJ-11* plug. The modem can be connected directly to the telephone line using ordinary telephone wire, unlike an *acoustic coupler* modem designed to cradle a telephone headset.

direct-map cache   A means of organizing *cache memory* by linking it to locations in *random-access memory (RAM)*. Though direct-map caches are simpler than other types of cache and easier to build, they are not as fast as other cache designs. See *full-associative cache* and *set-associative cache*.

direct memory access (DMA) channels   A channel that's used to transfer *data* from *memory* to *peripheral* devices, such as *hard disk controllers*, *network adapters*, and *tape backup* equipment. Requests for data are handled by a special chip called a *direct memory access (DMA) controller*, which operates at one-half the *microprocessor's* speed. When data is transferred using DMA channels, the microprocessor is bypassed completely, leaving it free to process other requests.

direct memory access (DMA) conflict   A problem that results when two *peripherals* try to use the same *direct memory access (DMA) channel*. A DMA conflict usually causes a system *crash*, and can be solved by assigning one of the conflicting peripherals a new DMA channel.

direct memory access (DMA) controller   A *chip* that controls the flow of *data* through the *direct memory access (DMA) channels*. By handling the work of regulating data flow through the channels, the DMA controller frees the *microprocessor* to do other work.

direct-to-drum imaging   Hewlett-Packard's design for *color laser printers*. The *drum* in HP Color LaserJets turns four times— once each for cyan, magenta, yellow, and black—and once more to fuse the various toners to the page. With this method, as many as five pages can be printed each minute. See *CMYK*.

directory   An index you can display of the files stored on a disk or on a portion of a disk. The contents of a disk aren't obvious to the eye. The operating system keeps an up-to-date record of the files stored on a disk, with ample information about the file's content, time of creation, and size.

See *current directory, directory markers, parent directory* and *subdirectory*.

directory markers   In DOS, symbols displayed in a directory table that represent the *current directory* (.) and the *parent directory* (..). See *directory* and *subdirectory*.

C
D
E

directory of servers   In *Wide Area Information Servers (WAIS)*, a *database* of WAIS database names, consisting of the names of current WAIS-accessible public databases and a short description of their contents. The first step in searching WAIS is to access the directory of servers, several copies of which are available by means of the *Internet*. (There is also a *WAIS gateway* accessible by means of the *World Wide Web (WWW)*.) You begin your search by using very general topical key words, such as "education" or "child psychology." The directory of servers then lists the databases that contain information pertinent to your topic.

directory sorting   The oganized display of the *files* in a *directory*, sorted by name, *extension*, or date and time of creation. The Windows Explorer can sort the contents of directories in several ways.

 directory title   In *Gopher,* an item on a Gopher menu that, when accessed, reveals another menu (rather than a *document, graphic,* or other item).

directory tree   A graphical representation of a disk's contents that shows the branching structure of *directories* and *subdirectories.* The *Microsoft Windows 95 Windows Explorer,* for example, displays a directory tree (see fig. D.6).

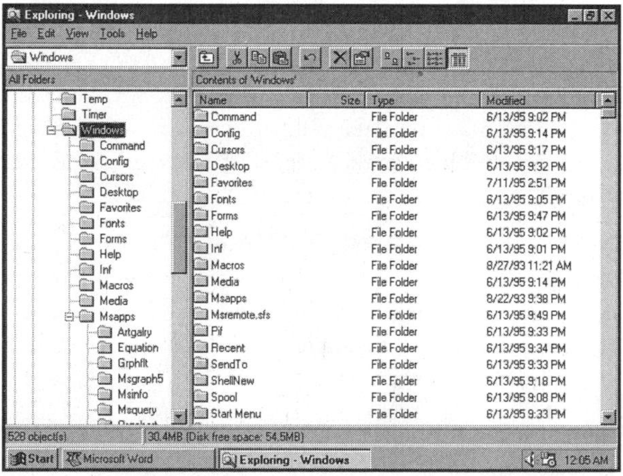

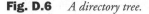

Fig. D.6   *A directory tree.*

dirty   Full of extraneous signals or noise. A dirty telephone line causes problems when you try to log on with a *modem* to a distant computer system or *BBS.* You'll know if the line's dirty: you'll see many *garbage characters* on the screen. Log off, hang up, and dial again.

Also, a *file* that has been changed but hasn't yet been saved.

disable   To temporarily disconnect a *hardware* device or *program* feature; to make it unavailable for use.

disk   See *floppy disk* and *hard disk.*

disk buffer   See *cache controller.*

disk cache   In a *Web browser,* a portion of your hard disk that has been set aside to store the *World Wide Web (WWW)* documents you have accessed recently. When you re-access these pages, the browser first checks with the server to find out whether the document has been changed; if not, the browser retrieves the document from the disk cache rather than the network, resulting in significantly faster retrieval.

In general personal computing, a portion of *random-access memory (RAM)* set aside to hold data recently retrieved from a disk. Disk caches can significantly speed up a system's performance.

disk capacity   The storage capacity of a *floppy disk* or *hard disk,* measured in *kilobytes (K)* or *megabytes (M).* The capacity of a floppy disk depends on the size of the disk and the *areal density* of the magnetic particles on its surface. The two most popular disk sizes are 5 1/4 inch and 3 1/2 inch. *Single-sided disks* were once common but are obsolete now; *double-sided disks* are the norm. Also standard today are *high-density disks. Extra-high density disks* are available, but aren't common.

The remaining variables are the *operating system* you use to *format* the disk and the capabilities of the disk drive you're using. The following table shows the relationship of the variables and the resulting capacity:

C
D
E

Size	Density	System	Drive	Capacity
3 1/2"	DD	MS-DOS	Standard	720K
3 1/2"	DD	Mac	Standard	800K
3 1/2"	HD	Mac	Superdrive	1.4M
3 1/2"	HD	MS-DOS	High density	1.44M
3 1/2"	HD	MS-DOS	Extra-high density	2.88M
5 1/4"	DD	MS-DOS	Standard	360K
5 1/4"	HD	MS-DOS	High density	1.2M

disk drive   A *secondary storage* device such as a *floppy disk drive* or a *hard disk*. This term usually refers to floppy disk drives.

A *floppy disk* drive is an economical secondary storage medium that uses a removable magnetic disk that can be recorded, erased, and reused over and over. Floppy disk drives are too slow to serve as the main data storage for today's *personal computers*, but are needed to copy software and disk-based data onto the system and for backup operations. See *random access, read/write head,* and *secondary storage.*

disk drive controller   The circuitry that controls the physical operations of the floppy disks and/or hard disks connected to the computer. With the advent of the *Integrated Drive Electronics (IDE)* standard, which transfers much of the controller circuitry to the drive itself, disk drive controller circuity is often included on the *motherboard* instead of on a plug-in card.

The disk drive controller circuitry performs two functions: it uses an interface standard (such as *ST-506/ST-412, Enhanced Small Device Interface [ESDI],* or *Small Computer System Interface [SCSI]*) to establish communication with the drive's electronics, as well as a data encoding scheme (such as *modified frequency modulation [MFM], run-length limited [RLL],* or advanced run-length limited *[ARLL]*) to encode information on the magnetic surface of the disk.

diskette   See *floppy disk.*

diskless workstation   In a *local area network (LAN)*, a *workstation* that has a central processing unit (CPU) and random-acccss memory (RAM) but lacks its own disk drives. Diskless workstations ensure that everone in an organization produces compatible data and helps reduce security risks. However, diskless workstations cause serious loss of speed, flexibility, and originality and with greater vulnerability to the effects of a disk or system *crash.* See *distributed processing system* and *personal computer.*

disk operating system   See *operating system.*

disk optimizer   See *defragmentation.*

display   See *monitor.*

display adapter   See *video adapter.*

display card   See *video adapter.*

display power management signaling (DPMS)   A system in which a specially equipped *video adapter* sends instructions to a compatible *monitor* telling it to conserve electricity. The video adapter can tell the monitor to assume any of three levels of power conservation.

display type   A *typeface,* usually 14 *points* or larger and differing in style from the *body type,* used for headings and subheadings.

TIP: *Use a sans serif typeface such as Avant Garde or Helvetica for display type. For body type, use serif fonts such as Times Roman or New Century Schoolbook, because serif fonts are more readable than sans serif fonts.*

distributed bulletin board   A collection of computer conferences, called *newsgroups,* automatically distributed throughout a wide area network (WAN) so that individual postings are available to every user. The conferences are organized by topic, embracing such areas as ecology, politics, current events, music, specific computers and computer programs, and human sexuality. See *follow-on post, Internet, moderated newsgroup, post, thread, unmoderated newsgroup,* and *UseNet.*

distributed processing system A *computer system* designed for multiple users that provides each user with a fully functional computer. In personal computing, distributed processing takes the form of *local area networks (LANs),* in which the *personal computers* of the members of a department or organization are linked by high-speed cable connections.

Distributed processing offers some advantages over *multiuser systems.* If the *network* fails, you can still work. You also can select software tailored to your needs. You can start a distributed processing system with a modest initial investment, since you need only two or three workstations and, if desired, a central *file server.*

 distribution In *UseNet,* the geographic area throughout which you want your *post* to be distributed. With most systems, you can choose from world distribution (the default in most systems), your country, your state, your local area, or your organization. Choose a distribution that is appropriate for your message, unless you really want your "Dinette Set for Sale in New Jersey" post to be read in Wollongong, Australia.

dithering In color or *grayscale* printing and *displays,* the mingling of dots of several colors to produce what appears to be a new color. With dithering, you can combine 256 colors to produce what appears to be a continuously variable color palette, but at the cost of sacrificing *resolution;* the several colors of dots tend to be mingled in patterns rather than blended well.

.DLL The *MS-DOS file name extension* attached to a collection of *library routines.*

DMI See *Desktop Management Interface (DMI).*

DO/WHILE loop In *programming,* a *loop* control structure that continues to carry out its function until a condition is satisfied. A DO/WHILE control structure establishes a condition that, if true, causes the program to wait until the test is false, then move on to the next instruction. See *loop, sequence control structure, software command language,* and *syntax.*

docking station A cabinet containing *disk drives,* video circuits, and special receptacles designed to house a portable computer. When the portable is inserted into the docking station, the portable can use devices attached to the docking station.

TIP: *If you have a high-speed notebook or laptop with a large hard drive and at least 4M of random-access memory (RAM), a docking station may be a less expensive alternative to purchasing a desktop computer.*

C
D
E

document   A file containing work you've created, such as a business report, a memo, or a worksheet. The term strongly connotes the authority of an original—that is, fixed text—with a clearly named author. However, with today's *network* technology, a document can become text in flux, constantly accessed and modified by many people and with *dynamic data exchange (DDE),* even by the computer itself, as it detects changes in supporting documents and updates dynamic links automatically. See *groupware* and *word processing.*

document base font   The *base font* you've told a *word processing* program to use for only one document. You can choose Times Roman as the *initial base font* for all documents, for example, but for a letter you're now writing, override that choice by choosing *Helvetica* as the document base font. You can choose other fonts within this letter, but the program uses Helvetica unless you give an explicit command to the contrary.

document comparison utility   A *utility program* or *word processing* command that compares two *documents* created with word processing programs. If the two documents aren't identical, the program displays the differences between them, line by line.

Document comparison utilities are useful in collaborative writing. In figure 4.7, for example, altered or added passages are shown as highlighted text, and the original version is shown in strikethrough text. See *redlining.*

document file icon   In *Microsoft Windows 95,* the *icon* of a *document* associated with an application program. You can open the document and launch the application simultaneously just by double-clicking a document file icon.

document format   In a *word processing* program, a set of formatting choices that control the page layout of the entire document. Examples of document formats include margins, headers, footers, page numbers, and columns.

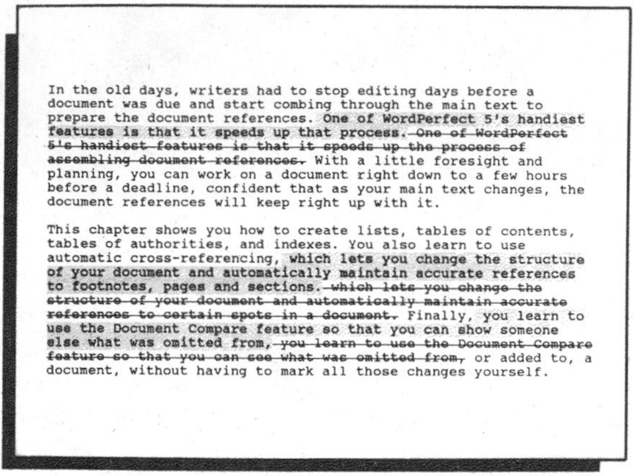

In the old days, writers had to stop editing days before a document was due and start combing through the main text to prepare the document references. One of WordPerfect 5's handiest ~~features is that it speeds up that process. One of WordPerfect 5's handiest features is that it speeds up the process of assembling document references.~~ With a little foresight and planning, you can work on a document right down to a few hours before a deadline, confident that as your main text changes, the document references will keep right up with it.

This chapter shows you how to create lists, tables of contents, tables of authorities, and indexes. You also learn to use automatic cross-referencing, which lets you change the structure of your document and automatically maintain accurate references ~~to footnotes, pages and sections. which lets you change the structure of your document and automatically maintain accurate references to certain spots in a document.~~ Finally, you learn to use the Document Compare feature so that you can show someone else what was omitted from, ~~you learn to use the Document Compare feature so that you can see what was omitted from,~~ or added to, a document, without having to mark all those changes yourself.

Fig. D.7 *Comparing two documents.*

document image processing (DIP)   A system for the imaging, storage, and retrieval of text-based documents that includes scanning documents, storing the files on optical or magnetic media, and viewing when needed using a *monitor, printer,* or *fax.* The goal of a document image processing system is a "*paperless office,*" but the goal probably will not be realized until *optical character recognition (OCR)* technology improves.

document processing   The use of computer technology during every stage of the production of *documents,* such as instruction manuals, handbooks, reports, and proposals. A complete document processing system includes all the *software* and *hardware* needed to create, organize, edit, and print such documents, including generating indexes and tables of contents. See *desktop publishing (DTP)* and *word processing program.*

document window   In multidocument *programs* as diverse as *Microsoft Word* and WordPerfect 6.0 for DOS, a *window* within an *application program* that displays the document you're creating or altering. You can open more than one document window within an application window.

documentation   The instructions, tutorials, and reference information that provide you with the information you need to use a *program* or *computer system* effectively. Documentation can appear in printed form or in on-line help systems.

domain   On the *Internet*, the highest subdivision, usually a country. However, in the United States, the subdivision is by type of organization, such as commercial (**.com**), educational (**.edu**), or government (**.gov** and **.mil**).

 domain name   In the system of *domain names* used to identify individual *Internet* computers, a single word or abbreviation that makes up part of a computer's unique name (such as **watt.seas.virginia.edu**). Reading from left to right, the parts of a domain name go from specific to general; for example, "watt" is a specific computer, one of several RS-6000 *minicomputers* in service at the School of Engineering and Applied Science (**seas**) at the University of Virginia (**virginia**). At the end of the series of domain names is the top level domain (here, **edu**), which includes hundreds of colleges and universities throughout the U.S. See *Domain Name Service (DNS)*.

C
D
E

Domain Name Service (DNS)   A *program* that runs on an *Internet*—connected *computer system* (called a DNS server) and provides an automatic translation between domain names (such as **watt.seas.virginia.edu**) and *IP addresses* (128.143.7.186) The purpose of this translation process, called *resolution,* is to enable Internet users to continue using a familiar name (such as **www.yahoo.com**) even though the service's IP address may change.

dongle   A small piece of *hardware* that plugs into a *port* and serves some purpose. Some very expensive programs use dongles as *copy-protection* devices—if you don't have the dongle plugged in, the program won't work. Other dongles provide infrared data transfer or *network* connectivity.

DOS   See *MS-DOS* and *operating system*.

Doskey   A personal utility provided with *MS-DOS* (5.0 and later) that allows you to type more than one DOS command on a line, store and retrieve previously used DOS commands, create stored macros, and customize all DOS commands.

DOS prompt   In *MS-DOS,* a letter representing the current *disk drive* followed by the greater-than symbol (>), which together inform you that the *operating system* is ready to receive a command. See *prompt*.

 dot address   See *IP address*.

dot file In *UNIX*, a *file* that has a name preceded by a dot. Such a file normally isn't displayed by UNIX file-listing *utility programs*. Dot files are frequently used for user configuration files, such as a file that lists the *newsgroups* the user regularly consults.

dot-matrix printer An impact printer that forms text and graphic images by hammering the ends of pins against a ribbon in a pattern (a matrix) of dots.

Dot-matrix printers are relatively fast, but their output is generally poor quality because characters aren't well-formed. Some dot-matrix printers use 24 pins instead of 9, to improve print quality, but the output is still inferior to that of an *inkjet* or *laser printer*. These printers also can be extremely noisy. See *font, near-letter quality (NLQ)*, and *non-impact printer*.

dot pitch The size of the smallest dot a *monitor* can display. Dot pitch determines a monitor's maximum *resolution. High-resolution* monitors use dot pitches of approximately 0.31 mm or less; the best monitors use dot pitches of 0.28 mm or less.

dot prompt In *dBASE*, the prompt, a lone period on an otherwise empty screen, for the command-driven interface of the program.

dots per inch (dpi) A measure of *printer resolution* that counts the dots that the device can fit into a linear inch.

In describing screen *resolutions*, the practice is to state the resolution in horizontal pixels (picture elements) by vertical lines, rather than state a dpi figure. The resolution of a *Super VGA* monitor, for example, is 800 horizontal *pixels* by 600 vertical lines.

double-click To click a *mouse* button twice in rapid succession. In many programs, double-clicking extends the action that results from single-clicking; double-clicking anywhere in a word, for example, selects the whole word rather than just one character. Double-clicking is also used to initiate an action. In a file list, for example, double-clicking a file name selects and opens the file.

double density A widely used recording technique that packs twice as much data on a *floppy* or *hard disk* as the earlier, single-density standard. See *high density, Modified Frequency Modulation (MFM), Run-Length Limited (RLL)*, and *single density*.

double-scanned passive matrix   See *dual-scanned passive matrix*.

double-sided floppy disk   A *floppy disk* that can store data on both its surfaces. Most floppy disks are double-sided—though a few obsolete floppy disks record data on only one side.

double-speed drive   A *CD-ROM disk drive* that can transfer data at up to 300 *K* per second. Though the maximum *data transfer rate* of double-speed disk drives is twice that of the first CD-ROM disk drives, the *access times* of the two are about equal.

 TIP: *Quad-speed drives, which cost only a little more, offer big gains in both access time and data transfer rate.*

Dow Jones News/Retrieval Service   An *on-line information service* from Dow Jones, the publishers of the Wall Street Journal and Barron's, that offers a computer-searchable index to financial and business publications and to up-to-date financial information, such as stock quotes.

download   To transfer a *file* from another computer to your computer by means of a *modem* and a telephone line. See *upload*.

downloadable font   A *printer font* that's transferred from the *hard disk* to the printer's *memory* at the time of printing. Often called soft fonts, downloadable fonts are the least convenient of the three types of printer fonts you can use. Downloading can consume from 5 to 10 minutes at the start of every operating session. See *bit-mapped font, built-in font, cartridge font, downloading utility, font, font family, outline font, page description language (PDL),* and *PostScript*.

TIP: *After you print a document that requires several downloadable fonts that you no longer need, switch your printer off and on before proceeding, especially if the next document contains graphics. The power interruption clears the printer's memory and makes room for the data needed to generate the graphic image.*

downloading   Transferring a copy of a *file* from a distant computer to a disk in your computer using data communication links. See *file transfer protocol (FTP)* and *modem*.

downloading utility   A *utility program* that transfers *downloadable fonts* from your computer or printer *hard disk* to the printer's *random-access memory (RAM)*. Downloading utilities usually are included with the downloadable fonts you buy. You may not need the utility if the *word processing* or *page layout program* you're using has downloading capabilities built in, as do *WordPerfect*, *Microsoft Word*, Ventura Publisher, and *PageMaker*.

downward compatibility   *Hardware* or *software* that runs without modification when using earlier computer components or files created with earlier software versions. *Video Graphics Array (VGA) monitors*, for example, are downward compatible with the original IBM PC if you use an 8-bit VGA *video adapter* that fits in the PC's 8-bit *expansion bus*.

dpi   See *dots per inch (dpi)*.

DPMA   See *Data Processing Management Association (DPMA)*.

drag   To move the *mouse* pointer while holding down a mouse button.

drag-and-drop   In *Microsoft Windows 95* and *Macintosh* programs running under *System* 7.5, a technique that allows you to perform operations on objects by *dragging* them with the mouse. You can open a document by dragging its *icon* to an *application icon*, or install icons in folders by dragging icons to them. Many *word processing* programs feature *drag-and-drop editing*, which speeds re-arrangement of text.

TIP: *Microsoft Windows 95 implements drag-and- drop in Windows Explorer, so you can copy and move files quickly and easily. To copy a file from one drive to another, click the file and drag the pointer to the file's destination (see fig. D.8).*

drag-and-drop editing   An editing feature that allows you to perform a *block move* or copy by *highlighting* a block of text and then using the *mouse* to *drag* the block to its new location. When you release the mouse button, the text appears in the new location. Some DOS programs, such as WordPerfect 6.0, allow drag-and-drop editing.

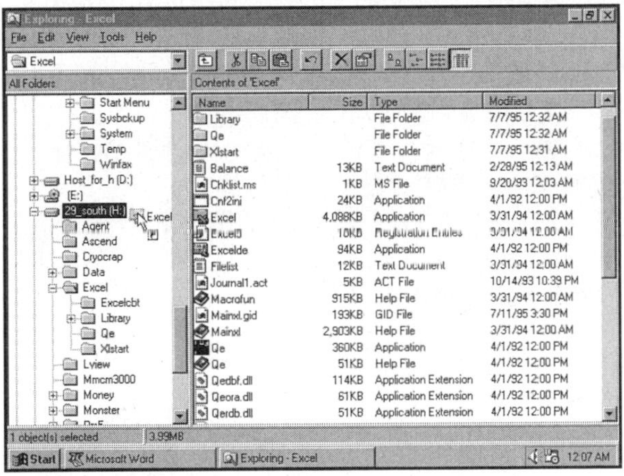

Fig. D.8 *Using drag-and-drop to copy a file from drive C to drive D in Windows Explorer.*

DRAM See *dynamic random-access memory (DRAM).*

draw program A *graphics program* that uses *object-oriented graphics* to produce *line art.* A draw program stores the components of a drawing, such as lines, circles, and curves, as mathematical formulas rather than as a configuration of bits on-screen, as *paint programs* do. Unlike images created with *paint programs,* line art created with a draw program can be sized and scaled without introducing distortions. Draw programs produce output that prints at a printer's maximum *resolution.*

draw tool In any program that includes graphics capabilities, a command that transforms the cursor into a "pen" for creating *object-oriented (vector) graphics.* Draw tools typically include options for creating lines, circles, ovals, polylines, rectangles, and *Bézier curves.*

drive See *disk drive.*

drive activity indicator   A small signal light, often mounted so it shows through the computer's *case*, that indicate when a *disk drive* is in use.

drive arrays   Groups of *hard disks* organized, often as *a redundant array of inexpensive disks (RAID)*, to improve speed and provide protection against data loss. Drive arrays may incorporate *data striping* schemes.

drive bay   A receptacle or opening into which you can install a *hard* or *floppy disk drive*. Half-height drive bays are common in today's IBM and IBM-compatible personal computers. See *half-height drive*.

drive designator   In *DOS*, an argument that specifies the drive to be affected by the command. The command FORMAT B:, for example, tells DOS to format the disk in drive B. B: is the drive designator.

driver   A *file* that contains information needed by a *program* to operate a *peripheral* such as a *monitor* or *printer*. See *device driver*.

DriveSpace   A disk compression program included with *Microsoft Windows 95*.

drop cap   An initial letter of a chapter or paragraph, enlarged and positioned so that the top of the character is even with the top of the first line, and the rest of the character descends into the second and subsequent lines (see fig. D.9). See *initial* and *stickup initial*.

This is a 24 point Helvetica Big First Char. with Space For Big First: Normal. Ventura automatically aligns the top of the character with the top of the first line of text and calculates the number of lines to indent.

Fig. D.9   *A drop cap created with Ventura Publisher.*

drop-down list box   In *industry-standard interface* and *graphical user interface (GUI),* a list of command options that displays as a single-item text box until you select the command, which causes a list of options to drop down (or pop up). After you "drop down" the list, you can choose one of its options. The drop-down list box lets a *programmer* provide many options without taking up much space on-screen.

dropouts   Characters lost in data transmission for some reason. On slower systems, for example, a fast typist may find that some typed characters don't make it into a *word processing* program's *data file*; this is caused by an interruption of user input when the program must access the disk for some reason. The user soon learns to pause when the *drive activity light* comes on.

dropout type   White characters printed on a black background.

drop shadow   A shadow placed behind an image, slightly offset horizontally and vertically, creating the illusion that the topmost image has been lifted off the surface of the page.

drunk mouse   A *mouse* whose *pointer* seems to jump wildly and irritatingly just as you're about to select something. Many users suspect that this malady is caused by a *virus,* but it's attributable to something far more mundane: plain old dirt.

About once every two weeks, pop the ball out of your mouse and take a look inside. On Microsoft-compatible mice, you'll see two metal rollers that are supposed to spin as the mouse ball moves. If you're experiencing the drunk mouse syndrome, chances are good that one or both of these bars is coated with finger grease. To remove it, dip a cotton swab in isopropyl alcohol and rub the rollers until the dirt is completely gone. Then wipe grease off the ball using a soft cloth dampened with isopropyl alcohol.

D-shell connector   The connector that plugs into the *video adapter* end of the cable between the video adapter and the *monitor. Video Graphics Array (VGA)* and *Super VGA* video adapters use 15-pin D-shell connectors; older *video standards* use 9-pin D-shell plugs.

DSMR   See *dual-stripe magneto-resistive (DSMR) head.*

DTE   See *Data Terminal Equipment (DTE).*

C
D
E

DTE speed   The rate, measured in *bits per second (bps)*, at which a *Data Terminal Equipment (DTE)* device such as a personal computer can send data to a *Data Communication Equipment (DCE)* device like a *modem*.

DTMF   See *Desktop Management Task Force (DMTF)*.

DTP   See *desktop publishing*.

dual-actuator hard disk   A *hard disk* design that incorporates two *read/write heads*. Dual-actuator hard disks have better *access times* than standard hard disks, since they have half the *latency*: a needed bit of data is always less than half a revolution away from one of the heads, instead of a full revolution away in a standard hard disk.

dual in-line package (DIP)   A standard packaging and mounting device for *integrated circuits*. DIP is the favored packaging for *dynamic random-access memory (DRAM)* chips, for example. The package, made of hard plastic material, encloses the circuit; the circuit's leads are connected to downward-pointing pins that stick in two parallel rows. The pins are designed to fit securely into a socket; you also can solder them directly to a circuit board. See *single in-line package (SIP)*.

 CAUTION: *Don't try to install or remove DIP circuits unless you know what you're doing. You can easily bend or break the pins.*

dual-issue processor   A type of *central processing unit (CPU)* that can process two instructions simultaneously, each in its own *pipeline*. See *superscalar architecture*.

dual-scanned passive matrix   An improved *passive-matrix LCD* design in which the *display* is *refreshed* twice as fast as standard passive-matrix *liquid-crystal displays (LCDs)*. Though dual-scanned passive matrix displays have better *brightness* and *contrast* than standard *passive-matrix displays*, they are generally inferior to *active-matrix LCDs*.

dual-stripe magneto-resistive (DSMR) head   A new *read/write head* design for *hard disks* that reduces their sensitivity to interference from the outside environment. DSMR heads have separate portions for reading and writing, and pack data tightly onto disks.

dual-tone multi-frequency (DTMF) tones The tones generated by a touch-tone telephone during dialing. Most *dialup modems* generate DTMF tones, as well.

dual y-axis graph In presentation and analytical graphics, a *line* or *column graph* that uses two y-axes (values axes) when comparing two sets of data measured differently. In figure D.10, for example, sales (of battery-operated hand warmers, perhaps?) are measured in dollars, and temperatures are measured in degrees. See *paired bar graph*.

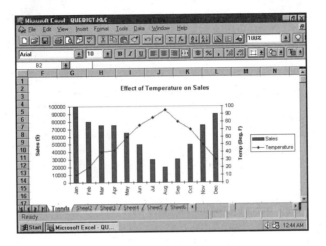

Fig. D.10 *A dual y-axis graph.*

dumb terminal See *terminal*.

dump To transfer the contents of *memory* to a *printer* or disk storage. *Programmers* use memory dumps while debugging programs to see exactly what the computer is doing when the dump occurs. See *core dump* and *Print Screen (PrtSc)*.

duplex See *full duplex* and *half duplex*.

duplex printing Printing or reproducing a document on both sides of the page so that the *verso* (left) and *recto* (right) pages face each other after the document is bound. (A document always begins on an odd-numbered recto page; verso pages have even numbers.) See *binding offset*.

duplication station A *printer/scanner* combination that can serve as a light-duty photocopier.

Dvorak keyboard An alternative *keyboard* layout in which 70 percent of the keystrokes take place on the home row (compared to 32 percent with the standard *QWERTY* layout). A Dvorak keyboard is easier to learn and faster to use. However, every time you return to a *QWERTY* keyboard, you must go back to the hunt-and-peck method.

dynamic astigmatism control See *dynamic beam forming*.

dynamic beam forming A *monitor* design that ensures that electron beams are perfectly round when they strike the *display*, no matter where on-screen the *yoke* steers them. Without dynamic beam forming, electron beams would be elliptical at the edges of the display—like a flashlight beam striking the ground at an angle—and poor focus would result.

dynamic data exchange (DDE) In *Microsoft Windows 95* and *Macintosh System 7.5*, an *interprocess communication channel (IPC)* based on the *client-server* model through which programs can exchange data and control other applications. To be capable of DDE, *programs* must conform to Microsoft Corporation's specifications.

DDE allows simultaneously running programs to exchange data as the information changes. Through the use of *object linking and embedding*, which makes using DDE easier, a DDE-capable *spreadsheet* program can receive real-time data from an *on-line information service*, record changes in the price of key stocks and bonds, and recalculate the entire worksheet as the change occurs. See *client application, dynamic link*, and *server application*.

dynamic link A method of linking *data* so it's shared by two programs. When data is changed in one program, the data is likewise changed in the other when you use an update command. See *hot link*.

dynamic object A *document* or portion of a document pasted or inserted into a destination document using *object linking and embedding (OLE)* techniques. A linked object is automatically updated if you make changes to the *source document*. An embedded object includes information to allow you to open the application used to create the object and edit the object.

dynamic random-access memory (DRAM) A *random-access memory (RAM)* chip that uses capacitors that store electrical charges. Because the capacitors eventually lose their charges, DRAM chips must refresh regularly (hence dynamic). DRAM chips are often used on inexpensive *videoadapter* cards to store video information. See *static random-access memory (SRAM)*.

dynamic range The range of colors a *scanner* can detect, and, along with *color depth* one of the main indicators of a scanner's quality. Though any 24-*bit* scanner can record 16.7 million colors and 265 levels of gray, a 24-bit scanner with a narrow dynamic range could not detect both pale shades of yellow and very dark indigo hues.

C
D
E

Easter egg A message or screen buried within a *program* and accessible only through an undocumented procedure.

Buried in the *Macintosh System* is the message "Help! Help! We're being held prisoner in a system software factory!" Reportedly, at least 12 Easter eggs are buried in Macintosh system software.

A notorious *Microsoft Word* Easter egg depicts *WordPerfect* as a green monster being vanquished by a tiny hero, who squashes the competing program with a Word *icon*, as other tiny figures cheer and celebrate.

EBCDIC See *Extended Binary Coded Decimal Interchange Code (EBCDIC)*.

echoplex A *communications protocol* in which the receiving station acknowledges and confirms the reception by echoing the message back to the transmitting station. See *full duplex* and *half duplex*.

ECP See *extended capabilities port (ECP)*.

edge connector The part of an *adapter* that plugs into an *expansion slot*.

edgelighting A scheme for shining light at a *liquid crystal display (LCD)* to improve readability in bright light conditions. Unlike *backlighting*, which shines light from behind the LCD, edgelighting relies on shining lights around the borders of an LCD. Edgelighting is considered less effective than backlighting.

EDI See *Electronic Data Interchange (EDI)*.

edit mode A *program* mode that makes correcting text and data easier. In *Lotus 1-2-3*, for example, you press F2 to display the contents of a cell in the second line of the control panel, where you can use editing keys to correct errors or add characters. Few programs have special edit modes anymore, since they allow editing in their normal modes.

editor See *text editor*.

edu   A *domain name* denoting a U.S. college or university.

edutainment   *Application programs* designed to tell the user about a subject but presented in the form of a game that is sufficiently entertaining or challenging to hold the user's interest.

A long-time best-selling example of edutainment is the Microsoft Flight Simulator, which many people buy to play as a game but which many flight schools use as a prelude to flight instruction in the air. Almost as well known is the Carmen Sandiego series of games, including Where in the World Is Carmen Sandiego? and Where in Europe Is Carmen Sandiego?

**C
D
E**

EEMS   See *Enhanced Expanded Memory Specification (EEMS)*.

effective resolution   The *resolution* of a *printer's* output on which *resolution enhancement* has been performed. Some *laser printers* claim effective resolutions of 1,200 *dots per inch (dpi)*, but their output is of lower quality than that of printers that can achieve 1,200 dpi without resolution enhancement.

effective transmission rate   The rate at which a *modem* that uses *on-the-fly data compression* communicates *data* to another modem. Data compression ensures that a given amount of data can be communicated at a given speed in a shorter amount of time than uncompressed data, so modems that use on-the-fly compression have higher *throughput* than modems that do not.

EGA   See *Enhanced Graphics Adapter (EGA)*.

EIDE   See *Enhanced IDE (EIDE)*.

Elnet Galaxy   In the *World Wide Web (WWW)*, a *subject tree* maintained by Enterprise Integration Network (EINet), a division of Microelectronics and Computer Technology Corporation. Like all *subject trees*, EINet Galaxy's coverage is limited by the ability of the staff responsible for maintaining it to find and classify useful new Web pages. The service also includes a *search engine* that helps users find the entries that the subject tree contains.

EISA   See *Enhanced ISA (EISA) expansion bus* and *Extended Industry Standard Architecture (EISA)*.

EISA-2   An improved version of the *Enhanced ISA (EISA) expansion bus* that can transfer *data* at 132*M* per second. The earlier EISA standard could transfer data at only 33M per second. Like

EISA, EISA-2 has been mostly replaced by the *Peripheral Component Interconnect (PCI)* standard, but it remains in some high-end *EtherNet* servers.

electrocutaneous feedback   A primitive method of providing *tactile feedback* in *virtual reality* systems by administering a low-voltage shock to the user's skin. The user feels a mild buzz. Varying the voltage and frequency of the current produces variations in the buzz that the user can learn to discriminate.

electron gun   A cathode (electron emitter) in the back of a *cathode ray tube (CRT)* that releases a stream of electrons toward the *display.* Steered by the *yoke,* the electrons "paint" an image on the display. *Color monitors* have three electron guns—one for each primary color—while *monochrome monitors* have only one.

Electronic Communications Privacy Act (ECPA)

A U.S. federal law, enacted in 1986, that prevents U.S. investigative agencies from intercepting *electronic mail* messages, or reading such messages that are temporarily stored in interim storage devices (up to 180 days) without first obtaining a warrant. In a major omission that might stem from the legislators' lack of technical knowledge, the act does not prevent such agencies from obtaining and reading copies of electronic mail permanently stored in *archives.* Investigators used this loophole to obtain Oliver North's e-mail messages to other White House officials involved in the Iran-Contra scandal. The act does not prevent any other persons or agencies from intercepting or reading e-mail. See *confidentiality.*

Electronic Data Interchange (EDI)   A standard for the electronic exchange of business documents, such as invoices and purchase orders. The Data Interchange Standards Association (DISA) developed the standard.

Using field codes, such as BT for Bill To or ST for Ship To, EDI specifies the format in which data is being transmitted electronically. By ensuring that all EDI-based communications have the same data in the same place, this protocol enables companies to exchange purchase orders and other documents electronically.

Electronic Frontier Foundation (EFF)   A nonprofit public advocacy organization dedicated to ensuring the survival of privacy and civil liberties in the computer age. Spurred by an ill-conceived but heavy-handed Secret Service program that resulted in the seizure of *hackers' computer systems* throughout the United States, the organization's founders—Mitchell Kapor and John Perry Barlowe—initially contributed to hackers' legal defense funds, and have since developed an extensive public education and lobbying program.

electronic mail   The use of a *network* to send and receive messages. Also called *e-mail* or *e-pistles*.

Linked by high-speed data connections that cross national boundaries, electronic mail lets you compose messages and transmit them in seconds to one or more recipients in your office, to headquarters in another state, or to a friend in another country.

The *Internet,* an extensive system of computer linkages, is making it easy to send mail worldwide. Electronic mail vendors such as *MCI Mail* and *CompuServe* now offer links to the Internet. See *freenet* and *netiquette.*

electronic mail address   A series of characters that precisely identifies the location of a person's electronic mailbox. On the *Internet,* e-mail addresses consist of a mailbox name (such as **rebecca)** followed by an at sign (**@**) and the computer's domain name (as in **rebecca@hummer.virginia.edu**).

electrostatic printer   A *printer* that relies on the attraction between oppositely charged particles to draw *toner* to paper. *Laser printers* and *LED printers* are electrostatic printers.

element   In the *HyperText Markup Language (HTML),* a distinctive component of a document's structure, such as a title, heading, or list. HTML divides elements into two categories: head elements (such as the document's title) and body elements (headings, paragraphs, links, and text).

elevator seeking   In *hard disks,* a way to sort *data* requests to minimize jumping between *tracks.* In an elevator-seeking scheme, the drive handles data requests in track order; that is, it gets needed data from inner tracks first, then from the outer tracks. Elevator seeking minimizes *access time.*

elite   A typeface that prints 12 *characters per inch (cpi).* See *pitch.*

emacs   A *UNIX*-based *text editor* that is sometimes configured as the default editor on UNIX systems. Programmed in *LISP,* emacs is an excellent *hacker's* tool, but can be a nightmare for users accustomed to *user-friendly word processing programs.*

em   A distance equal to the width of the capital letter M in a given *typeface*. An em dash often introduces parenthetical remarks. The following sentence contains em dashes:

> The butler—or someone who knows what the butler knows—must have done it.

An em space is a space one em wide. See *en*.

em fraction   A single-character fraction that occupies one *em* of space and uses a diagonal stroke (^{1}/4) rather than a piece fraction made from three or more characters (1/4). See *en fraction*.

e-mail   See *electronic mail*.

embed   In *Object Linking and Embedding (OLE)*, to place an object in a document. See *embedded object*.

embedded chart   In *Microsoft Excel*, a chart created within a *worksheet* rather than as a separate chart document.

embedded formatting command   A text formatting command placed directly in the text to be formatted. In some *programs*, the command doesn't affect the text's on-screen appearance, which can make the program more difficult to use. In other programs, such as *WordPerfect*, only a few embedded commands—full *justification* or a *font* change—do not change the screen display. *Microsoft Windows 95* applications include a graphical display that immediately displays formatting. Synonymous with *off-screen formatting*. See *hidden codes, on-screen formatting*, and *what-you-see-is-what-you-get (WYSIWYG)*.

embedded object   In *Object Linking and Embedding (OLE)*, an object wholly inserted, or embedded, into a *destination document* created by an application other than that which created the destination document. The object can be text, a chart, a *graphic*, or sound. See *linked object*.

EMM   See *expanded memory manager (EMM)*.

EMM386.EXE   In MS-DOS running on a computer with an *80386* or higher *microprocessor* and *extended memory*, an *expanded memory emulator* that enables DOS applications to use the extended memory as though it were *expanded memory (EMS)*. EMM386.EXE also enables the user to load *device drivers* and programs into the *upper memory area*.

emoticon In *electronic mail* and *newsgroups,* a sideways face made of *ASCII characters* that puts a message into context and compensates for the lack of verbal inflections and body language that plagues electronic communication.

To avoid finding yourself the object of a *flame* (or worse, a *flame war*) as a result of a misinterpreted message, learn all you can about *netiquette.* In particular, learn how to use emoticons effectively. The following are some commonly used emoticons:

:-)	I'm smiling as I make this joke.
:-D	I'm overjoyed about the last thing that I typed.
:-*	Here's a kiss.
:-O	I'm yawning; this thing is so boring.
;-)	I'm winking or flirting about this joke.
:-7	I say this tongue-in-cheek.
:-(	I'm sad about the thing that I just typed.
:-<	I'm really sad and frowning at this.
>:-(	I'm angry or annoyed about this.
:'-(	I'm crying; this is really sad to me.
:-9	I am licking my lips.
X-(	I'm dead; this has killed me.

See *ASCII art.*

emphasis The use of a non-Roman *type style*—such as underlining, italic, bold, or small caps typefaces—to highlight a word or phrase.

EMS See *Lotus-Intel-Microsoft Expanded Memory Specification (LIM EMS).*

emulation The duplication within a device of another device's functional capability, or a device designed to work exactly like another. In *telecommunications,* for example, a *personal computer* emulates a dumb *terminal*—a terminal without its own microprocessor—for on-line communication with a distant computer.

emulation sensing   See *automatic emulation switching* and *automatic network switching*.

emulation switching   See *automatic emulation switching*.

en   In typesetting, a unit of measurement that equals half the width of an *em* space, which is the width of the capital letter M in a typeface. En dashes are used in place of the English words *to* or *through,* as in *January 9–January 23* or *pp. 63–68.* They also are used as minus signs, as in *–30 degrees Farenheit.* See *em dash.*

Encapsulated PostScript (EPS) file   A *high-resolution graphic* image stored in the *PostScript* page description language. The EPS standard enables users to transfer high-resolution graphics images between applications. You can size EPS images without sacrificing image quality

A major drawback of EPS graphics is that to print them, you usually need a PostScript-compatible *laser printer.* A second drawback is that with most application programs, you cannot view the image on-screen unless you attach a screen image to it. To provide an alternative to expensive PostScript printers, developers have created programs, such as LaserGo, Inc.'s GoScript, that interpret and print EPS files on standard *dot-matrix printers* or non-PostScript laser printers.

encryption   In *cryptography,* the process of converting a message into a ciphertext (an encrypted message) by using a *key,* so the message appears to be nothing but gibberish. However, the intended recipient can apply the key to decrypt and read the message. See *decryption, public key cryptography,* and *rot-13.*

End key   A *key* on *IBM PC-compatible keyboards,* with functions that vary from program to program. Frequently, pressing the End key moves the cursor to the end of the line or the bottom of the screen, but the assignment of this key is up to the *programmer.*

endnote   A footnote positioned at the end of a *document* or section rather than the bottom of a page. Many *word processing programs* let the user choose between footnotes and endnotes.

end user   The person who uses a *computer system* and its *application programs* at home or at work to perform tasks and produce results.

Energy Star   A U.S. Environmental Protection Agency (EPA) program that seeks to reduce energy waste by encouraging *monitor* and *printer* manufacturers to reduce the amount of electricity that their devices require. Energy Star devices typically have a *sleep mode* that reduces their power consumption when they are not being used. Energy Star devices, identifiable by a blue and green EPA sticker, can save their owners hundreds of dollars in electrical costs each year.

en fraction   A single-character fraction that occupies one *en* of space and uses a horizontal stroke. See *em fraction.*

enhanced 101-key keyboard   See *enhanced keyboard.*

Enhanced ATA   See *ATA-2.*

Enhanced CD   A standard created by *Microsoft Corporation* for audio compact disks. This standard enables audio CD publishers to include digital information on compact disks; for example, a jazz disk could include information on each track's performers. The information about the performers could be read on a specially equipped CD player.

Enhanced Expanded Memory Specification (EEMS) A version of the original *Lotus-Intel-Microsoft Expanded Memory Specification (LIM EMS)* that is enhanced to enable DOS applications to use more than 640K of memory. See *bank switching* and *expanded memory (EMS).*

Enhanced Graphics Adapter (EGA)   A color, bit-mapped, graphics *video adapter* standard for *IBM PC-compatible* computers. The EGA adapter can display as many as 16 colors simultaneously with a resolution of 640 *pixels* horizontally by 350 lines vertically. You select the 16 colors from the EGA color palette, which contains 64 colors (including black and shades of gray). See *Color Graphics Adapter (CGA), Super VGA,* and *Video Graphics Array (VGA).*

Enhanced Graphics Display   A color *digital monitor* designed to work only with the IBM *Enhanced Graphics Adapter (EGA).*

Enhanced IDE (EIDE)   An improved version of the *integrated drive electronics (IDE)* disk-interface standard that dictates how *hard disks* and *CD-ROM drives* connect to the rest of the computer. The EIDE standard allows hard disk drives as large as 8.4*G,* while IDE supports hard disks no larger than 528*M.* Also, the EIDE standard enables you to connect four hard disks to your computer rather than two.

Enhanced ISA (EISA) expansion bus   A 32-bit *expansion bus* standard designed by a consortium of computer companies to compete with IBM's *Micro Channel Architecture (MCA) expansion bus.* The EISA expansion bus can move data at 33*M* per second, but has been replaced by the *EISA-2* standard and, to a greater extent, the *Peripheral Component Interconnect (PCI) expansion bus* standard.

enhanced keyboard   The modern *keyboard* standard. An enhanced keyboard has 101 *keys,* including a *numeric keypad,* 12 *function keys,* and several navigation keys.

Enhanced NCSA Mosaic   A *Web browser,* developed by Spyglass, Inc., that is based on *NCSA Mosaic* and specifically designed for commercial distribution. Most of the several million copies of Enhanced NCSA Mosaic now in existence have been distributed under license to software resellers (such as *IBM*) and book publishers. Enhanced NCSA Mosaic is designed for stability and uses the *Secure HTTP (S-HTTP)* protocol to provide secure communications capabilities.

enhanced parallel port (EPP)   An improvement on the *parallel port,* which enables two-way communication. Using an EPP, for example, a *printer* can tell a *microprocessor* how much paper or toner remains in its bins. The *extended capabilities port (ECP)* might eventually replace the EPP, but for now, many *motherboards* support both standards.

enhanced serial port (ESP)   A speedy *serial port* that uses dedicated *random-access memory (RAM)* to move data quickly.

Enhanced System Device Interface (ESDI)   An *interface standard* for hard disk drives. Drives that use the ESDI standard transfer at 10 to 15 *megabits of data per second (Mbps),* which is two to three times as fast as the earlier *ST-506/ST-412* interface standard. Faster, more flexible *Integrated Drive Electronics (IDE) drives* have almost totally replaced ESDI drives.

Enter/Return   A *key* that confirms a command, sending the command to the *central processing unit (CPU)*; synonymous with *carriage return.* In *word processing*, the Enter/Return key starts a new paragraph. Early IBM PC keyboards labeled this key with a hooked left arrow. On more recent AT and enhanced keyboards, the word *Enter* is printed on the key. (The word *Return* appears on *Macintosh* keyboards.)

Most *IBM PC-compatible* keyboards have an Enter key to the right of the typing area, and a second one in the numeric keypad's lower-right corner. These two keys have identical functions in most but not all programs.

entity   In the *HyperText Markup Language (HTML)*, a code that represents a non ASCII character, such as an accented character from a foreign language.

entry-level system   A *computer system* considered to be the minimal system for using serious computer *application programs*, such as *spreadsheet* programs or *word processing software.*

The definition of an entry-level system changes rapidly. Ten years ago, an entry-level system—incapable of running the latest versions of today's most popular software—had at least one 360*K floppy disk drive*, a *monochrome* text monitor, and 256K of *random-access memory (RAM)*. Modern entry-level systems have *486 DX/2 microprocessors*, *Video Graphics Array monitors*, and at least 8*M* of RAM.

entry line   In a *spreadsheet* program, the second line, on which the characters that you type appear. The program doesn't insert the characters into the current cell until you press Enter. If the cell has contents, the control panel's upper-left corner displays them.

envelope printer   A *printer* designed specifically to print names, addresses, and usually U.S. Postal Service POSTNET *bar codes* on business envelopes. Businesses that use the bar codes receive an attractive discount on postal rates and receive faster and more accurate delivery of their business correspondence.

You might not need an envelope printer if you already have a *laser* or *inkjet printer*, because many such printers can print POSTNET codes. Envelope printers, however, do a better job of handling high-volume printing jobs.

environment   The *hardware* and *operating system* for *application programs*, such as the *Macintosh* environment. In *MS-DOS*, the environment also is a space in memory reserved for storing variables that applications running on your system can use. See *environment variable*.

environment variable   An instruction stored in the *MS-DOS environment* that controls, for example, how to display the DOS *prompt*, where to store any temporary files, and the *path* of directories that DOS searches to find commands. The PATH, COMSPEC, PROMPT, and SET commands in the AUTOEXEC.BAT file all define environment variables.

EOF   Abbreviation for *end of file*.

EOL   Abbreviation for *end of line*.

e-pistle   See *electronic mail*.

EPP   See *enhanced parallel port (EPP)*.

EPP/ECP port   An improved version of the *parallel port* that supports both the *enhanced parallel port (EPP)* and *extended capabilities port (ECP)* standards. EPP/ECP ports can transmit data very fast—as fast as an *EtherNet network interface card*.

TIP: *If you're planning to run* Microsoft Windows 95, *look for a computer that offers one or more EPP/ECP ports. Windows 95 can use these ports to give you detailed information about a printer's status.*

EPROM   See *erasable programmable read-only memory (EPROM)*.

EPS   See *Encapsulated PostScript (EPS) file*.

equation typesetting   Codes in a *word processing* document that cause the program to print multiline equations, including mathematical symbols such as integrals and summation signs. The best word processing programs, such as *WordPerfect* and *Microsoft Word*, offer *what-you-see-is-what-you-get (WYSIWYG)* on-screen equation editors, which let you see the equation as you build it.

erasable optical disk drive   A *read/write* data storage medium that uses a laser and reflected light to store and retrieve data on an *optical disk*.

Unlike *CD-ROM disk drives* and *write-once, read-many (WORM)* drives, erasable *optical disk* drives can be used like *hard disks*. You can write and erase data repeatedly. Storage capacities are sizable;

current drives store up to 650*M* of information. They're expensive and much slower than hard disks, however. See *secondary storage*.

erasable programmable read-only memory
(EPROM)
A *read-only memory (ROM)* chip that can be programmed and reprogrammed with a special electronic device. EPROM chips are packaged in a clear plastic case so that the contents can be erased using ultraviolet light.

The erasability of EPROM chips matters to computer manufacturers, who often find that they need to reprogram ROM chips containing bugs. *Programmable read-only memory (PROM)* chips, which can't be reprogrammed, must be discarded when a programming error is discovered.

TIP: *Ultraviolet light can damage EPROM chips, so avoid exposing your computer's innards to bright sunlight.*

e rate   See *vertical frequency*.

ergonomic keyboard   A *keyboard* designed to reduce strain on the wrists, which can result in *repetitive stress injury (RSI)*. Some ergonomic keyboards, such as the Microsoft Natural Keyboard, angle keys away from the center, while others put keys in pits into which a naturally curved hand can fit.

ergonomics   The science of designing machines, tools, computers, and physical work areas so that people find them easy and healthful to use.

error-correction protocol   In *modems*, a method for filtering out *line noise* and repeating transmissions automatically if an error occurs. Error correction requires the use of sending and receiving modems that conform to the same error-correction protocols. When error correction is in use, a *reliable link* is established. Two widely used error-correcting protocols are *MNP-4* and *V.42*. See *CCITT protocol*.

error handling   The way that a *program* copes with errors, such as the failure to access data on a disk or a user's failure to press the right key. A poorly written program might fail to handle errors at all, leading to a system *crash*. The best *programmers* anticipate possible errors and provide information that helps the user solve the problem. See *error trapping*.

error message   In *application programs*, an on-screen message informing you that the program can't carry out a requested operation. Early computing systems assumed users to be technically sophisticated, and frequently presented cryptic error messages. Applications for general use should display more helpful error messages that include suggestions about how to solve the problem, such as the following:

```
You are about to lose work you have not saved.
Choose OK if you want to abandon this work.
Choose Cancel to return to your document.
```

error trapping   An application's capability to recognize an error and perform a predetermined action in response to that error.

Esc   A key that *application programs* can implement in various ways. In most applications, pressing Esc cancels a command or an operation.

escape character   In *Telnet,* a command (often Ctrl+[) that enables you to interrupt the link with the Telnet server so that you can communicate directly with your Telnet client. The escape character comes in handy when the Telnet server isn't responding.

escape code   A series of characters, combining Esc (ASCII value 27) with one or more *ASCII characters,* that you can use to change screen colors, control the *cursor,* create special *prompts,* reassign *keys* on the *keyboard,* and change your printer's settings (to compressed type or bold, for example). Also, the series of characters that engages a *modem's command mode.* In the *Hayes command set,* the escape sequence consists of three plus signs (+++). Synonymous with *escape sequence.*

escape sequence   See *escape code.*

ESDI   See *Enhanced System Device Interface (ESDI).*

ESP   See *enhanced serial port (ESP).*

EtherNet   A *local area network (LAN)* hardware, communication, and cabling standard, originally developed by Xerox Corporation, that can link up to 1,024 nodes in a *bus network.*

A high-speed standard using a *baseband* (single-channel) communication technique, EtherNet provides for a raw data transfer rate of 10 *megabits per second (Mbps),* with actual *throughput* in the range of 2 to 3 megabits per second. EtherNet uses *carrier sense multiple access with collision detection (CSMA/CD)* techniques to prevent network failures when two devices try to access the network at the same time. See *AppleTalk*.

CAUTION: *Several firms, such as 3Com and Novell, manufacture LAN hardware that uses EtherNet protocols, but the products of one firm often are incompatible with the products of another.*

EtherTalk An implementation of *EtherNet local area network (LAN)* hardware, jointly developed by Apple and 3Com, and designed to work with the *AppleShare* network operating system. EtherTalk transmits data through coaxial cables at the EtherNet rate of 10 megabits per second, in contrast to *AppleTalk's* rate of 230 kilobits per second.

ETX/ACK handshaking See *handshaking*.

 Eudora A popular *electronic mail program* that enables *Macintosh* and *Microsoft Windows 95* users to access *Internet* electronic mail by means of *SLIP/PPP* or network connections. Fully integrated with *Multipurpose Internet Multimedia Extensions (MIME)*, Eudora enables you to include *binary files* and *multimedia objects*, such as graphics and videos, with your electronic mail messages.

European Laboratory for Particle Physics (CERN)
A Geneva, Switzerland-based research center for advanced physics research. The center is more widely known by the acronym for its French name (CERN, Conseil European pour la Recherche Nucleaire). CERN is the birthplace of the *World Wide Web (WWW)*, which the center's high-energy physics researchers began in 1989 as a collaborative network.

even parity In *asynchronous communications*, an error-checking technique that sets an extra *bit* (called a *parity bit*) to 1 if the number of 1 bits in a one-byte data item adds up to an even number. The parity bit is set to 0 if the number of 1 bits adds up to an odd number. See *odd parity* and *parity checking*.

event In an *event-driven environment*, an action—such as moving the *mouse* or clicking a mouse button—that generates a message. See *event handler*.

event-driven environment   A *program* or *operating system* that normally functions in an idle *loop*, waiting for events, such as a *mouse click*, *keyboard* input, or a message from a device, to occur. When an event occurs, the program exits the idle loop and executes the program code designed to handle the specific event. This code is called an *event handler*. After handling the event, the program returns to the idle loop. *Microsoft Windows 95* and *Macintosh System* software are event-driven environments.

event-driven language   A *programming language* that creates *programs* that respond to events such as input, incoming data, or signals received from other applications. Such programs keep the computer in an idle *loop* until an event occurs, at which time they execute code that is relevant to the event. *HyperTalk*, the language included with the *HyperCard* application packaged with every *Macintosh*, is an event-driven language. See *object-oriented programming language*.

event-driven program   See *event-driven environment*.

event handler   In an *event-driven environment*, a block of *program* code designed to handle the messages generated when a specific kind of event occurs, such as a *mouse click*.

eWorld   An *on-line information service* introduced June 20, 1994, and designed specifically for the *Macintosh*. eWorld offers stock quotes, *electronic mail*, conferences, news, sports, weather, and *Apple* and Macintosh information such as names of dealers. Apple has merged its on-line business service, AppleLink, with eWorld. eWorld also provides a variety of conferences, files, and other information for the Macintosh.

Excel   See *Microsoft Excel*.

.EXE   In *MS-DOS*, a file name extension that indicates that the file is an executable *program*. To run the program with DOS, simply type the file name (but not the extension) and press Enter.

executable file   See *executable program*.

executable program   A *program* that is ready to run on a given computer. For a program to be executable, it first must be translated, usually by a *compiler*, into the *machine language* of a particular computer.

TIP: *In* MS-DOS, *you can tell whether a file is an executable program by looking at the extension: .EXE and .COM files are executable programs.*

C
D
E

execute   To carry out the instructions in an *algorithm* or *program*.

expand   In an *outlining utility* or a graphical file management utility (such as the *Windows Explorer*), to reveal all the subordinate entries below the selected outline heading or *directory*. In Explorer, for example, you can expand a directory quickly by double-clicking the directory *icon*—a folder.

expandability   The capability of a *computer system* to accommodate more *memory*, additional *disk drives*, or *adapters*.

Computers vary in their expandability. When shopping for a computer, consider systems configured the way that you want but with space for growth. Look for one or two empty *drive bays*, three to five empty *expansion slots*, and room for at least four times as much *random-access memory (RAM)* as comes installed.

expanded memory board   An adapter that adds *expanded memory* to an *IBM PC-compatible* computer.

expanded memory emulator   A *utility program* for Intel 80386 and *Intel 486* computers that uses *extended memory* to simulate *expanded memory* to accommodate older programs and the many games that require it. See *EMM386.EXE*.

expanded memory manager (EMM)   A *utility program* that manages *expanded memory* in an *IBM PC-compatible* computer equipped with an *expanded memory board*. See *EMM386.EXE*.

Expanded Memory Specification (EMS)   See *Lotus-Intel-Microsoft Expanded Memory Specification (LIM EMS)*.

expanded type   A *typeface* that places characters farther apart or makes the characters wider so that there are fewer *characters per inch (cpi)*.

expansion board   See *adapter*.

expansion bus   An extension of the computer's *data bus* and *address bus* that includes several *expansion slots* for *adapters*.

Peripheral Component Interconnect (PCI) and *Industry Standard Architecture (ISA)* are the most popular expansion bus designs available today. See *Micro Channel Bus, VESA local bus,* and *motherboard.*

expansion bus bottleneck   A phenomenon that occurs when the *microprocessor* performs far better than the *expansion bus,* and which results in poor overall *computer system* performance. The expansion bus bottleneck problem has been solved by fast expansion bus standards like the *Peripheral Component Interconnect (PCI)* standard.

expansion card   See *adapter.*

expansion slot   A receptacle connected to the computer's *expansion bus,* designed to accept *adapters.*

expect statement   In a *communication program's* login *script,* a statement that tells the dialer to wait for the service provider's computer to send certain characters (such as "Please type your password").

expert system   A *program* that contains much of the knowledge used by an expert in a specific field and that assists nonexperts as they try to solve problems.

Expert systems contain a *knowledge base* expressed in a series of IF/THEN rules and an engine capable of drawing inferences from this knowledge base. The system prompts you to supply information needed to assess the situation and come to a conclusion. Most expert systems express conclusions with a confidence factor, ranging from speculation to educated guess to firm conclusion. See *artificial intelligence (AI), backward-chaining, forward-chaining,* and *PROLOG.*

expiration date   In *UseNet,* the date at which a *post* is set to expire. The expiration date can be set in two ways: by the article's author, and by UseNet system administrators. Although an article's author usually can choose to set an expiration date, not all *newsreaders* support this capability; if the author doesn't set a date, the expiration date field (part of the article's header) remains blank. UseNet system administrators can also choose to set default expiration dates for all the articles in a given newsgroup, such as two weeks from the date of delivery. On the expiration date, the article is deleted to conserve disk space for incoming articles. See *expired article.*

expired article   In *UseNet,* an article that is still listed in the article selector, even though the UseNet system software has deleted the article because it has expired. You cannot read an expired article. See *expiration date.*

exploded pie graph   A pie chart in which one or more of the slices is offset slightly (exploded) from the others to emphasize the data represented by the exploded slice (see fig. E.1). See *pie graph.*

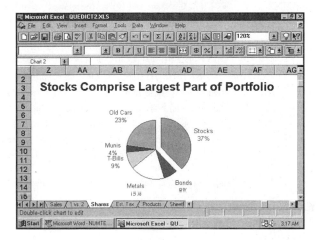

Fig. E.1   *An exploded pie graph.*

export   To save *data* in a *format* that another *program* can *read.* Most programs can export a document in *ASCII* format, which almost any program can read and use. When saving a *document* with a recent versions of a *word processing program,* you can choose a format from a list of dozens. See *import.*

Extended Binary Coded Decimal Interchange Code (EBCDIC)   A *character set* coding scheme that represents 256 standard characters. IBM *mainframes* use EBCDIC coding, while *personal computers* use *ASCII* coding. *Networks* that link personal computers to IBM mainframes must include a translating device to mediate between the two systems.

extended capabilities port (ECP) An improvement on the *parallel port* that supports two-way communication between the computer and a *peripheral* device. Using an ECP, for example, a *scanner* can tell the *central processing unit (CPU)* that it has a paper jam and needs attention. The ECP may eventually displace the competing *enhanced parallel port (EPP)* standard, although many *motherboards* currently support both standards.

extended character set In *IBM PC-compatible* computing, a 256-character *character set* stored in a computer's *read-only memory (ROM)* that includes, in addition to the 128 *ASCII* character codes, a collection of foreign language, technical, and block graphics characters. The characters with numbers above ASCII code 128 sometimes are referred to as higher-order characters.

eXtended Graphics Array (XGA) A *video standard* intended to replace the *8514/A* standard and to bring 1,024-*pixel* by 768-line *resolution* to IBM and *IBM PC-compatible displays*. An XGA board equipped with sufficient memory (1*M* or more) can display 65,536 colors at its low-resolution mode (640 × 480) and 256 colors at its high-resolution mode (1,024 × 768). For *downward compatibility* with *software* that supports earlier standards, XGA boards also support the *Video Graphics Array (VGA)* standard. The XGA standard faces stiff competition from makers of extended VGA (high-resolution *Super VGA*) *video adapters*.

Extended Industry Standard Architecture (EISA) A 32-bit *expansion bus* design introduced by a consortium of *IBM PC-compatible* computer makers to counter IBM's proprietary *Micro Channel Bus*. Unlike the Micro Channel Bus, the EISA bus is downwardly compatible with existing 16-bit peripherals such as disk drives and display adapters.

Once the state-of-the-art in personal computing, EISA machines have been eclipsed by the *Peripheral Component Interconnect (PCI) expansion bus*.

extended-level synthesizer In the *Microsoft Windows 95 Multimedia Personal Computer (MPC)* specification, a synthesizer that can play a minimum of 16 simultaneous notes on nine melodic instruments, and 16 simultaneous notes on eight percussive instruments. See *base-level synthesizer*.

extended memory In *Intel 80286* or later *IBM PC-compatible* computers, the *random-access memory (RAM)*, if any, above 1*M* (megabyte) that usually is installed directly on the *motherboard* and is directly accessible to the microprocessor. *Operating System/2 (OS/2)* and *Microsoft Windows 95* do not make distinctions among various portions of RAM.

extended memory manager A *utility program* that lets certain *MS-DOS* programs access *extended memory*. The programs must be written to conform to the *eXtended Memory Specification (XMS)* standard. See *conventional memory* and *HIMEM.SYS*.

eXtended Memory Specification (XMS) A set of standards and an operating environment that enables all programs to access *extended memory*.

XMS requires a *utility program* known as an *extended memory manager,* such as *HIMEM.SYS* (which is provided with DOS 5.0).

extended VGA See *Super VGA*.

extensible Capable of accepting new, user-defined commands.

extension A three-letter suffix (such as *.BMP*, *.RTF*, or *.ASM*) added to an *MS-DOS file name* that describes the file's contents. The extension is optional and is separated from the file name by a period.

external cache See *secondary cache*.

external command An *MS-DOS* command that executes a *program*. The program file must be present in the current *drive*, *directory*, or *path*. FORMAT and DISKCOPY are examples of external commands. See *internal command*.

eXternal CoMmanD (XCMD) In *HyperTalk programming*, a user-defined command (written in a language such as *Pascal* or *C*) that uses built-in *Macintosh library routines* to perform tasks not normally available within *HyperCard*.

A popular XCMD is ResCopy, which is widely available in *public domain* or *shareware* stack-writing *utility programs*. ResCopy enables a HyperTalk programmer to copy external commands and external resources from one program or stack to another. See *external function (XCFN)* and *ResEdit*.

external data bus A set of communications channels that facilitate communication between a *central processing unit (CPU)* and other components on the *motherboard,* including *random-access memory (RAM).*

external function (XCFN) In *HyperTalk programming,* a *program* function (written in a language such as Pascal or C) that is external to HyperTalk but returns values to the program that can be used within the HyperTalk program. For example, Resources, an XCFN widely available in *public domain* or *shareware* stack-writing utilities, returns a list of all named resources in a file of a specified type. See *external command (XCMD).*

external hard disk A *hard disk* equipped with its own case, cables, and power supply. External hard disks usually cost more than *internal hard disks* of comparable speed and capacity.

external modem A *modem* with its own case, cables, and power supply, designed to plug into a *serial port.* See *internal modem.*

external reference formula In *Microsoft Excel* and other *dynamic data exchange (DDE)*-capable *spreadsheet programs,* a *formula* placed in a cell that creates a link to another spreadsheet.

external table In *Lotus 1-2-3,* a *database* created with a *database management program* (such as *dBASE*) that 1-2-3 can access directly.

 extraction The process using *uudecode* to decode a *file* encoded for *network* transmission by *uuencode,* a *UNIX utility program.*

extra-high-density floppy disk A type of *floppy disk* that requires a special *floppy disk drive* (equipped with two heads rather than the usual one) and can hold 2.88*M* when formatted for *MS-DOS.*

extremely low-frequency (ELF) emission A magnetic field generated by commonly used electrical appliances such as *monitors,* electric blankets, hair dryers, and food mixers, and extending one to two meters from the source.

ELF fields have caused tissue changes and fetal abnormalities in laboratory test animals and might be related to reproductive anomalies and cancers among frequent users of computers. Despite repeated assurances that computer displays are safe, evidence continues to accumulate of reproductive disorders and miscarriages among pregnant computer users.

CAUTION: *Emissions are strongest at the back and sides of the monitor. Avoid sitting behind a monitor, and reduce exposure further by remaining an arm's length away from the screen. Better still, you might replace your current display with a low-emissions model that meets strict Swedish government standards. See* MPR II.

C
D
E

F2F In *electronic mail,* a common abbreviation that means "face to face"—a real-life meeting.

fabless Without large-scale fabrication facilities. A fabless *chip* maker, such as *Advanced Micro Devices (AMD),* must farm out chip-manufacturing jobs to other companies.

facing pages The two pages of a bound document that face each other when the document is open. See *recto* and *verso.*

facsimile machine See *fax machine.*

factory configuration The set of operating parameters built in to a *modem* that can be overridden with an *initialization string* that establishes an *active configuration.*

fall back In *modems,* to decrease the *data transfer rate* to accommodate communication with an older modem or across a *dirty* line. Some modems also *fall forward* if *line noise* conditions improve.

fall forward In *modems,* to increase the *data transfer rate* if the quality of a connection improves. Some modems that *fall back* due to *line noise* can fall forward again if noise abates.

false dependency In *microprocessors* that use *superscalar architecture,* a condition in which the results of two calculations are written to the same *register* if separate *pipelines* perform the calculations simultaneously. The more registers a microprocessor has, the fewer false dependencies are likely to occur. See *data dependency* and *register renaming.*

false drop In an information retrieval system, such as a *World Wide Web (WWW)*-based *search engine,* the retrieval of an item that does not bear any relation to the subject on which you are searching. This is a common flaw of keyword search systems. For example, suppose that you are searching for "gun control." The list of retrieved documents might contain some of interest to you, but it might also include "The Unofficial Guns & Roses Home Page."

FAQ See *Frequently Asked Questions (FAQ)*.

Fast ATA See *Enhanced IDE*.

FAT See *file allocation table (FAT)*.

fatal error An error in a program that, at best, causes the program to *abort*, and, at worst, causes a crash with loss of data. *Bulletproof* programs are supposed to be immune to fatal errors, but they usually are not.

fatware *Software* that is so laden with *features*, or is designed so inefficiently, that it monopolizes huge chunks of *hard disk* space, *random-access memory (RAM)*, and *microprocessor* power. Fatware is one of the undesirable results of *creeping featurism*.

fault tolerance The capability of a *computer system* to cope with internal *hardware* problems without interrupting the system's performance, often by automatically bringing backup systems on-line when the system detects a failure. Fault tolerance is indispensable whenever computers are assigned critical functions, such as guiding an aircraft to a safe landing or ensuring a steady flow of medicines to a patient. Fault tolerance also is beneficial for non-critical, everyday applications. See *bulletproof* and *Microsoft Windows NT*.

fax To send and receive printed pages between two locations using a telephone line. Fax is short for facsimile. See *fax machine*.

fax board A *circuit board* that fits into an *expansion slot* in a computer, providing many of the features of a *fax machine* at a lower cost, as well as crisper output and convenience. If you are traveling, or at a remote location, you can use a *portable computer* with a fax board to *fax* materials to and from any place with a phone.

Fax boards send a coded image of a *document* and receive that image in the form of a file that you can then print. Before using a fax board to send printed or handwritten material, you must use special video equipment to scan or record the material. Some fax boards are send-only; others can receive and send faxes. See *modem*.

fax machine A device that can send and receive images of pages through a phone line. A fax machine scans a sheet of paper and creates an image in a coded form that the machine can then transmit. A fax machine on the other end receives and translates the code, and then prints a replica of the original page. See *fax board*.

fax modem See *fax board*.

fax program An *application program* that enables you to use a *fax board*. Usually, a fax program enables you to compose, send, receive, and print faxes, and complete one of a variety of fax cover pages included with the program. When you receive documents that include text, the newest fax programs use *optical character recognition (OCR)* to convert the faxed image back into text so that you can edit the document by using any of the popular word processing programs.

fax server A computer or dedicated device that provides fax capabilities to all the *workstations* in a *local area network (LAN)*. See *fax board*.

fax switch A device that routes incoming telephone calls to the telephone, the *modem,* or the *fax machine,* whichever is appropriate. A fax switch can save the cost of extra telephone lines.

FCC certification An attestation, formerly made by the U.S. Federal Communications Commission (FCC), that a given brand and model of a computer meets the agency's limits for radio frequency emissions. There are two certification levels: *Class A certification,* for computers to be used in industrial and commercial locations (specifically, mainframes and minicomputers), and *Class B certification,* for computers to be used in home locations, including home offices. All personal computers are explicitly defined as Class B equipment. See *radio frequency interference (RFI)*.

FDD An acronym for *floppy disk drive* sometimes used in advertisements.

FDHD An acronym for *floppy drive high density*. See *SuperDrive*.

feathering Adding an equal amount of space between each line on a page or column to force *vertical justification*.

feature A capability of a *program*. Occasionally, programs contain undocumented features. Of recent concern is *creeping featurism* where, in an attempt to remain competitive, manufacturers load their programs with extra features that slow a program's operation and clutter the interface.

federated database   In scientific networking, a collaborative database (part of a *collaboratory*) in which scientists pool their knowledge and discoveries. Federated databases are one proposed solution to the *Grand Challenges*—problems that are so complex that they far outstrip the capabilities of individual scientists, or even individual research institutions, to tackle them independently.

female connector   A cable terminator and connection device with receptacles designed to accept the pins of a *male connector*.

femto-   A prefix indicating one quadrillionth, or a millionth of a billionth (10^{15}).

TIP: *Prefixes similar to femto- include atto- (a billionth of a billionth, or 10^{18}) and zepto- (quadrillionth of a billionth, or 10^{21}).*

Fiber Distributed Data Interface (FDDI)   A standard for creating high-speed computer networks that employ *fiber-optic cable*. The FDDI specification calls for networks up to 250km long that can transfer data at speeds of 100 million bits per second (Mbps).

fiber optic cable   A high-speed physical medium that can be used for transmitting *data*. Constructed from thin fibers of glass, fiber-optic cable guides the light of transmitting lasers without significant loss, despite twists and turns along the way. At the receiving end, optical detectors transform the light into electrical impulses. Fiber optics enables very high-speed networking (the *Fiber Distributed Data Interface [FDDI]* specification calls for data transfer at speeds of 100 Mbps), but is expensive and difficult with which to work.

fiber optics   A data transmission technology that uses *fiber optic cable* to convey information.

Fidonet   A set of data exchange standards and procedures that permit privately operated computer *bulletin board systems (BBSs)* to exchange data, files, and *electronic mail* internationally, using the world telephone system.

At an agreed-on time when telephone rates are low, subscribing BBSs send e-mail messages and files to a regional host, which in turn distributes them to other bulletin boards. Responses, or *echoes,* eventually find their way back to the host bulletin board. A popular Fidonet feature is EchoMail, a set of moderated conferences that cover a variety of popular subjects, such as *Star Trek,* model aircraft, and political issues. See *Internet* and *wide area network (WAN).*

field   See *data field.*

field definition   In a *database management* program, a list of the attributes that define the type of information that you can enter into a *data field.* The field definition also determines how the field's contents appear on-screen.

In *dBASE,* for example, the field definition includes the field name, the type and maximum length of data that can be entered, the number of decimal places if the field is numeric, and the index attribute, if any. See *data type* and *field template.*

field name   In a *database management* program, a unique name given to a *data field.* The name should help users identify the field's contents.

Keep field names short. That way, when you display data in a columnar format, you can see more columns of data on-screen.

TIP: *When naming fields, make sure that each name describes the data that its field contains, such as CITY. You see the field names on data-entry forms and data tables. Try creating two- or three-word field names by inserting underscore characters, as in LAST_NAME or P_O_BOX. If you name a field MX388SMRPS, nobody will know what the field contains.*

field privilege   In a *database management* program, a database definition that establishes what you can do with the contents of a *data field* in a protected database.

field template   In *database management* programs, a field definition that specifies the kind of data that you can type in the *data field.* If you try to type some data into a field that doesn't match the field template, the program displays an error message. Synonymous with *data mask.*

Use field templates as often as possible. They help prevent users from adding inappropriate information to the database. See *data type.*

file   A *document* or other collection of information stored on a disk and identified as a unit by a unique name. When you save a file, the disk may scatter the data among dozens or even hundreds of noncontiguous *clusters.* The *file allocation table (FAT)* is an index of the order in which those clusters are linked to equal a file. To the user, however, files appear as units on disk *directories* and are retrieved and copied as units. See *secondary storage.*

file allocation table (FAT)   A hidden table of every *cluster* on a *floppy* or *hard disk.* The FAT records how files are stored in distinct—and not necessarily contiguous—clusters. *Viruses* also like to hide out in the FAT; make sure your virus-checking software looks there for malicious programs.

A file allocation table uses a simple method, much like a scavenger hunt, to keep track of data. The directory file stores the address of the file's first cluster. In the FAT entry for the first cluster is the address of the second cluster used to store the file. In the entry for the second cluster is the address of the third cluster, and so on, until the last cluster entry, which contains an end-of-file code. Because this table provides the only means for finding data on a disk, DOS creates and maintains two copies of the FAT in case one is damaged. See *file fragmentation.*

file attribute   A *hidden code,* stored with a file's directory, that contains the file's read-only or archive status and whether the file is a system, hidden, or directory file. See *archive attribute, hidden file, locked file,* and *read-only attribute.*

file compression utility   A *utility program,* such as PKZIP, StuffIt or DriveSpace, that compresses and decompresses infrequently used files so that they take up 40 to 90 percent less room on a hard disk. You use another utility to decompress a file.

Specialty file compression utilities that compress only certain types of files, such as *downloadable font* files, are also available. These programs usually load a special driver that remains in memory to decompress and recompress the files as needed. See *archive, bulletin board system (BBS)*, and *compressed file*.

file conversion utility A *utility program* that converts text or graphics files created with one program to the file format used by another program. The best application programs now include a conversion utility that can handle a dozen or more file formats.

file defragmentation See *defragmentation*.

file deletion The process of rendering a *file* unusable. There are two types of file deletion: physical and logical. Logical deletion makes a file disappear, but ensures that it is recoverable. Dragging a file to the *Macintosh* Trash Can icon or the *Microsoft Windows 95* Recycling Bin logically deletes it.

Physical deletion removes a file's magnetic information from *secondary storage*, and makes the file irretrieveable. Emptying the Trash Can or Recycle Bin causes physical deletion of the files they contain. See *shareware, undelete utility*, and *utility program*.

CAUTION: *If you accidentally delete a file, stop working. Open the Recycling Bin or Trash Can and drag the file's icon out.*

file extension See *extension*.

file format The patterns and standards that a program uses to store data on disk. Few programs store data in *ASCII format*. Most use a *proprietary file format* that other programs cannot read, ensuring that customers continue to use the company's program and enabling programmers to include special features that standard formats might not allow. See *file conversion utility* and *native file format*.

TIP: *If you can't convert a document to a format that you can use, try a data conversion service. Look for these services in the Yellow Pages or in the advertising sections of personal computer magazines.*

file fragmentation The allocation of a file in noncontiguous sectors on a *floppy* or *hard disk*. Fragmentation occurs because of multiple file deletions and write operations.

File fragmentation can seriously reduce disk efficiency, because a disk drive's read/write head must travel longer distances to retrieve a file that's scattered all over the disk. Defragmenting can improve disk efficiency by as much as 50 percent by rewriting files so that they are placed in contiguous clusters. See *defragmentation.*

file locking   On a *network*, a method of *concurrency control* that ensures the integrity of data. File locking prevents more than one user from accessing and altering a file at the same time. See *local area network (LAN).*

file management program   A *program* that enables you to manage *files, directories,* and disks by displaying a disk's directory structure and listing existing files. Commands available on the program's menus are used to move and copy files, create directories, and perform other housekeeping tasks that help improve disk performance and protect your data. The *Windows Explorer* and XTree Gold are popular file management programs.

file name   A unique name assigned to a *file* when the file is written on a disk.

In *MS-DOS* and early versions of *Operating System/2 (OS/2)*, file names have two parts: the file name and the *extension*. These names must conform to the following rules:

• Length. You can use as many as eight characters for the file name and as many as three characters for the extension. The extension is optional.

• Delimiter. If you use the extension, you must separate the file name and extension with a period.

• Legal characters. You can use any letter or number on the keyboard for file names and extensions, but not spaces. You also can use the following punctuation symbols:

   ' ~ ! @ # $ ^ & ( ) _ { }

In the *Macintosh* and *Microsoft Windows 95* environments, you can use as many as 32 characters for file names, and file names can contain any character (including spaces) except the colon (:).

file privilege   In *dBASE*, an attribute that determines what you can do with a protected *database* on a *network*. The options are DELETE, EXTEND, READ, and UPDATE. See *field privilege.*

file recovery   Restoring an erased disk *file*. See *undelete utility*.

file server   In a *local area network (LAN)*, a computer that stores on its *hard disk* the *application programs* and *data files* for all the *workstations* in the *network*.

In a *peer-to-peer network*, all workstations act as file servers, because each workstation can provide files to other workstations. In the more common *client/server architecture*, a single, high-powered machine with a huge hard disk is set aside to function as the file server for all the workstations (clients) in the network. See *network operating system (NOS)*.

filespec   In *MS-DOS*, a complete statement of a file's location, including a drive letter, *path name*, *file name*, and *extension*, such as C:\REPORTS\REPORT1.WK1. Synonymous with path name.

file transfer protocol (ftp)   In *asynchronous communications*, a standard that ensures the error-free transmission of program and data files through the telephone system. *XMODEM*, *Kermit*, and *ZMODEM* are file transfer protocols.

File Transfer Protocol (FTP)   An *Internet* standard for the exchange of files. FTP (Uppercase letters) is a specific set of rules that comprise a *file transfer protocol (ftp*, note the lowercase letters).

To use FTP, you start an FTP client, an *application program* that enables you to contact another computer on the Internet and exchange files with it. To gain access to the other computer, you normally must supply a login name and password, after which you are given access to the computer's file *directory* system, and you can send (upload) and receive (download) files. An exception is *anonymous FTP,* which makes a file archive publicly accessible to any Internet user who possesses an FTP client; in response to the authentication prompts, you enter **anonymous** rather than a login name, and, as a courtesy, supply your *electronic mail* address as a password. Many *Web browsers* can function as FTP clients to download files from anonymous FTP file archives.

file transfer utility   A *utility program* that transfers files between different *hardware* platforms, such as the IBM Personal Computer and the *Macintosh*, or between a *desktop* and a *laptop* computer. Popular file transfer utilities include MacLink Plus, which links PCs and Macs through their serial ports, and Brooklyn

Bridge, which links desktop IBM computers with *IBM PC-compatible* laptops.

fill To enter the same text, *value* (numbers, dates, times, or formulas), or a sequence of values in a *spreadsheet* programs *worksheet*. In *Lotus 1-2-3*, for example, you use the Data Fill command to fill a *range* with values, indicating the value in the first cell, the amount to increase or decrease each number placed in the range, and the number where Lotus should stop filling. Synonymous with *data series*.

filter Any *utility program* that functions automatically to screen data. In *electronic mail*, you can use a filter to delete unwanted messages automatically.

filter command In MS-DOS, a command that takes input from a device or file, changes the input by passing it through a filter, then sends the result to the screen or printer. The DOS *filters* are MORE (which scrolls long output screen by screen), FIND (which searches for text), and SORT (which sorts in order of *ASCII* characters).

To send a file through a filter, use the less-than symbol (<). For example, the following command sorts the lines in a file called LIST.TXT:

```
SORT < list.txt
```

To route another command's output through a filter, use a pipe symbol (¦). The following command, for example, sends the output of the TREE command through the MORE filter:

```
TREE C:\ ¦ MORE
```

To redirect the output, use the greater-than symbol (>). To sort the file LIST.TXT and save the sorted result as the file ALPHA.TXT, for example, use the following command:

```
TYPE LIST.TXT ¦ SORT > ALPHA.TXT
```

Finder A file and memory management *utility program* provided by *Apple Computer* for *Macintosh* computers. This utility enables you to run one application at a time.

Often mistakenly referred to as the Macintosh's operating system, the Finder is nothing more than a *shell* that other shell programs such as XTreeMac can replace. Although the Finder's icons and menus have contributed to the Mac's success, the program's limitations quickly become apparent on systems equipped with large hard disks. An improved Finder that shipped with System 7 addresses many of the program's shortcomings. See *MultiFinder*.

FinePrint   A *resolution enhancement technology* that produces *effective resolution* of 600 by 600 *dots per inch (dpi)* in Apple *laser printers*. See *PhotoGrade*.

finger   An *Internet* utility that enables you to obtain information about a user who has an *electronic mail* address. Normally, this information is limited to the person's full name, job title, and address. However, the user can set up finger to retrieve one or more text files that contain information (such as a resume) that the user wants to make public.

firewall   A *security* procedure that places a specially programmed computer system between an organization's *local area network (LAN)* and the *Internet*. The firewall computer prevents *crackers* from accessing the internal network. Unfortunately, it also prevents the organization's computer users from gaining direct access to the Internet. The access that the firewall provides is indirect and mediated by programs called *proxy servers*.

FireWire   A standard established by the *Institute of Electrical and Electronic Engineers (IEEE)* that lays out specifications for a very fast *port* that may someday replace the *serial port*. FireWire ports have not yet appeared on any commercially available *computer systems*.

firmware   Broadly, the *system* software stored in a computer's *read-only memory (ROM)* or elsewhere in the computer's circuitry, such as the *basic input-output system (BIOS)* chips in *IBM PC-compatible* computers.

FIRST   See *Forum of Incident Response and Security Teams (FIRST)*.

fixed disk   A *hard disk,* in IBM parlance.

fixed-frequency monitor   An *analog monitor* designed to receive input signals at only one frequency. In contrast, a *multiscanning monitor* automatically adjusts to match the incoming signal. Most of the *Video Graphics Array (VGA)* monitors sold with inexpensive entry-level 486-class systems are fixed-frequency monitors.

fixed-length field   In a *database management program*, a field whose length is set and cannot vary, as opposed to a *variable-length field*, which can adjust to accommodate entries of different lengths.

fixed numeric format   In *spreadsheet* programs, a *numeric format* that rounds values to the number of decimal places that you specify. The format also inserts commas in numbers greater than 999.

Fkey   A *Macintosh utility program* that you execute by pressing the Command (") and Shift keys with a number key from 0 to 9— the keys that simulate the function keys on *IBM PC-compatible* keyboards. The *Macintosh System* software includes four Fkey utilities, *shareware* and commercial sources offer additional Fkey utilities (and *software* for managing them).

flag   A variable that serves as an indicator about the status of a *program* or some data. A flag in a *database record* might be true if the other fields in the record show that a videotape is overdue, for example.

flame   In *UseNet* and *electronic mail*, a message that contains abusive, threatening, obscene, or inflammatory language.

In electronic mail, a slang term meaning to lose your self-control by writing a message that uses derogatory, obscene, or inappropriate language. See *flame bait, flame war, moderated newsgroup,* and *rave.*

flame bait   In an *unmoderated newsgroup*, a posting that contains opinions that prompt *flames*—abusive remarks and personal attacks—and may ultimately launch a *flame war*. Flame-bait topics include abortion, homosexuality, and the desirability of using *Microsoft Windows 95*. True flame bait unintentionally elicits such responses; when such postings are made intentionally, the post is more properly called a *troll*. See *moderated newsgroup*.

flame war   In an *unmoderated newsgroup*, an unproductive and long-running debate marked by high emotion and little information. See *flame, flame bait,* and *unmoderated newsgroup*.

> **TIP:** *If a newsgroup that you're following erupts in a flame war, learn how to create a kill file that contains a list of subjects that you want to exclude automatically from the messages displayed on your screen.*

flash BIOS A *read-only memory (ROM) chip* storing the computer's *basic input-output system (BIOS)* that you can reprogram with software, instead of having to remove the BIOS chip, reprogram it in a special machine, and then replace the chip. With flash BIOS, a computer manufacturer can easily update BIOS chips simply by sending to users a properly encoded *floppy disk.* See *erasable programmable read-only memory (EPROM)* and *programmable read-only memory (PROM).*

flat Lacking elaborate structure. A file system without *subdirectories* in which you can group files is said to be flat. Such systems have not been used since the earliest days of personal computing.

flat address space A method of organizing a computer's memory so the *operating system* can allocate portions of the *memory* without restriction. The opposite of a flat address space is the *segmented memory architecture* of *MS-DOS* and Microsoft Windows 3.1, which divide memory into 64K sections (called segments). A flat memory space design is more efficient because the processor does not have to map each memory address to a specific 64K segment, but such a design requires the use of 32-bit memory addresses. *Microsoft Windows 95,* which employs 32-bit memory addresses, creates a flat address space for your applications.

flatbed scanner A *scanner* with a flat scanning area large enough to accommodate a letter-sized page (8 1/2 by 11 inches) of material. A sheet feeder to automate scanning multiple-page documents is an available option. See *digitize.*

flat-file database management program A *database management program* that stores, organizes, and retrieves information from one file at a time. Such programs lack *relational database management* features. See *data integrity.*

flat-panel display In *portable computers,* a thin display screen that uses one of several display technologies, such as electroluminescence, *gas plasma display, liquid crystal display (LCD),* or thin film transistor (TFT). A backlit display makes the display easier to read.

flat-square monitor　A *monitor* that is more gently curved than most, but really neither flat nor square. Although such monitors have less distortion than most displays, they are not free of spherical distortion, as *flat tension-mask monitors* are.

flat tension-mask monitor　A Zenith *monitor* design that includes an absolutely flat—and therefore distortion-free—*display.* Flat tension-mask monitors are the only truly distortion-free monitors available, but are too expensive for most computer users. See *flat-square monitor* and *vertically flat.*

flicker　A visible distortion that occurs when you scroll the screen of a *monitor* that uses a low *refresh* rate. Also, a visible distortion apparent in light areas on an interlaced monitor. See *interlacing.*

floating graphic　A graph or picture that hasn't been fixed in an absolute position on the page, so that it moves up or down on the page as you delete or insert text above it.

floating-point calculation　A method for storing and calculating numbers so that the location of the decimal isn't fixed but floating (the decimal moves around as needed so that the calculation takes into account significant digits). Numeric coprocessors or software can implement floating-point calculation to improve the accuracy of computer calculations.

floating-point unit (FPU)　A portion of a *microprocessor* that handles operations in which the decimal point moves left and right to allow for very high precision when dealing with very large or very small numbers. An FPU usually makes a microprocessor much faster. Early *Pentium* chips had flaws in their FPUs.

floppy disk　A removable and widely used data storage medium that uses a magnetically coated flexible disk of Mylar enclosed in a plastic envelope or case.

Software publishers sometimes distribute their applications on floppy disks. At one time, they also were the only medium for data storage for *personal computers,* but the availability of inexpensive *hard disks* has relegated floppy disks to the sidelines. See *double density, head slot, high density, read/write head, single-sided disk,* and *write-protect notch.*

floppy disk controller   The circuitry responsible for operating a *floppy disk drive.* Usually based on the *765* controller *chip,* the floppy disk controller moves the *read/write head* and operates the *spindle motor* under directions from the *host adapter.*

floppy disk drive   A mechanism that enables a computer to read and write information on *floppy disks.* Floppy disk drives come in two sizes—*3 1/2 inch* and *5 1/4 inch*—and several *densities,* to handle a variety of floppy disks. A *high-density* floppy disk drive can work with both high-density and *double-density* floppy disks, but a double-density floppy disk drive can use only double-density disks.

floptical disk   A removable *optical disk* the size of a *3 1/2-inch floppy disk* but with a capacity of 20*M* to 25M.

floptical drive   A data storage device that uses laser technology to illuminate optical tracts on a *floptical disk.*

The reflected light is sensed by a photodetector, which generates a signal that allows precise positioning of the *read/write heads.* The pattern of *tracks,* created when the disk is manufactured, is extremely compact, making it possible to create 3 1/2-inch floptical disks the same size as the familiar *3 1/2-inch floppy disks* but capable of storing 21*M* of information. Floptical drives manufactured by such companies as Iomega can read and write on standard 3 1/2-inch floppy disks.

flow   A feature that allows text in a page layout to wrap around graphics and to move automatically from column to column (called *newspaper columns* or snaking columns). *Page layout programs* and better word processing programs can format text this way.

flowchart   A chart that contains symbols referring to computer operations, describing how the program performs.

flow control   A method of ensuring that the data device such as a *modem* or a *computer system* sends does not overwhelm the receiving device, such as a modem. *Software handshaking* (also called *XON/XOFF* handshaking) regulates communications between two modems. *Hardware handshaking* (*CTS/RTS*) regulates data flow between the computer and the modem.

flush To clear or empty. Flushing a printer's *random-access memory (RAM)* by turning it off for a few seconds, then turning it on again may correct certain problems.

flush left In *word processing*, the alignment of text along the left margin, leaving a ragged right margin. See *justification*.

flush right In *word processing*, aligning text along the right margin, leaving a ragged left margin. Flush-right alignment is seldom used except to create decorative effects or cover pages. See *justification*.

FMD See *frequency division multiplexing (FMD)*.

FM synthesis In *sound boards* that use the *Musical Instrument Digital Interface (MIDI)* standard, a method of simulating musical instruments that is less costly than *wave-table synthesis* but also of much lower quality.

TIP: *When shopping for a sound board for your system, consider spending a bit more money and getting a* wave-table synthesis *sound board. Wave-table synthesis boards play MIDI music using simulated musical instrument sounds rather than digitally constructed FM-synthesis sounds, which sound like a cheap electronic organ.*

folder In the Macintosh *Finder* and *Microsoft Windows 95 desktop*, an on-screen representation of a file folder on the desktop and into which you can organize *files*.

follow-on post In an on-line *newsgroup*, a contribution posted in response to a previous posting. Unlike a reply, a follow-on post is public and can be read by everyone in the newsgroup. Follow-on posts form a *thread* of discussion. See *distributed bulletin board* and *netiquette*.

TIP: *Consider replying to a message (by personal electronic mail) instead of posting a follow-on message. In* UseNet, *posting a message worldwide eventually costs hundreds of dollars, which has to be paid for by government and organizational subsidies. Post a follow-on message only if you truly believe your response is of sufficient value to all the members of the newsgroup.*

F
G
H

follow-up post   See *follow-on post*.

font   One complete collection of letters, punctuation marks, numbers, and special characters with a consistent and identifiable *typeface, weight* (roman or bold), *posture* (upright or italic), and *type size*. The term often is used incorrectly in reference to a type-face or *font family*. Two kinds of fonts exist: *bit-mapped fonts* and *outline fonts*. Each comes in two versions: *screen fonts* and *printer fonts*. See *book weight*.

font cartridge   A plug-in *read-only memory (ROM)* cartridge—designed to fit into a receptacle on a *printer*—that contains one or more *fonts* and expands the printer's font capabilities. See *cartridge font*.

Font/DA Mover   A *utility program*, provided with *Macintosh System* software, that adds *fonts* and *desk accessories (DA)* to the *System Folder* of the computer's *startup disk*.

font downloader   See *downloading utility*.

font family   A set of *fonts* in several sizes and weights that share the same typeface. The following list illustrates a font family in the *Helvetica* typeface:

Helvetica Roman 10

Helvetica bold 10

Helvetica italic 10

Helvetica Roman 12

Helvetica bold 12

Helvetica italic 12

Helvetica bold italic 12

In *Microsoft Windows 95*, a font family includes several similar typefaces. Arial, Small Fonts, and MS Sans Serif are all considered part of the Swiss font family, for example.

font ID conflict   In the *Macintosh* environment, a system error caused by conflicts between the identification numbers assigned to the screen fonts stored in the *System Folder*.

The Macintosh System and many Mac *application programs* recognize and retrieve fonts by the identification number, not by name. The original Mac operating system let you assign only 128 unique numbers, so you could inadvertently assemble a repertoire of screen fonts with conflicting numbers, causing printing errors. Beginning with System 6, Macintosh introduced a New Font Numbering Table (NFNT) scheme that lets you assign 16,000 unique numbers, reducing—but not eliminating—the potential for font ID conflicts.

font metric   The width and height information for each character in a *font*. The font metric is stored in a width table.

F
G
H

font smoothing   In *high-resolution laser printers*, the reduction of *aliasing* and other distortions when text or *graphics* are printed.

font substitution   Substituting an *outline font* in place of a *bit-mapped screen font* for printing purposes. In the *Macintosh* environment, the Apple LaserWriter printer driver substitutes the outline fonts *Helvetica*, Times Roman, and Courier for the screen fonts Geneva, New York, and Monaco. To avoid unsatisfactory spacing, use screen fonts that are equivalent to the *printer font*.

footer   In a *word processing* or *page layout* program, repetitive material printed at the bottom of the documents pages. See *header*.

footnote   In a *word processing* or *page layout* program, a reference or note positioned at the bottom of the page. Most word processing programs number footnotes automatically and renumber them if you insert or delete a note. The best programs can float lengthy footnotes to the next page so that they take up no more than half the page. See *endnote*.

> **TIP:** *When creating documents that require elaborate footnotes, make sure that you can format the footnotes properly. For example, many publishers require double-spacing of all text, even footnotes, but some word processors cannot provide such spacing for footnotes.*

footprint   The amount of space occupied by a computer, printer, monitor, or other piece of equipment on a desk, shelf, or floor.

forced page break   A *page break* inserted by the user; the page always breaks at this location. Synonymous with *hard page break*.

forced perfect termination   Like *active termination* and *passive termination*, a way of ending a *Small Computer System Interface (SCSI) daisy chain*. Forced perfect termination is rarely used.

forecasting   In a *spreadsheet* program, a method of financial analysis that projects past trends into the future.

CAUTION: *Implementing a forecast with a spreadsheet program is easy, but remember that any model is only as good as the assumptions on which it is based. Such forecasts might overlook or fail to anticipate seasonal variables, a change in the prime rate, or other factors.*

foreground task   In a computer capable of *multitasking*, the *job* that the computer is performing in the *active window*.

In *networks* and *MS-DOS*, a foreground task is a job that receives priority status before *background tasks* are executed. *Background printing* or calculation, for example, takes place in brief pauses while the foreground task executes.

forgery   In *UseNet*, mailing lists, or *electronic mail*, a message written by someone other than the apparent author. *Internet* software enables any person with a modicum of technical knowledge to forge messages. An old USENET custom is a host of April Fool's Day forgeries, which are harmless enough, but many forgeries are intended to embarrass and harass.

A famous 1995 forgery faked a press release announcing that Microsoft Corporation had purchased the Roman Catholic Church. Microsoft had to issue a statement denying the forgery's allegations.

form   See *forms*.

format   The organization of information for storage, printing, or displaying.

The format of *floppy disks* and *hard disks* is the magnetic pattern laid down by the formatting utility. In a document, the format includes margins, the *font* and *alignment* used for text, headers, footers, page numbering, and the way that numbers are displayed. In a *database management program*, the format is the physical arrangement of field names and data fields in an on-screen data-entry form.

formatting   An operation that establishes a pattern for the display, storage, or printing of data. In operating systems, an operation that prepares a floppy disk for use in a particular computer system by laying down a magnetic pattern. See *format, high-level format,* and *low-level format.*

form factor   The physical size (usually just height) of a *hard disk* or *floppy disk drive.* Most modern hard and floppy disks fit into *half-height* drive bays, but a few high-capacity hard disks require *full-height* bays.

form feed   A command that forces the printer to eject the current page and start a new page.

forms   In *HyperText Markup Language (HTML)* and *World Wide Web (WWW)* documents, a set of document features (including fill-in text areas, drop-down list boxes, check boxes, and option buttons) that enable you to interact with a Web page. Not all *Web browsers* can interact with forms. See *forms-capable browser.*

forms-capable browser   A *Web browser* that can deal with *HyperText Markup Language (HTML) tags* that create on-screen, interactive *forms,* including fill-in text boxes, option buttons, and drop-down list boxes. Some early *Web browsers* could not interact with forms; the leading programs, such as *NCSA Mosaic* and *Netscape Navigator,* have no trouble with these features.

formula   In a *spreadsheet* program, a *cell definition* that defines the relationship between two or more *values.* In a database management program, an expression that tells the program to perform calculations on numeric data contained in one or more data fields. See *calculated field* and *precedence.*

formula bar   In *Microsoft Excel,* the bar, located below the *toolbar,* in which you enter or edit *formulas* and which displays the address of the *current cell.*

FOR/NEXT loop   In *programming*, a *loop* control structure that carries out a procedure a specified number of times. Suppose that you have a list of 10 items. A FOR/NEXT loop to change each item might read: "Set the count to 1. Select to the end of the line. Apply formatting. Move down one line. Then set the count to the previous count plus 1. Keep doing this until the count is equal to 10." See *macro*.

FORTH   A *high-level programming language* that offers direct control over hardware devices. Astronomer Charles Moore developed FORTH in 1970 to help him control the equipment at the Kitt Peak National Radio Observatory. FORTH (short for *fourth-generation programming language*) has been slow to gain acceptance as a general-purpose programming language. Because FORTH accepts user-defined commands, one FORTH programmer's code might be unintelligible to another programmer. FORTH sometimes is preferred for laboratory data acquisition, robotics, machine control, arcade games, automation, patient monitoring, and interfaces with musical devices.

FORTRAN   The first compiled *high-level programming language*. FORTRAN (short for *fo*rmula *tran*slator), which strongly resembles *BASIC,* enables programmers to describe and solve complex mathematical calculations. Still highly suited to mathematical applications, FORTRAN is widely used in scientific, academic, and technical settings. See *modular programming, Pascal,* and *structured programming.*

forum   See *newsgroup.*

Forum of Incident Response and Security Teams (FIRST)   A unit of the *Internet Society* that coordinates the activities of several *Computer Emergency Response Teams (CERTs)* worldwide. FIRSTs purpose is to bring these teams together to foster cooperation and coordination when security-related incidents occur, and to promote the sharing of information concerning the security perils facing the Internet.

forward chaining   In *expert systems,* an inference technique that requires the user to state all the relevant data before processing begins. A forward chaining system starts with the data and works forward through its rules to determine whether additional data is required and how to draw the inference. See *backward chaining* and *knowledge base*.

For Your Information (FYI)   A series of electronic publications that seek to explain *Internet* standards and technology in plain English. Distributed in the same manner as *Requests for Comments (RFCs)*, FYIs are not intended to establish new standards (as RFCs do). You can obtain FYI documents from any *Network Information Center (NIC)*.

FYI is often used in *electronic mail* and *UseNet newsgroups* as an abbreviation for your information in discussions.

four-way set-associative cache   The *set-associative cache* design that strikes the best balance between speed and cost control. Four-way, set-associative caches are faster than *two-way, set-associative caches* and *direct-map caches,* but are also more expensive.

FPU   See *floating-point unit (FPU)*.

fragmentation   See *file fragmentation*.

frame   A portion of data transmitted by a *modem* for purposes of checking for errors in other transmitted data.

In *desktop publishing (DTP)* and *word processing*, a rectangular area absolutely positioned on the page. The frame can contain text, graphics, or both.

frame buffer   A portion of *display memory* that stores the information used to generate an image on-screen. Usually, the *central processing unit (CPU)* writes data to the frame buffer, then the *video controller* reads it, but dual-ported *video random-access memory (VRAM)* allows simultaneous reads and writes. A frame buffer that can handle more information than the display might be used for *hardware panning*.

In *Lotus 1-2-3*, the shaded border across the top of the spreadsheet containing the column letters and down the left of the *spreadsheet* containing the row numbers.

free-form text chart   In *presentation graphics*, a text chart used to handle information difficult to express in lists, such as lengthy explanations, directions, invitations, and certificates (see fig. F.1).

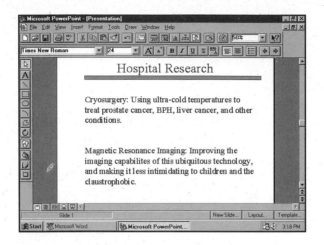

Fig. F.1 *A free-form text chart.*

freenet   A community-based *bulletin board system (BBS),* usually based in a public library, that attempts to make useful resources available to the local citizenry. Such resources include transcripts of city council meetings, access to the local library's card catalog, the names and addresses of community organizations, and—increasingly—access to the *Internet.* In keeping with the freenet's public-service orientation, access is free or very inexpensive.

Free Software Foundation (FSF)   A nonprofit organization, based in Massachusetts, that is devoted to the ideal of the free sharing of useful software for noncommercial purposes. To promote this goal, FSF supports a *UNIX*-compatible *operating system* (called GNU) and system utilities, which are freely redistributable under FSF's General Public License (GPL). See *copyleft.*

freestanding pointing device   A pointing device—such as a *mouse* or *trackball*—connected to the computer through the serial or mouse port that isn't otherwise attached to the computer. See *built-in pointing device* and *clip-on pointing device.*

freeware   Copyrighted *programs* that have been made available without charge for public use. The programs cannot be resold for profit. See *public domain software* and *shareware.*

freeze   To stop software development at a point at which the developer judges that the software is sufficiently stable for release.

frequency division multiplexing (FDM)   In *local area networks (LANs),* a technique for transmitting two or more signals over one cable by assigning each to its own frequency. *Broadband* (analog) networks use this technique. See *multiplexing.*

frequency modulation (FM) recording   An early, low-density method of recording digital signals on recording media such as *tape* and disks. Synonymous with *single-density* recording. See *Modified Frequency Modulation (MFM).*

frequency shift keying (FSK)   In *modems,* an obsolete way of communicating data by changing the frequency of the *carrier.* The *Bell 103* protocol employs FSK, but newer data transmission protocols use *group coding* or *trellis-code modulation.*

Frequently Asked Questions (FAQ)   In *USENET,* a document automatically posted to a *newsgroup* at regular intervals and designed to assist new users. A FAQ contains a list of the questions that are commonly posted to the newsgroup, together with the answers that have emerged from the newsgroup participants collective experience. FAQs are well worth reading, for two reasons: First, they can save you the embarrassment of posting a common question, and second, many FAQs are exceptionally well developed and may contain some of the best information that you will find anywhere on a subject.

friction feed   A *printer* paper-feed mechanism that draws individual sheets of paper through the printer by using a platen to exert pressure on the paper. See *cut-sheet feeder* and *tractor feed.*

fried   Burned out; short-circuited.

front end   The portion of a *program* that interacts directly with the user. A front end can also be a separate program that acts as a user-friendly *interface* for a more difficult environment; for example, HyperText Markup Language (HTML) has been called a front-end for the Internet.

A *local area network (LAN)* might distribute the front end to each workstation so that the user can interact with the *back-end* application on the *file server.* See *client/server architecture.*

FTP   See *File Transfer Protocol (FTP).*

full-associative cache   A *secondary cache* design that is superior to the *direct-map cache* design but inferior to the *set-associative cache* design. Full-associative caches require the *central processing unit (CPU)* to search the entire *cache* for a needed piece of information. See *four-way set-associative cache.*

full backup   A *hard disk* backup of every file on the entire hard disk. Synonymous with *global backup.* Although extremely tedious if you're backing up to floppy disks, the procedure is necessary for secure computing. If your full *backup procedure* takes too long, consider adding a tape drive to your system. See *incremental backup.*

full bleed   Text or graphics extending from one edge of a page to the other. See *bleed capability.*

full duplex   An *asynchronous communications* protocol that allows the communications channel to send and receive signals at the same time. See *communications protocol, echoplex,* and *half duplex.*

full-height drive bay   A mounting space in the computer's *case* for a component 3.38 inches tall. Designed to accept an old IBM *hard disk,* a single full-height drive bay can accept two modern hard disks. See *half-height drive* and *half-height drive bay.*

full justification   See *justification.*

full-motion video adapter   A video adapter that can display moving video images—prerecorded or live—in a *window* that appears on the display. To display video images, you connect the adapter to a videocassette recorder, laser disk player, or a camcorder.

Most full-motion video adapters come with software that enables users to develop a *multimedia* presentation, complete with wipes, washes, fades, animation, and sound. Full-motion video applications are expected to play a growing role in corporate and professional presentations and training applications.

full-page display   A *monitor* that can display a full page of text at a time. Such monitors are used most frequently with *computer systems* dedicated to *desktop publishing (DTP).* With a full-page display, you can view and edit an entire page of text, figures, or graphics at a time, providing a better overview of your documents structure and organization.

If you're thinking about equipping your DOS system with a full-page display, be aware that not all the programs that you're using can take advantage of it. Check your programs' documentation. The *Macintosh Finder* and *Microsoft Windows 95* support full-page displays.

full-screen editor   A *word processing* utility, often included with *application development systems,* designed specifically for creating and editing *programs.* Such utilities include special features for indenting lines of program code, searching for nonstandard characters, and interfacing with program interpreters or compilers. See *line editor* and *programming environment.*

full-travel keyboard   A *keyboard* on which the *keys* travel at least 1/8 inch. Full-travel keyboards provide good *tactile feedback* and enable professional typists to work quickly.

fully formed character printer   A *printer,* such as a *daisy-wheel printer,* that prints one character at a time.

function   In *programming* languages and *spreadsheet* programs, a named and stored procedure that returns one value. In *spreadsheets,* synonymous with *built-in function.*

function key   A programmable *key*—conventionally numbered F1, F2, and so on—that provides special functions, depending on the *software* that you're using. See *Fkey.*

fuser wand   In *laser printers,* a heated roller that melts *toner* onto the page. Dirty fuser wands sometimes cause unwanted vertical stripes on output.

FYI   See *For Your Information (FYI).*

G   Abbreviation for *gigabyte*.

game port   A socket that lets you connect a *joystick*, control yoke, or other game device to your computer. Without a game port—which may be included on your *sound board*—you'll find it's much harder to defeat the Empire of Galactic Doom.

gamut   In *graphics*, the range of colors that a color *monitor* can display.

garage   A special bracket in *ink jet printers* in which an unused ink cartridge may be stored without the ink drying out. Also, the place the *print head* goes when it is not in use.

garbage characters   In *modems*, meaningless characters caused by *line noise*. In *printers*, meaningless characters caused by line noise, a faulty *printer driver*, or some other communication problem.

garbage collection   A process by which a program goes through *random-access memory (RAM)*, decides which information stored there is no longer needed, and prepares the addresses housing the unneeded data for re-use. Garbage collection prevents programs from filling RAM with useless data and causing a *crash*.

gas plasma display   See *plasma display*.

gateway   A means by which users of one computer service or network may access certain kinds of information on a different service or network. This may be achieved by means of hardware devices called *bridges,* by computer programs that perform the necessary translation, or both. For example, *Internet* electronic mail users can exchange mail with *CompuServe* users by means of a gateway. Similarly, people using *Web browsers* can access the Archie service by means of a Web page that functions as an Archie gateway.

In *networks*, a device that connects two dissimilar *local area networks (LANs)* or connects a local area network to a *wide-area network (WAN)*, a *minicomputer*, or a *mainframe*. A gateway has its own microprocessor and memory and may perform *network protocol* conversion and *bandwidth* conversion. See *bridge*.

Gbps See *bits per second (bps)*.

GDI See *Graphical Device Interface (GDI)*.

GDI printer See *Graphical Device Interface (GDI) printer*.

general format In most *spreadsheet programs*, the default *numeric format* in which all the numbers on either side of the decimal point (up to the furthest number that isn't a zero) are displayed, but without commas or currency signs. When a number is too large to display with the current column width, scientific notation is used.

General MIDI (GM) In *multimedia*, a standard controlled by the *MIDI Manufacturers' Association (MMA)* that defines a set of 96 standard voices corresponding to traditional musical instruments, and an additional set of voices corresponding to non-melodic percussion instruments. When you use the standard code numbers from these sets to create a *MIDI* (Musical Instrument Digital Interface) *file*, any GM-compatible synthesizer will reproduce the sounds in the file the way you intended them.

general-purpose computer A computer that contains a sufficiently versatile *microprocessor* that a wide variety of *algorithms* can be devised for it. Personal computers are general-purpose computers.

generate To produce something by setting in motion an automatic procedure. For example, after marking the entries and indicating the table, list, and index locations, you can generate a table of contents, lists of figures, and an index in a *word processing program* when you choose the generate command.

GEnie Developed by General Electric, an *on-line information service* that, like *CompuServe*, offers many of the attractions of a *bulletin board system (BBS)* and up-to-date stock quotes, conferences, *Internet electronic mail*, home shopping, and news updates.

geometry The physical layout of a *hard disk's* surface, including number of *tracks*, number of *sectors*, tracks per sector and *landing zone* location. Disk geometry specifications are part of a disk's *setup parameters*.

ghost The effect of an image being displayed continuously on-screen. Such images "burn" into the screen *phosphors*, resulting in a ghost image. See *screen saver*.

F
G
H

GIF See *Graphics Interchange Format (GIF)*.

giga- A prefix indicating one billion (10^9).

gigabit A unit of measurement approximately equal to 1 billion bits (1,073,741,824). Usually used when indicating the amount of data that can be transferred or transmitted per second.

gigabyte A unit of measurement approximately equal to 1 billion bytes (1,073,741,824). Used when stating an amount of memory or disk capacity. One gigabyte equals 1,000M (megabytes).

GIGO Acronym for "garbage in, garbage out," which is usually said in response to fouled-up output that's attributable to erroneous input (such as a mistyped command).

glare Light reflected off the *display* from an outside source—such as a lamp or a window—and into your eyes. Glare makes the display hard to read and may cause eyestrain or headaches. Several *anti-glare* techniques exist, but the simplest one is to reposition the *monitor*.

glitch A momentary power interruption or some other unexpected fluctuation in electronic circuits, such as those caused by power *surges* or dirty connections, that causes computer systems to generate garbage output or, in the extreme, to crash. A glitch is a *hardware* problem; a *software* problem is called a *bug*.

global backup See *full backup*.

global format In a *spreadsheet program*, a *numeric format* or *label alignment* choice that applies to all *cells* in the worksheet. With most programs, you can override the global format by defining a format for certain cells.

TIP: *If you're working on a financial spreadsheet, the values in your worksheet may require dollar signs and two decimal places. Choose currency as the global format when you begin the worksheet. If some cells require, say, date formatting and others require currency formatting, use the range format command instead.*

global kill file In a *UseNet* newsreader program, a file containing words, phrases, names, or *network* addresses that you have identified as signals of an unwanted message (such as "Make Money Fast!"). The program screens incoming articles for these signals, and automatically deletes the articles before you even see them. A global kill file performs this function in all newsgroups, while a *newsgroup kill file* deletes unwanted messages only in specific newsgroups.

glossary In a *word processing program*, a feature used to store frequently used phrases and *boilerplate* text for later insertion into documents when needed.

glossy finish A quality of paper that reflects light harshly. Glossy finish paper is less popular for laser printer use than *matte finish* paper.

GM See *General MIDI (GM).*

Gopher In UNIX-based systems linked to the *Internet,* a menu-based program that helps you find files, programs, definitions, and other resources on topics you specify. Gopher was originally developed at the University of Minnesota and named after the school mascot.

Unlike *FTP* and *Archie,* Gopher doesn't require you to know and use the details of host, directory, and file names. Instead, you browse through menus and press Enter when you find something interesting. You usually see another menu, with more options, until finally you select an option that displays information. You can then read the information or save it to your disk storage area after retrieving it with *anonymous FTP.* The *World Wide Web (WWW)* has begun to make Gopher and other text-based Internet search tools obsolete.

 gopherspace In *Gopher,* the enormous computer-based "space" that is created by the global dissemination of Gopher-accessible resources. A search tool called *Veronica* enables you to search Gopherspace for *directory titles* and *resources* that match key words you supply.

gov A *domain name* denoting a government office or agency.

grabber hand In *graphics programs* and *HyperCard,* an on-screen image of a hand that you can position with the *mouse* to move selected units of text or graphics from place to place on-screen.

Grand Challenge An unsolved scientific or engineering problem of such fabulous complexity that no individual researcher, nor even an individual research institute, can hope to tackle it alone. Examples include mapping the human genome or understanding the astrophysics of the Milky Way. Advanced computer *networks* may help researchers tackle the Grand Challenges by fostering *collaboratory* research and resource sharing by means of *federated databases.*

granularity of allocation The smallest unit of storage space available. The granularity of *hard* and *floppy disks* is determined by the size of their *clusters*—if a disk has a cluster size of 100*K,* even files smaller than 100K will be assigned an entire cluster.

Graphical Device Interface (GDI) A programming resource—part of a graphical user interface—that enables programmers to generate dialog boxes and other graphical elements in a consistent style. GDIs handle the detail work of drawing such elements on-screen; the programmer need only tell the GDI what to draw and where to draw it.

Graphical Device Interface (GDI) printer Synonymous with Windows printer, a *printer* that has no *raster image processor (RIP)* and leaves much of the task of preparing a page for printing to *software.* GDI printers can be used only with *Microsoft Windows.* GDI printers tax the often already-burdened *central processing unit (CPU),* and may not be supported by future versions of Windows, so they're probably not a good buy.

Graphical User Interface (GUI) A design for the part of a program that interacts with the user and uses *icons* to represent program features. The Apple Macintosh and Microsoft Windows operating environments are popular GUIs.

Having found that people recognize graphic representations faster than they read words or phrases, a Xerox research team designed a user interface with graphic images called icons. GUIs typically work with *mousable interfaces* with *pull-down menus, dialog boxes, check boxes, radio buttons, drop-down list boxes, scroll bars, scroll boxes,* and the like. Programs with a GUI require a computer with sufficient speed, power, and memory to display a high-resolution, bit-mapped display.

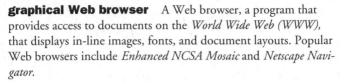 **graphical Web browser** A Web browser, a program that provides access to documents on the *World Wide Web (WWW)*, that displays in-line images, fonts, and document layouts. Popular Web browsers include *Enhanced NCSA Mosaic* and *Netscape Navigator*.

graphics In personal computing, the creation, modification, and printing pictures, as opposed to text. The two basic types of computer-produced graphics are *object-oriented graphics*, also called vector graphics, and *bit-mapped graphics*, often called raster graphics.

Object-oriented graphics programs, usually called *draw programs*, store graphic images in the form of mathematical representations that can be sized and scaled without distortion. Object-oriented graphics programs are well suited for architecture, computer-aided design, interior design, and other applications in which precision and scaling capability are more important than artistic effects.

Bit-mapped graphics programs, often called *paint programs*, store graphic images in the form of patterns of screen pixels. Unlike draw programs, paint programs can create delicate patterns of shading that convey an artistic touch, but any attempt to resize or scale the graphic may result in unacceptable distortion.

graphics accelerator See *graphics accelerator board*.

graphics accelerator board A *video adapter* that includes a *graphics coprocessor* and all the other circuitry normally found on a *video adapter*. The graphics accelerator handles the graphics processing, freeing the *central processing unit (CPU)* for other important tasks and thereby dramatically improving your system's capability to run *Microsoft Windows* and other graphical applications.

graphics adapter See *video adapter*.

graphics board See *video adapter*.

graphics card See *video adapter*.

graphics character In a computer's built-*in character set*, a character composed of lines, shaded rectangles, or other shapes. You can combine graphics characters to form *block graphics*: simple images, illustrations, and borders. Some programs, called *character-based programs,* use no graphics other than those made up of graphics characters.

F
G
H

graphics coprocessor   A *microprocessor* specially designed to speed the processing and display of *high-resolution* video images. A *graphics accelerator board* that includes a graphics coprocessor can speed the display of programs, such as Microsoft Windows, that use *graphical user interfaces (GUIs)*. Popular graphics coprocessors include the Weitek W5086 and W5186 and S3 Inc.'s 86C911.

graphics file format   In a *graphics program*, the way in which the information needed to display a graphic is arranged and stored on *disk*.

Little standardization exists for graphics file formats in the PC-compatible world. Programs such as AutoCAD, GEM Draw, *Lotus 1-2-3*, Windows Paint, and PC Paintbrush generate *files* in propri-etary *file formats* that other programs can read only if specially equipped to do so, as many programs are.

The Macintosh environment has a standard file format called *PICT* that uses routines drawn from the Mac's *QuickDraw* toolbox. This format, however, isn't satisfactory for many applica-tions. Additional formats include the MacPaint *file format* for bit-mapped graphics of up to 72 *dots per inch (dpi) resolution, tagged image file format (TIFF)* files for scanned images stored at up to 300 dpi, and *Encapsulated PostScript (EPS)*.

Graphics Interchange Format (GIF)   A *graphics* file origi-nally developed by *CompuServe* and widely used to encode and exchange graphics files on the Internet. The GIF format employs a *lossless compression* technique that reduces the size of the graphics file. Although GIF graphics are in widespread use, the *Joint Photo-graphic Experts Group (JPEG)* format (which uses *lossy compression*) reduces graphics files to a size roughly one-third the size of a corre-sponding GIF file, leading to speedier *Internet* transmission.

graphics mode   In video adapters, a display mode in which everything on-screen—including text and graphics—is drawn using *pixels* instead of characters from the *character set*. Many adapters also offer a *character mode*, which runs more quickly because it uses the computer's built-in, ready-made characters rather than composes them individually. Some programs allow you to switch between a *graphics view*, which uses graphics mode and accurately shows what printed output will look like, and character view, which is faster than graphics view.

TIP: *Windows users who frequently run graphics-intensive applications, such as desktop publishing programs, and find that Windows runs sluggishly should consider adding a graphics accelerator board, which will result in impressive performance gains.*

graphics primitive   In an *object-oriented graphics program*, the most basic unit of graphic expression, such as a line, arc, circle, rectangle, or oval.

graphics scanner   A *graphics* input device that transforms a picture into an image that can be displayed on-screen.

graphics spreadsheet   A *spreadsheet program* that displays the worksheet by using *bit-mapped graphics* instead of relying on the computer's built-in *character set*. Graphics spreadsheets such as *Microsoft Excel* and *Lotus 1-2-3* for Windows include *desktop publishing* tools such as multiple *typefaces*, type sizes, *rules*, and screens (grayed areas). Also, printouts can combine spreadsheets and business graphs on one page.

graphics tablet   An input device that lets you draw with an electronic pen on an electronically sensitive table. The pen's movements are relayed to the screen. See *pen computer*.

graphics view   In some DOS applications, a mode in which the program switches the display circuitry to its *graphics mode*. In graphics mode, the computer can display bit-mapped graphics. On all except the fastest computers, graphics mode is significantly slower than *character mode*. Some programs have a fast *character view* that does not offer the *what-you-see-is-what-you-get (WYSIWYG)* features of graphics view.

grayscale   In computer graphics, a series of shades from white to black.

grayscale monitor   A *monitor* (and compatible *display adapter*) that can display a full range of shades from white to black.

 TIP: *True grayscale monitors are expensive and, in comparison to color monitors, offer few benefits to most users. They're essential, however, for a few applications, such as photographic image processing and retouching. A video graphics array (VGA) monitor may suffice; VGA monitors can display at least 64 gray-scale levels.*

F
G
H

grayscale scanner A *scanner* that generates output in 256 levels of gray. Though grayscale scanners are less expensive than *color scanners*, the price difference is not as large as it once was.

greeking Displaying a simulated version of a page on-screen, showing lines or bars instead of text so that the overall page layout design is apparent. Some word processing and page layout programs use a print preview feature that's similar to greeking.

Greek text A block of simulated text or lines used to represent the positioning and point size of text in a designer's composition of a page, used so that the aesthetics of the page design can be assessed.

Green Book A Philips standard for packing text, sound, and video onto *a CD-ROM disk* that is best known as *CD-I (Compact Disc-Interactive)*.

green PC A computer system designed to operate in an energy-efficient manner.

Powerful green PCs typically draw from 90 to 130 watts, while standard systems draw 130 to 160 watts. Green PCs also include power-saving modes that dim *monitors* and stop *hard-disk* rotation when they are not in use. In *sleep mode*, green PCs draw between 28 and 36 watts. Electrical efficiency can quickly translate to big monetary savings in offices equipped with hundreds of machines.

Group 1 An obsolete, very slow standard for *fax* machines.

Group 2 An obsolete, very slow standard for *fax* machines.

Group 3 The most common standard for *fax* machines and *fax modems*, published by the *ITU-TSS*. The Group 3 specification dictates methods by which a page-long fax can be sent in a minute or less. Several other standards support Group 3, including the *V.27ter*, *V.29*, and *V.17* standards.

Group 4 A standard for *fax* transmission designed to work with digital transmission networks such as *Integrated Services Digital Network (ISDN)*. Group 3 will continue to reign until *digital communications* find their way into more homes and offices.

group coding   Like *frequency shift keying (FSK)*, a means used by a *modem* to transmit data by altering the character of the *carrier*. Unlike FSK, though, group coding enables the modem to convey more than one *bit* per change in the carrier. Group coding, which is used in most modern modems, uses *quadrature modulation* and other *modulation* techniques to modify the carrier.

groupware   Programs that increase the cooperation and joint productivity of small groups of co-workers. An example of groupware is ForComment (by Broderbund Software), designed to make collaborative writing easier. The program allows each member of the group to insert comments and make changes to the text, subject to the other members' approval.

Some industry observers thought that groupware was just a marketing gimmick after it was reported that Broderbund didn't use ForComment for internal collaborative writing. The success of *Lotus Notes*, a groupware program designed for *minicomputer* and *mainframe* computer systems as well as *local-area networks (LANs)* and *wide-area networks (WANs)*, may suggest otherwise.

guest   In a *local area network (LAN)*, an access privilege that allows you to access another computer on the network without having to provide a *password*.

GUI   See *graphical user interface (GUI)*.

guide   In a page layout program, a non-printing line that appears as a dotted line on-screen, showing the current location of margins, gutters, and other page layout design elements.

guru   In computing, an expert who can talk about highly technical subjects in an intelligible way (a rare quality) and doesn't mind doing so (even rarer).

gutter   See *binding offset*.

GW-BASIC   A version of the *BASIC programming language* often licensed to IBM-compatible (but not IBM-made) computers. GW-BASIC is nearly identical to the BASIC *interpreter* distributed with IBM PCs, but each manufacturer is free to customize the language.

F
G
H

hack   An inordinately clever rearrangement of existing system resources that results, as if by magic, in a stunning improvement in system performance—or an equally stunning prank. A hacker is one who uses computers to perform hacks. See *hacker ethic* and *phreaking*.

hacker   A computer enthusiast who enjoys learning everything about a computer system and, through clever *programming*, pushing the system to its highest possible level of performance.

During the 1980s, the press redefined the term to include hobbyists who break into secured computer systems—often called *crackers*. Sensationalist news accounts of the dangerous activities of "hackers" created a "hacker hysteria." In 1989, for example, the *New York Times* published an article headlined "Invasion of the Data Snatchers," culminating in a ridiculous series of Secret Service raids in which federal agents confiscated the computer systems of these "dangerous" individuals. See *hack, hacker ethic,* and *phreaking*.

hacker ethic   A set of moral principles that were common to the first-generation *hacker* community (roughly 1965–1982), described by Steven Levy in *Hackers* (1984). According to the hacker ethic, all technical information should, in principle, be freely available to all. Therefore gaining entry to a system to explore data and increase knowledge is never unethical. However, destroying, altering, or moving data in such a way that could cause injury or expense to others is always unethical. In increasingly more states, breaking into databases systems is against the law. See *cracker, cyberpunk, cyberspace, hack,* and *phreaking*.

half-duplex   An *asynchronous communications* protocol in which the communications channel can handle only one signal at a time. The two stations alternate their transmissions. Synonymous with *local echo*. See *communications protocol, echoplex,* and *full duplex*.

half-height drive   A disk drive half the size of the three-inch-high drives in the original IBM Personal Computer. *Half-height drive bays* and drives are standard in today's PCs.

TIP: *When shopping for a computer, make sure that you choose one with plenty of drive bays. You might want to add an extra* floppy disk drive *or a* second hard disk drive.

half-height drive bay   A mounting space for half-height devices, such as *half-height drives,* in a computer's *case.* A half-height drive bay is 1.625 inches tall. See *full-height drive bay.*

halftone   A copy of a photograph prepared for printing by breaking down the continuous gradations of tones into a series of dots with a special screen or a *scanner.* Dense patterns of thick dots produce dark shades, and less dense patterns of smaller dots produce lighter shades. See *Tagged Image File Format (TIFF).*

F
G
H

hand-held scanner   A *scanner* that you hold and move over the material that you are scanning. Hand-held scanners are somewhat less expensive than *flatbed scanners,* but often require more than one pass to scan page-size documents. Avoid hand-held scanners unless you plan to scan narrow material, such as *newspaper columns.*

handle   In memory management, an *access channel* to a block of *extended memory.* When a program requests extended memory, *HIMEM.SYS* gives the program a handle to an extended memory block. The parameter /NUMHANDLES–num informs HIMEM.SYS how many handles it must manage. In *Microsoft Windows 95,* the *global heap* consists of all the tasks, called *objects,* that have been allocated memory; each object is assigned a handle.

In a *graphical user interface (GUI),* the small, black squares around a selected object. You use these squares to drag, size, or scale the object. See *draw program* and *object-oriented graphic.*

handler   A driver, *utility program,* or subroutine that takes care of a task. The A20 handler, for example, is a routine that controls access to *extended memory.* If *HIMEM.SYS* cannot gain control of the A20 address line, you use the /MACHINE:code parameter to tell HIMEM.SYS what type of computer you are using, which usually solves the problem.

Handlers can also be a set of programming instructions attached to a *pushbutton.* The instructions control what happens when the user selects a button. See *event-driven program* and *object-oriented programming language.*

handshaking   A method for controlling the flow of serial communication between two devices so that one device transmits data only when the other device is ready. In *hardware handshaking*, a separate wire sends a signal when the receiving device is ready to receive the signal; *software handshaking* uses special control characters.

Devices such as *serial printers* use hardware handshaking because they are close to one another and can use a special cable. Because the telephone system doesn't have an extra wire available, the telephone connections that *modems* use require software handshaking. The two software handshaking techniques are ETX/ACK, which uses the *ASCII* character Ctrl+C to pause data transmission, and XON/XOFF, which uses Ctrl+S to pause and Ctrl+Q to resume transmission.

hanging indent   A paragraph indentation in which the first line is flush with the left margin, but subsequent lines (called turnover lines) are indented.

hard   Permanent, physically defined, permanently wired, or fixed, as opposed to soft (changeable or subject to redefinition). The printed document is hard, because changing the printed document is difficult. A document in the computer's memory is soft, because you can still make changes to it. See *hard copy, hard hyphen, hard return, hard space,* and *hard wired.*

hard card   A *hard disk* and *disk drive controller* that are contained on a single plug-in *adapter.* By using a hard card, you can easily add a hard disk to a system: you simply press the adapter into the *expansion slot* just as you would any other adapter.

Hardcard   See *hard card.*

hard copy   Printed output, distinguished from data stored on disk or in memory.

hard disk   A *secondary storage medium* that uses several rigid disks coated with a magnetically sensitive material and housed, together with the recording heads, in a hermetically sealed mechanism. Typical storage capacities range from $60M$ to 500M, although $2G$ hard disks are now available.

A hard disk includes two to five disks, the read/write head assembly, and the electronic interface that governs the connection between the drive and the computer (see fig. H.1).

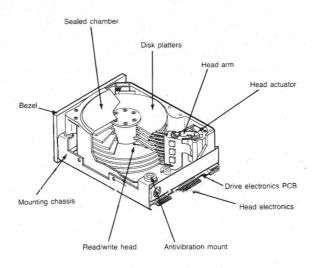

Sealed chamber

Disk platters

Head arm

Head actuator

Bezel

Drive electronics PCB

Head electronics

Mounting chassis

Read/write head   Antivibration mount

Fig. H.1 *The components of a hard disk drive.*

Hard drive *interface standards*—the means by which hard drives transmit their contents to other parts of a computer—include *ST506/ST-412, Integrated Drive Electronics (IDE), Enhanced System Device Interface (ESDI),* and *Small Computer System Interface (SCSI).* IDE and SCSI are most common today. See *access time, backup, backup utility, Bernoulli box, Run-Length Limited (RLL),* and *secondary storage.*

hard disk backup program   A *utility program* that backs up *hard disk* data and programs onto *floppy disks.* See *backup utility.*

TIP: *The best backup programs can perform incremental backups, in which the program backs up only those files that have changed since the last backup procedure.*

hard disk card   See *hard card.*

hard disk carrier   A somewhat *kludge*-like device that gives any *hard disk* some of the advantages of *removable hard disks*—*security* and easy data transfer. By attaching special fixtures to both the hard disk and the *drive bay* in which it fits, you can plug in the hard disk before *booting up* and remove it after shutting down, and meanwhile, use it in another computer or store it in a safe.

hard disk controller The circuitry, usually mounted on the *hard disk* itself, that controls the *spindle motor* and the *head actuator* of a hard disk. Under instructions from the *host adapter*, the hard disk controller searches for needed information and communicates it to the rest of the computer. *Integrated Drive Electronics (IDE)* hard disk controllers must be configured in different ways, depending on whether they are *master* or *slave* drives.

hard disk drive See *hard disk*.

hard disk interface An electronic standard for connecting a *hard disk* to the computer. See *Enhanced System Device Interface (ESDI), Integrated Drive Electronics (IDE),* and *Small Computer System Interface (SCSI).*

hard drive See *hard disk*.

hard hyphen In *word processing* programs, a special hyphen that acts as a regular character so that text can't word wrap at this hyphen. Synonymous with *nonbreaking hyphen.* See *soft hyphen*.

TIP: *Use a hard hyphen for hyphenated names, even if the names aren't positioned near the end of a line. Remember, you might later add or delete text in the paragraph, and these changes are likely to push the name to the end of a line.*

hard page A *page break*, inserted by the user, that remains in effect even after the user later adds or deletes text above the break. In contrast, the soft *page break* inserted by the program moves automatically as you add and delete text. Synonymous with *forced page break*.

hard return In *word processing* programs, a *line break* created by actually pressing the Enter key, as opposed to a *soft return*, which a program creates automatically at the end of a line. Unlike a soft return, a hard return stays in place when you insert and delete text.

hard space In *word processing* programs, a space specially formatted as a regular character so that the text can't word wrap at the space's location. Hard spaces often are used to keep two-word proper nouns or month and date together, such as *Key Biscayne, West Point,* and *January 25.*

hardware   The electronic components, boards, peripherals, and equipment that make up your computer system; distinguished from the programs (*software*) that tell these components what to do.

hardware cache   *Cache memory* on a *disk drive controller* or a *disk drive*. The cache memory stores frequently accessed program instructions and data, as well as additional *tracks* of data that a program might need next. A computer can access required data much more quickly from the hardware cache than from the disk. The data is then delivered as fast as the *expansion bus* can carry it, which is not very fast unless you have the controller on a *local bus*. Both 32-bit and 16-bit cached disk controller cards are available. See *disk drive controller*.

hardware error control   Encoding an *error-correction protocol*, such as *MNP4* or *V.42*, in the *modem* rather than in a *communications program*. Hardware error control frees the *central processing unit (CPU)* from the responsibility of catching and correcting errors.

hardware handshaking   See *Clear To Send/Ready To Send (CTS/RTS)*.

hardware panning   A *video adapter* feature that enables it to simulate a *display* larger than the one to which the video adapter is connected. By having extra *display memory* and being capable of changing the portion of display memory designated as the *frame buffer,* a video adapter enables you to drag the *mouse* to the edge of the screen and scroll into other parts of a large "virtual" display.

hardware platform   A *hardware* standard, such as *IBM PC-compatible* or *Macintosh*. Devices or programs created for one platform cannot run on others. See *device independence* and *platform independence*.

hardware reset   Restarting the system by pushing the computer's *reset button* or *programmer's switch*. A hardware reset might be necessary after a system crash so severe that you can't use the keyboard restart command (in DOS, Ctrl+Alt+Del) to restart the computer. See *warm boot*.

hardware sprite   A *video adapter* feature that enables the video adapter to draw a *cursor* or mouse *pointer* on the *display* without having to redraw the entire screen. Hardware sprites, included in all video standards since *Extended Graphics Array (XGA),* make *programming* easier because programs can move the cursor or pointer with very simple commands.

hardware tree   In Microsoft Windows 95, a graphical representation of the various devices and adapters installed in a computer.

hardware windowing   A method of improving video performance, employed by most *graphics accelerator boards*. A hardware windowing design is particularly well suited to *multitasking* environments like *Microsoft Windows 95* or *IBM's Operating System/2 (OS/2)*, because it keeps track of the screen area (or window) in which each program runs. Besides freeing the *central processing unit (CPU)* from managing windows, hardware windowing systems enable the graphics accelerator board to work faster because it has to alter only the window in which a change occurs, not the whole screen.

hard-wired   A processing function built in to the computer's electronic circuits instead of facilitated by *program* instructions. To improve computer performance, computer designers include circuits that perform specific functions, such as multiplication or division, at higher speeds. These functions are hard-wired. The term *hard-wired* also refers to the program instructions contained in the computer's *read-only memory (ROM)* or *firmware*.

Hayes command set   A standardized set of instructions used to control *modems*. Common Hayes commands include the following:

AT	Attention (used to start all commands)
ATDT	Attention, dial in tone mode
ATDP	Attention, dial in pulse mode
+++	Enter the command mode during the communication session
ATH	Attention, hang up

Hayes-compatible modem   A *modem* that recognizes the *Hayes command set*.

HDD   An acronym for *hard disk drive* frequently used in advertisements.

head   See *read/write head*.

head access aperture   The opening in a *floppy disk's shell* that enables the *read/write head* to work with the *recording medium*. In *3 1/2-inch floppy disks*, a sliding metal shutter covers the head access aperture, but *5 1/4-inch disks* expose the head access aperture whenever the disk is out of its protective sleeve.

head actuator   In a *disk drive*, a mechanism that moves the assembly containing the *read/write heads* across the surface of the disk to the location where data is to be written or read. See *random access* and *sequential access*.

head arm   In a *disk drive*, a rigid mechanical rod with a *read/write head* flexibly connected at one end and attached to a single moving assembly on the other end. Several head arms, one for each side of each platter in a hard disk, are attached to the same assembly so that they can move as a unit.

head crash   In a hard disk, the collision of a *read/write head* with the surface of the disk, resulting in damage to the disk surface and possibly to the head.

CAUTION: *Most disk drives can withstand some jostling, but you should avoid moving your computer or bumping its case while the drive is running. You should always* park *the head, if your drive does not do so automatically, before moving the computer.*

header   Repeated text, such as a page number and a short version of a document's title, that appears at the top of the pages in a document.

Some programs include both odd and even headers, so you can define mirror-image headers for documents printed on both sides of the page. Use this feature to place the page number on the outside corner of facing pages. You can suppress the printing of a header on the first page of a document or a section of a document, and change headers within the document. Synonymous with running head. See *footer*.

header   In *UseNet* and *electronic mail*, the beginning of a message. The header contains important information about the sender's address, the subject of the message, and other information.

head-mounted display (HMD)   A stereoscopic set of head-mounted goggles that produce a sensation of three-dimensional space. Head-mounted displays are an integral part of *virtual reality* systems, in which users feel as though they're exploring a real world that has actually been created within the computer system. See *stereoscopy.*

head parking   Positioning the *read/write head* over the *zone* to prevent a *head crash,* in which the head strikes and usually damages the disk surface. Older hard disks require you to issue a command to park the head, while newer hard disks feature *automatic head parking.*

head seek time   See *access time.*

head slot   An opening in a *floppy disk* case. The access hole exposes a portion of the disk surface so that a *read/write head* can read information or write new information on the disk.

heap   In early versions of Microsoft Windows, a special storage area in memory used for critical resources.

During normal Windows operations, several types of heaps are created, including a local heap, menu heap, and user heap, which are collectively called the system resources. These heaps are limited to a 64*K* size. When they're full, launching another application results in a "Not enough memory" message, even though plenty physical memory might be available.

Operating System/2 (OS/2) and *Microsoft Windows 95* do not need to worry about the 64K resource heap.

heat sink   A finned metal assembly that sits on top of a hot component, such as a *microprocessor,* and draws heat out of it, preventing it from overheating. *Pentium* microprocessors get very hot and often need a heat sink—and sometimes a CPU fan—to keep cool.

helper program   In a *Web browser,* a supplementary program that enables the browser to handle *multimedia* files, such as animations, videos, and sounds. Most helper programs are *freeware* or *shareware.* Few browsers come with helper programs, so users must go through the tedious process of locating the appropriate helper programs, downloading them from the *Internet,* and configuring the browser to start them automatically when it encounters a

multimedia file. You usually set up this configuration in a configuration dialog box, in which you match the program with the type
of file (the *MIME type*) that the program is designed to display.

Helvetica   A *sans serif typeface* frequently used for *display type*
and occasionally for *body type.* One of the world's most widely
used *fonts,* Helvetica is included in many *laser printers* as a *built-in
font.* The following are examples of Helvetica type:

ABCDEFGHIJKLMNOPQRSTUVWXYZ

abcdefghijklmnopqrstuvwxyz 1234567890

Hercules Graphics Adapter   A *monochrome display adapter*
for *IBM PC-compatible* computers. The Hercules Graphics
Adapter displays text and graphics on a monochrome *monitor* with
a resolution of 720 *pixels* horizontally and 320 lines vertically.
Hercules monitors are obsolete. See *monochrome display adapter
(MDA).*

hertz (Hz)   A unit of measurement of electrical vibrations; one
Hz is equal to one cycle per second. See *megahertz (MHz).*

heterogeneous network   A *local area network (LAN)* that
includes computers and devices from several manufacturers. Many
firms create heterogeneous networks that successfully link
Macintosh and *IBM PC-compatible* systems.

heuristic   A method of solving a problem by using rules of
thumb acquired from experience. Textbooks rarely state heuristics
formally, but they are part of the knowledge that human experts
use in problem solving. See *expert system* and *knowledge base.*

Hewlett-Packard Graphics Language   A *page description
language (PDL)* and *file format* for graphics printing with the HP
LaserJet line of printers, HP *plotters*, and high-end *inkjet printers*,
now widely emulated by HP-compatible laser printers. See
Hewlett-Packard Printer Control Language (HPPCL).

**Hewlett-Packard Printer Control Language
(HPPCL)**   The proprietary *printer control language (PCL)* that
Hewlett-Packard introduced in 1984 with the company's first
LaserJet printer. Like the *Hayes command set* in the *modem* world,
HPPCL has become a standard.

hex   See *hexadecimal*.

hexadecimal   A numbering system that uses a base (radix) of 16. Unlike decimal numbers (base 10), hexadecimal numbers include 16 digits: 0, 1, 2, 3, 4, 5, 6, 7, 8, 9, A, B, C, D, E, and F. Although *binary* numbers are ideally suited to the devices used in computers, they are inconvenient and hard to read. Binary numbers grow long quickly; for example, 16 is 1111 in binary and 10 in hexadecimal format. Therefore, *programmers* use hexadecimal numbers as a convenient way to represent binary numbers.

hidden codes   The hidden text formatting codes embedded in a document by an on-screen formatting program.

Even a *what-you-see-is-what-you-get (WYSIWYG)* word processing program generates and embeds codes in your text as a result of formatting commands. The codes are necessary because the screen imaging technique might not have any connection to the technique used to generate output to the printer. Most *word processing* programs hide these codes; in *WordPerfect*, however, you can view and edit the codes.

hidden file   In *MS-DOS,* a *file* with the hidden attribute set so that when users view a directory by using the DIR command, the file name isn't displayed. You can't erase or copy hidden files.

Hierarchical File System (HFS)   A *Macintosh* disk storage system, designed for use with *hard disks*, that stores files within folders so only a short list of files appears in *dialog boxes*.

HFS is similar to the directory organization of DOS disks, with one important exception: No path definition command exists, except for checking the *System Folder* when an application searches for a file. See *path*.

> **TIP:** *Macintosh users should avoid nesting too many levels of folders. Keeping the nested levels under two or three reduces the amount of pointing or clicking required to search for a file; if you have five or six levels, however, the tedium increases. To automate the process, consider buying a file-location utility such as Findswell (Working Software) or Boomerang (ZetaSoft).*

hierarchy   In *UseNet,* a category of *newsgroups.* Within the standard newsgroups, for example, seven hierarchies exist: *comp, misc, news, rec, sci, soc,* and *talk.* The term *hierarchies* suggests the way that newsgroups are internally categorized. For example, the rec.* hierarchy includes many newsgroups pertaining to hobbies and recreation; the rec.comics.* hierarchy contains several newsgroups for comic collectors; and the rec.comics.elfquest newsgroup focuses on Wendy and Richard Pini's Elfquest comics. See *alt, alternative newsgroup hierarchies, local newsgroup hierarchies,* and *standard newsgroup hierarchies.*

high density   A *floppy disk* storage technique that uses extremely fine-grained magnetic particles. High-density disks are more expensive to manufacture than *double-density* disks, but can store 1*M* or more of information on one 5 1/4- or 3 1/2-inch disk. Synonymous with *quad density.*

F G H

high-density disk   See *floppy disk.*

High-Density Multimedia CD (HDMMCD)   See *Multimedia Compact Disc (MMCD).*

high end   An expensive product at the top of a firm's offerings; includes features or capabilities likely to be needed only by the most discriminating users or professionals. See *low end.*

higher-order characters   See *extended character set.*

high-level format   A formatting operation that creates the *boot record, file allocation table (FAT),* and *root directory* on a disk.

When you use the DOS FORMAT command to format a floppy disk, the computer performs a *low-level format* (which creates tracks and sectors) in addition to the high-level format. When you use a hard disk, however, FORMAT performs just the high-level format, because hard disks are usually factory-formatted. See *boot sector.*

high-level programming language   A *programming language* such as *BASIC* or *Pascal* that crudely resembles human language.

Each statement in a high-level language corresponds to several *machine language* instructions. Using such languages, a programmer can write programs more quickly and concentrate on the problem that the program is designed to solve, instead of how the computer will carry out the program. However, programs written in a high-level language run slower than those written in a *low-level programming language*. See *assembly language*.

highlight   A character, word, text block, or command displayed in *reverse video*, indicating the current location of the cursor. This term sometimes is used synonymously with *cursor*.

highlighting   The process of marking characters or command names in *reverse video* on-screen. Synonymous with *selecting*.

high/low/close/open graph   In *presentation graphics*, a *line graph* in which a stock's high value, low value, closing price, and *open price* are displayed (see fig. H.2). The graph aligns the x-axis (categories) horizontally and the y-axis (values) vertically. Another application for a high/low/open/close graph is a record of daily minimum, maximum, and average temperatures. Synonymous with *HLCO chart*. See *column graph* and *line graph*.

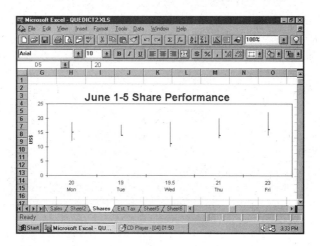

Fig. H.2   *A high/low/close/open graph.*

high memory   See *high memory area (HMA)*.

high memory area (HMA)   In a DOS computer, the first 64K of *extended memory* above 1M. Programs that conform to the *eXtended Memory Specification (XMS)* can use HMA as a direct extension of *conventional memory*. Beginning with *MS-DOS* 5.0, most of the portions of DOS that you must load into conventional memory can be loaded into the high memory area.

High Performance Computing Act of 1991 A U.S. federal legislative act that is intended to promote the development of gigabit networking (*wide area networks* capable of transferring a billion or more bits of information per second). The act calls for the construction of the *National Research and Education Network (NREN)*, the purpose of which is to link several supercomputer research centers. The act created the High Performance Computing and Communications (HPCC) program, which brings together several federal agencies in support of high-performance computing.

high resolution In computer systems, using a sufficient number of *pixels* in *monitors* or *dots per inch (dpi)* when printing to produce well-defined text characters as well as smoothly defined curves in graphic images. A high-resolution video adapter and monitor can display 1,024 pixels horizontally by 768 lines vertically; a high-resolution printer can print at least 300 dpi. See *low resolution.*

high-rez Slang for a technically savvy person. Unlike a *low-rez* individual, a high-rez person is both intelligent and technically proficient, and neither shuns new technology nor relies on it completely.

High Sierra An obsolete standard for encoding data onto *CD-ROMs.* Although similar to High Sierra, the widely used *ISO 9660* standard is incompatible with it.

high-speed modem Technically, a *modem* capable of *data transfer rates* of 9600 *bits per second (bps)* or faster. In reality, only 14,400 bps and 28,800 bps modems are considered to be high-speed. High-speed modems can drastically reduce the time that it takes to transmit data over a telephone line.

High Speed Technology (HST) A *proprietary* data transmission standard developed by U.S. Robotics for *modems.* HST allows for data transmission at 14,400 *bits per second (bps)* in the direction in which the most data is moving and 450 bps in the other direction. The universally accepted *V.32bis* protocol has replaced HST, which you should avoid.

HIMEM.SYS An *MS-DOS device driver* that configures *extended memory* and the *high memory area (HMA)* so that programs conforming to the *eXtended Memory Standard (XMS)* can access it.

See *CONFIG.SYS, eXtended Memory Specification (XMS)*, and *upper memory area*.

hinting   In digital *typography*, reducing the weight (thickness) of a *typeface* so that small-sized *fonts* print without blurring or losing detail on 300-*dots per inch (dpi)* printers.

histogram   A *stacked column graph* in which you place the columns close together to emphasize differences in the data items within each stack. See figure H.3.

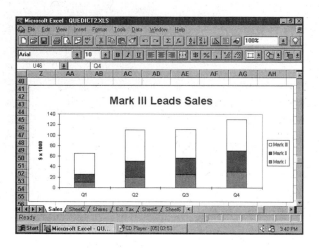

Fig. H.3   *A histogram.*

By stacking data in a column, you emphasize the contribution that each data item makes to the whole (as in a *pie graph*). By placing the columns next to each other, you lead the viewer to compare the relative proportions of one data item as it varies from column to column.

HLCO chart   See *high/low/close/open graph*.

holy war   A protracted and often incendiary debate within the computing community regarding the merits of a particular computer, operating system, or programming style. The term nicely captures the inflexible and often dogmatic positions that the various participants take in the debate. Famous holy wars include the debate between those who feel that the most significant bit in a unit of represented data should come first (little endian) or last (big endian). Holy wars tend to strike outsiders as rather ridiculous.

home computer   A *personal computer* specifically designed and marketed for home applications, such as educating children, playing games, balancing a checkbook, paying bills, and controlling lights or appliances.

Home key   A key on computer *keyboards* which in most programs moves the cursor to the beginning of the line or the top of the screen. However, the assignment of this key is up to the *programmer*.

home page   In any *hypertext* system, including the *World Wide Web (WWW),* a document intended to serve as an initial point of entry to a *web* of related documents. Also called a welcome page, a home page contains general introductory information, as well as *hyperlinks* to related resources. A well-designed home page contains internal *navigation buttons,* which help users find their way among the various documents that the home page makes available.

home server   In *Gopher,* the server that the Gopher client program is configured to display automatically when you start the program.

homophone error   A type of spelling error that involves using an incorrect word that sounds the same as the correct word (as in "Two Bee, Oar Knot Too Be"). Although many application programs' spell checking features fail to find homophone errors, grammar checking programs usually do find them.

hook   A feature included in a *software* or *hardware* product to enable hobbyists and *programmers* to add their own custom features. For example, *Microsoft Word* is loaded with hooks that enable experts to create custom *dialog boxes,* which greatly extends the program's functionality for specific applications. In hardware, an *open architecure* system might make it easy to design specialized monitoring tools or improved sound capabilities.

horizontal frequency   A measure (usually in *kilohertz [Khz]*) of how fast a *monitor* draws horizontal lines on its *display.* Unlike *vertical frequency,* horizontal frequency does not vary significantly from one monitor to another. Synonymous with line rate.

horizontal retrace   The process of the electron beam in a *cathode ray tube (CRT)* being directed by the *yoke* from the end of one horizontal scan line to the beginning of the next. *Video* *adapters* must allow time for horizontal retrace in preparing the video signal.

horizontal scroll bar See *scroll bar/scroll box.*

host In the *Internet,* any computer that can function as the beginning and end point of data transfers. An Internet host has a unique Internet address (called an *IP address*) and a unique *domain name.*

In *networks* and telecommunications generally, the computer that performs centralized functions such as making program or data files available to other computers.

host adapter The *adapter* that transfers data and instructions back and forth between a *hard* or *floppy disk drive controller* and the *central processing unit (CPU).* Usually an adapter that plugs into the *expansion bus,* the host adapter complies with a specification such as *Integrated Drive Electronics (IDE), Enhanced IDE (EIDE),* or *Small Computer System Interface (SCSI).*

hot key A keyboard shortcut that accesses a menu command. A *shortcut key,* in contrast, gives you direct access to a dialog box or other feature. Alt+key combinations are hot keys; function-key assignments are shortcut keys.

TIP: *In most programs, you can use keyboard shortcuts for many menu commands. If you see a bolded or an underlined character in a command or option name, you can access that command or option by holding down the Alt key and pressing that letter.*

hot link A method of copying information from one document (the *source document*) to another (the *destination document*) so that the target document's information is updated automatically when the source document's information changes.

In *Microsoft Windows 95* applications, you can create a hot link by using the Paste/Link command. In Macintosh *System 7,* open the Edit menu and choose Publish in the source document, and then paste the link by using Subscribe in the target document. See *dynamic data exchange (DDE), object linking and embedding (OLE),* and *warm link.*

hotlist In a *Web browser,* a list of favorite *World Wide Web (WWW) sites* that a user saves for future use while browsing. To retrieve hotlist items, you select the item that you want in a menu or dialog box and then choose the Go To command or its equivalent. In *Netscape Navigator,* the hotlist items are called bookmarks, and the hotlist is called the bookmark list.

HoTMetaL A stand-alone *Html editor,* created by SoftQuad Systems, for *Microsoft Windows 95* systems (see fig. H.4). Widely distributed as *shareware,* HoTMetaL is also available in a professional version called HoTMetaL Pro. The current version ruthlessly checks HTML *tags* for conformity to the original *HTML 1.0* specification, making it difficult to produce pages incorporating more recent additions to *HyperText Markup Language (HTML),* such as the *Netscape extensions.* HoTMetaL competes with *WebAuthor, Microsoft Internet Assistant,* and *HTML Assistant.*

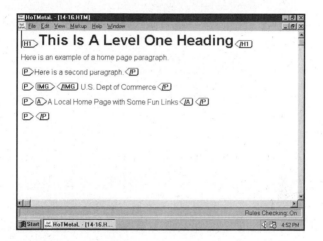

Fig. H.4 *HoTMetaL, a stand-alone HTML editor.*

HP-compatible printer A printer that responds to the Hewlett-Packard *printer control language (PCL),* which has become the standard for laser printing in the IBM and IBM-compatible computing world.

HPGL See *Hewlett-Packard Graphics Language (HPGL).*

HTML + An unofficial *HyperText Markup Language (HTML)* specification that has strongly influenced *HTML 2.0* and the forthcoming *HTML 3.0* standards. HTML + describes advanced features of the language, including forms and tables.

HTML 1.0   The original *HyperText Markup Language (HTML)* specification, drafted in 1990. Because it contains certain *tags* that are no longer used, this specification is considered obsolete. The *HTML 2.0* specification is now considered authoritative. Also known as HTML Level 1.

 HTML 2.0   A revised *HyperText Markup Language (HTML)* specification that describes current HTML practice, as of mid-1994, and formalizes these practices as an *Internet Draft*. The major updates from *HTML 1.0* are the inclusion of forms and the removal of certain little-used *tags*. The HTML 2.0 specification does not include many practices that have arisen since its release, including tables and the *Netscape extensions*.

HTML 3.0   A revised *HyperText Markup Language (HTML)* specification, still under development, that will provide support for tables and other advanced features.

HTML Assistant   A stand-alone *HTML editor,* created by Howard Harawitz at Brooklyn North Software Works, for *Microsoft Windows 95* systems (see fig. H.5). The *freeware* version has a file-size limit of 32K; a professional version, HTML Assistant Pro, allows unlimited-length files and provides full support and a printed manual. HTML Assistant competes with *Microsoft Internet Assistant, HoTMetal,* and *WebAuthor.* See *HyperText Markup Language (HTML).*

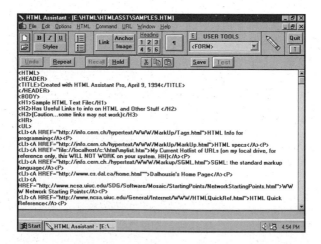

Fig. H.5 *HTML Assistant, a stand-alone HTML editor.*

HTML editor   A program that provides assistance in preparing documents for the *World Wide Web (WWW)* using the *HyperText Markup Language (HTML)*. The simplest HTML editor is simply a word processing program that enables you to type text and add HTML *tags* manually. Add-on packages for popular word processing programs enable you to view the effects of your HTML tags in a *what-you-see-is-what-you-get (WYSIWYG)* environment, but these add-ons tend to be slow and cumbersome. Stand-alone HTML editors provide automated assistance with HTML coding and display some formats on-screen. See *HoTMetaL, HTML Assistant, Microsoft Internet Assistant,* and *WebAuthor.*

HTTPS   A *Web server* for *Microsoft Windows NT* created and maintained by the European Microsoft Windows NT Academic Centre (EMWAC) project, at the University of Edinburgh. The server is available through *anonymous FTP* and incorporates several unique features, such as the capability to search *Wide Area Information Server (WAIS) databases* in response to browser queries.

hub ring   The ring of Teflon or plastic in the center of a *5 1/4-inch floppy disk.* The hub ring, which not all disks have, protects the disk from wear caused by contact with the *spindle.*

hung system   A computer that has experienced a system failure and is no longer processing data, even though the cursor might still be blinking on-screen. The only option in most cases is to restart the system, which means losing any unsaved work.

> **TIP:** *If you experience frequent computer crashes, try removing all the* terminate-and-stay-resident (TSR) *programs that you're using. These programs, called* INITs *in the Macintosh world, can cause conflicts that produce hung systems. Add the programs again, one by one, testing between each addition to determine whether one of them is causing the problem. Check the program documentation to see whether you must load TSRs or INITs in a specific order. Some operate in an unstable fashion unless they are the last program loaded at system startup.*

HyperCard   A software product, available with the Apple Macintosh computer, for developing information systems based on *hypertext.* See *HyperTalk.*

hyperlink   In a *hypertext* system, an underlined or otherwise emphasized word or phrase that, when clicked with the *mouse,* displays another document.

hypermedia   A *hypertext* system that employs multimedia resources (graphics, videos, animations, and sounds). The best hypermedia systems employ various media in ways that are more than just "window dressing," but materially support the presentation's objective.

HyperTalk   A *scripting* language provided with *HyperCard,* an accessory program shipped with every Macintosh. HyperTalk is an *event-driven language.* To create a HyperTalk program, you first use HyperCard to create screen objects (cards with text fields, *pushbuttons,* and other features). You then write short, English-like programs, called *scripts,* that tell HyperCard what to do when the program's user manipulates one of the screen objects. HyperTalk programming is fun and introduces a programming novice to the fundamental principles of *object-oriented programming.* The language is too slow, however, for professional program development, for which it was never intended. See *SmallTalk.*

hypertext   A method of preparing and publishing text, ideally suited to the computer, in which readers can choose their own paths through the material. To prepare hypertext, you first "chunk" the information into small, manageable units, such as single pages of text. These units are called *nodes.* You then embed *hyperlinks* (also called anchors) in the text. When the reader clicks on a hyperlink, the hypertext software displays a different node. The process of navigating among the nodes linked in this way is called *browsing.* A collection of nodes that are interconnected by hyperlinks is called a *web.* The *World Wide Web (WWW)* is a hypertext system on a global scale.

Hypertext applications are particularly useful for working with massive amounts of text, such as encyclopedias and multivolume case law reporters.

HyperText Markup Language (HTML)   A set of conventions for marking the portions of a document so that, when accessed by a program called a parser, each portion appears with a distinctive format. HTML is the markup language behind the appearance of documents on the *World Wide Web (WWW),* and the parser programs for accessing these documents are called *Web browsers.* A subset of *Standard Generalized Markup Language*

(SGML), HTML includes capabilities that enable authors to insert *hyperlinks,* which when clicked display another HTML document.

The process of composing HTML text is called authoring. You can author HTML text by editing a plain-text document with a stand-alone *HTML editor,* such as *HTML Assistant.* In addition, add-on programs are available that provide HTML editing capabilities to word processing programs such as Microsoft Word for Windows.

Unlike a word processing program's formatting codes, HTML codes—called *tags*—do not specify just how the tagged text should appear. They merely tell the parser that the text is a certain portion of a document, such as a title, heading, or body text. The parser decides how to format the text.

F
G
H

HyperText Transfer Protocol Daemon (httpd)   A *Web server* originally developed at the Swiss *Center for Particle Research (CERN)* and originally called CERN httpd. Subsequently, httpd was developed independently at the *National Center for Supercomputing Applications (NCSA)* for UNIX systems. An important innovation in the history of Web servers, NASA httpd introduced *forms,* clickable *imagemaps, authentication,* and *key word searches.* Most of these features are now taken for granted in other Web servers. An adaptation of the program for *Microsoft Windows 95,* called *Windows httpd,* is available.

HyperText Transport Protocol (HTTP)   The *Internet* standard that supports the exchange of information on the *World Wide Web (WWW).* By defining *Universal Resource Locators (URLs)* and how they can be used to retrieve resources (including not only Web documents but also *File Transport Protocol [FTP]*-accessible files, *UseNet newsgroups,* and *Gopher* menus) anywhere on the Internet, HTTP enables Web authors to embed *hyperlinks* in Web documents. When clicked, a hyperlink initiates a data transfer process that accesses and retrieves the document, without any further intervention from the user (or, indeed, without any knowledge of where the document is coming from or how it was accessed). In short, HTTP lays the foundation for transparent access to the Internet.

hyphenation   In *word processing* and *page layout programs,* an automatic operation that hyphenates words at the end of lines as needed. If you use it carefully and manually confirm each hyphen, a hyphenation utility can improve a document's appearance, especially when you are using *newspaper columns* or large margins. See *hard hyphen, hyphen ladder,* and *soft hyphen.*

CAUTION: *You must carefully check the work or programs that hyphenate automatically, because some programs break fundamental hyphenation rules. Some leave only one or two characters on one side of the hyphen or hyphenate words on several consecutive lines. Others have trouble with* homographs, *two words spelled the same but with different meanings and pronunciations, as in the following two examples:*

in-val-id and in-va-lid

min-ute and mi-nute

hyphen ladder A formatting flaw caused by the repetition of hyphens at the end of two or more lines in a row. Synonymous with *hyphen stack.*

Hyphen ladders distract the eye and disrupt the text's readability. If you use automatic hyphenation, proofread the results carefully for hyphen ladders. Adjust word spacing and hyphenation manually, if necessary.

Hytelnet A *hypertext*-based guide to the *Telnet*-based resources accessible on the Internet, including libraries, *freenets, bulletin board systems (BBS),* and other information sites (see fig. H.6). A *World Wide Web (WWW)* gateway version is available.

Fig. H.6 *The Hytelnet search engine for Telnet resources.*

Hz See *hertz (Hz).*

IAC See *Inter-Application Communication (IAC).*

I-beam pointer In Macintosh and *Microsoft Windows* applications, an I-shaped *mouse* pointer that appears when the pointer is moved over a screen area when you can edit text.

The I-beam pointer is thin enough that you can position the pointer between characters with precision.

IBM 486BLX See *IBM Blue Lightning.*

IBM 486BLX2 See *IBM Blue Lightning.*

IBM 486BLX3 See *IBM Blue Lightning.*

IBM 486SLC2 An energy-saving *microprocessor,* designed by IBM for use in *portable computers,* that is *pin-compatible* with *Intel 486* chips. The 486SLC2 boasts performance on par with the *Intel 486SX.*

IBM 8514 A *video adapter* for IBM Personal System/2 computers that, with the on-board *Video Graphics Array (VGA)* circuitry, produces a resolution of 1,024 *pixels* horizontally and 768 lines vertically. The adapter also contains its own processing circuitry that reduces demand on the *central processing unit (CPU).* The 8514 replaces the 8514/A and MCGA adapters, which have been discontinued. See *Super VGA.*

IBM Blue Lightning Low-power *microprocessors* that are *pin-compatible* with, and offer performance similar to, *Intel 486DX* chips. The IBM 486BLX runs at *clock speeds* of 33 *megahertz (MHz)* and lower. The *clock-doubled* IBM 486BLX2 runs at 66 MHz. The clock-tripled IBM 486BLX3 runs at 100 MHz.

IBM PC-compatible computer A personal computer that runs all or almost all the software developed for the IBM Personal Computer, and accepts the IBM computer's cards, adapters, and peripheral devices. Synonymous with clone.

ICCP See *Institute for Certification of Computer Professionals (ICCP).*

icon In a graphical user interface (GUI), an on-screen symbol that represents a *program*, data *file*, or some other computer entity or function (see fig. I.1).

Several icons might appear together on an icon bar, an on-screen row of *buttons*, usually placed just above the *document window*, that allows the user to choose frequently accessed menu options without having to use the *menus*. On each button is a icon that shows the button's function. For example, the Print button might display a tiny picture of a printer.

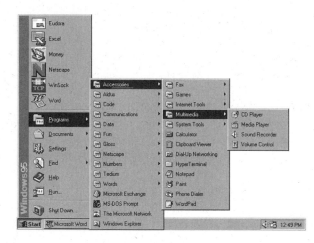

Fig. I.1 *On-screen icons representing shortcuts to Microsoft Windows 95 accessory programs.*

IDE See *Integrated Drive Electronics (IDE)*.

IDE drive On 80286 and more recent computers, a hard disk that contains most of the control circuitry within the drive itself. Synonymous with AT Attachment drives, IDE drives combine the speed of *Enhanced System Device Interface (ESDI)* drives with the integration of the *Small Computer System Interface (SCSI)* hard drive interface. This performance is offered at a price lower than most ESDI and SCSI drives. See *Integrated Drive Electronics (IDE)*.

identifier In *database management,* a *descriptor* used to specify the uniqueness of the information contained in the data record. For example, the descriptor Norway appears in the data record of the only travel films that depict scenery from that country.

TIP: *If you're shopping for a computer and value is uppermost in your mind, look for a machine that includes an IDE interface and IDE drive. You need an ESDI or SCSI drive only if you run applications that demand the highest possible performance from your computer.*

IEEE 802 standards   A series of telecommunications standards governing *local area networks (LANs)*. Established by the *Institute of Electrical and Electronic Engineers (IEEE),* the standards include 10Base2 and 10Base-T cabling, network *bridges,* and *topologies.* See *bridge, bus network, EtherNet, fiber optics,* and *star network.*

IEEE 1284   A standard developed by the *Institute of Electrical and Electronics Engineers (IEEE)* that governs the design of *bidirectional parallel ports.* Both the *enhanced parallel port (EPP)* and the *extended capabilities port (ECP)* conform to IEEE 1284.

IEEE Computer Society   See *Institute of Electrical and Electronic Engineers Computer Society (IEEE Computer Society).*

IF/THEN/ELSE   In programming, a structure that conducts a test to see whether a condition is true. If the condition is true, then the program branches to one option; if the condition is false, the program branches to another option. IF/THEN/ELSE structures, with slight variations in the language, are used when writing *macros,* as merge codes, as functions in *spreadsheet* software, and as part of all *high-level programming languages.*

The following example tests to see whether a file exists. If the file exists, the program tells the computer to open the file. If the file doesn't exist, the program tells the computer to create a file.

```
IF file_exists = true
    THEN open_file
    ELSE create_new_file
ENDIF
```

illegal character   A character that can't be used according to the syntax rules of command-driven programs and *programming languages.* Such characters usually are reserved for a specific program function. With DOS, for example, you can't assign a *file name* to a *file* if the name includes an asterisk (*). The asterisk is reserved for use as *a wild card* symbol. Commas, spaces, slashes, and several other punctuation characters also are illegal characters for file names.

image compression   The use of a compression technique to reduce the size of *graphics* files, which usually consume inordinate amounts of disk space. A single 100K *gray scale Taggeg Image File Format (TIFF)* file can be reduced by as much as 96 percent to 4K or 5K for *telecommunications* or storage purposes. Some graphics programs compress images automatically, but popular file compression programs such as PKZIP (PKWARE, Inc.) also can do the job.

image processing   In *graphics*, the use of a computer to enhance, embellish, or refine a graphic image. Typical processing operations include enhancing or reducing contrast, altering colors so that the image is more easily analyzed, correcting underexposure or overexposure, and outlining objects so they can be identified.

imagesetter   A professional typesetting machine that generates very high-resolution output on photographic paper or film.

Popular imagesetters include the Agfa Compugraphic, Linotronic, and Varityper models that recognize *PostScript* commands. All are capable of *resolutions* of 1,200 or more *dots per inch (dpi)*, unlike the 300-600 dpi resolution of *laser printers*. They also sell for $30,000 and up, so if you have a *PostScript*-compatible *word processor* or page layout program, take a disk to a *service bureau* that owns one of these machines to obtain high-resolution output.

imaging model   The method of representing output on-screen. In a *graphical user interface (GUI),* for example, the imaging model is for the *screen font* to closely resemble the way the text is printed.

IMHO   In *on-line* conferences, an *acronym* for In My Humble Opinion.

impact printer   A *printer* that generates output like typewriters, by actually striking the page with something solid. *Daisywheel* and *dot-matrix printers* are impact printers. Impact printers are slow and noisy, but they are inexpensive by printer standards and are necessary for filling out carbon-copy forms.

import   To load a file created by one program into a different program. Harvard Graphics, for example, can import the PIC files created by *Lotus 1-2-3*.

increment   To increase a value. See *decrement.*

incremental backup   A *backup* procedure in which a hard disk *backup utility* backs up only the *files* changed since the last backup procedure. See *archival backup.*

incremental update   See *maintenance release.*

indentation   The *alignment* of a paragraph to the right or left of the document margins.

CAUTION: *Don't use the space bar or Tab key to indent text. If a printer uses proportional typefaces, the text won't align properly. This method also doesn't change the indentation of all the lines; you must change each line individually. Finally, if you edit the text, it won't automatically reformat correctly.*

index   In *database management* programs, a compact file containing information about the physical location of records in a database file. When searching or sorting the database, the program uses the index rather than the full database. Such operations are faster than sorts or searches performed on the actual database.

In *word processing* programs, an index is an appendix that lists important words, names, and concepts in alphabetical order, and the page numbers where the terms appear. With most word processing programs, you must mark terms to be included in the index the program constructs. See *active index, concordance file, sort,* and *sort order.*

index hole   In a *floppy disk,* a hole that's electro-optically detected by the drive to locate the beginning of the first *sector* on the disk. Few disk drives use the index hole.

indexing   The method a *floppy disk drive* uses to locate the *track* on which needed information is located. Indexing involves moving the *read/write head* to the outermost track on a disk and moving inward, one track at a time, until the needed track is reached.

Industry Standard Architecture (ISA)   The *expansion bus* design of IBM's AT (Advanced Technology) computer, which uses a 16-bit bus with several 8-bit slots for downward compatibility.

I
J
K

The *AT bus* added more than a simple doubling of the width of the data bus. The *address bus* was increased to 24 lines, enough to address 16M of memory. Downward compatibility was assured by adding a supplemental connector to the original 8-bit, 62-pin connector. Several new *interrupt request (IRQ) lines* and *direct memory access (DMA)* control lines were added. See *channels, Extended Industry Standard Architecture (EISA), local bus,* and *Micro Channel Architecture (MCA).*

Industry Standard Architecture (ISA) expansion bus

A generally outmoded 16-bit *expansion bus* design developed in the early 1980s. The ISA expansion bus can transfer data at 8*M* per second, and was adequate for connecting adapters to the *central processing unit (CPU)* until, in the early 1990s, microprocessor performance created an *expansion bus bottleneck* with the ISA standard.

TIP: *The ISA standard has been replaced with the Peripheral Component Interconnect (PCI) standard, but most new computers still come with ISA slots to accommodate older adapters.*

industry standard user interface

An IBM standard for displaying programs on-screen; part of the company's Systems Application Architecture (SAA). The standard, called Common User Access (CUA), calls for many of the interface features found in *graphical user interfaces (GUIs)*: *pull-down menus*, dialog boxes with check boxes and option buttons, and highlighted accelerator keys for rapid keyboard selection of commands.

The CUA standard is now found in many character-based DOS applications. Strictly speaking, it isn't a graphical user interface (GUI) because it runs in *character mode* and doesn't represent computer resources as *icons*. But the CUA interface has just about every other GUI benefit, including a refreshing commonality of key assignments and procedures across applications. See *application program interface (API), Microsoft Windows,* and *mousable interface.*

infection

The presence of a *virus* within a computer system or on a disk. The infection may not be obvious to the user; many viruses, for example, remain in the background until a specific time and date, when they display prank messages or erase data. See *Trojan horse* and *worm.*

infinite loop   In *programming,* a *loop* whose condition for terminating is never fulfilled. For example, a loop designed to add 5 to an integer variable until the variable equaled 133.2 would never end—at least not until a *crash* occurred or the programmer invoked the *big red switch.*

Infobahn   A term preferred by some for the so-called *Information Superhighway,* a high-speed information system that would link homes, schools, and offices with high-bandwidth local delivery systems and backbone systems capable of gigabit-per-second speeds.

information   Data—whether in the form of numbers, graphics, or words—that has been organized, systematized, and presented so that the underlying patterns become clear. The temperature, humidity, and wind reports from hundreds of weather stations are data; a computer simulation that shows how this data predicts a strong possibility of tornados is information.

information kiosk   *See kiosk.*

information service   See *bibliographic retrieval service, bulletin board system (BBS),* and *on-line information service.*

Information Superhighway   An envisioned information infrastructure that will bring high-speed computer networking within the reach of homes, schools, and offices. The term is misleading in that the "freeways," high-speed backbone networks, already exist; what is lacking is a good system of "local roads." The current telephone system does not have the bandwidth to deliver high-speed digital services to the home; a capital investment on the order of $325 billion would be necessary to replace the existing telephone lines with high-speed fiber optic cables. The replacement will occur—but we will be decades into the 21st century before it is complete.

infrared port   A port that enables a PC to exchange data with infrared-capable *portable computers* or *peripheral* devices, without using cables. Usually created by attaching a *dongle* to a *serial port,* infrared ports can move data at more than 115,000 *bits per second (bps).*

inheritance   In object-oriented programming, the passing of a message up through the levels of objects until an object traps the message.

In *HyperTalk*, for example, the lowest-level object is a button. If the user produces a message by clicking on the *button*, and the button contains no programming code (called a handler) that traps this message, the message is passed up to the next level of the hierarchy, the card; if the card has no handler, the message is passed to the stack; finally, if there's still no *handler*, the message goes to the highest level, *HyperCard*. See *object-oriented programming language*.

INIT   In the Macintosh environment, a *utility program* that executes during a system start or restart, such as SuperClock, which displays the current system date and time in the *menu bar*, and Adobe Type Manager, which uses outline-font technology to display Adobe *screen fonts*.

CAUTION: *Like terminate-and-stay resident (TSR) programs in the IBM environment, INITs can conflict with each other and cause system crashes. If your system is behaving erratically, try removing INITs one at a time from the System Folder and restarting your system; you may be able to determine whether an INIT is the culprit.*

initial   In *typography*, an enlarged letter at the beginning of a chapter or paragraph. Initials set down within the copy are *drop caps*, and initials raised above the top line of the text are stickup initials (see fig. I.2).

initial base font   The *font* used by *word processing* programs for all documents unless you instruct otherwise. The initial base font is part of the *printer* definition. Whenever you select a different printer, the initial base font may change.

You can override the initial base font for a particular document by choosing a *document base font* using the document menu or using the base font menu, and you can override this choice by formatting individual characters or blocks of characters within the document.

OREM IPSUM dolor sit amet, consectetuer adipiscing elit, sed diam nonummy nibh euismod tincidunt ut laoreet dolore magna aliquam erat volutpat. Ut wisi enim ad minim veniam, quis nostrud exerci tation ullamcorper suscipit lobortis nisl ut aliquip ex

Y a commodo consequat. Duis autem vel eum iriure dolor in hendrerit in vulputate velit esse molestie consequat, vel illum dolore eu feugiat nulla facilisis at vero eros et accumsan et iusto odio dignissim qui blandit praesent luptatum zzril delenit augue duis

TELUM COMMODO consequat. Duis autem vel eum iriure dolor in hendrerit in vulputate velit esse molestie consequat, vel illum dolore eu feugiat nulla facilisis

Lorem ipsum dolor sit amet, consectetuer adipiscing elit, sed diam nonummy nibh euismod tincidunt ut laoreet dolore magna aliquam erat volutpat. Ut wisi enim ad minim veniam,

Fig. I.2 *Examples of drop caps (S and Y) and stickup initials (T and L).*

CAUTION: *You can create specially formatted initials with many word processing and page layout programs, but to avoid a common formatting error, make sure that the letter aligns precisely at the base of a line of text.*

I J K

initialization In *modems,* the establishment of an *active configuration* that, in whole or in part, supersedes the *factory configuration.* By using an *initialization string,* you can configure the modem to work well with your *communications program.*

In disks, the process of *formatting* a hard disk and floppy disks so that they are ready for use.

initialization string In *modems,* a group of *AT commands,* issued to the modem by a *communications program* at the beginning of a communication session, that establishes an *active configuration.* Initialization strings enable communications programs to work smoothly with a variety of modems, and often you can choose an initialization string appropriate for your modem from a list provided in your communications program. See *initialization.*

initialize To prepare *hardware* or *software* to perform a task. A *serial port* is initialized using the MODE command to set the *baud, parity, data,* and *stop bit* values, for example. In some programs, initializing can be setting a counter or *variable* to zero before running a procedure.

inkjet printer   A *non-impact printer* that forms an image by spraying ink from a matrix of tiny jets.

Inkjet printers are quiet and can produce excellent results. Hewlett-Packard's DeskJet and DeskWriter printers can produce text and *graphics* at resolutions of *300 dots per inch (dpi)* and better, rivaling the output of *laser printers* to the untrained eye.

CAUTION: *The ink used by most inkjet printers is water-soluble and smears easily.*

in-line image   In a document prepared for the *World Wide Web (WWW)*, a graphic that has been placed so that it appears on the same line with text. In *HyperText Markup Language (HTML)*, in-line images are defined by the IMG tag, which specifies the source of the graphic, its alignment (top, middle, or bottom), and the text to display if the document is accessed by a text-only browser.

in-place activation   In *Object Linking and Embedding (OLE)* in *Microsoft Windows 95,* the use of a *server application's* functions within the *client application*, without the need to switch to a *window* containing the server application.

input   Any *information* entered into a computer.

input device   Any *peripheral* that assists you in getting data into a computer, such as a *keyboard, mouse, trackball, voice recognition* system, *graphics tablet*, or *modem*.

input/output (I/O) redirection   In DOS and *UNIX,* the routing of a program's *output* to a *file* or device, or the routing of a program's input from a file rather than the *keyboard*.

Most DOS commands (such as DIR) send output to the screen, but you can easily redirect a command's output by using the greater-than sign (>). To redirect the output of DIR to the LPT1 (printer) port, for example, you type **DIR > lpt1** and press Enter. To redirect the command's output to a file, type **DIR > dir.txt** and press Enter. In DOS, input redirection is frequently used with filters. See *filter* and *MS-DOS*.

input/output (I/O) system   One of the chief components of a computer system's architecture, the link between the *microprocessor* and its surrounding components.

Insert (Ins) key   On IBM PC-compatible *keyboards*, a programmable key frequently (but not always) used to toggle between *insert mode* and *overtype mode* when entering text.

insert mode   In *word processing* programs, a program mode in which inserted text pushes existing text to the right and down. The Insert key is used to toggle between insert and *overtype modes.*

insertion point   In Macintosh and *Microsoft Windows* applications, the blinking vertical bar that shows the point at which text will appear when you start typing. The insertion point is similar to the *cursor* in DOS applications.

installation program   A *utility program* provided with an *application* that helps you install the program on a *hard disk* and configure the program so you can use it.

CAUTION: *In IBM PC-compatible computing, installation programs sometimes must change the* CONFIG.SYS *configuration file or the* AUTOEXEC.BAT *startup file on your hard disk. Some programs append instructions to the existing files, whereas others may actually delete files without asking you and write new ones in their place. If an old program stops working just after you install a program, the newly installed program may be the offender. Make a copy of both files before installing new programs in case the new program deletes the originals or modifies them so that they no longer work.*

Institute for Certification of Computer Professionals (ICCP)   An organization that sanctions examinations that establish professional competence in various computer fields. The ICCP awards data processing and computer programming certification, making people who pass its examinations *Certified Data Processors (CDPs)* and *Certified Computer Programmers (CCPs).* Though ICCP certification is recognized as a professional achievement, it is rarely required for employment or for the awarding of a contract.

Institute of Electrical and Electronic Engineers (IEEE) A membership organization of engineers, scientists, and students. IEEE has also declared standards for computers and communications. Of particular interest is the *IEEE 802 standard* for local area networks, although the IEEE drew up a complete set of specifications for the *AT bus,* also called the ISA bus. See *Industry Standard Architecture (ISA)*.

Institute of Electrical and Electronic Engineers Computer Society (IEEE Computer Society) A part of the *Institute of Electrical and Electronic Engineers (IEEE)* that specializes in computer issues. The IEEE Computer Society holds conferences and sponsors publications on computer-related topics.

instruction In *programming,* a program statement interpreted or compiled into *machine language*. See *interpreter* and *compiler.*

instruction cycle The time it takes a *central processing unit (CPU)* to carry out one instruction and move on to the next.

instruction set A list of keywords describing all the actions or operations that *a central processing unit (CPU)* can perform. See *complex instruction set computer (CISC)* and *reduced instruction set computer (RISC).*

integer A whole number. If a number contains decimal places, the numbers to the left of the decimal point are the integer portion of the number.

integrated accounting package An accounting program that includes all the major accounting functions: general ledger, accounts payable, accounts receivable, payroll, and inventory. Integrated programs update the general ledger every time an accounts payable or accounts receivable transaction occurs.

integrated circuit A *semiconductor* that contains more than one electronic component. Synonymous with chip.

Integrated Drive Electronics (IDE) A *hard disk interface* standard for 80286, 80386, 80486, and Pentium computers that offers high performance at low cost. The IDE standard transfers most of the controller electronics to the hard disk assembly. For this reason, the IDE interface can be contained on the computer's motherboard; no *controller card* or expansion slot is necessary. See *IDE drive.*

integrated program   A *program* that combines two or more software functions, such as *word processing* and *database management.* Microsoft Works for DOS or *Microsoft Windows* and ClarisWorks for Macintosh are examples of integrated programs.

Integrated Services Digital Network (ISDN)   A worldwide standard for the delivery of digital telephone and data services to homes, schools, and offices. Widely implemented in Europe and Japan, ISDN service has been delayed in the U.S. owing to the development of incompatible variations by the regional Bell operating companies (RBOC). This problem was solved by the 1991 publication of the ISDN-1 standard, to which the RBOCs agreed to abide. ISDN services fall into to three categories: *Basic Rate ISDN (BRI), Primary Rate ISDN (PRI),* and *Broadband ISDN (B-ISDN).* Designed as the basic option for consumers, Basic Rate ISDN offers two 64,000 bit per second channels for voice, graphics, and data, plus one 16,000 bit per second channel for signalling purposes. Primary Rate ISDN provides 23 channels with 64,000 bits per second capacity. Broadband ISDN, still under development, would supply up to 150 million bits per second of data transmission capacity.

Intel   The world's largest manufacturer of *microprocessors* and other *semiconductors,* based in Santa Clara, California. About three-fourths of the world's *microcomputers* have Intel *central processing units (CPUs).* Intel faces competition from several companies, including *Advanced Micro Devices (AMD), Cyrix,* and *NexGen.*

Intel 386DX   See *Intel 80386.*

Intel 386SL   A power-conserving variation of the *Intel 386SX* designed with *power management* features for use in *portable computers.* The 386SL includes a *sleep mode* that preserves work, while using very little electricity, during periods of disuse.

Intel 386SX   A slower but less expensive version of the *Intel 80386 microprocessor.* The 386SX uses a 16-bit *external data bus,* compared with the 386DX's 32-bit data pathway. The 386SX can address only 20*M* of *random-access memory (RAM),* compared to the 386DX's ability to handle 4*G* of RAM.

I
J
K

Intel 486DX   The *32-bit microprocessor* that, in its various modifications (such as the *Intel 486DX2* and *Intel 486DX4*), strikes the best balance between cost and performance today, though it is rapidly losing market share to the *Pentium.* Introduced in 1989, the 486DX offers a significant speed improvement over the Intel *386DX,* its predecessor. By using *pipelining* and an on-board *numeric coprocessor,* the 486DX can manage 4*G* of *random-access memory (RAM)* and 64*T* of *virtual memory.* The two versions of the 486DX operate at *clock speeds* of 25 *megahertz (MHz)* and 33 MHz, though *clock-doubled* and *clock-tripled* versions operate at higher clock speeds. See *Intel 486SX.*

Intel 486DX2   An improvement on the *Intel 486DX* that uses *clock-doubling* techniques to achieve *clock speeds* inside the *microprocessor* of 50 *megahertz (MHz)* or 66 MHz, while the microprocessor is installed on a *motherboard* running at half the chip's clock speed (25 MHz or 33 MHz, respectively). Though the performance of the microprocessor far outstrips the performance of the motherboard, good *external cache* design can minimize the time a clock-doubled microprocessor spends waiting for the motherboard to catch up with it.

Intel 486DX4   An improved version of the *Intel 486DX microprocessor* that, by means of *clock tripling,* operates at *clock speeds* of 75 *megahertz (MHz)* or 100 MHz. The 486DX4 boasts a larger *internal cache* than other 486s, and operates at 3.3 volts instead of 5 volts. 486DX4-equipped computers are valid alternatives to low-end *Pentium* machines.

Intel 486SL   A power-saving version of the *Intel 486DX microprocessor.* Designed for *portable computers,* the 486SL includes a *sleep mode* that lets you stop working and start again later without having to *reboot.*

Intel 486SX   A 32-bit *microprocessor* based on the *Intel 486DX,* but without the 486DX's *numeric coprocessor.* Designed to be a slower but more affordable alternative to the 486DX, the two versions of the 486SX run at *clock speeds* of 20 *megahertz (MHz)* and 25 MHz.

Intel 4004   The first *microprocessor,* unveiled in 1971. A 4-bit *chip* operating at about 0.1-*megahertz (MHz),* the 4004 was used in programmable calculators.

Intel 8080   The 8-bit *microprocessor* found in the Altair, a popular 1970s *microcomputer.* The Intel 8080, which runs at a *clock speed* of 2 *MHz,* has a 16-bit address bus and can handle one-half million instructions per second. The Intel 8080 was obsolete by the early 1980s.

Intel 8088   Essentially an Intel 8086 with an 8-bit data bus, the 4.77 megahertz (MHz) Intel 8088 was the engine in the earliest IBM personal computers. Though it was a 16-bit *microprocessor,* the 8086's 8-bit data bus enabled computer manufacturers to use inexpensive, off-the-shelf 8-bit *peripherals.*

Intel 80286   The now obsolete 16-bit *microprocessor* that was used in the IBM Personal Computer AT, unveiled in 1984, and compatible computers. The 80286 operates at *clock speeds* as fast as 20 *MHz,* and can use its 24-bit address bus to work with as much as 16 *M* of *random-access memory (RAM)* and 1 *G* of virtual memory. Unlike previous personal computer microprocessors, the 80286 has the ability to operate in both *real mode* and *protected mode.* Unfortunately, it cannot switch between the two modes without *rebooting*—a serious design flaw that led to the 80286's unseating by the Intel 80386.

Intel 80386   As the oldest *microprocessor* capable of taking full advantage of *Microsoft Windows,* the Intel 80386 boasts *32-bit processing* ability, the ability to switch from *real mode* to *protected mode* without *rebooting,* and a 32-bit *address bus* that lets it manage as much as 4 *G* of *random-access memory (RAM)* and 64 *T* of *virtual memory.* Various versions of the 80386 run at *clock speeds* of 16 *megahertz (MHz),* 20 MHz, 25 MHz, and 33 MHz. The 80386 was renamed the 386DX when the *Intel 386SX* (a cheaper version of the microprocessor, with a 16-bit data bus) was introduced. Make sure any 386 you buy has two sigmas printed on it—unmarked early versions of the *chip* had a flaw that Intel later corrected.

Intel P6   The as-yet-unreleased heir apparent to the *Pentium* and *x86* legacy. Said to employ *superscalar architecture, super-pipelining, reduced instruction-set computer (RISC)* technology, *speculative execution, register renaming,* and *out-of-order execution* capability, the P6 should have twice the integer-processing power of the Pentium. The first P6s, supposed to be unveiled in late 1995 or early 1996, are rumored to run at *clock speeds* of 133 *megahertz (MHz).*

interactive processing   A method displaying the computer's operations on a monitor so the user can catch and correct errors before the processing operation is completed.

Certain features of today's programs, however, recall the days when computer operations were performed in batches, invisible to the user. *Word processing* programs, for example, sometimes require you to embed formatting commands into the text without show-ing you their effects directly on-screen. See *batch processing.*

interactive videodisk   A *computer-assisted instruction (CAI)* technology that uses a computer to provide access to up to two hours of video information stored on a videodisk.

Like *CD-ROM*, videodisks are *read-only* optical storage media, but are designed for the storage and *random-access* retrieval of images, including stills and continuous video. You need a *front-end* pro-gram to access the videodisk information. With a videodisk of paintings in the National Gallery of Art, the user can demand, "Show me all the Renaissance paintings that depict flowers or gardens," and be led through a series of vivid instructional experi-ences while retaining complete control.

Inter-Application Communication (IAC)   In the Macintosh *System 7,* a specification for creating *hot links* and *cold links* between applications.

interface   The connection between two *hardware* devices, between two *applications*, or between a user and an application that facilitates the exchange of data.

interface standard   A set of specifications for the connection between the two *hardware* devices, such as the drive controller and the drive electronics in a hard disk. Common hard disk interface standards in personal computing include ST506, *Enhanced System Device Interface (ESDI),* and *Small Computer System Interface (SCSI).* Other standards exist for connections with serial and parallel ports, such as the *Centronics interface.* See *ST-506/ST-412.*

interlaced   See *interlacing.*

interlacing   A *monitor* technology that uses the monitor's electron gun to paint every other line of the screen with the first pass and the remaining lines on the second pass. When most of the screen display is a solid, light-color background, the eye perceives the alternating painted and fading lines as a slight flicker or shimmer. This technique provides higher resolution, but at the price of visual comfort.

TIP: *When you buy a monitor, make sure it's a non-interlaced monitor.*

interleaved memory   A method of speeding the retrieval of data from *dynamic random-access memory (DRAM)* chips by dividing all the RAM into two or four large banks; sequential bits of data are stored in alternating banks. The microprocessor reads one bank while the other is being refreshed. Naturally, this memory arrangement doesn't improve speed when the central processing unit (CPU) requests non-sequential bits of data. See *random-access memory (RAM)*.

interleave factor   The ratio of physical disk *sectors* on a hard disk that are skipped for every sector actually used for write operations.

With an interleave factor of 6:1, a disk writes to a sector, skips six sectors, writes to a sector, and so on. The computer figures out what it needs next and sends the request to the hard drive while the disk is skipping sectors. 80386SX and higher computers operate faster than hard disks, so a 1:1 interleave is standard today.

The interleave factor is set by the hard disk manufacturer but can be changed by software capable of performing a *low-level format.* Synonymous with sector interleave.

interleaving   A method of intentionally slowing down the reading of data from a *hard disk* to prevent the hard disk from outrunning other parts of the computer system. By placing sectors in non-sequential order, the read/write head has to jump around while collecting data. The *interleave factor* describes the amount of interleaving employed on a hard disk.

internal cache   An 8K holding area for data included as part of the *Intel 80486* and *Pentium microprocessor* design. Synonymous with primary cache.

The cache included on the 486 chip uses a *set-associative write-through* design, while the two caches on the Pentium chip use a more efficient set-associative *write-back* scheme. Although small,

I
J
K

these caches can achieve an excellent "hit" rate—that is, the number of times the data requested next is found in the cache.

To further improve performance, the cache feeds requested data directly to a *pipeline* designed to optimize delivery to the processing area. Part of the reason for the faster performance of the Pentium microprocessor is its use of two caches: one to handle data and the other for instructions. Each cache has its own direct pipeline. See *cache memory*.

internal command   In DOS, a command such as DIR or COPY that's part of COMMAND.COM, and therefore is in memory and available whenever the DOS prompt is visible on-screen. See *external command*.

internal data bus   The circuitry on which data moves inside a *microprocessor*. Internal data bus size is measured in *bits*: the more bits a bus can handle (the wider it is), the faster it can move data. The internal data bus is independent of the *external data bus*, which is often half as wide as the internal data bus.

internal font   See *printer font*.

internal hard disk   A *hard disk* designed to fit within a computer's case and use electricity from the computer's *power supply*.

TIP: *Because internal hard disks don't require their own power supply, case, or cables, they generally cost less than external hard disks of comparable quality.*

In printers, a hard disk drive in the printer that stores *font* information.

internal modem   A *modem* designed to fit into the *expansion bus* of a personal computer. See *external modem*.

internal navigation aid   In a series of related *World Wide Web (WWW)* documents (a web), the hyperlinks or clickable buttons that provide users with a way of navigating through the documents without getting lost. If you see a "Home" button on one of the pages in a web, for example, you can click it to return to the web's *welcome page.* This is different from clicking the browser's Home button, which displays the browser's default *home page*. See *home page*.

International Standards Organization (ISO)   A non-profit organization, headquartered in Geneva, Switzerland, that seeks technological and scientific advancement by establishing non-proprietary standards. An umbrella organization for the standards bodies of more than 90 nations, the ISO is responsible for the development of the Open System Interconnect (OSI) Reference Model, a means of conceptualizing computer networks that has proven extremely influential. In the U.S., the ISO is represented by the *American National Standards Institute (ANSI)*.

International Telecommunications Union-Telecommunications Standards Section (ITU-TSS)
An organization, sponsored by the United Nations, that sets standards for communications technology. In computers, ITU-TSS standards, such as the widely used *V.32bis* protocol that governs some *high-speed modem* communications, enable *modems* from different manufacturers to communicate with one another. The ITU-TSS is the successor the the Comité Consultatif International Téléphonique et Télégraphique (CCITT).

internet   A group of local area networks (LANs) that have been connected by means of a common communications protocol. Note the small "i"—many internets exist besides the *Internet,* including many TCP/IP based networks that are not linked to the Internet (the Defense Data Network is a case in point).

Internet   A system of linked computer networks, worldwide in scope, that facilitates data communication services such as remote login, file transfer, electronic mail, and newsgroups. The Internet is a way of connecting existing computer networks that greatly extends the reach of each participating system.

The Internet, in its first incarnation as the ARPAnet, was designed to serve military institutions, yet its technology allows virtually any system to link to it via an electronic gateway. In this way, thousands of corporate computer systems, as well as for-profit electronic mail systems such as MCI and CompuServe, have become part of the Internet. With more than 2 million host computers serving an estimated 20 million users, the Internet is exploding at the rate of a million new users each month.

TIP: *Almost anyone can gain access to the Internet. If you're a student or faculty member at a college or university, ask your campus computing center how to access the Internet. Many large- and medium-sized corporations with electronic mail systems have Internet gateways. Increasingly, for-profit electronic mail services (such as CompuServe and MCI) offer Internet gateways, as do some local bulletin-board systems (BBSs). In some areas, freenets provide Internet gateways at no charge.*

See *America Online, anonymous FTP, archie, ARPAnet, BITNET, BIX, Delphi, distributed bulletin board, electronic mail, FAQ, Fidonet, file transfer protocol (FTP), freenet, gateway, Gopher, host, MUD, net.god(dess), netiquette, NSFNet, packet-switching network, protocol, telnet, Transfer Control Protocol/Internet Protocol (TCP/IP), unmoderated newsgroup, UseNet, Wide Area Information Server (WAIS), World Wide Web (WWW),* and *wide area network.*

Internet Activities Board (IAB)   An organization, founded in 1983, that was charged with the development of TCP/IP; its activities have been taken over by the *Internet Architecture Board (IAB).*

Internet Architecture Board (IAB)   A unit of the *Internet Society* that provides broad-level oversight over the *Internet's* technical development and adjudicates technical disputes that occur in the standards-setting process. Among the units that the organization oversees are *Internet Engineering Task Force (IETF), Internet Research Task Force (IRTF),* and *Internet Assigned Numbers Authority (IANA).*

Internet Assigned Numbers Authority (IANA)   A unit of the *Internet Architecture Board (IAB)* that supervises the allocation of IP addresses, port addresses, and other numerical standards on the *Internet.*

Internet Draft   A working document of the *Internet Engineering Task Force (IETF),* a unit of the *Internet Architecture Board (IAB).* Internet Drafts are unofficial discussion documents, meant to be circulated on the *Internet,* that are not intended to delineate new standards.

Internet Engineering and Planning Group (IEPG) A unit of the *Internet Society* that promotes the technical coordination of day-to-day *Internet* operations. IEPG is composed of Internet backbone service providers and is not concerned with the development of new standards.

Internet Engineering Steering Group (IESG) A unit of the *Internet Society* that reviews proposed standards created by the *Internet Engineering Task Force (IETF),* in consultation with the *Internet Architecture Board (IAB);* standards are published in the form of *Requests for Comments (RFC).*

Internet Engineering Task Force (IETF) A unit of the *Internet Architecture Board (IAB)* that is concerned with the immediate technical challenges facing the *Internet.* The IETF's technical work is done in a number of working groups, which are organized by topics such as security, routing, and network management. Managed by the *Internet Engineering Steering Group (IESG),* the IETF convenes several meetings per year and publishes its proceedings.

Internet Experiment Notes (IEN) An obsolete publication series that was formerly used to report the results of research on the *TCP/IP* protocols.

Internet Monthly Report (IMR) A monthly publication of the *Internet Architecture Board (IAB)* that summarizes the current status of the Internet. The report includes statistical summaries of usage, descriptions of technical challenges and the steps being taken to meet them, and the reports of various technical committees.

Internet PCA Registration Authority (IPRA) A unit of the *Internet Society* that is devoted to the global implementation of *public key crytopography* applications on the *Internet,* both for the purposes of *authentication* and *privacy.*

Internet Protocol (IP) In *TCP/IP,* the standard that describes how an Internet-connected computer should break data down into packets for transmission across the network, and how those packets should be addressed so that they arrive at their destination. IP is the connectionless part of the TCP/IP protocols; the *Transmission Control Protocol (TCP)* specifies how two Internet computers can establish a reliable data link by means of *handshaking.* See *connectionless protocol* and *packet-switching network.*

I ◄
J
K

Internet Relay Chat (IRC)   A real-time, Internet-based chat service, in which one can find "live" participants from the world over. Created by Jarkko Oikarinen of Finland in 1988, IRC requires the use of an IRC client program, which displays a list of the current IRC "channels." The names of each channel, created by participants with the requisite technical knowledge to create and name them, sometimes indicate the channel's interest area, such as Elfquest comics. After joining a channel, you can see what other participants are typing on-screen, and you can type your own repartee. There is often a frustrating delay, however, before others see your message and respond. Also, many IRC channels are dominated by inconsiderate people who think IRC is the appropriate place to show off their technical talents.

Internet Research Task Force (IRTF)   A unit of the *Internet Architecture Board (IAB)* that deals with the long-range challenges facing the Internet, such as the lack of sufficient IP addresses.

Internet Society (ISOC)   An international, not-for-profit organization, headquartered in Reston, Virginia, that seeks to maintain and broaden the *Internet's* availability. Created in 1992, ISOC is governed by an elected board of trustees. Members include individuals and organizations (including service providers, product providers, Internet enterprise operators, educational institutions, computer professional organizations, international treaty organizations, and government agencies). The organization sponsors annual conferences and has numerous publication programs. Spearheading the Internet's technical operation and development, the Internet Society coordinates the activities of the *Internet Architecture Board (IAB),* the *Internet Engineering Task Force (IETF),* the *Internet Engineering Steering Group (IESG),* the *Internet Engineering and Planning Group (IEPG),* the *Internet Assigned Numbers Authority (IANA),* and the *Internet PCA Registration Authority (IPRA).*

Internet Talk Radio   An experiment in the distribution of high-quality audio programs, 30 minutes to one hour in length, via the *Internet.* Each program is disseminated as an audio file that can be downloaded via *file transfer protocol (FTP).* Popular programs include the Internet Hall of Flame (noteworthy instances of bizarre behavior on mailing lists) and the Geek of the Week. One drawback: a half-hour audio file in the *.au format consumes 15M of disk space.

Internet Worm   A rogue program, ostensibly designed as a harmless experiment, that propogated throughout the Internet in 1988, overloading and shutting down thousands of computer systems worldwide. Robert Morris, Jr., the author of the program and at the time a graduate student in computer science at Cornell University, was convicted under the *Computer Fraud and Abuse Act of 1986*. He was sentenced to 3 years of probation, 400 hours of community service, and a $10,000 fine.

InterNIC   A consortium of two organizations that provide networking information services to the *Internet* community, under contract to the *National Science Foundation (NSF)*. Currently, AT&T provides directory and database services, while Network Solutions, Inc., provides registration services for new *domain names* and *IP addresses*.

Intero   See *Networld + InterOp*.

interoperability   The ability of one computer system to control another, even though the two systems are made by different manufacturers. Interoperability is one of the chief technical achievements of the *TCP/IP* protocols; using *File Transfer Protocol (FTP)*, for instance, you can use a Macintosh to log on to a *Sun workstation*, and direct that workstation to send a file to you via the Internet. In another example, a U.S. Robotics *modem* can exchange data with a Zoom modem, as long as both conform to a common standard such as *v.32bis*.

Interpedia   A public-domain encyclopedia, still in the planning stages, that will provide *Internet* users with free access to information. A unique feature of the Interpedia project is that the planned encyclopedia will not be refereed; anyone who wishes to do so may contribute an article on any subject, or a commentary on an existing article, so long as they indicate their biases.

interpolated resolution   A means of improving the output of a *scanner* by means of a software *algorithm*. Instead of relying solely on closely spaced *charge-coupled devices (CCDs)*, scanners that use interpolated resolution average the readings of each pair of adjacent CCDs and insert an extra *pixel* between them. Though a given interpolated resolution is not as good as the same *optical resolution*, it can cost-effectively improve scan quality.

interpreter   A translator for a *high-level programming language* that translates and runs the program at the same time. Interpreters are excellent for learning how to program, because if an error occurs, the interpreter shows you the likely place (and sometimes even the cause) of the error. You can correct the problem immediately and execute the program again, learning interactively how to create a successful program. See *compiler.*

interprocess communication (IPC)   In a *multitasking* computing environment such as *Microsoft Windows* running in the *386 Enhanced mode*, the communication of data or commands from one program to another while both are running, made possible by *dynamic data exchange (DDE)* specifications. In *Microsoft Excel*, for instance, you can write a DDE command that accesses changing data, such as stock prices, that's being received on-line in a communications program.

interrupt   A signal to the *microprocessor* indicating that an event has occurred that requires its attention. Processing is halted momentarily so that input/output or other operations can take place. When the operation is finished, processing resumes.

interrupt controller   Part of the *motherboard's chip set* that distributes hardware *interrupt request (IRQ) lines.* The interrupt controller prevents more than one *peripheral* device from communicating with the *microprocessor* at one time.

interrupt request (IRQ) lines   For IBM PC-compatible computers, the hardware lines over which *peripherals* (such as printers or modems) can get the attention of the microprocessor when the device is ready to send or receive data.

InterSLIP   A *freeware* program, created by InterCon Systems Corp., that provides *Serial Line Internet Protocol (SLIP)* connectivity, including a dialer program, for Macintosh computers. InterSLIP requires *MacTCP.*

Intuit Quicken Deluxe   A personal-finance management *program* that keeps track of transactions in your savings, checking, and investment accounts, and can help you plan to meet savings goals. Intuit Quicken Deluxe can also generate a variety of reports about your monetary situation, such as your net worth, the status of your mortgage, or your progress in saving for retirement. Intuit Quicken Deluxe competes with Microsoft Money, which offers similar features.

A word of warning: personal-finance software can be addictive. A recent *Washington Post* article quoted an Intuit Quicken Deluxe user as saying, "I like to keep track of where my dimes go."

invisible file   See *hidden file.*

I/O   See *input/output (I/O) system.*

i/o adapter   An *adapter* that plugs into your computer's *expansion bus* and provides several ports to which peripheral devices may attach. Typically, an i/o adapter provides a *bidirectional parallel port,* a *serial port* with a *16550A Universal Asynchronous Receiver/ Transmitter (UART),* and a *game port.* Often, ports are built into the *motherboard* and an i/o adapter is not needed.

i/o buffering   A feature of *high-end network printers* that enables them to print one document while receiving information about another, which is to be printed next.

IP address   A 32-bit *binary number* that uniquely and precisely identifies the location of a particular computer on the *Internet.* Every computer that is directly connected to the Internet must have an IP address. Because binary numbers are so hard to read, IP addresses are given in four-part decimal numbers, each part representing 8 bits of the 32-bit address (for example, 128.143.7.226). On networks and *SLIP/PPP* connections that dynamically assign IP numbers when you log on, this number may change from session to session. See *domain name.*

IPC   See *interprocess communication (IPC).*

IRQ   See *interrupt request (IRQ) lines.*

IRQ conflict   A problem that results when two *peripheral* devices have been assigned the same *interrupt request (IRQ) line* and try to communicate with the *microprocessor* simultaneously. Assigning a new peripheral an unused IRQ line in order to prevent an IRQ conflict is usually done by trial and error, but the *Plug and Play* standard is supposed to eliminate guesswork in installing new *adapters.*

ISA   See *Industry Standard Architecture (ISA) expansion bus.*

ISA slot   A receptacle on the *motherboard* that accepts *peripherals* designed to conform to the *Industry Standard Architecture (ISA)* standard. ISA slots are not as fast as *VESA local bus slots* or

Peripheral Component Interconnect (PCI) bus slots, but they continue to appear alongside those faster slots on the expansion buses of modern computers. See *expansion bus*.

ISO 9660   The current standard for encoding data onto *CD-ROMs*. Practically all *CD-ROM disk drives* embrace the ISO 9660 standard, though a few cling to the obsolete, incompatible *High Sierra* standard on which ISO 9660 is based.

ISO Latin 1   A character set defined by the *International Standards Organization (ISO)*. ISO Latin 1 contains the characters needed for most Western European languages, and also contains a non-breaking space, a soft hyphen indicator, 93 *graphics characters*, and 25 control characters. With certain exceptions, ISO Latin 1 is the default character set used in *HyperText Markup Languge (HTML)*.

issue restrictions   In a *microprocessor* with *superscalar architecture* and multiple *pipelines*, the set of rules that determines whether two instructions may be processed simultaneously. Generally, the fewer issue restrictions a microprocessor has, the faster it processes instructions. See *data dependency* and *false data dependency*.

italic   A *typeface* characteristic, commonly used for emphasis, in which the characters slant to the right. Two words in the following sentence are in italic. See *oblique* and *Roman*.

iteration   The repetition of a command or program statement. See *loop*.

ITU-TSS   See *International Telecommunications Union-Telecommunications Standards Section (ITU-TSS)*.

jaggies See *aliasing*.

jitter In a *network*, an annoying and perceptible variation in the time it takes various workstations to respond to messages—some respond quickly, while some respond slowly, and some do not respond at all. Jitter is to be expected when the network cannot ensure fixed latency, the amount of time required for a message to travel from point A to point B in a network.

job A task for a computer. The word derives from the days when people had to take their *programs* to a computing department to be run on a *mainframe*, and thereby assign a job to the computing department.

job control language (JCL) In *mainframe* computing, a programming language that allows programmers to specify *batch processing* instructions, which the computer then carries out. The abbreviation JCL refers to the job control language used in IBM mainframes.

job queue A series of tasks automatically executed, one after the other, by the computer.

In *mainframe* data processing during the 1950s and 1960s, the job queue was literally a queue, or line of people waiting to have their programs run. With interactive, multi-user computing and personal computing, you usually don't need to line up to get your work done (although jobs can still back up at a busy *printer*). The term is still used in *WordPerfect*, for example, where you can assign a job number to several files you want to print, and the program prints the files in the order you assign.

join In a *relational database management program*, a data retrieval operation in which a new *data table* is built from data in two or more existing data tables.

To understand how a join works and why join operations are desirable in database applications, suppose that for your video store you create a database table called RENTALS that lists the rented tapes with the phone number of the person renting the tape and the due date. You create another database table, called CUSTOMERS, in which you list the phone number, name, and credit card number of all your customers. To find out whether any customers are more than two weeks late returning a tape, you need to join information from the two databases. Suppose that you want to know the title and due date of the movie and the phone number and name of the customer. The following *Structured Query Language (SQL)* command retrieves the information:

```
SELECT TITLE, DUE_DATE, PHONE_NO, L_NAME, F_NAME
FROM RENTALS, CUSTOMERS
WHERE DUE_DATE=<05/07/92
```

This command tells the program to display the information contained in the data fields TITLE, DUE_DATE, PHONE_NO, L_NAME, and F_NAME, but only for those records in which the data field DUE_DATE contains a date equal to or earlier than May 7, 1992. The result is the following display:

TITLE	DUE_DATE	PHONE_NO	L_NAME	F_NAME
Alien Beings	05/07/92	499-1234	Jones	Terry
Almost Home	05/05/92	499-7890	Smith	Jake

See *join condition*.

join condition   In a *relational database management* program, a statement of how two *databases* are to be joined together to form a single table. The statement usually specifies a field common to both databases as the condition for joining records. See *join*.

Joint Photographic Experts Group (JPEG)   A committee of computer graphics experts, jointly sponsored by the *International Standards Organization (ISO)* and the *Comité Consultif International de Télégraphique et Téléphonique (CCITT),* that developed the *JPEG graphics* standard.

Joint Photographic Experts Group (JPEG) graphic
A graphics format that is ideal for complex pictures of natural, real-world scenes, including photographs, realistic artwork, and paintings. (The format is not well suited to line drawings, text, or simple cartoons.) Developed by the *Joint Photographic Experts Group (JPEG)*, a committee created by two international

standards bodies, the JPEG graphic format employs lossy compression. Exploiting a known property of human vision, namely that small color changes are less noticeable than changes in brightness, JPEG compression is not noticeable unless very high compression ratios are chosen. Typically, JPEG can achieve compression ratios of 10:1 or 20:1 without noticeable degradation in picture quality—a much better compression ratio than that of the *Graphics Interchange Format (GIF)*.

joystick   A control device widely used, as an alternative to the keyboard, for computer games and some professional applications, such as computer-aided design.

JPEG   See *Joint Photographic Experts Group (JPEG)*.

JPEG graphic   See *Joint Photographic Experts Group (JPEG) graphic*.

Jughead   In *Gopher,* a search service that enables you to search all of *Gopherspace* for key words appearing in directory titles (not menu items). To search both directory titles and menu items, use *Veronica*.

jukebox   See *CD-ROM changer*.

jump line   A message at the end of part of an article in a newsletter, magazine, or newspaper, indicating the page on which the article is continued. *Desktop publishing programs* include features that make using jump lines for newsletters easier.

jumper   An electrical connector that allows the user to select a particular configuration on a *circuit board*. The jumper is a small rectangle of plastic with two or three receptacles. You install a jumper by pushing it down on two or more pins from a selection of many that are sticking up from the circuit board's surface. The placement of the jumper completes the circuit for the configuration you want to use.

jumper settings   The configuration of movable conductors on an *adapter*. Jumper settings dictate how an adapter interacts with the rest of a system—by determining its *interrupt request (IRQ) channel,* for example.

I
J
K

justification   The alignment of multiple lines of text along the left margin, the right margin, or both margins. The term justification often is used to refer to full justification, or the alignment of text along both margins. See *color*.

 CAUTION: *When using a* monospaced *font, programs justify both margins by placing extra spaces between words, creating an uneven appearance. Proportional spaced fonts can have space added between letters as well as words to create a more even appearance. Regardless, research has shown that text formatted with a ragged right margin is easier to read than fully justified text.*

K Abbreviation for *kilobyte* (1,024 bytes).

KB Alternative abbreviation for *kilobyte* (1,024 bytes).

Kbps See *bits per second (bps).*

Kermit An *asynchronous communications* protocol that makes the error-free transmission of program files via the telephone system easier. Developed by Columbia University and placed in the public domain, Kermit is used by academic institutions because, unlike *XMODEM,* Kermit can be implemented on mainframe systems that transmit 7 bits per byte. See *communications protocol.*

kernel In an operating system, the core portions of the program that reside in memory and perform the most essential operating system tasks, such as handling disk input and output operations and managing the internal memory.

kerning The adjustment of space between certain pairs of characters, so that the characters print in an aesthetically pleasing manner.

Kerning is used for the *body type* in this book. The underlined pairs of characters in the next paragraph illustrate the use of kerning to decrease the space between the character pairs.

Some page layout programs include an automatic kerning <u>fe</u>ature, relying on a built-in database of letter pairs that require kerning (such as AV, VA, WA, YA, and so on). Manual kerning is possible with most page layout and some <u>wo</u>rd processing programs (see fig. K.1).

Before   After

Fig. K.1 *Kerning with PageMaker.*

Kerr effect   The tendency of *polarized light* to shift its orientation slightly when reflected from a magnetized surface. *Magneto-optical disks* rely on the Kerr effect to read and write data.

key   In *cryptography,* the procedure that is used to encipher the message so that it appears to be just so much nonsense. The key also is required for *decryption.*

key assignments   The functions given to specific keys by a computer program. Most of the keys on a personal computer *keyboard* are fully programmable, meaning that a programmer can use them in different ways. The best programs, however, stick to an *industry standard user interface.*

key disk   A computer software protection scheme that requires the user to insert a specially encoded *floppy disk* before the program will start. This is intended to prevent the recipients of illegal copies of the program from running the program on their machines. Protection schemes that involve key disks are a hassle and are becoming rare. See *software piracy.*

key status indicator   An on-screen status message displayed by many application programs that informs you which, if any, *toggle keys* are active on the *keyboard.*

key variable   In a *spreadsheet* program, a constant placed in a *cell* and referenced throughout the spreadsheet using *absolute cell references.*

TIP: *The use of key variables is essential to good spreadsheet design. If you place a key variable, such as a tax or commission rate, in one cell and refer to the cell when its contents are needed in formulas, you need to make only one change if the rate changes. If you place the constant in all the formulas, you must change every formula to update your spreadsheet.*

keyboard   The most frequently used *input device.* The keyboard provides a set of alphabetic, numeric, punctuation, symbol, and control keys. When a character key is pressed, a coded input signal is sent to the computer, which echoes the signal by displaying a character on-screen. See *autorepeat key, keyboard layout,* and *toggle key.*

keyboard buffer   See *keystroke buffer*.

keyboard layout   The arrangement of keys on the computer's *keyboard*. A PC's keyboard layout uses the standard *QWERTY* layout that typewriters have used for a century. However, three different standards are used for arranging special computer keys such as Control and Alt: the original 83-key IBM PC keyboard (see fig. K.2), the 84-key IBM PC AT keyboard (see fig. K.3), and the current standard, the 101-key enhanced keyboard (see fig. K.4).

Fig. K.2 *The original PC keyboard.*

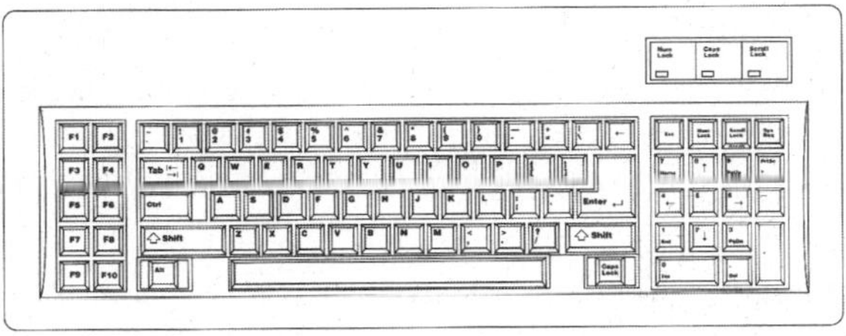

Fig. K.3 *The AT keyboard.*

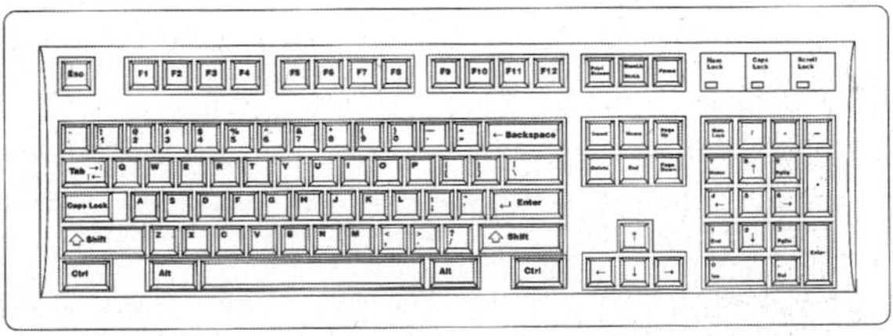

Fig. K.4 *The enhanced keyboard.*

➜ **TIP:** *Fast typists should make sure that the keyboard has N-key rollover, enabling you to press an additional key even while the previous key is still engaged at the end of a stroke. To find out whether a keyboard has N-key rollover, hold down the A key and press S D F in rapid succession. You may see several a characters, but you also should see the s, d, and f.*

keyboard template   A plastic card or strip with an adhesive backing that you can attach to the *keyboard* to explain the way a program configures the keyboard. Many applications provide keyboard templates, which are helpful when you're learning to use new programs.

keystroke   The physical action of pressing down a key on the *keyboard* so that a character is entered or a command is initiated.

keystroke buffer   A holding area in memory that's used to save your current *keystrokes* if you type something while the *microprocessor* is busy with something else. If, for example, you begin typing while a file is being saved, the characters you type are placed in the keystroke buffer. When it's full (usually the buffer holds 20 characters), you'll hear a beep each time you press another key, indicating that your input isn't being accepted. When the microprocessor completes its task, the characters in the buffer are sent to the screen.

keyword   In *programming languages* (including *software command languages*), a word describing an action or operation that the computer can recognize and execute. A *database query* might include several keywords.

In a document summary, one or more words that succinctly describe a document's contents. In the document summary of a letter inquiring about *green PCs*, a keyword might be electricity.

keyword search   In a *database* system, a search that begins by supplying the computer with one or more words that describe the topic of your search. To retrieve items on North Carolina's Outer Banks, for example, you could type "outer" and "banks." With most systems, you can use *Boolean operators* to focus or broaden the search. For example, if you type outer and banks, the system will retrieve only those documents in which both of these words appear.

kill   To stop an ongoing process. In the better UseNet *newsreaders,* to delete an article containing a certain word, name, or origin site so that articles containing this information do not appear subsequently in the article selector. See *article selector, global kill file, and kill file.*

kill file   In a *UseNet* newsreader, a file that contains a list of subjects or names that you don't want to appear on the list of messages available for you to read. If you no longer want to read messages from Edward P. Jerk, you can add Ed's name to your *newsreaders* kill file, and his contributions will be discarded automatically before they reach your screen.

Instead of posting a complaint to a *newsgroup,* use a kill file to keep offensive messages off your screen. That way, you won't receive angry messages that accuse you of ignorance, censorship, and worse. See *flame war.*

kilo-   A prefix indicating one thousand (10^3).

kilobit   1,024 bits of information. See *kilobyte (K).*

kilobyte (K)   The basic unit of measurement for computer memory and disk capacity, equal to 1,024 bytes. The prefix kilo-suggests 1,000, but the computer world is based on twos, not tens: 2^{10} = 1,024. Because one byte is the same as one character in personal computing, 1K of data can contain 1,024 characters (letters, numbers, or punctuation marks).

kiosk   A publicly accessible computer system that has been set up to allow interactive information browsing. In a kiosk, the computer's operating system has been hidden from view and the program runs in a full-screen mode, which provides a few simple tools for navigation. See *kiosk mode.*

kiosk mode   In a *Web browser,* a mode that zooms the program to full screen, permitting its use as an information navigation tool in a *kiosk.*

kludge   An improvised, technically inelegant solution to a problem, often a computer system assembled with poorly matched components. Also spelled kluge.

knowbot   See *agent.*

knowledge acquisition   In *expert system* programming, the process of acquiring and systematizing knowledge from experts.

A major limitation of current expert system technology is that *knowledge engineers* must aquire knowledge in a slow and painstaking process, called *knowledge representation,* that is designed to express the knowledge in terms of computer-readable rules.

knowledge base   In an *expert system*, the portion of the program that includes an expert's knowledge, often in IF/THEN rules. (Such as "If the tank pressure exceeds 600 pounds per square inch, then sound a warning".)

knowledge domain   In *artificial intelligence (AI)*, an area of problem-solving expertise. Current artificial intelligence technology works well only in sharply limited knowledge domains, such as the configuration of one manufacturer's computer systems, the repair of a specific robotic system, or investment analysis for a limited collection of securities.

knowledge engineer   In *expert system* programming, a specialist who obtains the knowledge possessed by experts on a subject and expresses this knowledge in a form that an expert system can use. See *knowledge domain.*

knowledge representation   In *expert system* programming, the method used to encode and store the knowledge in a *knowledge base.*

Although several alternative knowledge representation schemes are used, most commercially available expert systems use the production system approach in which knowledge is represented in the form of production rules, which have the following form:

IF {condition} THEN {action}

A given rule may have multiple conditions as in the following example:

IF {a person's intraocular pressure is raised}

AND {the person has pain in the left quadratic region}

THEN {immediate hospitalization is indicated}

L2 cache   See *secondary cache*.

label   In a spreadsheet program, text entered in a cell. A number entered in a cell, by contrast, is a *value*. In DOS batch files, a string of characters preceded by a colon that marks the destination of a GOTO command.

label alignment   In a *spreadsheet* program, the way *labels* are aligned in a cell (flush left, centered, flush right, or repeating across the cell). Unless you specify otherwise, labels are aligned on the left of the cell. See *label prefix*.

label prefix   In most *spreadsheet* programs, a punctuation mark at the beginning of a cell entry that tells the program that the entry is a label and specifies how the program should align the label within the cell.

TIP: *If you begin a cell entry with a number, the program interprets the number as a value rather than a label; however, you can make a number into a label by starting the entry with a label prefix. In Lotus 1-2-3, for example, if you type '1991, the program interprets the entry as a* label *and formats the label flush left. See* label alignment.

Programs that use prefixes enter the default label prefix—usually an apostrophe (')—when the cell entry begins with a letter. You can control the alignment of a label as you type it by beginning the label with one of these prefixes:

Label Prefix	Alignment
'	Flush left
^	Centered
"	Flush right
\	Repeating across the cell

label printer   A *printer* designed specifically to print names and addresses on continuous labels.

LAN backup program   A program designed specifically to back up the programs and data stored on a *local area network's (LAN's)* file server. The best LAN backup programs automatically back up the file server at scheduled times, without user intervention.

LAN memory management program   A *utility program* designed specifically to free *conventional memory* so that you can run applications on a network workstation. Every workstation must run local area network (LAN) software, which can consume as much as 100K of *conventional memory*. As a result, workstations may not be capable of running certain memory-hungry applications. *Local area network (LAN)* memory managers move the network software—as well as *device drivers, terminate-and-stay-resident (TSR)* programs, and other utilities—into the upper memory area, *extended memory,* or *expanded memory.* A popular and well-rated LAN management program is NetRoom by Helix Software. See *network operating system (NOS).*

LAN   See *local area network (LAN).*

LAN server   See *file server* and *print server.*

LAN-aware program   A version of an *application program* specifically modified so that the program can function in a *local area network (LAN)* environment.

Network versions of *transactional application* programs—such as database management programs—create and maintain shared files. An invoice-processing program, for example, has access to a database of accounts receivable. The network versions of *non-transactional programs*—such as word processing programs—include file security features to prevent unauthorized users from gaining access to your documents. LAN-aware programs boast such features as *concurrency control,* which manages multiple copies of files, and *file locking,* which prevents unauthorized users from accessing certain files. LAN-aware programs usually are stored on a *file server.* See *LAN-ignorant program.*

LAN-ignorant program   An *application program* designed for use only as a stand-alone program and that contains no provisions for use on a network (such as *file locking* and *concurrency control*).

landing zone   Ideally, the only area of a *hard disk's* surface that actually touches the *read/write head*. Through a process called *head parking*, the read/write head moves over the landing zone before the computer is shut off, and drifts to rest there. The landing zone, on which no data is encoded, is designed to prevent the read/write head from damaging portions of the disk used to store data—a *head crash*.

landscape font   A *font* in which the characters are oriented toward the long edge of the page. See *portrait font.*

landscape orientation   The rotation of a page layout so that text and/or graphics are printed sideways on the paper. See *portrait orientation.*

landscape printing   Printing so *graphics* and characters are oriented toward the long edge of the page. In landscape printing, the 11-inch sides of *A-size paper* are the top and bottom of the page.

laptop computer   A small, portable computer that's light and small enough to hold on your lap. Small laptop computers, which weigh less than 6 pounds and can fit in a briefcase, are called *note-book computers.* The smallest portable computers, weighing about 5 pounds, are called *subnotebook computers.*

Laptops aren't always a suitable replacement for desktop comput-ers, since they can't be expanded or modified easily should your computing needs change. Also, the display is inferior to standard *video graphics array (VGA)* displays, although *active matrix* displays compete well except for size. See *docking station.*

large-scale integration (LSI)   In integrated circuit technol-ogy, placing up to 100,000 transistors on a single chip. See *very large scale integration (VLSI).*

laser font   See *outline font.*

laser printer   A high-resolution printer that uses a version of the electrostatic reproduction technology of copying machines to fuse text and graphic images to paper.

To print a page, the printer's controller circuitry receives the printing instructions from the computer and builds a bit map of every dot on a page. The controller ensures that the *print engine's* laser transfers a precise replica of this bit map to a photostatically sensitive drum or belt. Switching on and off rapidly, the beam travels across the drum, and as the beam moves, the drum charges the areas exposed to the beam. The charged areas attract toner (electrically charged ink) as the drum rotates past the toner cartridge. An electrically charged wire pulls the toner from the drum onto the paper, and heat rollers fuse the toner to the paper. A second electrically charged wire neutralizes the drum's electrical charge. See *light-emitting diode (LED) printer* and *resolution*.

latency   In a computer network, the amount of time required for a message to travel from the sending to the receiving computer. This is far from instantaneous in a *packet-switching* network, given the fact that the message must be read and passed on by several *routers* before it reaches its destination, and results in *jitter*.

In disk drives, the time required for the portion of the disk containing needed information to rotate under the *read/write head*. The faster a disk drive spins, the lower its latency.

launch   To start a program.

layer   In some illustration and page-layout applications, an on-screen sheet on which you can place text or graphics so that they're independent of any text or graphics on other sheets. The layer can be opaque or transparent.

In SuperPaint, for example, you can create illustrations on two layers: a paint layer for bit-mapped graphics and a draw layer for object-oriented graphics. In FreeHand, you can draw or paint on up to 200 transparent layers. Commands typically named Bring to Front or Send to Back allow you to bring a background layer forward so that you can edit that layer.

layout   In *desktop publishing* and *word processing*, the process of arranging text and graphics on a page. In database management systems, the arrangement of report elements, such as headers and fields, on a printed page.

LBA   See *logical block addressing (LBA)*.

LCD printer   See *liquid crystal display (LCD) printer*.

LCD   See *liquid crystal display (LCD)*.

LCS printer   See *liquid crystal shutter (LCS) printer*.

leader In *word processing*, a row of dots or dashes that provides a path for the eye to follow across the page. Leaders often are used in tables of contents to lead the reader's eye from the entry to the page number. Most word processing programs let you define tab stops that insert leaders when you press the Tab key.

leading The space between lines of type, measured from *baseline* to baseline. Synonymous with line spacing. The term originated from letterpress-printing technology, in which lead strips were inserted between lines of type to add spacing between lines.

leading zero The zeros added in front of numeric values so that a number fills up all required spaces in a data field. For example, three leading zeros are in the number 00098.54.

leased line A permanently-connected and conditioned telephone line that provides *wide area network (WAN)* connectivity to an organization or business. Most leased lines transfer digital data at 56 *Kbps*.

LED indicator See *drive activity indicator*.

LED printer See *light-emitting diode (LED) printer*.

LED See *light-emitting diode (LED)*.

left justification Synonymous with ragged-right alignment. See *justification*.

legacy hardware An adapter that does not conform to the *Plug and Play* standard. *Microsoft Windows 95* can advise you about how to adjust the *jumper settings* on legacy hardware to get it to work with your system.

legend In *presentation graphics*, an area of a chart or graph that explains what data is being represented by the colors or patterns used in the chart.

letter-quality printer An *impact printer* that offers the fully formed text characters produced by a high-quality office typewriter.

As with office typewriter technology, many letter-quality printers use *daisywheels* or similar printing mechanisms. A major drawback of these mechanisms is that they can't print *graphics*. This fact ensured a brisk market for dot-matrix printers that, despite their

L
M
N

poorer quality for text output, can print charts and graphs. With the arrival of *laser printers*, the market for letter-quality printers has all but disappeared.

CAUTION: *If you plan to buy a letter-quality printer, make sure that your software includes a* printer driver *for the specific brand and model you're buying. Alternatively, check the printer manual to determine whether the printer can emulate a printer, usually a Diablo or Qume, that your software supports. Many letter-quality printers also recognize the Epson or IBM commands, but others don't.*

library   A collection of programs kept with a computer system and made available for processing purposes. The term often refers to a collection of *library routines* written in a given programming language such as C or Pascal.

library routine   In *programming*, a well-tested subroutine, procedure, or function in a given programming language. The library routine handles tasks that all or most programs need, such as reading data from disks. The programmer can draw on this library to develop programs quickly.

ligature   In *typography*, two or more characters designed and cast as a distinct unit for aesthetic reasons, such as æ.

Five letter combinations beginning with f (_fi, ff, *fl_, ffi, and ffl) and two diphthongs (æ and oe) commonly are printed as ligatures. Some *outline fonts* available for *PostScript laser printers* include ligatures for professional typesetting applications.

light pen   An *input device* that uses a light-sensitive stylus so that you can draw on-screen, draw on a graphics tablet, or select items from menus.

light-emitting diode (LED)   A small electronic device made from semiconductor materials. An LED emits light when current flows through it. LEDs are used for small indicator lights, but because they draw more power than *liquid crystal displays (LCD)*, they rarely are used for computer displays.

light-emitting diode (LED) printer   A high-quality printer that closely resembles the *laser printer* in that it electrostatically fuses toner to paper; however, the light source is a matrix of light-emitting diodes. To create the image, the diodes flash on and off over the rotating print drum. See *liquid crystal display (LCD) printer*.

LIM EMS   See *Lotus-Intel-Microsoft Expanded Memory Specification (LIM EMS)*.

line   In *programming*, one program statement. In data communications, a circuit that directly connects two or more electronic devices.

line adapter   In data communications, an electronic device that converts signals from one form to another so that you can transmit the signals. A *modem* is a line adapter that converts the computer's digital signals to analog equivalents so that they can be transmitted using standard telephone lines.

line art   In *graphics*, a drawing that doesn't contain *halftones* so that low- to medium-*resolution* printers can accurately reproduce the drawing.

line chart   See *line graph*.

line editor   A primitive *word processing* utility that's often provided with an operating system as part of its programming environment. Unlike with a *full-screen editor*, you can write or edit only one line of program code at a time. See *programming environment*.

> **TIP:** *Even if you're programming just for fun or for hobby purposes, obtain and use a full-screen editor. Line editors are murderously tedious to program with.*

line feed   A signal that tells the printer when to start a new line. See *carriage return* and *Enter/Return*.

line graph   In presentation and analytical graphics, a graph that uses lines to show the variations of data over time or to show the relationship between two numeric variables (see fig. L.1). In general, the *x-axis* (categories) is aligned horizontally, and the *y-axis* (values) is aligned vertically. A line graph, however, may have two y-axes. See *bar graph* and *presentation graphics*.

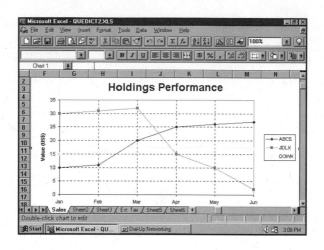

Fig. L.1 *A line graph.*

line interactive UPS   A type of *uninterruptible power supply (UPS)* that provides protection from brownouts as well as power failures. A line interactive UPS monitors electrical current from a wall outlet and provides full operating power if the line voltage drops or disappears. See *standby UPS*.

Line Mode Browser   A text-only *Web browser* created for *UNIX* computer systems and currently maintained by the *World Wide Web Consortium*.

line mode terminal   A terminal that is designed to communicate with the user with one line of text at a time, like an old-fashioned teletype machine (in fact, such terminals are often abbreviated TTY, which stands for "teletype"). You type a one-line command, and the *terminal* responds with a one-line conformation or error message. See *Network Virtual Terminal (NVT)* and *Telnet*.

line noise   Interference in a telephone line, caused by current fluctuations, poor connections in telephone equipment, crosstalk from adjacent lines, or environmental conditions such as lightning. Line noise may reduce the *data transfer rate* a *modem* can sustain, or may introduce *garbage characters* into the data stream.

line rate   See *horizontal frequency*.

line spacing   See *leading*.

liner   The cloth envelope that fits between the *recording medium* of a *floppy disk* and its *shell*. The liner reduces friction and keeps dust off the recording medium.

link   To establish a connection between two files or data items so that a change in one is reflected by a change in the second. A *cold link* requires user intervention and action, such as opening both files and using an updating command, to make sure that the change has occurred. A *warm link* occurs automatically. See *hot link* and *Object Linking and Embedding (OLE)*.

Link Access Protocol for Modems (LAPM)   An *error-correction protocol* included in the *V.42* standard. V.42 tries to establish a connection with LAPM, but will try *MNP4* if it fails. Like other error-correction protocols, LAPM exists to ensure that data is transmitted accurately and *garbage characters* are eliminated.

linked list   See *list*.

linked object   In *object linking and embedding (OLE),* a document or portion of a document (an object) created with one application that's inserted in a document created with another application.

Linking places a copy of the object, with hidden information about the source of the object, into the *destination document.* If you change the source document while the destination document is open, the object in the destination document is automatically updated. If the destination document isn't open, the object is updated the next time you open it. Object linking and embedding is possible only when you're using OLE-compatible applications on a *Microsoft Windows* system, or on a Macintosh system running System 7. See *embedded object*.

L M N

TIP: *To quickly edit a linked object, double-click the object. The computer automatically opens the application used to create the object. When you exit the source application, any changes you made appear in the object.*

linked pie/column chart   See *linked pie/column graph.*

linked pie/column graph   In *presentation graphics*, a pie graph paired with a column graph so that the column graph displays the internal distribution of data items in one slice of the pie (see fig. L.2).

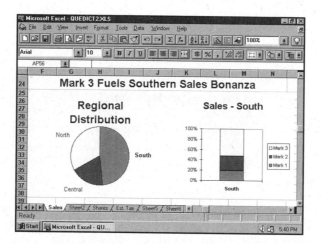

Fig. L.2 *A linked pie/column graph.*

liquid crystal display (LCD)   Low-power *display* technology used in *laptop computers* and small, battery-powered electronic devices such as meters, testing equipment, and digital watches. The display device uses rod-shaped crystal molecules that change their orientation when an electrical current flows through them. Some LCD designs use *backlit* screens to improve readability, but at the cost of drawing more power.

liquid crystal display (LCD) printer   A high-quality *printer* that closely resembles the *laser printer* in that it electrostatically fuses toner to paper; however, the light source is a matrix of liquid crystal shutters. The shutters open and close to create the pattern of light that falls on the print drum. See *light-emitting diode (LED) printer.*

liquid crystal shutter (LCS) printer   A *printer* that uses a light source and a series of shutters and lenses, instead of a laser beam, to create an electrostatic charge on a page. LCS printers may have longer lives than *laser printers* because they have fewer moving parts.

LISP A *high-level programming language*, often used for *artificial intelligence* research, that makes no distinction between the program and the data. This language is considered ideal for manipulating text.

One of the oldest programming languages still in use, LISP is a *declarative language;* the programmer composes lists that declare the relationships among symbolic values. Lists are the fundamental data structure of LISP, and the program performs computations on the symbolic values expressed in those lists.

Like other public domain programming languages, however, a number of mutually unintelligible versions of LISP exist. A standardized, fully configured, and widely accepted version is Common LISP. See *interpreter*.

list In *programming*, a data structure that lists and links each data item with a pointer showing the item's physical location in a database. Using a list, a programmer can organize data in various ways without changing the physical location of the data. For example, the programmer can display a database so that it appears to be sorted in alphabetical order, even though the actual physical data records still are stored in the order in which they were entered.

LISTSERV A commercial mailing list manager, originally developed in 1986 for BITNET mailing lists, that has since been ported to *UNIX*, *Microsoft Windows*, and *Windows 95*. LISTSERV is marketed by L-Soft International.

live copy/paste See *hot link*.

load To transfer program instructions or data from a disk into the computer's *random-access memory (RAM)*.

local area network (LAN) Personal and other computers within a limited area that are linked by high-performance cables so that users can exchange information, share peripherals, and draw on programs and data stored in a dedicated computer called a file server.

Ranging tremendously in size and complexity, LANs may link only a few personal computers to an expensive, shared peripheral, such as a *laser printer*. More complex systems use central computers (*file servers*) and allow users to communicate with each other via *electronic mail* to share multiuser programs and to access shared databases. See *AppleTalk, baseband, broadband, bus network, EtherNet, multiuser system, NetWare, network operating system (NOS), peer-to-peer network, ring network,* and *star network.*

local bus   A high-speed data path that directly links the computer's *central processing unit (CPU)* with one or more slots on the *expansion bus.* This direct link means the signals from an adapter (video or hard disk controller, for example) don't have to travel through the computer's expansion bus, which is significantly slower.

Expansion bus designs—such as the *Industry Standard Architecture (ISA) bus,* the *Extended Industry Standard Architecture (EISA) bus,* and IBM's proprietary *Micro Channel Architecture (MCA)* design)—all slow Windows down to an almost unacceptable level because redrawing the screen is held up while the video signals travel through the expansion bus. Although an Intel 80486 microprocessor can handle about 74M of data per second, the standard ISA expansion bus can move only 16M per second. A local bus design with circuits directly connected to the computer's processing unit can produce substantial performance gains. See *AT bus, Micro Channel Bus, Peripheral Component Interconnect (PCI) bus,* and *VL-Bus.*

local drive   In a *local area network (LAN),* a disk drive that's part of the *workstation* you are now using, as distinguished from a network drive (a drive made available to you through the *network*).

local echo   See *half duplex.*

local loop   The *copper pair* wire that connects a home or business to a telephone company switching station. Local loop wires have very low *bandwidth,* and need to be replaced before high-speed *digital* telecommunications, such as those provided by the *Integrated Services Digital Network (ISDN),* can be implemented.

local printer   In a *local area network (LAN),* a *printer* directly connected to the *workstation* you're using, as distinguished from a network printer (a printer made available to you through the *network*).

local UseNet hierarchy   In *UseNet,* a category of *newsgroups* that is set up for local distribution only—for example, within the confines of a company or university. Local *newsgroup*s are not ordinarily accessible outside the organization.

locale In *Microsoft Windows 95*, the geographical location of a computer. The locale determines the language in which messages appear, the formats for time, date, and money expressions, and the time of day.

LocalTalk The physical connectors and cables manufactured by Apple Computer for use in *AppleTalk* networks.

locked file In a *local area network (LAN)*, a file attribute that prevents applications or the user from updating or deleting the file.

log A record. In *communications programs*, a log feature can record everything that appears on the *monitor* for later review— which can save you money if you're paying a per-minute connection fee.

log off The process of terminating a connection with a computer system or *peripheral* device in an orderly way.

log on The process of establishing a connection with, or gaining access to, a computer system or *peripheral* device.

In MS-DOS, logging on refers to the process of changing to another drive by typing the drive letter and a colon, and then pressing Enter. In *networks*, you may be required to type a *password* to log on.

logarithmic chart See *logarithmic graph*.

logarithmic graph In *analytical* and *presentation graphics*, a graph displayed with a *y-axis* (values) that increases exponentially in powers of 10.

On an ordinary y-axis, the 10 is followed by 20, 30, 40, and so on. On a logarithmic scale, however, 10 is followed by 100, 1,000, 10,000, and so on. This makes a logarithmic graph useful when great differences exist in the values of the data being graphed. In an ordinary graph, you can hardly see a data series or data item with small values (see fig. L.3); on a logarithmic chart, however, the small values show up much better (see fig. L.4).

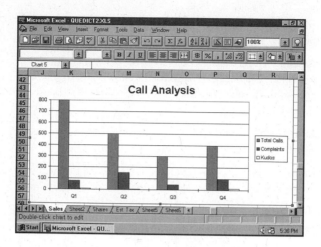

Fig. L.3 *A column graph with an ordinary y-axis.*

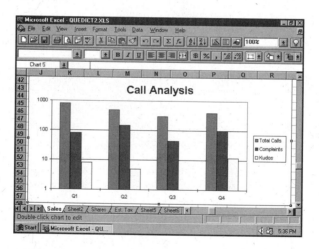

Fig. L.4 *A column graph with a logarithmic y-axis.*

logic board   See *motherboard.*

logic gate   An automatic switch, incorporated into *microprocessors* and other *chips,* that tests for certain conditions and takes certain actions if they are satisfied. Logic gates are at the center of a computer's ability to carry out instructions and solve problems. See *arithmetic-logic unit.*

logical   Having the appearance of, and treated as, a real thing. The difference doesn't matter to the user. For example, a sheet of mailing labels is a page. Each label on the page is a logical page. See *logical drive* and *physical drive.*

Logical Block Addressing (LBA)   Part of the *Enhanced IDE* standard, LBA permits *hard disks* to store up to 8.4*G* of data. Without LBA, hard disks could store only 528*M* of data.

logical drives   Sections of a *hard drive* that are formatted and assigned a drive letter, each of which is presented to the user as though it were a separate drive. Another way logical drives are created is by substituting a drive letter for a directory. Also, *networks* typically map directories to drive letters, resulting in logical drives. See *logical, partition,* and *physical drive.*

TIP: *Partitioning a hard drive is no longer necessary. However, creating separate partitions may make disk organization easier.*

logical format   See *high-level format.*

logical network   A *network* as it appears to the user. In fact, the network could be composed of two or more physical networks, or portions of these, which are linked and coordinated in such a way that they appear to be a unit. One of the most remarkable facts about the *Internet* is that, even though it links tens of thousands of physically heterogeneous networks, they nevertheless appear to the user to comprise a single, immense network of global proportions.

logical operator   A symbol used to specify the logical relationship between two quantities or concepts. In *query languages,* the inclusive logical operator (OR) broadens the number of data records retrieved, and the exclusive logical operators (AND and NOT) restrict the number retrieved. Synonymous with *Boolean operator.*

Each of these queries illustrates the use of a logical operator and produces a different list of video tape titles:

```
The field RATING contains PG or PG-13.
The field CATEGORY contains Adventure and the field
RATING includes PG.
The field CATEGORY contains Adventure, but not the ones
in which the field RATING includes R.
```

login ID   See *login name*.

login name   In a *network*, a unique name assigned to you by the system administrator that's used as a means of initial identification. You must type this name, and also your *password*, to gain access to the system.

login script   In *dialup access,* a list of instructions that guides the *dialer program* through the process of dialing the service provider's number, supplying the user's login name and password, and establishing the connection.

login security   A validation process that requires you to type a *password* before gaining access to a system.

Logo   A *high-level programming language* well-suited to teaching fundamental programming concepts to children.

A special version of *LISP*, Logo was designed as an educational language to illustrate the concepts of recursion, extensibility, and other concepts of computing, without requiring math skills. The language also provides an environment in which children can develop their reasoning and problem-solving skills and includes turtle graphics — a teaching aid that involves telling an on-screen "turtle" how to draw pictures.

logon file   In a *local area network (LAN)*, a batch file or configuration file that starts the network software and establishes the connection with the network when you turn on the *workstation*.

lookup function   A procedure in which a *program* consults stored data listed in a table or *file*.

lookup table   In a *spreadsheet* program, data entered in a range of cells and organized so that a lookup function can use the data— for example, to determine the correct tax rate based on annual income.

loop   In *programming*, a *control structure* in which a block of instructions repeats until a condition is fulfilled. See *DO/WHILE loop* and *FOR/NEXT loop*.

lossless compression   A *data compression* technique that reduces the size of a file without sacrificing any original data; used by programs such as Stacker to compress all the program and document files on a *hard disk*. In lossless compression, the expanded or restored file is an exact replica of the original file before it was compressed, while in *lossy compression,* data is lost in a way imperceptible to humans. Lossless compression is suitable for text and computer code, while lossy compression is good mainly for shrinking audio and graphics files.

lossy compression   A *data compression* technique in which some data is deliberately discarded to achieve massive reductions in the size of the compressed file. Lossy compression techniques can reduce a file to 1/50 of its former size (or less), compared to the average of one-third achieved by lossless compression techniques. Lossy compression is used for graphics files in which the loss of data—such as information about some of the graphic's several million colors—isn't noticeable. An example is the *JPEG* compression technique. See *lossless compression.*

lost chain   In *MS-DOS*, a group of clusters that are connected to each other in the *file allocation table (FAT)* but are no longer connected to a specific *file.*

lost cluster   A *cluster* that remains on the disk, even though the *file allocation table (FAT)* contains no record of its link to a file. Lost clusters can occur when the computer is turned off (or the power fails) or tries to perform other operations while a file is being written.

Lotus 1-2-3   A full-featured *spreadsheet program* known for its ability to work with *Lotus Notes* and *electronic mail* programs. Lotus 1-2-3 release 5 competes with *Microsoft Excel* and *Quattro Pro.* Though praised for its strength in managing multiple *what-if scenarios* and its ability to link spreadsheet information to maps, 1-2-3 is considered to be third in the pack of three major spreadsheet programs.

Lotus Approach   A *database management program* for *Microsoft Windows* that has the distinction of being both easy to use and capable of handling complex operations. A competitor of *Microsoft Access* and *dBASE for Windows*, Lotus Approach makes it possible to analyze *data* in a variety of forms (including dBASE, Microsoft Access, *Microsoft Excel,* and Borland Paradox) without performing any *programming.*

Using Lotus Approach is made easier by the Form Assistant, an automated helper that assists with organizing data, and a variety of templates set up for many common tasks. Critics, citing Lotus Approach's good balance of usability and power, usually put it near the top of the database rankings.

Lotus-Intel-Microsoft Expanded Memory Specification (LIM EMS)   An *expanded memory* standard that allows the programs that recognize the standard to work with more than 640K RAM under DOS. The LIM Version 4.0 standard, introduced in 1987, supports up to 32*M* of expanded memory and lets programs run in expanded memory.

CAUTION: *Software can't work with expanded memory unless specifically designed to do so. Applications such as* WordPerfect, Lotus 1-2-3, *and* dBASE *work with LIM 4.0 expanded memory, but less popular programs and shareware may not unless you use a windowing environment such as Quarterdeck's DESQview or* Microsoft Windows. *See* expanded memory (EMS) *and* extended memory.

Lotus Notes   A *groupware application* that brings *features* such as discussion tracking and database sharing to large and small workgroups. First released in 1988, Lotus Notes is the most popular groupware application available. Lotus Notes comes with an elaborate application-development language that enables it to be tailored to the needs of a particular workgroup. Lotus NoteÆs faces competition from *Microsoft Exchange*.

Lotus Organizer   A *personal-information manager (PIM)* designed to work well with *Lotus Notes*. With Lotus Organizer, the time of an appointment you enter is visible to other Notes users as a time you're not available, so they know not to try setting up meetings with you then. Lotus Organizer competes with ACT! and Ecco in the PIM market.

Lotus SmartSuite   A *suite* of *application programs*, published by Lotus, that includes *Lotus Word Pro*, *Lotus 1-2-3*, *Lotus Approach*, *Lotus Organizer*, and *Lotus Notes* for a single member of a Lotus Notes-equipped workgroup. Lotus SmartSuite competes with *PerfectOffice Professional* and *Microsoft Office Professional*.

Lotus Word Pro   Formerly called Ami Pro, Lotus Word Pro is a full-featured word processing program that competes with

Microsoft Word and *WordPerfect*. Lotus Word Pro trails its competitors, but offers several attractive features.

Designed to work with *Lotus Notes*, Lotus Word Pro allows the members of a workgroup to attach electronic "sticky notes" to documents. The program also features a novel spelling checker that lets you see all the misspelled words in a document at once. Some critics, though, have said Lotus Word Pro's automatic formatting features are weak.

low end   An inexpensive product at the bottom or near the bottom of a firm's offerings. Low-end products include only a few of the features available in more expensive products and may rely on obsolete or near-obsolete technology to keep costs down.

low-level format   Defining the physical location of magnetic *tracks* and *sectors* on a disk. This operation, sometimes called a physical format, is different from the *high-level format* that establishes the sections where DOS system files are stored and that records the free and in-use areas of the disk.

low-level programming language   In *programming*, a language, such as *machine language* or *assembly language*, that describes exactly the procedures to be carried out by the computer's central processing unit (CPU). See *high-level programming language*.

low-power microprocessor   A *microprocessor* that runs on 3.3 volts of electricity or less. Low-power microprocessors are often used in *portable computers* to conserve battery power. See *0.5-micron technology* and *complimentary metal-oxide semiconductor (CMOS)*.

low resolution   In *monitors* and *printers*, a visual definition that results in characters and graphics with jagged edges. The IBM *Color Graphics Adapter (CGA)* and monitor, for example, can display 640 pixels horizontally, but only 200 lines vertically, resulting in poor visual definition. *High-resolution* monitors and printers produce well-defined characters or smoothly defined curves in graphic images.

low-rez   Slang for a technically unsavvy person. Usage: "Our boss is nice enough, but he's kind of low-rez." See *high-rez*.

LPT In DOS, a device name that refers to a parallel port to which you can connect parallel printers.

LSI See *large-scale integration (LSI)*.

lurk To read a newsgroup or mailing list without ever posting a message. See *delurk*.

LViewPro A *shareware* graphics viewer program for Microsoft Windows, created by Leonardo H. Loureiro and widely available on the Internet. Often used as a *helper program* for Web browsers, the program can read JPEG, TIFF, Targa, GIF, PCX, Windows bitmap, OS/2 bitmap, PBM, PGM, and PPM files. A feature of LViewPro of interest to Web developers is the program's ability to create *transparent GIFs*.

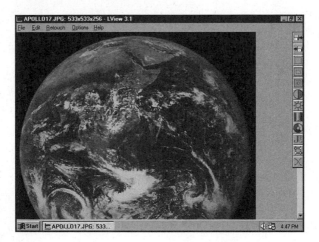

Fig. L.5 *LViewPro (graphical viewer).*

Lycos A *search engine* for locating *World Wide Web* documents that is provided by Carnegie Mellon University's Center for Machine Translation. Lycos, named after a particularly energetic night-hunting spider, relies on an automated search routine (called a *spider*) that prowls the Web, discovering new Web, *FTP*, and *Gopher* documents (about 5,000 per day). The additions become part of Lycos' huge database, currently approaching 5 million documents. For each document, Lycos indexes words in the title, headings, subheadings, all of the document's hyperlinks, the 100 most important words in the document, and the words in the first 20 lines of text. Although a typical Lycos search will retrieve many false drops (irrelevant documents), it is currently the best search engine on the Web.

TIP: *Fine-tune your Lycos search, and speed retrieval, by typing a period after each search term you use. The period instructs Lycos to ignore related forms of the search term (for example, if you type "safety." Lycos will ignore documents that contain "safetycenter," "safetyicon," and "safetynet").*

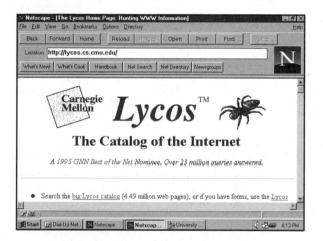

Fig. L.6 *Lycos search engine.*

LYNX A full-screen, text-only *Web browser* for *UNIX* computers, created by Lou Montoulli of the University of Kansas. LYNX is a full-featured Web browser but it cannot display *in-line images*.

M   Abbreviation for megabyte (1,048,576 *bytes*).

MacBinary   A *file transfer protocol (ftp)* for *Macintosh* computers that allows you to store Macintosh files on non-Macintosh computers without losing *icons*, graphics, and information about the file (such as the creation date). Most Macintosh *communication programs* send and receive files in MacBinary.

machine-dependent   Capable of running on only a specific kind of *hardware*.

machine language   The native *binary language* recognized and executed by a computer's *central processing unit (CPU)*. Machine language, a *low-level language* symbolized by 0s and 1s, is extremely difficult to use and read. See *assembly language* and *high-level programming language*.

Macintosh   A line of *personal computers* created by *Apple Computer*, released in 1984. The Macintosh pioneered the *graphical user interface (GUI)*, which was first developed—but never successfully marketed—by Xerox Corporation. The Macintosh also pioneered the concept of *Plug and Play* peripherals, built-in *Small Computer System Interface (SCSI)* device support, and built-in local area networking. However, the years since 1984 have seen a steady erosion of the Mac's technological lead, which Apple was never able to exploit successfully. Partly because Apple Computer refused until 1995 to license Macintosh technology to *clone* makers, who could have mass-marketed the Mac at low cost, Macintoshes generally cost more than comparably equipped *IBM PC-compatible* computers. Since there are approximately 9 IBM PC compatibles for every Macintosh, software developers naturally prefer to develop programs for the IBM PC and *Microsoft Windows 95* markets—and for this reason, far fewer programs are available for the Macintosh. Still, the Mac is the platform of choice for computer applications in the arts, including desktop publishing, illustration, graphics and photo processing, and music production. (See fig. M.1).

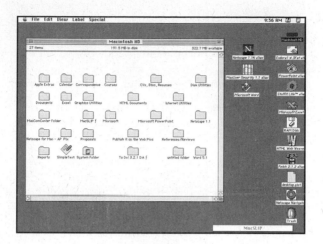

Fig. M.1 *The Macintosh desktop.*

macro A *program* consisting of recorded *keystrokes* and an application's *command language* that, when run within the application, executes the keystrokes and commands to accomplish a task. Macros can automate tedious and often-repeated tasks (such as saving and backing up a file to a floppy) or create special *menus* to speed data entry.

Some programs provide a macro-recording mode in which the program records your keystrokes and then saves the recording as a macro. Others provide a built-in macro editor, where you type and edit macro commands directly to create *IF/THEN/ELSE* statements and *DO/WHILE* loops.

MacTCP A *Macintosh utility program,* developed by *Apple Computer* and included with *System* 7.5, that provides the *TCP/IP* support needed to connect Macintoshes to the Internet. A separate *communications program* is needed to connect via *Serial Line Internet Protocol (SLIP)* or *Point-to-Point Protocol (PPP).*

magnetic disk In data storage, a *random-access* storage medium that's the most popular method for storing and retrieving computer programs and data files. In personal computing, common magnetic disks include *5 1/4-inch floppy disks, 3 1/2-inch floppy disks,* and *hard disks* of various sizes.

The disk is coated with a magnetically sensitive material. Magnetic *read/write heads* move across the surface of the spinning disk under the disk drive's automatic control to the location of desired information. The information stored on a magnetic disk can be repeatedly erased and rewritten, like any other magnetic storage medium.

magnetic medium   A *secondary storage medium* that uses magnetic techniques to store and retrieve data on disks or *tapes* coated with magnetically sensitive materials.

Like iron filings on a sheet of waxed paper, these materials are reoriented when a magnetic field passes over them. During write operations, the *read/write head* emits a magnetic field that orients the magnetic materials on the disk or tape to represent encoded data. During read operations, the read/write head senses the encoded data on the medium.

magnetic tape   See *tape* and *tape drive*.

magneto-optical (MO) cartridge   The removable storage device used in a *magneto-optical (MO) drive*. MO cartridges are either 5 $^1/_4$ inches across (with capacities up to 1300M) or 3 $^1/_2$ inches across (with capacities up to 230M). The data on a magneto-optical cartridge is highly stable, unlike the data on *floppy* and *hard disks*, which tends to self-erase if the data isn't rewritten regularly.

magneto-optical (MO) drive   A data storage device that uses laser technology to heat an extremely small spot on a *magneto-optical (MO) cartridge* so that the magnetic medium used in the MO disk becomes capable of having its magnetic orientation changed by the *read/write head*.

Though magneto-optical drives are slow (average *seek time* of 30 *ms*, compared to about 15 ms for hard drives) and expensive (the average internal drive costs about $750, including disks), they are highly suitable for backup storage and for storing large programs or data that's accessed infrequently.

magneto-resistive (MR) head   A technologically advanced kind of *read/write head* that uses a special metal alloy to improve *areal density* by packing *tracks* more tightly and increases *throughput* by having separate reading and writing portions. MR heads are often used in *hard disks* that employ *partial-response maximum-likelihood (PRML) read channel technology*.

mail bombing   A form of harassment that involves sending numerous large *electronic mail* messages to a person's electronic mailbox.

 mail bridge   A *gateway* that enables users of one *network* or *on-line information service* to exchange electronic mail with users of other networks or services. For example, *CompuServe* users can exchange mail with *Internet* users by means of a gateway.

mail exploder   See *mailing list manager.*

mail merge   In *word processing programs,* a utility that draws information from a *database*—usually a mailing list—and incorporates it into a form document to create multiple copies of the document. Each copy of the document includes information from one record from the database.

The most common application of mail merge utilities is to personalize form letters. Instead of generating "Dear Applicant" letters, you can use a mail-merge utility to generate letters that start, "Dear Mr. Bergman."

TIP: *Most programs let you perform conditional merging that prints an optional passage of text if a database record meets a specified condition.*

L
M
N

mail package   A *utility program* that manages the sending and receiving of *electronic mail* messages for a specific computer.

Some *networks* use a full-featured package such as *PerfectOffice* that includes an e-mail program. More friendly or full-featured mail programs can also be bought separately. *Microsoft Mail* and *cc:Mail* are two popular mail packages.

mail reflector   See *mailing list manager.*

mail server   A *program* that responds automatically to *electronic mail* messages. Mail server programs exist that enter or remove subscriptions to *mailing lists,* and that send information in response to a request.

mailbox   In *electronic mail,* the storage space that has been set aside to store an individual's electronic mail messages.

mailbox name   In an *Internet electronic mail* address, one of the two basic parts of a person's address: the part to the left of the *at sign* (@), which specifies the name of the person's *mailbox*. To the right of the @ sign is the *domain name* of the computer that houses the mailbox. A person's mailbox name often is the same as his or her *login name*. See *electronic name*.

 mailing list   On the *Internet* or any other *network*, a list of users who will receive copies of mail messages. Lists are usually divided by topic or work area. On the Internet, you can subscribe to mailing lists for topics that interest you.

mailing list manager   In a *mailing list,* the *mail server* software, such as *LISTSERV* or *Majordomo*, that receives incoming contributions to the list and sends out copies of them to all the subscribers. Synonymous with mail exploder.

main memory   See *random-access memory (RAM)*.

main program   In *programming*, the part of a *program* containing the master sequence of instructions, unlike the *subroutines*, procedures, and functions that the main program calls.

main storage   See *random-access memory (RAM)*.

mainframe   A multi-user computer designed to meet the computing needs of a large organization.

Originally, the term mainframe referred to the metal cabinet that housed the *central processing unit (CPU)* of early computers. The term came to be used generally to refer to the large central computers developed in the late 1950s and 1960s to meet the accounting and information-management needs of large organizations. The largest mainframes can handle thousands of *dumb terminals* and use terabytes of *secondary storage*. See *minicomputer, personal computer,* and *workstation*.

maintenance programming   Altering *programs* after they have been in use for a while. Maintenance programming may be performed to add *features*, correct *bugs* that escaped detection during testing, or update key variables (such as the inflation rate) that change over time.

maintenance release   A program revision that corrects a minor *bug* or makes a minor new feature available, such as a new *printer driver*. Maintenance releases are usually numbered in tenths

(3.2) or hundredths (2.01), to distinguish them from major program revisions. Synonymous with interim update.

Majordomo   A popular *freeware* mailing list manager for *UNIX*
computer systems. See *LISTSERV* and *mailing list manager.*

male connector   In cables, a cable terminator and connection
device in which the pins protrude from the connector's surface.
Male connectors plug into *female connectors.*

management information system (MIS)   A *computer*
system, based on a *mainframe, minicomputer,* local-area network
(LAN) or wide-area network (WAN), designed to provide business
managers with up-to-date information on the organization's performance.

manual recalculation   In a *spreadsheet program,* a recalculation method that suspends the recalculation of values until you
issue a command that forces recalculation to take place.

Most spreadsheet programs employ *automatic recalculation,* that is,
they recalculate all values within the spreadsheet after you change
the contents of any *cell.* If you're using a slow computer and creating a large spreadsheet, you may want to choose the manual recalculation mode as you enter data. When you're finished, be sure to
recalculate the spreadsheet and turn *automatic recalculation* on
again. The word CALC or a similar indicator appears at the bottom of the spreadsheet to remind you to recalculate.

TIP: *In the latest generation of spreadsheet software, such as Lotus
1-2-3, recalculation occurs in the background. With these spreadsheet programs you don't need to use manual recalculation.*

map   A representation of *data* stored in memory. See *bit map.*

MAPI   See *Messaging Application Program Interface (MAPI).*

mapping   The process of converting *data* encoded in one *format*
to another format. In *database management,* for example, the database index provides a way of mapping the actual *data records*
(which are stored on disk in a fixed order) to the display screen in
useful ways.

In a *local area network (LAN)*, mapping refers to assigning *drive* letters to specific volumes and directories.

marquee   In *Microsoft Excel*, a moving dotted line that surrounds a cell or a range of cells that you've cut or copied.

mask   A pattern of symbols or characters that, when imposed on a *data field*, limits the kinds of characters that you can type into the field. In a *database management program*, for example, the mask AZ lets you type any alphabetical character, uppercase or lowercase, but not numbers or other symbols.

mass storage   See *secondary storage*.

master document   In *word processing*, a *document* that contains commands that tell the program to print additional documents at the commands' locations. The program prints all the documents as though they were one. See *chain printing*.

master   The first disk in a string of two attached to *an integrated drive electronics (IDE) host adapter*. Though the master disk does not control the *slave* disk, it interprets commands from the host adapter for it.

masthead   In *desktop publishing (DTP)*, the section of a newsletter or magazine that gives the details of its staff, ownership, advertising, subscription prices, and so on.

math coprocessor   A secondary *microprocessor* that frees the *central processing unit (CPU)* from tedious, calculation-intensive chores. Math coprocessors can significantly speed up *computer-aided design (CAD)* drawing and *spreadsheet* calculation, but won't significantly improve *Microsoft Windows 95's* performance. Some CPUs, such as the *Intel 486DX* and *Pentium*, have math coprocessors built in. See *numeric coprocessor*.

matte finish   A quality of paper that does not reflect light as harshly as a *glossy finish*. Most users prefer matte finish paper to *glossy finish* paper, because it matches the light-absorbent qualities of *laser printer* text.

maximize   To zoom or enlarge a window so that it fills the screen.

In *Microsoft Windows 95*, you maximize a *window* by clicking the maximize button (the middle button in the upper right corner) or by choosing Maximize from the *control menu*. See *minimize*.

maximum RAM   The amount of *random-access memory (RAM)* that could possibly be installed on a particular *motherboard*. Maximum RAM specifications usually are expressed as "expandable-to" statements in advertisements, as in, "The motherboard has 8*M* RAM, expandable to 128M."

maximum transmission unit (MTU)   The largest *packet* that may be transmitted over a *packet-switching network*.

MB   Alternative abbreviation for megabyte (1,048,576 bytes).

Mbps   See *bits per second (bps)*.

MCA   See *Micro Channel Architecture (MCA)*.

MCD   See *magneto-optical drive*.

MCGA   See *MultiColor Graphics Array (MCGA)*.

MCI   See *Media Control Interface (MCI)*.

MDA   See *monochrome display adapter (MDA)*.

MDI   See *Multiple Document Interface (MDI)*.

mean time between failures (MTBF)   The statistical average operating time between the start of a component's life and the time of its first electronic or mechanical failure.

> **TIP:** *You shouldn't take MTBF figures too seriously when comparison shopping. The figures stem from laboratory tests performed under extreme conditions; the results are then statistically extrapolated to determine the MTBF. Little pressure exists for manufacturers to use an extrapolation procedure that revises the MTBF figure downward.*

mechanical mouse   Unlike an *optical mouse*, a mechanical *mouse* relies on metal rollers, which are turned by the mouse's rubberized ball, to communicate its movements to the *central processing unit (CPU)*. Though mechanical mice may be used almost anywhere, their internal mechanisms tend to get dirty and require cleaning.

mechanicals   In *desktop publishing (DTP)*, the final pages or boards with pasted-up galleys of type and *line art*, sometimes with acetate or tissue overlays for *color separations* and notes, which you send to the offset printer. See *camera-ready copy*.

Media Control Interface (MCI) In *Microsoft Windows 95*, the *multimedia extensions* that greatly simplify the task of *programming* multimedia device functions such as Stop, Play, and Record.

Media Player An accessory provided with *Microsoft Windows 95* that provides a control center for *multimedia* devices, such as *CD-ROM drives*. The buttons resemble the familiar controls of a cassette tape player (see fig. M.2).

Fig. M.2 *Microsoft Windows 95 Media Player.*

media The plural of medium. See *secondary storage medium*.

medium See *storage medium*.

meg Common abbreviation for *megabyte*.

mega- Prefix indicating 1 million.

megabyte (M) A measurement of storage capacity equal to approximately 1 million *bytes* (1,048,576 bytes).

megaflop A *benchmark* used to rate *professional workstations, mainframes,* and *minicomputers*. A megaflop is equal to 1 million floating point operations per second.

megahertz (MHz) A unit of measurement equal to 1 million electrical vibrations or cycles per second; commonly used to compare the *clock speeds* of computers.

One million cycles per second sounds impressive, but by today's standards, the 4.77 MHz clock speed of the original IBM Personal Computer is considered intolerable. Clock speeds of 66 MHz, 100 MHz, and even 133 MHz are increasingly common in *personal computing*. See *hertz (Hz)*.

membrane keyboard A flat and inexpensive *keyboard* covered with a dust- and dirt-proof plastic sheet on which only the two-dimensional outline of computer keys appears. The user presses the plastic sheet and engages a switch hidden beneath. Accurately typing on a membrane keyboard is more difficult, but such keyboards are needed in restaurant kitchens or other locations where users may not have clean hands.

memory   The computer's *primary storage,* such as *random-access memory (RAM),* as distinguished from its *secondary storage,* such as *disk drives.*

memory address   A code number that specifies a specific location in a computer's *random-access memory (RAM).*

memory cache   See *cache memory.*

memory check   Part of the *power-on self-test (POST)* that verifies that the computer's *random-access memory (RAM)* is properly plugged in and is functioning well. As the computer goes through its *boot-up* routine, you can often see the progress of the memory check on the *display.* If there is a problem in memory, be sure to record the *memory address* of the error and give it to a computer repair technician.

memory controller gate array   Synonymous with MultiColor Graphics Array (MCGA), a *video standard* once used in the *low-end* models of IBM's Personal System/2 computers.

memory-management program   A *utility program* that increases the apparent size of *random-access memory (RAM)* by making *expanded memory, extended memory,* or virtual memory available for the execution of programs.

Memory-management programs include utilities provided with expanded memory boards, windowing environments such as *Microsoft Windows 95,* and *virtual memory* programs that set aside a portion of a hard disk and treat it as a RAM extension. See *EMM386.EXE, expanded memory emulator,* and *HIMEM.SYS.*

memory map   An arbitrary allocation of portions of a computer's *random-access memory (RAM),* defining which areas the computer can use for specific purposes.

Although the *Intel 8088 microprocessor* can use 1*M* of RAM, a portion of this potential memory space is reserved for functions such as the *keyboard buffer* and *display adapters.* This decision, although arbitrary, is irrevocable if *MS-DOS* is involved, because MS-DOS and its application programs can't operate unless the memory map remains exactly the way it was laid out when IBM designed the Personal Computer.

memory-resident program   *See terminate-and-stay-resident (TSR) program.*

memory word   See *word.*

menu   An on-screen display that lists available command choices. See *menu bar* and *pull-down menu.*

menu bar   In a *graphical user interface (GUI)*, a bar stretching across the top of the screen (or the top of a *window*) that contains the names of available *pull-down menus.* See *industry standard user interface.*

menu-driven program   A *program* that provides you with menus for choosing program options so that you don't need to memorize commands. See *command-driven program.*

merge printing   See *mail merge.*

message queue   In Microsoft Windows, a special space in the memory that is set aside to list the messages that applications send each other. In Microsoft Windows 3.1, there is only one message queue. If an application hangs and prevents other applications from checking the queue, the entire system is frozen beyond recovery. In *Microsoft Windows 95,* each *32-bit application* has its own message queue. If one application *aborts,* the others are not affected.

Messaging Application Program Interface (MAPI)
The Microsoft implementation of an *application program interface* that provides access to messaging services for developers. MAPI Version 3.2 provides resources to programmers for cross-platform messaging that's independent of operating system and underlying hardware, and to make applications mail-aware. MAPI can send messages to and from *Vendor Independent Messaging (VIM)* programs.

metal-oxide semiconductor (MOS)   A *chip* based on the conductive and insulative properties of silicon dioxide, aluminum oxide, and other oxidized metals. MOS chips are electrically efficient but must be handled carefully, since static electricity can destroy them. See *complimentary metal-oxide semiconductor (CMOS)* and *semiconductor.*

metal-oxide varistor (MOV)   A device used to protect the computer from abnormally high line voltages. An MOV conducts electrical current only when it exceeds a certain voltage. An MOV in a *surge protector* conducts electrical current in excess of 350 volts away from the computer. See *power surge.*

MFM   See *Modified Frequency Modulation (MFM).*

MHz   Abbreviation for *megahertz.*

MIB/MI   See *Plug and Print.*

micro-   Prefix for small. Also a prefix indicating one millionth, and an abbreviation (increasingly rare) for microcomputer.

Micro Channel Architecture (MCA)   The design specifications of IBM's *proprietary Micro Channel Bus.* An MCA-compatible peripheral is designed to plug directly into a *Micro Channel Bus,* but won't work with other bus architectures. See *local bus.*

Micro Channel Bus   A proprietary 32-bit *expansion bus* introduced by IBM for its high-end PS/2 computers.

Almost all non-IBM 80386 computers use a 32-bit bus structure for the microprocessor, but otherwise use the 16-bit AT expansion bus, for which a huge supply of cheap peripherals is available. In an attempt to define a 32-bit bus standard, IBM introduced *Micro Channel Architecture (MCA)* in 1987 and used the Micro Channel Bus on its high-end PS/2 models.

The MCA bus has many technical advantages, but the MCA standard isn't downwardly compatible with existing peripherals and adapters designed for the AT expansion bus. Therefore, the major manufacturers of IBM compatibles offered their own 32-bit bus design, called *Extended Industry Standard Architecture (EISA),* and later embraced *local bus* technology and the *Peripheral Component Interconnect (PCI) expansion bus* scheme.

microcode   *Program* instructions embedded in the internal circuitry of a *microprocessor.* Microcode makes *software* programmers' jobs easier—they can remain a step removed from the nitty-gritty details of what physically happens inside a microprocessor—but makes the task of *chip* designers harder. Since chips equipped with microcode need extra internal components to translate external instructions into physical actions, they need to be bigger, slower, and more complex than they might otherwise be. See *complex instruction set computer (CISC)* and *reduced instruction set computer (RISC)*.

Microcom Networking Protocol (MNP)   Any of 10 *error-correction* and *data-compression protocols* used by *modems*. MNP1 is obsolete, while MNP2, MNP3, and *MNP4* are error-correction protocols used in the *V.42* international standard. *MNP5* is an on-the-fly data-compression protocol used by most modern modems, and MNP6 through MNP 10 are *proprietary communications standards*.

microcomputer   Any computer with its *arithmetic-logic unit (ALU)* and *control unit* contained on one *integrated circuit*, called a *microprocessor*.

When *personal computers*—often referred to as microcomputers because their *central processing units (CPUs)* were microprocessors—first appeared in the mid to late 1970s, they were designed as single-user machines. Multi-user computing was left to relatively large *minicomputers*.

Since the mid 1980s, the distinction between minicomputers (as multi-user computers) and microcomputers (as single-user computers) has become blurry. Many microcomputers are substantially more powerful than the *mainframes* of just 10 years ago, and *high-end* microcomputers, unlike mainframes, can easily be reconfigured to serve new purposes.

Differentiating among machines by the function they're designed to perform makes the most sense:

- Centralized computing systems. Designed for use by several users simultaneously, most mainframe and minicomputer systems meet the needs of an organization or a department within an organization. The emphasis in such computer systems is on keeping programs, data, and processing capabilities under central control.

- Stand-alone computers. Designed for single-user applications, a stand-alone computer such as a personal computer designed for personal, home, or private use, that doesn't rely on external resources such as a central *database* or share computing resources with other people.

- Distributed computing systems. A *network* of personal computers designed to get computing power to the user without giving up the means to share external computing resources, such as access to a central database.

- *Professional workstation.* An advanced microcomputer that contains the display and processing circuitry needed by professionals such as engineers, financial planners, and architects.

microfine toner   Special *toner* for *laser* and *liquid crystal shutter (LCS) printers* that consists of finer particles than standard toner, enabling it to render text and *graphics* with finer detail. See *buckyball toner.*

micron   One millionth of a meter (about 0.0000394 inch).

microphone   A device that converts sounds into electrical signals that may be processed by a computer. Commonly found on *Macintosh* computers but less often seen on *IBM PC-compatible* computers, microphones may be used to record new system sounds (to replace that insipid "beep," for instance), or to add voice annotations to *documents.*

microprocessor   An *integrated circuit* that contains the *arithmetic-logic unit (ALU), control unit,* and sometimes the *floating-point unit (FPU)* of a computer's *central processing unit (CPU).* Many microprocessors have been, are, or will be available, including the *Am386,* the *Am486,* the *Am486DX2,* the *Am486DX4,* the *AMD K5,* the *Cyrix 486DLC,* the *Cyrix 486DX2,* the *Cyrix 486SLC,* the *Cyrix CX486DRu2,* the *Cyrix M1,* the *IBM Blue Lightning,* the *Intel 80386,* the *Intel 386SL,* the *Intel 386SX,* the *Intel 486,* the *Intel 486DX/2,* the *Intel 486DX/4,* the *Intel 486SL,* the *Intel 486SX,* the *Intel P6,* the *Motorola 68000,* the *Motorola 68020,* the *Motorola 68030,* and the *Pentium.*

Microsoft Access   A *database management program* for *IBM PC-compatible* computers that features *Wizards,* automated assistants that help organize and locate data, and Access Basic, a very powerful *application programming language.* Though Microsoft Access is powerful and is well-integrated with other application programs in *Microsoft Office Professional,* it is usually rated lower than *dBASE* and *Lotus Approach* because its user interface is somewhat confusing.

L
M
N

Microsoft at Work   A *Microsoft* standard for controlling a variety of office machines, such as copiers, *printers, fax* machines, and telephones, with computers. A limited version of Microsoft at Work that can control printers and fax machines is included in *Microsoft Windows 95.*

Microsoft Bookshelf   A *CD-ROM*-based *application* that makes the *Original Roget's Thesaurus, The American Heritage Dictionary,* the *Columbia Dictionary of Quotations,* the *Hammond Intermediate World Atlas,* and *The World Almanac and Book of Facts* available on your computer. Considered a valuable resource for writers and other experts who need immediate access to reference data, Microsoft Bookshelf saves the time required to look up information in a bound volume.

Microsoft Corporation   The largest software publisher in the world, Microsoft makes such ubiquitous programs as *Microsoft Windows 95, Microsoft Word,* and *Microsoft Excel.* Based in Redmond, Washington, Microsoft got its big break in 1982 when IBM agreed to buy operating systems for its new personal computers exclusively from Microsoft. *MS-DOS* remains one of the company's top products today.

Microsoft commands such market share that its products, even when inferior to competing products, often become standards. Many experts thought *Operating System/2 (OS/2)* was superior to Microsoft Windows 3.1, but OS/2 sold poorly in comparison to Windows. Microsoft competes with IBM, Lotus, and Novell.

Microsoft Excel   A very powerful, very user-friendly *spreadsheet program.* Microsoft Excel boasts extensive *formatting* tools and some extremely powerful *built-in functions* for many disciplines, including finance, engineering, and statistics. Microsoft Excel competes with *Quattro Pro* and *Lotus 1-2-3.*

Microsoft Excel's *Wizards,* automated routines that help you perform tedious tasks, are one of the program's strong points. The ChartWizard, for example, will decide what sort of graphical presentation is best for your data and help you make a chart or graph. Microsoft Excel also will often recognize when you're having problems and tell you that it can assist.

Microsoft Exchange   A message-management program capable of managing faxes and several types of electronic mail. Though experts say Microsoft Exchange will work best with

Microsoft Exchange Server, due out in late 1995 or early 1996, it handles *Microsoft Mail* messages, Internet mail, and mail from a variety of on-line information services.

Microsoft Internet Assistant   An *HTML editor* and *Web browser* add-on for *Microsoft Word*. Distributed free of charge, Microsoft Internet Assistant transforms Microsoft Word into a *what-you-see-is-what-you-get (WYSIWYG)* HTML editor, in which you see the results of the HTML *tags* rather than the tags themselves. The version current at this writing could not handle recent additions to HTML, such as the *Netscape extensions,* but did not prevent you from adding these manually. Only limited forms capabilities are available.

Microsoft Mail   An electronic mail program especially adept at handling communications on a *local area network (LAN)*. Microsoft Mail consists of two components: a client, which allows network users to read, write and manage mail; and the server, which distributes mail to the various clients.

With the advent of *Microsoft Exchange*, Microsoft offers two electronic mail clients. Microsoft Exchange can send messages to and receive messages from Microsoft Mail clients via a Microsoft Mail Server.

Microsoft Mouse   A *mouse* and associated software for IBM and *IBM PC-compatible* personal computers, including IBM's PS/1 and PS/2 computers. Available in serial and bus versions, the Microsoft Mouse uses the *mechanical mouse* technology that most mouse users favor.

Microsoft Office Professional   A *suite* of *application programs*, published by *Microsoft Corporation*, that includes *Microsoft Access* in addition to the programs in *Microsoft Office Standard*. Microsoft Office Professional competes with *Lotus SmartSuite* and *PerfectOffice Professional*.

Microsoft Office Standard   A *suite* of *application programs*, published by *Microsoft Corporation*, that includes *Microsoft Word*, *Microsoft Excel, Microsoft PowerPoint,* and *Microsoft Mail*. Microsoft Office Standard competes with *PerfectOffice Standard* and *Lotus SmartSuite*. See *Microsoft Office Professional*.

L
M
N

Microsoft PowerPoint A *presentation graphics* program that enables you to incorporate information from *spreadsheets* and *word processors* (especially *Microsoft Excel* and *Microsoft Word*, with which Microsoft PowerPoint coexists in the *Microsoft Office Standard* and *Microsoft Office Professional suites*) into attractive, persuasive presentations. Microsoft PowerPoint makes it easy to jazz up dull numbers and lists with color, graphical elements, and *clip art*, but the program's *multimedia* capabilities are limited. There's no way to include a video clip in a slide show, for example, without resorting to *Object Linking and Embedding (OLE)*, a procedure that is quite tedious.

Microsoft Publisher A limited-capability *desktop publishing (DTP)* program for use by people who occasionally need to design *documents* but don't need a full-featured desktop publishing program like *QuarkXPress*. Microsoft Publisher can't compete with high-end DTP programs, but for less than $100, Microsoft Publisher offers a lot of hand-holding and makes it easy for people with a minimum of design skill to generate good-looking documents.

Microsoft Windows 95 An *operating system* for Intel-based *80386DX, 486*, and *Pentium microprocessors*. Windows 95 is designed for running Windows applications, including *multimedia* applications, in homes and offices. A completely redesigned *graphical user interface (GUI)* enhances ease of learning as well as day-to-day usability. Additional innovations include long *file names*, 32-bit disk and file systems, *preemptive multitasking*, improved handling of *system resource* problems and *general protection faults (GPF)*, built-in support for the *Microsoft Network* and the *Internet*. Combining 16-bit and 32-bit *source code* to ensure reliable operation of existing 16-bit applications, Windows 95 is not a true 32-bit operating system (like *OS/2 Warp* or Microsoft's own *Microsoft Windows NT*); nevertheless, users appreciate not having to upgrade their applications. For corporate environments, Windows 95 includes built-in network support, offering a consistent interface for accessing network resources on a variety of physical media. To aid in the often arduous task of installing new hardware components, Windows 95 incorporates *Plug and Play* capabilities, which allow nearly automatic installation and configuration of compatible accessories (such as sound cards and CD-ROM drives). See fig. M.3.

CAUTION: *Though Microsoft claims that Microsoft Windows 95 will run on a 386-class computer with 4M or random-access memory (RAM), don't believe it. An absolute minimum configuration is a 486SX with 8M of RAM, and with that configuration you'll probably see a productivity decrease instead of an increase since you'll spend time waiting on your computer. Think twice about installing Microsoft Windows 95 on anything but a fast 486 or Pentium with a 400M or larger hard drive, a 64-bit video adapter, and a CD-ROM disk drive.*

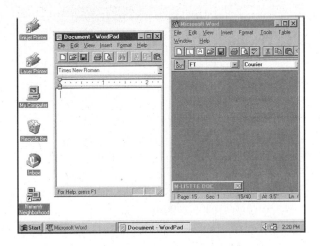

Fig. M.3 *The Microsoft Windows 95 desktop with several open applications.*

Microsoft Windows NT A *32-bit operating system*. On high-end *Pentium* systems, Windows NT provides the performance of *UNIX workstations* that cost far more money—and without sacrificing compatibility with personal productivity applications. Windows NT is designed for use by engineers, scientists, statisticians, and other professional or technical workers who carry out processor-intensive tasks. In addition to high-performance Intel processors, Windows NT runs on workstations based on the Alpha and MIPS processors.

Microsoft Word A full-featured *word processor*. Microsoft Word competes mainly with *WordPerfect* but also with *Lotus*

Word Pro. Several computer publications have reported that version 6.0 of Word has surpassed long-time favorite WordPerfect in terms of *feature*-richness and usability.

One of Microsoft Word's most useful advanced features is AutoCorrect, which automatically fixes spelling errors you make frequently (such as the common substitution of "teh" for "the"). *Wizards*, automated helpers that assist with such things as *mail merges* and *formatting*, and support for *object linking and embedding (OLE)*, are also included in Microsoft Word. Microsoft Word is highly customizable: *toolbars* and *menu bars* can be altered to suit individual tastes, and a very powerful *macro* language, called Word Basic, is included.

micro-to-mainframe   The linkage of *personal computers* to *mainframe* or *minicomputer networks.*

MIDI cueing   In *multimedia*, a set of *Musical Instrument Digital Interface (MIDI)* messages that determines the occurrence of events other than musical notes (such as recording, playing back, or turning on lighting devices).

MIDI file   A file containing musical data encoded according to *Musical Instrument Digital Interface (MIDI)* specifications. In *Microsoft Windows 95*, MIDI files use the extension .MID.

MIDI interface   See *MIDI port.*

MIDI port   A receptacle that allows you to connect a personal computer directly to a musical synthesizer. See *Musical Instrument Digital Interface (MIDI).*

MIDI   See *Musical Instrument Digital Interface (MIDI).*

migration   A change from an older *hardware* platform, *operating system*, or *software* version to a newer one. For example, industry observers expect corporations to migrate from Microsoft Windows 3.1 to *Microsoft Windows 95.*

milli-   Prefix indicating one thousandth.

million instructions per second (MIPS)   A *benchmark* method for measuring the rate at which a computer executes *microprocessor* instructions. A computer capable of 0.5 MIPS, for example, can execute 500,000 instructions per second.

CAUTION: *MIPS ratings are associated with sophisticated mainframes and supercomputers; only with the 80486 and Pentium systems has the performance of personal computers improved to the point that their processing speed can be described in MIPS. However, MIPS measurements inadequately state a computer system's throughput—a performance measurement that takes into account the speed of internal data transfer to and from the memory and the speed of important peripherals such as disk drives. See* Norton SI.

millisecond (ms)   A unit of measurement, equal to one-thousandth of a second, commonly used to specify the *access time* of hard disk drives.

MIME type   In the *Multipurpose Internet Multimedia Extensions (MIME)*, a code that specifies the content type of a multimedia file. The naming of MIME types is controlled by the *Internet Registered Numbers Authority (IANA)*. A Web browser detects MIME types by examining the file's extension; for example, a file with the extension *.mpg or *.mpeg contains an MPEG video.

mini-AT-size case   A desktop (horizontal) case that mounts the *motherboard* in the same way as the *AT-size case*, but takes up less space. Mini-AT-size cases are space-efficient, but sometimes have too few *expansion slots*. Before buying a mini-AT-size case, make sure it can handle any *adapters* you might add in the future. See *tower case*.

minicomputer   A multi-user computer designed to meet the needs of a small company or a department. A minicomputer is more powerful than a personal computer but not as powerful as a *mainframe*. Typically, about 4 to 100 people use a minicomputer simultaneously.

mini-driver   In *Microsoft Windows 95*, the portion of a *driver* that relates directly to *hardware*, such as a *printer* or *modem*. Mini-drivers take up less disk space than old-style drivers, since they share more resources with the *operating system*.

minimize   In a *graphical user interface (GUI)*, to shrink a window so that it collapses to an *icon* on the *desktop*. You minimize a window by clicking the minimize button (the left button in the upper-right corner) or by choosing Minimize from the *Control menu*. When you minimize an application in *Microsoft Windows 95*, the application appears as an icon on the *taskbar*.

L
M
N

mini-tower case A vertical case designed to fit into a smaller space than a full-sized *tower case*. Though they have less space for *disk drives* and other devices than tower cases, mini-tower cases can have an equal number of *expansion slots* and have smaller *footprints* than desktop cases. See *AT-size case* and *mini-AT-size case*.

MIPS See *million instructions per second (MIPS)*.

MIS See *management information system (MIS)*.

misc In *UseNet*, one of the *standard newsgroup hierarchies*, containing newsgroups that do not fit in the other categories (comp, sci, news, rec, soc, and talk). Examples of misc newsgroups include misc.consumers, misc.kids.computers, and misc.writing.

mixed cell reference In a *spreadsheet program*, a cell reference in which the column reference is absolute but the row reference is relative ($A9), or in which the row reference is absolute but the column reference is relative (A$9). See *absolute cell reference, cell reference,* and *relative cell reference*.

mixed column/line chart See *mixed column/line graph*.

mixed column/line graph In presentation and analytical graphics, a graph that displays one *data series* using columns and another data series using lines. You use a line graph to suggest a trend over time; a column graph groups data items so that you can compare one to another. In figure M.4, for example, the trends in manufacturing costs, represented by a line, are compared to expenses, shown as columns.

MNP See *Microcom Networking Protocol (MNP)*.

MNP-4 The most popular *error-correcting protocol*, which filters out *line noise* and eliminates errors that can occur during the transmission and reception of data via *modem*. For error correcting to function, both modems—the one sending as well as the one receiving the transmission—must have error-checking capabilities conforming to the same error-correcting protocol.

MNP-5 The same *error-correcting protocol* as *MNP-4*, as well as a data-compression protocol for computer *modems* that speeds transmissions by compressing (encoding, actually) data on the sending end and decompressing the data on the reception end. If the data isn't already compressed, gains in effective transmission speeds of up to 200 percent can be realized. See *data-compression protocol*.

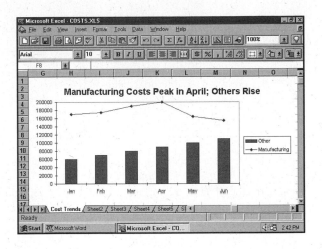

Fig. M.4 *A mixed column/line graph.*

mode The operating state in which you place a *program* by choosing among a set of exclusive operating options. Within a given mode, certain commands and *keystrokes* are available, but you may need to change modes to use other commands or keystrokes.

Lotus 1-2-3, for example, has numerous operating modes. Here are several:

Mode	Description
READY	1-2-3 is waiting for you to enter a command or make a cell entry.
VALUE	You're entering a number or formula.
LABEL	You're entering a label.
EDIT	You can edit the cell entry now displayed on the control panel.
POINT	You can use the arrow keys to expand the highlight and define a range.
HELP	1-2-3 is displaying a help screen.

continues

continued

Mode	Description
WAIT	1-2-3 is carrying out an operation and can't respond to additional commands or keyboard input.
STAT	1-2-3 is displaying the status of your worksheet.

A key step in learning a program is understanding its modes and how to switch from one mode to another. Beginners may reach a frustrating roadblock when they accidentally choose an unfamiliar mode and don't know how to exit it. Find out where the *mode indicator* is on-screen and learn what the messages mean.

mode indicator   An on-screen message that displays the program's current operating *mode*. In *Lotus 1-2-3*, for example, the mode indicator appears in the upper right corner of the screen.

model   A simulation of a system that exists in the real world, such as an aircraft fuselage or a business's cash flow. The purpose of constructing a model is to gain a better understanding of the prototype—the system being modeled. By examining or changing the characteristics of the model, you can draw inferences about the prototype's behavior.

CAUTION: *A model is only as good as its underlying assumptions. If these assumptions are incorrect, or if any information is missing from the model, it may not reflect the prototype's behavior accurately.*

modem   A device that converts the digital signals generated by the *serial port* to the modulated analog signals required for transmission over a telephone line and, likewise, transforms incoming analog signals to their digital equivalents. People frequently use modems to exchange programs and data with other computers or on-line information services.

The speed at which a modem (short for modulator/demodulator) transmits data is measured in units called *bits per second,* or *bps* (technically not the same as *baud,* although the terms are often used interchangeably). Modems come in various speeds and use various modulation protocols. Most 2400 bps modems use the

V.22bis protocol, while 9600 bps modems use the *V.32* protocol, 14,400 bps modems the *V.32bis* standard, and 28,800 bps modems use the *V.34*. Faster modems are usually *backward compatible* with slower ones.

Two common standards for *error-correcting protocols* eliminate errors attributable to noise and other *glitches* in the telephone system: *MNP-4* and *V.42*. For data-compression, two standards predominate: *V.42bis* and *MNP-5*. See *acoustic coupler, auto-dial/auto-answer modem, Bell 103A, Bell 212A, CCITT protocol, direct-connect modem, dirty, echoplex, external modem, full duplex, half duplex, Hayes command set, Hayes-compatible modem, internal modem, MNP-4, MNP-5, reliable link,* and *Universal Asynchronous Receiver/Transmitter (UART).*

moderated newsgroup   In a *distributed bulletin board* system such as *UseNet* or EchoMail, a topical conference in which contributions are screened by one or more moderators before the post appears. The moderator's job, often mistaken for censorship, is to ensure that postings adhere to the group's stated topic. A moderator also may rule out discussion on certain subtopics if postings on such subjects turn out to be *flame bait* (postings likely to cause an unproductive and bitter debate with low information content).

moderator   In *UseNet* and *mailing lists,* a volunteer who takes on the task of screening messages submitted to a *moderated newsgroup* or moderated mailing list.

Modified Frequency Modulation (MFM)   A method of recording digital information on a *magnetic medium* such as *tapes* and disks by eliminating redundant or blank areas. Because the MFM *data-encoding scheme* doubles the storage attained under the earlier frequency-modulation (FM) recording technique, MFM recording usually is referred to as *double density*.

MFM often is wrongly used to describe *hard disk controllers* conforming to the *ST-506/ST-412* standard. MFM actually refers to the method used to pack data on the disk and isn't synonymous with disk drive *interface standards* such as ST-506, *Small Computer System Interface (SCSI),* or *Enhanced Small Device Interface (ESDI).* See *Run-Length Limited (RLL).*

MO disk   See *magneto-optical (MO) disk.*

MO drive   See *magneto-optical (MO) drive.*

Modula-2   A *high-level programming language* that extends *Pascal* so that the language can execute program modules independently.

Developed in 1980 by computer wizard and *Pascal* creator Niklaus Wirth, Modula-2 supports the separate compilation of program modules and overcomes many other shortcomings of Pascal. A programmer working as part of a team can write and compile the module he or she has been assigned, and then test the module extensively before integrating it with other modules.

Although Modula-2 is increasingly popular as a teaching language at colleges and universities, *C* dominates professional software development. *See modular programming* and *structured programming.*

modular accounting package   A collection of accounting programs—one for each chief accounting function (general ledger, accounts payable, accounts receivable, payroll, and inventory, for example)—designed to work together, even though they aren't integrated into one program.

Modular accounting programs are computerized versions of traditional accounting operations, in which a firm keeps several ledgers. Modular packages require you to follow special procedures to make sure that all the modules work together. These programs haven't found a large market in personal computing for two reasons: they rarely mimic the way small-businesses operators keep their books, and they're often hard to use.

modular jack   Synonymous with RJ-11 jack, the standard receptacle for the connectors on telephone cable, found both in wall sockets and on *modems.* Wall sockets built before 1970 may have an incompatible, four-prong connector that can be connected to a RJ-11 plug with an RJA1X adapter.

modular programming   A *programming* style that breaks down program functions into modules, each of which accomplishes one function and contains all the *source code* and variables needed to accomplish that function.

Modular programming is a solution to the problem of very large programs that are difficult to *debug* and maintain. By segmenting the program into modules that perform clearly defined functions, you can determine the source of program errors more easily.

Object-oriented programming languages, such as *SmallTalk* and *HyperTalk,* incorporate modular programming principles.

modulation The conversion of a *digital* signal to its *analog* equivalent, especially for the purposes of transmitting signals using telephone lines and *modems.* See *demodulation.*

modulation protocol In *modems,* the standards used to govern the speed at which a modem sends and receives information over the telephone lines. See *Bell 103A, Bell 212A,* and *CCITT protocol.*

module In a *program,* a unit or section that can function on its own. In an integrated program, for instance, you can use the *word processing* module as though it were a separate, stand-alone program.

moiré effect An optical illusion, perceived as flickering, that sometimes occurs when you place high-contrast line patterns (such as cross-hatching in *pie graphs*) too close to one another.

CAUTION: *Many business graphics programs produce charts and graphs with undesirable moiré effects. You can avoid this problem by using no more than two or three cross-hatching patterns and separating them with solid white, gray, or black colors.*

monitor The complete device that produces an on-screen image, including the *display* and all necessary internal support circuitry. A monitor also is called a video display unit (VDU). See *analog monitor, digital monitor, Enhanced Graphics Display, monochrome monitor,* and *multiscanning monitor.*

monitor program A program that keeps track of and records the behavior of other programs, often for purposes of tracking bugs. Also, an obsolete synonym for *kernel.*

Monochrome Display Adapter (MDA) A single-color *display adapter* for *IBM PC-compatible* computers that displays text (but not *graphics*) with a resolution of 720 *pixels* horizontally and 350 lines vertically, placing characters in a matrix of 7 by 9. See *Hercules Graphics Adapter.*

Monochrome Display and Parallel Printer Adapter See *Monochrome Display Adapter (MDA).*

monochrome monitor   A *monitor* that displays one color against a black or white background. Examples include the IBM monochrome monitor that displays green text against a black background, and paper-white *Video Graphics Array (VGA)* monitors that display black text on a white background. See *paper-white monitor.*

monochrome printer   A printer that can generate output in black, white, and shades of gray, but not color.

monospace   A typeface such as Courier in which the width of each character is the same, producing output that looks like typed characters. The following is an example of monospace type:

```
The width of each character in this typeface is exactly
the same.
```

See *proportional spacing.*

monospaced font   See *monospace.*

monthly duty cycle   The number of pages a *printer* is designed to print each month. *Personal laser printers* may have monthly duty cycles as low as a few hundred pages, while *departmental laser printers* may have monthly duty cycles in excess of 200,000 pages.

morphing   Short for metamorphosing; a revolutionary animation technique used to "fill in the blanks" between dissimilar figures so that one seems to melt into another, such as changing a man to a werewolf, a bat to a vampire, or a rock singer to a panther.

Morphing, a common film industry special-effects technique, is related closely to another, more prosaic animation technique called tweening (short for in-betweening), which refers to the computer's capability to calculate and draw frames that are intermediate between the "key" frames hand-drawn by the artist. Morphing is the process of tweening to a different object.

Mosaic   A *Web browser* created by the *National Center for Supercomputing Applications (NCSA)* and placed in the *public domain.* Though Mosaic was one of the earliest Web browsers, it has been superseded by *Netscape Navigator.* See *World Wide Web (WWW).*

motherboard   A large circuit board that contains the computer's *central processing unit (CPU), microprocessor* support

chips, *random-access memory (RAM)*, and *expansion slots*. Synonymous with logic board.

Motorola   A Schaumburg, Illinois-based designer and manufacturer of electronic equipment, notably *semiconductors*. Motorola's
680x0 microprocessors are used in early *Macintosh* computers, and
the company collaborated with IBM and Apple to design the
PowerPC series of chips that are found in *Power Macintoshes*. See
PowerPC 601.

Motorola 68000   A *microprocessor* that processes 32 *bits* internally, although it uses a 16-bit *data bus* to communicate with the
rest of the computer. The 68000 can address up to 32 megabytes
of *random-access memory (RAM)*. Running at 8 MHz, the 68000
powers the entry-level Macintosh Classic.

Motorola 68020   A *microprocessor* electronically similar to the
Motorola 68000, except that this microprocessor uses a full 32-*bit*
architecture and runs at a *clock speed* of 16 *megahertz (MHz)*. The
68020 powers the original Macintosh II, displaced by newer models using the *Motorola 68030* chip.

Motorola 68030   A full 32-bit *microprocessor* that can run at
substantially higher *clock speeds* (16 to 50 *megahertz [MHz]*) than
the Motorola 68000 and 68020. The 68030 includes special features for *virtual memory management*.

The 68030 incorporates a chip that controls *page-mode RAM,* so
any 68030-equipped *Macintosh* can implement the advanced
memory management features of *System 7.5*.

Motorola 68040   A 32-bit *microprocessor* in *Motorola's* 680x0
family that represents an evolutionary advance over its immediate
predecessor, the *68030*. Analogous to the Intel 80486DX microprocessor, the 68040 packs more circuitry into its tiny confines,
reducing the need for support chips and improving performance.
For example, the 68040 includes a *numeric coprocessor*, eliminating
the need for a coprocessor chip. The 68040 powers the high-end
Quadra models of Apple Computer's *Macintosh* computers.

Motorola 68881   The *numeric coprocessor* used with the
Motorola *68000* and *68020 microprocessors*.

mount   To insert a *floppy disk* into a *floppy disk drive*. Installing
hardware, such as a *motherboard*, *disk drive*, and *adapters*, is also
referred to as mounting.

L
M
N

mousable interface   A *user interface* that responds to *mouse* input for such functions as selecting text, choosing commands from *menus*, and *scrolling* the screen.

mouse   An input device, equipped with one or more control buttons, that's housed in a palm-sized case and designed so that you can roll it about on the table next to your *keyboard*. As the mouse moves, its circuits relay signals that correspondingly move a *pointer* on-screen.

The simplest of all mouse functions is repositioning a *cursor*. You point to the cursor's new location and *click* the left mouse button. You also can use the mouse to choose commands from *menus*, select text for editing purposes, move objects, and draw pictures on-screen. Many typists don't like to take their fingers away from the keyboard, so programs that use the mouse often include keyboard equivalents.

A mouse is distinguished by the internal mechanism it uses to generate its signal and by its means of connection with the computer. Two types of internal mechanisms are popular:

- *Mechanical mouse.* This mouse has a rubber-coated ball on the underside of the case. As you move the mouse, the ball rotates and optical sensors detect the motion. You can use a mechanical mouse on virtually any surface, although a mouse pad made of special fabric gives the best results. A *trackball* mouse has the ball in the top of the case, and you use your thumb to move the ball.

- *Optical mouse.* This mouse registers its position by detecting reflections from a light-emitting diode that directs a beam downward. You must have a special metal pad to reflect the beam properly, and you can't move the mouse beyond the pad.

See *built-in pointing device, clip-on pointing device, freestanding pointing device, Microsoft mouse,* and *snap-on pointing device.*

mouse elbow   A painful *repetitive strain injury (RSI),* similar to tennis elbow, that's produced by lifting one's hand repeatedly to manipulate a *mouse.* Ostensibly ergonomic, the mouse turns out to be as severe a threat to one's health as the *keyboard,* which can cause carpal tunnel syndrome (another repetitive strain injury).

If you develop mouse elbow, learn to use the mouse with your other hand—or learn the keyboard shortcuts for mouse maneuvers. The latter isn't easy with *Macintosh* systems; *Microsoft Windows 95* and Windows applications, however, tend to offer excellent keyboard shortcuts for frequently used mouse techniques.

TIP: *Mechanical mice are prone to collect finger grease and dirt within their internal mechanisms. As this mixture hardens, the pointer may behave erratically. Remove the ball-retainer ring, freeing the ball, and clean the ball and the ball rollers with a cotton swab moistened in rubbing alcohol. Blow dust out of the ball chamber and reassemble the mouse.*

mouse port   Also called a PS/2 mouse port, a mouse port enables you to connect a *mouse* to the computer without tying up a *serial port.* A mouse port is a small, round socket into which you plug a PS/2-compatible mouse.

MOV   See *metal-oxide varistor (MOV).*

moving border   See *marquee.*

Moving Picture Experts Group (MPEG)   A working group of digital video experts who meet regularly under the auspices of the *International Standards Organization (ISO)* and the International Electro-technical Commission (IEC) to develop standards for compressed digital audio. The group's first standard, MPEG-1, compresses video to a rate of approximately 1.2 megabits per second and stereo audio to a rate of approximately 250 kilobits per second. The second standard, MPEG-2, will provide compression for higher-*bandwidth* distribution media, and has not yet been formalized. See *MPEG audio* and *MPEG video.*

MPC   See *Multimedia Personal Computer (MPC).*

MPC-2   See *Multimedia Personal Computer-2 (MPC-2).*

MPEG audio   A format for the compression of digitized stereo audio that employs the MPEG-1 *compression standard,* developed by the *Moving Picture Experts Group (MPEG).* Stereo MPEG files can deliver impressive-sounding stereo when played through a good *sound card* and speakers, although the sound is not up to the standards of audio compact discs.

MPEGPLAY An MPEG video player for *Microsoft Windows 95*, created by Michael Simmons. This *shareware* program is widely used as a *helper program* for *Web browsers*.

MPEG video A format for the compression of digitized videos and animations that employs the MPEG-1 *compression standard*, developed by the *Moving Picture Experts Group (MPEG)*. A disadvantage of MPEG video is that it does not incorporate sound, unlike the *QuickTime* and *AVI* movie formats.

MPR I An old Swedish standard—outmoded by the more stringent *MPR II* and *TCO* standards—for limiting *electromagnetic radiation* from monitors. Make sure any monitor you buy is MPR II- or TCO-compliant, not just "MPR-compliant" or "compliant with the Swedish standard."

MPR II A standard for monitor radiation developed by Sweden's National Board for Industrial and Technical Development in 1987 and updated in 1990. To meet MPR II standards, a monitor can't emit more than 250 nanoteslas of electromagnetic radiation at a distance of a half meter.

Scientists aren't sure whether *extremely low-frequency (ELF) emissions* are hazardous to your health, but you can stay on the safe side by selecting a monitor that conforms to MPR II standards. *TCO* standards are even tougher than MPR II.

MPU 401 The standard that governs the design of the *MIDI port*, which is used to connect musical instruments to computer *sound boards*. The MPU 401 standard dictates that the port have some of its own sound-processing circuitry, lessening the load on the rest of the computer.

MR head See *magneto-resistive head*.

ms See *millisecond (ms)*.

MS-DOS The standard, single-user *operating system* of IBM and IBM-compatible computers, introduced in 1981.

MS-DOS is a command-line operating system that requires you to enter commands, *arguments*, and *syntax* to use MS-DOS successfully. After mastering MS-DOS commands—or installing *utility programs* that do work for you—you can achieve a high degree of control over the operating system's capabilities—including setting *file attributes*, creating automatically executed *batch files*, and developing semi-automated backup procedures.

The most severe limitation of MS-DOS is the 640K *random-access memory (RAM)* barrier that the operating system imposes on *IBM PC-compatible* computing. Although many users are migrating to *Microsoft Windows 95* to use its memory-management capabilities and easier-to-use interface, millions of older IBM-compatible computers exist that can't run Windows well. MS-DOS is unquestionably the world's most widely used operating system and is likely to remain so for years to come. See *application program interface (API), CP/M (Control Program for Microprocessors), Microsoft Windows NT, MS-DOS QBasic, MS-DOS Shell, Operating System/2 (OS/2), PC-DOS, protected mode, real mode, terminate-and-stay-resident (TSR) program,* and *UNIX.*

MS-DOS QBasic　　An improved *BASIC* programming environment, supplied with *MS-DOS* 5.0 and later, that includes extensive on-line help.

MS-DOS Shell　　An improved, *menu*-driven user interface for the *MS-DOS operating system,* supplied with MS-DOS 5.0 and later, that conforms to the *industry-standard user interface.* MS-DOS Shell provides menu-driven access to most DOS commands, finally providing much of the functionality that has long been missing from MS-DOS. Users may find less need for utility *programs* such as PC Tools.

MTBF　　See *mean time between failures (MTBF).*

MTU　　See *maximum transmission unit (MTU).*

MUD, Object-Oriented (MOO)　　A type of Multi-User Dungeon (MUD) that incorporates a sophisticated, *object-oriented programming language,* which participants can use to construct their own personalized characters and worlds.

MOO worlds can be so realistic, they raise questions about what constitutes a crime. Julien Dibbell, in his famous essay *A Rape in Cyberspace,* describes an incident in LambdaMOO (the largest MOO) in which one LambdaMOO participant, a skilled hacker, made another LambdaMOO participant's character perform violent sex acts. Dibbell's essay discussed whether the hacker's actions were really rape, as the owners of the two characters were separated by many miles at the time of the virtual assault.

Multicast Backbone (Mbone)　　An experimental system that can deliver real-time audio and video delivery via the *Internet.* Capable of one-to-many and many-to-many transmission with low consumption of network resources, Mbone requires special software, which is installed on only a small number of the computers currently connected to the Internet. The Rolling Stones broadcast a concert on the Mbone during their 1994 Voodoo Lounge tour. See *multicasting*.

multicasting   In a *network*, the routing of a single message to two or more workstations.

MultiColor Graphics Array (MCGA)   A *video standard* of IBM's Personal System/2. MCGA adds 64 *grayscale* shades to the *Color Graphics Adapter (CGA)* standard and provides the *Extended Graphics Adapter (EGA)* standard *resolution* of 640 *pixels* by 350 lines with 16 possible colors.

MultiFinder   A *utility program*, included in *Macintosh System* 7.5, that extends the Finder's capabilities so that the *Macintosh* can run more than one application at a time.

With MultiFinder, the Macintosh becomes a multiloading operating system with some limited capabilities to perform tasks in the background, such as downloading information via telecommunications and carrying out *background printing*. Contrary to common belief, MultiFinder isn't a true *multitasking* operating system; when you activate one application, the other application freezes. See *context switching*, *multiple program loading*, and *shell*.

multilaunching   In a *local area network (LAN)*, the opening of an *application program* by more than one user at a time.

multilevel sort   In *database management*, a sort operation that uses two or more data fields to determine the order in which *data records* are arranged. To perform a multilevel sort, you identify two or more *data fields* as sort keys—fields used for ordering records.

In a membership database, for example, the primary sort key may be LAST_NAME, so all records are alphabetized by the member's last name. The second sort key, FIRST_NAME, comes into play when two or more records have the same last name. A third sort key, JOIN_DATE, is used when two or more records have the same last name and the same first name. Use a multilevel sort when one sort key can't resolve the order of two or more records in your database.

multimedia   A computer-based method of presenting information by using more than one medium of communication, such as text, *graphics* and sound, and emphasizing interactivity.

In *Microsoft Bookshelf,* for example, you can see portraits of William Shakespeare, see a list of his works, and follow *hyperlinks* to
related information (see fig. M.5). Advances in sound and video
synchronization allow you to display moving video images within
on-screen *windows.* However, because graphics and sound require
so much storage space, a minimal configuration for a multimedia
system includes a *CD-ROM disk drive.*

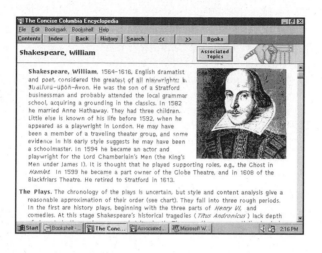

Fig. M.5 *A multimedia application.*

TIP: *Microsoft Windows 95 users should look for multimedia
products (including CD-ROM drives and software) that have the
MPC label. This label is your assurance that the product fully
conforms to the MPC standards and will function correctly with
Microsoft Windows 95. See* Multimedia Personal Computer
(MPC).

Multimedia Compact Disc (MMCD)   A proposed standard,
not supported by any mass-produced *CD-ROM disk drive,* that
describes a method for encoding 3.7 *G* of data on one side of a *CD-
ROM disk.* MMCD, which Sony calls High-Density Multimedia
Compact Disc (HDMMCD), is competing with *the CD-ROM/
Super Density (CD-ROM/SD)* standard for industry acceptance.

multimedia extensions   Additions to an *operating system* that allow *multimedia* software to synchronize graphics and sound. These extensions—called hooks in *programmers'* slang—allow multimedia software designers to access sound and video capabilities without extensive, non-standard programming. Apple's *QuickTime* is a multimedia extension to its System 7 software. *Microsoft Windows 95* includes the multimedia extensions (called *Media Control Interface [MCI]*) that were formerly available separately. See *application program interface (API)*.

Multimedia Personal Computer (MPC)   A standard for *multimedia hardware* and software jointly developed by the MPC Consortium, which includes *Microsoft Corporation*, Philips, Tandy, and Zenith Data Systems. Microsoft Windows 3.1 provides the foundation for MPC. The MPC standard assumes an IBM PS/2 or IBM-compatible hardware platform; Apple Computer, not surprisingly, has offered a competing standard (*QuickTime*) for its *Macintosh* computer. MPC has been replaced by the *Multimedia Personal Computer-2 (MPC-2)* standard.

Multimedia Personal Computer-2 (MPC-2)   A standard, developed by a consortium of computer-industry companies, that describes the minimum computer configuration needed to run *multimedia* applications. The standard calls for a 486SX-25 *microprocessor*, 8M of *random-access memory (RAM)*, a *Video Graphics Array (VGA) monitor*, and a *double-speed CD-ROM disk drive*.

multiple document interface (MDI)   In an *application program*, a user interface that allows the user to have more than one *document* or *worksheet* open at once. With its *Microsoft Windows 95 Application Program Interface (API)*, *Microsoft Corporation* discourages the use of MDIs. Instead, Microsoft favors running multiple copies of programs, each with a different document.

multiple program loading   An *operating system* that lets you start more than one program at a time; however, only one of the programs is active at any one time. You press a *key* to switch from one program to another. See *context switching* and *MultiFinder*.

multiple selection   In a *spreadsheet program*, a selection of two or more non-contiguous *ranges*. In figure M.6, for example, you see three ranges selected, making it possible for you to format and perform other operations on all three ranges at a time.

multiplex   To combine or interleave messages in a communications channel.

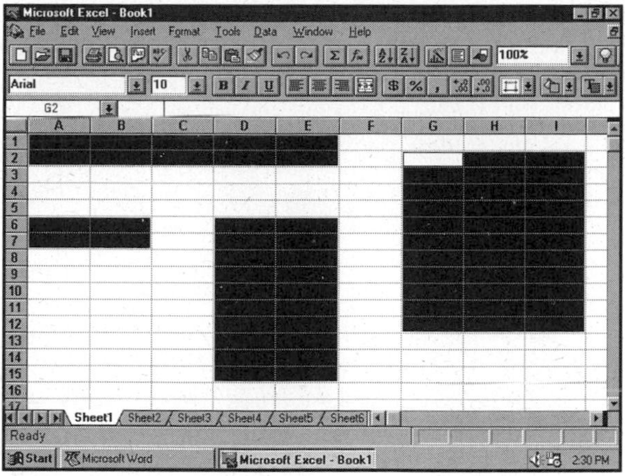

Fig. M.6 *Multiple selection of ranges.*

multiple zone recording (MZR) A way to pack more data onto *hard disks* that use *constant angular velocity (CAV)* recording. MZR drives pack extra data onto their edges, which would otherwise be filled to less than full capacity.

multiplexer (mux) A device that merges lower speed transmissions into one higher speed channel at one end of the link. Another mux reverses the process at the other end of the link.

multiplexing In *local area networks (LANs)*, the simultaneous transmission of multiple messages in one channel.

A network that can *multiplex* allows more than one computer to access the network simultaneously. Multiplexing increases the cost of a network, however, because multiplexing devices must be included that can mix the signals into a single channel for transmission. See *frequency division multiplexing, local area network (LAN),* and *time division multiplexing.*

Multi-Purpose Internet Mail Extensions (MIME) An *Internet* standard that specifies how tools, such as *electronic mail* programs and *Web browsers,* can transfer *multimedia* files (including sounds, graphics, and video) via the Internet. Prior to the development of MIME, all data transferred via the Internet had to be coded in *ASCII text.* See *uuencode/uudecode.*

multiscan monitor See *multiscanning monitor.*

multiscanning monitor   A color monitor that can adjust to a range of input frequencies so that it can work with a variety of *display adapters*. Multiscanning monitors are often called multisync monitors, but Multisync is a *proprietary* name of an NEC multiscanning monitor.

multisession PhotoCD   A standard for recording *PhotoCD* information onto a *CD-ROM disk* during several different recording sessions. Unlike standard *CD-ROM disk drives*, drives that are Multisession PhotoCD-compatible can read information recorded on a disk during several different pressings—an advantage for consumers who don't want to wait until they've taken enough pictures to fill a PhotoCD before having the photos processed, but don't want to waste PhotoCD capacity, either.

Multisync monitor   See *multiscanning monitor.*

multitasking   The execution of more than one program at a time on a computer system.

Multitasking shouldn't be confused with *multiple program loading,* in which two or more programs are present in *random-access memory (RAM)* but only one program executes at a time. When multitasking, the active, or foreground, task responds to the keyboard while the background task continues to run (but without your active control).

Among the operating systems or shells that provide multitasking are *Operating System/2 (OS/2),* DESQview, and *Microsoft Windows 95.*

multithreaded application   A *program* that can run two or more *threads* (independent portions of the program) at the same time. The advantage of dividing a program up into threads is that the operating system can decide which of the threads should get the highest priority for processing. See *preemptive multitasking.*

Multi-User Dungeon (MUD)   A MUD is a form of virtual reality designed for network use that offers participants an opportunity to interact with other computer users in real time. MUDs, originally developed to support on-line role-playing games, have mostly been replaced by more flexible *MUDs Object-Oriented (MOO).*

multi-user system   A *computer system* that can be used by more than one person to access programs and data at the same time.

In a multi-user system, each user is equipped with a terminal. If the system has just one central processing unit, a technique called *time-sharing* allocates access time to several terminals.

Personal computers with advanced microprocessors, such as the Intel 80486, are sufficiently powerful to serve as the nucleus of a multi-user system. Such systems typically are equipped with *UNIX, OS/2,* or *Microsoft Windows NT.* See *Appletalk, EtherNet, file server, local area network (LAN), mainframe, minicomputer, Netware,* and *Network Operating System (NOS).*

 TIP: *If you're considering installing a system that more than one person will use, familiarize yourself with the pros and cons of the two alternatives: multi-user systems and LANs.*

multiword DMA mode 1   The method *Enhanced IDE hard disks* use to transfer data to the rest of the computer. Multiword DMA mode 1 enables Enhanced IDE drives to transfer data three to four times faster than *integrated drive electronics (IDE)* hard disks.

Musical Instrument Digital Interface (MIDI)   A standard *communications protocol* for the exchange of information between computers and music synthesizers.

MIDI provides tools that many composers and musicians say are becoming almost indispensable. With a synthesizer and a computer equipped with the necessary software and a MIDI port, a musician can transcribe a composition into musical notation by playing the composition at the *keyboard.* After the music is placed into computer-represented form, virtually every aspect of the digitized sound—pitch, attack, delay time, tempo, and more—can be edited and altered.

My Computer   In *Microsoft Windows 95,* a file- and program-management utility that replaces the Windows 3.1 Program Manager and File Manager, combining the functions of the earlier utilities with a simple, consistent interface (see fig. M.7). The My Computer window displays files and programs as large *icons,* which can be double-clicked to access the files. In addition, the icons can be dragged and dropped to initiate functions such as printing or deletion (via the *Recycling Bin*).

L M N

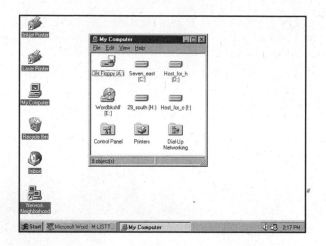

Fig. M.7 *Large icon view in My Computer (Windows 95)*

name server In an *Internet*-connected *local area network (LAN)*, a computer that provides the *Domain Name Service*, that is, the translation between alphabetical domain names and numerical *IP addresses*. To establish a connection with an Internet service provider, you need to know the *IP address* of the name server.

nano- A prefix indicating one billionth.

nanosecond (ns) A unit of time equal to one billionth of a second. Far beyond the range of human perception, nanoseconds are relevant to computers. An advertisement for 80 ns RAM chips, for example, means that the RAM chips respond to the central processing unit (CPU) within 80 nanoseconds. See *millisecond (ms)*.

National Center for Supercomputing Applications (NCSA) A supercomputer research center, affiliated with the University of Illinois at Urbana-Champaign, that specializes in scientific visualization. NCSA most recently achieved fame as the birthplace of *NCSA Mosaic,* the popular *Web browser*.

National Information Infrastructure (NII) A proposed high-speed, high-bandwidth *network* that can deliver voice, data, and video services throughout the United States. NII will be developed by private firms, cable television, and telephone companies, with minimal government funding. The major impetus is the delivery of on-demand movies to the home, fueled by good old-fashioned competition.

That NII will be built seems all but inevitable; whether this commercial venture will serve the public good is another matter. It may well end up being a television system that offers more channels, denying the use of the system for autonomous two-way communication and the construction of virtual communities. See *asynchronous digital subscriber loop (ADSL)*.

National Research and Education Network (NREN) Proposed backbone network capable of gigabit-per-second data transfer rates. NREN will link a number of supercomputer research centers and will not be available for public use.

National Science Foundation (NSF)   An independent agency of the U.S. government that seeks to promote the public good throughout the development of science and engineering. Until 1995, NSF subsidized and coordinated *NSFnet,* which at one time was the backbone network of the *Internet.*

National Television Standards Committee (NTSC)   A committee that governs physical standards for television broadcasting in the United States and most of Central and South America (but not Europe or Asia). NTSC television uses 525-line frames and displays full frames at 30 frames per second, using two interlaced fields at about 60 frames per second to correspond to the U.S. alternating-current frequency of 60 Hz. Most European and Asian countries use the PAL standard, which is based on their 50 Hz power-line frequencies.

native application   A *software program* designed to work with a particular type of *microprocessor;* in other words, a program that is *binary compatible* with a particular microprocessor. Non-native applications may run on a given microprocessor with the help of an *emulation* program, but native applications are almost always significantly faster than non-native applications.

native code   See *machine language.*

native file format   The default *file format* a program uses to store data on disk. The format is often a *proprietary file format.* Many popular programs today can retrieve and save data in several formats. See *ASCII.*

natural language   A naturally occurring language such as Spanish, French, German, or Tamil, as opposed to an artificial language such as a *programming language.*

Computer scientists are working to improve computers so that they can respond to natural language. Human languages are so complex that no single model of a natural language grammar system has gained widespread acceptance among linguists. The complexity of human languages, coupled with the lack of understanding about what information is needed to decode human sentences, makes it difficult to devise programs that recognize speech. Progress in solving these problems has been slow.

> **CAUTION:** *Computer programs, such as Lotus HAL, occasionally are marketed with the claim that they can accept natural language input, but your input must be phrased so that it conforms to fairly strict syntax guidelines.*

natural language processing   In *artificial intelligence*, using a computer to decipher or analyze human language.

natural recalculation   In a *spreadsheet* program, a *recalculation order* that performs worksheet computations in the manner logically dictated by the formulas you place in cells. If the value of a formula depends on references to other cells that contain formulas, the program calculates the other cells first. See *column-wise recalculation, optimal recalculation,* and *row-wise recalculation.*

navigation button   In a *Web browser,* a tool on the on-screen toolbar that enables the user to display the previously accessed document (Back), return to the document being displayed when the Back button was clicked (Forward), or return to the current default home page (Home). See *Web browser.*

NCSA Mosaic   A graphical *Web browser* created at the *National Center for Supercomputing Applications (NCSA).* Available as *freeware* for non-commercial uses, NCSA Mosaic is available in versions for *Microsoft Windows 95, UNIX,* and Macintosh computers. Because NCSA lacks the needed facilities and funding, technical support is unavailable and program bugs may go uncorrected for months. Because of these problems, NCSA has licensed Mosaic to Spyglass, Inc., which in turn licenses a fully supported version of the program (called *Enhanced NCSA Mosaic*) to book publishers, computer software firms, and other resellers. Much of the programming team that developed NCSA Mosaic joined Netscape Communications and produced the popular *Netscape Navigator* browser, today in use by an estimated 75 percent of the people roaming the *World Wide Web.*

near-letter quality (NLQ)   A *dot-matrix printer* mode that prints almost typewriter-quality characters. As a result, printing when using this mode is slower than other printing modes.

needle drop   In *multimedia,* using a short excerpt from a recorded musical piece instead of creating an original composition. The term stems from the days of vinyl phonograph needles.

L M N

> **CAUTION:** *Don't use recorded music in your multimedia presentations without first seeking permission and paying the required needle drop fee.*

negotiation   See *handshaking*.

nested structure   A structure in which one *control structure* is positioned within another. See *DO/WHILE loop*.

nested subtotal   In a *spreadsheet*, a *formula* that adds several *values* and is, in turn, included in a larger formula that adds several subtotals.

net.abuse   In *UseNet*, any action that interferes with peoples' right to use and enjoy UseNet, including flooding newsgroups with unwanted posts (also called *spamming*), conducting an organized forgery campaign, or carrying out an organized effort to prevent the discussion of an issue.

NetBIOS   See *Network Basic Input/Output System (NetBIOS)*.

net.god(dess)   In *UseNet*, an individual whose lengthy UseNet experience and savvy on-line demeanor elevates him or her to heroic status. An example of a net.god is James "Kibo" Parry, who is said to have developed a *Practical Extraction and Report Language (perl)* script enabling him to detect when and where his name was mentioned in any article throughout UseNet's thousands of *newsgroups*. His witty responses to these articles, and his ubiquity—at one time he claimed to post as many as two dozen articles per day—soon resulted in deification (and the creation of a newsgroup in his honor, called `alt.religion.kibology`).

netiquette   *Network* etiquette; a set of rules that reflect long-standing experience about getting along harmoniously in the electronic environment (*electronic mail* and *newsgroups*). The basics of netiquette are as follows:

- Keep your messages short and to the point, abbreviate whenever possible, and don't include an extravagant *signature* at the bottom of your message that lists your name and electronic mailing address.

- Don't use ALL UPPERCASE LETTERS. This is considered to be "shouting." To emphasize a word, use asterisks as you would quotation marks.

- If you want to criticize, criticize the idea, not the person. Don't criticize a person's spelling or grammatical errors. Today's worldwide networks encompass users willing to learn English and trying to participate; they deserve encouragement, not criticism.

- Don't overreact to something you read on-line. If you get angry, don't reply right away. Go take a walk or, better yet, sleep on it. Electronic mail is easily forwarded. Don't say anything that you don't want to wind up on your boss's desk.

- Don't ask members of a newsgroup to censor a particular person's contributions, or disallow discussion of a topic that you find offensive; instead, create a *kill file* so that those messages don't appear on your screen.

- If you ask a question in a newsgroup, request that replies be sent to you personally, unless you feel that the replies would be of interest to everyone who reads the newsgroup.

- In electronic mail, be cautious in replying to messages that were sent to more than one subscriber. In some systems, your reply will be sent to each person who received the original—which may include every subscriber.

- Don't *cross-post* a message (send it to more than one newsgroup), or reply to a cross-posted message, unless you're genuinely following the discussion in each newsgroup and believe your message would prove of interest to readers of each of them.

- If you're *posting* something that gives away the plot of a movie, novel, or television show, put *<SPOILER>* at the top of your message. That way, people can skip reading it if they don't want to know whodunnit.

- If you're posting something that some people may find offensive, such as an erotic story, use the command (available with most networks) that *encrypts* your text so that it looks like garbage characters. (In UseNet, for example, the command *rot-13* shifts each letter 13 characters, so that b becomes o.) To read such a message, use the command that *decrypts* the text. Any reader who is offended will have to take responsibility for having decrypted the message.

Also, use discretion when "getting personal" with other users. Stalking laws are now being interpreted to encompass e-mail messages. See *follow-on post, Internet,* and *net.police.*

net lag   In a *packet-switching network,* the delay in accessing a document that is caused by *latency* and other delivery problems.

NetManage Chameleon   A widely-distributed series of *TCP/IP* connectivity programs and *Internet* tools, created by NetManage, Inc. The Chameleon Sampler includes many Internet tools but lacks *local-area network (LAN)* connectivity (the package may be used for *Serial Line Internet Protocol (SLIP)* or *Point to Point Protocol (PPP)* connections only). A commercial version, called Internet Chameleon, includes a *Web browser* called WebSurfer.

netnews   A collective way of referring to the *UseNet newsgroups.*

NETNORTH   A Canadian *wide area network (WAN)* fully integrated with *BITNET* that performs the same functions as BITNET.

net.police   In *UseNet,* a person or group of persons who take upon themselves the enforcement of UseNet traditions and *netiquette.* For example, the famed *Cancelmoose* applies an automated program (called a *cancelbot*) that seeks out and destroys advertisements that are posted to excessive numbers of *newsgroups.* See *net.abuse* and *spamming.*

Netscape Commerce Server   A *World Wide Web (WWW)* server for *UNIX* and *Microsoft Windows NT* systems, created by Netscape Communications, that incorporates the firm's Secure Sockets Layer (SSL) Protocol security features. When users of Netscape Navigator log on to a site served by the Netsite Commerce Server, the browser's security icon indicates that a secure connection has been made; any information uploaded to the site (such as a credit card number and expiration date) is protected from interception while en route.

Netscape Communications Server   A *World Wide Web (WWW)* server for *UNIX* and *Microsoft Windows NT* systems, created by Netscape Communications, that lacks the security features of the *Netscape Commerce Server.*

Netscape Navigator A *Web browser* available free of charge via *File Transfer Protocol (FTP)* at ftp.mcom.com. Netscape Navigator offers support for advanced Web sites, including those that use forms and those that use flashing text. It also has an attractive, intuitive interface and operates faster than its main competition, *NCSA Mosaic*.

Fig. N.1 *Netscape Navigator (Web browser).*

Netscape News Server A *UseNet* server developed by Netscape Communications that incorporates the firm's Secure Sockets Layer (SSL) protocol. When users access the *newsgroup* with *Netscape Navigator,* the authenticity of the post is assured (*forgery* is a serious problem on UseNet). See *authentication.*

NetWare A *network operating system (NOS),* manufactured by Novell, for *local area networks (LANs).* NetWare accommodates more than 90 types of *network interface cards,* 30 network architectures, and several *communications protocols.* Versions are available for IBM PC compatibles and Macintosh computers.

network A communications and data exchange system created by physically connecting two or more computers with *network interface cards* and cables, and running a *network operating system (NOS).*

Personal computer networks differ in their scope. The smallest networks, called *local area networks (LANs),* may connect just two or three computers with an expensive peripheral, such as a *laser printer,* whereas others connect as many as 75 or more computers (see fig. N.2). Larger networks, called *wide-area networks (WANs),* use telephone lines or other communications media to link together computers separated by tens to thousands of miles. Networks have various topologies (such as bus or star), architectures (such as *client-server* or *peer-to-peer*), and communications standards (such as *AppleTalk, EtherNet,* or IBM's *token-ring*). See *baseband, broadband, bus network, network architecture, network protocol, network topology, star network,* and *token-ring network.*

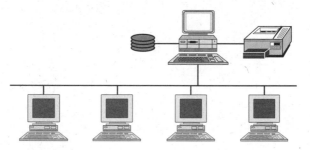

Fig. N.2 *An illustration of a local area network (LAN).*

network administrator In *local area networks (LANs),* the person responsible for maintaining the network and assisting its users.

network architecture The complete set of *hardware, software,* and cabling standards for a *local area network (LAN)* design. See *network topology.*

Network Basic Input/Output System (NetBIOS) A system program included in MS-DOS (Version 3.1 and later) that establishes standard methods for linking personal computers to *local area networks (LANs).*

network drive In a *local area network (LAN),* a disk drive made available to you through the network, as distinguished from a drive connected directly to the *workstation* you're using.

Network File System (NFS) A *network* file-access utility, developed by Sun Microsystems and subsequently released to the public as an *open standard,* that enables users of *UNIX* and

Microsoft Windows NT workstations to access files and directories on other computers as if they were physically present on the user's *workstation.*

Network Information Center (NIC)   A system that contains a repository of *Internet*-related information, including *File Transfer Protocol (FTP)* archives of Requests for Comments (RFCs), Internet Drafts, For Your Information (FYI) papers, and other documents, including handbooks on the use of the Internet. There are numerous Network Information Centers, but the official repository of network information is the Defense Data Network NIC (DDN NIC). See *InterNIC.*

network interface card   An *adapter* that lets you connect a network cable to a microcomputer. The card includes encoding and decoding circuitry and a receptacle for a network cable connection.

Because data is transmitted more rapidly within the computer's *internal bus,* a network interface card allows the network to operate at higher speeds than it would if delayed by the serial port. Networks such as *EtherNet* and *ARCnet* that use interface cards can transmit information much faster than networks such as *AppleTalk,* which uses serial ports.

network laser printer   A *laser printer,* often with a large *monthly duty cycle* and *remote management* features, that is designed to be connected to a *network* and serve the printing needs of several dozen people. See *automatic network switching.*

Network Neighborhood   In *Microsoft Windows 95,* a desktop *icon* that, when clicked, displays the PCs and other resources within the user's workgroup. With Network Neighborhood, files on other machines can be browsed and accessed just as if they were present on the user's computer.

Fig. N.3   *Network Neighborhood icon on desktop (Microsoft Windows 95).*

Network News Transfer Protocol (NNTP)   In *UseNet*, the standard that governs the distribution of UseNet newsgroups via the *Internet*. See *NNTP server*.

network operating system (NOS)   The system software of a *local area network (LAN)* that integrates the network's *hardware* components, usually adequate for connecting up to 50 workstations. Included, typically, are such features as a menu-driven administration interface, *tape backup* of *file-server* software, *security* restrictions, facilities for sharing *printers*, central storage of *application programs* and *databases*, remote log-in via *modem*, and support for *diskless workstations*.

A network operating system establishes and maintains the connection between the *workstations* and the file server; the physical connections alone aren't sufficient to support networking. The operating system consists of two parts: the file server software and workstation software. See *LAN memory management program*, and *NetWare*.

> **CAUTION:** *The workstation software can consume enough conventional memory to prevent you from running MS-DOS applications. When considering a network, find out how much workstation memory is required, and whether it's possible to store some or all of it in extended or expanded memory.*

network operations center (NOC)   An administrative and technical coordination office that is responsible for the day-to-day operation of a local, regional, or national *Internet* backbone service.

network printer   In a *local area network (LAN),* a printer made available to you through the network, as distinguished from a *local printer* (a printer connected directly to the workstation you're using).

network protocol   The method used to regulate a workstation's access to a computer network to prevent data collisions. Examples include *carrier sense multiple access with collision detection (CSMA/CD)* and *token passing*.

network server   See *file server*.

network termination 1 unit (NT-1)   In an *Integrated Services Digital Network (ISDN)* system, the device in a subscriber's home or office that is connected between ISDN devices (such as *digital modems* and digital telephones) and the telephone company's network. Users must usually buy their own NT-1s for $125-$300.

network topology   The geometric arrangement of nodes and cable links in a *local area network (LAN)*.

Network topologies fall into two categories: centralized and decentralized. In a centralized topology such as a *star network*, a central computer controls access to the network. This design ensures data security and central management control over the network's contents and activities.

In a decentralized topology such as a *bus network* or *ring network,* each workstation can access the network independently and establish its own connections with other workstations. See *star network.*

network virtual terminal (NVT)   A generic *terminal* standard that enables programmers to create applications without having to worry about all the different brands of terminals that are actually in use. The *Internet's* NVT standard is called *Telnet.* See *line mode terminal.*

 Networld + InterOp   An annual trade show sponsored by Novell, Inc., which has become a major showcase for new networking and *Internet* technology.

neural networks   An *artificial intelligence* technique that mimics the way nerve cells are connected in the human brain. Information is supplied to the neural network to train it to recognize patterns. The result is a program that can make predictions, useful in weather forecasting and stock market software.

 newbie   In *UseNet,* a new user who nevertheless makes his or her presence known, generally by pleading for information that is readily and easily available in *FAQs.*

news feed   In *UseNet,* a service that enables you to download the day's UseNet articles directly to your computer, and to upload all the articles contributed by people using your computer. Not for personal computer users, a news feed dumps as much as 100 MB of UseNet articles per day into your system—far more than one person could fruitfully read. A news feed is for organizations that want to set up a UseNet site, a computer—usually a minicomputer—with enough storage space to handle the huge influx of articles. Such a computer also has the multi-user capabilities that enable as many as dozens or even hundreds of people to take advantage of UseNet.

TIP: *If you're trying to gain access to* UseNet, *you don't need a news feed—you just need a* shell account *on a computer that receives a news feed. See* shell account *and* UseNet site.

newsgroup   In a *bulletin board system (BBS)* such as The WELL or a distributed bulletin board system such as EchoMail or *UseNet,* a discussion group that's devoted to a single topic, such as Star Trek, model aviation, the books of Ayn Rand, or the music of the Grateful Dead. Users *post* messages to the group, and those reading the discussion send reply messages to the author individually or post replies that can be read by the group as a whole.

The term newsgroup is a misnomer in that the discussions rarely involve "news;" discussion group would be more accurate, but the term newsgroup has taken root. Synonymous with forum. See *FAQ, follow-on post, local UseNet hierarchy, moderated newsgroup, net.god(dess), netiquette, thread,* and *unmoderated newsgroup.*

TIP: *Need information that's hard to find? Post a question on a newsgroup. Newsgroups offer an astonishingly rich information resource—much richer, according to some users, than the so-called "information databanks" that charge big bucks.*

newsgroup selector   In a *UseNet newsreader*, a program mode that presents a list of currently-subscribed newsgroups, from which you can select one to read.

news hierarchy   In *UseNet*, one of the seven standard newsgroup hierarchies. The news hierarchy is concerned with UseNet itself; the various newsgroups deal with administrative issues, new newsgroups, announcements, and UseNet software. See *local UseNet hierarchy* and *standard newsgroups.*

newspaper columns   A page format in which two or more columns of text are printed vertically on the page so that the text flows down one column and continues at the top of the next (see fig. N.4). High-end word processing programs such as *Microsoft Word* and *WordPerfect* do a good job of producing newspaper columns and can even balance the bottom margin of columns (called balanced newspaper columns) for a professional-looking effect.

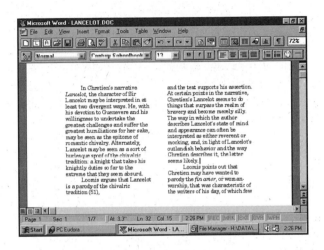

Fig. N.4   *Newspaper columns.*

> **TIP:** *Research on legibility demonstrates that a line should have approximately 55 to 60 characters (about 9 or 10 words) for optimum readability. If line lengths exceed this amount, break the text into two or more columns.*

newsreader   In *UseNet,* a client program that enables you to access a UseNet news server, subscribe to UseNet *newsgroups,* read the articles appearing in these newsgroups, and post your own articles or reply by electronic mail. Many *Web browsers* (such as *Netscape Navigator*) include newsreader functions.

news server   In *UseNet,* a computer that provides access to *newsgroups.* To read UseNet newsgroups, you must tell your *newsreader* program or *Web browser* the domain name of an *NNTP* server. Your Internet service provider can provide you with the name of this server, if one is available.

Newton   A *personal digital assistant,* driven by a 32-bit, 20Mhz *reduced instruction set computing (RISC)* processor with 640K of random-access memory (RAM), manufactured by *Apple Computer.*

The Newton includes a date book, address book, and freeform notebook in which you enter data using a *stylus* or an on-screen "*keyboard.*" The handwriting recognition engine can learn your writing, improving over time, although recognition is slow. Thirty built-in command words can be written directly on-screen, such as PRINT or SEND FAX.

The Newton is pricy at more than $700; however, if the antici-pated paging feature is delivered, it can bring the features more in line with the price. See *NewtonMail.*

NewtonMail   An on-line computer service providing the e-mail features of *eWorld* to *Newton* users with a modem. Regular eWorld users who have a Newton and NewtonMail can access NewtonMail from their *desktop computer.* See *Newton.*

NexGen   A *fabless* designer and marketer of *x86 central process-ing units (CPUs)* that is best known for the *NexGen Nx585,* which the company claims is *binary compatible* with the *Pentium.* Based in San Mateo, California, the company received a boost from early Pentiums' *floating-point unit (FPU)* troubles, and is trying to steal market share from *Intel* by offering its *chips* at relatively low prices.

NexGen Nx585   A *64-bit microprocessor* claimed to be *binary compatible* with the *Pentium* and offered at substantially lower prices by its manufacturer, *NexGen.* The Nx585, available in 70 *megahertz (MHz),* 75 MHz, 84 MHz, and 93 MHz versions, uses *register renaming* to get around the 8-*register* limit that slows the Pentium and uses *0.5-micron* and *CMOS technology* to reduce power consumption. The Nx585 boasts *throughput* on par with the Pentium, but the two *chips* are not binary compatible, which means the Nx585 requires a special *motherboard* and supporting *chip set.* See *AMD K5.*

nibble   Four *bits*, half of a *byte*. Sometimes cutely spelled "nybble."

Nikos   A *search engine* for locating *World Wide Web (WWW)* documents that is jointly funded by Rockwell Network Systems and California State Polytechnic University, San Luis Obispo. Nikos (short for New Internet Knowledge System) is based on an automated search routine (called a *spider*) that seeks to map 90 percent of the documents on the Web.

NLQ   See *near-letter quality*.

nn   In *UseNet*, a *UNIX newsreader* created by Kim F. Storm. A threaded *newsreader* that organizes articles and follow-up articles to show the thread of discussion, nn includes many advanced features but is not particularly easy to use. See *tin* and *trn*.

NNTP server.   See *news server*.

no parity   In *asynchronous communications*, a *communications protocol* that disables *parity checking* and leaves no space for the *parity bit*.

node   In a *local area network (LAN)*, a connection point that can create, receive, or repeat a message.

Nodes include *repeaters,* file servers, and shared peripherals. In common usage, however, the term node is synonymous with *workstation*. See *network topology*.

noise   In *data communications*, unwanted or random electrical signals on a communications channel, unlike the signal that carries the information you want. All communications channels have noise, but if the noise is excessive, data loss can occur.

Telephone lines are particularly noisy, requiring the use of communications programs that can perform error-checking operations to make sure that the data being received isn't corrupted.

non-adjacent selection   In *spreadsheets*, a selected *range of cells* that is separate from another selected range of cells. Non-adjacent selection is useful in *formatting* operations.

nondisclosure agreement   A contract designed to keep sensitive information confidential. Software publishers often establish nondisclosure agreements with their *beta test* sites so information about new products is less likely to leak out to the computer press.

non-impact printer   A *printer* that forms a text or graphic image by spraying or fusing ink to the page. Non-impact printers include *inkjet printers, laser printers,* and *thermal printers.*

All non-impact printers are considerably quieter than *impact printers,* but non-impact printers can't print multiple copies by using carbon paper.

non-interlaced monitor   A *monitor* that doesn't use the screen refresh technique called *interlacing* and, as a result, can display high-resolution images without flickering or streaking.

non-procedural language   See *declarative language.*

non-transactional application   In a *local area network (LAN),* a program that produces data that you don't need to keep in a shared database for all users to access. Most of the work done with *word processing* programs, for example, is non-transactional.

non-volatile memory   The memory specially designed to hold information, even when the power is switched off. *Read-only memory (ROM)* is non-volatile, as are all secondary storage units such as disk drives. See *random-access memory (RAM)* and *volatility.*

non-Windows application   A DOS *application program* that doesn't require *Microsoft Windows* to run.

DOS applications can also be run under Windows. Using *Standard* or *386 Enhanced modes,* you can switch from one non-Windows application to another without closing either program. In 386 Enhanced mode, you can multitask two or more DOS applications if each is running in a window and isn't *maximized.* Compared to running a DOS application under DOS, you may find that the mouse and the cursor aren't as responsive when running DOS applications in Windows. See *application program interface (API).*

Norton SI   In *IBM PC-compatible* computing, a widely used *benchmark* measurement of a computer's throughput.

Short for Norton System Information, Norton SI is a program included in Norton Utilities. The program's composite performance index provides a balanced picture of a computer system's *throughput,* including its internal processing speed and the speed of peripherals such as disk drives. See *million instructions per second (MIPS).*

NOS See *network operating system (NOS).*

notebook computer A *portable computer* that typically weighs less than 7 pounds and measures about 8" × 11" × 1^1/2" inches, easily fitting inside a briefcase. Notebook computers, unlike *subnotebook computers,* usually include a *floppy disk drive.* See *auxiliary battery* and *battery pack.*

Notes See *Lotus Notes.*

ns See *nanosecond.*

NSFnet A *wide area network (WAN)* developed by the Office of Advanced Scientific Computing at the *National Science Foundation (NSF).* NSFnet was developed to take over the civilian functions of the U.S. Defense Department's *ARPAnet,* which, for security reasons, has been closed to public access. NSFnet, until its abandonment in mid-1995, provided the communications hardware for the *Internet,* which is fast emerging as the world's *electronic mail* system.

NT-1 See *network termination 1 unit (NT-1).*

NTSC See *National Television Standards Committee (NTSC).*

NuBus The high-speed *expansion bus* of Macintosh II computers. NuBus requires adapters specifically designed for its 96-pin receptacles.

nuke To erase an entire *directory* or disk.

null modem cable A specially configured serial cable that allows you to connect two computers directly, without mediation by a modem.

null value In an accounting or *database management* program, a blank *field* in which you've never typed a value, as distinguished from a value of zero that you enter deliberately. In some applications, you need to distinguish between a null value and a deliberately entered zero; a null value doesn't affect computations, but a zero does.

number crunching A slang term for calculating, especially large amounts of data.

numeric coprocessor A *microprocessor* support chip that performs mathematical computations at speeds up to 100 times faster than the microprocessor alone.

TIP: *If you work with spreadsheets or any other application that performs calculations intensively, a numeric coprocessor will give you substantial gains in the apparent speed of your system without any changes to your software.*

numeric coprocessor socket A push-down socket on the *motherboard* of many personal computers into which you or a dealer can mount a *numeric coprocessor*, such as the Intel 80387. See *numeric coprocessor*.

numeric format In a *spreadsheet* program, the way in which the program displays numbers in a *cell*. With most spreadsheet programs, you can choose among the following numeric formatting options:

- Fixed. Displays values with a fixed number of decimal places, ranging from 0 to 15.

- Scientific. Displays very large or small numbers using scientific notation; for example, 12,460,000,000 appears as 1.25E+11.

- Currency. Displays values with commas and dollar signs and the number of decimal places you specify (0 to 15).

- Comma. Displays numbers larger than 999 with commas separating thousands.

- General. Displays numbers without commas and without trailing zeroes to the right of the decimal point. If the number of digits to the left of the decimal point exceeds the column width, scientific notation is used. If the number of digits to the right of the decimal point exceeds the column width, the number is rounded.

- +/−. Converts the number to a simple bar graph in the cell, with the number of plus or minus signs equaling the positive or negative whole number value of the entry; for example, 5 appears as +++++.

- Percent. Multiplies the value by 100 and adds a percent sign; for example, 0.485 appears as 48.5 percent. You specify the number of decimal places (0 to 15).

- Date. Converts a number to a date. The number 32734, for example, converts to the date August 14, 1989.

- Text. Displays the formula rather than the value computed by the formula.

- Hidden. Makes the cell entry invisible on-screen. Use the cell definition to see the contents.

numeric keypad   A group of keys arranged like the keys on an adding machine, usually located to the right of the typing area on a *keyboard*. The keypad is designed for the rapid touch-typing entry of numerical data.

Num Lock key   A toggle key that locks the *numeric keypad* into a mode in which you can enter numbers. When the Num Lock key is on, the cursor-movement keys are disabled.

On IBM PC-compatible *keyboards*, the keys on the numeric keypad are labeled with arrows and numbers. You can use these keys to move the cursor or to enter numbers. The Num Lock key toggles the keypad back and forth between these two modes.

n-way set associative cache   See *set-associative cache*.

nybble   See *nibble*.

object In *object linking and embedding (OLE),* a document or portion of a document that has been pasted into another document using the Paste Link, Paste Special, or Embed Object command. See *dynamic object* and *static object*.

object code In *programming,* the machine-readable instructions created by a *compiler* or *interpreter* from *source code*.

object linking and embedding (OLE) A set of standards, developed by Microsoft Corporation and incorporated into *Microsoft Windows* and Apple's Macintosh System software, that you use to create dynamic, automatically updated links between documents, and also to embed a document created by one application into a document created by another.

Unlike the *Clipboard,* OLE allows you to create a dynamic link between a *source document* (created by a *server application*) and a *destination document* (created by a *client application*) so that the changes you make to the source document are reflected in the destination document. Linking is useful when you want one authoritative version of a file, which you can include in many other documents and applications as *linked objects*. This source file can be edited as often as you want, but the location of the file must not be changed.

OLE also supports embedding. When you create an *embedded object,* you actually place a fully editable, independent copy of the source document (or a portion of the source document) into the destination file, resulting in a *compound file*. Double-click the embedded object to edit it.

object-oriented graphic A *graphic* composed of distinct objects—such as lines, circles, ellipses, and boxes—that you can edit independently.

Object-oriented graphics often are called vector graphics because the program stores them as mathematical formulas for the vectors, or directional lines, that compose the image. Unlike *bit-mapped graphics,* which distort when resized, you can resize object-oriented graphics without introducing distortions (see fig. O.1).

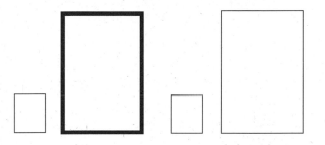

Fig. O.1   *A rectangle enlarged by a bit-mapped graphics program (left) and by an object-oriented graphics program (right).*

object-oriented programming language   *A non-procedural programming language* in which program elements are conceptualized as objects that can pass messages to each other. Object-oriented programming is the ultimate extension of the concept of *modular programming* and is especially suited to *graphical user interfaces (GUIs).*

In object-oriented programming, the modules are independent enough to stand on their own, so you can copy them into other programs. Rather than create an object again and again, you can copy it, add some new features, and then move the new object to another program. You can move objects around in chunks to compose new programs. See *declarative language, extensible,* and *script.*

Object Packager   In *Microsoft Windows 95*, an accessory that transforms an object into a package, which you can then insert in a *destination document* as a *linked object* or *embedded object.* The reader of this document sees an *icon,* which he can double-click to start the application that created the object. Using Object Packager, you can embed a *spreadsheet* as an icon in a *word processing*

O
P
Q
R

document with a note such as, "Jan, just double-click this icon to see our Excel worksheet showing the Fall Quarter figures I told you about."

Windows 95 users can make use of Object Packager for many purposes. Figure O.2 shows five packaged objects created by a variety of applications. This dynamic and interactive document plays a recording, displays text, runs through a worksheet "what-if" scenario, displays a chart, and displays a bit-mapped graphic image. It's often easier to use the *Windows Explorer* to embed objects in documents, but the Object Packager lets you embed partial documents as objects, too. See *annotation* and *object linking and embedding (OLE)*.

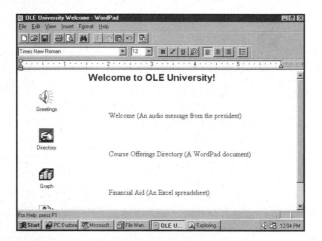

Fig. O.2 *An interactive document combining packages created by several server applications.*

oblique The italic form of a *sans serif* typeface.

octal A numbering system that uses a base (radix) of eight. There are eight octal digits: 0, 1, 2, 3, 4, 5, 6, and 7. Since octal notation is more compact than binary notation, it is sometimes used to represent binary numbers. Hexadecimal notation, though, is used even more often for that purpose.

octet A unit of *data* exactly eight *bits* in length—in other words, a *byte*. Internet people do not like to use the term byte because some of the computers connected to the Internet use data *word* lengths other than eight bits.

odd parity In *asynchronous communications,* an error-checking protocol in which the *parity bit* is set to 1 if the number of 1 digits in a one-byte data item adds up to an odd number. For example, the following byte has five 1s: 01011011. The parity bit therefore would be set to 1 in an odd *parity checking* scheme. If the parity bit indicates odd but the data transmitted actually contains an even number of 1s, the system will report that a transmission error has occurred. See *communications parameters, communications protocol, even parity,* and *parity checking.*

OEM See *original equipment manufacturer (OEM).*

off-line Not directly connected with a computer; for example, a device that isn't hooked up to your PC is off-line or has been switched to off-line mode. *In data communications*, not connected with another computer; for example, a workstation you've temporarily or permanently disconnected from a local area network is off-line.

office automation The use of computers and *local area networks (LANs)* to integrate traditional office activities such as conferencing, writing, filing, calculating, customer and merchandise tracking, and sending and receiving messages. Office automation rarely results in significant productivity gains.

Re-engineering, often undertaken along with office automation, seeks to identify ways to reorganize work so that people can do it more efficiently. Then computers are used to support the altered work roles. In re-engineering, the productivity gains really stem from the redesigned work roles, not from the computer.

O
P
Q
R

TIP: *If you automate a mess, you get an automated mess. Develop ways of working more efficiently, then automate.*

off-screen formatting See *embedded formatting command.*

offset See *binding offset.*

OK button A *pushbutton* you can activate in a *dialog box* to confirm the current settings and execute the command. If the OK button is highlighted or surrounded by a thick black line, you can press Enter to choose OK.

OLE client   See *client application.*

OLE server   See *server application.*

onboard audio   A circuit on the *motherboard* that simulates a *sound board* and is usually adequate only for *business audio* applications. Onboard audio circuits usually use crude *FM synthesis* techniques to produce sounds, and can be replaced, in a *desktop computer,* with a sound board of higher quality.

on-board cache   See *internal cache.*

on-board speaker   A small speaker located inside the computer's *case.* Though the on-board speaker can generate crude beeps, buzzes, and honks, it is entirely unsuitable for *multimedia applications.* A *sound board* and *auxiliary speakers* provide much better sound output than the on-board speaker.

on-line   Directly connected with and accessible to a computer; for example, after you successfully hook it up to your PC and turn it on. In *data communications,* connected with another, distant computer; for example, the successful connection with a *host* computer in a *client-server network.* On a bulletin board system (BBS), when a file or application is available to the users.

on-line help   A help utility available on-screen while you're using a *network* or an *application program.*

on-line information service   A for-profit firm that makes current news, stock quotes, and other information available to its subscribers over standard telephone lines. See *America Online, bibliographic retrieval service, CompuServe, Delphi, Dow Jones News/ Retrieval Service, GEnie,* and *Prodigy.*

on-screen formatting   In a *word processing* program, a formatting technique in which formatting commands directly affect the text that's visible on-screen. See *embedded formatting command* and *what-you-see-is-what-you-get (WYSIWYG).*

on-the-fly data compression   A method by which data to be sent by *modem* is packed into a tighter package during transmission rather than before, thereby increasing apparent transmission speed. Protocols such *V.42bis* and *MNP5* handle on-the-fly *data compression.*

one hundred (100) percent column graph   A *column graph* that resembles a pie graph in that each "slice" of the column displays the relative percentage of that data item compared to the total (see fig. O.3). See *stacked column graph.*

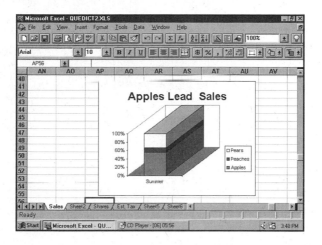

Fig. O.3   *A 100 percent column graph.*

one-shot program   A program designed to solve one problem, one time, and never be used again. One-shot programs often do not conform to the rules of style and *modular programming* that govern programs meant to be used over and over, which presents a problem if a one-shot program becomes widely popular. See *canonical form.*

OOPS   Acronym for object-oriented programming system. See *object-oriented programming language.*

open   Available for modification; not controlled by a single manufacturer.

open architecture   A system in which all the system specifications are made public so that other companies will develop add-on products such as *adapters* for the system. See *open bus system.*

O
P
Q
R

open bus system   A design in which the computer's *expansion bus* contains receptacles that readily accept *adapters*. An *open-architecture* system generally has an open bus, but not all systems with open buses have open architectures; the Macintosh is an example of the latter.

open-loop actuator   An obsolete mechanism for moving the *read/write head* over the *storage medium* of a *hard disk*. Open-loop actuators, unlike *closed-loop actuators*, provide no feedback about the head's position to the *hard disk controller*, therefore reducing the accuracy with which the controller can tightly pack data. Ultimately, open-loop actuators reduce *areal density*.

Open Software Foundation (OSF)   A consortium of computer companies that promotes standards and publishes specifications for programs operating on computers that run *UNIX*. OSF is perhaps best known for designing OSF Motif, a *graphical user interface (GUI)* for UNIX that provided much of the design inspiration for *Microsoft Windows 95*. OSF also developed the OSF Distributed Computing Environment (DCE) (a set of programs that supplement a vendor's *operating system* and enable cross-platform network interoperability, and the OSF/1 operating system, a publicly available variant of UNIX. See *proprietary*.

open standard   A set of rules and specifications, which collectively describe the design or operating characteristics of a program or device, that is published and made freely available to the technical community. Open standards may contribute to rapid market growth if they encourage interoperability (the ability of a device made by one manufacturer to work with a device made by a different manufacturer). The opposite of an open standard is a *proprietary standard,* which a company pushes in the hope that its standard, and no others, will come to dominate the market.

Open System Interconnection (OSI) reference model   An international standard for the organization of *local area networks (LANs)* established by *the International Standards Organization (ISO)* and the *Institute of Electrical and Electronic Engineers (IEEE)* that improves network flexibility. Synonymous with ISO/OSI reference model.

The OSI reference model separates the communication process into distinct layers insulated from each other, such as the physical hardware (the cabling, and so on), the transport layer (the method by which data is communicated), the presentation layer (the way the transmitted data interacts with programs in each computer), and the application layer (the programs available to all users of the network). Figure O.4 shows the OSI reference model divided into layers.

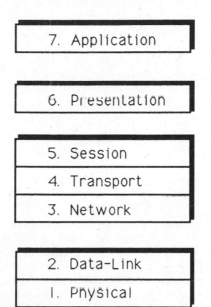

Fig. O.4 *The OSI reference model.*

Open Systems Interconnection (OSI) Protocol Suite A *wide-area network (WAN)* architecture that was developed by the *International Standards Organization (ISO)*, with heavy support from European state postal and telegraph organizations. The creation of a series of committees, the OSI protocol suite has proven to be unwieldy and brittle in practice, and would not pose a serious threat to the global dominance of the competing *TCP/IP* protocol suite were it not for the OSI's strong backing by European nations' postal and telegraph service bureaucracies. See *Open Systems Interconnection (OSI) Reference Model.*

operating system A master control program that manages the computer's internal functions and provides a means to control the computer's operations. The most popular operating systems for personal computers include *MS-DOS, OS/2, Microsoft Windows 95,* and the Macintosh *System.*

Operating System/2 (OS/2)   A *multitasking* operating system for IBM PC-compatible computers that breaks the 640K RAM barrier, provides protection for programs running simultaneously, and allows the dynamic exchange of data between applications.

The newest OS/2, Version 2.1, released in 1994, runs MS-DOS and Windows applications well, and takes full advantage of the 32-bit architecture of *Intel 80386* and later microprocessors. It also offers a new *graphical user interface (GUI)* similar to that of a NeXT *workstation* (see fig. O.5). OS/2 remains stymied by Windows' astonishing momentum, however, and whether it will ever gain wide acceptance remains to be seen. See *Microsoft Windows 95.*

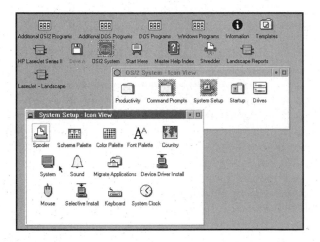

Fig. O.5   *The OS/2 Presentation Manager interface.*

OS/2 Warp   An *operating system,* designed and marketed by *IBM,* that offers most of the features of *Operating System/2 (OS/2)* and is optimized to run Windows applications as well as OS/2 programs. OS/2 Warp offered many exotic features—notably built-in *Internet* connectivity—several months before the release of *Microsoft Windows 95.*

operating voltage   The electrical voltage at which a *micropro-cessor* operates. Most microprocessors have operating voltages of 5 volts—a mostly arbitrary specification decided upon when the *transistor* was invented—but some chips run at 3.3 volts to save electricity (a real concern in *portable computers*) and reduce heat output.

optical character recognition (OCR)   Machine recogni-tion of printed or typed text. Using OCR software with a *scanner*, a printed page can be scanned and the characters converted into text in a *word processing* document format.

optical disk   A large-capacity data storage medium for com-puters on which information is stored at extremely high density in the form of tiny pits. The presence or absence of pits is read by a tightly focused laser beam.

Optical storage technologies are expected to play a significant role in the data storage systems of the 1990s. *CD-ROM* disks and disk drives offer an increasingly economical medium for read-only data and programs. *Write-once, read-many (WORM)* drives allow orga-nizations to create their own huge, in-house databases. Erasable optical disk drives offer more storage than *hard disks*, and the CDs are removable. They are, however, still more expensive and much slower than hard disks. See *interactive videodisk*.

optical mouse   A *mouse* that does not require cleaning, as a *mechanical mouse* does, but must be used on a special mouse pad. An optical mouse shines a beam of light into a grid in the mouse pad, which conveys the mouse's movements to the computer.

optical resolution   A measure of the sharpness with which a *scanner* can digitize an image without help from software. The more charge-coupled devices (CCDs) in a scanner (300 is about average, 600 is very good), the better its optical resolution. By means of *software interpolation*, output can be improved, but soft-ware interpolation is a poor substitute for high optical resolution.

optical scanner   See *scanner*.

optimal recalculation   In *Lotus 1-2-3* and other advanced *spreadsheet* programs, a method that speeds *automatic recalculation* by recalculating only those cells that have changed since the last recalculation.

O
P
Q
R

optimizing compiler A *compiler* that translates *source code* into *machine language* optimized to run as efficiently as possible on a particular *microprocessor*. Optimizing compilers are virtually essential when preparing programs to run on any microprocessor equipped with *superscalar architecture*.

option button See *radio button*.

ordered list In *HyperText Markup Language (HMTL),* a numbered list, created with <OL>...</OL> tags.

organization chart In *presentation graphics*, a text chart you use to diagram the reporting structure of an organization, such as a corporation or a club (see fig. O.6).

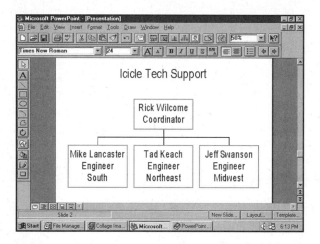

Fig. O.6 *An organization chart.*

Organizer See *Lotus Organizer*.

orientation See *landscape orientation and portrait orientation*.

original equipment manufacturer (OEM) The company that actually manufactures a given piece of *hardware*, unlike the *value-added reseller (VAR)*—the company that changes, configures, repackages, and sells the hardware.

For example, only a few companies such as Canon, Toshiba, and Ricoh make the *print engines* used in *laser printers*. These engines are installed in housings with other components and sold by VARs such as Hewlett-Packard.

originate mode In *modems*, a mode in which the modem will *originate* calls but not receive them. See *auto-answer mode*.

originate To make a telephone call, rather than receive one. In computers, the term usually applies to contacting another computer system via *modem*.

orphan A formatting flaw in which the first line of a paragraph appears alone at the bottom of a page. Most *word processing* and *page layout programs* suppress *widows* and orphans; the better programs let you switch widow/orphan control on and off and choose the number of lines for which the suppression feature is effective.

OS/2 See *Operating System/2 (OS/2)*.

OSF See *Open Software Foundation (OSF)*.

outline font A *printer font* or *screen font* in which a mathematical formula generates each character, producing a graceful and undistorted outline of the character, which the *printer* then fills in.

Mathematical formulas, rather than *bit maps*, produce the graceful arcs and lines of outline characters (see fig. O.7). The printer can easily change the type size of an outline font without introducing the distortion common with *bit-mapped fonts*. (You may need to reduce the weight of small font sizes by using a process called *hinting*, which prevents the loss of fine detail.)

O
P
Q
R

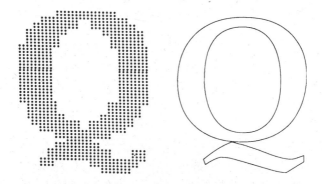

Fig. O.7 *A bit-mapped character (left) and an outline character (right).*

outline utility   In some full-featured *word processing* programs, a mode that helps you plan and organize a *document* by using outline headings as document headings. The program lets you view the document as an outline or as ordinary text.

When you view the document in outline mode, the headings and subheadings appear as they would in an outline (see fig. O.8). The text beneath the headings collapses (disappears) so that only the headings and subheadings are visible. In outline mode, you can move the headings and subheadings vertically; if you move a heading, all the hidden text positioned beneath it also moves. After you switch back to document mode, the outline format disappears, and the document appears normally (see fig. O.9).

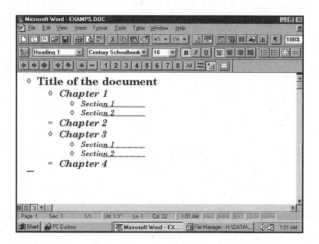

Fig. O.8   *Document headings viewed in outline mode.*

output   The process of displaying or printing the results of processing operations. See *input.*

OverDrive   Different from *Pentium OverDrive*, OverDrive *chips* are *microprocessors* that fit into special sockets on *Intel 486DX* and *Intel 486SX motherboards* and improve their performance to the level of *Intel 486DX/2 central processing units (CPUs).* The performance gain realized by installing an OverDrive chip is only about 20 percent, so installing one is not the most cost-effective *upgrade* route available.

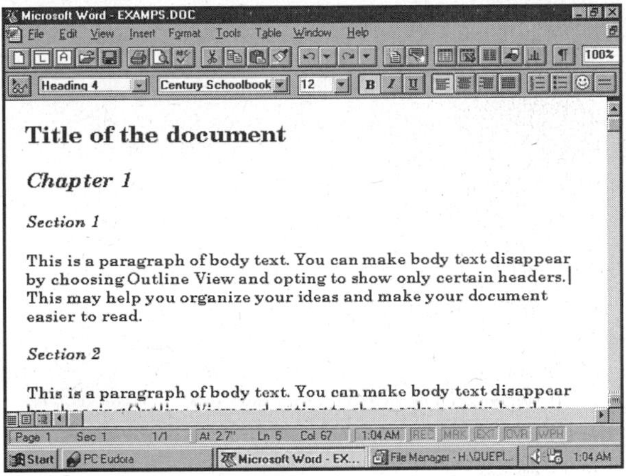

Fig. O.9   *Document headings viewed in document mode.*

overflow   A condition in which a program tries to put more data in a memory area than the area can accommodate, resulting in an error message.

overhead   In a *network*, the additional information that must be added to a message in order to ensure its error-free transmission. In *asynchronous communications,* for example, a *start bit* and *stop bit* must be added to every byte of transmitted data, producing a high, inefficient overhead of roughly 20 percent.

overlaid windows   In a *graphical user interface (GUI)*, a display mode in which windows are allowed to overlap each other. If you *maximize* the top window to full size, it completely hides the other windows. See *cascading windows* and *tiled windows.*

overlay   See *program overlay.*

overlay chart   In a business graphics program, a second type of chart that's overlaid on the main chart, such as a line chart on top of a bar chart. Synonymous with combination chart. See *mixed column/line graph.*

overrun error   A *serial port* error in which a *microprocessor* sends data faster than the *Universal Asynchronous Receiver/Transmitter (UART)* can handle it. An overrun error results in lost data.

overscan   A condition that exists when the image created on a *cathode ray tube (CRT) display* is larger than the visible portion of the display. Overscan helps relegate the relatively fuzzy perimeter of a CRT image to portions of the screen that are out of sight, and the overscan may disappear over time anyway. On the other hand, *monitors* with excessive overscan can allow you to lose *icons* and text at the edges of the display.

overstrike   Creating a character not found in a printer's character set by placing one character on top of another, such as using O and / to create zeros that can be easily distinguished from an uppercase letter O. Today's graphics-based computer systems eliminate the need for this printing technique; however, users of character-based DOS programs still need it sometimes.

overtype mode   An editing mode in *word processing* programs and other software that lets you enter and edit text. In overtype mode, the characters you type erase existing characters, if any. In *WordPerfect*, the overtype mode is called *typeover mode*. See *insert mode*.

overvoltage   Unusually high voltage, typically in the form of spikes or surges greater than 130 volts from a wall outlet. A surge protector provides overvoltage protection.

overwrite   To write data on a magnetic disk in the same area where other data is stored, thereby destroying the original data.

P24T socket A receptacle for the *Intel P24T microprocessor* on an *Intel 486 motherboard*. The P24T boosts the performance of a 486 to near-*Pentium* levels.

P60 Abbreviation for *Intel's* 60 *MHz* version of the *Pentium microprocessor*. Because it has a 5-volt *operating voltage*, the P60 runs very hot and should be avoided in favor of the *P75, P100,* and *P120*.

P66 Abbreviation for Intel's 66 *MHz* version of the *Pentium microprocessor*. Because it has a 5-volt *operating voltage*, the P66 runs very hot and should be avoided in favor of the *P75, P100,* and *P120*.

P75 Abbreviation for *Intel's* 75 *MHz* version of the *Pentium microprocessor*.

P90 Abbreviation for *Intel's* 90 *MHz* version of the *Pentium microprocessor*.

P100 Abbreviation for *Intel's* 100 *MHz* version of the *Pentium microprocessor*.

P120 Abbreviation for *Intel's* 120 *MHz* version of the *Pentium microprocessor*.

package In Microsoft Windows 95 and Microsoft Windows 3.1, an *icon*, created by Object Packager, that contains a linked object, *embedded object, file*, or part of a file. See *Object Linking and Embedding (OLE)*.

packaged software *Application programs* commercially marketed, unlike custom programs privately developed for a specific client. Synonymous with off-the-shelf software.

packet In a packet-switching unit, a unit of data of a fixed size—not exceeding the network's *maximum transmission unit (MTU)* size—that has been prepared for network transmission. Each packet contains a *header* that indicates its origin and its destination. See *packet-switching network*.

Packet Internet Groper (PING) A *diagnostic utility program* that is commonly used to determine whether a computer is properly connected to the *Internet.*

packet switching network One of two fundamental architectures for the design of a *wide-area network (WAN)*; the other is a *circuit switching network.* In a packet switching network such as the *Internet,* no effort is made to establish a single electrical circuit between two computing devices. Instead, the sending computer divides a message into a number of efficiently sized units called *packets,* each of which contains the address of the destination computer. These packets are simply dumped onto the network. They are intercepted by devices called *routers,* which read each packet's destination address and, based on that information, send the packets in the appropriate direction. Eventually, the packets arrive at their intended destination, although some may have actually traveled by different physical paths. The receiving computer assembles the packets, puts them in order, and delivers the received message to the appropriate application. Packet-switching networks are highly reliable and efficient, but they are not suited to the delivery of real-time voice and video.

page A fixed-size block of *random-access memory (RAM).* In word processing and *desktop publishing,* an on-screen representation of a printed page of text or graphics. See *paging memory.*

page break In *word processing,* a mark that indicates where the printer will start a new page.

Programs such as *WordPerfect* insert page breaks automatically (often a line of dots or dashes across the screen) when you've typed a full page of text. The automatic page break is called a soft page break because the program may adjust its location if you insert or delete text above the break. You can enter a hard page break, called a forced page break, which forces the program to start a new page at the hard page break's location.

page description language (PDL) A *programming language* that describes *printer* output in device-independent commands.

Normally, a program's printer output includes printer control codes that vary from printer to printer. A program that generates output in a PDL, however, can drive any printer containing an interpreter for the PDL. PDLs also transfer the burden of processing the printer output to the printer. See *PostScript*.

page layout program   In *desktop publishing*, an application program that assembles text and *graphics* from various files. You can determine the precise placement, sizing, scaling, and *cropping* of material in accordance with the page design represented on-screen.

Page layout programs such as *PageMaker* and Ventura Publisher display a graphic representation of the page, including non-printing guides that define areas into which you can insert text and graphics.

page-mode RAM   High-performance *dynamic random-access memory (DRAM)* chips found in *high-end* systems that include a buffer, called a column buffer, that stores data likely to be needed next by the *central processing unit (CPU)*.

DRAM chips store data in a matrix of rows and columns. When data is requested from page-mode RAM, the entire column, or page, of data is read into the buffer, since the next piece of data requested likely will be in the same column. If so, the data is read from the buffer, which is faster than accessing the matrix again. Page-mode RAM is not the same as *paging memory* systems. See *nanosecond (ns)*, *random-access memory (RAM)*, *virtual memory*, and *wait state*.

paged memory   See *paging memory*.

paged memory management unit (PMMU)   In *hardware*, a *chip* or circuit that enables *virtual memory*. Virtual memory allows your computer to use space on your *hard disk* to expand the apparent amount of *random-access memory (RAM)* in your system. With virtual memory, a computer with only 4*M* of RAM can function as though it were equipped with 16M or more of RAM, enabling you to run several programs simultaneously. See *Microsoft Windows* 95 and *System 7*.

page orientation   See *landscape orientation* and *portrait orientation*.

page printer   A *printer* that develops an image of a printed page in its memory, then transfers that image to paper in one operation. *Laser printers, liquid crystal shutter (LCS) printers*, and

O
P
Q
R

light-emitting diode (LED) printers are page printers, while *ink jet* and *dot matrix printers,* which print one line at a time, are not.

Page Up/Page Down keys   On *IBM PC-compatible computer* keyboards, the keys you press to move the cursor to the preceding screen (Page Up) or the next screen (Page Down). Because the precise implementation of these keys is up to the programmer, some *word processing* programs use Page Up and Page Down keys to move to the top of the preceding page, rather than to the preceding screen of text.

pages per minute (ppm)   A measurement of how many pages a *printer* can print in one minute. Manufacturers often inflate their printers' ppm rating, and the ratings are almost always inaccurate for print jobs that involve graphics or fonts other than the printer's *resident fonts.* Like automakers' gas-mileage figures, ppm ratings, although inflated, can serve as a point of comparison between models. Be sure to test a printer you're considering buying on print jobs like those you do frequently.

pagination   In *word processing,* the process of dividing a document into pages for printing. Today's advanced word processing programs use background pagination, in which pagination occurs after you stop typing or editing and the microprocessor has nothing else to do. See *page break.*

paging memory   A memory system in which the location of data is specified by the intersection of a column and row on the memory *page,* rather than by the actual physical location of the data. This makes it possible to store memory pages wherever memory space of any type becomes available, including disk drives.

Paging memory is used to implement *virtual memory,* in which your computer's hard drive functions as an extension of *random-access memory (RAM).* A chip or circuit called a *paged memory management unit* manages the movement of pages of data in and out of the memory devices. See *paged memory management unit (PMMU).*

paint file format   A bit-mapped graphics *file format* found in programs such as MacPaint and PC Paintbrush. See *paint program.*

paint program   A program that allows you to paint the screen by specifying the color of the individual dots or *pixels* that make up a bit-mapped screen display.

The first paint program (and the first program for the Macintosh) was MacPaint. Paint applications also exist for *IBM PC-compatible computers*; a leading program is PC Paintbrush.

pair kerning See *kerning*.

paired bar graph A *bar graph* with two different x-axes (categories axes). A paired bar graph is an excellent way to demonstrate the relationship between two *data series* that share the same y-axis values but require two different *x-axis* categories. Because the bars mirror each other, variations become obvious (see fig. P.1). See *dual y-axis graph*.

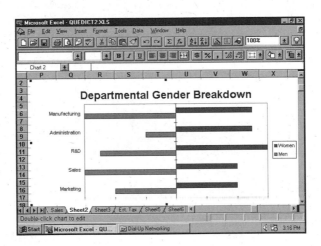

Fig. P.1 *A paired bar graph.*

paired pie graph A graphic containing two separate *pie graphs*. For example, a paired pie graph is appropriate for showing the breakdown of product sales in two different time periods. To show the difference in the size of the totals represented by each of the two pie graphs, a *proportional pie graph* is useful.

palette In computer video displays, the colors that the system can display. *Video Graphics Array (VGA) displays* offer a palette of 262,144 colors, although each screen can display a maximum of 256 colors simultaneously. In paint and draw programs, an on-screen display of options such as colors and drawing tools. See *draw program* and *paint program*.

pan In *multimedia,* the capability of a synthesizer or *sound board* to alter the left and right channel volumes to create the illusion of movement of the source of the sound.

Pantone Matching System (PMS) A *device-independent* way of describing and adjusting colors. When using PMS colors, you choose the color you want from a booklet, use that color's code in the *software,* and print to a specially calibrated printer. The output should closely match the color in the PMS book. See *device-dependent color.*

paper-white monitor A *monochrome* monitor that displays black text and graphics on a white background. Paper-white *monitors* are preferred for *word processing* and *desktop publishing* because the display closely resembles the appearance of the printed page. However, some users don't like the glare of a large expanse of white background.

TIP: *When shopping for a monitor, remember that color has its advantages. In a color display, you can locate menu names, accelerator keys, data entry fields, and other on-screen areas more easily. Moreover, most programs permit you to configure the on-screen colors, so you can simulate a paper-white monitor (black text on a white background) if you want.*

paperless office An office in which using paper for traditional purposes—such as sending messages, filling out forms, and maintaining records—has been reduced or eliminated. There are few paperless offices, in part since paper documents bear more psychological authority than electronic ones, paper documents have absolute legal status while the legal significance of electronic documents is unclear, and people are reluctant to trust electronic equipment with important information.

paradigm A way of looking at a situation or technology. For example, it isn't really fair to compare *MS-DOS* and *Microsoft Windows* in terms of ease-of-use because Windows is a *graphical user interface (GUI)* while MS-DOS is a command-line system. The two operating environments are based on entirely different modes of thinking.

parallel columns See *table columns.*

parallel interface   See *parallel port.*

parallel port   A connection for the synchronous, high-speed flow of data along parallel lines to a device, usually a *parallel printer.*

Parallel ports negotiate with *peripheral* devices to determine whether they're ready to receive data, and report error messages if a device isn't ready. Unlike the *serial port,* the parallel port provides an easy way to connect a printer to your computer. As the length of the cable increases, however, so does the risk of *crosstalk* (interference between the parallel wires). Parallel printer cables, therefore, are usually no longer than 10 to 15 feet.

parallel printer   A printer designed to be connected to the computer's *parallel port.*

If a printer is available in serial and parallel versions, the parallel version is the better choice unless you must position the printer more than 15 feet away from the computer. Parallel printers usually are easier to install and use than *serial printers.*

parallel processing   See *multitasking.*

parameter   A value or option that you add or alter when you give a command so that the command accomplishes its task the way you want. If you don't state a parameter, the program uses a *default setting.*

For instance, most programs let you type the name of the file you want to work with when you start the program. If you type **WORD report1.doc**, for example, Microsoft Word and the document file REPORT1.DOC load up at the same time. In this case, the file name is the parameter. If you don't type the file name, Word starts and opens a new, blank document file. See *argument.*

parameter RAM   In the Macintosh environment, a small bank of battery-powered memory that stores your *configuration* choices after you switch off the power.

parent directory   In DOS directories, the *directory* above the current *subdirectory* in the *tree structure.* You can move quickly to the parent directory by typing **CD..** and pressing Enter.

parity   Identity between data sent by one *modem* and data received by another modem. *Error-correction protocols* use *parity checking* and *parity bits* to determine if data needs to be re-sent.

parity bit   In *asynchronous communications* and primary storage, an extra *bit* added to a data word for *parity checking*.

TIP: *If you're using a* communications program, *setting the parity bit option to no parity and the data bits option to 8 bits is the most common configuration. If these settings don't work, try even parity with 7 data bits.*

parity checking   A technique used to detect memory or *data communication* errors. The computer adds up the number of bits in a one-byte data item, and if the *parity bit* setting disagrees with the sum of the other *bits*, the computer reports an error.

Parity-checking schemes work by storing a one-bit digit (0 or 1) that indicates whether the sum of the bits in a data item is odd or even. When the data item is read from memory or received by another computer, a parity check occurs. If the parity check reveals that the parity bit is incorrect, the computer displays an error message. See *even parity* and *odd parity*.

parity error   An error that a computer reports when *parity checking* reveals that one or more *parity bits* is incorrect, indicating a probable error in data processing or data transmission.

park   To position a *hard drive's* read/write heads over the *landing zone* so the disk isn't damaged by jostling during transport. Most hard drives now do this automatically when they are turned off.

parse   To break down into components. *Spreadsheet* programs, for example, often have parsing features that will break *ASCII* data into parts that will fit into *cells*.

parser   A program that breaks large units of data into smaller, more easily interpreted pieces.

For example, a *Web browser* reads documents prepared with a markup language (such as HTML). The markup language identifies the parts of the document (such as document headings, bulleted lists, or body text), but says nothing about how those portions of the document should appear on-screen. The parser reads the tagged text and formats the various portions of the document for on-screen display. See *HyperText Markup Language (HTML)*.

partial-response maximum-likelihood (PRML) read-channel technology A new design philosophy for *hard disks* that improves *throughput* and a real density. Typically used with *magneto-resistive heads*, PRML read-channel technology is very expensive and is found only on a few *high-end* hard disks for *network servers*.

partition A section of the storage area of a *hard disk* created for organizational purposes or to separate different *operating systems*. A partition is created during initial preparation of the hard disk, before the disk is formatted.

In *MS-DOS*, every hard disk has at least one DOS partition (Version of MS-DOS before version 4.0 required a separate partition for each 32M of disk space). Each partition is treated by DOS as though it were a separate drive.

Users may partition their drives to separate one operating system from another, but *utility programs,* such as MultiDisk, are available that let you create several system partitions. See *directory* and *subdirectory*.

.PAS The file name *extension* usually attached to a file containing *source code* written in *Pascal*.

Pascal A high-level, procedural *programming* language that encourages programmers to write well structured, modular programs that take advantage of modern *control structures* and lack *spaghetti code*. Pascal has gained wide acceptance as a teaching and application-development language, though most professional programmers prefer *C* or *C++*. Pascal is available in interpreted and compiled versions.

A major disadvantage of Pascal is that its standard version (Standard Pascal) contains many shortcomings. The language's inventor, Nicklaus Wirth, has offered a new language, *Modula-2,* as a successor to Pascal, that fixes some of the language's problems, and Borland International's Turbo Pascal makes Pascal easy for personal computer owners to use. See *BASIC* and *FORTRAN*.

passive matrix display In *notebook computers,* a *liquid-crystal display (LCD)* in which a single transistor controls an entire column or row of the display's tiny electrodes. Passive matrix displays are cheaper than *active matrix displays* but offer lower *resolution* and contrast.

O P Q R

passive termination   Like *active termination* and *forced-perfect termination*, a way of ending a chain of *Small Computer System Interface (SCSI)* devices. Passive termination is the simplest termination method and works best on *daisy chains* of four or fewer devices.

password   A security tool used to identify authorized users of a *program* or *network* and to define their privileges, such as read-only, reading and writing, or file copying.

TIP: *Computer* hackers *and saboteurs know that most people choose passwords based on their birthdays, nicknames, children's names, or easily remembered words such as password, secret, or even none. Choose a password randomly so that no one will associate the password with you. Open a book and run your fingers across a page until you come across a genuinely random word, such as wolf, porch, or capable. Then write it down somewhere (not under the keyboard or desk blotter) so that you don't forget it. Another suggestion is to misspell your password in an odd way; for example, instead of garnet, use garnit or garnete. Or vary your password from time to time by inserting a number in the middle of the word.*

password aging   In a computer network, a feature of the *network operating system (NOS)* that keeps track of the last time you changed your *password*. You should change your password frequently to help thwart computer *crackers*. When your password reaches the end of its "life," such as after six months, a message appears on-screen that encourages you to change your password.

password protection   A method of limiting access to a *program, file, computer,* or a *network* by requiring you to enter a *password*.

Some programs allow you to password-protect your files so they can't be read by others, but be sure to keep a record of the password. Many users have lost work permanently because they forgot the password and had no means to retrieve it. (If a method for retrieving a password were included in software programs, a clever *cracker* would quickly discover it, and your data wouldn't be secure.)

paste   In text editing, inserting at the location of the *cursor* text or *graphics* you've cut or copied from another location. In Windows and Macintosh systems, a temporary storage area called the *Clipboard* stores the cut or copied material while you move to the material's new location. When you paste, the material is copied from the Clipboard to its new location. See *block move*.

> **CAUTION:** *Bear in mind that the Clipboard stores only one unit of copied or cut text at a time. If you're not careful, you could copy or cut something else, accidentally deleting the Clipboard's contents. To avoid this problem, don't interrupt cut-and-paste operations.*

patch   A quick fix, in the form of one or more program statements, added to a *program* to correct *bugs* or to enhance the program's capabilities.

path   In DOS, the route the operating system must follow to find an executable program stored in a *subdirectory*.

DOS examines only the current subdirectory when you issue a command to start a program. If the program's executable file isn't in the current subdirectory, the message Bad command or file name appears.

To solve that problem, you can type the full *path name* when you issue a command, such as C:\WP51\WP, so DOS knows where to find the program. A much easier solution is to add a PATH statement to your hard disk's *AUTOEXEC.BAT* file, listing all the subdirectories in which programs are stored. DOS will then check each *directory* in the path to look for a file that matches the command you entered. See *current directory* and *path statement*.

path name   In DOS, a statement that indicates the name of a file and precisely where it's located on a *hard disk*. When opening or saving a file with most applications, you must specify the full path name to retrieve or store the file in a *directory* other than the *current directory*. Suppose that you're using WordPerfect, and you want to store the file REPORT9.DOC in the directory C:\DOCS. If C:\DOCS isn't the current directory, you must type C:\DOCS\REPORT9.DOC to name and store the file in the correct location.

O
P
Q
R

TIP: *Some applications permit you to define a permanent default directory for storing and retrieving the data files created by the application. If the application you're using permits you to define a default data directory, you don't need to type the full path name when retrieving and storing files.*

path statement In DOS, an entry in the *AUTOEXEC.BAT* file that lists the directories in which executable programs are listed. See *path*.

PC Abbreviation for *personal computer*. In practice, this abbreviation usually refers to IBM or IBM-compatible personal computers, as opposed to Macintoshes.

PC DOS The version of the *MS-DOS* operating system released by IBM. PC-DOS is functionally identical to MS-DOS.

PCI slot A socket for *adapters* in a *motherboard* equipped with a *Peripheral Component Interconnect (PCI) expansion bus*. PCI slots are preferred to *VESA local bus slots* and *ISA slots* because of their superior speed. PCI slots are found most often on motherboards housing the *Pentium microprocessor*.

PCL See *printer control language (PCL)*.

PCL3 The original, now-obsolete version of Hewlett-Packard's *Printer Control Language (PCL)*. PCL3 supports only *cartridge fonts* and restricts users to only one *font* per page.

PCL4 An improved and widely used version of Hewlett-Packard's *Printer Control Language (PCL)* that supports *downloadable fonts* and multiple *fonts* on single pages. PCL3 was used in HP LaserJet II printers.

PCL5 A version of Hewlett-Packard's *Printer Control Language (PCL)* that supports *vector graphics* and *scalable fonts*. PCL5 was first used on HP LaserJet III printers.

PCL5e The latest version of Hewlett-Packard's *Printer Control Language (PCL)*, used on HP LaserJet 4 printers. PCL5e is the first version of PCL to support *bi-directional communication* between printer and computer.

PCM See *pulse code modulation (PCM)*.

PCMCIA   See *Personal Computer Memory Card Interface Adapter (PCMCIA)*.

PCMCIA bus   An *expansion bus* specification used to connect a variety of credit-card-sized *peripherals* to computers, typically *portable computers*. PCMCIA (the acronym stands for Personal Computer Memory Card Interface Adapter) bus slots are being found with increasing frequency on *desktop computers*.

PCMCIA card reader   A peripheral device that enables a *desktop computer* to use devices designed to connect to a *PCMCIA bus*. PCMCIA card readers may be useful for computer users who only want to buy one of a particular peripheral, such as a *modem* or *network interface adapter*.

PCMCIA modem   A *modem* designed to connect to a *PCMCIA slot*, usually in a *portable computer*.

PCMCIA slot   A receptacle that's designed to connect devices to a *PCMCIA bus*. These slots can be used to plug in PCMCIA-compatible hardware such as *modems* and *network adapters*.

.PCX   A file *extension* indicating that the file contains a graphic in the PCX graphics file format, which was originally developed for the PC Paintbrush program but now is widely used by other applications. PCX files and *.BMP* files are usually functionally equivalent.

PD   See *public domain software*.

PDA   See *personal digital assistant (PDA)*.

PDL   See *page description language (PDL)*.

PDN   See *public data network (PDN)*.

Peachtree Accounting   A small-business *accounting package* that critics have lauded for its ease-of-use and power. Designed for companies with 100 employees or fewer, Peachtree Accounting features the ability to manage payroll, keep track of accounts payable and accounts receivable, and manage inventory in a variety of ways (first in, first out; last in, first out, etc.).

Peachtree Accounting, available in both Macintosh and *Microsoft Windows* versions, also has several *spreadsheet*-like analysis tools that let business managers develop several *what-if scenarios*.

O
P
Q
R

peer-to-peer file transfer   A file-sharing technique for *local area networks (LANs)* in which each user has access to the public files located on the *workstation* of any other network user. Each user determines which files, if any, he or she wants to make public for network access. See *TOPS*.

peer-to-peer network   A *local area network(LAN)* without a central *file server* and in which all computers in the network have access to the public files located on all other *workstations*. See *client/server network* and *peer-to-peer file transfer*.

pel   Abbreviation for *pixel*.

pen computer   A computer equipped with pattern recognition circuitry so that it can recognize human handwriting as a form of data input. Many *personal digital assistants (PDAs)* use pen technology.

To use a pen computer, you "write" on a screen with a special stylus that resembles a pen. Pen computing may find a market with people who need to fill out forms away from offices, such as police officers and census takers. Many delivery services already use pen computing devices. A special version of *Microsoft Windows* for pen-based computing systems is available.

Pentium   The fastest type of *microprocessor* currently available in IBM PCs and compatible computers. The Pentium, available with *clock speeds* of 60 *megahertz (MHz)*, 66 MHz, 90 MHz, 100 MHz, 120 MHz, 133 MHz and, soon, 155 MHz, uses a speedy version of *complex instruction-set computer (CISC)* technology, *superscalar architecture* (it has two *pipelines*), and a 64-bit *internal data bus*. Though early Pentiums had faulty *floating-point units (FPUs)*, Intel has corrected the problem and will replace bad parts for free. Note, though, that 60 MHz and 66 MHz Pentiums run very hot—hot enough to destroy themselves without *heat sinks* and *CPU fans*. Avoid buying 60 MHz and 66 MHz Pentiums.

Pentium OverDrive   A *microprocessor* that, as part of an upgrade, plugs into the *OverDrive socket* on the *motherboard* of an *Intel 486DX/2 central processing unit (CPU)*. The Pentium OverDrive improves the performance of an Intel 486DX/2 computer to *Pentium* levels.

Pentium-ready   Capable of being upgraded to near-*Pentium* performance levels. Pentium-ready 80486 motherboards have a

P24T socket, into which a *Pentium OverDrive microprocessor* may be inserted.

PerfectOffice Professional   A *suite* of *application programs,* published by Novell, that includes *Paradox,* a *database management* program, in addition to the programs in *PerfectOffice Standard.* PerfectOffice Professional competes with *Lotus SmartSuite* and *Microsoft Office Professional.*

PerfectOffice Standard   A *suite* of *application programs,* published by Novell, that includes *WordPerfect, Quattro Pro,* Presentations (presentation graphics), InfoCentral *(personal information manager [PIM]),* Envoy (publishing), and GroupWise (workgroup coordination). PerfectOffice Standard competes with *Microsoft Office Standard* and *Lotus SmartSuite.*

peripheral   A device, such as a *printer* or disk drive, connected to and controlled by a computer but external to the computer's *central processing unit (CPU).*

peripheral component interface (PCI) expansion bus   The fastest, most technically advanced, and most flexible *expansion bus* specification in wide use today. *Intel Corporation* released the PCI bus in 1992 to work with its *Pentium* microprocessor, but the design is flexible and should work with subsequent microprocessors as well. PCI has largely displaced the *VESA local bus* standard from the market and will likely soon do the same with the *Industry Standard Architecture (ISA)* expansion bus. PCI *supports Plug and Play,* which likely will help cement its hold on the expansion bus market for the next several years.

permanent font   A Hewlett-Packard term for a *font* that, when downloaded to a *laser printer,* stays in the printer's memory until the printer is shut off. See *downloadable font, temporary font.*

permanent swap file   In *Microsoft Windows,* a disk file composed of contiguous disk sectors that's set aside for the rapid storage and retrieval of program instructions or data in the program's 386 Enhanced mode. This storage space is used in *virtual memory* operations, which use disk space as a seamless extension of *random-access memory (RAM).* The permanent swap file, however, is slower than RAM and consumes a large amount of space on the disk. See *page memory management unit (PMMU), swap file,* and *temporary swap file.*

persistence A quality of the *phosphor* that coats the interior of a *cathode ray tube (CRT) display*. Persistence ensures that after being struck by the beam from an *electron gun,* a phosphor will continue to glow until the electron beam strikes it again. Persistence ensures that *displays* appear uniformly bright to human eyes.

persistent connection In *Microsoft Windows 95*, a network connection that lasts longer than a single working session. A *modem* call to CompuServe is usually not a persistent connection, while an *Ethernet* connection to a *network laser printer* is. Windows 95 tries to establish persistent connections every time it starts.

personal computer A small computer equipped with all the system, utility, and application software, and the input/output devices and other *peripherals* that an individual needs to perform one or more tasks. The term personal computer, or PC, is used today to refer collectively and individually to stand-alone IBM Personal Computers, *IBM PC-compatible computers,* Macintosh computers, Apple computers, Amiga computers, and others (such as the Commodore) that are no longer manufactured.

The idea of personal computing, at least initially, was to free individuals from dependence on tightly controlled *mainframe* and *minicomputer* resources. Yet in recent years, reasons have been found to reintegrate PCs into the data communications networks of organizations, and this goal can be achieved without forcing people to give up the autonomy that personal computing implies. See *local-area network (LAN)* and *professional workstation.*

Personal Computer Memory Card Interface Adapter (PCMCIA) An international trade association that has developed standards for devices, such as *modems* and external *hard disk* drives, that can be easily plugged into *notebook computers*. See *Plug and Play.*

personal digital assistant (PDA) A small, hand-held computer, capable of accepting input that the user writes on-screen with a stylus, that's designed to provide all the tools an individual would need for day-to-day organization. This would include, for example, an appointment calendar, an address book, a notepad, and a fax modem. See *Newton, pen computer,* and *transceiver.*

personal information manager (PIM) A *database management program* such as *Lotus Organizer* that stores and retrieves a variety of personal information, including notes, memos, names and addresses, and appointments.

Unlike a database management program, a PIM is optimized for the storage and retrieval of a variety of personal information. You can switch among different views of your notes, such as people, to-do items, and expenses. PIMs have been slow to gain acceptance, however, because they're hard to learn and because users often are away from their computers when they need the information.

personal laser printer   A *laser printer* designed to serve the printing needs of only one person, as opposed to a *departmental laser printer* which is designed to serve many people. Personal laser printers have *monthly duty cycles* of a few hundred pages.

PGA   See *professional graphics array (PGA)* and *pin grid array (PGA)*.

PgUp/PgDn keys   See *Page Up/Page Down keys*.

phono plug   A connector with a short stem used to connect home audio devices. In computers, phono plugs are used for audio and composite monitor output ports. Synonymous with RCA plug.

phosphor   An electrofluorescent material used to coat the inside face of a *cathode ray tube (CRT)*. After being energized by the electron beam that's directed to the inside face of the tube, the phosphors glow for a fraction of a second—long enough to make the display appear uniformly bright to human eyes. The beam refreshes the phosphor many times per second to produce a consistent illumination. See *raster display*.

PhotoCD   A standard for encoding photographs, taken with ordinary 35-millimeter cameras and film, onto *CD-ROMs*. Though PhotoCD technology has not become a big consumer hit, it is popular among publishers and some photographers. If you plan to work with PhotoCDs, make sure any *CD-ROM disk drive* you buy is *multisession PhotoCD*-compatible.

PhotoGrade   An Apple *resolution enhancement* scheme that improves the appearance of *grayscale* images, such as photographs, when they are printed on a *laser printer*.

photorealistic   Of photographic quality. *Printer* output is said to be photorealistic when its colors are well-saturated and blend smoothly with one another.

photorealistic output   *Printer* output that matches the quality of a chemically printed photograph. *Thermal dye transfer printers* can generate photorealistic output with *continuous tones,* but

O
P ◄
Q
R

they are very expensive and the *cost per page* exceeds $3.00, since they require special *coated paper.*

Photoshop   See *Adobe Photoshop.*

phototypesetter   See *imagesetter.*

phreaking   An illegal form of recreation that involves using one's knowledge of telephone system technology to make long-distance calls for free.

physical drive   The disk drive actually performing the current read/write operation.

A *hard disk* can be formatted into *partitions,* sections, and directories that have all the characteristics of a separate disk drive, but are *logical drives.* The data, however, is actually encoded either on the surface of a disk in a floppy drive or a hard disk drive, which is referred to as the physical drive. See *floppy disk,* and *secondary storage.*

physical format   See *low-level format.*

physical medium   In a computer network, the cabling through which network data travels. See *copper cable, coaxial cable, fiber optic, T1,* and *T3.*

physical memory   The actual *random-access memory (RAM)* circuits in which data is stored, as opposed to *virtual memory*—the "apparent" RAM that results from using the computer's *hard disk* as an extension of physical memory.

physical network   An actual physical *network* such as a *local area network (LAN),* generally constructed using the equipment and software of a single manufacturer, as opposed to a *logical network,* the network that users perceive when they use their *workstations.* At the University of Virginia, for example, there are several physical networks made by a number of different LAN hardware manufacturers. However, the differences among these networks are not apparent, or even discoverable, by the students, faculty, and staff who log on to these networks; so far as they are concerned, there is a single logical network that makes all of the University's computer resources available, and a broader global network (the *Internet*) that makes even more resources available.

.PIC   A file *extension* indicating that the file contains a graphic in the Lotus PIC format, used by *Lotus 1-2-3* to save business graphs.

pica   In *typography,* a unit of measure equal to approximately 1/6 inch, or 12 *points.* Picas are used to describe horizontal and vertical measurements on the page, with the exception of type sizes, which are expressed in points.

In formal typography, one pica is 0.166 of an inch, but many word processing and page layout programs, in the interest of simplification, define one pica as 1/6 inch.

In typewriting and letter-quality printing, pica is a 12-point monospace font that prints at a pitch of 10 *characters per inch (cpi)*.

pico- Prefix for one trillionth (10^{-12}). Abbreviated p.

picosecond One trillionth (10^{-12}) of a second.

PICT A Macintosh graphics *file format* originally developed for the MacDraw program. An *object-oriented graphic* format, PICT files consist of separate graphics objects, such as lines, arcs, ovals, or rectangles, each of which you can independently edit, size, move, or color. (PICT files also can store *bit-mapped graphics*.) Some Windows graphics applications can read PICT files.

picture element See *pixel.*

picture tube See *cathode ray tube (CRT).*

pie graph In *presentation graphics*, a graph that displays a *data series* as a circle to emphasize the relative contribution of each data item to the whole (see fig. P.2).

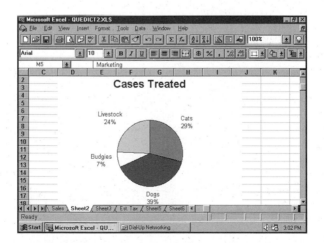

Fig. P.2 *A pie graph.*

Each slice of the pie appears in shades of gray or a distinctive pattern. Patterns can produce moiré distortions if you juxtapose too many patterns. Some programs can produce paired pie graphs that display two data series. For presentations, exploding a slice from the whole is a useful technique to add emphasis. See *exploded pie graph, linked pie/column graph, moiré effect,* and *proportional pie graph.*

PIF   See *program information file (PIF).*

PILOT   An authoring language for *computer-assisted instruction (CAI),* developed by John Starkweather at the University of California-San Francisco in 1968.

PILOT, short for Programmed Inquiry Learning Or Teaching, is exceptionally easy to learn because it has very few commands. Used primarily to develop on-screen instructional materials, PILOT is being displaced by new authoring languages that use graphical user interfaces such as *HyperTalk.*

PIM   See *personal information manager (PIM).*

pin-compatible   Able to fit and operate in the same socket as another *chip,* especially one made by another manufacturer. See *zero-insertion force (ZIF) package.*

pin feed   See *tractor feed.*

pin grid array (PGA)   On the bottom side of a *chip,* the collection of protruding pins that enable the chip to connect to a socket or *circuit board.*

Pine   An *electronic mail* program for *UNIX* computer systems. Unlike predecessor programs, such as *Elm,* the program contains its own easy-to-use full screen editor, thus freeing users from dependence on the not-very-easy-to-use default editors on UNIX systems (such as *emacs* and *vi*). (The name "Pine" is actually an acronym of the self-referential sort: Pine Is Not Elm.)

PING   See *Packet Internet Groper (PING).*

pingable   Able to respond to *PING*; an *Internet* site that is "alive" and should be able to respond to Internet tools such as *FTP* and *Gopher.*

pipe   In DOS and *UNIX,* a symbol that tells the operating system to send the output of one command to another command, rather than display this output.

In the following example, the pipe (represented by the ¦ symbol) tells DOS to send the output of the TREE command to the MORE command; the MORE command then displays the TREE result page by page on-screen:

```
TREE C:\ ¦ MORE
```

See *filter* and *input/output (I/O) redirection.*

pipeline   In computer design, an "assembly line" in the micro-processor that dramatically speeds the processing of instructions through retrieval, execution, and writing back. Long supported by *UNIX,* the pipeline included in the *Intel 80486* allows it to process an instruction every *clock cycle.* The *Intel Pentium* microprocessor features two pipelines, one for data and one for instruction, and can therefore process two instructions (one per pipeline) every clock cycle. A microprocessor with two or more pipelines is said to employ *superscalar architecture.*

pipeline stall   An error in a *superscalar architecture*-equipped *microprocessor* that delays the processing of an instruction. In a microprocessor with *an in-order execution* design, such as the *Pentium,* instructions must be processed in a precise order, and a pipeline stall in one *pipeline* will delay processing in the other pipeline, as well. In an *out-of-order execution* scheme, a pipeline stall in one pipeline would not hold up the other.

pipelining   A *microprocessor* design method that allows a micro-processor to handle more than one instruction at a time. There are typically five sequential steps to a microprocessor's handling of an instruction, and a pipelining scheme allows each of five instruc-tions to be undergoing one of the steps during a *clock cycle.* Micro-processors with *superscalar architecture* have two or more *pipelines,* increasing efficiency further.

piracy   See *software piracy.*

pitch   A horizontal measurement of the number of characters per linear inch in a *monospace* font, such as those used with type-writers, *dot-matrix printers,* and *daisywheel printers.*

By convention, *pica* pitch (not to be confused with the printer's measurement of approximately 1/6 inch) is equal to 10 characters per inch, and elite pitch is equal to 12 characters per inch. See *point.*

O
P
Q
R

pixel   The smallest element (a picture element) that a device can display and out of which the displayed image is constructed. See *bit-mapped graphic*.

Plain Old Telephone Service (POTS)   An *analog* communications system, adequate for voice communication and slow data communication with *modems*, but without sufficient *bandwidth* to handle high-speed *digital* communications. Technologies like the *Integrated Services Telecommunications Network (ISDN)* may replace POTS someday and provide higher bandwidth.

plain text document   A document that contains nothing but standard *ASCII* text, number, and punctuation characters.

TIP: *In many applications, you can save a plain text document in two ways: with or without Enter keystrokes at the end of each line. If you're exporting the document to another word processor, choose the option that saves the document without Enter keystrokes (carriage returns) at the end of each line; after you import the document, paragraphs will word wrap and reformat automatically. Choose the Enter keystroke option only when you need to save plain text for an application, such as uploading a file through telecommunications links.*

planar board   See *motherboard*.

plasma display   A *display* technology used with *high-end laptop* computers. The display is produced by energizing ionized gas held between two transparent panels. Synonymous with gas plasma display.

platen   In *dot-matrix* and *letter-quality impact printers,* the cylinder that guides paper through the printer and provides a backing surface for the paper when images are impressed onto the page.

platform   See *hardware platform*.

platform independence   The capability of a *local area network (LAN)* to connect computers made by different makers, such as connecting an IBM PC-compatible computer with a Macintosh computer.

plating   A means of coating a *hard disk platter* with a thin-film magnetic medium. By submerging an electrically charged bare platter in a liquid containing oppositely charged molecules of the recording medium, the platter is evenly coated with the medium. See *sputtering*.

platter   Synonymous with disk.

plot   To construct an image by drawing lines.

plotter   A printer that produces high-quality graphical output by moving ink pens over the surface of the paper. The printer moves the pens under the direction of the computer, so that printing is automatic. Plotters are commonly used for *computer-aided design (CAD)* and presentation graphics.

plotter font   In *Microsoft Windows*, a vector font designed to be used with a plotter. The font composes characters by generating dots connected by lines.

Plug and Play   An emerging industry-wide hardware standard for add-in hardware that requires the hardware be able to identify itself, on demand, in a standard fashion. *Microsoft Windows 95* supports Plug and Play, and should help create a market for Plug and Play peripherals, which are expected to overshadow older peripherals in short order.

With Plug and Play, you don't need to "install" devices; you don't fuss with *jumper settings* and *dual in-line package (DIP)* switches, or printer drivers for the newest printers. Instead, Plug and Play uses both hardware (a Plug and Play *BIOS [PnP BIOS]*) and software (a Plug and Play-compatible *operating system*) to do its job.

Plug and Play BIOS (PnP BIOS)   A *basic input-output system (BIOS)* compatible with the *Plug and Play* standard, which, when used in conjunction with a Plug and Play compatible *operating system* (such as *Microsoft Windows 95*) and Plug and Play compatible *adapters*, enables you to install adapters in the *expansion bus* without creating *interrupt request (IRQ) conflicts* or *port conflicts*. Note that a "plug and play" BIOS is not necessarily the same as a "Plug and Play" (capital letters) BIOS, which precisely conforms to the Plug and Play standard.

Plug and Print   A standard designed to improve the way *printers* and computers communicate. Developed by the *Desktop Management Task Force (DMTF)*, Plug and Print creates a Management Information Base (MIB) or Management Information File

O
P
Q
R

(MIF) that contains details about a printer's operation. Plug and Print, an open standard, competes with *Microsoft at Work*, a standard designed to be used only by systems running Microsoft Windows. Synonymous with MIB/MI.

plug-compatible   See *pin-compatible*.

PMJI   In on-line communications, shorthand for Pardon Me for Jumping In.

PMMU   See *paged memory management unit (PMMU)*.

PMS   See *Pantone Matching System (PMS)*.

PnP BIOS   See *Plug and Play BIOS (PnP BIOS)*.

pocket modem   An *external modem* about the size of a pack of cigarettes, designed for use with *portable computers*. Pocket modems have been largely replaced by *PCMCIA* modems.

point   To move the mouse pointer on-screen without clicking the button. In *typography*, a fundamental unit of measurement (72 points equal approximately one inch). Computer programs usually ignore this slight discrepancy, making a point exactly equal to 1/72 inch. See *pica* and *pitch*.

point of presence (POP)   In a *wide-area network (WAN)*, an area where it is possible to gain access to the network by means of a local telephone call.

point-of-sale software   A *program*, such as a *bar-code reader*, that automatically makes adjustments to accounting and inventory databases as a business sells merchandise.

A typical point-of-sale software package such as Retail Store Controller (Microbiz) brings virtually all the functionality of large business systems to a single-user, PC-based point-of-sale workstation. Included are such features as automatic credit card verification, customer history tracking, bar code label printing, sales tracking by employee, reorder reports, flexible sales analysis and reports, and export links to accounting software. Available accessories include a compatible cash drawer and a receipt printer.

Point to Point Protocol (PPP)   One of the two standards for directly connecting computers to the *Internet* via dialup telephone connections (the other is SLIP). Unlike the older SLIP protocol, PPP incorporates superior data negotiation, compression, and error correction. However, these features add overhead to data transmission, and are unnecessary when both the sending and receiving modems offer hardware error correction and on-the-fly data compression. See *Serial Line Internet Protocol (SLIP)*.

pointer   An on-screen symbol, usually an arrow, that shows the current position of the *mouse*. In *database management* programs, a record number in an index that stores the actual physical location of the data record.

The pointer doesn't necessarily indicate the position of the *cursor*. To move the cursor with the mouse, you must click the pointer on the desired cursor position.

TIP: *If you use* Microsoft Windows, *learn the meaning of the various pointer shapes. They tell you when the application is ready to select something, jump to related information, or size a graphic object.*

In *programming*, a variable that contains directions to (points to) another variable. Pointers enable programmers to set many variables equal to one another without lots of *assignment statements*.

pointing device   An input device such as a *mouse*, trackball, or *graphics tablet* used to manipulate a pointer on-screen.

pointing stick   An eraser-sized, rubberized device in the center of the *keyboard*, moved with the fingertip to relocate the cursor on-screen. Though pointing sticks originated in *portable computers* and are often used in them, pointing sticks appear on some *desktop computers* as well.

polarity   In electronics, the negative or positive property of a charge.

In *graphics*, the tonal relationship between foreground and background elements. Positive polarity is the printing of black or dark characters on a white or light background; negative polarity is the printing of white or light characters on a black or dark background.

polarization   A physical phenomenon, in which light waves vibrate in a single plane, that is part of the foundation of *magneto-optical (MO) disk drive* technology. Along with the *Kerr effect*, polarization is at the core of how MO drives read and write data.

O
P
Q
R

Polish notation See *reverse Polish notation (RPN).*

polling In *local area networks (LANs),* a method for controlling channel access in which the central computer continuously asks or polls the workstations to determine whether they have information to send.

With polling channel access, you can specify how often, and for how long, the central computer polls the workstations. Unlike CSMA/CD and token-ring channel-access methods, the network manager can give some nodes more access to the network than others. See *carrier sense multiple access with collision detection (CSMA/CD)* and *token-ring network.*

polyline In *graphics,* a drawing tool used to create a multisided, enclosed shape. To use the tool, draw a straight line to a point, and then continue the line in a different direction to a point. By continuing this operation until you return to the starting point, you can create a complex object of your own design. The result is a *graphics primitive,* which the program treats as a single object. Like the more familiar primitives (squares or circles), the polyline object can be independently edited, sized, moved, or colored. Some programs call this tool a polygon. See *object-oriented graphic.*

polyphony In *sound boards,* the reproduction of multiple sounds at one time. *High-end* sound boards can put out 20 or more sounds at once.

pop-up menu A *menu* that appears when you select a certain on-screen item, such as text, a *scroll bar,* or a *dialog box* option. The name doesn't truly reflect a direction. If a pop-up menu will appear too close to the top of the screen, it pops down. *Microsoft Windows 95* makes extensive use of pop-up menus, both for editing and tutorial tasks. See *pull-down menu.*

port An *interface* that governs and synchronizes the flow of data between the *central processing unit (CPU)* and external devices such as printers and modems. Also, reprogramming an application so that it runs on another type of computer. See *parallel port* and *serial port.*

portable Capable of working on a variety of *hardware* platforms.

UNIX is a portable *operating system.* Most operating systems are designed around the specific electronic capabilities of a given *central processing unit (CPU).* UNIX, in contrast, is designed with a predetermined, overall structure. Instructions are embedded within the program that allow it to function on a given CPU.

portable computer   A computer with a screen and keyboard built in and designed to be transported easily from one location to another.

The first portable personal computers, such as the Osborne I and Compaq II, are best described as "luggables." These computers weighed in at more than 25 pounds and couldn't be carried comfortably for more than a short distance. Today's battery-powered laptop and notebook computers are much smaller and lighter. See *laptop computer* and *notebook computer.*

portable document   A richly formatted document, which may contain *graphics* as well as text, that can be transferred to another type of computer system without losing the rich formatting. To create portable documents, you need *portable document software (PDS),* such as *Adobe Acrobat,* that is designed to save the formatting information to a file that can be easily transferred to a different type of computer system. To read the document, you need a file viewer program that is specifically designed to work on the type of computer you are using. For example, you can create an Adobe Acrobat document on a Macintosh, and give the file to somebody using a Sun workstation. To read the file, the Sun user needs a copy of the Adobe Acrobat reader program.

O P Q R

portable document software (PDS)   *Application programs* that create *portable documents,* which can be transferred to different types of computer systems without losing their rich formatting and graphics. Two types of software are required: the document publishing program and a file viewer. The document publishing program creates a coded *ASCII* file that retains *fonts,* graphics, and layout information. This file can be distributed electronically by means of on-line services such as *CompuServe* or the *Internet.* File viewers, which are designed to run on a specific type of computer, enable users to read these files and to see a replica of the original document's fonts, graphics, and layout. The most popular PDS is *Adobe Acrobat,* thanks to the widespread Internet availability of free file viewers for a wide variety of computer systems. Additional PDS solutions include Common Ground (No Hands Software), Replica (Farallon Computing) and Envoy (WordPerfect).

port address   A number that identifies the location of a particular *Internet* application, such as *FTP*, a *World Wide Web (WWW)* server, or *Gopher*, on a computer that is directly connected to the Internet. Regulated by the *Internet Assigned Numbers Authority (IANA)*, port numbers are included in the headers of every Internet packet; the numbers tell the receiving software where to deliver the incoming data. See *well-known ports*.

port conflict   An error that occurs when two devices, such as a *mouse* and a *modem*, try to access the same *serial port* at one time. If you can, set your mouse to serial port COM1, your modem to serial port COM2, and disable all other serial ports, since using them may cause problems.

portrait font   A *font* oriented toward the short edges of a page. This page is printed with a portrait font.

portrait monitor   See *full-page display*.

portrait orientation   The default printing orientation for a page of text by which the height of the page is greater than the width (see fig. P.3). See *landscape orientation*.

Fig. P.3   *Examples of portrait orientation (top) and landscape orientation (bottom).*

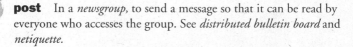

post   In a *newsgroup*, to send a message so that it can be read by everyone who accesses the group. See *distributed bulletin board* and *netiquette*.

In database management, to add data to a *data record*.

POST   See *Power-On Self-Test (POST)*.

postmaster   In a *network*, the human administrator who configures the electronic mail manager and handles problems that arise.

Post Office Protocol (POP)   An Internet electronic mail standard that specifies how an Internet-connected computer can function as a mail-handling agent. Messages arrive at a user's electronic mailbox, which is housed on the service provider's computer. From this central storage point, you can access your mail from different computers—a networked workstation in the office as well as a PC at home. In either case, a POP-compatible electronic mail program, which runs on your workstation or PC, establishes a connection with the POP server, and detects that new mail has arrived. You can then download the mail to the workstation or computer, and reply to it, print it, or store it, as you prefer.

postprocessor   A *program* that performs a final, automatic processing operation after you finish working with a file. Postprocessing programs include text formatters that prepare a document for printing, and *page description languages* that convert an on-screen document into a set of commands that the printer's interpreter can recognize and use to print the document.

PostScript   A sophisticated *page description language (PDL)* that's used for high-quality printing on laser printers and other *high-resolution* printing devices.

Though PostScript is a *programming language* and you can learn to write page descriptions in it, PostScript is usually invisible and automatic. Programs generate PostScript code that goes to the

O
P ◄
Q
R

printer, where a PostScript interpreter follows the coded instructions to generate an image of the page precisely according to these instructions.

A major benefit of PostScript is its device independence; you can print the PostScript code generated by an application on any printer with a PostScript interpreter. You can take PostScript files generated on your PC to a service bureau, which can print the document using expensive typesetting machines with resolutions of up to 2,400 dots per inch (dpi). See *PostScript font,* and *PostScript printer.*

PostScript font   A scalable *outline font* that conforms to Adobe Software's specifications for *Type 1 fonts*, which require a *PostScript printer.*

Unlike bit-mapped fonts, which often print with crude edges and curves, PostScript's outline font technology produces smooth letters that your printer renders at its maximum possible resolution. A *PostScript* font comes with a *screen font,* which simulates the font's appearance on-screen, and a *printer font,* which must either be built-in to your printer or downloaded to the printer before printing.

Note that the type may look jagged on-screen unless you buy Adobe Type Manager, which brings PostScript *scalable font* technology to the display screen.

> **TIP:** TrueType *font technology, jointly developed by Apple Computer and Microsoft Corporation, provides a cost-effective alternative to PostScript fonts and PostScript laser printers. TrueType fonts are scalable outline fonts that don't require a pricy PostScript printer. Moreover, if you're using TrueType with Microsoft Windows 3.1, or with the Mac's System 7, the scaling technology is built in so you also don't need Adobe Type Manager.*

PostScript Level 2   An improved version of *PostScript* that is faster and supports color printing and file *compression.*

PostScript printer   A *printer,* generally a *laser printer,* that includes the processing circuitry needed to decode and interpret printing instructions phrased in *PostScript,* a *page description language (PDL)* widely used in *desktop publishing.*

Because PostScript printers require their own microprocessor circuitry and at least 1*M* of random-access memory (RAM) to image each page, they're more expensive than non-PostScript printers. However, they can print text or graphics in subtle gradations of gray. They can also use *Encapsulated PostScript (EPS)* graphics and outline fonts, both of which you can size and scale without introducing distortions.

posture   The slant of the characters in a *font.* Italic characters slant to the right, but the term italic is reserved by conservative typographers for custom-designed (as opposed to electronically produced) *serif* typefaces.

POTS   See *Plain Old Telephone Service (POTS).*

power down   To turn off a device.

power line filter   An electrical device that smoothes out the peaks and valleys of the voltage delivered at the wall socket.

Every electrical circuit is subject to voltage fluctuations, and if these are extreme, they may cause computer errors and failures. If you're using a computer in a circuit shared by heavy appliances, you may need a power line filter to ensure error-free operation. See *surge protector.*

Power Macintosh   Any Macintosh computer that uses a PowerPC *microprocessor,* such as the *PowerPC 601.*

power management   A *microprocessor* feature that reduces a computer's consumption of electricity by turning off *peripherals* during periods of non-use. Though power management features are not part of all microprocessors, they are commonly found in chips used in *portable computers,* since energy savings equates to longer battery life in those machines. See *green PC* and *sleep mode.*

power supply   A device that provides the power to electronic equipment. In a computer system, the power supply converts standard AC current to the lower voltage DC current used by the computer.

O
P
Q
R

CAUTION: *The power supply of early IBM PC-compatible computers (63.5 watts) often proved inadequate to power several adapters, a hard disk, and other system upgrades. An overloaded power supply can cause erratic operations, such as read or write errors, parity errors, and unexplained system crashes. For systems with hard disks and several adapters, users should have a power supply of at least 200 watts.*

power surge   See *surge.*

power up   To turn on a device.

power user   A computer user who has gone beyond the beginning and intermediate stages of computer use. Such a person uses the advanced features of application programs, such as software command languages and macros, and can learn new *application programs* quickly.

Power-On Self-Test (POST)   Internal testing performed when you start or reset your computer. Encoded in *read-only memory (ROM)*, the POST program first checks the *microprocessor* by having it perform a few simple operations. Then it reads the *CMOS* ROM, which stores the amount of memory and type of disk drives in your system. Next, the POST writes, then reads, various data patterns to each byte of memory (you can watch the bytes count off on-screen and often end the test with a keystroke). Finally, the POST communicates with every device; you see the keyboard and drive lights flash and the printer resets, for example. The BIOS continues with hardware testing, then looks in drive A for an *operating system;* if drive A isn't found, it looks in drive C. See *basic input/output system (BIOS)* and *boot sector.*

PowerPC   A *reduced instruction set computer (RISC) microprocessor* developed by *Motorola* that's competitive with the *Pentium.* The PowerPC is being used by *IBM* for its RS/6000 line and by Apple Corporation as the next-generation processor for the Macintosh. The PowerPC will support Windows NT, OS/2, and UNIX, based on a promise of industry commitment to PowerOpen, a standard for PowerPC operating systems.

PowerPC 601   The first of the *PowerPC microprocessors* jointly developed by *IBM, Apple,* and *Motorola.* The PowerPC 601 is a *32-bit microprocessor* that employs *superscalar architecture* and a portion of *reduced instruction-set computer (RISC)* technology. The PowerPC 601 was used in the first *Power Macintoshes*. Designed to challenge the *Pentium* and *Intel Corporation's* dominance of the personal computer microprocessor market in general, the Power-PC and its brethren—the *PowerPC 601v, PowerPC 602, PowerPC 603, PowerPC 603e, PowerPC 604, PowerPC 615*, and *PowerPC 620*—are some of the fastest microprocessors available today.

PowerPC 601v   A version of the *PowerPC 601* that uses *0.5-micron technology* and an increased *clock speed* of 100 *megahertz (MHz)* to improve performance and reduce power consumption.

PowerPC 602   A 32-bit *microprocessor* designed for budget-minded computer users. The PowerPC 602 runs at a *clock speed* of 66 *megahertz (MHz)*, uses *reduced instruction-set computer (RISC)* technology, and achieves a *CINT92* score of 40. See *PowerPC 601*.

PowerPC 603   A *32-bit microprocessor*, similar in performance to the *PowerPC 601*, designed for situations—such as *portable computing*—in which power conservation is key. Available with *clock speeds* of 66 *megahertz (MHz)* and 80 MHz, the PowerPC 603 has a smaller *internal cache* than the PowerPC 601, but uses *0.5-micron technology* to reduce its power demand to only 2 watts. The PowerPC 603's *CINT92* rating is 75. See *PowerPC 601* and *PowerPC 603e*.

PowerPC 603e   A version of the *PowerPC 603* that includes even more *power-management* features.

PowerPC 604   A *64-bit microprocessor* that *incorporates reduced instruction-set computing (RISC)* technology and *branch-prediction* techniques to achieve a *CINT92* score of 160. The PowerPC 604, which runs at a *clock speed* of 100 *megahertz (MHz)*, is faster than the *PowerPC 601*, but considerably slower than the *PowerPC 620*. The PowerPC 604 earns a *CINT92* score of 160. See *PowerPC 601*.

PowerPC 615   A version of the PowerPC *microprocessor* under development by IBM, independent of Apple and Motorola (which collaborated with IBM in developing the other PowerPC micro-processors), that may be *binary compatible* with *x86* software. See *PowerPC 601*.

PowerPC 620   The speediest PowerPC *microprocessor* available today, the PowerPC 620 is twice as fast as the *PowerPC 604*

O
P
Q
R

thanks to a *pre-decode* step in the *pipeline*, a large *internal cache*, and excellent *branch-prediction* capabilities. A *64-bit microprocessor* that employs *reduced instruction-set computer (RISC)* technology, the PowerPC 620 runs at 133 *megahertz (MHz)* and, due in part to its use *of 0.5-micron technology*, draws only 3.3 volts. The PowerPC 620's *CINT92* rating is 225. See *PowerPC 601*.

PowerPoint   See *Microsoft PowerPoint*.

ppm   See *pages per minute (ppm)*.

Practical Extraction and Report Language (perl)   In *UNIX*, an interpreted *scripting language* that is specifically designed for scanning text files, extracting information from these files, and preparing reports summarizing this information. Written by Larry Wall, perl is widely used to create *Common Gateway Interface (CGI)* scripts that handle the output of HTML *forms*. See *HyperText Markup Language (HTML)* and *interpreter*.

PRAM   See *parameter RAM*.

precedence   The order in which a *program* performs the operations in a formula. Typically, the program performs exponentiation (such as squaring a number) before multiplication and division, and then performs addition and subtraction.

precision   The number of digits past the decimal that are used to express a quantity. See *accuracy*.

pre-decode stage   In *microprocessors* that employ *superscalar architectures*, a step in the processing of instructions in which the microprocessor determines what resources, such as *registers*, will be needed to process a particular instruction. A pre-decode stage allows instructions to move through a *pipeline* faster.

preemptive multitasking   In an *operating system*, a means of running more than one program at a time. In preemptive multitasking, the operating system decides which application should receive the processor's attention. In contrast to *cooperative multitasking*, in which a busy application could monopolize the computer for as much as several minutes, a computer with a preemptive multitasking system seems much more responsive to user commands. *Microsoft Windows 95* employs preemptive applications for *32-bit applications*, but not for *16-bit applications*.

presentation graphics   The branch of the graphics profession that's concerned with the preparation of slides, transparencies, and handouts for use in business presentations. Ideally, presentation graphics combines artistry with practical psychology and good taste; color, form, and emphasis are used intelligently to convey the presentation's most significant points to the audience. See *analytical graphics*.

presentation graphics program   An *application program* designed to create and enhance charts and graphs so that they're visually appealing and easily understood by an audience.

A full-featured presentation graphics package such as Lotus Freelance Graphics or *Microsoft PowerPoint* includes facilities for making a wide variety of charts and graphs and for adding titles, legends, and explanatory text anywhere in the chart or graph. A presentation graphics program also includes a library of *clip art*, so you can enliven charts and graphs by adding a picture related to the subject matter—for example, an airplane for a chart of earnings in the aerospace industry. You can print output, direct output to a film recorder, or display output on-screen as a computer slide show.

pretty print   In *programming*, a feature of *source code* editors that makes printouts of source code easier to read and understand. By indenting nested *loops* and inserting blank lines around *modules*, for example, a pretty print feature makes studying source code less tedious.

primary cache   *Cache memory* built into the *microprocessor*, instead of located on the *motherboard* like *secondary cache* memory, which is also called L2 cache. Primary cache is synonymous with *internal cache* and on-board cache.

primary storage   The computer's main memory, which consists of the *random-access memory (RAM)* and the *read-only memory (ROM)* that's directly accessible to the *central processing unit (CPU)*.

print engine   In a *laser printer*, the mechanism that uses a laser to create an electrostatic image of a page and fuses that image to a sheet of paper. You can distinguish print engines by their *resolution*, print quality, longevity, paper-handling features, and speed:

- Resolution. The print engine used in most laser printers generally produces resolutions of 300 and 600 *dots per inch (dpi)*. Professional typesetting machines called imagesetters use chemical photo-reproduction techniques to produce resolutions of up to 2,400 dpi.

- Print quality. Write-white *print engines* expose the portion of the page that doesn't receive ink (so that toner is attracted to the areas that print black) and generally produce deeper blacks than write-black engines, but this quality varies from engine to engine. Although dozens of retail brands of laser printers are on the market, the print engines are made by a few original equipment manufacturers (OEM) such as Canon, Ricoh, Toshiba, and Casio. Canon engines are highly regarded within the desktop publishing industry.

- Longevity. Most print engines have a life of 300,000 copies, but the life span ratings among brands vary from 180,000 to 600,000 copies. Because printer longevity is estimated from heavy use over a short period of time, you should consider a printer's longevity rating only if the printer will be used in heavy-demand network applications. The amount of use a printer is designed to handle often is expressed as a *monthly duty cycle*.

- Paper-handling features. Early laser printers vexed users with thin paper trays that could hold only 50 or 60 sheets of paper. For convenient use, you should consider a paper tray capacity of at least 200 to 250 sheets.

- Speed. Print engines often are rated (optimistically) at speeds of up to 10 *pages per minute (ppm)*. Such speeds, however, are attained only under ideal conditions; the same sparse page of text is printed over and over again. When printing a real manuscript with different text on each page, the printer must pause to construct the image. If the printer encounters a graphic, printing may halt for as long as a minute. What really determines a print engine's speed is the controller's microprocessor. The speed demons of laser printing use third-generation microprocessors (such as the Motorola 68020) running at clock speeds of up to 16.7 MHz.

print head   The mechanism that actually does the printing in a *printer*. There are several kinds of print head technology, including impact (found in *impact printers*), thermal (found in *thermal printers*), ink jet (found in *ink jet printers*), and electrostatic (found in *laser printers*).

print queue A list of files that a *print spooler* prints in the *background* while the computer performs other tasks in the *foreground*.

Print Screen (PrtSc) On IBM PC-compatible *keyboards*, a key you can use to print an image of the screen display.

> **TIP:** *If the screen display is in graphics mode, you must run the MS-DOS program* GRAPHICS.COM *before the screen prints properly.*

print server In a *local area network (LAN)*, a PC that has been dedicated to receiving and temporarily storing files to be printed, which are then doled out one by one to a *printer*. The print server, accessible to all the workstations in the network, runs *print spooler* software to manage a *print queue*.

print spooler A *utility program* that temporarily stores files to be printed in a *print queue* and doles them out one by one to the printer. See *background printing,* and *print server*.

printer A computer *peripheral* designed to print computer-generated text or graphics on paper or other physical media.

Printers vary significantly in their quality, speed, noise, graphics capabilities, *built-in fonts*, and paper usage. The following list provides a brief overview of the types of printers available today:

- *Letter-quality printers* (also called *daisywheel printers*) form an image the same way office typewriters do—by hammering a fully formed image of a character against a ribbon, thus producing an inked image on the paper. Letter-quality printers can't print graphics, and are quite slow.

- *Dot-matrix printers* form an image by extruding a pattern (or matrix) of wires against a ribbon, producing an inked image on paper. Dot-matrix printers print rapidly (100 or more characters per second), but printing speeds degrade considerably when you choose high-resolution modes. Some dot-matrix

O
P
Q
R

printers come with several fonts and font sizes, and all can print graphics.

- *Ink jet printers* form an image by spraying ink directly on the paper's surface, producing what appears to be a fully formed image. Ink jet printers, which often are rated at 4 to 6 *pages per minute (ppm)*, are slower than *laser printers*, but they produce text and graphics output that seem comparable to laser printer quality, are less expensive than laser printers, and produce little noise. Like laser printers, most ink jet printers come with a selection of built-in fonts and can use *font cartridges* or *downloadable fonts.*

- *Laser printers* use copy-machine technology to fuse powdered ink to paper, producing high-quality output at relatively high speeds (most are rated at eight or more pages per minute), use cut sheets or letterhead, and operate quietly. Most come with a selection of built-in fonts and can easily accommodate font cartridges or downloadable fonts. Their major drawback was high cost, but laser printers are now available for less than $700.

- LED and LCD printers closely resemble laser printers, except that these printers don't use lasers to form the image. *LED printers* use an array of light-emitting diodes (LEDs) for this purpose; *LCD printers* use a halogen light, the illumination of which is distributed by means of liquid crystal shutters.

- *Thermal printers* operate quietly, but that's their only advantage. They operate by pushing a matrix of heated pins against special heat-sensitive paper, which means that you must use the right kind of paper. They produce output that resembles that of a cheap dot-matrix printer, except that the paper's surface is shiny and smells bad; even worse, they print slowly. Thermal printers are relegated to minor applications in calculators, fax machines, and portable computer systems.

TIP: *What's the best printer for you? Because ink jet and laser printers are quiet and well supported by most application programs, one of these is probably your best bet. For a home system or for light office use, an ink jet printer may prove ideal. For a busy office, you'll need a laser printer's faster printing speed.*

printer control language   A set of commands that tell a
printer and *printer driver* how to print a document. Printer control
languages are usually proprietary—Hewlett-Packard's *Printer
Control Language* (note the capital letters) for *laser printers* is a very
common example—and are different from *page description languages (PDLs)* such as PostScript, which are somewhat limited
programming languages recognized by many manufacturers. See
PCL3, PCL4, PCL5, and *PCL5e.*

Printer Control Language (PCL)   The printer control
language used by Hewlett-Packard *laser printers.* See *PCL3, PCL4,*
and *PCL5e.*

printer driver   A file that contains the information a *program*
needs to print your work with a given brand and model of *printer.*

A major difference between the DOS environment and the
Macintosh/Windows environments is the way printer drivers are
handled. In the *MS-DOS* environment, printer drivers are the
responsibility of application programs. Each program must come
equipped with its own printer drivers for the many dozens of
printers available, and if a program doesn't include a driver for
your printer, you may be out of luck.

The *Microsoft Windows* and Macintosh operating environments,
on the other hand, provide printer drivers for all Windows applications, freeing application software from that responsibility.

printer emulation   The capability of a *printer* to recognize the
printer control language of a different printer. Widely emulated are
Epson, Hewlett-Packard, and Diablo printers.

printer font   A font that doesn't appear on-screen and is available for use only by the *printer.* When using a printer font, you see
a generic screen font on-screen; you must wait until printing is
complete to see your document's fonts.

Ideally, screen and printer fonts should be identical; only then can
a computer system claim to offer *what-you-see-is-what-you-get
(WYSIWYG)* text processing. Character-based programs, such as
WordPerfect 5.1, running under DOS can't display typefaces
other than those built into the computer's ROM. With *Microsoft
Windows* and Macintosh systems, you can use *TrueType* or Adobe
Type Manager (ATM) outline (scalable) fonts, which appear on-
screen the way they appear when printed. See *outline font.*

O
P
Q
R

printer maintenance   Regular procedures, such as cleaning, that keep a *printer* operating without problems. *Laser printers* require periodic cleaning of their rollers, *corona wires*, and lenses.

printer port   See *parallel port* and *serial port*.

privacy   On a *network*, a presumed right that your disk storage area, *electronic mail*, and files will not be scrutinized by persons to whom you have not given permission. However, privacy on a computer network does not exist. Although the federal *Electronic Communications Privacy Act (1986)* prohibits federal agencies from accessing your e-mail while it is in transit or temporary storage, no federal law prevents employers or other persons from doing so. Many employers believe that they may read employees' mail with impunity; after all, employees are using the employer's equipment. You can protect your privacy by encrypting your messages. See *encryption* and *Privacy Enhanced Mail (PEM)*.

Privacy Enhanced Mail (PEM)   An *Internet* standard that ensures the privacy of *electronic mail*. PEM uses *public key encryption* techniques to assure that only the intended recipient of the message will be able to read it.

PRML read-channel technology   See *partial-response maximum-likelihood read-channel technology*.

procedural language   A *programming language* such as *BASIC* or *Pascal* that requires the programmer to specify the procedure the computer has to follow to accomplish the task. See *declarative language*.

process color   One of the four colors—cyan, magenta, yellow, and black—that are mixed to create other colors. See *CMYK*, *color model*, and *spot color*.

processing   The execution of program instructions by the computer's *central processing unit (CPU)* that in some way transforms data, such as sorting it, selecting some of it according to specified criteria, or performing mathematical computations on it.

processor upgrade   A *chip* designed to replace or complement a *microprocessor* and provide improved performance. Intel's *OverDrive* chip is a processor upgrade for the *Intel 486*. Also, the act of installing such a chip.

Prodigy   An *on-line information service* jointly developed by Sears and *IBM* that offers (via modem) personal computer users home shopping, news, stock quotes, hobbyist conferences, and so on.

Innovative features of Prodigy include the use of a bit-mapped *graphical user interface (GUI)* and unlimited use of the system for a flat fee. (An exception is *electronic mail* usage, for which a surcharge may be added based on the number of messages sent.) Prodigy was the first commercial on-line service to offer access to the World Wide Web (WWW).

Prodigy, however, has no provisions for software *uploading* and has limited *downloading*. Also, part of the screen is occupied by commercial advertisements.

professional workstation   A high-performance personal computer optimized for professional applications in fields such as digital circuit design, architecture, and technical drawing.

Professional workstations typically offer excellent screen *resolution,* fast and powerful microprocessors, and lots of memory. Examples include the workstations made by Sun Microsystems and NeXT, Inc. Professional workstations are more expensive than personal computers and typically use the *UNIX operating system.* The boundary between *high-end personal computers* and professional workstations, however, is eroding as personal computers become more powerful.

program   A list of instructions, written in a *programming language,* that a computer can execute so that the machine acts in a predetermined way. Synonymous with software. The world of computer programs can be divided into system programs, utility programs, and application programs:

- System programs include all the programs the computer requires to function effectively, including the operating system, memory management software, and command-line interpreters. The MS-DOS operating system is an example of system software.

- *Utility programs* include all the programs you can use to maintain the computer system. MS-DOS includes several utility programs, such as CHKDSK. Most users equip their systems with utility packages (such as Norton Utilities or PC Tools) that go beyond the basics that MS-DOS provides.

O
P
Q
R

- *Application programs* transform the computer into a tool for performing a specific kind of work, such as word processing, financial analysis (with an electronic spreadsheet), or desktop publishing.

Additional software categories include programming languages, games, educational programs, and a variety of *vertical market programs.* See *executable program, high-level programming language,* and *machine language.*

program generator   A *program* that creates the program code automatically from a description of the application. In *database management programs,* for example, you can use simple program generation techniques to describe the format you want graphically. The program generator then uses your input as a set of *parameters* by which to build the output program code.

program information file (PIF)   A *file* available for *non-Windows application* programs that tells Windows how to run them. *Microsoft Windows 95* can run DOS applications even without a PIF file.

program overlay   A portion of a program kept on disk and called into memory only as required.

programmable   Capable of being controlled through instructions that can be varied to suit the user's needs.

programmable read-only memory (PROM)   A *read-only memory (ROM)* chip programmed at the factory for use with a given computer.

Unlike standard ROM chips, which have their programming included in the internal design of the chip circuits, programmable ROM chips are easy to modify. Though programmable ROM chips can be programmed, or burned, just once, after which the programming becomes permanent, it is easier to change the way the chips are programmed than to change their internal design. See *erasable programmable read-only memory (EPROM).*

programmer   A person who designs, codes, tests, debugs, and documents a computer program.

Professional programmers often hold B.S. or M.S. degrees in computer science, but a great deal of programming (professional and otherwise) is done by individuals with little or no formal training. More than half the readers of a popular personal computer magazine, for example, stated in a survey that they regularly programmed their personal computers using languages such as *BASIC*, *Pascal*, and *assembly language*.

programmer/analyst   A person who performs system analysis and design functions as well as *programming* activities. See *programmer*.

programmer's switch   A plastic accessory included with pre-1991 Macintosh computers that, when installed on the side of the computer, allows you to perform a hardware reset and access the computer's built-in debugger.

TIP: *If you use the MacPlus, SE, or SE/30, you should install the programmer's switch so you can restart the computer after a system crash without flipping the power switch on and off, thus subjecting your system to the stress of a startup power surge. You can perform a soft boot by choosing Restart from the Finder menu, but only if you can get to the Finder. More recent Macs allow you to restart the system from the keyboard.*

programming   The process of providing instructions to the computer that tell the *microprocessor* what to do.

Stages in programming include design, or making decisions about what the program should accomplish; coding, or using a programming language to express the program's logic in computer-readable form and entering internal documentation for the commands; testing and debugging, in which the program's flaws are discovered and corrected; and documentation, in which an instructional manual for the program is created, either in print or on-screen.

It's easiest to begin programming with an event-driven language such as *HyperTalk* (Macintosh systems) or *Visual BASIC* (Windows systems), where you can embed a few lines of programming code in an on-screen object, such as a window or button. Using an event-driven language, you can produce impressive results in short order. You can then move on to a more flexible but somewhat more difficult language like *QuickBASIC* or *Pascal*. To produce professional-quality programs, learn the details of specific

O
P
Q
R

microprocessors and work with assembly language, *C,* or *C++.* See *event-driven environment, object-oriented programming language, spaghetti code,* and *well-structured programming language.*

programming environment A set of tools for programming that's commonly provided with a computer's *operating system.* Minimally, the tools include a *line editor,* a *debugger,* and an *assembler* to compile *assembly language* programs. These tools usually are not sufficient for professional program development, however, and often are replaced by an *application development system.*

programming language An artificial language, consisting of a fixed vocabulary and a set of rules (called *syntax*), that you can use to create instructions for a computer to follow. Most programs are written using a text editor or word processing program to create *source code,* which is then interpreted or compiled into the machine language that the computer can actually execute.

Programming languages are divided into high-level languages and low-level languages:

- *High-level programming languages,* such as *BASIC, C,* or *Pascal,* allow the programmer to express the program using keywords and syntax that crudely resemble natural human language. These languages are called "high level" because they free the programmer from detailed concerns about just how the computer will physically carry out each instruction. Each statement in a high-level language corresponds to several machine language instructions, so you can write programs more quickly than in lower-level languages, such as assembly language. However, the translation is inefficient, so programs written in high-level languages run more slowly than programs written in low-level languages.

- Low-level programming languages, such as *assembly language,* allow the programmer to code instructions with the maximum possible efficiency. But using low-level languages requires detailed expertise in the exact capabilities of a given computer system and its microprocessor. Also, assembly language programming requires far more time.

Another way of differentiating programming languages is to distinguish between procedural and declarative languages. In a *procedural language,* such as C, the programmer spells out the procedure the computer will follow to accomplish a given goal. In a *declarative language* (also called a non-procedural language), such as *COBOL,* the language defines a set of facts and relationships and allows you to query for specific results. See *C++, compiler, expert system, FORTRAN, interpreter, Modula-2, modular programming, object code, object-oriented programming language,* and *PROLOG.*

project management program   *Software* that tracks individual tasks that make up an entire job.

Managing a big project, such as building a submarine or rebuilding the World Trade Center in New York, is far from easy. Thousands of little jobs must be finished at the same time that thousands of other little jobs are finished, because both groups are needed for the next phase of the project. Project management techniques exist to help managers find the critical path—that is, the jobs that must be completed on time if the whole project is to be finished as scheduled. Though project management software gives PC users access to advanced project management techniques, it is likely that anyone who can cost-effectively use such techniques will have access to more powerful computers.

PROLOG   A *high-level programming language* used in *artificial intelligence* research and applications, particularly expert systems.

PROLOG, short for PROgramming in LOGic, is a *declarative language;* rather than tell the computer what procedure to follow to solve a problem, the programmer describes the problem to be solved.

The language resembles the query language of a *database management system* such as *Standard Query Language (SQL)* in that you can use PROLOG to ask a question such as, "Is Foster City in California?" But an important difference exists between PROLOG and a database management system (DBMS). A database contains information you can retrieve; a PROLOG program, in contrast, contains knowledge, from which the program can draw inferences about what is true or false.

PROM   See *programmable read-only memory (PROM).*

prompt   A symbol or phrase that appears on-screen to inform you that the computer is ready to accept input.

property In *Microsoft Windows 95*, a characteristic or attribute of an *embedded object*. An object's properties are contained in its *property sheet*, which may be seen by *right-clicking* on the object.

property sheet In *Microsoft Windows 95*, a central location in which all of an *embedded object's properties* are recorded. To see an object's property sheet, *right-click* on the object.

proportional pie graph In *presentation graphics,* a paired *pie graph* in which the size of each pie is in proportion to the amount of data the pie represents. Proportional pie graphs are useful for comparing two pies when one is significantly larger than the other.

proportional spacing In *typefaces,* setting the width of a character in proportion to the character shape, so that a narrow character such as i receives less space than a wide character such as m. The text you're reading now uses proportional spacing. See *kerning* and *monospace.*

proprietary Privately owned; based on trade secrets, privately developed technology, or specifications that the owner refuses to divulge, thus preventing others from duplicating a product or program unless an explicit license is purchased. The Macintosh system architecture, though there are now a few carefully selected makers of Macintosh *clones*, is proprietary. The opposite of proprietary is open (privately developed but publicly published and available for emulation by others). The IBM PC system architecture, with the exception of the *basic input-output system (BIOS),* is open.

From the user's perspective, proprietary designs or formats entail risk. If the company prospers and the design or format is widely emulated or accepted, the user benefits. But if the company doesn't prosper or fails, the user could be stuck with a computer system or with data that can't be upgraded or exchanged with others. See *proprietary file format.*

proprietary file format A *file format* developed by a firm for storing data created by its products. A proprietary file format usually is unreadable by other companies' application programs. The popular programs all include the capability to convert the files of several other file formats.

proprietary local bus A *local bus* standard developed by one company for use on its machines. Never buy a computer with a proprietary local bus—they require you to buy adapters from one manufacturer.

proprietary protocol   Any set of rules adopted by a particular manufacturer but not adopted by the rest of the industry or an international standards-setting body like the *International Telecommunications Union-Telecommunications Standards Section (ITU-TSS)*. Proprietary standards let only pieces of equipment from one manufacturer be used together. In *modems*, for example, proprietary standards such as *High Speed Technology (HST)* should be avoided in favor of global standards like *V.32bis*.

proprietary standard   An unpublished and sometimes secret design or specification for a device or program. The company that owns the standard refuses to permit other firms to emulate it, in the hope that the standard will eclipse all others and become the industry norm. Taken to the extreme, the use of a proprietary standard could force users to buy not just one, but a whole series of the firm's products (since nothing else will work with them). But this strategy is often self-defeating in that it retards the development of a market. Users do not like to be forced into buying products from a single manufacturer. *Open standards* promote a growing market, thus benefiting all the corporate participants, and benefit users by encouraging competition and *interoperablity*.

protected mode   In *Intel 80286* and later *microprocessors*, an operating mode that supports *virtual memory* (which uses space on your *hard drive* to simulate memory and accesses other memory using techniques such as paging) and enables multi-tasking, in which two or more programs can run and use the computer's memory simultaneously without conflict.

In protected mode, the computer can use memory beyond the 640K conventional memory barrier. To run *MS-DOS* programs in this *extended memory, Intel 80386* and higher microprocessors can simulate two or more 640K DOS computers, up to the limits of the available extended memory. These simulated "machines," called virtual machines, give each DOS application what amounts to its own 640K computer in which to run, and each 640K "machine" is protected from interference by the others. See *386 Enhanced mode, memory-management program, Microsoft Windows 95, Microsoft Windows NT, paging memory, real mode,* and *terminate-and-stay-resident (TSR) program.*

protocol   A set of standards for exchanging information between two computer systems or two computer devices. See *communications protocol, file transfer protocol (FTP),* and *Internet.*

protocol suite   In a *network*, a set of related standards that, taken together, define the architecture of the network. For example, the *Internet* is based on the *TCP/IP* protocol suite, a collection of more than 100 standards that are all designed to work smoothly together.

protocol switching   See *automatic network switching.*

prototype   A demonstration version of a proposed *program* or *hardware* device. In software, a prototype is usually a mock-up of a program's user interface, without much *back-end* code to support it. In hardware, a prototype is usually a cumbersome device with lots of wires and components that, if the prototype is mass produced, will be replaced by *circuit boards* and *integrated circuits.*

PrtSc   See *Print Screen (PrtSc).*

PS/2 mouse   A *mouse* with a special connector that fits into a *mouse port.* PS/2 mice don't require a serial port to operate.

PS/2 mouse port   See *mouse port.*

pseudocode   An *algorithm* expressed in English to conceptualize the algorithm before coding it in a *programming language.*

public data network (PDN)   A *wide area network (WAN)* that makes long-distance data communication services available to organizations and individuals. Most of the PDNs in the U.S. offer services based on the X.25 and *TCP/IP* protocols.

public domain software   *Software* not copyrighted that can be freely distributed without obtaining permission from or paying a fee to the programmer. See *freeware* and *shareware.*

public key cryptography   In cryptography, a revolutionary new method of *encryption* that does not require the message's receiver to have received the key in a separate transmission. The need to send the key, required to decode the message, is the chief vulnerability of previous encryption techniques. In public key cryptography, there are two keys, a public one and a private one. The public key is used for encryption, and the private key is used for *decryption.* If John wants to receive a private message from

Alice, John sends his public key to Alice; Alice then uses the key to encrypt the message. Alice sends the message to John. Anyone trying to intercept the message en route would find that it is mere gibberish. When John receives the message, he uses his private key to decode it. Because John never sends his private key anywhere or gives it to anyone, he can be certain that the message is secure. Public key cryptography places into the hands of individuals a level of security that was formerly available only to the top levels of government security agencies.

pull quote   In *desktop publishing,* a quotation extracted from the *copy* of a newsletter or magazine article and printed in larger type in the column, often blocked off with ruled lines, and sometimes shaded.

pull-down menu   An on-screen *menu* of command options that appears after you select the command name on the menu bar (see fig. P.4).

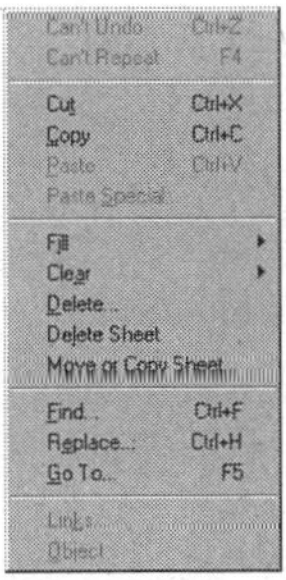

Fig. P.4   *A pull-down menu.*

The term pull-down comes from the Macintosh implementation of this idea, in which the menu doesn't stay on-screen unless you hold down the mouse button as you drag the pointer down the menu. In *MS-DOS* and *Microsoft Windows* programs, however, the menu stays on-screen after you click the menu name.

pulse code modulation (PCM)   A technique used to transform an incoming analog signal into a noise-free, digital equivalent. In *multimedia,* PCM is used to *sample* sounds digitally.

purge   To remove unwanted or outdated information, usually from the *hard drive,* in a systematic—and ideally automatic—manner. Also, in systems using a form of delete protection, purge refers to deleting protected files so that they no longer can be undeleted. See *undelete utility*.

pushbutton In industry-standard and *graphical user interfaces (GUIs)*, a large button in a dialog box that initiates actions after you choose an option. Most dialog boxes contain an *OK button*, which confirms your choices and carries out the command, and a Cancel button, which cancels your choices and closes the dialog box (see fig. P.5). The button representing the option you're most likely to choose, called the default button, is highlighted.

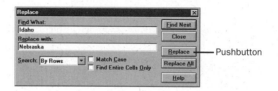

Pushbutton

Fig. P.5 *The pushbuttons in a Microsoft Windows 95 dialog box.*

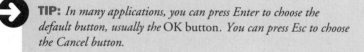

TIP: *In many applications, you can press Enter to choose the default button, usually the* OK *button. You can press Esc to choose the Cancel button.*

QBasic   See *MS-DOS QBasic.*

QEMM 386   A *memory-management program* by Quarterdeck Office Systems that moves *network* drivers, disk cache programs, device drivers, and *terminate-and-stay-resident (TSR) programs* to the *upper memory area,* thus freeing *conventional memory* for DOS programs.

QIC   See *quarter-inch cartridge.*

QIC-wide   A variation on *quarter-inch cartridge (QIC)* technology that uses tape 0.32 inches wide instead of 0.25 inches wide to increase data capacity.

quad density   See *high density.*

quad-speed drive   A *CD-ROM disk drive* capable of transferring data at 600 *K* per second. Quad-speed drives are, overall, not four times faster than single-speed drives since *access time* acts as a bottleneck that cannot be reduced as easily as data transfer rates can be increased. Quad-speed drives are about 40 percent faster than *double-speed drives.*

quad-issue processor   A *microprocessor* with a *two-pipeline superscalar architecture* that can begin handling four instructions at the same time.

quadrature modulation   A *group coding* technique used in *modems* to modulate the *carrier.* Modems that use quadrature modulation can exchange data at 2400 *bits per second (bps). Trellis-code modulation* enables higher *data transfer rates.*

QuarkXPress   A very powerful *desktop publishing (DTP) program* that is known for both its *typography* features and its customizability. QuarkXPress competes with *Aldus PageMaker,* which many believe lacks QuarkXPress's flexibility.

Though considered difficult to learn by some critics, QuarkXPress can complete tasks much faster than competing programs once its conventions are understood. QuarkXTensions, similar to *macros,* offer the ability to do repetitive tasks quickly and easily. Though

Microsoft Publisher is much less expensive, it is not a full-featured DTP program and does not compete with QuarkXPress.

quarter-inch cartridge (QIC)   A tape cartridge using quarter-inch-wide *magnetic tape* widely used for *backup operations.*

Quattro Pro   A full-featured *spreadsheet program* that includes more *built-in functions*—370—than *Microsoft Excel* or *Lotus 1-2-3*. If you work in an obscure discipline or need to do complex calculations, it's likely that Quattro Pro 6.0 has a function to do a lot of your work for you.

Many critics consider Quattro Pro a close second-place finisher to Excel, primarily because Quattro Pro's *pull-down menus* can be confusing and needed options are not all intuitively placed on the *menu bar.* On the other hand, Quattro Pro retails for only $99, several hundred dollars less than Excel and 1-2-3, making it an excellent value.

query   In *database management*, a search question that tells the program what kind of *data* should be retrieved from the *database.* An effective database management system lets you retrieve only the information you need for a specific purpose. A query specifies the characteristics (criteria) used to guide the computer to the required information. See *data independence, declarative language, query language,* and *Structured Query Language (SQL).*

query by example (QBE)   In *database management programs,* a query technique, developed by IBM for use in the QBE program, that prompts you to type the search criteria into a template resembling the *data record.*

The advantage of query-by-example retrieval is that you don't need to learn a *query language* to frame a query. When you start the search, the program presents a screen that lists all the *data fields* that appear on every data record; enter information that restricts the search to just the specified criteria. The fields left blank, however, will match anything.

Suppose that you are searching for the titles of all the Western video tapes rated PG or PG-13 that you have in stock. Using QBE techniques, you can type the following query:

CATEGORY	RATING	TITLE
Western	PG or PG-13	

This query says, "Find all records in which the CATEGORY field contains Western and the RATING field contains PG or PG-13."

query language   In *database management programs,* a retrieval and data-editing language you use to specify what information to retrieve and how to arrange the retrieved information on-screen or when printing. The dot-prompt language of dBASE is a full-fledged query language, as is *Structured Query Language (SQL),* which is used for minicomputer and mainframe databases and is growing in popularity in the world of personal computers

The ideal query language is a *natural language,* such as English, where you could tell the computer, "Using the database called VIDEOS, show me all the records in which the CATEGORY field contains Western and the RATING field contains PG or PG-13." A good query language, although rigid in syntax, approximates English, as the following example suggests:

SELECT title

FROM videos

WHERE CATEGORY = Western

AND RATING = PG

OR RATING = PG13

See *query* and *query by example (QBE).*

question mark   The *wild-card* symbol (?) that stands for a single character at a specific location, unlike the *asterisk* (*), which can stand for one or several characters. In AB?DE, for example, only file names or character strings that are five characters long with AB as the first two characters and DE as the last two characters are selected.

queue   See *job queue* and *print queue.*

QuickBASIC   A high-performance *compiler* for programs written in Microsoft *BASIC.* QuickBASIC recognizes modern *control structures* and allows programmers to create structured programs, complete with indentations and a full set of control structures, and to omit line numbers.

QuickBASIC was designed to compile any program written in *BASICA* or *GW-BASIC,* the versions of BASIC supplied with most

IBM Personal Computers and compatibles. Programs compiled with QuickBASIC execute much faster, making the compiler suitable for the creation of commercial *software*.

QuickDraw   The *object-oriented graphics* and text-display technology stored in every Macintosh's *read-only memory (ROM)*. When creating Macintosh programs, programmers achieve a common look by drawing on the QuickDraw resources to create on-screen windows, *dialog boxes, menus*, and shapes.

Quicken   See *Intuit Quicken Deluxe*.

QuickTime   An extension to the Macintosh *System* software that allows applications that support QuickTime to display animated or video sequences precisely synchronized with high-quality digital sound. In a training document, for instance, you can click an icon to see a QuickTime video sequence (a "movie") that visually shows a specific technique or procedure.

quit   To exit a *program* properly so that all your configuration choices and data are properly saved.

CAUTION: *With many programs, switching the computer off while the program is still open is a bad idea. Not only can you lose configuration choices, but you won't be warned to save your work. Also, programs that create temporary files won't have a chance to delete them, as is usually done when you exit the program.*

Microsoft Windows *exercises control over every part of your system. Don't end your Windows session by just switching off the computer; you can cause problems as severe as losing the computer hardware settings stored in* complementary metal oxide semiconductor (CMOS) chips. *Press Alt+F4 and return to DOS before you switch off the computer.*

QWERTY   (Pronounced *kwer-tee*) The standard typewriter keyboard layout, also used for computer keyboards. The keyboard name comes from the six keys on the left end of the top row of letter keys. Alternative keyboard layouts, such as the *Dvorak keyboard*, are said to speed typing by placing the most commonly used letters on the home row.

radio button   In a *graphical user interface (GUI)*, the round option buttons that appear in *dialog boxes*. Unlike *check boxes*, radio buttons are mutually exclusive; you can pick only one radio button option within a group.

radio frequency interference (RFI)   The radio noise generated by computers and other electronic and electromechanical devices. Excessive RFI generated by computers can disrupt the reception of radio and television signals. See *FCC certification*.

ragged-left alignment   See *justification*.

ragged-right alignment   See *justification*.

RAID   A group of *hard disks* under the control of array management *software* that work together to improve performance and decrease the odds of losing data due to mechanical or electronic failure by using such techniques as *data striping*. RAID implementations, because of their complexity and steep cost, are most often used on *network servers*. Several RAID levels exist, each with advantages and disadvantages. See *RAID level 0* through *RAID level 53*.

RAID level 0   A *redundant array of inexpensive disks (RAID)* scheme that includes *data striping* to improve disk performance but offers no protection against data loss due to drive failure.

RAID level 0 & 1   See *RAID level 10*.

RAID level 1   A *redundant array of inexpensive disks (RAID)* scheme involving an array of two *hard disks* with identical contents. RAID level 1 does not employ data striping, so it offers no speed advantage and is not economical.

RAID level 2   A *redundant array of inexpensive disks (RAID)* scheme that uses *data striping* over an array of as many as a dozen *hard disks*. Several of the drives in the array have copies of data that exist elsewhere, enabling them to catch and fix errors in the outgoing data stream. RAID level 2 is one of the most popular RAID implementations.

RAID level 3   A *redundant array of inexpensive disks (RAID)* implementation very similar to *RAID level 2,* in which the *hard disks* that contain the copies of data that appears elsewhere can detect but not fix errors in the outgoing data stream. Though RAID level 3 is slightly slower than RAID level 2 when errors occur, modern *hard disks* rarely make errors.

RAID level 4   A *redundant array of inexpensive disks (RAID)* implementation that distributes copies of *sectors* across an array of *hard disks* and uses one drive to check for, but not correct, errors in the outgoing data stream. RAID level 4's sector-copying technique is a special type of *data striping*.

RAID level 5   The most commonly used *redundant array of inexpensive disks (RAID)* implementation. RAID level 5 uses a sector-based data striping scheme like *RAID level 4*, but does not require a special data-checking disk since it distributes that function across the entire array, as well.

RAID level 6   A *redundant array of inexpensive disks (RAID)* implementation that allows two *hard disks* to fail without loss of *data* and boasts very good data-reading performance, but also has poor data-writing performance. RAID level 6 is similar to *RAID level 5*, except that it distributes two copies of the error-checking data across the array.

RAID level 10   A *redundant array of inexpensive disks (RAID)* implementation that combines the data striping of *RAID level 0* with the data-redundancy of *RAID level 1*. RAID level 10 arrays have high performance, but are not economical.

RAID level 53   A *redundant array of inexpensive disks (RAID)* scheme that uses data striping on two separate *RAID level 3* arrays. RAID level 53 arrays are very fast and quite *fault-tolerant*.

RAM cache   See *cache memory*.

RAM disk   An area of *random-access memory (RAM)* configured by a *utility program* to emulate a *hard disk drive*. Data stored in a RAM disk can be accessed more quickly than data stored on a disk drive, but this data is erased whenever you turn off or reboot the computer. See *configuration file*, *device driver*, and *RAMDRIVE.SYS*.

> **CAUTION:** *Many users have lost hours of important work by failing to copy a document from a RAM disk to a real disk at the end of a session.*

RAM   See *random-access memory (RAM)*.

RAMDRIVE.SYS   In *MS-DOS*, a *configuration file* provided with the *operating system* that sets aside part of your computer's *random-access memory (RAM)* as a *RAM disk*, which is treated by MS-DOS as though it were a *hard disk drive*. RAMDRIVE.SYS is a *device driver* that must be loaded using a DEVICE or DEVICEHIGH statement in your *CONFIG.SYS file*.

random access   An information storage and retrieval technique in which the computer can access information directly, without having to go through a sequence of locations. A better term is direct access, but the term "random" access has become enshrined in the acronym *random-access memory (RAM)*. To understand the distinction between random and *sequential access*, compare a cassette tape (sequential access) with a vinyl record (random access).

random-access memory (RAM)   The computer's primary working *memory*, in which *program* instructions and *data* are stored so that they can be accessed directly by the *central processing unit (CPU)* via the processor's high-speed *external data bus*.

RAM often is called read/write memory to distinguish it from *read-only memory (ROM)*, the other component of a personal computer's *primary storage*. In RAM, the CPU can write and read data. Most programs set aside a portion of RAM as a temporary work space for your data, so you can modify (rewrite) as needed until the data is ready for printing or storage on *secondary storage* media, such as a *hard* or *floppy disk*. RAM doesn't retain its contents when the power to the computer is switched off, so save your work frequently.

random-access memory digital-to-analog converter (RAMDAC)   A *chip* in the *video adapter* that converts three *digital* signals (one for each primary color) into one *analog* signal that is sent to the monitor. RAMDACs use on-board *random-access memory (RAM)* to store information before processing it.

O
P
Q
R

range In a *spreadsheet program,* a *cell* or a rectangular group of adjacent cells. Valid ranges include a single cell, part of a column, part of a row, and a block spanning several *columns* and several *rows* (see fig. R.1). Ranges allow you to perform operations, such as *formatting,* on groups of cells. See *range expression* and *range name.*

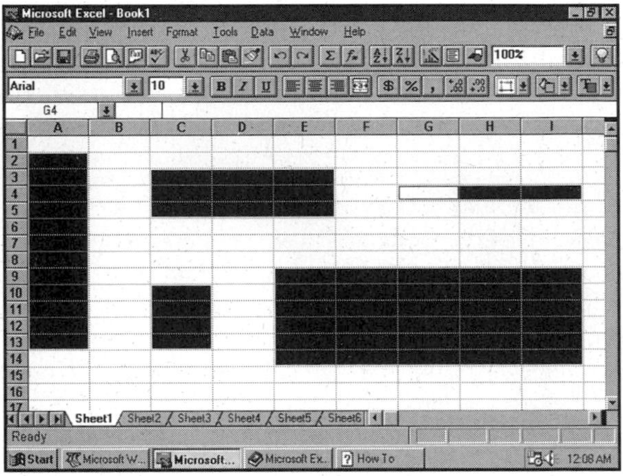

Fig R.1 *Valid ranges.*

range expression In a *spreadsheet program,* an expression that describes a *range* by defining the *cells* in opposing corners of a rectangle.

In *Lotus 1-2-3,* for example, you write a range expression by typing the beginning cell address, two periods, and the ending cell address A9..B12, for example. *Microsoft Excel* uses a colon in place of the two periods. See *range name.*

range format In a *spreadsheet program,* a *numeric format* or *label alignment* format that applies only to a *range* of *cells* and overrides the *global format.*

range name In a *spreadsheet program,* a title you assign to a *range* of *cells.* A range name, such as "Total Rainfall," is easier to remember than a *range expression.* Also, when you refer to the range by entering its name, *formulas* more clearly describe what's being calculated.

Another advantage of range naming is that you can move the *data* in the range to a new location and the range name stays the same. If you type the title of the range, the program unfailingly refers to the present location of the data in the range.

raster   On a *monitor* or television screen, the horizontal pattern of lines that forms the image. Within each line are dots, called *pixels*, that can be illuminated individually.

raster font   See *bit-mapped font*.

raster graphics   See *bitmapped graphics*.

raster image processor (RIP)   A device that converts *object-oriented graphics* into *raster graphics* before printing to output devices. See *vector-to-raster conversion*.

rave   In *electronic mail* and *newsgroups*, to carry on an argument in support of a position beyond all bounds of reason and sensitivity. Raving is annoying but isn't considered to be worthy of a *flame* unless the argument is couched in offensive terms.

raw data   Unprocessed or unformatted *data* that hasn't been arranged, edited, or represented in a form for easy retrieval and analysis.

RCA plug   See *phono plug*.

RDBMS   See *relational database management system (RDBMS)*.

read   To retrieve *data* or *program* instructions from a device such as a *hard* or *floppy disk* and place the data into the computer's *random-access memory (RAM)*.

README file   A *text file*, often included on the installation disk of *application programs*, that contains last-minute information not contained in the program's *documentation*. Typical README file names are README.1ST, README.TXT, and READ.ME.

O P Q R

TIP: *Be sure to look for* README *files, and read them; they may contain information that can save you trouble and headaches when installing and using a new program.*

read-only   Capable of being displayed or used, but not deleted. If a display of read-only data can be edited, *formatted*, or otherwise modified, it can't be saved under the same *file name*. See *file attribute*, *locked file*, and *read/write*.

read-only attribute   In *Microsoft Windows 95* and *Operating System/2 (OS/2)*, a *file attribute* stored with a file's *directory* entry that indicates whether the file can be changed or deleted. When the *read-only* attribute is on, you can display the file, but you can't modify or erase it. When the read-only attribute is off, you can modify or delete the file.

read-only memory (ROM)   The portion of a computer's *primary storage* that doesn't lose its contents when you switch off the power. ROM contains essential system programs that neither you nor the computer can erase.

Because the computer's internal memory is blank at powerup, the computer can perform no functions unless given startup instructions. These instructions are stored in ROM. A growing trend is toward including substantial portions of the *operating system* on ROM chips instead of on disk. See *erasable programmable read-only memory (EPROM)*, *programmable read-only memory (PROM)*.

read/write   The capability of a *primary* or *secondary storage* device to record *data* (write) and to play back data previously recorded or saved (read).

read/write file   In *MS-DOS*, *Microsoft Windows 95*, and *Operating System/2 (OS/2)*, a file whose *read-only file attribute* is set so that the file can be deleted and modified. See *locked file*.

read/write head   In a *hard disk* or *floppy disk*, the magnetic recording and playback device that travels back and forth across the surface of the disk, storing and retrieving *data*.

read/write memory   See *random-access memory (RAM)*.

real mode   An operating mode of *Intel microprocessors* in which a *program* is given a strictly defined area of *random-access memory (RAM)* and direct access to *peripheral* devices.

Real mode allocates memory so programs have direct access to actual memory locations, but have no way of managing more than one program loaded into memory simultaneously. See *protected mode*.

real time   The immediate processing of *input*, such as a point-of-sale transaction or a measurement performed by an *analog* laboratory device. The computers used in your car are real-time systems.

real-time clock   A battery-powered clock contained in the computer's internal circuitry. The real-time clock keeps track of the time of day even when the computer is switched off. This clock should be distinguished from the *system clock* that governs the *microprocessor's* cycles.

reboot   To restart. Rebooting is often necessary after a *crash*. In most cases, you can restart the system from the *keyboard*, but especially severe crashes may require you to push the *reset button*, or if no such button exists, turn off the computer and turn it on again. See *programmer's switch*.

rec   One of the seven *standard newsgroup hierarchies* in *UseNet*, this category includes newsgroups relating to recreational interests, such as movies, comics, science fiction, audio systems, sports cars, aviation, backpacking, collecting, brewing, cooking, board games, humor, hunting, kites, music of all kinds, pets, ham radio, skiing, sports, and more.

recalculation method   In a *spreadsheet program*, the way the program recalculates *cell values* after you change the contents of a cell. See *automatic recalculation*, *manual recalculation*, and *recalculation order*.

recalculation order   In a *spreadsheet program*, the sequence in which calculations are performed when you enter new *values*, *labels*, or *formulas*. Options for recalculation order usually include *column-wise recalculation*, *row-wise recalculation*, and *natural recalculation*. See *optimal recalculation*.

record   See *data record*.

record pointer   In a *database management program,* an on-screen status message that states the number of the *data record* now visible (or in which the cursor is positioned).

recover   To bring a *computer system* back to a previous stable operating state or to restore erased or misdirected *data*. Recovery is needed after a system or user error occurs, such as telling the system to *write* data to a drive that doesn't contain a disk. See *undelete utility*.

O
P
Q
R

record-oriented database management program   A *database management program* that displays *data records* as the result of *query* operations, unlike a *table-oriented database management program*, in which the result of all data query operations is a table. See *data retrieval, database management system (DBMS),* and *Structured Query Language (SQL).*

recoverable error   An error that doesn't cause the *program* or system to *crash* or to erase *data* irretrievably.

recto   The right-hand (odd-numbered) page in facing pages. In a book or magazine, the recto page is the right-hand, odd-numbered page. See *verso.*

recursion   In *programming,* a *program* instruction that causes a *module* or *subroutine* to call itself. A recursive function may be used to implement search strategies or perform repetitive calculations.

recycle bin   In *Microsoft Windows 95,* an on-screen icon where deleted files are stored. From the recycle bin, you can restore deleted files or discard them permanently (fig. R.2).

Fig. R.2   *The Recycle Bin (Microsoft Windows 95).*

Red Book   An International Standards Organization (ISO) standard (number 10149) that describes the way in which music is recorded on *Compact Disc-Digital Audio (CD-DA)* disks.

redirection   See *input/output (I/O) redirection.*

redirection operator   In *MS-DOS,* a symbol that routes the results of a command from or to a device other than the *keyboard* and video display (*console*), such as a *file* or a *printer.* See *input/ output (I/O) redirection.*

redlining   In *word processing*, a display attribute, such as *reverse video* or double underlining, that marks the text co-authors have added to a document. The redlined text is highlighted so that other authors or editors know exactly what has been added to or deleted from the document.

reduced instruction set computer (RISC) risk   A *central processing unit (CPU)* in which the number of instructions the *microprocessor* can execute is reduced to a minimum to increase processing speed.

The idea of RISC architecture is to reduce the instruction set to the bare minimum, emphasizing the instructions used most of the time and optimizing them for the fastest possible execution. A RISC processor usually runs 50 to 75 percent faster than its CISC counterpart. RISC processors also are cheaper to design, and debug.

redundant array of inexpensive disks (RAID)   See *RAID*.

re-engineering   Redesigning the way work is done, then choosing computer tools that enhance the redesigned work process.

Computerization of a process doesn't automatically make it more efficient. To realize big productivity gains, managers must re-think the way work is done and alter the process to be more efficient. In many companies, for example, after the credit department grants credit, the receiving department receives goods and the accounting department writes checks. The re-engineering strategy for this kind of setting may be to put computers in the receiving department, so that the receiving staff can confirm what's received and write the checks on the spot.

reflective liquid-crystal display (reflective LCD)   *A liquid-crystal display (LCD)* with no *edgelighting* or *backlighting* to enhance readability in bright-light conditions. Reflective LCDs are generally unsuitable for outdoor use.

reformat   In *operating systems*, to repeat a *formatting* operation on a *floppy* or *hard disk*. In *word processing* or *page layout programs*, to change the arrangement of text elements on the page.

refresh To repeat the display or storage of *data* to keep it from fading or becoming lost. The *monitor* and *random-access memory (RAM)* must be refreshed constantly.

refresh rate See *vertical refresh rate*.

Regional Bell Operating Companies (RBOCs) The regional telephone companies (Baby Bells) that were created as a result of the 1982 breakup of AT&T, which forced the former telephone monopoly to leave the local and regional telephone business.

register A *memory* location within a *microprocessor*, used to store values and external memory addresses while the microprocessor performs logical and arithmetic operations on them. A larger number of registers enables a microprocessor to handle more information at one time.

register renaming A means of enabling *software* designed to run on *x86 microprocessors*, which can recognize only 8 *registers*, to use the 32 or more registers available in more advanced microprocessors with *superscalar architecture*. A microprocessor capable of register renaming differentiates between the registers a x86 program can address and the actual number of registers available, and will divert information sent to an occupied register to one that is not in use.

Registry In *Microsoft Windows 95*, a *program* (see Fig. R.3) that enables the user to choose configuration options (and for applications to set them). The Registry replaces the confusing, text-based *.ini files used with Windows 3.1 applictions.

relational database management An approach to *database management*, employed by *Microsoft Access* and other *database management programs*, in which data that's stored in two-dimensional data *tables* of *columns* and *rows* can be related if the tables have a common column or field. The term relational as applied to database management refers to the storage and retrieval of data in tables.

Suppose a bookstore has a customer database that looks like this:

Name	Cust._No.
B. Gates	12
J. Morrison	13

Suppose also that the bookstore has a database of customers' favorite types of book, organized by customer number:

Cust._No.	Favorite_Category
12	Cookbooks
13	Gothic Novels

Now suppose that the store's owner wants to mail the right promotional literature to each customer. She enters a query that says, "Show me the names of each customer and their favorite type of book." Since she uses a *relational database management system*, the result of the query is a table that looks like this.

Cust._No.	Name	Favorite_Category
12	B. Gates	Cookbooks
13	J. Morrison	Gothic Novels

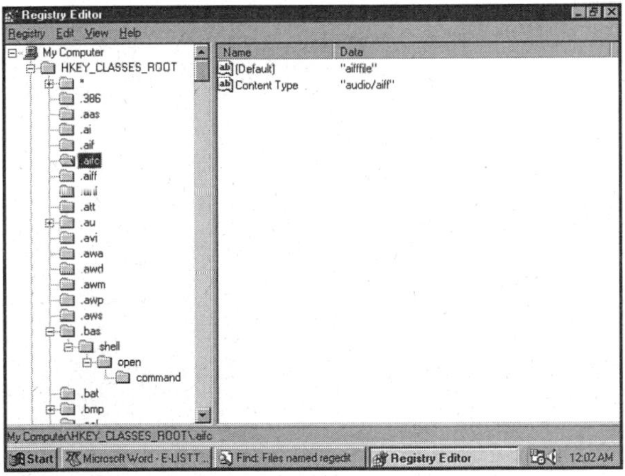

Fig.R.3   *The Registry (Microsoft Windows 95).*

relational database management system (RDBMS)

A *relational database* management program, especially one that comes with all the necessary support programs, *programming* tools, and *documentation* needed to create, install, and maintain custom *database* applications.

relational operator   A symbol used to specify the relationship between two numeric *values*. The result of a calculation using a relational operator is either true or false.

In *query languages*, relational operators often are used in specifying search criteria. For example, a video store manager may want to tell the computer, "Show me all the telephone numbers of customers with overdue tapes that are due on a date less than or equal to May 7, 1995."

In *spreadsheets*, relational operators are used, for example, in @IF formulas to perform tests on data so that different values are displayed, depending on whether the result of the test is true or false.

To permit the expression of logical operators in the character-based world of computing, many programs use the following conventions:

=   Equal to

<   Less than

>   Greater than

<=   Less than or equal to

>=   Greater than or equal to

<>   Not equal to

relative addressing   In a *program,* specifying a *random-access memory (RAM)* location using an expression so that the address can be calculated instead of using an *absolute address*.

relative cell reference   In a *formula* in a *spreadsheet program,* a reference to the contents of a *cell* that's adjusted by the program when you copy the formula to another cell or *range* of cells.

To understand what happens when you copy a relative cell reference, you need to know how a spreadsheet program actually records a cell reference. Suppose that you type the formula @SUM(C6..C8) in cell C10. The program records a code that means, "Add all the values in the cells positioned in the second, third, and fourth rows up from the current cell." When you copy this formula to the next four cells to the right (D10..G10), it still reads, "Add all the values in the cells positioned in the second, third, and fourth rows up from the current cell," and sums each column correctly (see fig. R.4). See *absolute cell reference* and *mixed cell reference*.

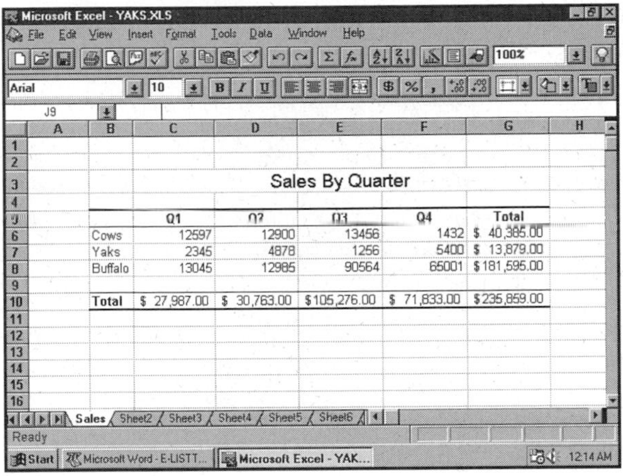

Fig. R.4 *The formulas in cells D10..G10 contain a relative cell reference copied from the first column.*

Relative URL (RELURL) One of two basic kinds of *Uniform Resource Identifiers (URIs)*, a string of characters that gives a resource's file name (such as merlot.html), but does not specify its type or exact location. *Parsers* (such as *Web browsers*) will assume that the resource is located in the same directory that contains the RELURL. See *Uniform Resource Locator (URL)*.

release number See *version*.

relevance feedback In *Wide Area Information Servers (WAISs)*, an innovative search feature that enables you to select a highly relevant *document*, which the search *software* subsequently uses in an attempt to discover additional relevant documents. Usually, you provide relevance feedback by *clicking* a *check box* next to a document that contains just the sort of information you are looking for.

reliability The capability of *hardware* or *software* to perform as the user expects and to do so consistently, without failures or erratic behavior. See *mean time between failures (MTBF)*.

O
P
Q
R

reliable connection   See *reliable link.*

reliable link   An error-free connection established via the telephone system (despite its high *line noise* and low *bandwidth*) by two *modems* that use *error-correction protocols.*

remark   In a *batch file, macro,* or *source code,* explanatory text that's ignored when the computer executes the commands.

remote control program   A *utility* program that lets you link two computers so you can use one to control the other.

remote management   A feature of newer *departmental laser printers* that transmits information about *toner* level, paper supply, and mechanical problems across a network to the person responsible for maintaining the printer.

remote system   The computer or *network* to which a computer is connected by a *modem* and a telephone line. The computer connected to the remote system is a *remote terminal.*

remote terminal   See *terminal.*

removable mass storage   A high-capacity data storage device, such as a *Bernoulli box* or a *tape drive,* in which the disk or tape is encased in a plastic cartridge or cassette so it can be removed from the drive for safekeeping.

removable storage media   See *removable mass storage.*

rendering   In *graphics,* the conversion of an outline drawing into a fully formed, three-dimensional image.

repagination   See *pagination.*

repeat key   A *key* that continues to enter the same character as long as you hold it down.

repeater   In *local area networks (LANs),* a *hardware* device used to extend the length of network cabling by amplifying and passing along the messages traveling through the network. See *bridge* and *router.*

repeating field   In *database design,* a *data field* in which the user must type the same few *data* items repeatedly—such as suppliers' names and addresses—thus creating many possibilities for errors due to typos or misspellings. See *data integrity* and *data redundancy.*

repeating label   In a *spreadsheet program*, a character preceded by a *label prefix* that causes the character to be repeated across a *cell*. For example, *Lotus 1-2-3* uses \ to repeat one or more characters across a cell. The entry \= would produce a line of equal signs across the cell.

repetitive strain injury (RSI)   A serious and potentially debilitating occupational illness caused by prolonged repetitive hand and arm movements that can damage, inflame, or kill nerves in the hands, arms, shoulders, or neck.

Also known as cumulative trauma disorder (CTD), RSI occurs when constantly repeated motions strain tendons and ligaments, resulting in scar tissue that squeezes nerves and eventually may kill them. With the proliferation of computer *keyboards*, RSI is increasingly noted among office workers and poses a genuine threat to personal computer users who work long hours at the keyboard. Specific RSI disorders include carpal tunnel syndrome (CTS).

TIP: *You can prevent RSI. Adjust your chair height to eliminate any unnecessary extension or flexing of the wrist. Take frequent breaks, use good posture, and vary your daily activities so you perform a variety of actions with your wrists. Finally, don't rest the heel of your hands on the base of the keyboard.*

replace   In *word processing* programs, a feature that searches for a *string* and replaces it with another string. Always save your work before performing a replace operation.

O
P
Q
R ◄

With most programs, you can improve the accuracy of the replacement operation by specifying capitalization and whole-word options. If you tell the program to match the capitalization pattern in the search string, such as Tree if you want the change only when tree begins a sentence, the program replaces only those strings that match the characters and the capitalization pattern (Tree is replaced, but not TREE or tree).

replaceable parameter   In *MS-DOS*, a symbol used in a *batch file* that MS-DOS replaces with information you type. The symbol consists of a percent sign and a number from 1 through 9, such as %1.

Suppose that you create a *batch file*, PRINTNOW.BAT, that contains the statement COPY %1 PRN. If you type the command PRINTNOW LETTER.DOC, MS-DOS replaces the %1 symbol with the file name you typed and copies LETTER.DOC to the printer.

report　In *database management,* printed output that usually is formatted with page numbers and headings. With most programs, reports can include *calculated fields,* showing subtotals, totals, averages, and other figures computed from the data. See *band.*

report generator　A *program* or *function* that allows a non-programmer to request printed output from a *database.*

Request for Comments (RFC)　An *Internet* publication that constitutes the chief means by which standards are promulgated (although not all RFCs contain new standards). More than 1,000 RFCs are accessible from *network information centers (NIC).* The publication of RFCs is currently controlled by the *Internet Architecture Board (IAB).*

research network　A *wide area network (WAN),* such as *ARPAnet* or *NSFnet,* developed and funded by a governmental agency to improve research productivity in areas of national interest.

ResEdit　A *Macintosh utility program,* available free from *Apple Computer* dealers, that lets you edit (and copy to other programs) many program features, such as *menu* text, *icons,* and *dialog boxes.*

reserved memory　See *upper memory area.*

reserved word　In a *programming language* or *operating system,* a word—also called a *keyword*—that has a fixed function and can't be used for any other purpose. In *BASIC,* for example, the word REM is reserved to indicate the beginning of a *remark.* You can use a reserved word only for its intended purpose; you can't use the word for naming files, *variables,* or other user-named *objects.*

reset button　A button, usually mounted on the system unit's front panel, that lets you perform a *warm boot* if the *reset key* doesn't work. On older *Macintoshes,* the reset button is part of the *programmer's switch.* Synonymous with *hardware reset.*

reset key   A *key* combination that, when pressed, restarts the computer. This key combination (Ctrl+Alt+Del on IBM-compatible machines) provides an alternative to switching the power off and on after a *crash* so severe that the keyboard doesn't respond. See *hardware reset, programmer's switch,* and *warm boot.*

resident font   As opposed to a *downloadable font* or a *cartridge font,* a *font* that is present in a *printer's* memory whenever it is turned on.

resident program   See *terminate-and-stay-resident (TSR) program.*

resolution enhancement technology   A way of reducing *aliasing* and smoothing the curves in *laser printer* output. Resolution enhancement technology, which inserts small dots between large ones, increases *effective resolution.*

resolution   In *printers,* a measurement usually expressed in linear *dots per inch (dpi),* horizontally and vertically of the sharpness of a printed image.

In *sound boards,* the number of *bits* used to encode sounds. Resolution determines the number of sound levels with which recorded sounds must be represented. Higher resolutions ensure greater fidelity to the original sound. Though a resolution of 8 bits is minimally acceptable for voice reproduction, 16-bit resolution is required to reproduce the range of sounds in complex pieces of music.

In *monitors,* resolution is expressed as the number of *pixels* horizontally and *lines* vertically on-screen. For example, a *color graphics array (CGA)* monitor displays fewer lines than a *video graphics array (VGA)* monitor, and therefore, a CGA image appears more jagged than a VGA image. The following table lists the resolutions of common video adapters for IBM PCs and compatibles:

Resolution Adapter	Pixels×Lines
Monochrome Display Adapter (MDA)	720×350
Color Graphics Adapter (CGA)	640×200

continues

continued

Resolution Adapter	Pixels×Lines
Enhanced Graphics Adapter (EGA)	640×350
MultiColor Graphics Array (MCGA)	640×480
Video Graphics Array (VGA)	640×480
Super VGA (extended VGA)	800×600
Super VGA (VGA Plus)	1,024×768

Macintoshes with 9-inch screens display 512×342, whereas Macs with 12- or 13-inch monitors display 640×480.

Low-end dot-matrix printers print approximately 125 dpi, whereas *laser printers* typically print 300 or 600 dpi. Professional *imagesetters* print at resolutions of 1,200 dpi or more.

response time   The time a computer needs to carry out a request. Response time is a better measurement of system performance than *access time* because it more fairly states the system's *throughput.*

retrieval   All the procedures involved in finding, summarizing, organizing, displaying, or printing information from a *computer system* in a form useful for the user.

Return   See *Enter/Return.*

reverse engineering   The process of systematically taking apart a *chip* or *application program* to discover how it works, with the aim of imitating or duplicating some or all of its functions.

Reverse Polish Notation (RPN)   A means of describing mathematical operations that makes calculations easier for computers. Many *compilers* convert arithmetic expressions into RPN. In RPN, the expression "a b +" adds the variables a and b, and would be written as "a + b" in standard notation. Synonymous with Polish notation.

reverse video   In *monochrome monitors*, a means of *highlighting* text on the *display* so that normally dark characters are displayed as bright characters on a dark background, or normally bright characters are displayed as dark characters on a bright background.

rewrite   Synonymous with *overwrite*.

RGB monitor   A color *digital monitor* that accepts separate inputs for red, green, and blue, and produces a much sharper image than *composite color monitors*.

Although the *Enhanced Graphics Adapter (EGA)* standard uses RGB techniques, RGB monitor is synonymous with the *Color Graphics Adapter (CGA)* standard.

Rich Text Format (RTF)   A text *formatting* standard developed by *Microsoft Corporation* that allows a *word processing program* to create a file encoded with all the document's formatting instructions, but without using any special *hidden codes*. An RTF-encoded document can be transmitted over *telecommunications* links or read by another RTF-compatible word processing program, without loss of the formatting.

right justification   See *justification*.

ring network   In *local area networks (LANs),* a decentralized *network topology* in which a number of *nodes* (including workstations, shared *peripherals,* and *file servers*) are arranged around a closed loop cable (see fig. R.5).

Like a *bus network,* a ring network's workstations can send messages to all other workstations. Each node in the ring has a unique address, and its reception circuitry constantly monitors the bus to determine whether a message is being sent. The failure of a single node can disrupt the entire network; however, *fault-tolerance* schemes have been devised that allow ring networks to continue to function even if one or more nodes fail.

RIP   See *raster image processor (RIP)*.

ripple-through effect   In a *spreadsheet program,* the sudden appearance of ERR values throughout the cells after you make a change that breaks a link among *formulas*.

If this happens, you may think that you've ruined the entire spreadsheet, but after you locate and repair the problem, all the affected formulas are restored.

O
P
Q
R

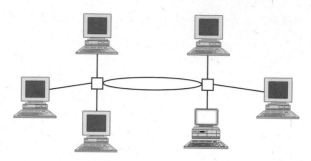

Fig. R.5 *An illustration of a ring network.*

RISC   See *reduced instruction set computer (RISC).*

river   In *desktop publishing (DTP)*, a formatting flaw that results in the accidental alignment of *white space* between words in sequential lines of text, encouraging the eye to follow the flow down three or more lines. Rivers injure what typographers refer to as the *color* of the page.

RJ-11 jack   See *modular jack.*

RLL   See *Run-Length Limited (RLL).*

rn   In *UseNet*, a non-threaded *newsreader* for *UNIX* systems. Written by Larry Wall in the mid-1980s, rn has been supplanted by *threaded newsreaders* such as *trn, tin,* and *nn.*

ROM   See *read-only memory (ROM).*

Roman   In *typography*, an upright *serif typeface* of medium *weight.* In proofreading, characters without emphasis.

root directory   On a *hard* or *floppy disk*, the top-level *directory* that *MS-DOS* and *Microsoft Windows 95* creates when you format the disk. See *parent directory* and *subdirectory.*

root name   The first, mandatory part of a *MS-DOS file name*, using from one to eight characters. See name *extension.*

rot-13   In *UseNet newsgroups,* a simple *encryption* technique that offsets each character by 13 places (so that an e becomes an r, for example). Rot-13 encryption is used for any message that may spoil someone's fun (such as the solution to a game) or offend some readers (such as erotic poetry). If the reader chooses to decrypt the message by issuing the appropriate command, then the reader—not the author of the message—bears the responsibility for any discomfort that may be caused by reading the message. Lately, rot-13 has fallen into disuse. See *netiquette* and *spoiler.*

rotated type   In a *graphics* or *desktop publishing (DTP) program,* text that has been turned vertically from its normal, horizontal position on the page. The best graphics programs, such as CorelDRAW!, allow you to edit the type even after you rotate it.

rotation tool   In a *graphics* or *desktop publishing (DTP)* program, a command option, represented by an *icon,* you can use to rotate type from its normal, horizontal position. See *rotated type.*

roughs   In *desktop publishing (DTP),* the preliminary page *layouts* that the designer creates using rough sketches to represent page design ideas. Synonymous with thumbnails.

router   In a *packet-switching network* such as the *Internet,* one of two basic devices (the other is a *host*). A router is an electronic device that examines each packet of data it receives, and then decides which way to send it onward toward its destination.

row   In a *spreadsheet program,* a block of *cells* running horizontally across the spreadsheet. In most programs, rows are numbered sequentially from the top. In a *database,* a row is the same as a record or *data record.*

row-wise recalculation   In *spreadsheet programs,* a *recalculation order* that calculates all the values in row 1 before moving to row 2, and so on.

> **CAUTION:** *If your spreadsheet program doesn't offer natural recalculation, use row-wise recalculation for worksheets in which rows are summed and the totals are forwarded.*

See *column-wise recalculation* and *optimal recalculation.*

RPN   See *reverse Polish notation.*

RS-232C   A standard recommended by the Electronic Industries Association (EIA) concerning the transmission of *data* between computers using *serial ports*. Most *personal computers* are equipped with an RS-232-compatible serial port, which you can use for external *modems, printers, scanners,* and other *peripheral* devices. RS-232C may someday be supplanted by the *FireWire* standard.

RS-422   A standard recommended by the Electronic Industries Association (EIA) and used as the *serial port* standard for *Macintosh* computers. RS-422 governs the asynchronous transmission of computer data at speeds of up to 920,000 bits per second. Like *RS-232C*, RS-422 may someday be supplanted by the *FireWire* standard.

RS232C port   See *serial port.*

RSI   See *repetitive strain injury (RSI).*

.RTF   The *MS-DOS file name extension* usually attached to a file containing text and *graphics* encoded in *Rich Text Format (RTF).*

RTFM   In *on-line communications,* an acronym for Read the "Frigging" Manual.

rule   In *graphics* and *desktop publishing (DTP),* a thin horizontal or vertical line.

ruler   In many *word processing* and *desktop publishing (DTP)* programs, an on-screen bar that measures the page horizontally, showing the current margins, *tab stops,* and paragraph *indents.*

run   To *execute* a *program.*

Run-Length Limited (RLL)   A method of storing and retrieving information on a *hard disk* that, compared to *double-density* techniques, increases by at least 50 percent the amount of *data* a hard disk can store. The improvement in storage density is achieved by translating the data into a digital format that can be written more compactly to the disk. See *Advanced Run-Length Limited (ARLL)* and *Modified Frequency Modulation (MFM).*

run-time version   A limited version of a supporting *program* that's bundled with an *application program.* For example, early versions of *Microsoft Excel* were sold with run-time versions of Microsoft Windows for users who didn't yet own Windows.

running head   See *header*.

r/w   A common abbreviation for *read/write*, indicating that the *file* or device is configured so you can write *data* to it as well as read data from it. See *read/write file*.

O
P
Q
R

SAA   See *Systems Application Architecture (SAA)*.

safe format   A disk *formatting* method that doesn't destroy the data on the disk so you can recover it if necessary. To format safely with *MS-DOS*, use the FORMAT command without the /u switch.

sampling rate   The frequency with which a recording device, such as a *sound board,* takes readings of the sound it is recording. High-quality sound boards, like the equipment used to record audio compact disks, have sampling rates of 44.1 *kilohertz (KHz)* or higher. Although sound boards with lower sampling rates might be adequate for recording simple noises or even voice clips, they are not adequate for recording music.

sans serif   A *typeface* that lacks *serifs,* the ornamental straight or curved lines across the ends of the main strokes of a character (see fig. S.1). *Helvetica* and Arial are two readily available sans serif fonts.

A B C D E F

Fig. S.1   *Example of a sans serif font.*

Sans serif typefaces are preferable for *display type* but, when used for *body type,* are harder to read than serif typefaces such as Times Roman.

SASI   See *Shugart Associates Standard Interface (SASI)*.

satellite   In a *multi-user system,* a *terminal* or *workstation* linked to a centralized *host* computer.

In the output of *ink jet* and *laser printers,* an extraneous spot of ink in the area around characters in which no ink should be present.

save   To transfer *data* from the computer's *random-access memory (RAM),* where the data is vulnerable to erasure, to a storage medium such as a *disk drive.*

By far the most common source of computer-realted grief is work loss resulting from power failures, user errors, or system *crashes*. Your work resides in the computer's RAM, and thus disappears if the power fails or the computer crashes. To protect your data, save it repeatedly as you work (every five minutes or so) or use an *autosave* feature to save the work for you. See *backup procedure* and *volatility*.

sawtooth distortion   See *aliasing*.

scalable font   A *screen font* or *printer font* that you can enlarge or reduce to any size, within a specified range, without introducing unattractive distortions. *Outline font* technology is most commonly used to provide scalable fonts, but other technologies—including stroke fonts, which form characters from a matrix of lines—are sometimes used. The most popular scalable fonts for *Macintosh* and *Microsoft Windows 95* systems are *PostScript* and *TrueType* fonts. See *bit-mapped font*.

TIP: *If you are shopping for a Macintosh or Windows system with scalable fonts, choose a Mac that's* System 7 *capable, or a Windows system with Windows 95. Both systems include TrueType capabilities, and thus display scalable fonts on-screen. The systems also yield good results from a variety of printers, which will save you from having to buy an expensive* PostScript-compatible printer.

scalar architecture   The design of a *microprocessor* with only one *pipeline*. Microprocessors with multiple pipelines have *superscalar architecture*.

scale-up problem   In a *network*, a technical problem caused by the system expanding far beyond its projected maximum size. For example, every computer connected to the *Internet* must have its own unique address, called an *IP address*. However, the Internet's designers allowed for a limited number of IP addresses.

scaling   In *presentation graphics,* the adjustment of the *y-axis* (values) that the program chooses to make differences in the data more apparent. Most *presentation graphics* programs scale the y-axis, but the programs' scaling choice can be unsatisfactory (see fig. S.2). Manually adjusting the scaling produces better results (see fig. S.3).

S
T
U
V

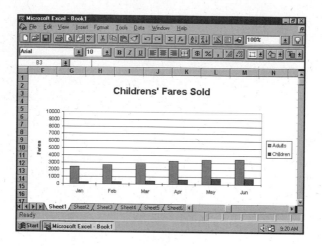

Fig. S.2 *A column graph with unsatisfactory scaling.*

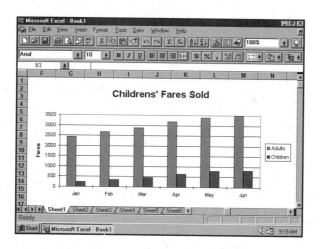

Fig. S.3 *A column graph with manually adjusted scaling.*

scanner A *peripheral* device that digitizes artwork or photographs and stores the image as a *file* that you can merge with text in many *word processing* and *page layout programs* (see fig. S.4). Scanners produce either *dithered* output, which somewhat crudely approximates a photographic *halftone*, or output in *Tagged Image File Format (TIFF)*, which is better than dithering but still inferior to professional *halftoning*. See *bit-mapped graphic*.

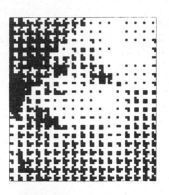

A 150 dpi digital-halftone scan,
printed on an Apple LaserWriter.

A 150 dpi gray-scale scan with
16 shades of gray, printed on
an Apple LaserWriter.

Fig. S.4 *A digital-halftone image (top) and a gray-scale image (bottom).*

scanning pass A trip made by a *scanner's charge-coupled devices (CCDs)* over the material being scanned. Although more popular than *triple-pass scanners, single-pass scanners* are not always faster.

scan rate See *vertical refresh rate.*

scatter diagram An analytical *graphic* that plots *data* items as points on two numeric axes; also called a scattergram.

Scatter diagrams show clustering relationships in numeric data. Computer magazines often use a scatter diagram to compare similarly configured computer systems, with price on one axis and the result of performance testing on the other axis to make slow, expensive computers and fast, inexpensive computers stand out.

scatter plot See *scatter diagram.*

S
T
U
V

sci In *UseNet's standard newsgroup hierarchy,* a category of *newsgroups* devoted to topics in the sciences. The category includes newsgroups that cover astronomy, biology, engineering, geology, mathematics, psychology, and statistics.

scientific notation A method for expressing very large or very small numbers as powers of 10, such as $7.24'10^{23}$. *Spreadsheet* programs usually express scientific notation with the symbol E, which stands for exponent, as in the following example: 7.24E23.

scissoring In *graphics*, an editing technique in which you crop an image to a size determined by a frame that you place over the image.

Scrapbook On the *Macintosh*, a *desk accessory (DA)* that can hold frequently used *graphic* images, such as company letterhead, which you can then insert into new *documents* as required.

screen blanking A crude electricity-conservation scheme, far inferior to *display power management signaling (DPMS)*. Screen blanking-capable *monitors* go blank when they recognize that a *screen-saver* utility has begun to operate, saving some electricity but not nearly as much as a DPMS monitor and *video adapter*.

screen capture A copy of a screen display that is saved as a text or graphics file on disk. Screen captures are usually *Tagged Image File Format (TIFF)* files. Many of the illustrations in this book are screen captures.

screen dump See *Print Screen (PrtSc)*.

screen element In *Microsoft Windows 95*, a component of the displayed image, such as a *dialog box,* border, *pushbutton, check box*, or *scroll bar*.

screen flicker See *flicker*.

screen font A *bit-mapped font* designed to mimic the appearance of *printer fonts* when displayed on medium-resolution monitors. Modern *laser printers* can print text with a *resolution* of 300 *dots per inch (dpi)* or more, but video displays, except for the most expensive professional units, lack such high resolution and can't display *typefaces* with such precision. What you see on screen usually isn't as good as what you get from the printer.

Adobe International's Adobe Type Manager (ATM) and the *TrueType* standard developed by *Apple Computer* and *Microsoft Corporation* provide screen fonts that closely mimic printer fonts. See *outline font.*

screen memory   See *video memory.*

screen pitch   In *Trinitron*-type monitors, the distance by which *phosphors* on the *display* are separated. Screen pitches of 0.31 mm and less are good. See *slot pitch.*

screen saver   A *utility program* that prolongs the life of your *monitor* by changing the screen display—to an aquarium scene, or a variable pattern of line   while you are away from your computer.

Monitors degrade with use, particularly when they continuously display a particular image. Such images "burn" into the screen phosphors, resulting in a *ghost* image. *Green PC* monitors don't require screen savers, because they already go blank when not in use.

TIP: *If you're running* Microsoft Windows 95, *don't bother buying a screen-saver utility. Windows 95, like Microsoft Windows 3.1, has a built-in screen saver.*

script   A series of instructions, similar to a *macro,* that tells a program how to perform a specific procedure, such as logging on to an *electronic mail* system.

Some programs have built-in script capabilities. You must learn how to write the script using a rather limited *programming language.* Some programs write the script automatically by recording your keystrokes and command choices as you perform the procedure. See *HyperTalk* and *scripting language.*

scripting   The process of creating a *handler*—a brief program that traps messages that you initiate—for an object in an *object-oriented programming language* such as *HyperTalk.* See *inheritance.*

scripting language   A simple *programming language* designed to enable computer users to write useful programs quickly. Examples of scripting languages are *HyperTalk* (the scripting

S
T
U
V

language for the *Macintosh HyperCard* application) and Practical
Extraction and Report Language (*perl*), which is widely used to
write *Common Gateway Interface (CGI)* scripts for *World Wide
Web (WWW)* forms processing.

script language   A limited *programming language* included in
an *application program* that enables you to automate certain tasks.
Some script languages "record" commonly performed tasks, such
as *logging on* to an *on-line information service*, so that you can play
it back later.

scroll   To move a *window* horizontally or vertically so its position over a *document* or *worksheet* changes.

In some programs, scrolling is clearly distinguished from *cursor*
movement; when you scroll, the cursor stays put. In other programs, however, scrolling the screen also moves the cursor.

scroll arrow   In a *graphical user interface (GUI),* an arrow
(pointing up, down, left, or right) that you can click to scroll the
screen in the desired direction. The scroll arrows are located at the
ends of *scroll bars.*

scroll bar/scroll box   A *graphical user interface (GUI)* feature
that enables the user to scroll horizontally and vertically using
rectangular scrolling areas on the right and bottom borders of the
window. You scroll the *document* horizontally or vertically by
clicking the scroll bars or *scroll arrows* or by dragging the scroll
boxes.

Scroll Lock key   On *IBM PC-compatible keyboards,* a *toggle
key* that, for most programs, switches the *cursor-movement keys*
between two different modes. The exact function of this key varies
among programs.

TIP: *If the cursor-movement keys seem to move the document
rather than the cursor, you might have accidentally pressed the
Scroll Lock key. Toggle it off and try again.*

SCSI   See *Small Computer System Interface (SCSI).*

SCSI-2 The current version of the *Small Computer System Interface (SCSI)* standard. SCSI-2 reduces the number of conflicts among devices in a *daisy chain* and includes *the common command set* to enable the devices to work together smoothly.

SCSI-3 A developmental standard that soon will likely succeed the *SCSI-2* standard as the current *Small Computer System Interface (SCSI)* standard. *SCSI-3* likely will alter the *common command set* and increase the number of devices allowed in a *daisy chain* from 8 to 16.

search and replace See *replace*.

search engine Any *program* that locates needed information in a *database*, but especially an *Internet*-accessible search service that enables you to search for information on the Internet. To use a search engine, you type one or more key words; the result is a list of *documents* or *files* that contain one or more of these words in their titles, descriptions, or text. The databases of most Internet search engines contain *World Wide Web (WWW)* documents; some also contain items found in *Gopher* menus and *File Transfer Protocol (FTP)* file *archives*. Compiling the database requires an automated search routine called a *spider*, forms filled out by Web authors, or a search of other databases of Internet documents. See *Aliweb*, *DA-CLOD*, *InfoSeek*, *Lycos*, *WebCrawler*, and *World Wide Web Worm (WWWW)*.

secondary cache *Cache memory* that is on the *motherboard* rather than inside a *microprocessor*. Also called L2 cache memory, secondary cache memory dramatically improves system performance and is essential to every *computer system*. Several kinds of secondary cache memory are available, ranging from the slow but inexpensive *direct-map cache* to fast and expensive *four-way set-associative cache*. *Write-back* secondary cache memory is better than *write-through* secondary cache memory. See *full-associative cache*.

S
T
U
V

TIP: *Don't buy a computer system that lacks at least 256K of secondary cache. Without secondary cache, a 486DX2-66 system runs at 386 speeds.*

secondary storage A nonvolatile storage medium, such as a *disk drive* that stores program instructions and data even after you switch off the power. Synonymous with *auxiliary storage*. See *primary storage*.

second-person virtual reality A *virtual reality (VR)* system that doesn't try to immerse the user in a computer-generated world through the use of goggles and gloves, but instead presents the user with a high-definition video screen and a cockpit with navigation controls, as in a flight simulator program.

sector A segment of one of the concentric tracks encoded on a *floppy* or *hard disk* during a *low-level format*. In *IBM PC-compatible* computing, a sector usually contains 512 *bytes* of information. See *cluster*.

sector interleave factor See *interleave factor*.

Secure HyperText Transport Protocol (Secure HTTP) An extension of the *World Wide Web's HyperText Transport Protocol (HTTP)* that supports secure commercial transactions on the Web. Secure HTTP provides this support in two ways: by assuring vendors that the customers attempting to buy the vendors' wares are who they say they are (authentication) and by encrypting sensitive information, such as credit-card numbers, so that it cannot be intercepted while en route. Secure HTTP was developed by Enterprise Integration Technology (EIT) and the *National Center for Supercomputer Applications (NCSA)*, with subsequent commercial development by Terisa Systems. Netscape Communications developed a competing security technology, the *Secure Sockets Layer (SSL)* protocol. The two security protocols are incompatible, and for a time it was feared that no single, widely accepted security protocol would emerge. In early 1995, however, Netscape invested heavily in Terisa Systems and announced that it would integrate Secure HTTP and SSL to provide the Web community with a single security protocol that will work with any security-capable browser.

Secure Socket Layer (SSL) An *Internet* security standard proposed by Netscape Communications and incorporated into its *Netscape Navigator* browser and *Netscape Commerce Server* software. Unlike its chief competition, *Secure HyperText Transport Protocol (Secure HTTP)*, SSL is application-independent—it works with all Internet tools, not just the *World Wide Web (WWW)*.

Applications that use SSL use public key encryption to ensure that, while information is being conveyed through the Internet, no one can intercept that information. Netscape Communications has released the SSL specification to the Internet community as an open standard. Terisa Systems is currently developing a hybrid SSL/Secure HTTP specification that ensures that any browser with security features can access any secure Web site. See *public key cryptography*.

security The protection of *data* so unauthorized users cannot examine or copy it.

Mainframe computer systems ensured security by keeping the computer and its mass storage media under lock and key, and allowing access only through remote *terminals* equipped with *displays* but no *disk drives*. Although some experts argue that personal computer *local area networks (LANs)* should be set up the same way, the excessive centralization of mainframe computer systems was one of the main reasons for the development of personal computers.

Concern for security shouldn't prevent a manager from distributing computing power—and computing autonomy—to subordinates. Sufficiently advanced *data encryption* and *password-protection* schemes can foil even the most skilled and determined *hacker*.

Security Administrator Tool for Analyzing Networks (SATAN) A *program* designed to assess the security status of a computer or *local area network (LAN)* connected to the *Internet*. The program determines whether Internet-related software is misconfigured in a way that could render the system vulnerable to a *cracker*. The program is controversial because intruders as well as *system administrators* can use it to find loopholes. The controversy deepened when the program's authors, Dan Farmer and Wietse Venema, made the program publicly available through the Internet.

seek In a *disk drive*, to locate a specific region of a disk and to position the *read/write head* so that the computer can retrieve *data* or *program* instructions.

seek time In a *secondary storage* device, the time that it takes the *read/write head* to reach the correct location on the disk. See *access time*.

segmented memory architecture In *MS-DOS* and early versions of Microsoft Windows, a method of addressing the full memory capabilities of *Intel 80386* and later *microprocessors*. These *16-bit operating systems* do not take full advantage of the *32-bit architecture* of the 386 and later microprocessors, which can perform operations on 32 bits of information at a time. Because DOS and Windows 3.1 can work with only 16 bits of information at a time, they must use 16-bit memory addresses. Each location in memory must have its own, unique address. However, under the 16-bit address scheme, only 64K address locations can be uniquely identified. The solution to this problem is to divide the memory into 64K segments, each with its own identifying code. However, this solution—the segmented memory architecture—has a heavy performance penalty, because the microprocessor must process the segment's identifying code as well as the memory code each time that the computer accesses the memory. A *32-bit operating system*, such as *Microsoft Windows 95* or *Operating System/2 (OS/2)*, provides a much better solution to this problem. A 32-bit memory address can uniquely identify up to 4G (four billion bytes) of memory locations without requiring segmentation.

select To *highlight* part of a *document* so the *program* can identify the material on which you want to perform the next operation. In addition to selecting text, you can highlight or select an item from a *list box* or select a *check box* item to *toggle* it on or off.

selection Part of a document, ranging from one character to many pages, highlighted for formatting or editing purposes. In programming, a branch or conditional control structure. In *database management programs*, the retrieval of records by using a *query*. See *branch control structure*.

self-powered speaker An *auxiliary speaker* that uses power from outside the computer—such as from a battery or from an AC line adapter—to boost the power of an audio signal from a *sound board* and make sounds louder.

semantic net In *hypertext* theory, a set of connections among the ideas in a *document*. To create a hypertext document, you first "chunk" the document—breaking the document into "chunks" or units of meaning. For example, a hypertext document on California wines might break the subject down into the following categories: wineries, wine varietals, history of California wine, climate of wine-growing areas, and scientific research on wine growing. A separate document would cover each of these topics. *Hyperlinks* within the document exploit every possible connection with every other document in the series of linked documents, which is called a semantic net (this term is synonymous with *web,* spelled with a small *w*). See *chunking.*

semiconductor   A material, such as silicon or germanium, that is less electrically conductive than excellent electrical conductors, such as copper, and insulating materials. Semiconductor wafers or *chips* of varying resistance can be assembled to create a variety of electronic devices. In *personal computers,* semiconductor materials are used for *microprocessors, memory,* and other circuits. See *integrated circuit.*

send statement   In a *Serial Line Internet Protocol (SLIP)* or *Point-to-Point Protocol (PPP) dialer program's script language,* a statement that tells the program to send certain characters. Send statements follow *expect statements,* which tell the program to wait until the service provider's computer sends certain characters to your computer.

sensor glove   In *virtual reality (VR)* systems, an interface that is worn on a hand and enables the user to manipulate and move *virtual* objects in a virtual reality environment. See *head-mounted display.*

sequence control structure   A *control structure* that tells the computer to execute program statements in the order in which the statements were written.

One of three fundamental *control structures* that govern the order in which *program* statements are executed, the sequence control structure is the default in all *programming languages.* You can use loops and *branch control structures* to alter the sequence.

sequential access   An *information* storage and retrieval technique in which the computer must move through a sequence of stored data items to reach the desired one. Sequential access media such as cassette tapes are much slower than *random-access* media, such as *hard disk drives.*

serial   See *asynchronous communication, multitasking, parallel port,* and *serial port.*

S
T
U
V

serial communication A type of electronic communication that, unlike *parallel communication,* requires that *data bits* be sent one after the other. *Modems* rely on serial communication to send data over telephone lines. See *serial port.*

Serial Line Internet Protocol (SLIP) One of two standards specifying how a *workstation* or *personal computer* can link to the *Internet* by means of a *dialup connection* (the other standard is the *Point-to-Point Protocol [PPP]*). SLIP defines the transport of data *packets* through an *asynchronous* telephone line. Therefore, SLIP enables computers not directly connected to *local area networks (LANs)* to be fully connected to the Internet. This mode of connectivity is far superior to *shell access* (a dialup, text-only account on a UNIX computer) because it enables you to use the Internet tools of your choice (such as a graphical *Web browser*) to run more than one Internet application at a time and to download data directly to your computer, with no intermediate storage required.

serial mouse A *mouse* designed to be connected directly to one of the computer's *serial ports.* See *bus mouse.*

serial port A *port* that synchronizes and manages *asynchronous communication* between the computer and devices such as *serial printers, modems,* and other computers.

The serial port not only sends and receives asynchronous data in a one-bit-after-the-other stream, it also negotiates with the receiving device to ensure that no data is lost when it is sent or received. The negotiation occurs through *hardware* or *software handshaking.* See *FireWire, RS-232C* and *Universal Asynchronous Receiver/Transmitter (UART).*

serial printer A *printer* designed to be connected to a computer's *serial port.*

CAUTION: *When using a serial printer with an IBM PC-compatible system, you must give the correct MODE command to configure your system at the start of each operating session—preferably in the AUTOEXEC.BAT file (for DOS users) or STARTUP.CMD file (for OS/2 users), which the respective operating systems consult when you start up your computer. See your printer's manual for more details.*

serif   The fine, ornamental cross strokes across the ends of the main strokes of a character (see fig. S.5).

A B C D E F

Fig. S.5   *Example of a serif font.*

Serif fonts are easier to read for *body type,* but most designers prefer to use *sans serif* typefaces for *display type.*

server   See *file server, print server,* and *Web server.*

server application   In *object linking and embedding (OLE),* the *program* that creates a *source document.* Data from a source document is linked or embedded in one or more *destination documents* created by *client applications.*

server-based application   A *network* version of a *program* stored on a network's *file server* and available to more than one user at a time. See *client-based application.*

service bureau   A business that provides a variety of publication services such as *graphics file format* conversion, optical scanning of graphics, and typesetting on high-resolution *imagesetters* such as Linotronics and Varitypes.

service provider   An organization that provides access to the *Internet* or some other *wide area network (WAN).* Some service providers are for-profit companies, while others (including *freenets*) are publicly subsidized.

servo-controlled DC motor   An electric motor used to turn the *spindle* of a *hard disk.* Unlike *synchronous motors,* servo-controlled DC motors are inexpensive and can operate at whatever speed the disk's designers want, because the motor's rotation speed is independent of the frequency of the wall outlet's current.

servo-voice coil actuator   The most popular kind of *head actuator* used in modern *hard disks.* Servo-voice coil actuators are *closed-loop actuators* that operate by using an electromagnet to pull the *read/write head* against tension created by a spring.

set-associative   A *cache* design used in the fastest *random-access memory (RAM)* caches and in the *internal caches* included on

S
T
U
V

486-class and *Pentium* chips. This design divides the cache into two to eight sets, or areas. Data stored in the cache is distributed in bits to each set in sequence. In most instances, data from each set in the cache is read sequentially. Therefore, the set just read or written to can prepare to be read or written to again while data is being read from or written to the next set. The *set-associative cache* design enables the *microprocessor* to complete an instruction in one *clock cycle*. A *four-way set-associative cache* provides the best compromise between cost and performance.

setup parameters   Information about a *computer system* encoded as part of the *basic input-output system (BIOS)*. Setup parameters include the amount of *random-access memory (RAM)* in the computer, the type of *keyboard* used, and the hard disk's *geometry*. To change the setup parameters, use the *setup program*.

setup program   A program, recorded as part of the *basic input-output system (BIOS)*, that changes the *setup options*. To run the setup program, you press a special *key* combination (usually shown on-screen) as the computer *boots* up.

setup string   A series of characters that a *program* conveys to a *printer* so the printer operates in a specified mode.

setup switches   *Dual in-line package (DIP) switches* in older *modems* that enabled you to set certain options, such as whether to answer incoming calls. Modern modems have no setup switches; instead, the *communications program* handles the setup.

shadowing   Copying the contents of *read-only memory (ROM)* into *random-access memory (RAM)* to enable the microprocessor to access them more quickly. See *shadow RAM*.

shadow mask   A metal screen located just inside a *cathode ray tube's (CRT's) display* that prevents electron beams from striking *phosphors* that glow in the incorrect color. The shadow mask, which is very carefully aligned with the *electron guns* and the phosphors on the inside of the display, causes the red electron gun to strike only red phosphors and the blue electron gun to strike only blue phosphors, for example.

shadow RAM   In 386- and 486-class computers, a portion of the *upper memory area* between 640K and 1M set aside for programs ordinarily retrieved from *read-only memory (ROM)*. *Random-access memory (RAM)* is faster than ROM, so shadow RAM increases performance.

CAUTION: *Computer manufacturers like to equip their machines with shadow RAM to improve the machines' performance on benchmark tests. However, using shadow RAM can cause problems with programs that try to use upper memory as extended memory.*

shareware   Copyrighted *programs* made available free of charge on a trial basis. If you like a shareware program and decide to use it, you are expected to pay a fee to the program's author. See *public domain software.*

CAUTION: *Always pay shareware registration fees. Shareware programmers work very hard on their creations and deserve compensation.*

sheet-fed scanner   A *flatbed scanner* that can automatically load a series of documents for scanning. Sheet-fed scanners are useful for *optical character recognition (OCR)* work.

sheet feeder   See *cut-sheet feeder.*

shell   A *program* that puts an easy-to-use *user interface* between the user and an *operating system.* Though *COMMAND.COM* is technically a shell (it works between the user and the inner workings of *MS-DOS*), the term usually applies to a program that replaces a *command line* with a set of *menus.*

A cover, usually of plastic, that protects the recording surface of *floppy disks.* The *read/write head* gets to the medium through the *head access aperture.*

In *UNIX,* the *at sign (@),* often used in *electronic mail* addresses.

 shell account   An inexpensive but limited type of *Internet dialup access.* A shell account does not directly connect your computer to the Internet. Instead, you use a *communications program* to access a computer, usually a *UNIX* computer, on which you have established an account. After logging on to this computer, you get text-only access to this UNIX computer's operating system (its *shell*). From the shell, you can run the Internet tools that are available on the *service provider's* computer, such as a text-only *UseNet* newsreaders or the text-only *Web browser* called Lynx.

A major disadvantage of these tools becomes obvious when you try to download some of the information that these tools help you discover. The downloaded data goes to a separate storage area on the service provider's computer. You must quit the Internet application and, in a separate and tedious operation, download the data to your own system. You can overcome these two limitations—the text-only limitation and the two-step downloading process—by using *Serial Line Internet Protocol (SLIP)* or *Point-to-Point Protocol (PPP)*, or by using applications such as *SlipKnot* that disguise the shell. Shell accounts, though, are usually much less expensive than SLIP and PPP accounts.

shielded speaker   An *auxiliary speaker* designed to protect the *monitor* and other computer components from the magnetic field that generates sounds. Magnetic fields, if unshielded, can distort a monitor's image or even erase data on disks.

Shift+click   A *mouse* maneuver accomplished by holding down the Shift key while you click the mouse. Applications implement Shift+clicking differently, but in most, the action extends a selection.

Shift key   The key that you press to enter uppercase letters or punctuation marks.

Early IBM *keyboards* labeled the Shift key only with a white arrow. Later keyboards label this key with the word *Shift*. See *Caps Lock key*.

shortcut   In *Microsoft Windows 95*, an icon (see fig. S.6) that provides fast access to a program. After you create the shortcut, you see the program's icon on the desktop, where you can start it quickly by double-clicking the icon.

Fig. S.6   *Shortcut icon on desktop (Microsoft Windows 95).*

shortcut key A *key* combination that provides one-stroke access directly to a command or *dialog box*, bypassing any intermediate *menus*. See *hot key*.

Shugart Associates Standard Interface (SASI) An early-1980s standard for connecting *hard disks* to personal computers. SASI later became *the Small Computer System Interface (SCSI)* standard.

side-by-side columns See *table columns*.

SIG See *special interest group (SIG)*.

signal The portion of a transmission that coherently represents information, unlike the random and meaningless *line noise* that occurs in the transmission channel.

signal-to-noise ratio In *UseNet*, the ratio between meaningful content and noise (ranting, raving, and *flaming*). A good *newsgroup* has a high signal-to-noise ratio; a poor newsgroup has a low one. A major advantage of *moderated newsgroups* is to ensure a high signal-to-noise ratio. The term was originally used in electrical engineering to describe the ratio of information to background noise in an electronic circuit.

signature In *electronic mail* and *UseNet newsgroups,* a brief file (of approximately three or four lines) that contains the message sender's name, organization, address, e-mail address, and (optionally) telephone numbers. You can configure most systems to add this file automatically at the end of each message you send. *Netiquette* advises against long, complicated signatures, especially when posting to UseNet. See *ASCII art*.

In virus-protection utilities, program code identifiable as belonging to a known *virus*.

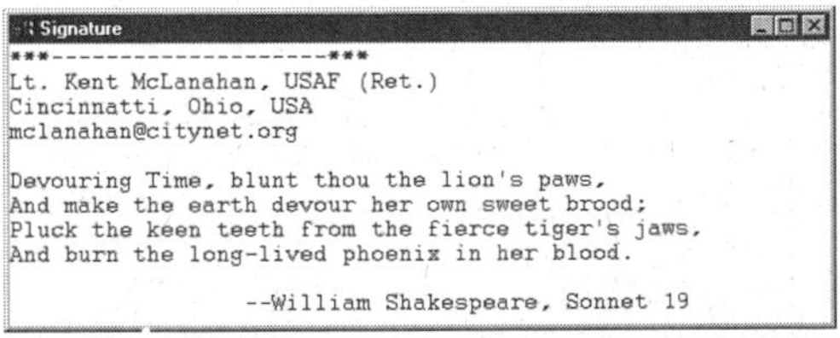

Fig. S.7 *An electronic mail signature.*

silicon chip   See *chip*.

Silicon Valley   An area in California's Santa Clara Valley with one of the largest concentrations of high-technology businesses in the world. The word silicon suggests the area's prominence in *chip* design and manufacturing.

SIM   See *Society for Information Management (SIM)*.

SIMM   See *single in-line memory module (SIMM)*.

simple list text chart   In *presentation graphics,* a text chart used to display items in no particular order, with each item given equal emphasis (see fig. S.8).

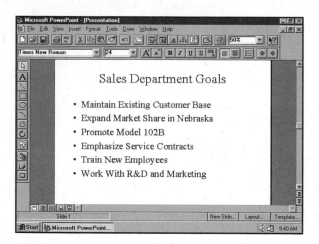

Fig. S.8   *A simple list text chart.*

Simple Network Management Protocol (SNMP)   A method for keeping track of various *hardware* devices, such as *printers,* connected to a *network*. SNMP can tell network administrators when printers are low on paper or *toner,* or when a paper jam has occurred. SNMP seems destined to be replaced by the *Microsoft at Work* standard or *the Desktop Management Interface (DMI)* standard.

simulation   An analytical technique in which an analyst investigates an item's properties by creating a *model* of the item and exploring the model's behavior.

Aeronautical engineers, for example, use computer simulation techniques to design and test thousands of alternative aircraft models quickly, pushing the wind tunnel toward obsolescence in modern aerospace firms. Simulation is also applied in education (to perform virtual science experiments) and in business (to perform financial *what-if analyses*).

As with any model, however, a simulation is only as good as its underlying assumptions. If these assumptions aren't correct, the model doesn't accurately mimic the behavior of the real-world system being simulated.

single density   A magnetic recording scheme for digital data that uses a technique called *frequency modulation (FM) recording.*

Single-density disks, common in early personal computing, use large-grained magnetic particles. Such disks have low storage capacity, such as 90K per disk, and are rarely used today. They have been superseded by *double-density* disks with finer grained partitions, and high-density disks with even finer partitions. See *Modified Frequency Modulation (MFM).*

single in-line memory module (SIMM)   A plug-in memory unit that contains all the chips required add 256*K*, 1*M*, or 2M of *random-access memory (RAM)* to a computer.

single in-line package (SIP)   A set of *random-access memory (RAM)* chips encased in hard plastic and attached to the *motherboard* with pins. Modern computers have replaced SIPs with *single in-line memory modules (SIMMs).*

single in-line pinned packages (SIPPs)   See *single in-line package (SIP).*

single-pass scanner   Any *scanner* that scans a document in one *scanning pass,* but especially a *color scanner* that does so. Single-pass color scanners collect data about all three primary colors on a single trip, unlike *triple-pass scanners,* which require three trips. Single-pass scanners are not necessarily faster than triple-pass scanners, however.

single-sided disk   A *floppy disk* designed so that only one side of the disk can be used for read/write operations. See *single density.*

SIP   See *single in-line package (SIP).*

S
T
U
V

SIPP   See *single in-line package (SIP)*.

site license   An agreement between a software publisher and a buyer that permits the buyer to make copies of specific software for internal use. Often a company using a *local area network (LAN)* buys a site license for a program so that all the users on the LAN can access the program. Most site licenses limit the number of copies that the purchasing organization can make. The cost per copy is much less than that of individually purchased copies.

sixteen-bit   See *16-bit computer*.

skip factor   In a *presentation graphics program*, an increment that specifies how many *data* items the program should skip when it labels a chart or graph. Use a skip factor when the categories axis is too crowded with headings. If you are labeling an axis with months, for example, a skip factor of three displays the name of every third month.

slave   The second *hard disk* in a series of two connected to an *Integrated Drive Electronics (IDE) host adapter*. The first disk in the series, the *master* disk, does not control the disk, but decodes instructions from the host adapter before sending them to the slave.

sleep mode   In computers equipped with *power-management* features, a state in which the *microprocessor* shuts down nonessential components during periods of disuse. Often, computers in sleep mode write the contents of their *random-access memory (RAM)* to a *hard disk* to save the energy required to refresh memory chips. See *Display Power Management System (DPMS)* and *green PC*.

slider   See *write-protect tab*.

slide show   In *presentation graphics,* a predetermined list of charts and graphs displayed one after the other.

Some programs can produce interesting effects, such as fading out one screen before displaying another. You can add *pushbuttons* that enable the viewer to alter the sequence in which the program displays the slides, jump to a specific slide, or exit the slide show.

SLIP   See *Serial Line Internet Protocol (SLIP)*.

SlipKnot   A *shareware Web browser,* designed for Microsoft Windows, that does not require a *Serial Line Internet Protocol*

(SLIP) or *Point-to-Point Protocol (PPP)* connection. MicroMind, Inc. specifically designed the program for Internet users who have *shell accounts* on *UNIX* systems. Running only slightly slower than a Web browser using a SLIP connection, SlipKnot enables the user to view in-line images and to download files directly, without an intermediary storage step. SlipKnot therefore overcomes the two chief limitations of shell account access, which is often available at a low monthly cost.

SLIP/PPP   A commonly used abbreviation for the two types of dialup Internet access that directly integrate your computer with the Internet: *Serial Line Internet Protocol (SLIP)* and *Point-to-Point Protocol (PPP)*. See *shell account.*

slot   See *expansion slot.*

slot pitch   The distance between the wires of a *Trinitron*-type *monitor's aperture grille.* Although slot pitch is an important specification for Trinitron-type monitors, *screen pitch* is even more important.

slow mail   A "polite" term for the postal service. See *snail mail.*

slug   In *word processing* and *desktop publishing (DTP)*, a code inserted in headers or footers to generate page numbers when the document is printed.

Small Computer System Interface (SCSI)   An interface amounting to a complete *expansion bus* in which you can plug devices such as *hard disk drives, CD-ROM disk drives, scanners*, and *laser printers.*

The most common SCSI device in use is the SCSI hard disk, which contains most of the controller circuitry, leaving the SCSI interface free to communicate with other peripherals. You can *daisy chain* as many as seven SCSI devices to a single SCSI port. See *Enhanced System Device Interface (ESDI)* and *ST-506/ST-412.*

SmallTalk   A *high-level, declarative programming language* and *programming environment* that treats computations as *objects* that send messages to one another. SmallTalk encourages the *programmer* to define objects in terms relevant to the intended application. The language is highly extensible because it enables you to create objects, which can be reused, quite easily.

S
T
U
V

SmallTalk inspired *HyperTalk,* the *software command language* of *HyperCard,* an application provided with every *Macintosh* produced since 1987. In this new guise, SmallTalk fulfills its goal of making programming more accessible; tens of thousands of Macintosh users have learned how to program in HyperTalk. See *object-oriented programming language.*

smart machine   Any device containing *microprocessor*-based electronics that enables the device either to branch to alternative operating sequences depending on external conditions, to repeat operations until a condition is fulfilled, or to execute a series of instructions repetitively. Microprocessors are so inexpensive that they can be embedded in even the most prosaic of everyday devices, such as toasters, coffee makers, and ovens.

smart terminal   In a *multi-user system,* a *terminal* that contains its own processing circuitry so that it not only retrieves data from the *host* computer, but also carries out additional processing operations and runs host-delivered programs.

smiley   See *emoticon.*

SMIS   See *Society for Information Management (SIM).*

snaf   The messy strips of waste paper that litter the office after you remove the perforated edge from continuous, *tractor-fed printer* paper.

The term *snaf* was the winning entry in a contest sponsored by National Public Radio's *All Things Considered.* The runner-up, *perfory,* is worthy of mention.

snail mail   A derogatory term for the postal service. In an *electronic mail* message, you might say "I'm sending the article to you by snail mail."

snaking columns   See *newspaper columns.*

snap-on pointing device   In *portable computers,* a *pointing device* that snaps on to the side of the computer's *case* in a special port. No *serial port* or *mouse* port cable is required. Snap-on pointing devices are convenient because they save you from having to connect the serial or mouse port cable every time that you want to use the computer. Instead, you simply snap the *trackball* into its receptacle. See *built-in pointing device* and *clip-on pointing device.*

snapshot   See *Print Screen (PrtSc)*.

sneakernet   A *network architecture* in which a person physically carries a data-laden *floppy disk* or *tape* from one computer to another. Although sneakernets usually are small, they sometimes involve transcontinental air travel.

SNOBOL   A *high-level programming language* designed for text-processing applications.

SNOBOL (String-Oriented Symbolic Language), which has particularly strong text pattern-matching capabilities, has been used for research work in fields such as language translation, the generation of indexes or concordances to literary works, and text reformatting. However, SNOBOL tends to generate inefficient, hard-to-read *source code*, and thus is rarely used. See *BASIC* and *FORTRAN*.

snow   See *video noise*.

soc   In *UseNet,* one of the *standard newsgroup hierarchies*. The soc newsgroups deal with social issues, social groups, and world cultures.

Society for Information Management (SIM)   A professional society for executives in information-systems fields that has branches in many cities. The SIM was formerly called the Society for Management Information Systems (SMIS).

Society for Management Information Systems (SMIS)   See *Society for Information Management (SIM)*.

socket   An *Internet* address that combines an *IP address* (the four-part numerical address that uniquely identifies a particular computer on the Internet) and a *port number* (which identifies a particular Internet application, such as *File Transfer Protocol [FTP]*, *Gopher,* or the *World Wide Web [WWW]*). See *well-known port*.

soft   Temporary or changeable, as opposed to *hard* (permanently wired, physically fixed, or inflexible). Compare *software, soft return,* and a page break inserted by a *word processing program* and subject to change if you add or delete text, to *hardware,* a *hard return,* and a page break that you insert manually and that remains fixed in place despite further editing.

S
T
U
V

soft cell boundary   In a *spreadsheet program*, a feature of *cells* that enable you to enter labels that are longer than the cell's width (unless the adjacent cells are occupied).

soft font   See *downloadable font.*

soft hyphen   A hyphen formatted so that it doesn't take effect unless the word that contains the hyphen otherwise *word wraps* to the next line. In that event, the word is hyphenated to improve the *kerning* of the line. Synonymous with optional hyphen. See *hard hyphen.*

soft page break   In a *word processing program*, a page break that the program inserts based on the current format of the text. This page break could move up or down if you insert or delete text or change margins, page size, or fonts. See *forced page break.*

soft return   In a *word processing program*, a line break that the program inserts to maintain the margins. The location of soft returns changes automatically if you change the margins or insert or delete text. See *hard page* and *word wrap.*

soft-sectored disk   A disk that, when new, contains no fixed magnetic patterns of tracks or sectors. *Tracks* and *sectors* are created during *formatting.*

soft start   See *warm boot.*

software   *System*, *utility*, or *application programs* expressed in a *machine language*. See *firmware* and *hardware.*

software cache   A large area of *random-access memory (RAM)* that a program such as SMARTDRV.EXE sets aside to store frequently accessed data and program instructions. A 1M to 2M software cache can speed up disk-intensive applications such as *database management programs.*

To prevent the slowdowns caused by hard disk *seeking*, many types of caches have been developed. If you have a *hardware cache,* a cache on your hard drive, and a *secondary cache* (or external cache), duplicate data and instructions can accumulate and actually bog down your system's performance. To optimize your system's speed, a single software cache usually suffices. *File servers* benefit from a large cache on the hard disk.

software command language   A *high-level programming language* developed to work with a *program*, such as a *spreadsheet* or *database management program*.

Software command languages range from the *macro* capabilities of *word processing* and spreadsheet programs to full-fledged programming languages, such as the *dBASE* command language. Like stand-alone programming languages, most software command languages include *control structures* that perform iteration, logical branching, and conditional execution of operations. Because the application program already manages all details for saving and retrieving information, controlling the user interface, maintaining data structures, handling errors, and so on, you can use a software command language to write custom programs that are fairly simple and yet extremely powerful. See *HyperTalk*.

software compatibility   The capability of a computer system to run a specific type of software. The Commodore 64, for example, isn't software-compatible with software written for the Apple II, even though both computers use the MOS Technology 6502 microprocessor.

software engineering   An applied science devoted to improving and optimizing the production of *software*.

software error control   An *error-correction protocol* that resides partly or entirely in a *communications program* rather than in *modem* hardware. Software error control makes modems cheaper, but also taxes the rest of the *computer system* and is supported by very few communications programs. For these reasons, you should avoid software error control.

software handshaking   A method of *flow control* that ensures that the data that a *modem* sends does not overwhelm the modem with which it is communicating. In a software handshaking scheme, such as *XON/XOFF handshaking*, modems exchange special codes when they are ready to send and receive data.

software license   A legal agreement included with commercial programs that specifies the rights and obligations of the program's purchaser and limits the liability of the software publisher. See *site license*.

S
T
U
V

software package A *program* delivered to the user in a complete and ready-to-run form, including all necessary *utility programs* and *documentation*. See *application software*.

software piracy The illegal duplication of copyrighted software without the permission of the software publisher.

Because anyone can duplicate software in a matter of seconds, software piracy is extremely common and seems to be an endemic problem of personal computing. When software publishers try to stop software pirates by using *copy-protection* schemes, legitimate users often resist buying the copy-protected programs.

The arguments of defenders of software piracy usually amount to little more than thinly veiled excuses for self interest. With today's pricing competition, the proliferation of discount houses, and the availability of inexpensive integrated packages such as Microsoft Works, affordable software is within the reach of any user.

CAUTION: *Although software piracy is always illegal, prosecution is far more common for infractions in the workplace than in the home. Companies have been sued for damages attributable to unauthorized software duplication, and an industry consortium has established a toll-free hotline through which violations, which carry penalties of $100,000 per occurrence under federal law, can be reported.*

software program An *application program*. Despite its redundancy, this term is used frequently, especially in advertisements, articles, books, and manuals written for a computer-illiterate audience. See *application software* and *software*.

software protection See *copy protection*.

sort An operation that rearranges data so it is in a specified ascending or descending order, usually alphabetical or numerical.

Most programs can perform sorts. Full-featured *word processing* programs, such as *WordPerfect*, provide commands that sort lists, and *spreadsheets* provide commands that sort the contents of the *cells* in a *range*.

Database management programs distinguish sorts from *index* operations. A sort physically rearranges *data records*, resulting in a new, permanently sorted file—consuming much disk space in the process. An index operation creates an index to the records and sorts the index rather than the records. The index file consumes less disk space than a new copy of the whole database. See *data integrity* and *sort order*.

sort key   In *sort* operations, the data that determines the order in which the operation arranges data records.

A *database* sort key is the *data field* by which to sort; in a *spreadsheet*, the sort key is the column or row used to arrange the data in alphabetical or numerical order. In a word processing program, the sort key is a word, but the word can be in any position. *WordPerfect's* sort utility can count the position from left or right. To sort a mailing list by ZIP code, for example, the sort key is the first word from the right in the last line of the address. See *multi-level sort*.

sort order   The order, such as ascending and descending, in which a program arranges data when performing a *sort*. Most programs also sort data in the standard order of ASCII characters. Synonymous with *collating sequence*. See *ASCII sort order* and *dictionary sort*.

sound board   An *adapter* that adds digital sound reproduction capabilities to an *IBM PC-compatible personal computer*, making it more competitive with *Macintosh* computers and better suited to *multimedia applications*.

TIP: Microsoft Windows 95 *users should look for a sound board that's fully supported by Windows' multimedia extensions. These sound boards include Ad Lib Gold Card, Soundblaster, Soundblaster Pro, Thunderboard, and others.*

sound card   See *sound board*.

Sound Recorder   A *Microsoft Windows 95* accessory that you use to record and play back sounds (see fig. S.9). To operate Sound Recorder, your system must have a *Multimedia Personal Computer (MPC)*-compatible *sound board* with recording capabilities, including a microphone. Sound Recorder serves as a control device, turning your computer into a digital tape recorder and

S
T
U
V

saving recordings in .WAV files that other MPC-compatible programs can access.

Fig. S.9 *The Sound Recorder window in Microsoft Windows 95.*

source   The record, *file*, *document*, or disk from which information is taken or moved, as opposed to the *destination*.

source code   In a *high-level programming language*, the typed program instructions that *programmers* write before the program is *compiled* or *interpreted* into *machine language* instructions the computer can execute.

source document   In *dynamic data exchange (DDE)* and *Object Linking and Embedding (OLE)*, the *document* that contains data linked to copies of that data in other documents, called *destination documents*.

source file   In many *MS-DOS* commands, the file from which data or program instructions are copied. See *destination file*.

source worksheet   In *Microsoft Excel*, a *worksheet* containing a *cell* or *range* linked to one or more *dependent worksheets*. The dependent worksheets reflect the changes that you make to the source worksheet.

SPA   See *Association for Systems Management (ASM)*.

spaghetti code   A poorly organized *program* that results from excessive use of GOTO statements, making the program almost impossible to read and debug. The cure is to use a well-structured programming language, such as *QuickBASIC, C,* or *Pascal,* that offers a full set of control structures. See *structured programming*.

spamming   In *UseNet,* posting a message to dozens or even hundreds of *newsgroups* in such a way that it rarely, or never, fits into the newsgroups' subject coverage, or posting a message too many times to the same newsgroup. Speculation on the term's origin invariably mentions the lunchmeat of the same name, but the term apparently stems from a Monty Python song with the lyrics, "Spam spam spam spam, spam spam spam spam, lovely spam, wonderful spam…" Some UseNet observers distinguish between *spam* (articles that are posted separately with the same or nearly the same wording, to an excessive number of newsgroups) and velveeta (articles that are cross-posted to an excessive number of newsgroups). Spam is worse because posting messages separately drains more disk space and network bandwidth. The newsreading software needs only one copy of a cross-posted message, even though it appears in many newsgroups. See *Cancelmoose* and *cancelbot*.

SPEC   See *Standard Performance Evaluation Corporation (SPEC)*.

special interest group (SIG)   A subgroup of an organization or *network*, consisting of members who share a common interest. Common SIG topics include software, hobbies, sports, and literary genres such as mystery or science fiction. See *user group*.

speculative execution   A method of analyzing instructions entering a *microprocessor* with *superscalar architecture* and determining how to route the instructions through the *pipelines* as efficiently as possible. Speculative execution, supposedly employed on Intel's *P6* microprocessor, greatly increases a microprocessor's *throughput*.

speech synthesis   Computer production of audio output that resembles human speech. Such output is particularly useful to visually impaired computer users.

Unlike *voice recognition*, speech synthesis technology is quite well developed. Existing speech synthesis boards are inexpensive and can do an impressive job of reading virtually any file containing English sentences in ASCII script—although, to some listeners, the English sounds as though it's being spoken with a Czech accent.

spell checker   A *program*, often a feature of *word processing* programs, that checks for the correct spelling of words in a *document* by comparing each word against a file of correctly spelled words.

A good spell checker displays suggestions for the correct spelling of a word and enables you to replace the misspelled word with the correct one. You usually can add words to the spell checker's dictionary.

> **TIP:** *Because of the way that they work, spell checkers can't tell when you have committed a common error, such as using a correctly spelled word in the wrong place. There's no substitute for a final, human proofreading of an important document—though grammar-checking software helps reduce the burden.*

spider   A program that prowls the *Internet,* attempting to locate new, publicly accessible resources such as *World Wide Web (WWW)* documents, files available in public *File Transfer Protocol (FTP) archives,* and *Gopher* documents. Also called wanderers or robots, spiders contribute their discoveries to a *database,* which Internet users can search by using an Internet-accessible *search engine* (such as *Lycos* or *WebCrawler*). Spiders are necessary because the rate at which people are creating new Internet documents greatly exceeds manual indexing capacity.

spike   See *surge.*

spindle   The "axle" on which a *hard* or *floppy disk* turns. The spindle, which is turned by a *spindle motor,* is not permanently attached to floppy disks but is permanently attached at the center of hard disk *platters.*

spindle motor   The electric motor—either a *synchronous motor* or a *servo-controlled DC motor*—that turns *hard* and *floppy disks.* Floppy-disk spindle motors turn only when you are writing data to a disk in your drive, but hard-disk spindle motors turn whenever your computer is on.

split bar   In a *graphical user interface (GUI)* such as *Microsoft Windows 95* or the *Macintosh Finder,* a bar that you can drag to split the *window* horizontally or vertically.

split screen   A display technique that divides the screen into two or more *windows.* In *word processing programs* that have split-screen capabilities, you can usually display two parts of the same document independently or display more than one document. Splitting the screen is useful when you want to refer to one document, or part of a document, while writing in another. The technique also facilitates cut-and-paste editing.

To split a window into two panes, you drag the split bar—a thick black line—down the vertical scroll bar. In this example, the Document2 window is split into two panes.

spoiler   In a *UseNet newsgroup,* a message that contains the ending of a novel, movie, or television program, or the solution to a computer or video game. Network etiquette (or *netiquette*) requires that you encrypt such messages so that users can't read them unless they choose to do so. In *UseNet* newsgroups, the *encryption* technique is called *rot-13*.

spooler   A *utility program,* often included with an *operating system,* that routes *printer* commands to a file on disk or in *random-access memory (RAM)* rather than to the printer, and then doles out the printer commands when the *central processing unit (CPU)* is idle.

A print spooler provides *background printing;* your program thinks that it's printing to a super-fast printer, but the spooler is actually directing the printer output to RAM or a disk file. You can continue working with your program, and the spooler guides the printer data to the printer whenever the CPU isn't busy handling your work.

spot color   A color defined by the *Pantone Matching System (PMS).* Spot color is a form of *device-independent color.*

spreadsheet   See *worksheet.*

spreadsheet program   A *program* that simulates an accountant's *worksheet* on screen and lets you embed hidden *formulas* that perform calculations on the visible data. Many spreadsheet programs also include powerful *graphics* and presentation capabilities to create attractive products.

A spreadsheet is a matrix of rows (usually numbered) and columns (usually assigned alphabetical letters) that form individual *cells.* Each cell has a distinct *cell address,* such as B4 or D19. Into each cell, you can place a value, which is a number or a hidden formula that performs a calculation, or a *label,* which is a heading or explanatory text.

A formula can contain constants, such as 2+2, but the most useful formulas contain cell references, such as D9+D10. By placing

S
T
U
V

formulas in a spreadsheet's cells, you can create a complex network of links among the parts of a spreadsheet. After embedding formulas, you can adjust constants—like the tax rate or acceleration due to gravity—to see how the bottom line changes.

CAUTION: *Spreadsheets often are used to simulate real-world business conditions, but remember: a spreadsheet is just a model of a business. Any model includes only some of the significant determinants of a firm's behavior, and manipulating the model can lead to serious errors. In your spreadsheets, avoid the temptation to tweak your model's assumptions to get the answers that you want.*

sputtering Like *plating,* a means of coating *hard disk substrate* with *thin-film magnetic media.* Sputtering uses heat and the attraction of oppositely charged particles to coat the platters evenly.

SQL See *Structured Query Language (SQL).*

squelch In a *network,* to suspend or cancel a *problem user's* access privileges. A network might squelch such privileges after a user repeatedly violates the terms under which the *account* was created.

S register *Memory* inside a *modem* that contains alterations to the *AT command set,* such as the number of rings to wait before answering a call or the time to wait for the *carrier* to be established.

ST-506/ST-412 A hard disk *interface standard* once widely used in IBM and IBM-compatible computers.

These drives, virtually unavailable today, are slower and cheaper than drives that use more recent interface standards, such as *Enhanced System Device Interface (ESDI), Integrated Drive Electronics (IDE),* and *Small Computer System Interface (SCSI).* The ST-506/ST-412 interface uses the *Modified Frequency Modulation (MFM)* and *Run-Length Limited (RLL)* standards.

stack In *programming,* a *data structure* in which the first items inserted are the last ones removed. Programs that use *control structures* use the Last In First Out (LIFO) data structure. A stack enables the computer to track what it was doing when it branched or jumped to a procedure. In *HyperCard,* the term *stack* refers to a file that contains one or more cards that share a common background.

stacked column chart See *stacked column graph*.

stacked column graph A column graph that displays two or more data series on top of one another. See *histogram*.

STACKS In *MS-DOS*, an area set aside to store information about the current task when an interrupt instruction is issued. After processing the interrupt, DOS uses the information in the stack to resume the original task. If you are running an *application program* that requires stacks, include a STACKS command in the *CONFIG.SYS* file to specify the size and number of stacks that you want set aside.

staggered windows See *cascading windows*.

stale link In the *World Wide Web (WWW)*, a *hyperlink* to a document that has been erased or moved. Synonymous with black hole.

stand-alone computer A *computer system* dedicated to meeting all the computing needs of an individual user. The user chooses just the *software* needed for his or her daily tasks. Links with other computers, if any, are incidental to the system's chief purpose. See *distributed processing system, multiuser system,* and *professional workstation*.

standard In computing, a set of rules or specifications which, taken together, define the architecture of a hardware device, program, or operating system. See *open standard* and *proprietary standard*.

Standard Generalized Markup Language (SGML) A means of describing markup languages, such as the *HyperText Markup Language (HTML),* the markup language widely used on the *World Wide Web (WWW)*. SGML is an open, international standard defined by the International Standards Organization (ISO).

standard newsgroup hierarchy In *UseNet*, a collection of categories that every UseNet site is expected to carry, if sufficient storage room exists. The standard *newsgroup hierarchy* includes the following newsgroup categories: *comp.*, misc.*, news.*, rec.*, sci.*, soc.*,* and *talk**. A voting process creates new newsgroups within the standard newsgroup hierarchies. See *alternative newsgroup hierarchies* and *call for votes (CFV)*.

standard parallel port   A *parallel port* that transfers *data*, in one direction only, at about 200*K* per second. Used since the days of the first IBM Personal Computers, standard parallel ports connect computers to *peripherals* such as *printers*. However, *bidirectional parallel ports* such as the *enhanced parallel port (EPP)* and the *extended capabilities port (ECP)* have made the standard parallel port obsolete.

Standard Performance Evaluation Corporation (SPEC)   A consortium of computer-industry companies that works to establish fair *benchmark* tests for evaluating computers. SPEC has developed two tests thus far: the CINT92 test, which measures integer calculations, and the CFP92 test, which tests *floating-point* computations.

standby UPS   An *uninterruptible power supply (UPS)* that protects against complete power failure but does not protect against reductions in line voltage (brownouts). Standby units are less expensive than *line interactive UPS* devices, but their inability to protect against brownouts might render them generally useless. See *surge protector*.

star network   In *local area networks (LANs)*, a centralized *network topology* with a physical layout that resembles a star. At the center is a central network processor or wiring concentrator; the nodes are arranged around and connected directly to the central point. A star network's wiring costs are considerably higher than those of other network topologies because each *workstation* requires a cable that links the workstation directly to the central processor.

start bit   In *serial communications*, a *bit* inserted into the data stream to inform the receiving computer that a byte of data is to follow. See *asynchronous communication* and *stop bit*.

starting point   In the *World Wide Web (WWW)*, a Web document that contains useful starting points for Web navigation, such as introductions to the *Internet* and to the Web, *subject trees, search engines,* and interesting Web sites.

startup disk   The disk that you normally use to boot your computer. The disk—often a *hard disk*—contains portions of the *operating system*. Synonymous with boot disk and system disk.

startup screen   A text or *graphics* display at the beginning of a program. Usually, the startup screen includes the program name and version and often contains a distinctive program logo.

statement   In a *high-level programming language,* an expression that can generate *machine language instructions* when the program is interpreted or compiled.

state-of-the-art   Technically sophisticated, representing the highest level of technical achievement.

static object   A *document* or portion of a document pasted into a *destination document* using standard copy-and-paste techniques. The object doesn't change if you make changes to the *source document.* To update the information in the object, you make changes to the source document and copy from it again. See *embedded object, linked object,* and *object linking and embedding (OLE).*

static random-access memory (SRAM)   A *random-access memory (RAM) chip* that holds its contents without constant *refreshing* from the *central processing unit (CPU).*

Although as *volatile* as *dynamic random-access memory (DRAM)* chips, SRAM doesn't require the CPU to refresh its contents several hundred times per second. These chips are substantially faster but also are significantly more expensive than DRAM chips and are therefore most often used for RAM *caches.* See *cache memory.*

station   See *workstation.*

statistical software   An *application program* that makes conducting statistical tests and measurements easier.

status line   A line of an *application program's* display screen, usually at the bottom, that describes the state of the program. The information presented in the status line often includes the name of the *file* that you are modifying, the cursor location, and the name of any toggle keys that you have pressed, such as *Num Lock* or *Caps Lock.*

stem   In *typography,* the main vertical stroke of a character.

stepper motor   A motor that makes a precise fraction of a turn each time that it receives an electrical impulse. Stepping motors are used as part of *head actuator* mechanisms in *hard* and *floppy disk drives*.

stepping motor   See *stepper motor*.

stereoscopy   A technology that presents two pictures taken from slightly different perspectives that, when viewed together using a stereoscope, creates a profound illusion of three-dimensional space. Stereoscopic viewers were popular in the last century, and the technology lives on today as one of the foundations of *virtual reality (VR)*. See *head-mounted display (HMD)*.

stickup initial   See *initial*.

stop bit   In *serial communications*, a *bit* inserted into the data stream to inform the receiving computer that the transmission of a *byte* of data is complete. See *asynchronous communication* and *start bit*.

storage   The retention of program instructions and data within the computer so that this information is available for processing purposes. See *primary storage* and *secondary storage*.

storage device   Any optical or magnetic device capable of information storage functions in a computer system. See *secondary storage*.

store-and-forward network   A *wide area network (WAN)* created by means of the telephone system. Each of the computers in the network stores messages received during the day. At night, when telephone rates are low, the computer's automatic software dials a central distribution site. The computer uploads those messages addressed to other computers on the system, and downloads messages from other computers. Store-and-forward technology is the basis of the *UNIX-to-UNIX Copy Program (UUCP)*, a UNIX network, and *FidoNet*, one of several wide area networks that link computer *bulletin board systems (BBS)*.

stored program concept   The idea, which underlies the *architecture* of all modern computers, that programs should be stored in *memory* with *data*.

This concept suggests that a program can jump back and forth through instructions instead of executing them sequentially. This insight launched virtually the entire world of modern computing. See *von Neumann bottleneck.*

storefront   In the *World Wide Web (WWW),* a Web document that establishes a commercial enterprise's presence on the Web. Typically, a storefront does not attempt to provide a complete catalog, but instead illustrates a few items or services that typify what the firm has to offer. Web marketing experience demonstrates that the most successful storefronts are those that offer some interesting "freebies," such as information or downloadable *software.* As security protocols become more widely used, customers will be able to use their credit cards safely to place orders. See *Secure HTTP* and *Secure Sockets Layer (SSL).*

streaming tape drive   A *secondary storage device* that uses continuous tape, contained in a cartridge, for *backup* purposes.

stress test   An *alpha test* procedure in which the manufacturer tries to determine how a program will behave under heavy demands. By pushing lots of data into a program, a manufacturer can determine whether, when, and how the program will fail under real-life conditions.

strikeout   A font attribute where text is struck through with a hyphen, as in the following example:

~~This text has strikeout formatting.~~

Strikeout is often used to mark text to be deleted from a coauthored document so that the other author can see changes easily. Also called *strikethrough.* See *overstrike, overtype mode,* and *redlining.*

string   A series of alphanumeric characters.

string formula   In a *spreadsheet program,* a *formula* that performs a *string operation* such as changing a label to upper- or lowercase.

string operation   A computation performed on alphanumeric characters.

S
T
U
V

Computers can't understand the meaning of words, and therefore can't process them like people do; however, computers can perform simple processing operations on textual data, such as comparing two *strings* to see whether they're the same, calculating the number of characters in a string, and arranging strings in *ASCII order*.

String-Oriented Symbolic Language   See *SNOBOL*.

stroke weight   The width of the lines that make up a character. "Light," "medium," and "bold" are designators of stroke weight for *fonts*.

structured programming   A set of quality standards that make *programs* more verbose but more readable, reliable, and easily maintained.

The goal of structured programming is to avoid *spaghetti code* caused by overreliance on GOTO statements, a problem often found in *BASIC* and *FORTRAN* programs. Structured programming—such as that promoted by *C, Pascal, Modula-2,* and the *dBASE software command language*—insists that the overall program structure reflect what the program is supposed to do, beginning with the first task and proceeding logically. Indentations help make the logic clear, and the *programmer* is encouraged to use *loops* and *branch control structures* and named procedures rather than GOTO statements.

Structured Query Language (SQL)   In *database management systems,* an IBM-developed *query language* widely used in *mainframe* and *minicomputer* systems. SQL is gaining acceptance on *local area networks (LANs)*.

SQL is an elegant and concise query language with only 30 commands. The four basic commands (SELECT, UPDATE, DELETE, and INSERT) correspond to the four basic functions of *data manipulation* (*data retrieval, data modification, data deletion,* and *data insertion,* respectively). SQL queries approximate the structure of an English *natural-language* query. A data table consisting of columns (corresponding to data fields) and rows (corresponding to data records) displays a query's results. See *table-oriented database management program*.

style In *fonts,* a defining characteristic such as italics, underlining, or boldface.

In *word processing,* a saved definition consisting of formatting commands that you regularly apply to specific kinds of text, such as main headings. Styles can include alignment, font, line spacing, and any other text-formatting features. After creating and saving a style, you can quickly apply it to the text by using one or two keystrokes. See *style sheet.*

style sheet In some *word processing* and *page layout programs,* a collection of styles frequently used in a specific type of *document,* such as newsletters, that are saved together. Synonymous with *style library.*

For example, you can have a style sheet entry for normal body text paragraphs that includes the following formats: Palatino, 10-point type size, left-justification, single line spacing, and 1/2-inch first-line indentation. When you create a document, you can use a style sheet that contains the styles that you want available. You can have separate style sheets for annual reports, memos, letters, or any other routine documents.

TIP: *By using style sheets, you can reformat a document much more quickly. Suppose that you decide to change the body type from Palatino to New Century Schoolbook. If you don't use styles, you must manually change the font everywhere that you originally applied it, carefully skipping over headings and other formats. If you have defined a body paragraph style in an attached style sheet, you make just one change to the style sheet and the program automatically changes all the text linked to that style.*

stylus A pen-shaped instrument used to select menu options on a monitor screen or to draw *line art* on a *graphics tablet.*

subdirectory In *MS-DOS* and *UNIX,* a *directory* structure created in another directory. A subdirectory can contain files and additional subdirectories.

When a *hard disk* is formatted, a fixed-size *root directory* area is created that's only large enough to contain the information for 512 files. To add more files to the hard drive, you create subdirectories in which you can store other files. By using subdirectories, you can create a treelike, hierarchical structure of nested directories so you can group programs and files, and organize your data to suit your needs (see fig. S.10). You can create subdirectories within subdirectories, up to a maximum of nine levels.

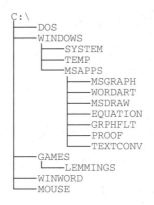

```
C:\
    ├──DOS
    ├──WINDOWS
    │      ├──SYSTEM
    │      ├──TEMP
    │      └──MSAPPS
    │             ├──MSGRAPH
    │             ├──WORDART
    │             ├──MSDRAW
    │             ├──EQUATION
    │             ├──GRPHFLT
    │             ├──PROOF
    │             └──TEXTCONV
    ├──GAMES
    │      └──LEMMINGS
    ├──WINWORD
    └──MOUSE
```

Fig. S.10 *An example of a hierarchical subdirectory structure.*

subject drift In *UseNet newsgroups,* the tendency of the subject lines of follow-up articles to become increasingly irrelevant to the articles' contents. Subject drift is an unintended consequence of *newsreader* software, which automatically echoes the original article's subject (a brief one-line description) when you write a follow-up article. As the discussion progresses into new territory, newsreaders keep echoing the same subject line, even though it soon becomes irrelevant to the subject actually being discussed.

TIP: *If you notice the occurrence of subject drift, edit the subject line when you post a follow-up article. Suppose that the subject was "Backpacking in the Sierra Nevada," but the thread is now talking about camping in Point Reyes, California. Type a new subject line that includes the old subject but stresses the change, such as "Camping in Pt. Reyes, Was: Backpacking in the Sierra Nevada."*

subject selector In a *UseNet newsreader,* a program mode in which you have a list of articles, sorted by subject. Note that sorting by subject is not the same thing as sorting by threads; a *threaded newsreader* shows the precise relationship among articles and *follow-on posts,* while a subject-sorted newsreader merely alphabetizes the subjects (thus obscuring some of the relationships among articles in a thread). See *thread selector.*

subject tree In the *World Wide Web (WWW),* a guide to the Web that organizes Web sites by subject. The term originates from many of the subject classifications (such as Environment or Music) having "branches," or subcategories. At the lowest level of the tree, you find *hyperlinks,* which you can click to display the cited Web document. See *EINet Galaxy, Global Network Navigator (GNN), Virtual Library,* and *Yahoo.*

submenu A subordinate *menu* that may appear when you choose a command from a pull-down menu. The submenu lists further choices (see fig. S.11).

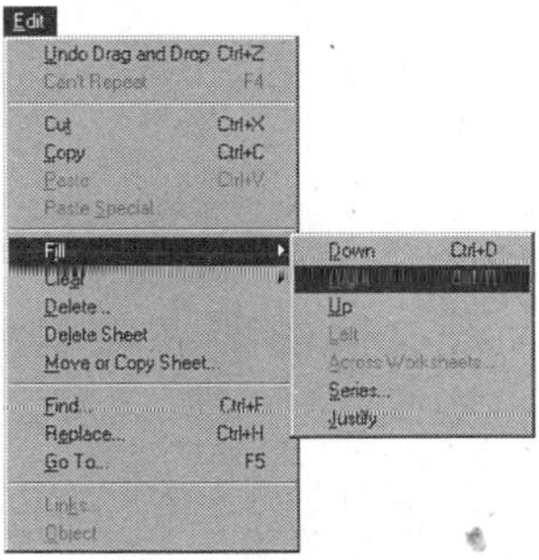

Fig. S.11 *The submenu that appears after you choose the menu option Fill in Microsoft Excel.*

Not all menu commands display submenus. Some carry out an action directly; others display *dialog boxes.*

TIP: *In many programs, you can tell which commands display submenus by the right-pointing triangle (→) at the right edge of the menu. Command names followed by an ellipsis (…) display dialog boxes.*

subroutine   A portion of a *program* that performs a specific function and is set aside so that more than one section of the program can use it. A subroutine performs tasks needed frequently, such as writing a file to disk. In *BASIC* programs, GOSUB statements reference subroutines.

subscribe   In *UseNet,* to add a *newsgroup* to the list of groups that you're reading regularly. Subscribed newsgroups appear in the *newsgroup selector,* enabling you to choose them easily. If you stop reading a newsgroup, you can *unsubscribe* to remove the newsgroup name from your subscription list.

subscript   In *word processing,* a number or letter printed slightly below the typing line, as in the following example: n_1. See *superscript.*

substrate   The material to which the *recording medium* of a *hard* or *floppy disk* is affixed. Floppy disks usually have plastic substrates, which are coated with a mixture of recording medium and *binder,* and hard disks have aluminum or glass substrates that, by *plating* or *sputtering,* are coated with *thin-film magnetic media.*

suitcase   In the *Macintosh* environment, an icon containing a *screen font* or *desk accessory (DA)* not yet installed in the *System Folder.*

suite   A group of *applications programs,* sold in a single package, that are designed to work well together. Suites, such as *Microsoft Office Standard* and *PerfectOffice Standard,* usually include a *word processing* program, a *spreadsheet,* and an *electronic mail* program. High-end suites, such as *PerfectOffice Professional, Microsoft Office Professional,* and *Lotus SmartSuite,* include *database management programs.* Suites cost less than the individual applications would if you purchased them separately.

supercomputer   A sophisticated, expensive computer designed to execute complex calculations at the maximum speed permitted by state-of-the-art technology. Supercomputers are used for scientific research, especially for modeling complex, dynamic systems, such as the world's weather, the U.S. economy, or the motions of a galaxy's spiral arms. The CrayY-MP is an example of a supercomputer.

SuperDrive   An innovative *3 1/2-inch floppy disk drive* now standard on *Macintosh* computers. SuperDrives can read all Macintosh formats (400K, 800K, and 1.4M). With the aid of Apple's Apple File Exchange software, included with all Macintosh system software, the drive also can read and write to 720K and 1.44M *MS-DOS* disks. SuperDrives also can format disks in the MS-DOS format.

TIP: *SuperDrive enables you to move data files easily between IBM PC and Macintosh systems. To achieve a higher level of data compatibility, choose the same applications for both systems. Suppose that you run the Macintosh version of Microsoft Word on your Mac and the Windows version on your PC. The Mac version of Word can read and write to the Windows format without losing any formatting.*

superpipelining   *Cyrix Corp.'s* modification of the *pipelining* process. Although the pipelining process usually consists of five steps, superpipelining changes it to a seven-step process. Cyrix claims that by having more, simpler steps, the process improves *throughput.*

superscalar architecture   A design that enables the *microprocessor* to take a sequential instruction and send several instructions at a time to separate execution units so that the processor can execute multiple instructions per *clock cycle.*

The *architecture* includes a built-in scheduler, which looks ahead in the instruction queue, identifies a group of instructions that do not conflict with one another or require simultaneous use of a particular service, and passes the group along for execution. The two *pipelines* available in the *Pentium* chip enable the processor to execute two instructions per clock cycle. The *PowerPC,* with three execution units, can handle three instructions simultaneously.

superscript   A number or letter printed slightly above the typing line, as in the following example: a^2. See *subscript.*

Super VGA   An enhancement of the *Video Graphics Array (VGA)* display standard. Super VGA can display at least 800 pixels

S
T
U
V

horizontally and 600 lines vertically, and up to 1,280 pixels by 768 lines with 16 colors, 256 colors, or 16.7 million colors simultaneously displayed. The amount of *video memory* required to display 16 colors is nominal, but as much as 3.9M of video memory is required to display 16.7 million colors.

TIP: *Do you really need 1,024 by 768 or higher resolution? With most Windows application programs, such higher resolution doesn't result in a sharper version of the same image; instead, you see more of the image—as much as 50 percent more than an 800-by-600 resolution display. However, the items on the screen are smaller. The higher resolution is most useful for spreadsheet users who want to see more of their worksheet, writers who want to see several paragraphs of text at a time, and desktop publishers who want to lay out an entire page.*

support   To offer assistance with a device, file format, or program. For example, *WordPerfect* supports all the latest *PostScript printers* and *EPS* files.

Also, a noun for the capability to use or work with a device, file format, or program. For example, WordPerfect offers PostScript and EPS support. See *technical support.*

surge   A momentary and sometimes destructive increase in the amount of voltage delivered through a power line. A surge is caused by a brief and often very large increase in line voltage resulting from appliances being turned off, lightning striking, or power being reestablished after a power outage. See *power line filter* and *surge protector.*

surge protector   An inexpensive electrical device that prevents high-voltage *surges* from reaching a computer and damaging its circuitry. See *power line filter.*

SVID   See *System V Interface Definition (SVID).*

swap file   In Microsoft Windows 3.1, a large, hidden system file that stores *program* instructions and *data* that don't fit in the computer's *random-access memory (RAM).* See *permanent swap file, temporary swap file,* and *virtual memory.*

swash   A character that sweeps over or under adjacent characters with a curvilinear flourish.

switch   An addition to an *MS-DOS* command that modifies the way that the command performs its function. The switch symbol is a forward slash (/), which is followed by a letter. For example, the command DIR /p displays a directory listing one page at a time.

switchable power supply   A *power supply* that lets you use both U.S. and European electrical power to run the computer. Unlike cheap "travel converters," which can ruin a PC's electronics, switchable power supplies enable a computer to use either 115-volt, 60-Hertz U.S. electricity or 230-volt, 50-Hertz European electricity.

symbolic coding   Expressing an *algorithm* in coded form by using symbols and numbers that people can understand (rather than the *binary* numbers that computers use). All modern *programming languages* use symbolic coding.

synchronous communication   Sending *data* at very high speeds by using circuits in which electronic clock signals synchronize the data transfer. Computers in high-speed *mainframe* computer networks use synchronous communication. See *asynchronous communication*.

synchronous motor   An obsolete kind of electric motor that some *hard disks* once used as a *spindle motor*. Now replaced by the *servo-controlled DC motor,* synchronous motors ran on high-voltage alternating current and could not be designed to run at different speeds.

syntax   The rules that govern the structure of commands, statements, or instructions.

syntax error   An error resulting from stating a command in a way that violates a program's *syntax* rules.

Syquest drive   A type of cartridge drive that is compatible with the *Small Computer System Interface (SCSI)* standard and very popular among both *Macintosh* and IBM *PC-compatible* computer users. Syquest Technology was the first company to market such products.

S
T
U
V

sysop Abbreviation for *system operator*. A person who runs a *bulletin board system (BBS)*.

system See *computer system*.

System The *operating system* for *Apple Macintosh* computers, contained in the *Macintosh's read-only memory (ROM)* and the System File in the *System Folder*.

system administrator The human being responsible for running and maintaining a *computer system,* especially a *mainframe, minicomputer,* or *local area network (LAN)*. System administrators, sometimes called *network* administrators, issue *login names,* maintain *security,* fix failures, and advise management about *hardware* and *software* purchases.

system board IBM's term for *motherboard*.

system clock A timer circuit on the *motherboard* that emits a synchronizing pulse at a regular interval, such as 33,000,000 times per second on a 33 *megahertz* (MHz) motherboard. The pulses of the system clock help synchronize processing operations. See *clock cycle*.

system date The calendar date that a computer system maintains.

Not all personal computers maintain the system date after you switch off the computer, which can make it difficult to determine which of several files is the newest. To enable such a system to maintain the system date, you must equip the system with a battery or a *clock/calendar board*. Otherwise, you can use the DATE command to set the system date manually.

system disk A disk that contains the *operating system* files necessary to start the computer. *Hard disk* users normally configure a hard disk to serve as the system disk.

system file A *program* or *data file* that contains information that the *operating system* needs; distinguished from the program or data files that the *application programs* use.

System Folder A *folder* in the *Macintosh* desktop environment that contains the *System* and *Finder* files, the two components of the Mac's *operating system*.

In addition to the System and Finder files, the System Folder also contains all the *desk accessories (DAs), INITs, control panel devices (CDEVs), screen fonts,* downloadable printer fonts, and *printer drivers* available during an operating session. See *blessed folder* and *downloadable font.*

System V Interface Definition (SVID)   A standard for *UNIX operating systems,* established by AT&T Bell Laboratories and demanded by corporate buyers, and based on UNIX Version 5. See *Berkeley UNIX.*

system prompt   In a *command-line operating system,* the text that indicates that the *operating system* is available for tasks such as copying files, formatting disks, and loading programs. In *MS-DOS,* the system prompt (a letter designating the disk drive, followed by a greater-than symbol) shows the current drive. When you see the prompt C>, for example, drive C is the current drive, and DOS is ready to accept instructions. You can customize the system prompt by using the PROMPT command.

systems analysis   A professional specialty that involves determining an organization's computing needs and designing *computer systems* to fit those needs. Systems analysis is less structured than *programming* or other aspects of computer science, because it is often difficult to determine whether the analyst has found the best system for an organization, or even whether the analyst has completely solved an organization's computing problems.

Systems and Procedures Association (SPA)   See *Association for Systems Management (ASM).*

Systems Application Architecture (SAA)   A set of standards for communication among various types of IBM computers, from *personal computers* to *mainframes.*

Announced in 1987, SAA was IBM's response to criticisms that its products didn't work well together, and to the competitive pressure exerted by Digital Electronic Corporation (DEC), which claimed that it had optimized its products for easy interconnection. SAA calls for a consistent *user interface* and consistent system terminology across all environments. The standard influenced the

S
T
U
V

design of Presentation Manager, the windowing environment jointly developed by Microsoft and IBM for *Operating System/2 (OS/2).* See *windowing environment.*

system software All the software used to operate and maintain a computer system, including the *operating system* and *utility program;* distinguished from *application programs.*

system time The time of day maintained by the computer system and updated while the system is operating.

Only computers equipped with a *clock/calendar board* or a battery-powered clock on the *motherboard* can keep the system time when the computer is turned off. If your IBM PC-compatible computer lacks this battery-powered system date circuitry, you can use the TIME command to set the system time manually.

TIP: *Be sure to set the system time. When you create and save files, the* operating system *records the date and time that you save each file. This information can be important when you are trying to determine which version of a file is the most recent.*

system unit The *case* that houses the computer's internal processing circuitry, including the *power supply, motherboard, disk drives, plug-in boards,* and a speaker. Some personal computer system units also contain a *monitor.*

The case often is called the *central processing unit (CPU),* but this usage is inaccurate. Properly, the CPU consists of the computer's *microprocessor* and memory (usually housed on the motherboard) but not *peripherals* such as disk drives.

T1   A high-bandwidth telephone trunk line that is capable of transferring 1.544 *megabits per second (Mbps)* of data. See *physical media, T3*.

T3   A very-high-bandwidth telephone trunk line that is capable of transferring 44.21 *megabits per second (Mbps)* of computer data. See *physical media, T1*.

TA   See *terminal adapter (TA)*.

Tab key   A *key* used to move a fixed number of spaces or to the next *tab stop* in a document. The Tab key often is used to guide the cursor in on-screen command menus.

TIP: *In a* word processing program, *don't use the space bar to indent the first line of a paragraph. Instead, press Tab or activate the first-line indent command found in most word processing programs. If you change your mind about the amount of the indentation, you can change all the first-line indentations in one keystroke by resetting the amount of the first-line indent or changing the tab settings.*

tab stop   The place where the *cursor* stops after you press the *Tab key*. Most *word processing programs* set default tab stops every 1/2 inch, but you can set tabs individually anywhere you want, or you can redefine the default tab width. Also, most programs allow you to set flush-right, centered, and *decimal tab* stops in addition to the default flush-left tab stops, as shown in the following examples:

Flush Right	Centered	Decimal
aligns at right	aligns at center	$2,110.56
		.50986
		54

tab-delimited file   A *data file*, usually an *ASCII file*, in which the data items are separated by tab keystrokes. See *comma-delimited file*.

table   In a *relational database management system*, the fundamental structure of data storage and display in which data items are linked by the relations formed by placing them in rows and columns. The rows correspond to the *data records* of record-oriented database management programs, and the columns correspond to *data fields*.

In a *word processing program*, a *spreadsheet* of columns and rows with mathematical capabilities, usually created using a *table utility*. In some word processing programs, the data document created when using the *mail merge* feature organizes the merge data in a table. See *table-oriented database management program*.

table columns   Unequally sized blocks of text positioned side by side on a page so that the first block is always positioned next to the second one. Synonymous with parallel columns with block protect.

Side-by-side columns, often called parallel columns, are used for paragraphs meant to be positioned near one another. *Newspaper column* formats can't handle this formatting task, because no relationship exists between the paragraphs in one column and the paragraphs in another.

An easy way to create side-by-side paragraphs is to use the *table utilities* included in some *word processing programs* (see fig. T.1).

table of authorities   A table of legal citations generated by a *word processing program* from references that have been marked in a *document*.

table-oriented database management program   A *database management program* that displays *data tables* (rather than *data records*) as the result of query operations. See *data retrieval, record-oriented database management program,* and *Structured Query Language (SQL)*.

table utility   In a *word processing program*, a utility that makes the typing of tables easier by creating a spreadsheet-like matrix of rows and columns, into which you can insert text without forcing word wrapping.

When you create a table with tabular columns, you must type the table line by line. If you later want to add a few words to one of the items, the words may not fit, and the rest of the line wraps down to the next line, ruining the column alignment. Table utilities solve this problem by making the cell, not the line, the unit of word wrapping (refer to fig. T.1).

![Microsoft Word document window showing a table titled "World Wide Web Search Tools"]

World Wide Web Search Tools	
Lycos	A search engine at Carnegie-Mellon University, Lycos has a large database.
Yahoo	Newly commercialized, Yahoo offers excellent organization based on subject trees.
Infoseek	Accessible from the Netscape home page, Infoseek is fast and very powerful.

Fig. T.1   *Side-by-side columns created using a table utility.*

tabloid printer   See *B-size printer.*

tactile feedback   Any information gained through the sense of touch. Typically, tactile feedback applies to the way a *keyboard's* keys feel to a typist, but the term also applies to *mouse* and *joystick* design and a variety of *virtual reality* applications.

tag   In *HyperText Markup Language (HTML)*, a code that identifies an element (a certain part of a document, such as a heading or list) so that a *Web browser* can tell how to display it. Tags are enclosed by beginning and ending delimiters (angle brackets). Most tags begin with a start tag (delimited with <>), followed by the content and an end tag (delimited with </>), as in the following example:

<H1>Welcome to my home page</H1>

Tagged Image File Format (TIFF)   A *bit-mapped graphics* format for scanned images with resolutions of up to 300 *dots per inch (dpi)*. TIFF simulates *gray-scale* shading.

S
T
U
V

talk In *UseNet*, one of the seven *standard newsgroup hierarchies*. The talk newsgroups are expressly devoted to controversial topics, and are often characterized by acrimonious debate. Topics covered include abortion, drugs, and gun control.

tape A strip of thin plastic, coated with a magnetically sensitive recording medium. In *mainframe* computing and minicomputing, tape is widely used as a *backup* medium. Thanks to a dramatic price drop in cartridge *tape backup units,* tape has become increasingly common in personal computing for backing up entire *hard drives.* See *backup procedure, backup utility, quarter-inch cartridge (QIC), random access, sequential access,* and *tape drive.*

tape backup unit A device that reads and writes data on a magnetically sensitive *tape.* Tape backup units are useful for performing *backups* on *hard disks*—thus protecting data from loss by accidental erasure—and for storing important but rarely needed data that would otherwise take up space on a hard disk. *Quarter-inch cartridge (QIC)* tape drives are the most common tape backup units for personal computers.

tape drive See *tape backup unit.*

taskbar In *Microsoft Windows 95,* an application launcher and task switcher that (by default) remains visible at the bottom of the screen (see fig. T.2). After launching a program with the Start menu, the program's *task button* appears on the taskbar, allowing the user to switch to it by clicking the button.

Start	Microsoft Word	Clipboard Viewer	CD Player	11:27 AM

Fig. T.2 *Taskbar (Microsoft Windows 95).*

task button In *Microsoft Windows 95,* a button that appears on the taskbar after an *application program* is launched. The user can switch to the application by clicking the task button.

TCM See *trellis-code modulation (TCM).*

TCO The Swedish white-collar labor union. In *monitors,* TCO is known for its very stringent regulations regarding *electromagnetic radiation*—even stricter than *MPR II* rules. Not many TCO-certified monitors are available in the United States, but the TCO standards are the toughest in the world.

TCP/IP   *See Transfer Control Protocol/Internet Protocol (TCP/IP).*

techie   An often derogatory term for a *programmer* or other computer expert. Like "bit twiddler," "computer jock," and "computer nerd," the term sometimes connotes a lack of interpersonal skills but does not convey the maliciousness of *"hacker."*

technical support   Providing technical advice and problem-solving expertise to registered users of a *hardware* device or *program.*

technocentrism   An overidentification with computer technology, often associated with a preference for factual thinking, denial of emotions, a lack of empathy for other people, and a low tolerance for human ambiguity. First noted by the psychotherapist Craig Brod, technocentrism stems from the stress individuals encounter as they try to adapt to a computer-driven society.

telecommunications   The transmission of information, whether expressed by voice or computer signals, via the telephone system. See *asynchronous communication* and *modem.*

telecommuting   Performing your work at home while linked to the office by means of a telecommunications-equipped *computer system.*

Telecommuting reduces pollution and allows people more time with their families, but few offices have adopted telecommuting policies. Managers are reluctant to trust employees to work unsupervised, and employees seem to like the social interaction an office environment provides. However, as urban transport becomes increasingly difficult and expensive and telecommunication technology improves, more and more people probably will work one or more days per week at home. See *remote control program.*

telemedicine   The provision of high-quality, up-to-date medical information to medical practitioners.

In rural areas and community health centers, doctors who are out of touch with the latest knowledge may make faulty diagnoses or prescribe an out-of-date therapy. A telemedicine system that can provide these practitioners with high-quality information could indeed save lives—perhaps thousands of lives in the case of an epidemic. Physicians are already transmitting X-rays and other information to specialists for consultation.

Telenet   A commercial *wide-area network (WAN)* with thousands of local *dialup* numbers. Telenet provides log-on services to various commercial *on-line information services,* such as *Dialog Information Services* and *CompuServe.*

telepresence   A psychological sensation of being immersed in a *virtual reality* that's persuasive and convincing enough to pass for the real world.

Riders of the Disneyland attraction Star Tours may have already experienced telepresence. In Star Tours, you board a "ship"— actually, a vehicle that travels on a track at low speeds, simulating turns, spins, acceleration, and braking—and view a high-resolution movie of interstellar travel, which is precisely coordinated with the vehicle's movements. The resulting telepresence convinces you that you're moving at fantastic speeds.

teletype (TTY) display   A method of displaying characters on a *monitor* in which characters are generated and sent, one by one, to the video display; as the characters are received, the screen fills, line by line. When full, the screen scrolls up to accommodate the new lines of characters appearing at the bottom of the screen.

Teletype display mode should be familiar to *DOS* users. DOS uses a teletype display for accepting commands and displaying messages. See *character-mapped display.*

Telnet   An *Internet* protocol that enables Internet users to log on to another computer linked to the Internet, including those that cannot directly communicate with the Internet's *TCP/IP* protocols. Telnet establishes a "plain vanilla" computer terminal called a *network virtual terminal.* This capability is frequently used to enable communications with *bulletin board systems (BBSs)* and *mainframe* computers. For example, you will often see *hyperlinks* to Telnet sessions while browsing the *World Wide Web (WWW).* If you click such a hyperlink, your browser starts a Telnet *helper program,* and you see a text-only command window. In this window, you type commands and see the remote system's reponses.

template   In a *program,* a *document* or *worksheet* that includes the text or formulas needed to create standardized documents. The template can be used to automate the creation of these documents in the future.

In *word processing*, templates frequently are used for letterheads; the template version of the file contains the corporate logo, the company's address, and all the formats necessary to write the letter, but no text. You use the template by opening it, adding text to it, and printing. In *spreadsheet* programs, templates are available for repetitive tasks such as calculating and printing a mortgage amortization schedule.

temporary font   A Hewlett-Packard term for a *font* that, when downloaded to a *laser printer*, stays in the printer's memory only until the printer is reset. See *downloadable font,* and *permanent font.*

tensioning wire   A very thin wire that stretches across an *aperture grille*, perpendicular to the other wires, to keep them steady. Sometimes, tensioning wires cast shadows on the *display*. The shadows are most visible in solid white images.

tera-   Prefix indicating one trillion (10^{12}).

terabyte   A unit of *memory* measurement equal to approximately 1 trillion *bytes* (actually, 1,099,511,627,776 bytes). One terabyte is equal to 1,000 *gigabytes*, or 1 million *megabytes*. See *gigabyte* and *kilobyte (K)*.

terminal   An input/output device, consisting of a *keyboard* and *monitor*, commonly used with *multiuser systems*.

terminal adapter (TA)   A device, functionally equivalent to a *modem*, that connects a computer or *fax* machine to an *Integrated Services Digital Network (ISDN)* system. TAs typically plug into the *expansion bus* like other *adapters*, though external versions exist.

A terminal lacking its own *central processing unit (CPU)* and disk drives is called a *dumb terminal* and is restricted to interacting with a distant multiuser computer. A *smart terminal*, on the other hand, has some processing circuitry and, in some cases, a disk drive so that you can download information and display it later. A *personal computer* is a terminal when it is connected to a *network*, either by a cable or a *modem*. See *terminal emulation*.

terminal emulation   The use of a *communications program* to transform a computer into a *terminal* for the purpose of *data communication*.

S
T
U
V

terminal mode   A state of a *communications program* in which the computer on which it is running becomes a *remote terminal* of another computer, to which it is linked by *modem*.

terminate-and-stay-resident (TSR) program   An accessory or *utility program* designed to remain in *random-access memory (RAM)* at all times so that you can activate it quickly, even if another program also is in memory.

CAUTION: *If you're using DOS, use TSR programs with caution because they may cause conflicts that result in system lockups. When running* Microsoft Windows 95, *you usually don't have to run TSRs.*

test driver   A program that tests another program, often as part of an *alpha test*. Test drivers typically send every conceivable input to a program and monitor the results.

test message   In *UseNet*, a message that is posted just to see whether one's *newsreader* software and UseNet connection are really working.

TIP: *Please don't post test messages to ordinary newsgroups—there are several test newsgroups that exist for this purpose alone. They include alt.test and misc.test.*

Texas Instruments Graphics Architecture (TIGA)   A *high-resolution* graphics standard for *IBM PC-compatible* personal computers. TIGA boards and monitors display 1,024 *pixels* horizontally by 786 lines vertically with 256 simultaneous colors. See *Super VGA*.

text   Data composed only of standard *ASCII* characters, without any *formatting codes*.

text chart   In *presentation graphics*, a slide, transparency, or handout that contains text, such as a bulleted list. See *bulleted list chart, column text chart, free-form text chart, organization chart,* and *simple list text chart.*

text editor   In *programming*, a program designed for altering sequences of words and numbers, but without the features of a full-fledged *word processing program*. Text editors are used for writing *source code* as well as creating basic text documents.

text file   A file consisting of nothing but standard *ASCII* characters (with no *control codes* or characters from the *extended character set*).

text mode   An operating mode of *IBM PC-compatible video boards* in which the computer displays images constructed using the built-in 256-character *ASCII character set*. Text mode is synonymous with character mode and the opposite of *graphics mode*. Because the character set includes several graphics characters, text mode can display graphic images such as boxes and lines. Also, text can be displayed in *bold* and *reverse video*. Text mode is much faster than graphics mode.

TFT   See *active matrix*.

thermal dye sublimation printer   A *high-end color printer* capable of generating *photorealistic output*—but at a very high price. By focusing a precisely controllable heat source on a special ribbon containing dyes, the dyes can be transferred to the special coated paper that thermal dye-sublimation printers require. Thermal dye-sublimation printers have very good color *saturation*, but can cost more than $15,000, plus a *cost per page* of $3 or more.

thermal fusion printer   A *printer* that melts dye from a special ribbon onto plain paper to form sharp text. Thermal fusion printers are often designed to be portable.

thermal printer   A *non-impact printer* that forms an image by moving heated styluses over specially treated paper. Although quiet and fast, thermal printers have one disadvantage: most of them require specially treated paper that smells odd and has an unpleasant, waxy feel.

thermal wax-transfer printer   A *printer* that heats wax-based dyes and deposits them on the page in a very dense pattern. Though thermal wax-transfer printers cannot generate *photorealistic output*, as *thermal dye-sublimation printers* can, they produce excellent *saturation* and output that is nearly *photorealistic*. Thermal wax transfer printers are much less expensive than *thermal dye-sublimation printers* (they can be had for less than $1,000) and the *cost per page* is lower, too—about 50 cents.

S
T
U
V

thin-film magnetic medium   A recording medium used in *hard disks* that is not composed of tiny bits of metal oxide, but instead is made up of thin layers of special metal alloys. Thin-film magnetic media, applied to disk *substrates* by *plating* or *sputtering*, allow higher *areal densities* and increased *coercivities* than oxide-based media.

thin-film transistor (TFT)   See *active matrix*.

third-party vendor   A firm that markets an accessory *hardware* product for a given brand of computer equipment. Many companies act as third-party vendors of *Machintosh* accessories.

thirty-two bit computer   See *32-bit computer*.

thread   In a *UseNet* newsgroup, a chain of postings on a single subject. Most *newsreaders* include a command that lets you follow the thread (that is, jump to the next message on the topic rather than display each message in sequence).

Also, a portion of a *program* that can operate independently. In a *multithreaded application*, a running program may have two or more threads running at the same time. The operating system decides which of these threads should receive the processor's attention. In this way, an operation such as printing or downloading a file can occur in the background, without tying up other threads or other applications. This is called *preemptive multitasking*. See *cooperative multitasking*.

thread selector   In a *UseNet newsreader*, a program mode in which you see articles sorted by *threads*. Many newsreaders use indentation to indicate that the indented article is a response to the one positioned above it. In the following example, there are three *follow-on posts* in response to the original "Australian Cabernet-Shiraz blends—great" post. The second follow-up article contains a response to the first follow-up article in the thread, and so on, so that the third follow-up article contains comments on all the previous posts on the subject:

Australian Cabernet-Shiraz blends—great

   Re: Australian Cabernet-Shiraz blends—great

      Re: Australian Cabernet-Shiraz blends—great

         Re: Australian Cabernet-Shiraz blends—great

What's the best cellar temperature for whites?

   Re: What's the best cellar temperature for whites?

Note that sorting articles by threads is not the same as sorting by subject. Were these articles sorted by subject, the newsreader might obscure the thread of discussion in the three "Re: Australian Cabernet-Shiraz blends—great" articles. See *subject selector* and *threaded newsreader*.

threaded newsreader A *UseNet newsreader* program that can group articles by topic of discussion, and then show where a given article stands in the chain of discussion. Often, this is done using indentation. See *thread selector*.

TIP: *Don't settle for anything less than a threaded newsreader; without threading capabilities, you're missing out on the dialogue that makes UseNet so fascinating.*

three-dimensional graph A business or scientific chart that depicts information using three axes: width (*x-axis*), height (*y-axis*), and depth (*z-axis*). In *Microsoft Excel*, the vertical axis—the one that measures the data items—is called the value (y) axis, and the horizontal axis is called the category (x) axis (see fig. T.3). The axis that shows depth—the one that seems to go "back" into the page—is the series (z) axis. 3-D graphs are very useful when you're showing more than one *data series*.

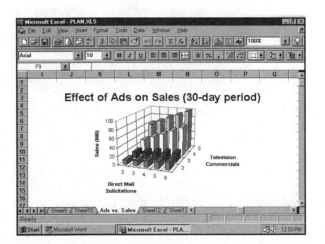

Fig. T.3 *A three-dimensional business graph.*

S
T
U
V

> **TIP:** *A three-dimensional graph can show the relationship among three values, as shown in figure T.3. This graph reveals the effectiveness of coupling television advertising with direct mail solicitation. In general, the more television advertising, the better the revenue.*

three-dimensional spreadsheet A *spreadsheet program* that can create a *worksheet* file made up of multiple stacked pages, each page resembling a separate worksheet.

Suppose that your organization has three divisions, each with its own income statement. You create four spreadsheets, one for each division, and one to summarize the quarterly income amounts. In the summary spreadsheet, you place formulas that use three-dimensional statements. Shown in the formula bar above the spreadsheet window in figure T.4, the statement in cell B4 of spreadsheet Consolidation is

```
@SUM(Northeast..Central:B4)
```

This statement says, "Sum the amounts shown in cell B4 of spreadsheets Northeast, Southeast, and Central, and place the total here."

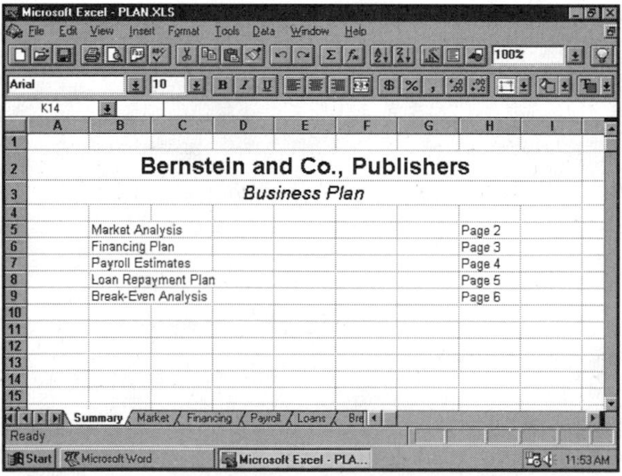

Fig. T.4 *A three-dimensional spreadsheet.*

three-gun tube   A color *cathode ray tube (CRT)*. Each of the three *electron guns* emits electrons that paint one of the primary colors on the *display*. So-called *one-gun tubes* in color *monitors* really have three guns, but the three guns are assembled into one unit. A *monochrome* monitor truly has only one gun.

throughput   A measure of a computer's overall performance, as measured by its capability to send data through all components of the system, including data storage devices such as disk drives.

Throughput is a much more meaningful indication of system performance than some of the *benchmark* speeds commonly reported in computer advertising, which involve the execution of computation-intensive *algorithms*. A computer equipped with slow *random-access memory (RAM)* chips, no *cache memory*, or a slow *hard disk* may not perform as well as its processor speed would indicate.

TIP: *Before you make a purchasing decision based on benchmarks, find out whether the benchmark includes a full range of computer tasks.* PC Magazine, *for example, tests CPU instruction mix, floating-point calculation, conventional memory, DOS file access (small and large records), and BIOS disk seek. Look also for benchmarks that measure the system's performance under Microsoft* Windows 95 *and* Operating System/2 (OS/2), *for which video speed is critical.*

In *modems*, the rate at which data moves from one modem to another, including the effects of *data-compression* and *error-correction protocols*.

thumbnails   See *roughs*.

thunking   The means by which a 32-bit *operating system*, such as *Microsoft Windows 95* or *Operating System/2 (OS/2)*, communicates with a 16-bit *application program*. A computer system slows significantly when it must pause to thunk, which is why 32-bit application programs will soon become the norm.

.TIF   The *MS-DOS file name extension* usually attached to a file containing *graphics* in *Tagged Image File Format (TIFF)*. .TIF files often are used to hold scanned photographic images.

TIFF   See *Tagged Image File Format (TIFF)*.

tiled windows   In a *graphical user interface (GUI)*, a display mode in which all windows occupy an equal portion of screen space (see fig. T.5). If you open additional windows, the others are automatically sized so that you still see all of them. See *cascading windows* and *overlaid windows*.

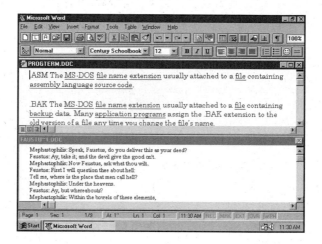

Fig. T.5   *Tiled windows in Microsoft Windows.*

timebomb   A *program*, either existing independently or built into a larger program, that waits until a specific day and time to come out of hiding and be disruptive. The famous Michelangelo *virus* activated itself on the birthday of the artist Michelangelo. See *Trojan horse*.

timed backup   A desirable *application program feature* that saves your work at a specified interval, such as every five minutes. Synonymous with autosave.

If a power outage or system *crash* occurs and a timed backup of your work has been performed, you'll be notified when you next start the program that a timed backup is available and asked whether you want to keep it. The best word processing programs include timed backup features that let you specify the interval.

CAUTION: *Using a timed backup feature is no substitute for saving your work to disk regularly. The files created by timed backup utilities are temporary files that are deleted when you exit the program properly. Use timed backups, but don't forget to save your work. See* backup procedure, save, *and* tape drive.

time division multiplexing In *local area networks (LANs),* a technique for transmitting two or more signals over the same cable by alternating them, one after the other. Time division is used in *baseband* (digital) networks. See *frequency division multiplexing.*

time out An interruption, resulting in a frozen *keyboard,* that occurs while the computer tries to access a device (or a remote computer) that isn't responding as it should. The computer keeps trying for a predetermined time and then gives up, returning control to you.

time-sharing A technique for sharing a *multiuser system's* resources in which each user has the illusion that he or she is the only person using the system. In the largest *mainframe* systems, hundreds or even thousands of people can use the system simultaneously without realizing that others are doing so. At times of peak usage, however, system response time tends to decline noticeably.

 tin A *UseNet newsreader program* for *UNIX* computers. Developed by Iain Lee, this *threaded newsreader* offers powerful features like its other UNIX *newsreader* counterparts, but is much easier to use. See *nn* and *trn.*

title bar In *graphical user interfaces (GUIs)* such as *Operating System/2 (OS/2),* a bar that stretches across the top of a *window,* indicating the name of the document displayed in that window. The color of the title bar indicates whether the window is active.

toggle To switch back and forth between two modes or states. On the *IBM PC-compatible keyboard,* for example, the Caps Lock key is a toggle key. When you press the key the first time, you switch the keyboard into a capitals-only mode. When you press the key the second time, you switch the keyboard back to the normal mode, in which you must press the Shift key to type capital letters.

**S
T
U
V**

toggle key   A *key* that switches back and forth between two modes. See *Caps Lock key, Num Lock key, Scroll Lock key,* and *toggle.*

token passing   In *local area networks (LANs),* a *network protocol* in which a special *bit* configuration, called a token, is circulated among the *workstations.* A *node* can send information across the network only if the node can obtain a free token, in which case the node converts the token into a data frame containing a network message. Nodes constantly monitor the network to catch tokens addressed to them.

Because token passing rules out the data collisions that occur when two devices begin transmitting at the same time, this channel access method is preferred for large, high-volume networks. See *carrier sense multiple access with collision detection (CSMA/CD), contention, local area network (LAN),* and *polling.*

token-ring network   A *local area network (LAN)* architecture that combines *token passing* with a hybrid star/ring topology.

Developed by *IBM* and announced in 1986, the IBM Token-Ring Network uses a Multistation Access Unit at its hub. This unit is wired with *twisted-pair* cable in a star configuration with up to 255 workstations, but the resulting network is actually a decentralized ring network.

toner   The electrically charged ink used in *laser printers* and photocopying machines. To form the image, toner is applied to an electrostatically charged drum and fused to the paper by a heating element. See *toner cartridge.*

toner cartridge   In *laser printers,* a cartridge containing the *toner* that the printer fuses to the page.

toolbar   A bar across the top of a *window* containing *push-buttons*, each with a distinctive *icon* (see fig. T.6). These icons represent frequently accessed commands.

Fig. T.6   *A toolbar.*

Only *Microsoft* and *Macintosh* use the term toolbar. The bar of buttons with icons found in other applications may be called speedbars, SmartIcons, powerbars, and button bars. See *icon bar.*

toolbox   A set of *programs* that helps *programmers* develop *software* without having to create basic *routines* from scratch. Some software publishers call these sets developer's toolkits.

In programs such as drawing and *presentation graphics* applications, the on-screen *icon* bar of drawing tools is called the toolbox.

toolkit   See *toolbox.*

top-down programming   A method of *program* design and development in which the design process begins with a statement (in English) of the program's fundamental purpose. This purpose is broken into a set of subcategories that describe aspects of the program's anticipated functions. Each subcategory corresponds to a specific program module that can be coded independently. *Structured programming* languages (such as *Pascal, C,* and Modula-2) and object-oriented programming languages (such as *C++*) are especially amenable to the top-down approach.

topology   See *network topology.*

TOPS   A file-serving program for *local area networks (LANs)* that allows *IBM PC-compatible* and *Macintosh* computers to be linked in an *AppleTalk* or *EtherNet network.* TOPS allows Macintosh and PC users to share *files* more or less seamlessly.

File-serving software provides peer-to-peer file transfer in which each user has access to the public files located on the workstations of all other users in the network. When a TOPS user decides to make a file public, he or she publishes the file on the network. Every *node* on the network, therefore, is potentially a *file server.*

S
T
U
V

touch screen   See *touch-sensitive display.*

touch-sensitive display   A *display* designed with a pressure-sensitive panel mounted in front of the screen; synonymous with touch screen. You select options by pressing the screen at the appropriate place.

Hewlett-Packard championed the touch-sensitive display concept in the mid 1980s, but users disliked it because the screen quickly became smudged and unreadable. Touch-sensitive displays are now used for public-access information purposes in such settings as museums, supermarkets, and airports.

tower case   A *system unit case* designed to stand vertically on the floor rather than sit horizontally on a desk. Tower cases usually have much more room for accessories than *desktop cases* and permit you to move noisy components, including cooling fans and hard disks, away from the immediate work area. They allow you more flexibility in positioning your *monitor* carefully, but they're inconvenient if you must frequently insert *floppy disks* or *CD-ROMs* into your system.

tpi   See *tracks per inch (tpi).*

track   On a *floppy* or *hard disk,* one of many concentric rings that are encoded on the disk during the low-level format and that define distinct areas of data storage on the disk. See *cluster* and *sector.*

trackball   An input device, designed to replace the *mouse,* that moves the mouse pointer on-screen as you use your thumb or fingers to rotate a ball embedded in the *keyboard* or in a case near the keyboard. Unlike a mouse, a trackball doesn't require a flat, clean surface to operate; as a result, trackballs are often used with portable or notebook computers. See *built-in pointing device, clip-on pointing device, freestanding pointing device,* and *snap-on pointing device.*

CAUTION: *If you're shopping for a portable computer, watch out for keyboard arrangements that place the trackball in an extra-wide area below the space bar. This space provides a convenient and inviting area to rest your hands while you type, a practice that may eventually lead to repetitive strain injury (RSI).*

track buffering   A *hard disk* design feature in which the entire contents of a hard disk *track* are read into a memory area, regardless of how much of the information on the track is requested by the *hard disk controller* and *host adapter*. Track buffering eliminates the need for *interleaving*, so all track-buffered disks (all modern hard disks and most *Enhanced Small Device Interface (EDSI)* drives are track-buffered) should have *interleave factors* of 1.

trackpad   A pointing device that allows you to move the mouse pointer by sliding a finger around on a touch-sensitive surface. To click, you tap your finger on the surface or press a button.

tracks per inch (tpi)   A measurement of the data-storage density of magnetic disks, such as *floppy disks*. The greater the tpi, the more data the disk can hold. In *DOS*, *double-density 5 1/4-inch floppy disks* are formatted with 48 tpi, and *high-density* 5 1/4-inch disks are formatted with 96 tpi. High-density *3 1/2-inch floppy disks* are formatted with 135 tpi.

track-to-track seek time   The time a hard or floppy disk drive requires to move the *read/write head* from one *track* to the next. Track-to-track seek time is much less important than *access time* in comparing disk drives.

tractor feed   A *printer* paper-feed mechanism in which *continuous paper* is pulled (or pushed) into and through the printer with a sprocket wheel. The sprockets fit into pre-punched holes on the left and right edges of the paper. *Dot-matrix printers* normally come with tractor-feed mechanisms. Tractor-feed printers require you spend time carefully separating the pages after printing.

traffic   The volume of messages sent over a *network*.

transactional application   In a *local area network (LAN)*, a program that creates and maintains a master record of all the transactions in which *network* participants engage, such as filling out invoices or time-billing forms. If a system *crash* results in the loss of data, this record can be used to restore data files to an earlier state. See *non-transactional application*.

transceiver   In *wireless wide-area networks (WANs)*, a *modem* that can send and receive data via radio frequencies. See *personal digital assistant (PDA)*.

**S
T
U
V**

transfer rate The number of *bytes* of data that can be transferred per second from a disk to the *microprocessor,* after the *read/write head* reaches the data.

The maximum transfer rate is limited by how fast the disk rotates and the *areal density* of the data on the disk (or how fast data passes under the drive head). These inflexible hardware limitations can be overcome by caching disk information. See *access time, Enhanced System Device Interface (ESDI), hardware cache,* and *Small Computer System Interface (SCSI).*

transient See *power surge.*

transient command See *external command.*

transistor-transistor logic (TTL) monitor An obsolete type of *monochrome monitor* that accepts *digital video signals.* TTL monitors work only with *Hercules* and *MDA video adapters,* and have been replaced by monitors that conform to *Video Graphics Array (VGA)* and *Super VGA* display standards.

translate To convert a *data file* from one *file format* to another, or to convert a *program* from one *programming language* or *operating system* to another.

Transmission Control Protocol (TCP) On the *Internet,* the protocol (standard) that permits two Internet-connected computers to establish a reliable connection. TCP ensures reliable data delivery with a method known as Positive Acknowledgment with Re-Transmission (PAR). The computer that sends the data continues to do so until it receives a confirmation from the receiving computer that the data has been received intact. See *Internet Protocol* and *Transmission Control Protocol/Internet Protocol (TCP/IP).*

Transmission Control Protocol/Internet Protocol (TCP/IP) The set of standards (protocols) for data transmission and error correction that allows the transfer of data from one *Internet*-linked computer to another. See *Transmission Control Protocol (TCP)* and *Internet Protocol (IP).*

transparency A see-through piece of acetate that can be displayed during presentations by overhead projection. *Laser* and *ink jet printers* can both print transparencies, but be sure to get the right kind of transparency material—ink jet transparency material will melt inside a laser printer.

transparency adapter   A *scanner* attachment that lets it scan slides and *transparencies*.

transparent   A computer operation or entity that programmers have made invisible so that you don't have to deal with it.

A transparent computer function is present, but you can't see it; a *virtual* computer function isn't present, but you can see it. *Microsoft Word*, for example, inserts formatting codes in your document, but they're transparent—you see only your formatted text. A *random-access memory (RAM)* disk drive, in contrast, isn't a disk drive at all; it's just part of your computer's memory, set aside to act like a disk drive.

transpose   To change the order in which characters, words, or sentences are displayed. Some *word processing programs* include commands that transpose text.

trapping   See *error trapping*.

tree structure   A way of organizing *information* into a hierarchical structure with a root and branches, much like a family tree or genealogy chart. See *directory* and *subdirectory*.

trellis-code modulation (TCM)   A *group coding modulation* technique employed by *high speed modems*. By enabling a modem to alter the *carrier* in a variety of ways, TCM enables modems to communicate at *data transfer rates* of 9600 *bits per second (bps)* or faster.

Trinitron   A *cathode ray tube (CRT)* design that, instead of a *shadow mask*, has an *aperture grill* to ensure that electrons from the *electron guns* hit the proper *pixels* on the *display*. An invention of Sony, Trinitron monitors are uniformly bright all over the display, unlike other monitor designs that are less bright around the edges. On the down side, Trinitron monitors have *tensioning wires* that sometimes cast shadows on the display.

triple-pass scanner   A *color scanner* that gathers data about one of the primary colors on each of three *scanning passes*. Triple-pass scanners are not necessarily slower than *single-pass scanners*, but the extra scanning passes can put extra wear on the scanning mechanism.

trn   A *UseNet newsreader* for *UNIX computer systems*. A *threaded newsreader* that is able to show the chain of discussion in a newsgroup, trn is a successor to the widely used *rn*. Somewhat difficult to learn and use, trn is a powerful program that offers many advanced features (such as the ability to decode binary postings).

Trojan horse   A *program* that appears to perform a valid function but contains, hidden in its code, instructions that cause damage (sometimes severe) to the systems on which it runs.

Trojan horses, unlike computer *viruses,* can't replicate themselves, but that may be small consolation indeed to someone who has just lost days or weeks of work.

trolling   In *UseNet*, posting a facetious message containing an obvious exaggeration or factual error. The troller hopes to trick a gullible person into posting a follow-up article pointing out the error.

troubleshooting   The process of determining why a *computer system* or specific *hardware* device is malfunctioning.

> **CAUTION:** *Many users automatically reboot the system whenever there is a problem. Rebooting may overwrite the very data you need to solve the problem. Always have a floppy disk formatted as a system disk readily available so that it can be used if you need to reboot the system.*

When a computer fails, most people panic and assume that a huge bill is on the way. Most likely, however, the problem is a minor one, such as a loose connection. Turn off the power and carefully inspect all the cables and connections. Remove the *case* lid and press down on the *adapters* to make sure that they're well seated in the *expansion slots.* You also should check connections at *peripheral* devices.

True BASIC   A modern, structured version of the *BASIC programming language* developed by its originators, John Kemeny and Thomas Kurtz, in response to criticism of earlier versions of BASIC.

With modern control structures and optional line numbers, True BASIC is a well-structured language used to teach the principles of *structured programming.* The language, which is interpreted rather than compiled, isn't frequently used for professional programming purposes.

TrueType A *font* technology, included with *Apple Computer's System 7* and *Microsoft Windows 95*, that brings *scalable fonts* to the screens and *printers* of *Macintosh* and Windows systems. Jointly developed by Apple Computer and Microsoft Corporation, TrueType offers a cost-effective alternative to *PostScript* font technology. TrueType doesn't require an add-on *utility program* or an expensive, *microprocessor*-driven *interpreter*. The TrueType fonts you see on-screen are exactly the same as the ones you see when you print your document.

With TrueType, you can print your documents on other systems or printers without going through the hassle of reformatting the fonts. Even programs such as WordPerfect 6.0 for DOS now can use the TrueType fonts stored in the Windows SYSTEM subdirectory.

Trumpet Winsock A widely used *shareware* program that provides *TCP/IP* support for early Microsoft Windows systems. Written by Peter Tattam (a trumpet player, incidentally, and a programmer at an Australian university), the program includes a dialer utility and is compatible with the *Winsock* specification.

truncate To cut off part of a number or character string.

truncation error A rounding error that occurs when part of a number is omitted from storage because it exceeds the capacity of the *memory* set aside for number storage. See *floating-point calculation*.

TSR See *terminate-and-stay-resident (TSR) program*.

TTL monitor See *transistor-transistor logic (TTL) monitor*.

TTY See *teletype (TTY) display*.

Turbo Pascal A high-performance *compiler* developed by Borland International for *Pascal*. The compiler comes with a full-screen *text editor*, and creates executable programs (*object code*). Outperforming compilers that cost 10 times as much, Turbo Pascal took the world of DOS programming by storm when released in 1984 and is now one of the most popular compilers ever written.

S
T
U
V

Turbo Pascal is used in hobby and academic environments, and some professional *programmers* use Turbo Pascal to prepare short- to medium-sized programs. See *interpreter*.

turnkey system   A *computer system* developed for a specific application, such as a point-of-sale terminal, and delivered ready to run, with all the necessary *application programs* and *peripherals*.

tutorial   A form of instruction in which the student is guided step-by-step through the application of a program to a specific task, such as developing a budget or writing a business letter. Some *programs* come with on-screen tutorials.

tweak   To adjust a program or computer system slightly to improve performance. An unethical researcher might alter an underlying variable slightly so *program* output is more in line with what is expected.

twisted pair   An improved physical medium for *local area networks (LANs)* and telephone service to homes and offices. Twisted pair wiring consists of two insulated copper cables that are twisted together like a braid, thus randomizing interference from other electrical circuits. Unlike the plain copper cable used in pre-1970 telephone installations, twisted pair can handle computer data and is sufficient for *Basic Rate ISDN (BRI)*. See *Integrated Services Digital Network (ISDN)*.

two-way set-associative cache   A *secondary cache* memory design that is faster than the *direct-map cache* design, but less ex- pensive than the *four-way set-associative cache*, which is the fastest of the three.

.TXT   The *MS-DOS file name extension* usually attached to a file containing *ASCII* text.

Type 1 font   A *PostScript*-compatible font that includes Adobe Systems' proprietary font-scaling technology, which improves type legibility at low resolutions and small type sizes. See *PostScript font*.

type size   The size of a *font*, measured in *points* (approximately 1/72 inch) from the top of the tallest *ascender* to the bottom of the lowest *descender*. See *pitch*.

type style   The weight (such as bold) or posture (such as italic) of a font distinguished from a font's typeface design and type size. See *attribute* and *emphasis*.

typeface   The distinctive design of a set of type, distinguished from its weight (such as *bold*), posture (such as *italic*), and *type size*.

Many *laser printers* come with as many as a dozen or more typefaces available in the printer's *read-only memory (ROM)*, and literally hundreds more can be downloaded. Notice that professional graphic artists rarely use more than two typefaces in one document. They choose one typeface for *display type* and a second for *body type*. See *font* and *font family*.

typeover   See *overtype mode*.

typeover mode   See *overtype mode*.

typesetter   See *imagesetter*.

typesetting   The production of *camera-ready copy* on a high-end *imagesetter*—such as a Linotronic or Varityper.

The current crop of office-quality *PostScript laser printers* can produce 1200-*dots-per-inch (dpi)* output, which is considered crude by professional typesetting standards, but which may be acceptable for applications such as newsletters, textbooks, instructional manuals, brochures, and proposals. See *resolution*.

typography   The science and art of designing aesthetically pleasing and readable *typefaces*.

S
T
U
V

UART   See *Universal Asynchronous Receiver/Transmitter (UART)*.

ultra-large scale integration (ULSI)   In *integrated circuit* technology, the fabrication of a chip containing more than one million transistors. The *Pentium* chip, for example, includes more than three million transistors.

unauthorized access   A computer break-in, done by a computer *cracker* for criminal or ego-boosting purposes. Unauthorized access is a crime in most states.

undelete utility   A *utility program* that can restore a file that was accidentally deleted from a disk.

Available from commercial and *shareware* sources, undelete utilities work because files aren't actually erased from disk drives; DOS changes the first letter of the file's name in the directory list to a non-displaying character. This makes the clusters used by the file available to the operating system for additional write operations. If such operations occur, the file can be erased irretrievably. The *Macintosh, Operating System/2 (OS/2),* and *Microsoft Windows 95* environments make file recovery easy—just drag the "deleted" file out of the Trash Can or Recycle Bin.

undo   A command that restores a *program* and your data to the stage they were in just before the last command was given or the last action was initiated. Undo commands let you reverse the often catastrophic effects of giving the wrong command.

unformat utility   A *utility program* that can restore the data on an inadvertently formatted disk. If the disk has been formatted using a safe-format technique, the data is restored quickly. If the disk hasn't been *safe formatted,* you can recover the data if you've been using the Mirror utility, provided with DOS beginning with Version 5.0 and with PC Tools.

unformatted text file   See *plain text document*.

Uniform Resource Identifier (URI)   A string of characters that identifies an Internet resource, including the type of resource and its location. There are two types of URIs: U*niform Resource Locators (URLs)* and *Relative URLs (RELURL).*

 Uniform Resource Locator (URL) One of two basic kinds of *Universal Resource Identifiers (URI),* a string of characters that precisely identifies an *Internet* resource's type and location. For example, the following fictitious URL identifies a *World Wide Web* document (http://), indicates the domain name of the computer on which it is stored (www.wolverine.virginia.edu), fully describes the document's location within the directory structure (~toros/winerefs/), and includes the document's name and extension (merlot.html).

```
http://www.wolverine.virginia.edu/~toros/
winerefs/merlot.html
```

See *Relative URL (RELURL).*

uninterruptible power supply (UPS) A battery that can supply continuous power to a *computer system* in the event of a power failure. The battery, charged while your computer is switched on, kicks in if the power fails and provides power for 10 minutes or more, during which time you can save files and shut down the computer to preserve the integrity of crucial data.

TIP: *An uninterruptible power supply is mandatory equipment if a sudden power outage will result in the loss of crucial data.*

Universal Asynchronous Receiver/Transmitter (UART) An integrated circuit that transforms the parallel data stream within the computer to the serial, one-after-the-other data stream used in *asynchronous communications.*

Serial communication requires, in addition to the UART, a serial port and modem. See *modem, motherboard,* and *serial port.*

UNIX An *operating system* used on a wide variety of computers, from *mainframes* to *personal computers,* that supports multitasking and is ideally suited to multiuser applications. UNIX is a very flexible operating system, well-suited to the needs of advanced computer users.

With more than 200 commands, inadequate error messages, and a cryptic command *syntax,* however, UNIX imposes heavy burdens on occasional users and the technically unsophisticated. With the development of UNIX *shells* such as NeXTStep, the operating system may play a much wider role in computing.

Because Bell Laboratories was prohibited from marketing UNIX by the antitrust regulations governing AT&T before the 1980s, UNIX was provided without charge to colleges and universities throughout North America, beginning in 1976. In 1979, the University of California at Berkeley developed a popular version of UNIX for VAX computers. In the early 1980s, AT&T gained the right to market the system and released System V in 1983. See *Berkeley UNIX, System V Interface Definition (SVID)* and *Linux, Wide Area Information Server (WAIS)*.

UNIX-to-UNIX Copy Program (UUCP) A *network*, based on long-distance telephone *uploads* and *downloads*. UUCP allows *UNIX* users to exchange files, *electronic mail*, and *UseNet* articles. In the 1980s, when *Internet* connectivity was hard to come by, UUCP played an important role in providing support for the UNIX *operating system*.

unmoderated newsgroup In a distributed *bulletin board system (BBS)* such as *EchoMail* (*FidoNet*) or *UseNet* (Internet), a topical discussion group in which postings aren't subject to review before distribution. Unmoderated newsgroups are characterized by spontaneity, but some postings may be inflammatory or inconsiderate, and *flame wars* may erupt. See *moderated newsgroup* and *newsgroup*.

unordered list In *HyperText Markup Language (HTML)*, a bulleted list created with <UL>...</UL> tags. Text tagged as an unordered list often appears bulleted.

unsubscribe In *UseNet*, to remove a *newsgroup* from your subscription list, so that it does not appear on the list of newsgroups you are actively following. You can also unsubscribe from a mailing list, so things sent to the list no longer come to you. See *subscribe*.

update In *database management*, a fundamental data manipulation that involves adding, modifying, or deleting data records so that data is brought up-to-date.

upgrade To buy a new release or version of a *program*, or a more recent or more powerful version of a *microprocessor* or *peripheral*.

upload   To send a file by *telecommunications* to another computer user or a *bulletin board system (BBS)*.

upper memory area   In an *IBM PC-compatible* computer running *MS-DOS*, the memory between the 640K limit of *conventional memory* and 1024K. In the original PC system design, some of the memory in this area was reserved for system use, but most was actually unused. Memory management programs, as well as *HIMEM.SYS,* available with MS-DOS 6.2, can configure the upper memory area so that it's available for system utilities and application programs. See *Microsoft Windows 95.*

UPS   See *uninterruptible power supply (UPS).*

upward compatibility   Software that functions, without modification, on later or more powerful versions of a *computer system.*

UseNet   The leading *distributed bulletin board,* widely available on *UNIX*-based *computer systems,* and linked through the *Internet* and other computer networks. Offering more than 1,500 *newsgroups,* UseNet is accessed daily by more than 15 million people in more than 100 countries.

Within UseNet is a discussion group (newsgroup) on every conceivable topic and some you haven't thought of. Each newsgroup focuses on a particular subject, such as sports cars, firearms, U.S. history, model aircraft, politics, or jazz. Well-represented subjects are hobbies, politics, scientific disciplines, and topics of current public debate. UseNet users can read and reply to posted messages.

The following is a sample of UseNet newsgroups:

- `alt.alien.visitors`   Unidentified flying objects, saucer watches, contact of prehistoric civilizations with alien intruders, tales of UFO abductions, secret government UFO files retrieved from top-secret computers by hackers, technical description of an alien warp drive engine under study at a secret Air Force base, and disturbing reports of phantom helicopters.

- `alt.rush-limbaugh`   Transcriptions of broadcasts, commentary, and debate on points raised by Mr. Limbaugh, such as whether the death of White House aide Vince Foster had anything to do with President and Mrs. Clinton's alleged involvement in the Whitewater affair.

**S
T
U
V**

- `clari.news.disasters` UPI news reports (the same ones the newspapers get) computer-sorted by topic on disasters of all kinds: tornadoes, hurricanes, earthquakes, typhoons, elevators dropping like stones, 50-gallon water heaters exploding and bursting through the roof "like a rocket," plane crashes, Autobahn pile-ups, the works.

- `rec.arts.drwho` Episode titles and summaries, endless discussions of plot loopholes and blunders, parodies, and occasional notes on related subjects, such as Sinbad movies and trivia regarding the sinking of the Titanic.

See distributed bulletin board, Internet, moderated newsgroup, and newsgroup.

UseNet site A *computer system*—one with lots of disk storage—that receives a news feed and enables dozens or hundreds of people to participate in UseNet. Currently, there are approximately 120,000 UseNet sites in existence, providing an estimated four million people with access to UseNet newsgroups.

user See *end user*.

user agent (UA) In the terminology established by the *Open System Interconnection (OSI) Reference Model*, a client program that runs on the user's machine and assists in contacting a server. You may run across this term in references to electronic mail clients such as Eudora or Pegasus Mail.

user default A user-defined program operating preference, such as the default margins for every new *document* that a *word processing program* creates. Also called preferences, options, or setup in various applications.

user-defined Selected or chosen by the user of the *computer system*.

user-friendly A *program* or *computer system* designed so that individuals who lack extensive computer experience or training can use the system without becoming confused or frustrated.

In a user-friendly program, *menus* are used instead of commands you have to memorize; on-screen help is available easily; error messages contain an explanation of what went wrong and what to do; and intermediate and advanced features are hidden from view so that they don't clutter the screen and confuse beginners. User-friendly programs also make it hard to accidentally delete data and often include *tutorials*.

user group   A voluntary association of users of a specific *computer system* or *program* who meet regularly to exchange tips and techniques, hear presentations by computer experts, and obtain *public domain software* and *shareware*.

user interface   All the features of a program or computer that govern the way people interact with the computer. See *command-driven program* and *graphical user interface (GUI)*.

> **TIP:** *Inexperienced users should be assured that user-friendly doesn't guarantee success. Don't give up too soon, learn to read the documentation, and expect to be challenged—even frustrated—from time to time no matter how experienced you become.*

utility program   A *program* that assists you in maintaining and improving the efficiency of a *computer system*.

Microsoft Plus! includes the *System Agent,* a utility program that defragments your hard disk, compresses rarely used files, and corrects minor disk problems. You can set the System Agent to work any time you leave your computer alone for a certain period of time, or to run early in the morning every day.

UUCP   See *UNIX-to-UNIX Copy Program (UUCP).*

uudecode   A *UNIX utility program* that decodes a *uuencoded ASCII file*, restoring the original *binary file* (such as a program or graphic). A uudecode utility is needed to decode the binary files posted to *UseNet*. Programs with uudecoding capabilities are available for *Macintosh* and *Microsoft Windows 95* systems, and are often built into UseNet *newsreaders*.

uuencode   A *UNIX utility program* that transforms a *binary file*, such as a program or *graphic*, into coded *ASCII text*. This text can be transferred by means of the *Internet* or posted to a *UseNet newsgroup*. At the receiving end, the *uudecode* utility decodes the message and restores the binary file. Programs with uuencoding capabilities are available for *Macintosh* and *Microsoft Windows 95* systems, and are often built into UseNet *newsreaders*.

S
T
U
V

V.17   An *International Telecommunications Union-Telecommunications Standards Section (ITU-TSS) modulation protocol* for transmitting and receiving *faxes* at speeds up to 14,400 *bits per second (bps).*

V.21   An *International Telecommunications Union-Telecommunications Standards Section (ITU-TSS) modulation protocol* for *modems* transmitting and receiving data at 300 *bits per second (bps).* V.21 conflicts with the *Bell 103* standard once widely used in the United States and Canada.

V.22   An *International Telecommunications Union-Telecommunications Standards Section (ITU-TSS) modulation protocol* for *modems* transmitting and receiving data at 1200 *bits per second (bps).* V.22 conflicts with the *Bell 212A* standard once widely used in the United States and Canada.

V.22bis   An *International Telecommunications Union-Telecommunications Standards Section (ITU-TSS) modulation protocol* for *modems* transmitting and receiving data at 2400 *bits per second (bps).* V.22 bis modems can *fall back* to slower data transfer rates if necessary, but they are obsolete—replaced by the *V.32 bis* standard that costs little, if at all, extra.

V.27ter   An *International Telecommunications Union-Telecommunications Standards Section (ITU-TSS) modulation protocol* for *fax modems* and *fax* machines transmitting and receiving fax information at 4800 *bits per second (bps).* V.27ter *modems* can *fall back* to 2400 bps if necessary.

V.29   An *International Telecommunications Union-Telecommunications Standards Section (ITU-TSS) modulation protocol* for *fax modems* and *fax* machines transmitting and receiving data at 9600 *bits per second (bps).* V.29 modems can *fall back* to 7200 bps if *line noise* dictates such a switch.

V.32   An *International Telecommunications Union-Telecommunications Standards Section (ITU-TSS) modulation protocol* for *modems* transmitting and receiving data at 9600 *bits per second (bps).*

Modems compliant with the v.32 standard can *fall back* to 4800 bps if needed, but use *trellis-code modulation* only at 9600 bps.

V.32bis An *International Telecommunications Union-Telecommunications Standards Section (ITU-TSS) modulation protocol* for *modems* transmitting and receiving data at 14,400 *bits per second (bps)*. Modems that use the v.32 bis standard are very common, and can transfer data at 12,000 bps, 9600 bps, 7200 bps, and 4800 bps if needed.

V.32 terbo A *proprietary* modulation protocol developed by AT&T to regulate *modems* transmitting and receiving data at 19,200 *bits per second (bps)* and *fall back*, if needed, to the *data transfer rates* supported by the *v.32 bis* standard. Despite its sneaky name, v.32 terbo is not recognized by the *International Telecommunications Union-Telecommunications Standards Section (ITU-TSS)*. The *V.34* standard has replaced v.32 terbo.

V.34 An *International Telecommunications Union-Telecommunications Standards Section (ITU-TSS) modulation protocol* for *modems* transmitting and receiving data at 28,800 *bits per second (bps)*. V.34 modems adjust to changing line conditions to achieve the highest possible *data transfer rate*.

V.42 An *International Telecommunications Union-Telecommunications Standards Section (ITU-TSS) error-correction protocol* designed to counter the effects of *line noise*. A pair of V.42-compliant *modems* will check each transmitted piece of data to make sure they arrive error-free, and retransmit any faulty data. The V.42 standard uses *the Link Access Protocol for Modems (LAPM)* as its default error-correction method, but will switch to *MNP4* if needed.

V.42bis An *International Telecommunications Union-Telecommunications Standards Section (ITU-TSS) compression protocol* that increases the *throughput* of *modems*. V.42bis is an o*n-the-fly compression* technique that reduces the amount of data a modem needs to transmit.

vaccine A *program* designed to offer protection against *viruses*. By adding a small amount of code to files, an alert sounds when a *virus* tries to change the file. Vaccines are also called immunizing programs.

**S
T
U
V**

CAUTION: *The malevolent authors of computer viruses are aware of vaccines and antivirus programs and are busy creating new viruses to thwart them. If you use your computer for vital business or professional applications, protect your data by introducing to your computer only fresh, previously unopened copies of software obtained directly from computer software publishers or reputable retailers.*

validation   In *programming*, proving that a program does its job. Many programmers prefer the term "validation" to "testing" or "debugging," since it has a more positive ring.

value   In a *spreadsheet* program, a numeric cell entry.

Two kinds of values exist. The first kind, called a constant, is a value you type directly into a *cell*. The second kind of value looks like a constant but is produced by a *formula* placed into a cell. Be careful not to confuse the two and type a constant over a formula. See *cell protection* and *label*.

value-added reseller (VAR)   A business that repackages and improves *hardware* manufactured by an *original equipment manufacturer (OEM)*. A value-added reseller typically improves the original equipment by adding superior *documentation*, packaging, system integration, and exterior finish. Some VARs, however, do little more than put their name on a device.

vanilla   Plain and unadorned, without bells, whistles, or advanced *features*, as in, "I'm using a plain vanilla 486." See *bells and whistles*.

vaporware   A *program* that's heavily marketed even though it's still under development, and no one knows whether its development problems will be solved.

variable   In *programming*, a named area in *memory* that stores a value or string assigned to that variable.

VBA   See *Visual Basic for Applications (VBA)*.

VDT   Abbreviation for video display terminal. Synonymous with *monitor*.

VDT radiation   See *cathode ray tube (CRT)* and *extremely low-frequency (ELF) emission*.

VDU   Abbreviation for video display unit. Synonymous with *monitor.*

vector font   See *outline font.*

vector graphics   See *object-oriented graphic.*

vector-to-raster conversion program   A *utility program* available with many professional illustration programs, such as CorelDRAW!, that transforms object-oriented (vector) graphics into *bit-mapped (raster) graphic* images. See *object-oriented graphic.*

vendor   A seller or supplier of *computers systems*, peripherals, or computer-related services.

Vendor Independent Messaging (VIM)   In *electronic mail* programs, an *application program interface (API)* that lets electronic mail programs from different manufacturers exchange mail with one another. The consortium of developers that designed VIM did not include *Microsoft Corporation*, which uses the *Messaging Application Program Interface (MAPI)*. A VIM-to-MAPI *dynamic link library (DLL)* file makes it possible for the two interfaces to exchange messages.

verify   To determine the accuracy and completion of a computer operation.

Veronica   In *Gopher*, a search service that scans a database of Gopher directory titles and resources (such as *documents*, *graphics*, movies, and sounds), and generates a new Gopher menu containing the results of the search. See *Jughead.*

version   A specific release of a *software* or *hardware* product.

A larger version number indicates a more recent product release. For example, MS-DOS 6.22 is a more recent product than MS-DOS 5.0. In many cases, version numbers are skipped, such as 3.4 to 3.9 in the MS-DOS example. Revisions that repair minor bugs, called bug fixes or *maintenance releases,* often have small intermediate numbers such as 1.02 or 1.2a.

It's unclear what the effect will be of *Microsoft Corporation's* decision to name its new *operating system* "*Microsoft Windows 95*" instead of "Microsoft Windows 4.0." It's possible that as the market for computer products broadens—and encompasses people unfamiliar with technical conventions, such as version numbers—programs will be named like cars. Changing the name of products each year could encourage sales to buyers who *must* have the latest thing on their computers.

verso   In printing, the left-side, even-numbered page in a two page spread. See *recto*.

vertical application   An *application program* created for a narrowly defined market, such as the members of a profession or a specific type of retail store, usually designed to provide complete management functions such as scheduling, billing, inventory control, and purchasing.

vertical centering   The automatic centering of graphics or text vertically on the page. *WordPerfect*, for example, includes a Center Top to Bottom command that centers text vertically.

vertical frequency   See *vertical refresh rate*.

vertical justification   The alignment of *newspaper columns* by means of *feathering* (adding vertical space) so all columns end evenly at the bottom margin. A *page layout program* capable of vertical justification inserts white space between frame borders and text, between paragraphs, and between lines to even the columns at the bottom margin.

vertical market program   See *vertical application*.

vertical refresh rate   The rate at which a *monitor* and *video adapter* pass the *electron guns* of a *cathode ray tube (CRT)* from the top of the display to the bottom. Measured in *Hertz (Hz)*, refresh rate determines whether a display appears to *flicker*. At a *resolution* of 1280 *pixels* by 1024 lines, a refresh rate of 72 Hz or more will eliminate visible flicker.

vertical retrace   The process of the electron beam in a *cathode ray tube (CRT)* being directed by the *yoke* from the end of one vertical scan to the beginning of the next. *Video adapters* must allow time for vertical retrace in preparing the video signal. During vertical retrace, *blanking* is in effect.

vertically flat   A *monitor* design, used in *Trinitron*-type and other monitors, that somewhat reduces image distortion. Vertically flat displays are curved like cylinders, instead of like spheres, as most *cathode ray tubes (CRTs)* are. See *flat-square* and *flat tension-mask*.

very high-level language (VHL) A *declarative language* that is used to solve a particular kind of problem. VHLs, nearly all of which are *proprietary*, are used to generate *reports* in *spreadsheets* and *database management programs*.

very large scale integration (VLSI) A level of technological sophistication in the manufacturing of semiconductor *chips* that allows the equivalent of more than 100,000—and up to 1 million—transistors to be placed on one chip.

VESA Acronym for Video Electronics Standards Association. See *video standard* and *VL-Bus*.

VESA bus See *local bus* and *VL-Bus*.

VESA local bus A *local bus* design designed to work with the *Intel 486* and provide a standard to compete with incompatible *proprietary local buses*. VESA local bus *adapters* typically are used to connect *video adapters* and *network adapters* to the *expansion bus*.

CAUTION: *VESA local bus designs have been rendered obsolete for Pentium-based systems by Peripheral Component Interconnect (PCI) expansion buses, but are fine for 486-equipped systems.*

VESA local bus slot A socket for *adapters* found on *expansion buses* compatible with the *VESA local bus* standard. VESA local bus slots provide 32-bit communication between the *microprocessor* and *adapters*, and were common in computers based on various versions of the 486-class microprocessor. However, *Peripheral Component Interconnect (PCI) slots* are much more flexible than VESA local bus slots and are expected to be the standard used for the next several years. See *Industry Standard Architecture (ISA)* and *ISA slot*.

V.Fast Class (V.FC) A *proprietary* modulation protocol used by several *modem* manufacturers before the *V.34* standard was published. Most V.FC modems can be upgraded to comply fully with V.34.

V.FC See *V.Fast Class (V.FC)*.

VGA See *Video Graphics Array (VGA)*.

VHL See *very high-level language (VHL)*.

vi   A text editor that is configured to be the *default editor* on many *UNIX* systems. Notoriously difficult to learn, vi has little in common with *Macintosh* and *Microsoft Windows 95* word processing programs. To avoid vi, many UNIX users prefer to use applications that have their own, built-in text editors, such as the *electronic mail* program *pine*. See *emacs*.

video accelerator   See *graphics accelerator board*.

video adapter   The *adapter* that generates the output required to display text and *graphics* on a *monitor*.

When you select a video adapter, you also must choose a compatible monitor. Most modern computers have *Super VGA* video adapters and monitors. See *Color Graphics Adapter (CGA), Enhanced Graphics Adapter (EGA), Hercules Graphics Adapter, IBM 8514/A display adapter, monochrome display adapter (MDA), MultiColor Graphics Array (MCGA),* and *Video Graphics Array (VGA)*.

> **TIP:** *Video adapters are not the place to scrimp when shopping for a computer. Especially with modern* graphical user interfaces (GUIs), *a good video adapter can really speed up a system by taking some load off the central processing unit (CPU). Get a video adapter with at least 1M of* video random-access memory (VRAM); *dual-ported VRAM is best.*

video amplifier   Part of the *monitor* circuitry that increases the weak signal received from the *video adapter* to a level high enough to drive the *electron guns. Monochrome* monitors have one video amplifier while color monitors have three, carefully tuned to work together.

video board   See *video adapter*.

video capture camera   A video camera device that records data in the form of digitized images. The images are saved as *files* that later can be retrieved using appropriate *software*, making it possible to run the movies on-screen.

video capture card   An *adapter* that plugs into the computer's *expansion bus* and enables you to control a video camera or videocassette recorder (VCR) and manipulate its output.

Video capture cards usually *compress* the video input to a manageable size and are useful for developing *multimedia* presentations.

video card   See *graphics accelerator board.*

video controller   A *microprocessor* on the *video adapter* that reads the information in *display memory*, arranges it into a continuous stream, and sends it to the *monitor.*

videodisk   See *interactive videodisk.*

video driver   A *program* that tells other programs how to work with a particular *video adapter* and *monitor.* Video drivers often have user-accessible controls that determine *resolution, refresh rate,* and *color depth.*

Video Graphics Array (VGA)   A color *bit-mapped graphics* display standard, introduced by IBM in 1987 with its PS/2 computers. VGA *video adapters* and *analog monitors* display as many as 256 continuously variable colors simultaneously, with a resolution of 640 *pixels* horizontally by 480 lines vertically. VGA circuitry is downwardly compatible with all previous display standards, including *Color Graphics Adapter (CGA), monochrome display adapter (MDA),* and *Enhanced Graphics Adapter (EGA).*

The IBM VGA standard has been pushed to new heights by third-party vendors, who offer VGA adapters that can display two additional graphics modes—an enhanced *Super VGA* resolution of 800 pixels by 600 lines and even more advanced adapters with a resolution of 1,024 by 768—with up to 256 colors displayed simultaneously.

video memory   A set of memory *chips* to which the *central processing unit (CPU)* writes display information, and from which the *video controller* reads data prior to sending it to the *monitor.* Video memory often uses inexpensive *dynamic random-access memory (DRAM)* chips, but *high-end* video adapters use much faster *video random-access memory (VRAM).*

video monitor   See *monitor.*

video noise   Random dots of interference on a *display.* Synonymous with "snow." Video noise is rarely a problem in modern displays, but it caused problems for users of *Color Graphics Array (CGA) video adapters* and *monitors.*

S
T
U
V ◄

video RAM (VRAM)   Specially designed *dynamic random-access memory (DRAM)* chips that maximize the performance of video adapters. The central processing unit (CPU) loads display information into VRAM, which is then read by the video system. *High-end* VRAM, called dual-ported VRAM, allows simultaneous reading and writing of data. *See random-access memory (RAM)* and *video adapter.*

video signal   See *analog video signal and digital video signal.*

video standard   A standard for *displays* developed so *software* developers can anticipate how their *programs* will appear on-screen.

Video standards, such as *color graphics adapter (CGA), enhanced graphics adapter (EGA)* and *video graphics array (VGA),* are defined by industry groups and include specifications on, among other things, screen resolution and color capability. The VGA standard, for example, allows for resolution of 640 *pixels* by 480 lines, and 256 simultaneous colors. See *Extended Graphics Array (XGA), Hercules Graphics Adapter, MultiColor Graphics Array (MCGA),* and *Super VGA.*

videotext   The transmission of information—such as news headlines, stock quotes, and movie reviews—through a cable television system. See *on-line information service.*

view   In *database management programs,* an on-screen display of the information in a *database* that meets the criteria specified in a *query.* With most database management programs, you can save views; the best programs update each view every time you add or edit *data records.*

Also, to display an image on-screen from a different perspective, particularly with three-dimensional *computer-aided design (CAD)* drawings.

VIM   See *Vendor Independent Messaging (VIM).*

virtual   Not real; a computer representation of something that is real.

Virtual 8086 mode   A mode available with 80386 and higher *microprocessors,* in which the *chip* simulates an almost unlimited number of *Intel 8086* machines.

virtual community   A group of people who, although they may have never met, share interests and concerns and communicate with each other via *electronic mail* and *newsgroups*. The people who see themselves as members of such communities feel a sense of belonging and develop deep emotional ties with other participants, even though the relationships that develop are mediated by the computer and may never involve face-to-face interaction.

virtual corporation   A means of organizing a business in which the various units are geographically dispersed, but actively and fruitfully linked by the *Internet* or some other *wide-area network (WAN)*.

virtual device   The simulation of a computer device or *periph eral*, such as a *hard disk drive* or *printer*, that doesn't exist—at least not nearby.

In a *local area network (LAN)*, a computer may appear to have an enormous hard disk, which actually is made available to the *workstation* by means of the network links to *the file server*.

Virtual Device Driver (VxD)   In *Microsoft Windows 95*, a 32-bit program that manages a specific system resource, such as a sound card or printer. Unlike the device drivers used in Windows 3.1, Virtual Device Drivers run in the processor's *protected mode*, where they are less likely to conflict with other applications and cause system crashes. The abbreviation "VxD" covers a range of devices, including virtual printer devices (VPD), virtual display devices (VDD), and virtual timing devices (VTD).

Virtual Library   In the *World Wide Web (WWW)*, a subject tree in which volunteers take on the responsibility of maintaining the portion of the tree that is devoted to a specific subject, such as astronomy or zoology. The Virtual Library is a good place to look for academically oriented information on the Web. See *subject tree.*

virtual machine   In 80386 and higher *microprocessors*, a protected memory space created by the microprocessor's *hardware* capabilities. Each virtual machine can run its own *programs*, completely isolated from other machines. The virtual machines can also access the *keyboard*, *printer*, and other devices without conflicts. Virtual machines are made possible by a computer with the necessary processing circuitry and a lot of *random-access memory (RAM)*. See *Virtual 8086 mode.*

**S
T
U
V**

virtual memory   A method of extending the apparent size of *random-access memory (RAM)* by using part of the *hard disk* as an extension of RAM. Many application programs, such as *Microsoft Word*, routinely use the disk instead of memory to store some data or program instructions while you're running the program. See *virtual memory management*.

virtual memory management   The management of *virtual memory* operations at the *operating system* level rather than the *application program* level.

An advantage to implementing virtual memory at the operating system level rather than the application level is that any program can take advantage of the virtual memory, with the result that memory extends seamlessly from random-access memory (RAM) to the computer's secondary storage. *Microsoft Windows 95* can take full advantage of the virtual memory capabilities of virtual memory. In the *Macintosh* world, *Apple's System 7.5* makes virtual memory management available for users of 68030-based Macintoshes.

virtual reality (VR)   A *computer system* that can immerse the user in the illusion of a computer-generated world and permit the user to navigate through this world at will. Typically, the user wears a *head-mounted display (HMD)* that displays a stereoscopic image, and wears a *sensor glove*, which permits the user to manipulate "objects" in the virtual environment.

The range of potential applications includes architecture, for example, where VR systems will allow architects to present clients with three-dimensional VR "walkthroughs" of proposed structures; and physicians will be able to try out new surgical techniques within three-dimensional, simulated "patients."

VR's greatest commercial potential undoubtedly lies in the entertainment area. An example: NEC Corporation is demonstrating a "virtual skiing lab," in which virtual skiers don goggles, poles, and virtual skis. See *cyberspace, electrocutaneous feedback, second-person virtual reality, sensor glove, stereoscopy, teledildonics,* and *telepresence*.

 Virtual Shareware Library (VSL)   A popular *World Wide Web (WWW)* page that provides a search interface for several *File Transfer Protocol (FTP)* software *archives*, including the *Center for Innovative Computer Applications CICA,* SIM-WIN, SIMTEL,

GARBO, and many more. The service currently indexes 110,000 files totaling 13.6M.

virus A *program,* designed as a prank or as sabotage, that replicates itself by attaching to other programs and carrying out unwanted and sometimes damaging operations.

When viruses appear, the effects vary, ranging from prank messages to erratic system software performance or catastrophic erasure of all the information on a *hard disk.* Don't ever assume that a prank message means that's all the virus will do. See *antivirus program, Trojan horse,* and *vaccine.*

TIP: *To protect your system from computer viruses, observe the following rules:*

- *Don't download executable programs from public* bulletin board systems (BBSs) *unless you're certain they're virus free (you actually have seen someone else use the program without problems).*

- *Don't obtain executable programs from mail-order vendors of* public domain *or* shareware *programs unless they specifically promise to check each program they sell.*

- *Never download a recently uploaded program on a bulletin board until the* sysop *has checked it. When you do download the program, download it to a* floppy disk *so the program can't get near your hard disk.*

- *Don't copy pirated disks of commercial programs, because these disks may contain viruses.*

- *Buy and use virus-checking software.*

- *Install a memory-resident virus-checking program, such as PC Tools VSafe, which will examine files as you copy them onto your computer.*

Visual Basic A *high-level programming language* for developing applications designed to run in *Microsoft Windows 95.*

Using Visual Basic, the *programmer* uses a screen designer to set up the contents of a window, selecting control objects (*pushbuttons,* list boxes, etc.) from an on-screen *toolbox* and placing them in your design. You then write procedures for the objects using a modern version of *BASIC*.

Visual Basic 3.0 includes *Object Linking and Embedding (OLE)* 2.0 support and the *Microsoft Access* 2.0 *database* engine, which makes it easy for you to write a *graphical user interface (GUI)* front end for a database. See *event-driven program*.

Visual Basic for Applications (VBA)   A version of the *Visual Basic* programming language included with *Microsoft Windows 95* applications, such as *Microsoft Excel*, also called Visual Basic Programming System, Applications Edition.

Visual Basic for Applications is used to create procedures as simple as basic *macros* and as complex as custom *application programs*, complete with *dialog boxes, menus, pushbuttons*, and unique commands. See *event-driven program*.

VL-Bus   See *VESA Local Bus*.

VLSI   See *very large scale integration (VLSI)*.

voice actuation   Computer recognition and acceptance of spoken commands as instructions to be processed. See *voice recognition*.

voice coil actuator   See *servo-voice coil actuator*.

voice mail   In *office automation*, a communications system in which voice messages are transformed into digital form and stored on a *network*. When the person to whom the message is directed logs on to the system and discovers that a message is waiting, the system plays the message. Synonymous with voice store and forward.

voice recognition   Computer recognition of human speech and transformation of the recognized words into computer-readable digitized text or instructions.

Computers and people share an unfortunate characteristic: they talk much better than they listen. In the most advanced research systems, computers can recognize only about 100 or 200 words, and even this capability is achieved only after the speaker has trained the system to recognize his or her specific voice pattern. Still, many see voice recognition as the input method of the future. See *natural language* and *voice synthesis*.

voice store and forward   See *voice mail.*

voice synthesis   The audible output of computer-based text in the form of synthesized speech that people can recognize and understand.

Voice synthesis is much easier to achieve than voice recognition; you can equip virtually any personal computer to read *ASCII text* aloud with few errors. This capability has helped blind people gain increased access to written works not recorded on cassette tape. See *voice recognition.*

voice-capable modem   A *modem* that, like a *fax switch*, can distinguish between *fax* transmissions, *data* transmissions, and voice telephone calls, and route each to the proper device. Voice-capable modems can serve as *voice-mail* systems for small offices.

volatility   The susceptibility of a computer's *random-access memory (RAM)* to the complete loss of stored information if power is interrupted.

volume label   In *MS-DOS*, an identifying name assigned to a disk and displayed on the first line of a *directory*. The name can be no longer than 11 characters and is assigned when you *format* the disk.

von Neumann bottleneck   The limitation on processing speed imposed by computer architectures linking a single *microprocessor* with *memory*. John von Neumann discovered that a program will spend more time retrieving data from memory than it spends actually processing it.

One proposed solution to the von Neumann bottleneck is *parallel processing*, in which a program's tasks are divided among two or more microprocessors. Existing *programming languages* and techniques, however, can't handle parallel processing very well. The *Pentium* microprocessor minimizes the von Neumann bottleneck by incorporating separate *caches* for data and instructions. See *stored program concept.*

VR   See *virtual reality.*

VRAM   See *video RAM (VRAM).*

Vulcan nerve pinch   A poorly conceived *keyboard* command that requires the user to contort the hands in an uncomfortable way.

S
T
U
V

W3   See *World Wide Web (WWW)*.

WAIS   See *Wide Area Information Server (WAIS)*.

wait state   A *microprocessor clock cycle* in which nothing occurs. A wait state is programmed into a *computer system* to allow other components, such as *random-access memory (RAM)*, to catch up with the *central processing unit (CPU)*. The number of wait states depends on the speed of the processor in relation to the speed of memory.

Wait states can be eliminated—resulting in a "zero wait state" machine—by using fast (but expensive) *cache memory, interleaved memory,* page-mode RAM, or static RAM chips.

wallpaper   See *desktop pattern*.

warm boot   A system restart performed after the system has been powered and operating. A warm boot is performed by using a special key combination or by pressing a *reset button,* while a *cold boot* involves actually turning the *big red switch* off and on.

A warm boot is preferable to a cold start because a warm boot places less strain on your system's electrical and electronic components. See *programmer's switch.*

warm link   In *Object Linking and Embedding (OLE)* and dynamic data exchange (DDE), a dynamic link that's updated only when you explicitly request the update by choosing an update link command. Warm links have also been available in *Lotus 1-2-3* since Release 2.2 and in *Quattro Pro* since Version 1.0. See *hot link.*

WAV   A sound file format jointly developed by *Microsoft* and *IBM,* and prominently featured in *Microsoft Windows 95's* accessories for storing wave sounds. The format's specification calls for both 8-bit and 16-bit storage formats, in both monaural and stereo, but most of the *.WAV sounds you'll encounter on the *Internet* are 8-bit mono sounds.

waveform sound   Like *MIDI sound,* a type of digitized audio information. Waveform sound, especially when recorded with 16-bit *resolution,* can produce startlingly good fidelity, but it takes up monstrous amounts of storage space. Each minute of sound recorded in the *Microsoft Windows 95* .WAV format, for example, takes up 27*M.*

wave sound   One of the two types of sounds recorded in computer-readable files; contains a digitized recording of an actual sound. Wave sound files tend to be voluminous; in the Windows *.WAV format, for example, as many as 5*M* of storage may be required to store a 4-minute popular tune. Popular *Internet* wave file formats include *.AU, *.AIFF,* and *.MPEG* sounds. See *MIDI sound.*

wave table synthesis   A method, far superior to *FM synthesis,* of generating and reproducing music in a *sound board.* Wave table synthesis uses a pre-recorded sample of dozens of orchestral instruments to determine how particular notes played on those instruments should sound.

TIP: *Though sound boards that use wave table synthesis cost more than FM-synthesis boards, the improved quality may be worth it.*

web   In the *World Wide Web (WWW)* or any *hypertext* system, a set of related documents that together make up a hypertext presentation. The documents do not have to be stored on the same *computer system,* but they are explicitly interlinked, generally by providing internal *navigation buttons.* A web generally includes a *welcome page* that serves as the top-level document (*home page*) of the web.

WebAuthor   An *HTML* editor add-on for *Microsoft Word,* created by Quarterdeck Systems. Like Microsoft's own *Microsoft Internet Assistant,* WebAuthor transforms Word into a *what-you-see-is-what-you-get (WYSIWYG) HTML editor,* in which you see the results of the HTML *tags* rather than the tags themselves. Excellent facilities for forms are included.

Web browser   A program that runs on an *Internet*-connected computer and provides access to the riches of the *World Wide Web (WWW).* Web browsers are of two kinds: *text-only browsers* and *graphical Web browsers* such as *NCSA Mosaic* and *Netscape Navigator.* Graphical browsers are preferable because you can see *in-line images,* fonts, and document layouts.

WebCrawler   A *search engine* for locating *World Wide Web (WWW)* documents that is based at the University of Washington and supported by DealerNet, Starwave Corporation, and Satchel Sports. Relying on an automated search routine (called a *spider*) that indexes all the words in the documents it finds, WebCrawler is slow to compile its database (which contains only 300,000 documents at this writing). However, the fact that it retrieves and indexes all the words in the document makes it unusually accurate when you're searching for words that may not appear in document titles or headings.

Web server   In the *World Wide Web (WWW),* a *program* that accepts requests for information framed according to the *HyperText Transport Protocol (HTTP).* The server processes these requests and sends the requested document. Web servers have been developed for most computer systems, including *UNIX* workstations, *Microsoft Windows 95* and *Microsoft Windows NT* systems, and *Macintoshes.* See *HyperText Transport Protocol Daemon (HTTPD), MacHTTP, Netscape Commerce Server, Netscape Communications Server,* and *Windows HTTPD.*

Web site   In the *World Wide Web (WWW),* a *computer system* that runs a *Web server,* and has been set up for publishing documents on the Web.

weight   The overall lightness or darkness of a *typeface* design, or the gradations of lightness to darkness within a font family. A type style can be light or dark, and within a type style, you can see several gradations of weight: extra light, light, semilight, regular, medium, semibold, bold, extra bold, and ultrabold. See *book weight.*

Weitek coprocessors   *Numeric coprocessors* created for computers that use *Intel 80386* or *80486* microprocessors.

These coprocessors offer faster performance than the *Intel 80387* and 80487SX and are widely used for professional *computer-aided design (CAD)* applications. The Weitek 4167 can perform floating-point math three to five times faster than a 486 alone, but programs often require special modifications to use Weitek coprocessors.

welcome page In the *World Wide Web (WWW),* a Web-accessible document that is meant to be the point of entry to a series of related documents, called a *web.* For example, a company's welcome page typically includes the company's logo, a brief description of the web's purpose, and links to the additional documents available at that site. Welcome pages are also called *home pages,* because they are the home page (the top-level document) of the series of related documents that makes up the web.

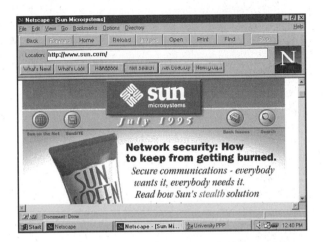

Fig. W.1 *The Sun Microsystems Welcome Page.*

well-known port An *Internet* port address that has been permanently linked with a certain application by the *Internet Assigned Numbers Authority (IANA).* A *port address* enables the *TCP/IP* software to direct incoming data to a certain application. The port address 80, for example, directs the incoming data to a Web server. Because IANA fixes port numbers for frequently used Internet applications (such as *Telnet, File Transfer Protocol [FTP],* and the *World Wide Web [WWW]*), it is not generally necessary to include port addresses when you are trying to locate data; the *domain name* is sufficient.

well-structured programming language A *programming language* that encourages programmers to create logically organized programs that are easy to read, debug, and update. Poorly structured programming languages allow *programmers* to create illogically organized programs, based on *spaghetti code,* that are almost impossible to debug or alter.

W
X
Y
Z

Modular programming languages encourage *structured programming:* clear, logical code by allowing the programmer to break down the program into separate modules, each of which accomplishes just one function. More recently, *object-oriented programming (OOP) languages,* such as SmallTalk and *C++,* have introduced another approach to modularity. The languages are structured by a hierarchy of objects, such as option buttons, *dialog boxes,* and *windows.*

what-if analysis   In *spreadsheet* programs, an important form of data exploration in which you change key variables to see the effect on the results of the computation. What-if analysis provides businesspeople and professionals with an effective vehicle for exploring the effect of alternative strategies.

what-you-see-is-what-you-get (WYSIWYG)   A design philosophy for word processing programs in which formatting commands directly affect the text on-screen, so the screen shows the appearance of the printed text. See *embedded formatting command.*

whipuptitude   A *programming language's* suitability for creating quick and easy solutions; *Practical Extraction and Report Language (PERL)* is considered to have much greater whipuptitude than *C.*

white pages   A computer version of the white pages section of a telephone book. White pages services are set up by organizations, such as corporations or universities, to provide computer assistance to people looking for a person's phone number or electronic mail address. Many white pages services are accessible via the *Internet.* See *Netfind,* and *X.500.*

white space   The portion of the page not printed. Good page design involves the use of white space to balance the areas that receive text and graphics, and also to improve the readability of the document.

white-write technique   See *print engine.*

whois   A *UNIX* utility, run by a *whois server,* that enables users to locate the *electronic mail* address, and often the telephone number and other information, of people who have an account on the same computer system. In Novell *networks,* a command that displays a list of all users logged on the network.

whois server An *Internet* program that accepts incoming requests for *electronic mail* addresses and telephone numbers, and tries to provide this information by searching a database of account holders. See *whois.*

Whole Internet Catalog In the *World Wide Web (WWW),* a subject tree maintained by O'Reilly & Associates, a book publisher. The Whole Internet Catalog contains hyperlinks to Web documents concerning arts and entertainment, business and finance, computers, education, government, health and medicine, the *Internet,* recreation, sports, hobbies, science and technology, the social sciences, and travel. See *subject tree.*

Wide Area Information Server (WAIS) A *UNIX*-based system linked to the *Internet;* also, a program that permits the user to search worldwide archives for resources based on a series of *key words.*

Users familiar with personal computer *database* programs are likely to find WAIS a less-than-satisfactory search tool, since WAIS generates a list of documents that's sure to contain many "false drops" (irrelevant documents that don't really pertain to the search subject). See *anonymous FTP.*

wide area network A *network* that uses high-speed, long-distance communications networks or satellites to connect computers over distances greater than those traversed by local area networks (LANs)—about 2 miles. See *ARPAnet, Fidonet,* and *Internet.*

widow A formatting flaw in which the last line of a paragraph appears alone at the top of a new column or page.

Most word processing and page layout programs suppress widows and *orphans;* better programs let you switch widow/orphan control on and off and to choose the number of lines at the beginning or end of the paragraph that you want kept together.

wild card Characters, such as asterisks and question marks, that stand for any other character that may appear in the same place.

Microsoft Windows 95 uses two wild cards: the asterisk (*), which stands for any character or characters, and the question mark (?), which stands for any single character. Note the following examples:

W
X
Y
Z

Wild card	Stands for
REP*.DOC	REPORT1.DOC
	REPOS.DOC
	REPORT2.DOC
REPORT?.DOC	REPORT1.DOC
	REPORT2.DOC

Win32   The 32-bit Windows *application programming interface (API)*. Programs that are written following the Win32 API guidelines will run only on *Microsoft Windows 95* and *Microsoft Windows NT*.

Win32s   A *freeware* utility, developed by *Microsoft Corporation*, that upgrades Microsoft Windows 3.1 and Microsoft Windows for Workgroups 3.11 so they can run *32-bit applications*.

Winchester drive   See *hard disk*.

window   A rectangular, on-screen frame through which you can view a *document*, worksheet, *database*, drawing, or *application program*.

In most programs, only one window is displayed. This window functions as a frame through which you can see your document, database, or worksheet. A windowing environment carries multiple windowing even further by enabling you to run two or more applications concurrently, each in its own window. See *application program interface (API), graphical user interface (GUI),* and *Microsoft Windows 95*.

windowing environment   An *application program interface (API)* that provides the features commonly associated with a *graphical user interface (GUI)* (such as windows, pull-down menus, on-screen fonts, and scroll bars or scroll boxes) and that makes these features available to programmers of application packages. See *graphical user interface (GUI)* and *Microsoft Windows*.

window menu   In *Microsoft Windows 95,* a synonym for *control menu*.

Windows   See *Microsoft Windows 95.*

Windows 95   See *Microsoft Windows 95.*

Windows accelerator   See *graphics accelerator board.*

Windows application   An application that can run only within the Microsoft Windows windowing environment, taking full advantage of Windows' *application program interface (API)*, its capability to display *fonts* and *graphics* on-screen, and its capability to exchange data dynamically between applications. See *non-Windows application.*

Windows Explorer   In *Microsoft Windows 95,* a file management program that replaces the Windows 3.1 File Manager. Most users will find it easier to manage files and programs by clicking the *My Computer* icon (see fig. W.2).

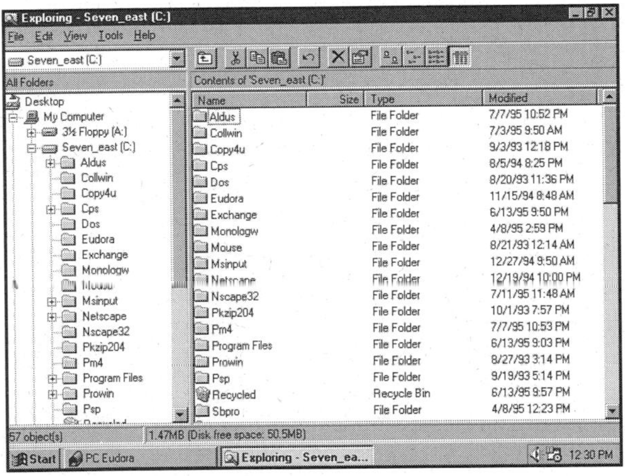

Fig. W.2   *Windows Explorer (Microsoft Windows 95).*

Windows Metafile Format (WMF)   An object-oriented (vector) graphics *file format* for *Microsoft Windows 95* applications. All Windows applications that support *object-oriented graphics* can read graphics files saved with the WMF format.

Windows printer   See *Graphical Device Interface (GDI) printer.*

W
X
Y
Z

Winsock   An open standard that specifies how a dynamic link library (DLL) should be written to provide *TCP/IP* support for *Microsoft Windows 95* systems. An outgrowth of a "birds of a feather" session at a *UNIX* conference, the Winsock standard—currently in version 2.0—is actively supported by *Microsoft Corporation.*

Winstone   A *benchmark* test developed by Ziff-Davis Publishing's PC Labs that attempts to simulate real-world conditions and test all aspects of a system's performance. By making a computer system execute *scripts* in more than a dozen popular *application programs,* the Winstone gives an idea of how well a system performs.

WinVN   A respected, public domain *UseNet newsreader* for *Microsoft Windows 95* and earlier Windows versions. Originally developed by Mark Riordan, this *threaded newsreader* is now developed and supported by programmers at NASA's Kennedy Space Center.

wireless wide area network   A radio network for computers equipped with *transceivers* that are used to receive (or, in two-way systems, to send and receive) *electronic mail* messages, news broadcasts, and *files.* Coverage is now limited to a few large metropolitan areas, but future satellite-based systems, which offer saturation coverage, may make wireless data communications more common.

wizard   An interactive help utility, originally developed by Microsoft for its Windows applications (and now widely imitated). The wizard guides the user through each step of a multi-step operation, offering helpful information and explaining options along the way (see fig. W.3).

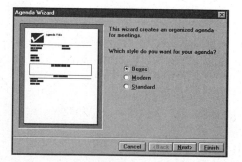

Fig. W.3   *Wizard (Microsoft Windows 95).*

.WMF A file name extension indicating that the file contains a graphic saved in the Windows Metafile Format (WMF).

word A unit of information, composed of characters, *bits* or *bytes*, that's treated as an entity and can be stored in one location. In *word processing* programs, a word is defined as including the space, if any, at the end of the characters.

Word See *Microsoft Word.*

WordPad In *Microsoft Windows 95,* a small *word processing program* that can directly read the files created by *Microsoft Word* and Microsoft Write (see fig. W.4). The program replaces the Notepad and Write accessories included with Windows 3.1.

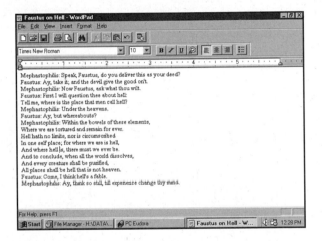

Fig. W.4 *WordPad (Microsoft Windows 95).*

WordPerfect A full-featured *word processor* published by Novell. WordPerfect is running neck-and-neck with *Microsoft Word* in the competition for the title of best word processor, and is generally considered superior to *Lotus Word Pro.*

WordPerfect is noted for PerfectSense, a *feature* that works with its *search-and-replace* utility. Instead of just replacing every instance of one word with another word, PerfectSense replaces words with the proper tense of a new word. For example, instructions to replace "sing" with "dance" also cause "singing" to be replaced with "dancing" and "sang" to be replaced with "danced."

W
X
Y
Z

word processing   Using the computer to create, edit, proofread, format, and print documents.

By a wide margin, word processing is the most popular computer
application and is probably responsible for the dramatic growth of
the personal computer industry. Unlike typewriters, computer
word processing programs allow users to change text before printing it and provide powerful editing tools. The most popular word
processing programs include WordPerfect and Microsoft Word.

> **TIP:** *A full-page display provides a better view of your document's
> paragraph-by-paragraph logic. Outlining utilities that are fully
> embedded within your word processing program can help you see
> and restructure your document's overall organization. Bear in
> mind, as you write, that the best cure for a poor sentence or para-
> graph is to delete the offending passage and rewrite it from scratch.
> As for wasting time with fonts and formatting, finish all text
> editing first, and then just remember to keep it simple.*

word processing program   A program that transforms a
computer into a tool for creating, editing, proofreading, formatting, and printing documents, such as *Lotus Word Pro*, *Microsoft
Word*, or *WordPerfect*. *Word processing* programs top the best-seller
lists, and for a simple reason: of all computer applications, people
have found word processing the most useful.

Modern word processors include many features to make writers'
and editors' jobs easier. Search-and-replace features help ease
revising documents, while spell-checkers and thesauruses ensure
clean, readable output. Various formatting tools make words
graphically appealing.

With the rise of *graphical user interface (GUI)* systems such as the
Macintosh and IBM PC-compatible computers running *Microsoft
Windows 95*, programs acquired the capability to display fonts and
font size choices on-screen. Today's word processing software can
take on light desktop publishing duties, such as newsletter production. See *what-you-see-is-what-you-get (WYSIWYG)*.

word wrap   A feature of *word processing programs*, and other
programs that include text-editing features, that wraps words

down to the beginning of the next line if they go beyond the right margin.

CAUTION: *If you're just getting started in word processing, remember that you shouldn't press Enter until you're ready to start a new paragraph. If you press Enter at the end of every line, you may find that changing the margins or performing editing operations is difficult after you type the text.*

workaround   A way of circumventing a *bug* without actually fixing it. Workarounds may be desirable when time is short or *programmers* are unavailable.

workbook   In a *spreadsheet* program, a collection of related *worksheets* kept in a single *file*. Workbooks make it easy to create *hot links* among worksheets.

workgroup   A small group of employees assigned to work together on a specific project.

Much of the work accomplished in large businesses is done in workgroups. If this work is to be done well and quickly, the workgroup needs to communicate effectively and share resources. *Personal computer* technology, especially when linked in a *local area network (LAN)*, is thought to enhance workgroup productivity by giving the group additional communication channels (in the form of *electronic mail*), facilities for the group editing of *documents* (such as *redlining* and *strikeout*), and shared access to a common *database*.

working model   See *crippled version*.

worksheet   In *spreadsheet programs*, the two-dimensional matrix of rows and columns within which you enter headings, *values*, and formulas. The worksheet resembles the ledger sheet used in accounting. Synonymous with spreadsheet.

worksheet window   In spreadsheet programs, the portion of the worksheet visible on-screen (see fig. W.5). With up to 8,192 rows and 256 columns, modern electronic spreadsheets are larger than a two-car garage in size. The worksheet window displays only a small portion of the total area potentially available.

W
X
Y
Z

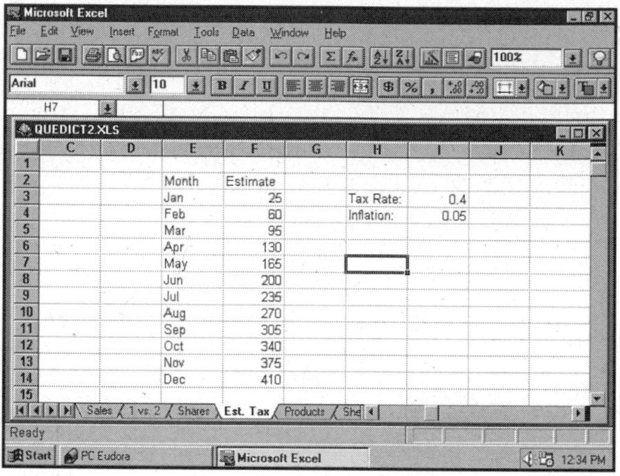

Fig. W.5   *A worksheet window.*

workstation   In a *local area network (LAN)*, a desktop computer that runs *application programs* and serves as an access point to the network. See *file server*, *personal computer*, and *professional workstation*.

World Wide Web (WWW)   A global *hypertext* system that uses the *Internet* as its transport mechanism. In a hypertext system, you navigate by clicking hyperlinks, which display another document (which also contains hyperlinks). What makes the Web such an exciting and useful medium is that the next document you see could be housed on a computer next door—or halfway around the world. The Web makes the Internet easy to use.

Created in 1989 at the *European Laboratory for Particle Physics (CERN)*, a research institute in Switzerland, the Web relies upon the *HyperText Transport Protocol (HTTP)*, an Internet standard that specifies how an application can locate and acquire resources (such as a *document*, sound, or *graphic*) stored on another computer on the Internet. HTTP provides transparent, easy-to-use access to Web documents, *FTP (File Transfer Protocol)* file archives, *Gopher* menus, and even *UseNet newsgroups*; users of Web navigation software, called Web browsers, simply click on an underlined word or phrase, and HTTP takes care of locating and downloading the desired document. Most Web documents are created using the *HyperText Markup Language (HTML)*, a *markup language* that is easy to learn and will soon be supplanted by automated tools. Incorporating *hypermedia* (graphics, sounds, animations, and video), the Web has become the ideal medium for publishing information on the Internet. A key 1995 agreement on security protocols ensures that the Web will quickly become an important commercial medium, in which consumers can browse on-line catalogs and place orders without worrying about anyone intercepting the supplied credit card information. See *Secure HTTP, Secure Sockets Layer (SSL),* and *Web browser.*

World Wide Web Worm (WWWW)   A *search engine* for locating *World Wide Web (WWW)* documents that is provided by the Department of Computer Science at the University of Colorado. Relying on an automated search routine (called a *spider*), WWWW retrieves *graphics*, video, and audio files as well as document titles and words in document hyperlinks.

CAUTION: *Because WWWW does not index words within the document, it may fail to retrieve many documents that are relevant to your interests; try* WebCrawler, Lycos, *or* InfoSeek *instead. However, WWWW is an excellent place to hunt for graphics, video, and audio files*

worm   A *virus* that's designed to find all *data* in memory or on disk and alter any data it encounters. The alteration may be to change certain characters to numbers or to swap bytes of stored memory. A few programs may still run, but usually data is irretrievably corrupted.

WORM   See *write-once, read-many (WORM).*

wrap-around type   Type contoured so that it surrounds a *graphic* (see fig. W.6). Because wrap-around type is harder to read than non-contoured type, use wrap-around type sparingly.

W
X
Y
Z

The selected graphic showing
its custom text-wrap boundary.

Dragging the graphic
into place on the page.

Surrounding text automatically
reflows itself around the graphic.

The final page after enlarging
and repositioning the graphic

Fig. W.6 *Text wrapped around a graphic.*

write A fundamental processing operation in which the *central processing unit (CPU)* records information in the computer's *random-access memory (RAM)* or the computer's *secondary storage* media, such as disk drives. In personal computing, the term most often refers to storing information on disks.

write-back cache A type of *cache memory* that stores information written to memory as well as information read from memory. Write-back caches, particularly those used in *secondary caches*, are considered to be technically superior to *write-through caches*.

write-black engine See *print engine.*

write head See *read/write head.*

write-once, read-many (WORM) An optical disk drive with storage capacities of up to 1 *terabyte*. After you write data to the disk, it becomes a read-only storage medium.

WORM drives can store huge amounts of information and have been touted as an excellent technology for organizations that need to publish large *databases* internally (such as collections of engineering drawings or technical documentation). The advent of fully read/write-capable optical disk drives, however, has greatly diminished the appeal of WORM technology. See *CD-ROM* and *erasable optical disk drive*.

write precompensation   A *hard disk's* increasing of the magnetic field with which the *read/write head* records data near the *spindle*, where data must be closely packed. The disk *geometry* includes the *cylinder* at which write precompensation begins.

write-protect   To modify a *file* or disk so no one can edit or erase its data.

write-protect notch   On a *5 1/4-inch floppy disk*, a small notch cut out of the disk's protective jacket that, when covered by a piece of tape, prevents the disk drive from performing erasures or write operations to the disk.

write-protect tab   On a *3 1/2-inch floppy disk*, a tab located in the disk's upper left corner as you hold the disk with the label facing away from you. When you slide the tab up to open the hole, you've write-protected the disk.

write-through cache   A *cache memory* scheme in which memory read operations are cached, but not memory write operations. Write operations are cached in *random-access memory (RAM)*, which is much slower than cache memory. Experts consider write-through caches to be inferior to *write-back* caches, which record both read and write operations.

write-white engine   See *print engine*.

WYSIWYG   See *what-you-see-is-what-you-get (WYSIWYG)*.

W
X
Y
Z

x86   The *microprocessor* architecture, developed by *Intel Corporation*, that is *binary compatible* with *MS-DOS* and *Microsoft Windows 95* programs.

x-axis   In a graph, the categories axis, which usually is the horizontal axis. See *bar graph*, *column graph*, *y-axis*, and *z-axis*.

Xbase   A generic term denoting any of the *programming* environments derived from the original *dBASE programming language* created by Ashton-Tate, Inc. Because the word dBASE is a registered trademark, the term Xbase has come to be used as a description for any programming language based on the dBASE programming language. Examples of the Xbase language would include FoxPro, dBASE, Clipper, Arago, and Force.

XCFN   See *external function (XCFN)*.

XCMD   See *external command (XCMD)*.

XENIX   An *operating system* developed by *Microsoft Corporation* that conforms to the *UNIX System V Interface Definition (SVID)* and runs on *IBM PC-compatible* computers.

XGA   See *Extended Graphics Array (XGA)*.

x-height   In *typography*, the height of a *font's* lowercase letters, measured from the *baseline* up. Because many fonts have unusually long or short *ascenders* and *descenders*, the x-height is a better measurement of the actual size of a font than the type size, measured in points. In figure X.1, for example, notice the variation in x-height in the letter y.

Fig. X.1   *Letters with the same nominal type size that have different x-heights.*

XMODEM   An asynchronous *file-transfer protocol* for *personal computers* that makes the error-free transmission of files through the telephone system easier. Developed by Ward Christiansen for 8-bit computers running *Control Program for Microprocessors (CP/M)* and placed in the public domain, the XMODEM protocol is included in most personal computer *communications programs* and commonly is used to download files from *bulletin board systems (BBSs)*.

XMODEM-1K   A *data transmission protocol* that retains *XMODEM/CRC's* error-checking capabilities but has higher *throughput*. By performing a *cyclic redundancy check (CRC)* only on 1,024-*byte blocks* of data, transmission overhead is reduced. See *YMODEM* and *ZMODEM*.

XMODEM/CRC   A version of the *XMODEM data transmission protocol* that reduces *throughput* but also reduces errors. XMODEM/CRC performs a *cyclic redundancy check (CRC)* on every two *bytes* transmitted—a more reliable scheme than the *checksum* technique employed by *XMODEM*. See *XMODEM-1K, YMODEM,* and *ZMODEM*.

XMS   See *eXtended Memory Specification (XMS)*.

XON/XOFF handshaking   See *handshaking*.

X Windows   A *network windowing environment* commonly used on *UNIX*-based *workstations*.

X Windows is a *device-independent application program interface (API)* that can run under *operating systems* ranging from disk operating systems to a *mainframe* operating system. It's used most frequently on UNIX machines. Unlike *Microsoft Windows 95* and other PC-based windowing environments, X Windows is designed for use on a *minicomputer*-based network.

x-y graph   See *scatter diagram*.

W
X
Y
Z

y-axis   In a graph, the values axis, which normally is vertical. See *bar graph, column graph, x-axis,* and *z-axis.*

Yahoo   In the *World Wide Web (WWW),* a popular subject tree created by David Filo and Jerry Yang of the Department of Computer Science at Stanford University. With a keen eye for the popular as well as the useful, Filo and Yang have created a directory of Web resources that currently includes nearly 35,000 Web documents. In 1995, Yahoo moved out of Stanford to **www.yahoo.com**, where it is supported by advertising. Yahoo reportedly performs 10 million searches each week.

Yellow Book   An *International Standards Organization (ISO)* standard that describes the way data is encoded on CD-ROMs. The Yellow Book standard includes CD-XA specifications.

YMCK   See *CMYK.*

YMODEM   A *file transfer protocol* that is an improved version of *XMODEM-1K.* YMODEM transfers data in 1,024-*byte blocks* and performs a *cyclic redundancy check (CRC)* on each *frame.* Also, YMODEM supports sending more than one file in sequence. See *YMODEM-g* and *ZMODEM.*

YMODEM-g   A *file transfer protocol* that leaves *error-checking* to protocols encoded on modem hardware, such as *V.42* and *MNP4,* and is best used with *high-speed modems* in low *line noise* conditions. *ZMODEM* is usually a better choice than YMODEM-g.

yoke   The collection of electromagnets precisely arrayed around the outside of a *cathode ray tube (CRT).* The yoke, controlled by the *monitor* circuitry and *video adapter,* steers electrons from the *electron guns* to the proper *pixels* on the *display.* If the yoke gets out of alignment, the monitor is useless. Make sure any monitor you buy has a 30-day guarantee, especially if you purchase by mail.

Z39.50   A protocol for the *network* retrieval of bibliographic data that was developed by the National Information Standards Organization (NISO), a unit of the *American National Standards Institute (ANSI)*. Using a Z39.50-compatible application, a user can frame a query that can be processed on any other computer attached to a *network*, even if it is made by a different manufacturer. The protocol precisely specifies the format of the query in a way that is ideal for searching bibliographic databases, such as library card catalogues. Z39.50 applications are being developed to allow Internet applications to retrieve data from databases stored on IBM *mainframe* computers, which house most of the on-line library catalogues currently in existence.

Zapf Dingbats   A set of decorative symbols developed by Herman Zapf, a German typeface designer (see fig. Z.1). Dingbats originally were ornamental symbols used between columns or, more commonly, between paragraphs, to provide separation.

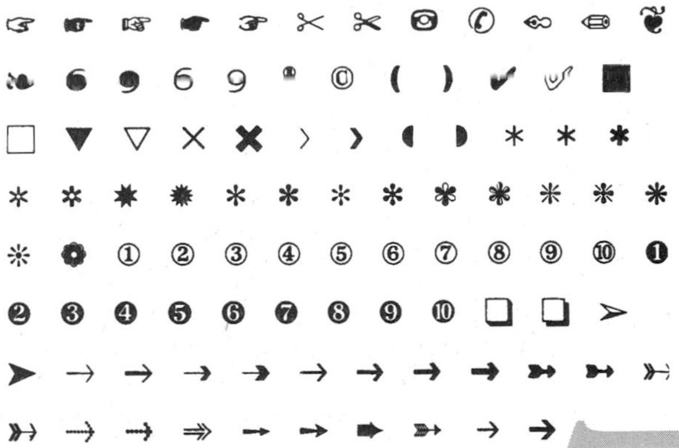

Fig. Z.1   *Zapf Dingbats.*

z-axis   In a three-dimensional graphic image, the third dimension, usually depth. See *three-dimensional graph, x-axis,* and *y-axis.*

zero-insertion force (ZIF) package A socket for large *chips,* such as *microprocessors,* that makes it easy to remove and install *parts* without bending pins. By raising a lever at the side of the ZIF package, the pins are released and the chip may be easily removed. When another chip is installed, the lever may be moved back to clamp the pins in place again.

Zero Insertion Force (ZIF) socket See *zero insertion force (ZIF) package.*

zero-slot LAN A *local area network (LAN)* designed to use a computer's *serial port* rather than require the user to buy a *network interface card.*

CAUTION: *Zero-slot LANs are considerably slower than systems that use network interface cards that take advantage of the computer's high-speed internal bus. Zero-slot LANs are therefore best used for applications in which network applications are limited to occasional access to an infrequently used, shared peripheral (such as a plotter) or electronic mail.*

zero wait state computer An *IBM PC-compatible* computer with memory speed optimized by using a scheme such as *cache memory, interleaved memory, page-mode random-access memory* (RAM), or *static random access memory (SRAM)* chips, so that the microprocessor doesn't have to wait—enter a *wait state*—for the memory to catch up with processing operations.

ZIF See *zero-insertion force (ZIF) package.*

ZIF socket See *zero-insertion force (ZIF) package.*

.ZIP The *MS-DOS file name extension* usually attached to a file, generated by PKZIP, that contains several compressed files. ZIP files often are found on *bulletin board systems (BBSs).*

ZMODEM An asynchronous *file transfer protocol* for personal computers that makes the error-free transmission of computer files with a *modem* easier. ZMODEM is a very fast protocol that lets you use wild-card file names for transfers. It's also well-liked because you can resume the transfer of a file if the first attempt is interrupted before completion. Next to *XMODEM,* ZMODEM is the most popular file transfer protocol and is included in most communications applications.

zone   In a *local area network (LAN)*, a subgroup of networked computers set aside and named by the network administrator so that these computers can be treated as a group. If an administrator sets up zones called Marketing, Design, and Manufacturing, for example, someone in manufacturing can address an *electronic mail* message to everyone in marketing by sending the message to the marketing zone.

zone-bit recording   A *Multiple-Zone Recording (MZR)*, in Seagate Technologies parlance.

Zoned Constant Angular Velocity (ZCAV)   See *Multiple-Zone Recording (MZR)*.

zoom   To enlarge a *window* or part of a document or image so it fills the screen.

zoom box   In a *graphical user interface (GUI)*, a box—usually positioned on the window border—that you click to zoom the window to full size or restore the window to normal size. Synonymous with *maximize button*.

W
X
Y
Z

Add terms to:

Que's Computer and Internet Dictionary, 6th Edition

Que's Computer and Internet Dictionary defines and describes terms of interest to the typical user of computers. We have tried to include all terms appropriate to a general audience, but we know that we must have missed some that you think should be in this book. Please help us improve the next edition. Write down the terms you think we should include, and send the list to:

> *Que's Computer and Internet Dictionary,* 6th Edition
> Que Corporation
> c/o Mark Cierzniak
> 201 West 103rd St.
> Indianapolis, IN 46290

Your feedback is important to us. Thanks for your help!